Second Edition

A FINAL RIVER TO CROSS

The Underground Railroad at Youngstown, NY

You will be missed ... but enjoy your new home! Keep in touch!

Gretchen Duling, Ph.D. and Dennis Duling, Ph.D.

The Dulings

Gretchen and Denny

A CITY OF LIGHT IMPRINT

First edition published by Buffalo Heritage Press in 2017
Second edition published by City of Light Publishing in 2021

A CITY OF LIGHT IMPRINT

City of Light Publishing
266 Elmwood Avenue, #407
Buffalo, NY 14222
www.CityofLightPublishing.com

Chapter heading images are from E. T. Foote's *Antislavery Scrapbook*. We are grateful to John Paul Wolfe, Curator of the Chautauqua County Historical Museum, for finding them and for permission from the New York Chautauqua County Historical Society to use them.

Book design by Dennis Duling & Goulah Design Group, Inc.
Cover image: A Horse Boat at Empy's Ferry, Osnabruck, Ontario, 1898 (see **Image 4.8**, p. 93)

First edition ISBN: 978-1-942483-40-3 (softcover)
Second edition ISBN: 978-1-952536-01-4 (softcover)

Printed in the U.S.A.

10 9 8 7 6 5 4 3 2 1

Library of Congress Cataloging-in-Publication Data

Names: Duling, Gretchen A., author. | Duling, Dennis C., author.
Title: A final river to cross : the Underground Railroad at Youngstown, New York / Gretchen Duling, Ph.D. and Dennis Duling, Ph.D.
Other titles: Underground Railroad at Youngstown, New York
Description: Second edition. | Buffalo, NY : New Idea Press, a City of Light imprint, 2021. | Includes bibliographical references and index. | Summary: "The second edition of A Final River to Cross: The Underground Railroad at Youngstown, New York offers further proof of the existence of, support for, and operation of the Underground Railroad in Western New York. The revised and enhanced second edition contains newly discovered primary source materials and includes an extensive bibliography and a comprehensive index. It clearly demonstrates the connection of Youngstown, New York to regional and national UGRR networks, and tells the compelling stories of the Village and its citizens-an agent, boaters, ferrymen-who were linked with other persons and villages in a broader network. Seven accounts document eighteen fugitive slaves who made the perilous crossing to freedom in Canada from Youngstown. The final chapter is an Underground Railroad database based on the Wellman Scale. This thoroughly documented book is exactly the kind of local and regional study that UGRR experts currently recommend and fills a gap in research on the Underground Railroad in New York State. "Thoroughly researched, with solid information, this book explores the fascinating people, places, and stories relating to the Underground Railroad in Youngstown, NY." -- Provided by publisher.
Identifiers: LCCN 2020047279 (print) | LCCN 2020047280 (ebook) | ISBN 9781952536014 (paperback) | ISBN 9781952536021 (epub) | ISBN 9781952536021 (kindle edition) | ISBN 9781952536021 (mobi) | ISBN 9781952536021 (pdf)
Subjects: LCSH: Underground Railroad--New York (State)--Youngstown. | African Americans--New York (State)--Youngstown--History--19th century. | Fugitive slaves--New York (State)--Youngstown--History--19th century. | Youngstown (N.Y.)--History--19th century.
Classification: LCC E450 .D84 2021 (print) | LCC E450 (ebook) | DDC 974.7/980496073--dc23
LC record available at https://lccn.loc.gov/2020047279
LC ebook record available at https://lccn.loc.gov/2020047280

Image 0.1

Away to Canada[1]

I've served my master all my days

Without a dime's reward,

And now I'm forced to run away

To flee the lash abhored.

The hounds are baying on my track—

The master's just behind,

Resolved that he will bring me back

Before I cross the line.

> Farewell old master,
>
> Don't come after me,
>
> I'm on my way to Canada
>
> Where colored men are free!

---

[1]"Away to Canada," a slave song. Library of the University of Michigan: Henry Bibb's paper, "The Voice of the Fugitive," file of 1851—1852; *Dalhousie Review* (January, 1926) 531. Quoted by Wilbur H. Siebert, "The Underground Railroad in Massachusetts," *The New England Quarterly* 9/3 (1936) 448 (Online at JSTOR).

Dedication

*This book was researched and written
to honor the memory of the
freedom seekers and free colored people
who lived in or passed through nineteenth-century
Youngstown, New York,
and to its local people, most especially the ferrymen who helped keep
them safe, guided them further, and ferried many of them across the
Niagara River to freedom in Canada.*

Youngstown, New York, early 1900s
(Courtesy of the Town of Porter Historical Society)
Image 0.2

CONTENTS

IMAGES

PREFACE
to the Second Edition

The second edition of *A Final River to Cross* is an international edition by New Ideas Press, City of Light Publishing that avoids international publishing and sales complications. It features many minor changes and a new, more detailed Index. The project required meetings, communication, and cooperation between the authors, the publisher, and Goulah Design Group. Gretchen and Dennis Duling, the authors, thank the publisher Marti Gorman of New Ideas Press for her initiative in implementing this new edition. We also give Pauline Goulah and her staff of Goulah Design Group special thanks for their patience, professionalism, and detailed work.

ACKNOWLEDGMENTS

There are many people we want to acknowledge for their assistance, both in particular and in general. We first want to thank Dr. Judith Wellman who was engaged by the Niagara Falls Underground Railroad Commission to do an Underground Railroad survey and research for Niagara Falls, New York. Gretchen's Underground Railroad (UGRR) research about Youngstown, New York, had already begun, so she attended most of the Commission's public meetings and was able to speak with Dr. Wellman several times. Gretchen did not influence Dr. Wellman, but was certainly pleased when she and her team of researchers expanded their efforts into Niagara County, which included Youngstown. Gretchen's and Wellman's research data were closely matched. (We have studied, credited, and often used her material since then, but in following up her work on Youngstown we have found more details and discovered additional local and regional information.) Through e-mails, Dr. Wellman gave Gretchen reassurance and positive feedback. Wellman also produced a short paper on Youngstown entitled "Site of the Ferry Landing at Youngstown." It noted four major sources that are researched and developed in greater detail in this book.[1] Her extensive survey data and analysis, indispensable for Underground Railroad research in Niagara County, can be found on the website www.niagarafallsundergroundrailroad.org. The site also contains many valuable articles on persons and sites in Niagara Falls, as well as across Niagara County. Together our efforts are the first time Youngstown's involvement in the Underground Railroad has been studied to such an extent. We are grateful to her for including our little village along the Niagara River. It was exciting to us that she agreed to be a reader of our manuscript! That

---

[1] See the following Preface for location of the "Site of the Ferry Landing at Youngstown" and the Database for Niagara Falls and Niagara County. For discussion of the Youngstown Ferry, see Ch. 6 and especially Ch. 16.

certainly set the standards high. We have communicated off and on for several years and followed her suggestions and appreciated her clarifications.

At a conference sponsored by the Niagara Falls Underground Railroad Commission at Niagara University in Lewiston, New York, several invited scholars known for their Underground Railroad research and publications made presentations. Gretchen attended and was particularly fascinated by the work of Dr. Kate Clifford Larson. She purchased and had Dr. Larson sign her book, *Bound for the Promised Land. Harriet Tubman, Portrait of an American Hero* (2004).[2] Gretchen spoke briefly with her about her research and asked for suggestions on where to look for local sources of information. Dr. Larson encouraged her to keep researching and to examine the census reports of the 1800s, which we have pursued and included. Gretchen kept in contact with Dr. Larson and she agreed to be a reader for our manuscript, for which we owe her our most sincere gratitude.

Impressive to Gretchen was a Niagara University Department of History master's thesis entitled *History of the Underground Railroad along the Niagara Frontier,* written in 1947 by Carl J. Constantino, a history student. He considered the Niagara River to be the "last river to cross" in the long and torturous journey to freedom.[3] His project is concise, well written, and is a pleasure to read. For information about Niagara University's History Department, go to www.niagara.edu/history.

Gretchen has had deep respect for the late Carol Murphy, who died on May 22, 2014. She was a woman farmer with a background in science who became the owner of the McClew Farm/Murphy Orchards in Burt, New York. Carol believed that her farm had been involved in the Underground Railroad. She created an inspirational walking tour of her property, mostly for school children. She also established an educational program on the history of farming. She was a member of the Niagara Falls National Underground Railroad Commission. She asked Gretchen to join her McClew Education and Interpretative Center, Inc., of Murphy Orchard's Board of

---

[2] Kate Clifford Larson, *Bound for the Promised Land. Harriet Tubman, Portrait of an American Hero* (New York, NY: Ballantine Books, 2004).
[3] Carl J. Constantino, *History of the Underground Railroad along the Niagara Frontier* (M.A. Thesis Niagara University; Lewiston, NY: Niagara University History Department, 1947).

Trustees.[4] Throughout her relatively short illness, Carol was always positive, looking forward to the future. The Board continued to meet and she welcomed its counsel. Her untimely death is a great loss of support for researching and documenting the history of the Niagara County Underground Railroad. Murphy Orchards is now an UGRR educational site of the National Park Service and it is listed as an UGRR "local tradition" in the Niagara Falls Underground Railroad database.[5] A link to a *Buffalo News* article about Murphy Orchards written by reporter Teresa Sharp was found for a while on the website of the Niagara Falls National Underground Railroad Commission.[6] Her family and staff have made every effort to continue Carol's vision. For more information about Murphy Orchards, see www.murphyorchards.com.[7]

There are many images throughout this book (see the List of Images). We are especially grateful to John Paul Wolfe, Curator of the Chautauqua County Historical Society/McClurg Museum, for finding the images from E. T. Foote's *Antislavery Scrapbook*, which are chapter headings with permission from the New York Chautauqua County Historical Society. The Public Library of Cincinnati and Hamilton County in Ohio graciously gave us permission to use two images of horse ferries that were in their collection. Rebecca Foster assisted us in receiving permission to use a horse boat [horse ferry] image from the Umatilla County Historical Society Museum in Pendleton, Oregon. The McElfresh Map Company LLC, in Olean, New York, gave us permission to use a section of their *Freedom's Tracks: Map of the Underground Railroad*. Karen S. Shafts, Assistant Keeper of Prints, Print Department, and Sean Casey, Rare Books and Manuscripts Department, both from the Boston Public Library in Boston, Massachusetts,

---

[4] On March 5, 2012, a private email from Carol to Gretchen included these comments: "It is my plan within the next five years to turn over all of Murphy Orchard's real property and operations to The McClew Interpretive Center, Inc., which was formed as a 501(c)(3) organization in 2005. In order to make that transition, we need passionate, knowledgeable, dedicated, and intelligent people who believe that this farm should be preserved and enhanced as an educational facility of significant worth to our community."

[5] Judith Wellman, "People and Sites Relating to the Underground Railroad, Abolitionism, and African American Life, 1820-1880 Niagara Falls and Niagara County." http://www.niagarafallsundergroundrailroad.org/assets/Uploads/Niagara-Falls-Underground-Railroad-Project-Database.pdf. Search "McClew."

[6] Teresa Sharpe, "Take a Step Back in Time at Historic McClew Farmstead in Burt," *The Buffalo News* (Sept. 1, 2013). http://www.buffalonews.com/city-region/all-niagara-county/take-a-step-back-in-time-at-historic-mcclew-farmstead-in-burt-20130901 See also, "Children Vow to Continue Murphy's Devoted Work," *The Buffalo News* (June 1, 2014) http://www.buffalonews.com/city-region/all-niagara-county/children-vow-to-continue-murphys-devoted-work-20140601.

[7] See Ch. 16.

located the original 1851 "broadside" (poster) titled "Caution!! Colored People of Boston . . . ." archived in the Rare Books Department of the Theodore Parker Collection. The Trustees of the Boston Public Library/Rare Books granted us permission to reproduce this broadside. Murphy Orchards gave permission to use the two photo images Dennis took while visiting the farm and Tea Room. Jim Reynolds of Niagara-on-the-Lake, Ontario, sent us a photo of Edward Walsh's 1804 painting Fort George/Navy Hall/and New Niagara, as well as 1810 and 1819 maps of Fort George, Navy Hall, and New Niagara. These were in the Niagara Museum in Niagara-on-the-Lake and, with information from the Niagara Museum's Managing Director, Sarah Kaufman, we gained official permission to use them (below). The Reverend Dr. Rex Stewart gave us permission to use an old photo of the First Presbyterian Church of Youngstown, now found in the church's 175th Anniversary Booklet (1998). Thanks also to Deborah Fox, John Carter's great, great, great granddaughter, for information about Carter's family and a photo of Carter that she gave to the Town of Porter Historical Society, which has granted us permission to use.

There are others to acknowledge. Jean Siddall, Curator, and Anne Brett, Museum Director, from the Town of Porter Historical Society Museum provided timely answers to our questions; the historical museum and society Board of Trustees gave us permission for the use of images. Jean spent time with us in searching through the census records' booklets and Internet time on Ancestry.com. Ann Marie Linnabery, Assistant Director and Education Coordinator of the Niagara County Historical Society, assisted in sending and interpreting a Lockport handbill opposing immediate abolition. Catherine Emerson, the Niagara County Historian, took time to assist us in dating an image from the Park Presbyterian Church at Newark, New York, and to inform us about Betsy Doyle. She and Deputy Historians, Ronald Cary and Craig Bacon, helped us navigate the Niagara County Historian's Office archives. Mr. and Mrs. Herman Erbacher of Warrens Corners helped us understand the geographical environment of Warrens Corners, and Brooke Morse, Cambria Town Historian, clarified several features of the same area, including information about local families. Pamela Hauth, the recent, past Historical Association of Lewiston's Curator and Executive Director, provided timely clarifications, dated images, and shared old maps of Lewiston. Michelle Kratts, the Lewiston Public Library Genealogist and former Historian of Niagara Falls, New York, had collaborated previously with us on another local history project representing the four bi-national river villages on the Lower Niagara River. Her education, experience, research skills, and the software available to her were extremely important. She managed to locate some citizens in Youngstown and the Town of Porter for us. She had also previously assisted Dr. Wellman with her research on the Underground Railroad in Niagara Falls, New York, and Niagara County, and had further information about a key Niagara Falls image, John Morrison. Clyde L. Burmaster, Vice-Chairman of the Niagara County Legislature, was helpful in our search for historical information about ferrymen.

We want to recognize a local historian colleague, Karen Noonan, Ph.D. Over the years, she has collaborated with us on a number of successful local history projects. We developed a professional understanding that we would join forces by sharing information we came across that was relevant to each other's individual research. Karen's attitude towards this research style—cooperation without competition—has been impressive. There are many images in the book that were taken by photographers, Karen Noonan, Dennis Duling, and Gretchen. Glenn Clark, a professional photographer from Youngstown, took the photo of King's Wharf below Fort George in Canada.

Special mention must be made again about three of the above persons. Each undertook the task—an imposing one—of reading and commenting on our manuscript: Karen Noonan, Judith Wellman, and Kate Clifford Larson. Karen made editorial and historical comments in great detail and then discussed them with us; as a result, we made a number of important changes. Judith Wellman is an acknowledged expert about the New York State UGRR. Her methods and research are abundantly scattered throughout this book and she read and critiqued a draft of it. Kate Clifford Larson, also a draft critic, is known nationally for her biographical research and as an author of a highly-praised work on Harriet Tubman. As noted, Gretchen has kept in contact with her and she was a natural choice for comments. We are also much indebted to our deeply informed fourth reader, Bill Bradberry, a lawyer, activist, *Niagara Gazette* editorial writer, and Chair of the Niagara Falls Underground Railroad Heritage Area Commission. Yet, we, not they, are finally responsible for the content of this book.

Finally, there are many museums, historical societies, research centers, consultants, archivists, curators, and historians, as well as public, college, and university libraries that provided service and information. It was a distinct pleasure to have worked with these professionals who shared their interest and expertise. Unfortunately, we cannot thank them all in detail; instead, we have cited them in the following list of institutions and professionals.

Museums, Historical Societies, Directors, Archivists, Curators, and Historians

Buffalo History Museum Research Library, Buffalo, New York. Cynthia M. Van Ness, MLS, Director and Research Librarian, Library and Archives.

Cambria. Thanks to Mr. and Mrs. Herman Erbacher of Warrens Corners for initial clarification of the area (confusing to outsiders) and to Brooke Morse, Cambria Town Historian.

Chautauqua Co. Historical Society/McClurg Museum, Westfield, New York. Curator, John Paul Wolfe.

Firelands Museum, Norwalk, Ohio. Curator, Mary Carabin.

Gallia County Genealogical Society, Gallipolis, Ohio. Research Assistance. President, Henny Evans.

H. Lee White Maritime Museum, Oswego, New York. Director and Curator, Michael Pittavino.

Historical Association of Lewiston, Lewiston, New York. Recent past Curator and Executive Director, Pamela Hauth.

John P. Parker Museum and Historical Society, Ripley, Ohio. Docent, Dewey Scott.

Landmark Society of the Niagara Frontier, President (1988-2002), John H. Conlin.

Library and Archives Canada, Ottawa, Ontario.

Newark-Arcadia Historical Society Museum, Newark, New York. Director, Christopher Davis.

Niagara County Historian's Office, Lockport, New York. Historian Catherine Emerson; Deputy Historians, Ronald Cary and Craig Bacon.

Niagara Falls Historian's Office, Niagara Falls, New York. Historian, Daniel L. Davis.

Niagara Historical Society's Museum, Niagara-on-the-Lake, Ontario, Canada. Managing Director, Sarah Maloney Kaufman.

Old Fort Niagara Association, Youngstown, New York. Past Executive Director, Brian Dunnigan, and current Assistant Director and Curator, Jerome P. Brubaker.

Presbyterian Historical Society, National Archives of the Presbyterian Church (U.S.A.), Philadelphia, Pennsylvania. Reference Archivist, David Koch, and Researcher, Anita Sheahan Coraluzzi.

Ransomville Historical Museum, Hamlet of Ransomville, New York. Director, Millie Hillman.

Smithfield Town Historian, Smithfield, New York. Historian, Donna Burdick.

Town of Porter, New York. Historian, Suzanne Simon Dietz.

Town of Porter Historical Museum in Youngstown, New York. Curator, Jean Siddall; Museum Director, Anne Brett.

Umatilla County Historical Society Museum, Pendleton, Oregon. Assisted by Rebecca Foster.

Wayne County Historian's Office, Lyons, New York. Historian, Peter K. Evans.

Western New York Heritage Press, Buffalo, New York. Editor, Douglas DeCroix.

Public, College, and University Libraries, Special Collections, and Librarians

Boston Public Library, Boston, Massachusetts. Assistant Keeper of Prints, Karen S. Shafts; Rare Books and Manuscripts, Sean Casey; Curator of Newspapers and Microtexts, Department of Rare Books & Manuscripts of the Theodore Parker Collection, Henry Scannell.

Burke Library (Auburn Theological Seminary Records) at Union Theological Seminary, Columbia University in the City of New York, New York.

Cincinnati Public Library and Hamilton County in Ohio, Cincinnati, Ohio.

Gerrit Smith Estate National Historic Landmark, Peterboro, New York. Co-Chairs, Steward and Dot Willsey; Gerrit Smith biographer and tour guide, Norman K. Dann.

Lewiston Public Library, Lewiston, New York. Librarian and Genealogist, Michelle Kratts.

McElfresh Map Company, LLC, Olean, New York. Head of Permissions, Michiko McElfresh.

New York Public Library, New York, New York. Research and Reference Division, Jean Blackwell Hutson. Schomberg Center for Research in Black Culture, Astor, Lenox and Tilden Foundations, Michael Siegel. Library Division: Schomburg Center for Research in Black

Culture, Manuscripts, Archives and Rare Book Division & Collection: Slavery and Abolition, 1700-1890. Permissions and Reproduction Services, Manager, Thomas Lisanti.

Niagara Falls Public Library, Niagara Falls, New York. Local History Room Historian.

Niagara University Library, Niagara University, Lewiston, New York.

Ohio History Connection and State Library of Ohio, Department of Special Collections, Ohio History Connection of the Ohio Historical Society, Columbus, Ohio. Wilbur H. Siebert Collection: Questionnaire and Letters, regarding Thomas Birnmore (VMF 156). Permissions and Digital Projects Coordinator, Lily Birkhimer.

St. Catharines Public Library, St. Catharines, Ontario, Canada. Special Collections, Sandra Enskat.

Swarthmore College, Friends Historical Library. Swarthmore, Pennsylvania. Curator, Christopher Densmore (formerly with the University Archives, University at Buffalo, Buffalo [Amherst], New York).

Syracuse University Libraries, Special Collections Research Center, Gerrit Smith Papers, Syracuse, New York. Reading Room Supervisor, Nicole C. Dittrich.

Toronto Public Library, Reference Library and Intellisearch, Toronto, Ontario, Canada.

University of Saskatchewan, College of Law. Saskatoon, Saskatchewan, Canada. Ariel F. Sallows Visiting Professor of Human Rights Law Democracy, Citizenship and Constitutionalism Program, University of Pennsylvania Senior Fellow, Paul Finkelman.

University of Virginia, Steve Railton, Professor of English, and Heather Riser, Clifton Waller Barrett Collection, the Special Collections Library.

William L. Clements Library, University of Michigan, Ann Arbor, Michigan. Associate Director and Curator of Maps, Brian Dunnigan; Curatorial Assistant and Reading Room Supervisor, Jayne Ptolemy.

Church Officials and Miscellaneous Historians

First Presbyterian Church, Youngstown, New York. William Siddall, Historian; the Reverend Dr. Rex Stewart.

K & D Action Photo Historic Youngstown, New York. Photographers, Kevin and Dawn Cobello.

Park Presbyterian Church, Newark, New York. Pastor, the Reverend Kirk Baker; Office
Administrator, Bethany Comella.

St. John's Episcopal Church, Youngstown, New York. Archival Research, Permission from the
Vestry, Coordinated by Mary Ellen Aureli.

Youngstown and Town of Porter, Youngstown, New York. Local Historian, Researcher, Writer,
Author, and Photographer, Dennis Duling.

Youngstown and Town of Porter, New York, Youngstown, New York. Local Historian,
Researcher, Writer, Author, and Photographer, Karen Noonan.

Youngstown and Town of Porter, Youngstown, New York. Local Historian, Researcher, Writer,
Author, and Photographer, Gretchen Duling.

Youngstown, New York. Professional Photographer, Glenn Clark.

Fulton History

A special thanks to Tom Tryniski who administers http://www.Fultonhistory.com.
Without his work, it would be impossible to find most of 19th century newspapers in this study.

Chapter Headings and E. T. Foote's *Antislavery Scrapbook*

The images at the beginning of each chapter were taken from Elial Todd Foote's
Antislavery Scrapbook, so named by one of his and Anne Cheney Foote's five children, Horace
Foote, in 1893. Judge E. T. Foote (1796 – 1877) was a physician, legislator, jurist, and historian
who settled in Jamestown, New York, from New Haven, Connecticut, in 1815. He was active in
the Chautauqua County anti-slavery movement in 1843 and backed the abolitionist Liberty
ticket in 1844 before returning to New Haven to resume his medical practice. His *Scrapbook* is
the largest known collection of antislavery materials from Chautauqua County.[8] It is archived in
the Chautauqua County Historical Society/McClurg Museum, Westfield, New York. Thanks again
to John Paul Wolfe, Curator.

---

[8] "Elial Todd Foote," 1800s Antislavery Activists. http://ugrr.orbitist.com/content/foote.

This book contains a great deal of information about the Lower Niagara River, Youngstown, and the Underground Railroad. We hope that our study will make a contribution, and where we have fallen short, that others will correct our work and move forward in the historical reconstruction of the Underground Railroad in this region. There is still much to be discovered.

Terms to Designate Persons of Color

Terms used to designate persons of color in this book are based on both primary sources and on more recent historical studies. It is hoped that readers will take no offense at these terms: fugitives, fugitive slaves, escapees, Underground Railroad passengers, colored (or coloured), people, negro (Negro), whites, blacks (Blacks), African Americans, African Canadians, mulattos, friends, passengers, strangers, and freedom seekers.

PREFACE

Youngstown and the Underground Railroad

The "Underground Railroad" (UGRR) is a metaphor for the secret, loosely connected, interlocking network of black and white activists who risked helping fugitive slaves from slavery in the southern slave states of the United States to freedom in northern free states and on to Canada in the decades prior to the Civil War.[1] The metaphor includes terms such as "passengers," "packages," "cargo," and "freight" to refer to the fugitive slaves who sought freedom; "stations" or "depots" to refer to secret safe houses, barns, churches, and other places to hide along the way, usually about eight or ten miles apart; "station masters" to indicate local central persons who knew most about the local UGRR network; "agents" or intermediary contacts who helped to plan, organize, and communicate routes; "conductors" to refer to those who guided fugitive slaves, sometimes from one station to another; and "tracks" as routes. Although the activity of helping fugitive slaves to escape, whether by whites, blacks, or indigenous peoples, had antecedents that extended back into the colonial period, the origin of the name seems to have surfaced in the 1830s. One of several originating legends is that in 1831, when an escaping fugitive slave named Tice Davids swam across the Ohio River to the free state at Ripley, Ohio, the slave catcher who attempted to catch him along the Ohio shoreline said that his disappearance happened so suddenly that "he must have gone on an underground road."[2] There were other, similar stories of origin.[3] Whatever the case, the

---

[1] An exception to the Underground Railroad as only a metaphor is found in the recent, prize winning novel, *The Underground Railroad* (New York, NY: Doubleday Books, 2016) by Colson Whitehead, who imaginatively interprets it as also a *literal* railroad under the ground.

[2] Wilber H. Siebert, *The Underground Railroad from Slavery to Freedom: A Comprehensive History* (New York, NY; London, England: The Macmillan Co., 1898; reprint Mineola, NY: Dover Publications, 2006) 45-46. Siebert thought that such anecdotes had some general validity, but their specificity could not be trusted.

Underground Railroad network grew and flourished in the decades before the Civil War (1861-1865). It helped thousands of slaves on their way to freedom, especially in the border or free states of the North. A little more detail about the UGRR will be noted at the end of Chapter 1.

There is a long list of studies and other sources about the UGRR, some of it in the Bibliography of this book. In the older literature, the Village of Youngstown is rarely mentioned and when it is, the village is usually considered in passing as a minor Niagara River crossing place to Canada. One of the most cited early writers was Eber M. Pettit, who was an UGRR conductor who kept a station and eating house at a river crossing of the Cattaraugus River in Cattaraugus County, New York. He collected and published his reminiscences and interviews, first anonymously as "the Conductor" in the Fredonia (New York) *Censor* in 1868 and then, under pressure by his newspaper editor, in an 1879 book under his own name. For Pettit, the main line to Canada went to the Niagara River via Buffalo and Black Rock (near Buffalo);[4] Youngstown was important only in connection with the Youngstown Ferry in a story about a fugitive slave named Cassey.[5] Another early work that became authoritative was Wilbur H. Siebert's *The Underground Railroad from Slavery to Freedom: A Comprehensive History"* (1898). Siebert clearly knew about Youngstown and referred to Underground Railroad sites not far away,[6] but he never discussed Youngstown.[7] From these authoritative accounts, it would be easy to conclude that Youngstown had little, if any, role in the Underground Railroad.

These opinions were not without some foundation. Youngstown did not have the status in the Underground Railroad that larger, more populated towns such as Syracuse, Rochester, Lockport, Buffalo, and Niagara Falls had. Yet, this little river village should not be ignored. Certainly, local historians have not forgotten it. An example is *The Youngstown Centennial Magazine 1854-1954* published in 1954. Its articles were written by local authors, most of

---

[3] See Alan White, "Origins [of the Underground Railroad]," http://www.undergroundrailroad.org.uk/ur-origins.htm.

[4] Eber M. Pettit, *Sketches in the History of the Underground Railroad* (Westfield, NY: Chautauqua Region Press, 1879, Introduction by Willard McKinstry); reprinted with an Introduction with Notes by Paul Leone (Westfield, NY: Chautauqua Region Press, 1999).

[5] See Ch. 13.

[6] See Ch. 11.

[7] Siebert, *The Underground Railroad,*

whom lived their lives in Youngstown, some of whom could claim descent from early settlers. The following two statements appeared in this commemorative magazine:

> Youngstown figured in the slavery days when it served as a station in [on] the Underground Railway in which run-away slaves were transferred north from point to point and at this location crossed the river to Canada.

> Youngstown once had a horse ferry.[8]

Several years ago, these statements piqued Gretchen Duling's historical curiosity. She was inspired to dig deeper into the history of the UGRR and get information about the ferries of Youngstown that freedom seekers used to cross the Niagara River.

More recent historians have briefly mentioned Youngstown and we shall draw upon them later. At this point we highlight the most important published work to date. Not long after Gretchen began researching the UGRR in 2010, Judith Wellman and her research team (see Acknowledgements) were at work assembling UGRR information about the city of Niagara Falls, New York, most of the results of which were written by Wellman herself. By 2012, the team had developed an informative, fact-filled website about the city. The effort was sponsored by the Niagara Falls Underground Railroad Heritage Commission and managed by Tanya Lee Warren.[9] Eventually, the team extended its research into Niagara County as a whole and assembled some of the same UGRR information about Youngstown that Gretchen had found. At this Niagara Falls site, redesigned by Ally Spongr in 2016, three sections are especially important for Youngstown's role in the Underground Railroad.

> 1) "Site of the Ferry Landing at **Youngstown**" (**Judith Wellman**). Go to the Underground Railroad Heritage Area site (http://www.niagarafallsundergroundrailroad.org/), click on "UGRR SITES" and scroll down to "Site of the Ferry Landing at Youngstown," then click

---

[8] Edwin L. and Virginia M. Howard, "The History of Youngstown," *The Youngstown Centennial Magazine 1854-1954,* 19 and 15, respectively.
[9] For Tanya Lee Warren's management of the Cayuga County database, see the footnote on David Green Wheelbanks, Ch. 7 in this book.

on "READ MORE" and "Click here."[10] Wellman's article briefly summarizes material about Thomas James, Samuel Ringgold Ward, John P. VanDeusen, and Cassey, four of the persons we discuss in more detail in this book.[11]

2) This article is also found at the site as pages 177-81 under *Niagara Falls Underground Railroad Heritage Area Management Plan Appendix C: Survey of Sites Relation to the Underground Railroad. Abolitionism and African American Life in Niagara Falls and Surrounding Area, 1820-1880. Historic Resources Survey Report* (April 2012). *Part II*. Go to the Underground Railroad Heritage Area site (http://www.niagarafallsundergroundrailroad.org/), click on "HISTORY," then click on "HISTORICAL RESOURCES SURVEY," and then "Click here" to download Appendix C (PDF).[12]

3) "People and Sites Relating to the Underground Railroad, Abolitionism, and African American Life, 1820-1880 Niagara Falls and Niagara County" (The Wellman Team Database managed by Tanya Lee Warren). Go to the Underground Railroad Heritage Area site (http://www.niagarafallsundergroundrailroad.org/), click on "HISTORY," then "DATABASE," then "Click here" to download the Database (PDF). Seventy pages of data will load, which can be searched with "Control F." This site includes the four Youngstown sources; it also notes the saga of fugitive slave Ben Hockley[13] and has a brief comment about Thomas Birnmore (spelled as "Binmore," as is usually the case in UGRR literature[14]), both important for this book.

In early 2014, Gretchen's husband Dennis was drawn into her studies of Youngstown and the Underground Railroad. It has evolved into a joint project, and so the plural "we" is

---

[10] One can go there directly. http://www.niagarafallsundergroundrailroad.org/assets/Uploads/24-Site-of-the-Ferry-Landing-at-Youngstown.pdf.

[11] Judith Wellman, "Site of the Ferry Landing at Youngstown," http://www.niagarafallsundergroundrailroad.org/assets/Uploads/Niagara-Falls-Underground-Railroad-Project-Database.pdf. The name is spelled "VanDeusen" (one word), not as one would expect, "Van Deusen"; VanDeusen wrote his *Diary* in Newark, New York, not Palmyra, New York. See Ch. 10.

[12] One can go there directly. http://www.niagarafallsundergroundrailroad.org/assets/Uploads/NF-HAMP-Report-Appendix-C-1.pdf.

[13] For John P. VanDeusen, see Ch. 12 and Appendix 6.

[14] For a brief discussion of the two spellings, see Ch. 11.

normally used.[15] We have not only pursued the materials mentioned by the Wellman team in greater detail, but we have developed more information about them and their historical contexts, made a number of new historical discoveries along the way, and attempted to document the fuller story of Youngstown and some of its citizens as part of a more extensive regional and local Underground Railroad network in Western New York.

History, Historians, and the Underground Railroad

This book is primarily a historical study. In the late Nineteenth Century, there was a reaction against both abstract, grand philosophical theories of history on the one hand, and undocumented, opinionated, and romanticized versions of history on the other.[16] The so-called "science" of history was born. This meant that the object of historians was to reconstruct "what really happened" by investigating the written and material remains of the past ("primary sources") and to reconstruct an "objective" account that had no presuppositions. Their legacy mostly survives: professional historians still take objective, factual "historial accuracy" very seriously. That is also the case among UGRR historians. It appears especially with their rejection of fanciful speculations about supposed UGRR sites, such as secret tunnels.

Yet, most contemporary historians recognize that writing history is not a totally objective, scientific enterprise. Historians cannot repeat controlled experiments in the laboratory to test the validity of their theories and reconstructions; they must interpret—and interpretation always includes subjective opinion. They understand that their primary sources are what *some* people in the past remembered, selected, and preserved—usually a few educated, literate men from the dominant ruling classes. This means that much, perhaps most, of human history has been lost forever. Yet, some information from the past survives and some has been rediscovered by careful research, the discovery of lost documents, archaeology, and new methods of research. Intepretation remains. For example, there are competing images of

---

[15] More detail about the team is found in the description of the authors at the end of the book.

[16] The "father of modern historiography," Leopold von Ranke (1795–1886), believed the historian's main task was to gather and correlate facts from primary sources and then describe "what really happened" (*wle as eigentlich gewesen* [*ist*]) as neutrally as possible without resorting to any interpretative theory. See Leopold von Ranke, "*Vorrede der ersten Ausgabe, Okt. 1824,*' in *Geschichte der romanischen und germanischen Völker von 1494 bis 1514 zur Kritik neuerer Geschichtsschreiber* (3. Ausgabe; *Leipzig, Germany: Verlag Duncker und Humblot,* 1885) 5.vii.

George Washington: the aristocratic, slave-owning Washington; the democratic, manumitting Washington; and the synthesized Washington.[17] Interpretation of the past has often been manipulated as a powerful tool for ethnic, racial, and nationalistic propaganda. More recently, histories that highlight politically and militarily powerful men have been counterbalanced by a more inclusive, diversified revisionist "social studies" history: "the common people's history," "black history," "Native American/Canadian history," and "women's history." David Lowenthal, author of a classic called *The Past is a Foreign Country* (1985; 2015), has added to these more inclusive revisions the subjectivity of the historian's own human imperfections:

> It is salutary to be reminded that we [historians] are perforce fallible not only epistmically [how we know what we think we know] but also personally, subjugated not only to our slippery subject matter but to our slippery selves. To the genre's own insuperable limitations—data that are always selective and never complete; the unbridgeable gulf between actual pasts and any accounts of them; bias stemming from temporal distance, from hindsight, and from narrative needs—we must add, and keep in mind, human frailty. Hence we rightly accede to perpetual revision of our work. Continual correction is mandatory not only because new data keep coming to light, new insights keep arising, and the passage of time outdates earlier judgments, but also because we recognize that we never wholly live up to the demanding tenets of our trade.[18]

UGRR historical study mirrors the attempt to be factually objective and the recognition of subjectivity and therefore, the need for constant revision. As noted, Wilbur H. Siebert wrote an important, classic work, *The Underground Railroad from Slavery to Freedom, A Comprehensive History* (1898 [reprint 2006]);[19] it is full of detailed information, some from

---

[17] Barry Schwartz, "Social Change and Collective Memory: The Democratization of George Washington," *American Sociological Review* 56/2 (1991) 221–236; Schwartz holds that the past is not a foreign country, but a familiar country (see following note).

[18] David Lowenthal, "The Frailty of Historical Truth: Learning Why Historians Inevitably Err," *Perspectives on History. Magazine of the American Historical Association.* https://www.historians.org/publications-and-directories/perspectives-on-history/march-2013/the-frailty-of-historical-truth. See Lowenthal, *The Past is a Foreign Country* (Cambridge, UK: Cambridge University Press, 1985; revised 2015).

[19] See Appendix 2.

participant-observers. The work is still a valuable source for historical reconstruction. However, in 1961 Larry Gara argued in his book *The Liberty Line* that Siebert had focused far too much on mostly white European American abolitionists, agents, and conductors helping African American fugitive slaves escape and not enough on the role that African Americans themselves played. For Gara, earlier historians had transformed the Underground Railroad into a "legend." What in his view was missing? Recognition that "[i]t was often the *slaves themselves* who took things into their own hands."[20] Gara's revisionist history of the UGRR emerged as an extremely important corrective. Indeed, for many years Gara's work was normative.[21]

Yet, Gara's revisionist version of the UGRR has, as one might expect, been subject to revision. New York Underground Railroad historian Judith Wellman gladly accepts Gara's major criticism, but she also draws attention to Gara's lament in a reprint of his book some thirty-five years later (1996), namely, that, ". . . were I to write the book again, I would give more recognition to the abolitionists."[22] Wellman argues that Gara's 1961 corrective was absolutely necessary, but it was typified by too many broad, sweeping generalizations at the *national* level and needs to be corrected by research at the *local* level.[23]

Using sources related to Oswego County, New York, this essay will suggest that, while the legendary version of the underground railroad exaggerates (or omits) parts of the story, Gara's revisionist version does not give the whole picture, either. In fact, any attempt to generalize about the underground railroad nationally cannot account for its tremendous diversity over time and place. In order to develop a more sophisticated understanding of the underground railroad, we need to develop detailed studies of specific events and people in specific places. Only then can we begin to discover how these related to the larger whole . . . We can transform [Gara's] conclusions into hypotheses to test at the local level. We may find, for example, that sometimes

---

[20] Larry Gera, *The Liberty Line* (Lexington, KY: The University Press of Kentucky, 1961; reprint 1996) 42 (italics ours).
[21] For more critiques, see Lauren Elizabeth Burton, *Evaluating the National Underground Railroad Network to Freedom Program of the National Park Service* (M.A. Thesis; Philadelphia, PA: University of Pennsylvania, 2014); Gara's perspective is reaching the public in award-winning television programs, for example, Henry Louis Gates, Jr.'s instructive *Many Rivers to Cross*. http://www.pbs.org/wnet/african-americans-many-rivers-to-cross/history/who-really-ran-the-underground-railroad/. See http://en.wikipedia.org/wiki/Henry_Louis_Gates, Jr.
[22] Gara, *The Liberty Line* (Reprint 1996) xii.
[23] This is a well known critique by ethnologists about overly generalized theorizing.

underground railroad activities were secret, sometimes not. Sometimes they were organized, sometimes not. Sometimes whites were involved as helpers, sometimes African Americans were helpers, sometimes both. Sometimes large numbers of fugitives found assistance, sometimes few. Sometimes fugitives found their way North with little or no help; sometimes guides accompanied them every step of the way. Sometimes the underground railroad was an important "propaganda device"; sometimes it was more important as an aid to fugitives. Finally, neither the traditional legend nor Gara's revisionist version dealt with gender or with the experience of freedom seekers who settled on the U.S. side of the border.[24]

In recent years, *local* UGRR studies like Wellman's have become more and more common. Underground Railroad historian Eric Foner emphasizes that Wilbur Siebert's image of a highly organized, "'great and intricate network' of stations leading to Canada," buttressed with many maps, was overdrawn. To be sure, Siebert ". . . laid the groundwork for all future study of the subject" and that therefore the information generated by Siebert's questionnaires "cannot be entirely discounted."[25] Yet, like Wellman, Foner stresses the necessity of collecting information about *local* networks of both European Americans and African Americans—whites and blacks—and determining how they were *loosely* organized. He is favorably disposed to Fergus M. Bordewich's work *Bound for Canaan*, which also respects Gara's revisionism, but nonetheless stresses the necessity of local research.[26]

> The picture that emerges from recent studies [of the Underground Railroad] is not of the highly organized system with tunnels, codes, and clearly defined routes and stations of popular lore, but of an *interlocking series of local networks*, each of whose fortunes rose and fell over time, but which together helped a substantial number of fugitives reach safety in the free states and Canada . . . The "underground railroad"

---

[24] Judith Wellman, "Larry Gara's Liberty Line in Oswego County, New York, 1838—1854: A New Look at the Legend," *Afro-Americans in New York Life and History*, 2001. https://www.questia.com/read/1P3-494776751/larry-gara-s-liberty-line-in-oswego-county-n.

[25] Foner, *Gateway to Freedom*, 12, 14.

[26] Ibid. Fergus M. Bordewich, *Bound for Canaan: The Epic Story of the Underground Railroad, American's First Civil Rights Movement* (New York, NY: Amistad, 2005; New York, NY: HarperCollins, 2006).

should be understood not as a single entity but as *an umbrella term for local groups* that employed numerous methods to assist fugitives, some public and entirely legal, some flagrant violations of the law.[27]

Even though exact UGRR routes are difficult to determine, a useful attempt to find regional networks and various routes in a general way is William J. Switala's *Underground Railroad in New York and New Jersey*.[28]

Wellman, Foner, Bordewich, and Switala emphasize that local histories of the Underground Railroad, particularly in the North, can be partially reconstructed based on surviving sources—if they are carefully and cautiously sifted and weighed. These sources would include genealogical and census data (names, ages, gender, boarders, tenants, workers, race, slaves, free, trade, education); documents in state and local archives, museums, and libraries; autobiographies and memoirs; state and county records; newspapers; periodicals; directories; almanacs; gazetteers; calendars; foreign records; records of anti-slavery societies and "vigilance committees"; benevolent groups and churches; legal documents and court records; records and stories about ferries and steam boats; manuscript collections; historic maps; cemetery records; and "Negro spirituals." There are also secondary sources such as state, regional, and town/village histories, histories of the early UGRR historians such as Pettit and Siebert, and more recent, critical histories.[29]

---

[27] Foner, *Gateway to Freedom*, 15. It should be noted that Siebert, too, sometimes emphasized local networks, e.g., *The Underground Railroad*, 30: "With the growth of a thing so unfavorable as was the Underground Railroad, local conditions must have (had) a great deal to do. The characteristics of small and scattered localities and even of isolated families, are of the first importance in the consideration of a movement such as this. These little communities were in general the elements out of which the underground system built itself up."

[28] William J. Switala, *Underground Railroad in New York and New Jersey* (Mechanicsburg, PA: Stockpole Books, 2006).

[29] Judith Wellman and Marjory Allen Perez, with Charles Lenhart and others, "Uncovering Sites Related to the Underground Railroad, Abolitionism, and African American Life in Wayne County, New York, 1820-1880," Wayne County Historian's Office, Peter Evans, Historian; also, Wellman, "Bibliography." Wellman, *Uncovering the Freedom Trail. The Underground Railroad, Abolitionism, and African American Life Syracuse and Onondaga County, 1820-70*. Project sponsored by the Preservation Association of Central New York, with funding from Preserve New York, Preservation League of New York State, 2001-2002.
http://www.oswego.edu/Acad_Dept/a_and_s/history/uggr/guide/html; National Park Service, "Exploring a Common Past." Researching and Interpreting the Underground Railroad. Part II: Using Primary Sources: the Historians' Toolbox." https://www.nps.gov/parkhistory/online_books/ugrr/exugrr3.htm.

Given all these variables and revisions, are there criteria to evaluate the sources of the UGRR past, which was so secretive? One way that has become normative for many UGRR historians is the "Wellman Scale," put forward by Judith Wellman. A short version of her scale for evaluting sources looks like this:[30]

Oral Tradition contradicted by evidence;	Oral Tradition; no written evidence;	Oral Tradition plus circumstantial evidence; (e.g., physical)	Some written evidence, but no direct primary source;	Conclusive written evidence with primary sources;
probably not true	possibly true	probably true	almost certainly true	almost certainly true

Image 0.3. The Wellman Scale

The Wellman Scale uses the word "true," but truth is qualfied by the terms "possibly," "probably," and "almost certainly." It is not a scale of absolute truth, but a *scale of ascending probability*—from oral tradition that is contradicted; to oral tradition with no written evidence; to oral tradition supported by circumstantial evidence (often physical—artifacts and professional archaeological judgments); to some written, indirect evidence; and finally to written primary sources. Note that this probability/improbability scale is not simply the value of the *source*, which is implied, but also the value of its historical *content*. While these two dimensions usually reinforce each other—the most valuable information is usually found in the most valuable sources—some sources give valuable information about persons and places in the UGRR, but no direct information about the UGRR itself. One example is census data.

With respect to sources, it is clear that in the Wellman Scale *written* primary evidence is valued most highly. Yet, oral tradition, carefully analyzed, is not discarded; even without written evidence, or with only circumstantial evidence, it can be evaluated as "possibly true" or "probably true." Wellman underscores this point in her recent study, "Oral Traditions and

---

[30] For the long version, see Ch. 17.

Beyond: A Guide to Documenting the Underground Railroad." With a nod in the direction of social (as contrasted with individual) memory, it assumes

> . . . as a working hypothesis that most Underground Railroad stories contain at least a nugget of historical fact and that historians can use oral traditions as one of many essential sources to help bring the past into clearer focus . . . Underground Railroad stories are exactly those kinds of events most likely to be kept alive through oral history. They were generally local, personal, and unofficial, exactly the kinds of experiences that were not likely to be recorded in written documents. To those involved, however, whether as freedom seekers or as helpers, such events were etched into their memories as defining moments of their lives—dramatic, often traumatic, and certainly for freedom seekers, at least, life-changing.[31]

From this persepctive, oral *tradition* handed down from generation to generation—stories, legends, anecdotes, slogans, tall tales, personal names, place names, and the like—can sometimes be very valuable. Oral *history*—the information derived from oral interviews with living informants, whether participants or descendants of participants—must be taken seriously and evaluated. Some oral stories are preserved secondarily in writing and in the case of the UGRR some of those are testimonies that come from fugitive slaves themselves. Analysis often makes it possible to find in such sources Wellman's "nuggets of historical truth" that compliment written sources. Especially important in her view is trauma memory, individual or collective.[32] Sorting out probability and improbability in the various kinds of sources, including oral sources, then, is difficult, but not impossible and potentially rewarding. That task is important for UGRR historians.

---

[31] Judith Wellman, "Oral Traditions and Beyond: A Guide to Documenting the Underground Railroad" (unpublished manuscript). For the UGRR and memory theory, see also David W. Blight, *Passages to Freedom: The Underground Railroad in History and Memory* (Washington, DC: Smithsonian Books in Association with the National Underground Railroad Freedom Center, 2004). We add that oral tradition research has a more than 200-year history. See Gretchen A. Duling, *Voices From The Recitation Bench: Oral Life Histories of Rural One-Room School House Retired Career Teachers from Southeastern Ohio* (Lewiston, NY: Edwin Mellen Press, 19970; in Biblical research; see Dennis C. Duling, "Memory, Collective Memory, Orality, and the Gospels," *HTS Teologiese Studies/Theological Studies* 67/1 (2011) 103-113 (The A.G. van Aarde *Festschrift*) online at http://www.hts.org.za/index.php/HTS/article/view/915/1496 Art. #915, 11 pages. DOI: 10.4102/hts.v67i1.915.
[32] Trauma memory is a debated topic in memory research, much discussed in relation to repressed memory, false memory, and Post-Traumatic Stress Disorder (PTSD); see Dennis C. Duling, ibid.

Underground Railroad Networks

As noted previously, Judith Wellman, Eric Foner, Fergus M. Bordewich, and William J. Switala think that Siebert's notion of a *national, highly organized* UGRR network is overdrawn, but that they nevertheless maintain and stress the strategic importance of *local, loose, interlocking* UGRR networks, particularly in the North, that can be carefully and cautiously researched and at least partially reconstructed. A further word about networks is worth consideration.

There is a difference between the *activity* of social networking, such as on Facebook or Twitter, and carefully *analyzing and describing* networks of persons and places, which consists of the connections between or among them, and how they operate. This analysis is an academic field of study called Social Network Analysis (SNA). Contemporary SNA can generate massive amounts of data—polls and hashtags, for example—and analyze it with sophisticated logarithms in software programs. One well known conclusion, now increasingly accepted, is that people tend to share views with people with whom they agree. They reinforce their views, whether factual or not: "birds of a feather flock together" (clusters). Historians cannot electronically generate massive new data sets from the past and analyze them with such mathematically articulated precision. Yet, they do make new discoveries and they can construct network diagrams or "sociograms," however crude, as heuristic models that simplify and aid in explanation and understanding complex information.[33] These illustrate persons and places, the connections between and among them, and what is being passed on through the network.

In short, it is possible to imagine the Underground Railroad as a large, loosely connected umbrella network made up of smaller, local, loosely connected, networks of persons (agents, conductors, or station masters) and places ("stations" or safe houses at crossroads or in villages, towns), and what is passed on *to* fugitive slaves passing through it whether material (food, clothing, shelter) or immaterial (information, routes, modes of transportation, the next station, slave catcher density, and the like)—or passing on *the fugitive slaves themselves*. These

---

[33] See Dennis C. Duling, "Paul's Aegean Network: The Strength of Strong Ties," *Biblical Theology Bulletin* 43/3 (2013) 135-54; "The Jesus Movement and Social Network Analysis," pp. 301-32 in Bruce J. Malina, Wolfgang Stegemann, and Gerd Theissen, editors, *The Social Setting of Jesus and the Gospels* (Minneapolis, MN: Fortress Press, 2002) (published also in German and Italian translations).

networks help fugitive slaves reach their ultimate goal: freedom from slavery. More detail about SNA in general is found in Appendix 1. Part of the regional network in which Youngstown is a part will be illustrated with simplified sociograms in Chapters 10 and 17.

Summary

This book attempts to solidify the historical fact that the Village of Youngstown in the Town of Porter in Niagara County in New York State had a legitimate place in the Underground Railroad network. It will tap a wide variety of sources, including oral traditions, and it will use the Wellman Scale to evaluate them. It will suggest that within the surviving materials that we investigate and analyze, both written and oral, Youngstown had a role in Underground Railroad history, one that is more significant than has often been acknowledged. It is a role that should not be ignored.

PART I
Contexts

The first six chapters of this book attempt to prepare the way for understanding the role of the Niagara River village of Youngstown, New York, in the Underground Railroad. **Chapter 1** offers a general introduction to slavery and abolition, comparing and contrasting Canada with the United States. **Chapter 2** gives sketches of the American Anti-Slavery Society, the New York Anti-Slavery Society, and the Niagara County Anti-Slavery Society, with lists of 1855 anti-slavery meeting locations that include Youngstown. Three New York State Underground Railroad leaders are noted. **Chapter 3** presents some nineteenth-century census data for Niagara County, including African Americans, and compares this data to similar data in Niagara, Lower Canada (Niagara-on-the-Lake, Ontario); it concludes with a brief discussion of some possibilities about the United States military position on capturing and returning escaped slaves, especially after 1850, in relation to nearby Fort Niagara. **Chapter 4** opens up the problems of, and solutions to, crossing inland waterways in the United States, illustrating them with various kinds of watercraft with a special emphasis on ferries; it includes watercraft that were built at, used at, or put in to, Youngstown. **Chapter 5** details trains and bridges that were important for crossing the Niagara River and the short-lived trains that went to Youngstown. **Chapter 6** presents unpublished sources about Youngstown's ferrymen—and a ferrywoman!

CHAPTER 1

Slavery, Fugitive Slaves, and the Underground Railroad: Canada and the United States

From E. T. Foote's *Antislavery Scrapbook*
Used by permission from the New York Chautauqua County Historical Society[1]
Image 1.1

From the *Life of the Rev. Thomas James by Himself* (1886)

. . . I was born a slave at Canajoharie, this state [New York], in the year 1804. I was the third of four children, and we were all the property of Asa Kimball, who, when I was in the eighth year of my age, sold my mother, brother and elder sister to purchasers from Smithtown, a village not far distant from Amsterdam in the same part of the state. My mother refused to go and ran into the garret [small attic room] to seek a hiding place. She was pursued, caught, tied hand and foot and delivered to her new owner. I

---

[1] Images from E. T. Foote's *Antislavery Handbook* will be used with permission from the New York Chautauqua County Historical Society at the beginning of each chapter, but hereafter without repeating the source and permission.

caught my last sight of my mother as they rode off with her. My elder brother and sister were taken away at the same time. I never saw either my mother or sister again. Long years afterwards my brother and I were reunited, and he died in this city a little over a year ago. From him I learned that my mother died about the year 1846 in the place to which she had been taken. My brother also informed me that he and his sister were separated soon after their transfer to a Smithport [Tennessee] master, and that he never heard of her subsequent fate. Of my father I never had any personal knowledge, and, indeed, never heard anything. My other sister, the youngest member of the family, died when I was yet a youth.

While I was still in the seventeenth year of my age [1821?], Master Kimball was killed in a runaway accident; and at the administrator's sale I was sold with the rest of the property, my new master being Cromwell Bartlett of the same neighborhood. As I remember, my first master was a well-to-do but rough farmer, a skeptic in religious matters, but of better heart than address; for he treated me well. He owned several farms and my work was that of a farmhand. My new master had owned me but a few months [late 1821 to March 1822?] when he sold me, or rather traded me, to George H. Hess, a wealthy farmer of the vicinity of Fort Plain [New York]. I was bartered in exchange for a yoke of steers, a colt and some additional property, the nature and amount of which I have now forgotten. I remained with Master Hess from March until June of the same year, when I ran away. My master had worked me hard, and at last undertook to whip me. This led me to seek escape from slavery. I arose in the night, and taking the then newly staked line of the Erie Canal for my route, traveled along it westward until, about a week later, I reached the village of Lockport [New York]. No one had stopped me in my flight. Men were at work digging the new canal at many points, but they never troubled themselves even to question me. I slept in barns at night and begged food at farmers' houses along my route. At Lockport a colored man showed me the way to the Canadian border. *I crossed the Niagara [River] at Youngstown on the ferry boat, and was free!*[2]

Some sixty-five years had passed when Thomas James recalled these dramatic events from his past. Behind them lay a transnational history related to the horrendous experience of the enslavement of human beings, a history in the United States and a history in Canada. Those histories converged at that one moment in 1821 when James crossed the Niagara River on the Youngstown Ferry and set foot in Niagara[on-the-Lake], Canada.

It is important to back up and recall what was happening not only in the decades before Thomas James wrote in 1886, but even before he was born in 1804. It is a transnational story.

Slavery and Abolition of Slavery in Upper Canada

One way to illustrate the move toward abolition of slavery in Upper Canada (Ontario) is to tell the well known story of the slave Chloe Cooley.

Chloe Cooley, Queenston, Ontario, Canada, 1793

A succinct account of the tragic story of the slave Chloe Cooley has been summarized by Queenston, Ontario, resident and local historian, Linda Fritz.

On the crisp spring morning of March 14, 1793, near the village of Queenston, screams were heard coming first from a nearby farm and later, down by the river. Her body bound, Chloe Cooley, a young enslaved girl, was forced onto a boat against her will and taken across the Niagara River [to Lewiston, New York] to be sold to an American.

On Wednesday, March 21, 1793, Peter Martin, a free black and former Butler's Ranger, and William Grisley, a neighbour who had witnessed the event, appeared before members of the government's executive council. Present at the meeting were Lieutenant Governor John Graves Simcoe, Chief Justice William Osgoode and the Honourable Peter Russell, a prominent slave owner. Martin told the council that a

---

[2] Thomas James, *Life of Rev. Thomas James, by Himself* (Rochester, NY: Post Express Printing Company, 1886) 5-6 (italics ours). Thomas James's story is developed in Ch. 7.

violent outrage had occurred to an African Canadian woman named Chloe Cooley, who had worked for him. A resident of Queenston named William Vrooman, Chloe's master, had decided to sell her in New York State. When she resisted, Vrooman forcibly transported her across the Niagara River to her new owner.

At the time, Vrooman was acting within his rights and could not be prosecuted. Since other [Canadian] slave owners were about to do the same thing with their slaves, Simcoe, an abolitionist, was concerned. He was determined that something must be done to prevent further acts of this nature.

Simcoe passed the first piece of legislation in the British Empire to limit slavery in 1793. . . [3]

Chloe's ultimate fate is unknown; however, witnesses and reports of her brave, heroic resistance by free black Peter Martin and William Grisley influenced Lieutenant Governor John Graves Simcoe to move forward a 1793 act to prohibit the further importation of slaves into Upper Canada, which was one step toward the abolition of slavery in the British Empire and Canada several decades later. The Ontario government has commissioned a historical plaque to honor Chloe Cooley. It is located on the Niagara Parkway at Vrooman's Point between Queenston and Niagara-on-the-Lake.

---

[3] Linda Fritz, "Chloe Cooley 1793," in Linda Fritz with Susan Allen, Helena Copeland, Maureen Ott, and Paulette Peggs, "Queenston," 49 (full reference below); See Michael Power, "Simcoe and Slavery," in Michael Power and Nancy Butler (with Joy Ormsby), *Slavery and Freedom in Niagara* (Niagara-on-the-Lake, ON: The Niagara Historical Society, 1993; reprint 2000) 9-39. This 1993 booklet celebrated the 1793 progress toward abolition in Upper Canada; it is online. For documented detail on Chloe Cooley and Solomon Moseby, see William Renwick Riddell, "Slave in Upper Canada," *Journal of Criminal Law and Criminology* (No. 249, May 1923 to February 1924) 14/2, Article 6 (1923) 249-78; for clear and succinct accounts, see Natasha L. Henry, "Chloe Cooley and the Act to Limit Slavery in Upper Canada," *The Canadian Encyclopedia* at the Historical Canada Learning Center. http://www.thecanadianencyclopedia.ca/en/article/chloe-cooley-and-the-act-to-limit-slavery-in-upper-canada/. James Reynolds, "American Canadians and the Underground Railroad" in James Reynolds and Jim Smith with Phebe Appleton and Terry Boulton, "Niagara-on-the-Lake," in Gretchen A. Duling, Dennis Duling, Karen Noonan, Toby Jewett, James Reynolds, James Smith, Linda Fritz, Michelle Kratts, and Teresa Sharp Donaldson, *From the Mouth of the Lower Niagara River: Stories of Four Historic Communities, Commemorating 200 Years of Peace on the Border*. Niagara Greenway Approved Projected funded by the Niagara County Host Community (Buffalo, NY: Goulah Design Group, 2012) 94.

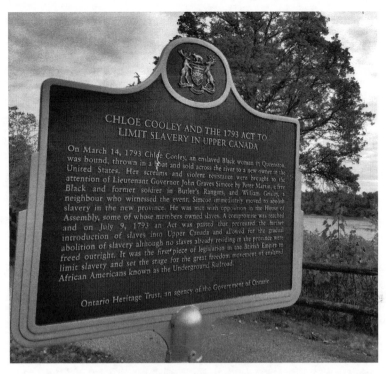

Chloe Cooley and the 1793 Act to Limit Slavery in Upper Canada
Queenston, Ontario, Canada, 1793
Photo by Dennis Duling
Image 1.2

Solomon Moseby in Niagara, [Niagara-on-the-Lake], 1837

Chloe Cooley's sacrifice and Simcoe's actions meant the beginnings of the abolition in Upper Canada. Canadian historian Nancy Butler reminds us, however, that the vestiges of slavery, which had been practiced in Upper Canada prior to 1793, did not suddenly and totally disappear. "In Niagara, [freedom seekers] . . . did not find a paradise. From the perspective of white society, their black skin still bore the imprint of shackles. Acceptance of blacks as equals came slowly. The blacks, dependent on good will, had to struggle to become truly free."[4]

---

[4] Butler, "Starting Anew: The Black Community of Early Niagara," in Power and Butler, *Slavery and Freedom in Niagara*, 72-73.

The act that abolished slavery throughout virtually the whole British Empire, including Upper Canada, was passed some forty years later in 1833 and activated in 1834.[5] Some Canadian slave owners, fearful of losing a considerable slave investment, were willing to sell their slaves to American slave owners, as had already happened, as in the case of Chloe in 1793. Even after 1834, a fugitive slave, now an African Canadian, could be extradited back to the United States if convicted of a crime. In the words of Butler again, ". . . the lieutenant governor [had] the power [in Upper Canada] to decide each case individually. A Slave could not be returned, however, unless he had committed a crime serious enough that under Canadian law he would have been punished with death, corporal punishment, or imprisonment with hard labour."[6]

So it happened that slave owners and their agents sought to have former slaves who had escaped to Canada tried for crimes such as murder or theft rather than as fugitives from slavery. This was the case of Solomon Moseby as summarized by local Canadian historian James Reynolds of Niagara-on-the-Lake, Ontario.

Slavery was abolished through the British Empire in 1833 but the law of Upper Canada continued to allow the extradition of slaves to the United States if it could be proven that they had committed a crime to make good their escape. Often slave hunters would appear before Canadian courts with documents purporting to prove that refugee slave was a horse thief or a murderer. In such cases the Canadian authorities seemed more than willing to cooperate in returning the victim of these allegations to his fate. Such was the case of Solomon Moseby.

Moseby was accused of stealing his master's horse in order to make good his escape from Kentucky. David Castleman, his former owner, arrived in Niagara in 1837 with a grand jury indictment from a Kentucky court. A Canadian official, with the blessing of the Lieutenant Governor Francis Bond Head, jailed Moseby and was ready to deport him. Castleman was abetted in his efforts by his brother-in-law Peter B. Porter of

---

[5] Exceptions to the 1833 law were territories possessed by the East India Company, the Island of Saint Helena, and the Island of Ceylon. Abolition of slavery took place in these areas in 1843. The celebration of the 1834 emancipation of the West Indies in Niagara Falls, New York, in 1856 is noted again in Ch. 14.
[6] Butler, "Starting Anew," 49-51.

Niagara Falls, New York, who lobbied Canadian officials upon the written advice from his friend Castleman to pursue Moseby as a criminal and not as an escaped slave. . .

Under the leadership of Herbert Holmes, the pastor of the local Baptist congregation, several hundred members of the black community rallied and surrounded the jail, holding a vigil which lasted for several days. This group, made up in large measure of African-Canadian women, was determined that the captive should not be handed over. The Riot Act was read but the crowd refused to disperse and as Moseby came out of the jail, the crowd surged. Aided perhaps by sympathetic jailers, he slipped out of his shackles and disappeared. The soldiers fired upon the throng, killing two members of the community, Pastor Holmes and Jacob Green. Moseby made his way to freedom in England and it is said that he eventually returned to Niagara.[7]

We note that in some accounts of the Moseby episode, Deputy Sherriff Alexander McLeod attempted to enlist the captains of Niagara River steamboats to take Moseby to Lewiston, New York, but they refused.[8] One of those captains was purportedly Captain Hugh Richardson, known for his aid to fugitive slaves.[9] Another version by William Renwick Riddell

---

[7] James Reynolds, "American Canadians and the Underground Railroad," in Gretchen Duling *et al*, *From the Mouth*, 95. For more about the black experience of arrival in Canada, see Butler, "Starting Anew." For detail on Cooley and Moseby, see Patricia Frazier, "Niagara's Negroes Kept Vigil at Jail," *Niagara Advance, Historical Issue* (1976); Riddell, "Slave in Upper Canada," 249-78.

[8] Hiram Wilson, Letter dated October 26, 1837, published in *Friend of Man* (November 22, 1837), cited in Breaking the Chains. Tubman Institute.
http://breakingthechains.tubmaninstitute.ca/sites/breakingthechains.tubmaninstitute.ca/files/Report%20moseby.pdf.

[9] Janet Carnochan, "Slave Rescue in Canada Sixty Years Ago," *Niagara Historical Society* 2 (1897) 13-14, cited in Breaking the Chains. Tubman Institute.
http://breakingthechains.tubmaninstitute.ca/sites/breakingthechains.tubmaninstitute.ca/files/Report%20moseby.pdf; see further, David Murray, *Colonial Justice: Justice, Morality, and Crime in the Niagara District, 1791-1849* (Toronto, ON: University of Toronto Press, 2003) 208, cited in Judith Wellman, "Lewiston Landing," *Niagara Falls Underground Railroad Heritage Area Management Plan Appendix C: Survey of Sites Relation to the Underground Railroad. Abolitionism, and African American Life in Niagara Falls and Surrounding Area, 1820-1880. Historic Resources Survey Report* (April 2012). *Part II*, 181-92 and n. 326.
http://www.niagarafallsundergroundrailroad.org/assets/Uploads/NF-HAMP-Report-Appendix-C-1.pdf. This same Sherriff McLeod was tried for the murder of an African American in relation to the *Caroline* Affair of 1837; see Appendix 8.

says simply that McLeod wanted Moseby ". . . to go to the Ferry across the Niagara River," which could have been the ferry from Queenston to Lewiston or from Niagara to Youngstown.[10]

Despite the mixed experiences of African Americans in Canada, a sizeable African American Community developed in Upper Canada, perhaps about 30,000 by 1852.[11] Once across the Niagara River some purchased land and settled in the Town of Niagara (changed to Niagara-on-the-Lake by the postal service in the late nineteenth century to avoid confusion with the region below the escarpment, also called Town of Niagara). Within Niagara an area with cheaper lots evolved into what became known as "the colored village." Most of these villagers arrived before 1840 and were well known by members of the general population. The small houses they built on their lots allowed for large gardens. Some black immigrants purchased a cow, or a horse, or both. Members of the colored village looked after each other and took in single people who had no home. Jobs were sought outside of the village when they became available. There was a rather high level of illiteracy among these new immigrants and schooling issues had to be addressed. St. Andrew's Presbyterian Church in Niagara started the first Sunday School for black children in order to address what they believed was their lack of moral development. Even though there were local anxieties about these new black people arriving in British North America, it needs to be emphasized that in the majority of cases they were exemplary community residents, especially because many of them yearned to become citizens of the country they now embraced.

After the *1850 Fugitive Slave Act* in the United States there was an increase in the number of black fugitives entering British North America, but in Niagara the black population changed modestly in nineteen years (82 in 1842 and 104 in 1861). The main reason for slow growth seems to have been that Niagara's economy was in decline and so was its population. Perhaps the reason was that a fugitive slave chose not to remain in Niagara after crossing the

---

[10] Riddell, Slave in Upper Canada, 263.

[11] The First Report of the Anti-Slavery Society of Canada cited in Benjamin Drew, *The Refugee or the Narratives of Fugitive Slaves in Canada Related by Themselves with an Account of the History and Condition of the Colored Population of Upper Canada* (Boston, MA: John P. Jewett and Company, 1856) estimated about 30,000 Africans in Upper Canada (Preface, v). Drew noted about 800 for St. Catharines (p. 17) or 13.33% of the inhabitants. Population estimates for Canada as a whole have ranged widely from 11,000 to 60,000. See William J. Switala, *Underground Railroad in New York and New Jersey* (Mechanicsburg, PA: Stackpole Books, 2006) 146.

river when other towns like St. Catharines could offer work and larger black communities that could provide familiar churches.

Yet, some of people of the "colored village" remained in Niagara and prospered.

William and Susannah Steward House in the "Coloured Village" (ca. 1835), Niagara-on-the-Lake, Ontario, Canada[12]
Photo by Dennis Duling
Image 1.3

Headstone   **Historical Marker (1830)**
Negro Burial Ground
Niagara-on-the-Lake, Ontario, Canada
Photos by Dennis Duling
Images 1.4a & 4b

---

[12] "William and Susanna Steward House," http://www.heritagetrust.on.ca/CMSImages/be/beef58ca-f187-4930-89a3-67d62ffeed70.pdf. William Steward and sixteen other blacks signed a petition to Lieutenant Governor Sir Francis Bond not to extradite ex-slave Solomon Moseby to the United States. Although they came from the United States, it is not known whether they were fugitive slaves.

Because of the location of Youngstown across the Lower Niagara River from Niagara, its history is interwoven with Niagara[-on-the-Lake], Canada. The history of the area is therefore transnational, a fact that is reflected in the timeline at the end of this chapter.[13]

Slavery in the United States

The first slaves were brought to Jamestown, Virginia, by the Dutch in 1619.[14] When the Declaration of Independence was signed on July 4, 1776, there were about 500,000 slaves, about one-fifth of the American population. The rich southern agricultural economy based on tobacco, rice, indigo, and sugar—cotton did not become profitable until 1793, after the advent of the cotton gin—utilized slave labor and, although many founding fathers detested the institution in theory, in practice many of them owned slaves.

The first United States Constitution, the Articles of Confederation of 1781, was silent on the subject of slavery. States rights were a continual area of contention and the new government left the delicate and divisive matter of slavery to the individual states. The 1781 Articles were weak and in the years following several key issues arose between northern and southern states. One of them was representation in Congress. After much debate, a Constitutional Convention in 1787 settled on the "Great Compromise": there would be a Senate with two elected members from each state and a House of Representatives with members from each state based on population; a slave would count as three-fifths a person, a tilt toward the southern states which had heavy slave populations; and an end to the slave trade by 1808. Tragically, the new Constitution contained a "slave clause"—a Fugitive Slave Law—that was put into practice on February 12, 1793—the year of Canada's move to prohibit the importation of slaves and Chloe's tragic sale to a United States master. This law stated:

> No person held to service or labour in one state, under the laws thereof,
> escaping into another, shall, in consequence of any law or regulation therein, be

---

[13] Reynolds, "American Canadians and the Underground Railroad," 94-95. The timeline is modified from "Black History Canada," www.blackhistorycanada.ca/timeline.php?id=1800.
[14] The National Geographic interactive timeline of slavery, http://nationalgeographic.org/interactive/slavery-united-states/ and "Abolition of Slavery Timeline," *Wikipedia*, https://en.wikipedia.org/wiki/Abolition_of_slavery_timeline.

discharged from such service or labour, but shall be delivered up on claim of the party to whom such service or labour may be due.[15]

Although some interpreters think that the inclusion of the phrase "under the laws thereof" meant simply that slavery was an issue of the individual states, in principle this law required that people in all states, including non-slave states, were obligated to return fugitive slaves to the service and labor of their owners. Slave owners or their agents from slave states could search for fugitive slaves in free states, apprehend them, bring them before a judge, give proof that they were property of a slave owner (usually by an affidavit), and if officials agreed, could be returned to owners in slave states or territories (Section 3). Persons who harbored, or helped to harbor, fugitive slaves were subject to a $500 fine (Section 4). However, northern states that gradually abolished the slave trade and slavery itself did not enforce this first fugitive slave law; indeed, some northern states countered by passing "personal liberty laws" that forbad cooperation in the capture or jailing of fugitive slaves and permitted trials for fugitive slaves. In short, the law was not strictly enforced in the North. Southern states were angered by this development.[16]

The slavery issue was not resolved and it surfaced again in relation to the admittance to the Union of the new states in the Southwest, that is, Texas (annexed) and the New Mexico and Utah Territories won in the Mexican-American War (1846-1848). As part of the *Compromise of 1850* Congress attempted to satisfy the North and appease the South. California could enter the Union as a non-slave state and the citizens of Utah and New Mexico could decide the issue themselves. However, as a conciliation to the South, officials, such as marshals, who did not carry out their obligations, for example, aiding escaping slaves from slave or non-slave states, were to be fined $1,000; citizens doing the same could be fined up to $1,000 and were liable to be incarcerated up to six months. Although a trial was permitted, a slave was not allowed to

---

[15] United States Constitution, Article IV, Section 2.3, superseded by Amendment XIII."The Avalon Project. Documents in Law, History and Diplomacy," Yale Law School, Lillian Goldman Law Library. http://avalon.law.yale.edu/18th_century/art4.asp.

[16] "The Constitution and Slavery," Constitutional Rights Foundation, http://www.crf-usa.org/black-history-month/the-constitution-and-slavery. These laws were ultimately superseded by the Thirteenth Amendment of the Constitution.

testify on his or her own behalf. The law also required that if the slave was found and captured, he or she should be sent back to the South, usually to the slave owner, because the slave was legally a form of personal property (chattel). In this case, a slave was most likely badly beaten and perhaps sold as an example to other slaves who might consider trying to escape to freedom.

There had been fugitive slaves who escaped to Canada, but others felt reasonably safe living in non-slave states in the northern United States. However, the new *Fugitive Slave Act of 1850* was more rigidly enforced than the 1793 Act. Moreover, anyone who helped fugitive slaves was disobeying federal law. Therefore, after 1850 many more African Americans left the States and fled to Canada. Yet, as before, many northerners, particularly abolitionists, resisted the new *Fugitive Slave Law*. Some more anti-kidnapping and personal liberty laws were passed. Vigilance Committees sought to protect fugitive slaves or rescue them from slave catchers or jails. In the wake of the famous Dred Scott decision, the Kansas-Nebraska Act,[17] and the widely publicized return of Anthony Burns from Boston,[18] sentiment against the new law in the North grew and by the mid-1850s opposition in the North was strong. On January 1, 1863, Lincoln's Emancipation Proclamation freed the slaves in the rebellious states and his reconstruction plan offered amnesty to white Southerners who took a loyalty oath to the Union. Lincoln repealed the *Fugitive Slave Act of 1850* in 1864.

---

[17] *The Kansas-Nebraska Act* established popular sovereignty, that is, the right of each state to choose whether to be a slave or non-slave state; it repealed the Missouri Compromise of 1820, which prohibited slavery in these territories. See pp. 28, 58, 75 (n.57).

[18] In 1853, Fugitive slave Anthony Burns was captured, tried, and found guilty in Boston. The decision provoked public protest and unrest. Subsequently, Boston sympathizers raised funds and ransomed him.

[18] Stanley W. Campbell, *The Slave Catchers. Enforcement of the Fugitive Slave Law, 1850-1860* (Chapel Hill, NC: The University of North Carolina Press, 1970) 79. https://www.questia.com/read/104468881/the-slave-catchers-enforcement-of-the-fugitive-slave.

Slavery and Resistance to Slavery in New York State

The Dutch West India Company began importing slaves from Africa into its New Netherlands colony in 1626 and the British continued the practice in its New York colony when it assumed control in 1664. By 1746, the number of slaves in the colony was almost 10,000, about 20% of the population. A number of slave laws, some stimulated by slave insurrections in 1712 and 1741, were passed. Some early examples were the prevention of more than three slaves assembling together away from the master's service (1673); an act that allowed masters or mistresses to punish slaves at their own discretion, providing that they did not maim or kill them (1702); an act forbidding the practice permissible for indentured servants, that is, of baptizing Negroes, Indians, or Mulattoes as a means to set them free (1706); the implementation of the ancient Roman principle that the status of the child was determined by the status of the mother (1706; *partus sequitur ventrem*[19]). After the Insurrection of 1712, the Assembly reacted by passing "An Act for the suppressing and punishing the conspiracy and insurrection of Negroes and other Slaves," by which slaves convicted of murder, rape, arson, or assault were to "suffer the pains of Death in such manner and with such circumstances as the aggravation or enormity of their Crimes. . . " In this case, twenty-three insurrectionists were executed. This 1712 law included prohibiting free blacks from owning property; forbad freeing slaves by paying the government L200 (British pounds) and an annuity of L20 to the slave; and provided for a "Public Whipper" to enforce its provisions with lashes. The colony also enacted its own Fugitive Slave Law (1717).[20]

The legal status of African Americans in New York began to change in the late eighteenth century. All free propertied men could vote regardless of color or previous servitude

---

[19] *The Institute of Gaius*, 86.

[20] "Slaves" in the Index to *Journal of the Legislative Council of the Province of New York*, https://books.google.com/books?id=BMT04vmAoR8C&pg=PA2066&lpg=PA2066&dq=%22An+Act+for+the+suppre ssion+and+punishment+the+conspiracy+and+insurrection+of+Negroes+and&source=bl&ots=CezcG0BFux&sig=H6r tS7R7eBfTXoGrE8iomC4TmB8&hl=en&sa=X&ved=0ahUKEwi8_PS1nfbPAhUBMz4KHdyHDbIQ6AEIKDAC#v=onepage &q&f=false; Marc Newman, "Slavery and Insurrections in the Colonial Province of New York," *Social Education* 59/3 (1995) 125-29, http://www.socialstudies.org/sites/default/files/publications/se/5903/590301.html; "New York Slave Laws: Colonial Period." http://law2.umkc.edu/faculty/projects/ftrials/negroplot/slavelaws.html. See also Edgar J. McManus, *A History of Negro Slavery in New York* (Forward by Richard B. Morris; Syracuse, NY: Syracuse University Press, 1966). For further bibliography, see "Slavery in New York, The New York Historical Society," http://www.slaveryinnewyork.org/bibliography.htm.

(1777); slaves could no longer be imported and could be emancipated without masters posting bonds (1785); and the slave trade was banned (1788—there were loopholes). Yet, a comprehensive slave law that remained maintained that current slaves were slaves for life (1788). A key shift came with *An Act for the Gradual Abolition of Slavery* in 1799. It freed children born to a slave woman after July 4, 1799, although not at once: male slaves would be free at age 28, females at age 25. This age stipulation bowed to slave owners' economic investment; moreover, some slaves could be reclassified as indentured servants.

Finally, two critical changes appeared. First, in 1817, in contrast to 1799, slaves born before July 4, 1799, were free, but—note the gradualism that supported the economic interests of slave owners—not until July 4, 1827.[21] In the meantime, nonresidents could bring their slaves into New York State for up to nine months, the famous "nine months law." Second, New York State finally abolished slavery in 1827, but it still allowed that that slave children born between 1799 and 1827 could be indentured until age 25 (females) and age 28 (males). Nonetheless, this was considered enough of an advance that on July 5—note the deliberate protest about July 4th!—4,000 African Americans in New York City celebrated this law as Emancipation Day.[22]

The *Fugitive Slave Act of 1850*[23]

The abolition of slavery in New York State in 1827 was not the end of the matter. In 1850, President Millard Fillmore, hoping to preserve the Union, signed into law the *Compromise of 1850* which attempted to mediate between the North and the South about whether new states added to the Union would be slave states or free states. Most important, it included the *Fugitive Slave Act of 1850*. It was a concession to the South. There had been a similar, but less stringent, act in 1793, but it had been generally ignored in the North. The new 1850 law, however, had teeth and Fillmore energetically sought to have it enforced by including a charge of treason and consequent execution. The courts rejected that extreme option, but the new law did allow slave owners or their agents to enter free states and territories and, helped by federal

---

[21] "When Did Slavery End in New York?" New York Historical Society, Museum and Library; http://www.nyhistory.org/community/slavery-end-new-york-state.
[22] "Happy Fifth of July, New York!" *New York Times* (July 3, 2005).
[23] For excerpts from the *Fugitive Slave Act of 1850*, see Appendix 3.

marshals, professional slave catchers, and posses, to seize alleged fugitive slaves, take them before a federal judge or magistrate, as well as "commissioners" specially appointed by the *Act*, identify them and prove that they were runaways, and receive a "certificate of rendition" that permitted them to be removed from the free state and be returned to their masters in a slave state. As already noted, the officially appointed federal marshals charged with implementing the *Act* were subject to a $1,000 fine and six months in jail if they did not carry out their charge and if they allowed fugitive slaves to escape their custody they were subject to pay the value of the slave. Citizens who hid or helped fugitive slaves with food or instructions were also subject to up to a $1,000 fine and up to six months in jail. Those blacks detained were not allowed to defend themselves verbally or by a writ of habeas corpus.[24] If the person was judged guilty as a fugitive slave, the commissioners received a fee of $10; if innocent, a fee of $5.[25] Finally, federal troops were sometimes called upon to enforce the law.[26]

The anti-slavery movements that had been growing in the 1830s and 1840s in the northern, free states offered resistance to the law, which included attempts such as these:

1. A failed attempt to repeal the *Act* by members of the abolitionist Free Soil Party;

2. Many African Americans fleeing to Canada, perhaps more than doubling their numbers in Ontario (estimates vary);

3. The charge that commissioners were not judges and their activities not legal;

4. The claims that the *Act* denied trial by jury, writ of habeas corpus, and cross-examination of accusers;

5. The objection that the federal government's involvement in rendition of fugitive slaves was unconstitutional;

6. Physical, sometimes violent, resistance to the law by African Americans, abolitionists, members of Vigilance Committees who harassed slave catchers; and

---

[24] A writ of habeas corpus (literally, "produce the body") allows a defendant who wishes to challenge the legality of the detainment to have a court order that requires those who hold the person captive to bring the person to the court issuing that order.

[25] For more detail, see "Fugitive Slave Act 1850." http://www.nationalcenter.org/FugitiveSlaveAct.html.

[26] For the full law: http://www.nationalcenter.org/FugitiveSlaveAct.html.

7. Individual states passed "personal liberty laws" that affirmed trial by jury and habeas corpus: Vermont, Main, Massachusetts, Rhode Island, Connecticut, Ohio, Wisconsin, and Michigan (New York State did not pass such a law, but resistance was still strong).

New York State did not pass a personal liberty law, but resistance to the Fugitive Slave Act included citizens of the State of New York. An example was the "Great Fugitive Slave Law Convention," Cazenovia, New York, in August 1850, less than a month before the law was passed. The Convention was supported by the wealthy abolitionist Gerrit Smith.[27] In this Daguerreotype group image, several famous abolitionists are recognizable: Theodore Weld

The "Great Fugitive Slave Law Convention," Cazenovia, New York, August 22, 1850
From the Daguerreotype Photo by Ezra Greenleaf Weld[28]
Permission from Mr. Set Charles Momjian, owner
Image 1.5

---

[27] For more information about Gerrit Smith, see Chs. 2, 8, 9, 10, 14.
[28] Ezra Greenleaf Weld, who took the photo, was the abolitionist brother of Theodore Weld. http://www.getty.edu/art/collection/objects/49687/ezra-greenleaf-weld-fugitive-slave-law-convention-cazenovia-new-york-american-august-22-1850/. See Hugh Humphreys, *Agitate! Agitate! Agitate! The Great Fugitive Slave Law Convention and its Rare Daguerreotype* (Madison County Heritage, 1994). The negative original is in the Madison County Historical Society (Heritage No. 19, 1994). The Getty Museum photo has the correct positioning. For this version see Daniel H. Weiskotten, The "Great Cazenovia Fugitive Slave Law Convention" at Cazenovia, NY, August 21 and 22, 1850. http://www.rootsweb.ancestry.com/~nyccazen/Shorts/1850Convention.html.

(front, left),[29] Frederick Douglass (behind Weld), Gerrit Smith (standing behind Douglass), J. C. Hathaway (sitting on the right), and black women, Mary and Emily Edmonson (plaid dresses). The image is interesting also for showing diversity: both men and women, both black and white. Another immediate response was the David Green Wheelbanks lecture and *Fugitive Slave Act* discussion on November 9, 1850, at Newark, New York. [30]

Who were the Freedom Seekers and How Did They Travel?

Freedom seekers, known in perhaps less neutral terms as runaways, fugitive slaves, and escapees, were African Americans escaping slavery and seeking freedom. It was common that freedom seekers planned their own escape and summoned the courage to do it. Many had little, if any, knowledge of the states that were free. Fleeing from beatings and mistreatments did motivate slaves to run away.[31] But this might not have been the situation in some cases. A slave could be very intelligent, highly skilled, with a certain amount of freedom. Some secretly knew how to read and enjoyed a high level of sophistication. An individual slave was quite capable of planning and implementing his or her own escape.[32] There is also evidence that groups of slaves planned their escape together. Camp Meetings could provide time for communications, time to hear about successful escapees, and information about how to head north or how and where to find UGRR stations and conductors or agents who would assist them along their way. African Americans who wanted to be free from slavery, no matter what the reason, surely became inspired at these meetings. Above all . . . courage was needed.

Usually slaves, especially those on the move, were required to produce some type of identification. If they did not have passes from their masters to travel, or if free Negroes did not have papers stating that they were not slaves, they could be in great danger, especially from slave catchers and kidnappers. Slaves or sympathizers often stole, borrowed, or made fake

---

[29] The identification that Theodore Weld is in the foreground of the photo is argued by Daniel H. Weiskotten, "The 'Great Cazenovia Fugitive Slave Law Convention' August 21 and 22, 1850." For the photo of Theodore Weld, see Ch. 2. http://www.rootsweb.ancestry.com/~nyccazen/Shorts/1850Convention.html.

[30] For Gerrit Smith see Chs. 8, 10, 11, 14; for Theodore Weld and Frederick Douglass, see Ch. 2; for David Green Wheelbanks, see Ch. 10.

[31] For harsh images of slavery portrayed in anti-slavery propaganda, see Ch. 2.

[32] Larry Gara, *The Liberty Line*, 43.

passes. If they could not be made or obtained, then their bravery often inspired them to leave without the necessary identifying papers.[33]

Creativity was important in order to survive. Fugitives used disguises, made up reasons for a light-skinned slave (Mulatto) to travel with a dark-skinned companion, or used other creative means to escape and continue the journey northward. Some fugitives felt prepared to take care of themselves when facing threatening situations.

Many fugitives traveled for days or months and for great distances before they actually came upon those who were willing to help them. Moreover, it was not unusual for freedom seekers to fear and mistrust white people; therefore, they would normally hide by day and travel by night, perhaps using the one piece of information they all seemed to know and understood—following the North Star.

The majority of the fugitive slaves were men or young boys.[34] They could travel more quickly than women and children. Sometimes grandparents, wives, and children had to be left behind with the hope that their fathers and sons would make it through to safety, become free men, work to pay for their freedom, and then come back and use their experience in bringing them to safety and freedom. However, there were also whole family units who escaped together. There were cases of women traveling with a child but finding it necessary to leave him or her with trusted friends. There was always present the hope that families would be reunited.

When slave masters realized that slaves had escaped there was always the chance that those left behind would be exposed to the burdens of retaliation. The worst of all retaliations would be against a captured fugitive who was brought back to his master and the plantation of his origin by a slave catcher. He was used to set an example for the other slaves to not attempt to escape. After beatings, he would often be sent further into the Deep South where it was said that slaves were actually worked to death.

---

[33] For an image of a "Manumission Certificate for a Slave named 'George,' April 24, 1817," see Ch. 3.
[34] "Fugitive Slave," *Encyclopedia Britannica* on line: "One study that examined advertisements in newspapers in the early 1800s calling for the return of fugitive slaves noted that 76 percent of all fugitive slaves were younger than age 35, and 89 percent were male," https://www.britannica.com/topic/fugitive-slave.

Free blacks in the North could also be in danger. David Wilson in an 1853 book, *Twelve Years a Slave*, records the memoir of Solomon Northrup (1803—1863?), a free African American living in New York State, who was drugged, illegally abducted in 1841, and taken to Louisiana where he became a slave for twelve years. Finally, he was identified by a Canadian abolitionist and freed under the authority of a New York State official.[35]

However, there were slave owners who agreed or came to understand that slavery was not appropriate for any human being. They freed their slaves and permitted them to leave and go off on their own if they so pleased. There were cases where the slaves who were freed just did not know where to go! They knew only one way of life and were afraid to leave the security of familiarity. Some masters actually had strong feelings towards protecting their slaves; other slave owners wanted to educate them and became very attached to them (not meaning the sexual abuse often experienced by African American women and girls with the possible mixed-race children born from these encounters).

After the *Fugitive Slave Act of 1850* many escaping slaves continued their dangerous and difficult journey to freedom in Canada rather than consider settling in northern states such as New York State. Indeed, some who had presumably settled safely in the northern states decided to go on to Canada. In Canada, freed slaves often moved further north away from the border with the United States. They had the right to keep their freedom, but the United States *Fugitive Slave Law of 1850* regenerated their fears of capture on the charge of murder or theft in Canada. Even so, some fugitive slaves returned to the United States when they believed that it was safe.

Many escaping slaves traveled at night through forests and waded in creeks so the search dogs could not follow their trail. Along the way there were at times UGRR stations with secret rooms where freedom seekers could hide, rest, eat, and regain strength to continue their journey.

---

[35] David Wilson, *Twelve Years a Slave* (Auburn, NY: Derby & Miller, 1853), dedicated to Harriet Beecher Stowe's *Uncle Tom's Cabin*, published the previous year, 1852 (Boston, MA: John P. Jewett & Company; Cleveland, OH: Jewett, Proctor & Worthington, 1852; reprinted as a Dover Thrift Edition, Mineola, NY: Dover Publications, Inc., 2005). *Twelve Years a Slave* has been examined for accuracy and passed the test. There is also a critically acclaimed Academy Award-winning film *Twelve Years a Slave* in 2013 based on the book, directed by Steve McQueen and starring Chiweter Ejiofor. See "Twelve Years a Slave," https://en.wikipedia.org/wiki/Twelve_Years_a_Slave.

The means of transportation varied most often according to what might be available. New York State had an excellent road system. Roads were in good repair and extended out into rural areas. Railroad lines were also extended to locations that enabled the fugitive slaves to move more quickly across the state. Waterways such as streams, creeks, rivers, and canals were abundant, most especially in Niagara County in western New York. The canal systems throughout New York State were a very important means of travel within the UGRR escape system. The tow-paths were especially useful for self-reliant freedom seekers. Canals were often safer than public roads.

The Underground Railroad and Western New York

As stated in the Preface, the name "Underground Railroad" is a metaphor that referred to the secret, loosely connected, interlocking network of blacks and whites who risked breaking the law and possible imprisonment to help fugitive slaves to freedom. Although it had antecedents going back to the late Eighteenth Century, UGRR activity expanded greatly in the decades leading up to the Civil War (1861-1865). Freedom-seeking passengers in the network moved from station to station, each station only a few miles away, where they sought refuge and help to move on to the next station, assisted by station masters, agents, and conductors, both black and white. Most freedom seekers did not know about geography and often they did not come into contact with the UGRR network until they reached northern states. After the *Fugitive Slave Act of 1850*, UGRR networks helped thousands of slaves to escape.[36]

Many people are not aware that the importance of the efforts of cities, towns, and hamlets in the outlying areas of the UGRR system in western New York is undisputed. This has been known for well over a century. Wilbur H. Siebert already commented in 1898:

> Lake Ontario had only a few comparatively insignificant routes; at the upper end
> of the Lake were two, one joining Rochester and St. Catharines, the other, joining St.
> Catharines and Toronto . . . Within that region the terminals were numerous, being
> scattered from the southern shore of Georgian Bay to Lake Erie, and from the Detroit

---

[36] An exception to the metaphorical description of the Underground Railroad is found in Colson Whitehead's best-selling, prize-winning novel, *The Underground Railroad* (New York, NY: Doubleday Books, 2016). Whitehead imaginatively interjects a *literal* underground railroad into his story.

and Huron Rivers to *the Niagara* [River] . . . A full record would take into account the localities in the outlying country, districts as well as those adjoining or forming a part of the hamlets, towns, and cities of the whites.[37]

[The eleven crossing-places to Canada] were Ogdensburg, Cape Vincent, Port Ontario, Oswego, Rochester, Lewiston, Suspension Bridge, Black Rock, Buffalo, Dunkirk Harbor and Erie. Doubtless the most important of these crossing-places were the four along the *Niagara River* [Lewiston, Suspension Bridge, Black Rock, and Buffalo], *for here the most travelled of the routes in New York terminated*.[38]

In 1903, historian Frank Hayward Severance (1856-1931) added the importance of ferries: "[T]he most active part in the Underground Railroad operations in New York State was borne by the *western counties* . . . The most vital part of the Underground Railroad was the *over-water ferry*." [39] Research on the UGRR has advanced dramatically since Siebert and Severance made their comments. In the rest of this book, we present evidence to show how these early statements can be documented in much greater detail in Niagara County and especially the Village of Youngstown as a fugitive slave crossing place on the Lower Niagara River.

Precise routes of the Underground Railroad are often impossible to determine—they often changed—but it will be helpful to visualize major directions with a map.

---

[37] Siebert, *The Underground Railroad from Slavery to Freedom,* 148-149 [italics ours].
[38] Ibid., 145-46.
[39] Frank Hayward Severance, *Old Trails on the Niagara Frontier* (Buffalo, NY: The Matthews Northrup Co., 1899; Cleveland, OH: Burrows Brothers, 1903), 230, 231, 229 (italics ours).

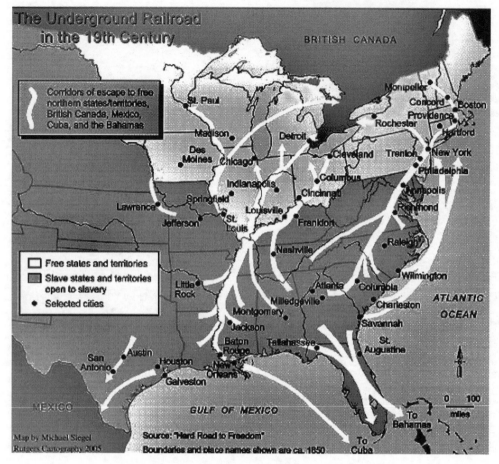

The Underground Railroad in the 19th Century

Original Map (in color) by Mike Siegel, Rutgers University. Permission from the New York Public Library

(Thomas Lisanti, Manager, Permissions & Reproduction Services)

Image 1.6

UGRR historians often refer to UGRR networks. Much can be said about networks in general. Here, following recent UGRR historians, we imagine the UGRR network as a large, loosely connected umbrella network made up of smaller, local, loosely connected, networks of persons—abolitionists, agents, conductors, station masters, free blacks—and stations or safe houses that offered refuge and passed on valuable content *to fugitive slaves*—material (food, clothing, shelter) and immaterial (information, routes, modes of transportation, the next station, slave catcher density)—or *the fugitive slaves themselves*. These networks helped fugitive slaves reach their ultimate goal: freedom from slavery. Such networks are not mathematically precise, as in formal Social Network Analysis[40]—we are dealing with secretive history—but a network sociogram can nevertheless help to visualize in a general way local and regional networks of the UGRR. In Chapter 10, we offer simplified network sociogram and in Chapter 17, another from our study in Part II, the heart of the book. In them, one will see networked links between persons or groups that helped fugitive slaves to cross the Niagara River at Youngstown.[41]

In summary, analysis of historical information in this book will document the Village of Youngstown and some of her residents as connected to a local UGRR network which is further connected to other local UGRR networks at Newark, Palmyra, Lyons, Lockport, Lewiston, Ransomville, and Niagara Falls. This network is embedded in a still larger umbrella Underground Railroad network in the northern United States and "Upper Canada" (Ontario). Our goal is to offer substantive proof to solidify the historical fact that the Village of Youngstown in the Town of Porter in Niagara County in New York State had a legitimate social and geographical place in the Underground Railroad.

Addendum:
A Transnational Timeline of Slavery, the Abolitionist Movement, and the Underground Railroad[42]

1619 – The First Twenty African slaves arrived at Jamestown, Virginia, in a Dutch boat.
1758 – Philadelphia Quakers prohibited slave owning.
1771 – Nearly 20,000 enslaved people in the New York Colony, one of every eight people.
1775 – First Abolition Society formed in Philadelphia.
1777 – Vermont banned slavery.
1781 – Massachusetts banned slavery.
1786 – Letters of George Washington indicate a fugitive slave network, Quaker involvement.

---

[40] See the Preface; Appendix 1.
[41] In Chapter 15 there is a map of possible sites in Niagara County, New York.
[42] "Underground Railroad." African American Studies Center. http://aasc.oupexplore.com/undergroundrailroad/#!/timeline; "New York," http://aasc.oupexplore.com/undergroundrailroad/#!/location/new-york; "A History of Slavery in the United States," National Geographic Society, http://nationalgeographic.org/interactive/slavery-united-states/.

1787 – The U.S. Constitutional Convention. Voted to ban the slave trade (not slavery) until 1808; as a compromise to the Senate's two senators per state, the House of Representatives would be population-based and could count each **slave as three-fifths of a person**, thereby giving the southern slave states more representative power.

1787 – The U.S. Constitution "Slave Clause," Article IV, Section 2, Clause 3. "No person held to service or labor in one state, under the laws thereof, escaping into another, shall, in consequence of any law or regulation therein, be discharged from such service or labor, but shall be delivered up on claim of the party to whom such service or labor may be due."

1788 – New York State banned the slave trade (but not slavery; with loopholes).

1790 – The Naturalization Act denied naturalization to all those who were not free whites.

1790-1860 – The Second Great Awakening. Religious revivalism, powerful in western New York ("the burned over district"), viewed slavery as a sin and contributed to northern Christian abolition, especially from **1830 to 1860**.

1792 – African Americans were not permitted to be in the military.

1793 – Congress passed a Fugitive Slave Law. Slave owners or their agents could search for fugitive slaves in free states, apprehend them, bring them before a judge, give proof that they were property of a slave owner (usually by an affidavit), and if officials agreed, slaves could be returned to owners in slave states or territories (Section 3). Persons who helped to harbor or harbored fugitive slaves were subject to a $500 fine (Section 4).

1793 – Upper Canada (the western portion of the old Province of Quebec, today Ontario) abolished importing of slaves (the slave trade), but not slavery itself. Chloe Cooley (pp. 5-6).

1799 – New York State passed "An Act for the Gradual Abolition of Slavery." It freed children born to a slave woman after July 4, 1799, but not immediately; they would remain property of the mother's master, males until age 28, females until age 25 (their most productive years). Slaves born before July 4, 1799, remained slaves, but were reclassified "indentured servants."

1803 – Lower Canada (The eastern portion of the old Province of **Quebec**, Canada) abolished slavery.

1804 – A Quaker ferry family named Wright ferried slaves across the Susquehanna River, which flows from eastern New York and Pennsylvania south into Chesapeake Bay. When a bridge was built, a black abolitionist William Whipper, whose house was at the end of the bridge, became a conductor, anticipating a role that would become central to the Underground Railroad.

1807 – United States – Act Prohibiting Importation of Slaves, or the slave trade (effective 1809), was passed. It made international slave trade a felony. It was not strongly enforced.

1807 – British Empire – Abolition of Slave Trade Act abolishes slave trading in the Empire, but not slavery itself (see **1833/1834**).

1812 – 1815 – Upper Canada (Ontario). The "Colored Troops," as well as African Canadians in regular regiments (1000's volunteered), were promised freedom and land, trained at Fort George, and fought valiantly for the British in the War of 1812. Those who were rewarded received one hundred acres of poor land and the grant was half that given to white veterans.

1815 – 1862 – The Underground Railroad in the United States assisted thousands of freedom seekers to get to Upper and Lower Canada.

1817 – New York Law – In contrast to 1799, a new slave law freed slaves born *before* July 4, 1799, to be effective July 4, 1827.[43] However, nonresidents could bring their slaves into the state for up to nine months (the **"nine months law"**). The **1841** law changed this law.

1821 – Thomas James was ferried across Niagara River at Youngstown.

1826-1846 – Newport, Indiana. An Early Underground Railroad Station. Quakers Levi and Catharine Coffin take fugitive slaves into their home, helping perhaps as many as 2,000.

1827 – New York State – The new Law abolished slavery in New York State, but declared that slave children born between 1799 and 1827 could be indentured until age 28 (males) and 25 (females). On *July 5*, 4,000 Blacks celebrated this law in New York City as "Emancipation Day."

1830 – Federal Census data indicated that there were only 75 slaves left in New York State.[44]

1833 – Emancipation Act, British Parliament (enforced 1834) – enacted a law that abolished slavery throughout most of its colonies, including Canada, West Indies, Mauritius, and South Africa. In Ontario, this superseded the 1793 law which only restricted importing slaves.

1837 – Newark/Niagara (Niagara-on-the-Lake) – when Solomon Moseby, a free slave in Canada, was going to be transferred back to his former master in Kentucky, who accused him of stealing a horse (a felony in Ontario), a riot ensued. (He was supposedly to have been ferried from Niagara, Ontario, to Lewiston, New York [to Youngstown?]). Two people were killed in the riot, but Moseby escaped.

1840 – Federal Census data indicated that there were four slaves in New York State, none in New York City.[45]

1840 – Anti-Slavery Society Schism. William Lloyd Garrison, founder of *The Liberator*, and his followers argued that the Constitution was pro-slavery, that if the South would not change the North should secede from the Union, and that women should have a prominent role in the abolitionist movement. Many thought his views too radical and formed the Liberty Party which held that the Constitution was anti-slavery. It fought slavery more gradually. See 1847.

1841 – New York State – the "nine months law" (part of the 1817 Law) repealed. The repeal resulted in New York State abolitionists informing slaves in transit that they were legally free in New York State.

1842 – *Prigg vs. Pennsylvania.* The Supreme Court: federal slave law superseded Pennsylvania State's "personal liberty law," which prohibited slaves from being removed from the state.

1847 – Frederick Douglass found *The North Star* weekly newspaper; it competed with Garrison's *The Liberator* and this move, along with Douglass' joining the pro-Constitutional Liberty Party and Free Soil Party, contributed to the dissolution of their close friendship and cooperation. See 1840 Anti-Slavery Society Schism.

1847 –African American William Still, born a slave under Maryland law, was very active as a free man in Philadelphia, and has been called "Father of the Underground Railroad."

1848-1852 – The Free Soil Party absorbed the **Liberty Party**; it opposed slavery's westward expansion in new states.

---

[43] "When Did Slavery End in New York?" New York Historical Society, Museum and Library; http://www.nyhistory.org/community/slavery-end-new-york-state.

[44] *A Century of Population Growth in the United States, From the First Census of the United States to the Twelfth (1790-1900)* (Washington, D.C.: Government Printing Office, 1909), 138-33. https://www2.census.gov/prod2/decennial/documents/00165897ch14.pdf.

[45] *A Century of Population Growth,* 132-33; "When Did Slavery End in New York State?"

1849 – Harriet Tubman began her heroic activity as an Underground Railroad conductor who guided family and others to freedom in Canada.

1850 – United States *Fugitive Slave Act of 1850* – as part of the *Compromise of 1850* between slave and non-slave states, it stated that accused fugitive slaves could be arrested on the claims of slave owner agents and tried by a special commissioner in every county. See the description above. This Act went against New York State law enacted in 1827.

1850 – United States near the Canadian border - Hundreds of black freed people living in the United States uprooted and crossed into Canada in fear that if they were captured by slave catchers and bounty hunters, they would be illegally returned to the southern states as slaves and suffer severe consequences.

1850 – Federal Census data indicated that there were no slaves in New York State.[46]

1851 – Anti-Slavery Society of Canada. Canadian response to the *1850 Fugitive Slave Act*. Its goal was to extinguish all slavery everywhere.

1852 – *Uncle Tom's Cabin,* best seller by Harriet Beecher Stowe, originally published in serial form in the *National Era* weekly newspaper (June 5, 1851-April 1, 1852) stimulated abolitionism.

1853 – Upper Canada (Ontario) – The Canadian Steamer *Chief Justice Robinson* picked up a stranded fugitive slave floating on a wooden gate in Lake Ontario. See Chapter 9.

1853-1863 – Most evidence for fugitive slaves crossing at Youngstown, New York.

1857 – Dred Scott vs. Sanford Case. Dred Scott sued for his freedom. The Supreme Court ruled that slaves, ex-slaves, and descendants of slaves were not United States citizens.

1859 – John Brown's Unsuccessful Raid at Harpers Ferry, Virginia. Brown, a white man, was executed for treason, but became a symbol for abolitionists.

1861 – 1865 – The Civil War in the United States. It started with the attack on Fort Sumter, April 12–14, 1861, and ended with the surrender of Robert E. Lee of the Confederacy to Ulysses S. Grant of the Union at Appomattox Courthouse, April 9, 1865.

1863 – Emancipation Proclamation – On January 1, President Lincoln issued a statement that all persons held as slaves within any State or designated part of a State ". . . shall be then, thenceforward, and forever free."[47] In "border states" most slaves had been freed by state laws.

1863 – Emancipation in Washington, D. C.

1865 – Abraham Lincoln assassinated on April 15th.

1865 – December 18th - Thirteenth Amendment to the United State Constitution was ratified. It stated that slavery is abolished throughout the United States. See Appendix 8.[48]

---

[46] *A Century of Population Growth,* 132-33.

[47] "The Emancipation Proclamation," Featured Documents, National Archives & Records Administration. http://www.archives.gov/exhibits/featured_documents/emancipation_proclamation/transcript.html.

[48] *The Constitution: Amendment XIII*: http://constitutioncenter.org/constitution/the-amendments/amendment-13-slavery-abolished.

CHAPTER 2

The Anti-Slavery Society and the Abolitionists in Niagara County and Youngstown, New York

Image 2.1

The *Fugitive Slave Act of 1850* was shocking to many white Northerners. They were learning more about the violent and sometimes lethal encounters between southern slave catchers and African Americans, whether they were fugitive slaves or free. The opposition to slavery grew.[1] A Broadside (poster) posted in Boston by the influential white Transcendentalist abolitionist Unitarian minister, Theodore Parker, in 1851 dramatically illustrates the changing mood.

---

[1] For detailed historical analysis showing that the law was enforceable, but was nonetheless not successful for economic reasons, see Stanley W. Campbell, *The Slave Catchers: Enforcement of the Fugitive Slave Law, 1850-1860* (Chapel Hill, NC: The University of North Carolina Press, 1970). https://www.questia.com/read/104469009/the-slave-catchers-enforcement-of-the-fugitive-slave.

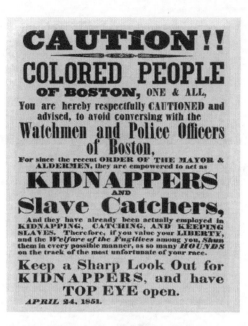

The Broadside of Boston Abolitionist Theodore Parker, 1851
(Courtesy of the Trustees of the Boston Public Library/Rare Books)[2]
Image 2.2

What drove this anti-slavery attitude?

The American Anti-Slavery Society and William Lloyd Garrison

In 1832, William Lloyd Garrison (1805 – 1879) supported by businessmen Arthur and Lewis Tappan[3] and lawyer Wendell Phillips, founded the New England Anti-Slavery Society and was the inspiration for the formation of the American Anti-Slavery Society at Philadelphia in 1833. Garrison was an abolitionist, a suffragist, a reformer, and a journalist who published an influential abolitionist weekly, *The Liberator*, from 1831 to 1865. He was radical, hard-nosed, and uncompromising. His first issue declared: "I am in earnest—I will not equivocate—I will not

---

[2] "Caution, Colored People of Boston." Thanks to Karen S. Shafts, Assistant Keeper of Prints, Print Department, and Sean Casey, Rare Books and Manuscripts Department, both from the Boston Public Library in Boston, Massachusetts. http://chnm.gmu.edu/lostmuseum/lm/307/.
[3] For the Tappan brothers, see also Ch. 7, p. 180 and n. 13.

excuse—I will not retreat a single inch— AND I WILL BE HEARD."[4] He believed that the United States Constitution was a pro- slavery document (recall the Slave Clause), that the American

William Lloyd Garrison (1805 – 1879)
(Image in the public domain)[5]
Image 2.3

Anti-Slavery Society should not be aligned with any political party, and that women should be allowed to participate. It is noteworthy that Lucretia A. Mott (1793-1880), a white, "quiet Quaker" minister and mother attended the first anti-slavery meeting in Philadelphia in 1833. Possessed of oratory skills, she quickly launched an auxiliary called the Philadelphia Female Anti-Slavery Society and became an ardent activist in the Underground Railroad, as well as in the women's rights movement and other areas of social reform.[6]

The ideology of the American Anti-Slavery Society's "Declaration of Sentiments" on December 3, 1833, offers insight. It was composed largely by Garrison and was rooted in the Bible and the religious philosophy of Enlightenment Rationalists and Deists, such as Jefferson, Franklin, and Thomas Paine. For these intellectuals, certain basic truths are natural and self-evident, particularly, as the Declaration of Independence states, "that all men are created

---

[4] Accessible Archives, "The Liberator," http://www.accessible-archives.com/collections/the-liberator/.
[5] William Lloyd Garrison photo, www.blackpast.org.
[6] See Carol Faulkner, *Lucretia Mott's Heresy. Abolition and Women's Rights in Nineteenth Century America* (Philadelphia, PA: University of Pennsylvania Press, 2011).

equal, that they are endowed by their Creator with certain unalienable Rights, that among these are Life, Liberty and the pursuit of Happiness."[7] The Anti-Slavery Society's "Declaration of Sentiments" also stated that slavery is a crime and a sin, specifically,

> . . . [that] all those laws which are now in force, admitting the right of slavery, are . . . before God utterly null and void; being an audacious usurpation of Divine prerogative, a daring infringement on the law of nature, a base overthrow of the vary foundations of the social compact . . . and a presumptuous transgression of all the holy commandments, and that therefore they ought instantly to be abrogated.[8]

In short, the American Anti-Slavery Society promoted the *immediate* abolition of slavery throughout the United States. It supported state and local auxiliaries, sponsored meetings, adopted resolutions, signed antislavery petitions to be sent to Congress, published journals and enlisted subscriptions to them, printed them, and sent out agents and lecturers—seventy in 1836 alone—to carry the anti-slavery message to Northern audiences.[9] It distributed strong anti-slavery propaganda illustrating the horrors of slavery.

---

[7] See the Rationalist views of the Lockport, New York, Quaker Lyman Spalding in Ch. 11.

[8] "The Declaration and Constitutions of the American Anti-Slavery Society" (New York, NY: Anti-Slavery Society, 1835), 5. http://scua.library.umass.edu/digital/antislavery/016.pdf.

[9] Editors of the *Encyclopedia Britannica*, http://www.britannica.com/EBchecked/topic/19269/American-AntiSlavery-Society; Fergus M. Bordewich, *Bound for Canaan: The Epic Story of the Underground Railroad, American's First Civil Rights Movement* (New York, NY: Amistad, 2005; HarperCollins, 2006), 143-46.

Illustrations from the *American Anti-Slavery Almanac* for 1840
(New York: NY, 1840; the Library of Congress; images in the public domain)[10]
Image 2.4

---

[10] Library of Congress, Portfolio 248, Folder 1 as part of "Broadsides, Leaflets, and Pamphlets from America and Europe." Online at "An American Time Capsule: Three Centuries of Broadsides and Other Painted Ephemers," http://memory.loc.gov/cgi-bin/query/h?ammem/rbpebib:@field(NUMBER+@band(rbpe+24800100). The *Almanac* circulated in major cities such as Boston, New York, and Pittsburgh, beginning in 1836. To read the 1840 *Almanac* archived in the Boston Public Library, see https://archive.org/details/americanantislav1840chil.

Here are enlargements of two images in the *Almanac*.

Showing how slavery improves the condition of the female sex.

Image 2.5

Hunting Slaves with dogs and guns. A Slave drowned by the dogs.

Image 2.6

It should be added that many within the American Anti-Slavery Society disagreed with Garrison's uncompromising stance and in 1840 a major rift occurred. It is also important to note the changing relationship between Garrison and Frederick Douglass (1818-1895).[11] In his early years in Maryland, Douglass was a slave under several masters, one of whom beat him, and he tried to escape several times. Yet, with some help, he taught himself to read. Meanwhile, he met a fine, free black woman, Anna Murray in 1838, and after he fled to New York City, she joined him and they married. Then, they migrated to New Bedford, Massachusetts. He began reading Garrison's *The Liberator,* was taken with Garrison, and joined the Massachusetts Anti-Slavery Society. In 1841, he went to Nantucket to an anti-slavery meeting where he gave an inspired speech about his life.[12] Garrison, much impressed, arose and complimented him and afterward hired him as an agent of the Anti-Slavery Society. The two men became friends and often shared the stage at anti-slavery meetings.

Frederick Douglass (1818 –1895)
Image in public domain[13]
Image 2.7

Gradually, however, Douglass' complicated relationship with Garrison and his followers deteriorated. In 1845, Douglass published his memoir, the *Narrative of the Life of Frederick*

---

[11] 'Garrison and Douglass: Friendship and Estrangement." Pilgrim Pathways: Notes for a Diaspora People. https://pilgrimpathways.wordpress.com/2010/07/29/garrison-and-douglass-friendship-and-estrangement/; "Frederick Douglass." https://en.wikipedia.org/wiki/Frederick_Douglass#Life_as_a_slave; https://en.wikipedia.org/wiki/Anna_Murray-Douglass.

[12] Nantucket was heavily populated with Quakers. Abolitionist and women's right activist, Quaker minister Lucretia Mott, was from Nantucket.

[13] Frederick Douglass photo. www.history.com/topics/abolitionist-movement.

Douglass, an American Slave. It was first printed in Garrison's *The Liberator*,[14] but the work displayed Douglass' fine literary talents and, after Douglass' successful lecture and money raising tour in Britain, the Scots purchased his freedom, which did not sit well with some American Garrisonites because it could be interpreted to acknowledge the legality of slavery. Douglass returned to the United States a free man in 1847 and, although there were other black newspapers, started his own newspaper, *The North Star*, in Rochester. Garrison complimented the paper, but it naturally competed with Garrison's *The Liberator*, especially among blacks. In that same year, Douglass wrote that the United States Constitution could be used as a weapon *against* slavery, a view not shared by Garrison. When Douglass repeated his view at a meeting of the American Anti-slavery Society in 1851, Garrison, apparently feeling betrayed, disagreed with Douglass in *The Liberator*. Douglass, who merged his paper with *The Liberty Party Paper* of Syracuse and renamed it the *Frederick Douglass' Paper* (1851 – 1859), responded. The disagreements intensified. Eventually, Douglass became increasingly influential in the anti-slavery cause and gained the ear of President Abraham Lincoln.

Although Garrison continued to publish Douglass' activities in *The Liberator*, he and Douglass never reconciled their differences.[15]

Gerrit Smith and the New York Anti-Slavery Society (NYASS), 1835

When delegates from around New York State came to the Bleeker Street Presbyterian Church in Utica, New York, on October 21, 1835, the atmosphere was tense. Anti-abolitionists, including Utica's mayor and Democrats, fearful of civil war, opposed the gathering. As proceedings commenced, a wild mob threatened. Then, Gerrit Smith of Peterboro, the wealthiest land owner in New York State,[16] was introduced. Smith rose and shouted above the

---

[14] "Garrison and Douglass: Friendship and Estrangement" at *Pilgrim Pathways. Notes for a Diaspora People*, https://pilgrimpathways.wordpress.com/2010/07/29/garrison-and-douglass-friendship-and-estrangement/; Tyrone Tillery, "The Inevitability of the Douglass-Garrison Conflict," *Phylon* 37/2 (1976), 137-49.

[15] "PBS Online Resource Bank," http://www.pbs.org/wgbh/aia/part4/4p1561.html.

[16] Norman K. Dann, *Practical Dreamer. Gerrit Smith and the Crusade for Social Reform* (Hamilton, NY: Log Cabin Books, 2009); also,"The Gerrit Smith Estate National Historic Landmark, Peterboro, New York," http://www.gerritsmith.org/; "National Abolition Hall of Fame and Museum Gerrit Smith (1797-1874)," http://www.nationalabolitionhalloffameandmuseum.org/gsmith.html. The former Presbyterian Church in Peterboro, now the Smithfield Community Center, became the home of the National Abolition Hall of Fame and

din that the convention was welcome to move its location to his mansion in Peterboro, thirty miles away. The assembly immediately dispersed. The carriages of the abolitionists were pursued by an angry mob. Some delegates hopped a freighter on the Erie Canal part way. Others, inspired by prayer and song, marched through the night to Peterboro. Smith, hastening ahead, prepared food for about three hundred delegates who then met across the square at the Peterboro Presbyterian Church. The New York Anti-slavery Society was formed.[17]

Gerrit Smith (1797-1874)
Image in public domain
Image 2.8

Who was Gerrit Smith? In his earlier years, Smith was influenced by the Second Great Awakening, a religious revivalism, the most famous leader of which was the Presbyterian-rooted revivalist, social reformer, and abolitionist, Charles G. Finney. Although Smith eventually shifted to a religion of reason, he continually backed the temperance movement. He initially supported the American Colonization Society, formed in 1817, which emphasized the emancipation of slaves in order that they could return free to Liberia in West Africa. After the Utica-to-Peterboro affair, Smith turned away from the Colonization Society and dedicated himself and his great wealth wholly to the anti-slavery movement. He bought slaves and freed them; he arranged for their passage to Canada; he sponsored anti-slavery conventions; he developed a relationship with Frederick Douglass; he paid for abolitionists' travel expenses and publications; and he gave away 120,000 acres of land to 3,000 African American males in an area dubbed "Timbuctoo" at North Elba, New York (near Lake Placid in the Adirondacks), hoping that they would improve the land. It is estimated that

---

Museum. We thank Norman K. Dann, our richly informed guide to the Gerrit Smith Estate. For more on Smith as indirectly related to Youngstown, see Chs. 8, 9, 10, 14.

[17] *Proceedings of the New York Anti-slavery Convention held at Utica, New York, October 21, and New York Anti-slavery State Society, held at Peterboro, October 22, 1835* (Utica, NY: Standard & Democratic Office, 1835). https://archive.org/stream/proceedingsofnew00newy#page/n1/mode/2up.

Smith donated millions (perhaps a billion in today's dollars) to the anti-slavery movement. The Smith Estate in Peterboro, New York—his home was destroyed by fire in 1936—was an Underground Railroad Station and meeting place for abolitionists. He was nominated for President of the United States four times on abolitionist tickets, particularly the abolitionist Liberty Party,[18] and served in Congress for eighteen months (1852 – 1854). However, he grew disenchanted with politics as a means to abolish slavery, became more and more militant, involving himself in the famous "Jerry Rescue" at Syracuse,[19] and was one of the "Secret Six"

Gerrit Smith's Land Office (center) and Carriage House (Far Left) on the Gerrit Smith Estate, Peterboro, New York
Photo by Dennis Duling
Image 2.9

who supported the radical John Brown's attack on Harpers Ferry, Virginia, October 16-18, 1859. Smith had given Brown farm land near Lake Placid, New York. When Brown's revolt/raid failed, and Brown was executed, he attempted to distance himself from Brown's vision.[20] Brown's

---

[18] Smith supported women's rights—Elizabeth Cady met Henry Stanton of the Liberty Party at the Smith home—but that was negatively affected by his backing the 16th Amendment to the Constitution, the right to vote for African American men.

[19] See detail about the "Jerry Rescue" in Ch. 8.

[20] Federal authorities found on John Brown's person a letter from Smith dated June 4, 1859, and a bank draft for $100 dated August 22, 1859. After Brown's raid on Harpers Ferry failed and Brown was executed for treason, Smith suffered a temporary physical and mental breakdown and was institutionalized at the State Asylum for the Insane at Utica, New York, for a few months. See Gordon-Omelka, "Militant Abolitionist Gerrit Smith"; Dann, *Practical Dreamer*, Ch. 18.

widow then took his body to the John Brown Farm and buried him there. Most important here, Gerrit Smith was a major figure in the formation of the New York State Anti-Slavery Society and later we note that he had indirect connections with Youngstown.[21]

John Brown's House and Grave (far right) on the John Brown Farm, North Elba, New York, near Lake Placid
Photo by Dennis Duling
Image 2.10

In 1836, The Fourth Annual Report of the American Anti-Slavery Societies listed all the Anti-Slavery Societies in the United States. Some 607 societies reported, 399 did not, for a total of 1,006 societies with an average of about ninety in each society; that is almost 100,000 members. The results for New York State included Niagara County:

Number of societies: 274; number of members in 173 [reporting societies], 17,664; average number [in each society], 102; one state society; 19 county societies – Allegany, Chautauqua, Clinton, Cortland, Delaware, Erie, Genesee, Jefferson, Lewis,

---

[21] See Chs. 8, 9, 10, 14. Smith owned property in Lewiston, New York, and had land transactions with agent Myron J. Pardee, abolitionist Samuel Ringgold Ward, fugitive slave Ben Hockley, and abolitionist Jordan Gaines, all of whom played roles in the Youngstown story.

Madison, Monroe, **Niagara,** Oneida, Orleans, Oswego, Otsego, Suffolk, Tompkins, Washington; 2 young men's [societies]; 16 female [societies] and three juvenile [societies]. [22]

Map: Nineteen Anti-Slavery Society Counties in New York State, 1836
(Census Finder; public domain; counties darkened by Dennis Duling)[23]
Image 2.11

According to historian Fergus M. Bordewich, who also drew on the annual reports of the American Anti-Slavery for 1837 and 1838, the New York Anti-Slavery Society in 1837 had 21,000 members (about .009% of the total state population of about 2,300,000) and branches in nine of the county's twelve townships.[24] In the fourth Annual Report of the American Anti-Slavery

---

[22] *The Plaindealer* (New York City), Vol. 1, No. 1 (Dec 3, 1836), 590-91.
https://books.google.com/books?id=2y4ZAAAAYAAJ&pg=PA590&lpg=PA590&dq=1836+List+of+Anti-Slavery+societies+in+the+United+States,+fourth+annual+report+of+the+American+Anti-Slavery+society&source=bl&ots=o6TJwVSbRM&sig=EFpen3Yts8iIolTpIgnnTnamKKo&hl=en&sa=X&ei=9f1TVanNGZPtggTvu4HgBQ&ved=0CDAQ6AEwAw#v=onepage&q=1836%20List%20of%20Anti-Slavery%20societies%20in%20the%20United%20States%2C%20fourth%20annual%20report%20of%20the%20American%20Anti-Slavery%20society&f=false.

[23] http://www.censusfinder.com/mapny.htm.

[24] See Bordewich, *Bound for Canaan*, 147-165, especially 159. The New York State population in 1840 was 2,438, 921 (*The New York State Legislature for 1845* [New York, NY: J. Disturnell, 1845] 36). The "American Anti-Slavery Society Branches in Western New York, 1837—1838," at the State University of New York at Buffalo (U.B.), University Archives, in an archive titled "Reform, Religion and the Underground Railroad in Western New York," derived from the *Daily Commercial Advertiser* (Buffalo, New York), July 13, 1835, lists twelve societies, but three are in Lockport, and Niagara County as a whole is listed as a society. This could equal nine. Some society secretaries are also listed, for example, Lyman A. Spalding of Lockport is the secretary for all of Niagara County (for Spalding, see Ch. 11). http://library.buffalo.edu/archives/exhibits/old/urr/PDFs/ASS-WNY.pdf (the work of Christopher Densmore). The Town of Wilson is listed, but Porter and Lewiston are not; see, however, the meeting locations in the following section.

Society just noted, the average number of members in each of the 173 societies that reported across New York State was better than the national average, 102, and the total number of societies was 274 (some did not report); therefore, perhaps the total number was larger than 21,000 (102 x 274 = 28,000).[25] An estimate is that Niagara County's nine branch societies had roughly 900 to 1000 members (102 x 9).

The Anti-Slavery Society in Niagara County, New York

Niagara County lies in the extreme northwestern corner of New York State. Here are its current towns, villages, cities, and a hamlet.

Towns – 12		Villages – 5	Cities – 3	Hamlet -1
1. Cambria	7. Pendleton	1. Barker	1. Lockport	1. Ransomville
2. Hartland	8. Porter	2. Lewiston	2. Niagara Falls	
3. Lewiston	9. Royalton	3. Middleport	3. Tonawanda	
4. Lockport	10. Somerset	4. Wilson		
5. Newfane	11. Wilson	5. Youngstown		
6. Niagara	12. Wheatfield			

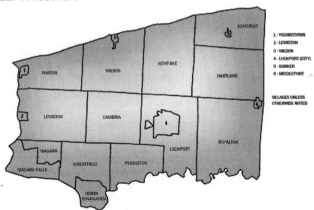

Map: Niagara County, New York
(Public Domain)[26]
Image 2.12

[25] Fourth Annual Report of the Anti-Slavery Society in "Miscellaneous News. Anti-Slavery Societies," from *The Liberator* reprinted in *The [New York] Plaindealer* (December 3. 1836), 590; see Appendix 3 for a transcription.
[26] File: Niagara County, NY map labeled png. Wikimedia Commons made black and white. https://commons.wikimedia.org/wiki/File:Niagara_County_NY_map_labeled.png.

1803 – 1895
Image in the public domain[27]
Image 2.13

Theodore Dwight Weld (1803 – 1895) arrived in Lockport, the seat of Niagara County, in mid-April of 1836. By this time, Weld was well known as a fine orator and qualified for his task. Reared in a family that boasted distinguished Congregationalist ministers, he attended Phillips Academy, was converted in 1825 by the revivalist Charles G. Finney, and studied at the integrated Oneida Institute of Science and Industry in Whitestown, New York, which was established to train ministers and educate them in physical education and manual labor ("industry"). Disenchanted, Weld led several students to transfer to Lane Theological Seminary (Presbyterian) in Cincinnati, whose president was the prominent theologian and abolitionist, Lyman Beecher, father of Harriet Beecher Stowe, author of *Uncle Tom's Cabin* (1852). At Lane, Weld became radicalized and organized the "Lane Debates" on abolition. When President Beecher and cautious members of the Board of Trustees judged that the movement was interfering with theological studies, they sought to curb it. As a result, Weld and several students, administrators, and faculty members transferred in 1835 to the newly formed, interracial Oberlin Seminary at Oberlin, Ohio, whose president was none other than Weld's spiritual father, the famed Charles G. Finney. The transferred students from Lane became the Seminary's first graduating class in 1836.[28] Meanwhile, the talented Weld had been appointed an agent of the American Anti-Slavery Society. Indeed, he helped to form more than one hundred local anti-slavery societies and had signed up thousands of abolitionists in Ohio. After graduation, he was summoned to western New York.[29]

---

[27] The print (wood engraving) of Weld is in the Library of Congress, http://www.loc.gov/pictures/item/2006687237/. Weld is probably portrayed in the old Daguerreotype group photo of the 1850 Fugitive Slave Law Convention at Cazenovia, New York. See Ch. 1.

[28] On Samuel Ringgold Ward and Hiram Wilson among the graduates, see Ch. 8.

[29] John L. Myers, "The Beginning of Anti-Slavery Agencies in New York State, 1833-1836," *New York History* 43/2 (April 1962): 173-174.

In 1836, Weld was invited to help galvanize a Niagara County Anti-Slavery Society. He was scheduled to give ten or eleven public lectures at the Lockport Presbyterian Church beginning on April 11 and to engage in a debate about slavery, although his two lawyer debate opponents failed to show.[30] The last scheduled day of Weld's anti-slavery lectures was on Saturday, April 23, 1836. It was also the day the Niagara County Anti-Slavery Society was to be officially organized. On the previous day, April 22, handbills were being handed out by opponents of these so-called "Immediate Abolitionists." They stated that they, too, would meet at the Presbyterian Church, the site of the anti-slavery lectures, on Saturday, April 23rd ("tomorrow afternoon"), precisely at 1 o'clock in order to express their opinion.

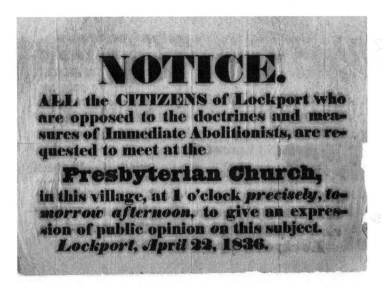

Handbill Urging Anti-Abolitionists to Organize for Opposing "Immediate Abolitionism"
at the Lockport, New York, Presbyterian Church, April 23, 1836
(Used with permission, Niagara County Historical Society, Lockport, NY)[31]
Image 2.14

---

[30] John Janitz, "Lyman A. Spalding, the Samuel Pepys of Lockport, New York," *The Courier* 8/3 (April 1971) 16 (3-19), quoting from the Spalding's Journal in the Spalding Family Papers at the George Arents Research Library, Syracuse University.
[31] Thanks to Ann Marie Linnabery, Assistant Director and Education Coordinator, The Niagara County Historical Society for her assistance in sending the handbill copy and helping with the dating (April 22 is the probable date the handbill was passed out, not the date of the meeting; if so, "tomorrow afternoon" would have meant April 23).

A large contingent of anti-abolitionists gathered that afternoon in the church. It included a judge, lawyers, and the sheriff. Weld gave the invocation and announced the subject of his lecture, but immediately the anti-abolitionists shouted, stamped their feet, and hissed. Unable to speak, Weld sat down. Over the objections of church officials, the anti-abolitionists then organized a counter-meeting and, after four hours, adopted anti-abolition resolutions, adjourned, and withdrew. The anti-slavery group, still present, proceeded to organize the Niagara County Anti-Slavery Society and adopted a Constitution, which was signed by 157 members. Lockport Quaker and UGRR activist Lyman A. Spalding wrote about the day: "1836 April 23. Formed the Niagara County Antislavery Society—after a great tumult & the most high handed encroachments upon [sic] private rights."[32] Weld, unable to lecture that day, was invited to stay longer, abandoned his plan to leave on Sunday, April 24th, and on Monday, April 25th he lectured again for four to five hours. About forty or fifty opponents appeared, but did not speak. At the end of the day, the Niagara County Anti-Slavery Constitution had 440 signatures. Within a year, it boasted 2,100 members.[33]

William J. Watkins and the 1855 Anti-Slavery Meetings in Niagara and Orleans Counties (Including Youngstown)

In the spring and summer of 1855, several advance announcements of forthcoming Anti-Slavery meetings in Orleans and Niagara Counties were published in the *Frederick Douglass' Paper*.[34] The advance notices gave the upcoming meeting dates and their locations, each location hosting two meetings that were about ten weeks apart. The announcement for the second set of meetings claimed that Douglass himself was also involved in this venture (the reference is vague), but the main organizer seems to have been Douglass' associate and friend,

---

[32] Janitz, "Lyman A. Spalding," 16, quoting from Spalding's journal.

[33] Bordewich, *Bound for Canaan*, 158-159.

[34] "Anti-Slavery Meetings in Niagara and Orleans Counties," African American Newspapers Collection at "Accessible Archives: Frederick Douglass' Paper," http://www.accessible-archives.com/2011/02/african-american-newpapers/ (membership required; last accessed May 1, 2015). The advance announcements of this first list of meeting times and places were published weekly (four times: May 4, 11, 18, and 25) in 1855 in *Frederick Douglass' Paper*, Rochester, New York. The second set of meeting times and places was published weekly (five times; see following note). Michelle Kratts, Genealogist Librarian at the Lewiston, NY, Public Library, initially found two announcements, one for each meeting. For Frederick Douglass, see above; Chs. 1, 3.

William J. Watkins (ca. 1803-ca. 1858).[35] Originally from Baltimore, Maryland, Watkins married Henrietta Russell sometime before 1826 and according to the 1850 Federal Census the couple

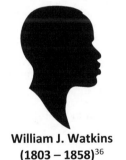

William J. Watkins (1803 – 1858)[36]
Image 2.15

had seven children living with them. Described as a teacher, he created Watkins' Academy for Negro Youth in Baltimore, educated Negro youth in rhetoric, wrote anti-colonization and anti-slavery essays, and was especially effective as an eloquent, itinerant anti-slavery lecturer in Massachusetts, Pennsylvania, and New York State. He was also the editor-in-chief of the *Freedman's Journal*, was active in African American conventions,

was influenced by his friend Frederick Douglass, and took up women's rights.[37] In 1852, he moved to Toronto, but was also an agent for the Rochester Ladies Anti-Slavery Society, which existed from 1851-1868. In a letter to Mrs. Armstrong, presumably an officer of the society, he listed fugitive slaves he had facilitated in their escape to Canada in 1856-1857:

Mrs. Armstrong, I find upon examination, that from Dec. 15th to Aug. 9th, '57, I passed 59 fugitives to Canada, as follows. 6 to Toronto, and 53 to Suspension Bridge [near Niagara Falls, New York], St. Catharines, Hamilton [Ontario], etc.

Respectfully,
Wm. J. Watkins
P. S. Expended on behalf of the Society, $90.00. W. J. W.[38]

---

[35] See "William Watkins (b. circa 1803 - d. circa 1858) (Biographical Series, "Archives of Maryland" at http://msa.maryland.gov/megafile/msa/speccol/sc5400/sc5496/002500/002535/html/002535bio.html and "Our Rights as Men," Black Abolitionist Archives 13923 at http://research.udmercy.edu/digital_collections/baa/Watkins_13923spe.pdf.

[36] There is no known photo of William J. Watkins.

[37] William Watkins and his spouse raised Frances Ellen Watkins Harper (1825 – 1911), who became a noted African American poet, author, abolitionist, and lecturer for women's rights. Thanks to Judith Wellman for this notice.

[38] Watkins' letter is cited in Wellman, "Site of the International Suspension Bridge, 1848, 1855," *Niagara Falls Underground Railroad Heritage Area Management Plan Appendix C,* 171-72. The letter is archived in the "Rochester Ladies Anti-Slavery Society and Papers, 1851-1868," William L. Clements Library Manuscripts Division, University of Michigan, Ann Arbor Michigan. See Chs. 5, 10 for Suspension Bridge Village.

Announcement of Locations of the First Series of Anti-Slavery Meetings in Orleans and Niagara Counties during May and June 1855

As is clear by now, abolitionist ideas since the 1830s became increasingly prominent in the North, especially in the northern churches, and particularly among those of the Quakers, Congregationalists, Methodists, Baptists, and Presbyterians.[39] We do not always know where the anti-slavery meetings were held, but often they were in churches. Here are the Churches of Niagara County that were in some way involved with the Anti-Slavery movement in 1850.

Quaker Meeting Houses – 4

Methodist Churches – 16[40]

Baptist Churches – 9

Presbyterian Churches – 10

Episcopal Churches – 1[41]

Advance notices of the first series of anti-slavery meetings were published four times, May 4, 11, 18, and 25, in the 1855 *Frederick Douglass' Paper*, Rochester, New York. Youngstown is one of the sites.

---

[39] Ibid., 128, Table 7. In Ch. 11, we note the development of the anti-slavery Wesleyan Methodist Church. Not only Methodists, but Baptists and Presbyterians were divided on the slavery issue, resulting in schisms.

[40] The Wesleyan Methodist Church split off from the Methodist Episcopal Church in 1842, primarily because of their anti-slavery position, theology of holiness, and church polity. It should be noted, however, that the parent Methodist Episcopal Church itself split between North and South in 1844 and most of the larger Protestant denominations did the same, primarily because of slavery. There were Wesleyan Methodist churches in Olcott and Ransomville; today they are in Appleton and Lockport. See our speculations about the Methodist circuit rider, the Reverend Glezen Fillmore, who helped to dedicate the Lockport Wesleyan church (Ch. 15).

[41] The first four denominations are listed in William J. Switala, *Underground Railroad in New York and New Jersey* (Mechanicsburg, PA: Stackpole Books, 2006), 128. We have added an Episcopal Church, St. Peter's of Niagara Falls, which had some prominent members who were probably in some way associated with the UGRR, e.g., European Americans Peter A. Porter and Elizabeth Porter, and Parkhurst and Celinda Whitney. Prominent African Americans Samuel Edwards and Charles Kersey Jackson were also members. Edwards, a "colored man" and waiter, is buried in the Niagara Falls Oakwood Cemetery and the burial service was officiated by St. Peters. Abolitionist Elizabeth Porter is also buried there. For detail, see Michelle Kratts, "Bringing Lost Souls Home: John Morrison, a Hero of Niagara" in "Hearts of War Part One: The War of 1812 at Oakwood Cemetery," Oakwood Cemetery, Niagara Falls, Series. Online at Kratt's Corner, March 26, 2013. http://myoakwoodcemetery.com/kratts-korner/. Peter A. Porter and Parkhurst Whitney are candidates for the mysterious "Col. P___" of Cassey's supposed escape to Youngstown; see Ch. 12. The Episcopal Church in Youngstown was not yet founded.

The following example is the May 4 announcement. The Youngstown meeting was on Monday, June 4, 1855.

[The NOTICE:]

WM. J. WATKINS intends to hold a series of Anti-Slavery meetings in the above named Counties. He proposes to devote four weeks to this object, commencing on MONDAY, MAY 21st. The following places have been, already, named by MR. LEMUEL PRATT, of *North Ridgeway, Orleans Co.*[42]; and any friends in these Counties, who desire Mr. WATKINS to give a lecture in the town in which they reside, are requested to communicate with him, (Mr. W.,) by letter, addressed to Rochester, or with *Mr. L. Pratt*, as promptly as possible.

[Meeting locations listed on MAY 4, 1855]

Holly, Monday, May 21.

Rendell Corners, Tuesday, May 22.

West Rendall, Wednesday, May 23.

Two Bridges, in the town of Carlton Thursday, May 24.

Yates Centre, Friday, May 25.

County Line Corners, Saturday, May 26.

Somerset, Monday, May 28.

West Somerset, Tuesday, May 29.

Charlottsville, Wednesday, May 30.

Olcott, Thursday, May 31.

Wilson, Friday, June 1.

Ransomville, Saturday June 2.

---

[42] Lemuel Pratt is a documented abolitionist. The Wellman Team Database managed by Tanya Lee Warren, "People and Sites Relating to the Underground Railroad, Abolitionism, and African American Life, 1820-1880, Niagara Falls and Niagara County" contains the following comment from Pratt's obituary: "Obit.: Died, in Somerset, Niagara County, New York [about 27 miles east of Youngstown on Lake Ontario], of typhoid fever, September 16, 1856, Deacon LEMUEL PRATT, aged sixty-five years. The subject of this notice embraced religion in his youth, and up to his death [he] lived a practical Christian. He was a pioneer in the cause of Temperance as well as the Anti-Slavery cause."
http://www.niagarafallsundergroundrailroad.org/documents/Niagara%20Falls%20Underground%20Railroad%20Project%20Database.pdf.

Youngstown, Monday, June 4.

Lewiston, Tuesday, June 5.

Pekin, Wednesday, June 6.

Lockport, Thursday, June 7.

Chestnut Ridge, Friday, June 8.

Royalton Centre, Saturday, June 9.

Shelby Centre, Monday, June 11.

Millville, Tuesday, June 12.

Eagle Harbor, Wednesday, June 13.

Gaines, Thursday, June 14.

Clarendon, Friday, June 15.

The friends, in each of these places, are called upon to make immediate arrangement for the meetings, and they are at liberty to fix the *hour* for the Lecture. Mr. WATKINS will address them in the afternoon, or evening, as they deem best. Many *urgent calls*, from ORLEANS and NIAGARA Counties, have been sent to *Frederick Douglass' Office*, for an Anti-Slavery lecturer. AN able and *efficient* man is now to be sent out to those counties one who draws large audiences wherever he lectures. The friends of the holy cause for which he labors, (who reside there) are, therefore, *especially called on to exert themselves, and to see that nothing be wanting on their part, towards rendering the meetings successful, in every respect.*

Note again the claim that Frederick Douglass himself was involved in this venture, and that the local sequence included Olcott—Wilson—Ransomville—Youngstown—and Lewiston. The Youngstown date was scheduled for Monday, June 4, 1855. The exact location in Youngstown is unknown, but might have been the Town of Porter [today First] Presbyterian Church.[43]

---

[43] The Reverend Thomas James, a former fugitive slave who crossed to Canada at Youngstown in 1821, returned to speak to Methodists and Presbyterians at the Porter (First) Presbyterian Church of Youngstown in 1883. See Ch. 7 in this book.

Announcement of Locations of the Second Series of Anti-Slavery Meetings in Orleans and Niagara Counties Meetings, August and September 1855

[Advance notice of the second series of meetings was published five times in the 1855 *Frederick Douglass' Paper*, Rochester, New York: July 27; August 3, 17, 24, and 31. It clearly included the planning of Frederick Douglass! The following example is the second, or August 3, announcement of the second series of meetings, again from the newspaper. LeRoy, the last location, missing from the July 27th announcement, was added on August 3. The Youngstown meeting was scheduled for August 28, 1855 (a Tuesday).

[The NOTICE:]

Frederick Douglass and Wm. J. Watkins, contemplate holding a series of Anti-Slavery Meetings in the above named counties, commencing on WEDNESDAY, August 15th. The following places have been already named by Mr. Lemuel Pratt, of North Ridgeway, Orleans County.[44] The friends in each of these places are called upon to make immediate arrangements for the meetings, and they are at liberty to fix the hour for the lectures. We hope nothing will be wanting on their part, towards rendering them successful in every respect: [*Note that some of the spellings are not consistent and that this second list indicates that meetings were held on Sundays; days of the week were omitted, as well.]

[Meeting locations listed on the Announcement of August 3, 1855 (unedited)]

Holly, Aug. 15th.

Kendall Corners, 16th.

West Kendall, 17th.

Two bridges in town of Carlton, 18th.

Yates Centre, 19th.

County Line Corners, 21st.

Somerset, 22nd.

West Somerset, 23rd.

---

[44] See a previous note for Pratt's obituary.

Charlottsville, 24th.

Olcott, 25th.

Wilson, 26th.

Ransomville, 27th.

Youngstown, 28th.

Lewiston, 29th.

Pekin, 30th.

Lockport, 31st.

Chestnut Ridge, Sept. 1st.

Royalton Centre, 2nd.

Shelby Centre, 3rd.

Millville, 4th.

Eagle Harbor, 5th.

Gaines, 6th.

Clarendon, 7th.

LeRoy 8th.

For further information, the friends in these places, can confer, by letter, with Mr. LEMUEL PRATT, *North Ridgeway, Orleans County*.

[Meeting locations listed on the Announcement of August 31, 1855]. LeRoy, which had been added on August 3, was now removed from the last five meetings. Again, the Youngstown meeting was scheduled for Tuesday, August 28, 1855.

> Holly, Wednesday, August 15
>
> Kendall Corners [Rendell Corners], Thursday, August 16
>
> West Lendall [Rendall] Friday, August 17
>
> Two Bridges, in the town of Carlton, Saturday, August 18
>
> Yates Centre, [Meeting scheduled on Sunday] August 19
>
> [No meeting scheduled for Monday, August 20]

County Line Corners, Tuesday, August 21

Somerset, Wednesday, August 22

West Somerset, Thursday, August 23

Charlottsville, Friday, August 24

Olcott, Saturday, August 25

Wilson, [Meeting scheduled on Sunday], August 26

Ransomville, Monday, August 27

Youngstown, Tuesday, August 28

Lewiston, Wednesday, August 29

Pekin, Thursday, August 30

Lockport, Friday, August 31

Chestnut Ridge, Saturday, September 1

Royalton Centre, [Meeting scheduled on Sunday], September 2

Shelby Centre, Monday, September 3   *[The actual last meeting]*

Millville, Tuesday, September 4   *[Taken off the August 31st announcement]*

Eagle Harbor, Wednesday, September 5   *[Taken off the August 31st announcement]*

Gaines, Thursday, September 6   *[Taken off the August 31st announcement]*

Clarendon, Friday, September 7   *[Taken off the August 31st announcement]*

LeRoy, Saturday, September 8   *[Taken off the August 31st announcement]*

For further information, the friends in these places can confer, by letter, with Mr. LEMUEL PRATT, *North Ridgeway, Orleans County*.

In short, the Youngstown meetings were scheduled for Monday, June 4, 1855, and Tuesday, August 28, 1855. The exact location of the meeting in the village is unknown, but might have been the Methodist or Presbyterian Church.

In summary, under the influence of prominent abolitionists, there appeared abolitionist publications, anti-slavery conventions, and anti-slavery movements in the 1830s, 1840s, and 1850s. The anti-slavery movements had national, state, and county organizations in the northern states, including New York State and Niagara County. Meetings were held in the towns and villages, and membership grew. The examples above show that one of the sites was Youngstown. The date, 1855, is very important. As we shall see, surviving primary sources about Youngstown's UGRR involvement date mostly from the 1850s and early 1860s.

We turn in the next chapter to a major primary source, census data about African Americans, focusing on Niagara County's Town of Porter, including Youngstown, New York, and compare it to similar data across the Niagara River in Niagara, Canada.

Addendum: Petitions to End Slavery

The right to petition Congress is one of the five freedoms of the Constitution (1st Amendment). When anti-slavery societies began to appear in the 1830's, there were an increasing number of petitions to end slavery.[45] Judith Wellman cites such petitions and some who signed them are in the Niagara Falls and Niagara County Data Base.[46] Michelle Kratts, Lewiston Public Library Librarian collected this data for Gretchen Duling who analyzed it from 1836 to 1850. Although there were signers in the hundreds from several Niagara County communities, petitions from Youngstown to Congress to end slavery have not yet been found.

---

[45] http://study.com/academy/lesson/the-impacts-of-anti-slavery-petitions-to-congress.html. See Ch.7.
[46] Wellman and Tanya Warren, Data Base Manager, "People and Sites . . . 1820-1880." http://www.niagarafallsundergroundrailroad.org/assets/Uploads/Niagara-Falls-Underground-Railroad-Project-Database.pdf.

CHAPTER 3

African Americans in the Town of Porter

Image 3.1

The Village of Youngstown is in the Town of Porter, one of twelve townships in Niagara County, New York. Most of the key information in this chapter comes from Federal Census data for the Town of Porter, which includes not only Youngstown, but also part of the Hamlet of Ransomville. [1]

Authorizing Legislation for the United States Census; Original Questions

Congress assigned responsibility for the first Federal Census in 1790 to the marshals of the United States judicial districts under an act which, with minor modifications and extensions, governed census taking through 1840.[2] It required information about the head of each household and requested answers to five questions to determine the general age, gender, free or slave living in that household. In summary:

1. Names of heads of families

---

[1] See Ch. 2, Image 2.12 for a map of Niagara County and a list of its political divisions and municipalities.
[2] United States Census Bureau, "History. 1790 Overview."
https://www.census.gov/history/www/through_the_decades/overview/1790.html.

2. Free White males of 16 years and upward, including heads of families (to assess the country's industrial and military potential)

3. Free White males under 16 years

4. Free White females, including heads of families

5. All other free persons

6. Slaves

Census forms in 1840 introduced the category of "free colored persons" as distinct from "slaves," and added other categories such as "deaf," "dumb," "blind," "idiot," and education. Age categories were by decade and related to three major categories. Summarizing:

1) Free White Persons   Heads of families, males and females, age by decade

2) Free Colored Persons   Heads of families, males and females, age by decade

3) Slaves   Heads of families, males and females, age by decade

In 1850, the categories "White" ("W"), "Black" ("B"), and "Mulatto" ("M") appeared. Other categories were from time to time included such as job classification, level of education, and whether children were in school.

Number of Slaves Reported in the U.S. Census Data, 1790 – 1860

"The first slaves brought to this country were sold from a Dutch vessel at Jamestown, Va., in 1619."[3] According to United States Census records, nationally, the number of slaves increased dramatically from 1790 to 1860.

In 1790 (first United States Census) the slaves numbered 697,897.

In 1800, there were   893,000.

In 1810, there were 1,191,364.

In 1820, there were 1,538,038.

In 1830, there were 2,009,043.

In 1840, there were 2,487,455.

In 1850, there were 3,204,313.

In 1860, there were 3,952,608.[4]

Census Data for the Town of Porter in Niagara County, New York, 1814 – 1850

Niagara County was created from Genesee County in 1818 and Erie County was created from Niagara County in 1821. The Town of Porter in Niagara County, named for Judge Augustus S. Porter of Niagara Falls, was created from the Town of Cambria on June 1, 1812, by an act of the New York State Legislature. It is situated in the northwest corner of Niagara County (and New York State) and bounded on the north by Lake Ontario, on the west by the Niagara River, on the east by Ransomville, and on the south by Lewiston.[5]

---

[3] Pettit, *Sketches,* 1.

[4] McKinstry, "Introduction," in Pettit, *Sketches*, 1.

[5] See "About Porter" http://townofporter.net/about.porter; https://www.genealogyinc.com/newyork/niagara-county/; Suzanne Simon Dietz, "History of Porter," http://townofporter.net/history-of-porter, who derived her data from the Niagara County Historian's Office, Lockport, New York. For more on Augustus Porter, see Ch. 9; for maps of Niagara County, see Ch. 2 (Images 2:11; 2:12).

Year:	Population:	Year:	Population:
1814	148	1855	2,643
1820	**850**	**1860**	**2,353**[6]
1825	925	1865	2,366
1830	**1,490**	1870	2,042
1835	1,838	1875	2,102
1840	**2,177**	1880	2,278
1845	2,303	1885	2,700
1850	**2,455**	1890	2,104

These population numbers do not give information about the number of slaves, free colored people, or Mulattos living in the Town of Porter. Before taking up this information in Porter, we ask basic questions about Census categories not yet considered, free colored or Black and Mulatto persons.

Free Colored (Black) and Mulatto Persons

The category "free colored persons" was added to the Federal Census in 1840. Changes were made again in 1850: household members were now listed individually in one of two major categories, "Free" or "Slave." These two categories were subdivided with further options by racial categories: White, Black, Mulatto. The "Free" category could be left open or blank (indicating "White"), filled in with "M" (Mulatto), or filled in with "B" (Black); the "Slave" category could be filled in with "M" (Mulatto) or "B" (Black).[7]

Chapters 1 and 2 contained in this book take up "slavery." In this chapter, we briefly consider the new Census categories "free colored" ("free Black") and "Mulatto."

---

[6] If these statistics are correct, we have no certain explanation for the drop in population between 1855 (2,643) and 1880 (1880: 1880: 2,278). Perhaps some left because two railroads to Youngstown did not succeed; see Ch. 5. Perhaps some were casualties of the Civil War; https://dmna.ny.gov/historic/reghist/civil/dornbusch/niagara.htm. For shifts in the military population at Fort Niagara, see the Addendum at the end of this chapter.

[7] https://www.census.gov/history/www/through_the_decades/index_of_questions/1850_1.html,

These categories, of course, were added by the White persons who constructed the Census forms.[8] The terms "free colored" or "free Black" could refer to several sub-categories. Free Blacks were free African American immigrants such as sailors; the children of free Black women (*partus sequitur ventrem*[9]); mixed-race children of free Native Americans; and slaves manumitted by their masters, whether by the master's beliefs or by a will. Free light-skinned "colored" whose mothers were normally White indentured servants were called "Mulattos" in 1850 and they could be either free or slave.

The category "Mulatto" to describe human beings, added to the Census in 1850, had for some persons a stigma;[10] certainly, its offensiveness to persons so described has grown to the degree that it has generally fallen out of use.[11] However, it was common in the antebellum period. Some Whites considered Mulattos to be a superior to darker skinned Blacks because their "blood" was mixed with supposedly genetically superior Whites; some Mulattos accepted these views and considered themselves to be superior to Blacks.[12] Some officials accepted the category and held that Mulatto status was higher than Black status—evolutionary theories of racial superiority and inferiority related to skin color were common—but they were in the minority. Some officials believed that the category implied "miscegenation," or racial mixing in marriage or breeding and since they disapproved of miscegenation—anti-miscegenation laws were common—they preferred not to acknowledge the term. Northern travelers in the South were often struck by what they perceived to be the relatively high number of Mulattos, impressions that came primarily from the cities rather than the plantations. According to the

---

[8] In trying to categorize categories such as "race" and "ethnicity," the Federal Census forms have changed every census; recent forms include an undefined category "Other" as a choice. Despite DNA, categories of race and ethnicity are as much social and cultural as they are biological, if not more so.

[9] For the ancient Roman law *partus sequitur ventrem*, see Ch. 1.

[10] The term comes from Arabic *muwallad* and Latin *Mulatto*, terms for mule, a hybrid or "mixed breed" between a horse and a donkey. It entered English through Spanish (*mulato; mestizo*). Attitudes about racial purity analogous to the breeding of animals were common. From the biological perspective of the human gene pool, all humans are Mulattos; however, social identity categories tend to rule.

[11] Robert Brent Toplin, "Between Black and White: Attitudes toward Southern Mulattos, 1830-1861," *The Journal of Southern History* 45/2 (1979), 185-200. Negative labels by outsiders have sometimes become acceptable to insiders, for example, "Christian"; African-Americans once preferred "Negro" over "Black," but at this writing that has reversed, and indeed, the more inclusive "people of color" (as contrasted with "White") is now common.

[12] Lighter-skinned Creoles in antebellum New Orleans often joined Whites, but that gradually changed after the Civil War. It is noteworthy that most of Harriet Beecher Stowe's heroes were Mulattos, including Eliza; see the Eliza sketch in Ch. 9.

1860 Federal Census, Mulattos made up 10.4% of the slave population and 36.2% of the free population; however, such figures were skewed by several factors, such as selective inclusion in the Census and Census takers' unschooled opinions. However, it cannot be denied that male sexual promiscuity and sexual oppression of women were involved and underlying such relationships were what we would call racist attitudes.

Census categories "slave," "free," "Black," and "Mulatto" were, or course, complicated by social contexts and social identity. Black or Mulatto fugitive slaves who escaped to free states or to free Canada might be termed "free," but they risked their freedom if they voluntarily returned to slave states, especially after 1850. They also lost their freedom if they were kidnapped by slave catchers and returned to their masters. Legally "free colored" (Black or Mulatto) were sometimes kidnapped and sold into slavery; if they then escaped, they could *become* fugitive slaves. Living in free states and free territories was no guarantee of perpetual freedom. Dred Scott, a slave from the slave state of Missouri according to the Missouri Compromise of 1820, had been living with his family in the non-slave states Illinois and Wisconsin, and sued for his freedom. However, by a 7–2 decision of the Supreme Court in 1856 (effective March 6, 1857), he lost his case on the principle that persons of African American descent were not United States citizens with rights in a federal court.[13] Moreover, the term "free" did not mean free *and equal*. Most Black males were limited to farming and the various trades, such as boatman, laborer, teamster, Blacksmith, or carpenter;[14] and most African American women were limited to domestic work. There were, of course, notable exceptions to these generalities: highly prominent and educated Black men such as William Still and ex-slaves Frederick Douglass and John P. Parker,[15] or the Quaker-educated journalist Mary Ann Shadd Cary (1823-1893).

---

[13]U.S. Supreme Court. *Scott v. Sandford*. 60 U.S. (19 How.) 393 (1856): "4. A free negro of the African race, whose ancestors were brought to this country and sold as slaves, is not a 'citizen' within the meaning of the Constitution of the United States." *Justia US Supreme Court* at https://supreme.justia.com/cases/federal/us/60/393/case.html. Legal scholars often say that this decision was the worst (most unjust) Supreme Court decision ever made.

[14] See comments on barbers below.

[15] For Frederick Douglas, see Ch. 2; on Still, Tubman, and Parker, see below; on Mary Ann Shadd Cary, see Shirley J. Yee, *Black Women Abolitionists: A Study in Activism, 1828-1860* (Knoxville: Univ. of Tennessee Press, 1992); Jane Rhodes, *Mary Ann Shadd Cary: The Black Press and Protest in the Nineteenth Century* (Bloomington, IN: Indiana University Press, 1998). See Blackpast.org: http://www.Blackpast.org/gah/cary-mary-ann-shadd-1823-1893#sthash.2JQFdMdh.dpuf.

Here is an interesting and instructive quotation from a 1937 interview with a free Black man working for the Works Progress Administration during the New Deal:

> We was known as "Free Niggers." Master said he didn't believe it was right to own human beings just because dey was Black, and he freed all his slaves long before de War. He give 'em all freedom papers and told dem dat dey was as free as he was and could go anywhere dey wanted. Dey didn't have nowhere to go so we all stayed on wid him. It was nice though to know we could go where we pleased 'thout having to get a pass and could come back when we pleased even if we didn't take advantage of it.[16]

This quotation mentions *freedom papers*. It important to recall that Blacks and Mulattos who freely moved about were well advised to carry freedom papers, or if they were ex-slaves, manumission certificates that detailed their terms of manumission.[17] An early example from the City of New York is the manumission certificate of George by his master John [Delaney?].

---

[16] "Slave to Free Before General Emancipation. Selections from 19th- & 20th-Century Slave Narratives," National Humanities Center Resource Toolbox. The Making of African American Identity: Vol. I, 1500-1865, http://nationalhumanitiescenter.org/pds/maai/identity/text2/slavetofreenarr.pdf.
[17] Larry Gara, *The Liberty Line*, 46-47.

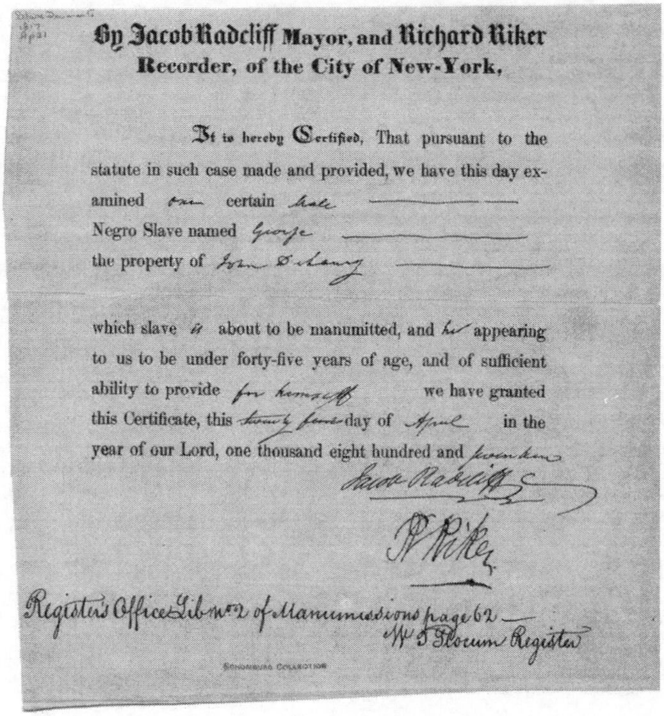

Manumission Certificate for a Slave named "George," April 24, 1817
(Permission of the New York Public Library)[18]
Image 3.2

A transcription reads (hand-written words italicized):

> By Jacob Radcliff Mayor, and Richard Riker / Recorder, of the City of New-York,

> It is hereby Certified, That pursuant to the statute in such case made and provided, we

> have this day examined *one* certain *hale* [healthy; able-bodied] --- Negro Slave named

> *George* --- the property of *John Delaney* --- which slave is about to be manumitted, and

> *he* appearing to us to be under forty-five years of age, and of sufficient ability to provide

---

[18] "Manumission certificate for a slave named George, signed by Radcliffe and Riker, New York City, 24 April 1817." Reproduced by permission of the New York Public Library, Slavery and Abolition Collection, Thomas Lisalnti, Manager, Permissions and Reproduction Services. For other examples of Deeds of Manumission from several states, see the New York Heritage Digital Collections, Slavery Collection, at http://cdm16694.contentdm.oclc.org/cdm/search/searchterm/manumission; also, Dernoral Davis, "A Contested Presence: Free Black in Antebellum Mississippi, 1820—1860," Mississippi Historical Society, http://mshistorynow.mdah.state.ms.us/articles/45/a-contested-presence-free-Blacks-in-antebellum-mississippi-18201860.

for himself we have granted this Certificate, this *twenty fourth* day of *April* in the year of

our Lord, one thousand eight hundred and *seventeen.*

[Signed] *Jacob Radcliffe*
P Riker
Register's Office Lib No. 2 of Manumissions page 62 ---
W. T. Slocum Register[19]

The Importance of Free Blacks and Mulattos for the Underground Railroad: William Still, Harriet Tubman, and John P. Parker

Free Blacks and Mulattos often helped freedom seekers, sometimes in Black or mixed

Black-White UGRR networks. Three famous examples were William Still, Harriett Tubman, and

John P. Parker.

William Still (1821 – 1902)
Image in the Public Domain
Image 3.3

Under Maryland state law, William Still was a slave because, although his father, Levin

Still, was manumitted in 1796 in the slave state of Maryland, his mother, Charity, was a slave

(*partus sequitur ventrem*). Still escaped to New Jersey and then in 1844 he moved to

---

[19] *Register's office Lib no. 2 of manumissions page 62 - / W F Slocum Register.*
http://nationalhumanitiescenter.org/pds/maai/identity/text2/text2read.htm.

Philadelphia in the non-slave state of Pennsylvania.[20] There, he became a clerk for the Pennsylvania Anti-Slavery Society and chairman of its committee to help fugitive slaves who arrived in Philadelphia. It is estimated that from 1844 to 1865, he helped at least sixty freedom seekers a month, an accomplishment that led some to honor him with the title, "Father of the Underground Railroad."[21] His work, *Still's Underground Railroad,* is a classic and considered to contain reliable accounts of fugitive slave experiences.[22]

The best-known example is Harriet Tubman. She was born a slave under Maryland state law, escaped from Maryland in 1849 to the free states of Pennsylvania and New York. Tubman was an UGRR conductor who led approximately seventy individuals to freedom into Canada between 1849 and 1860. She also became active in the women's suffrage movement. Kate Clifford Larson writes in praise of Tubman's courageous life:

> The true facts of Tubman's long life, including her years under slavery, her family life, her profound spirituality, and her accomplishments as a freedom fighter from her Underground Railroad days to her Civil War exploits and then later her suffrage and community activism, reveal a remarkably powerful and influential life endured during some of the darkest days in American history. Motivated by a deep love of family, Tubman struggled against great odds to bring scores of relatives and friends to freedom in the North. Necessarily shrouded in secrecy at the time, the details of her escape missions have been buried in the historical record for generations.[23]

---

[20] New Jersey passed gradual abolition laws in 1798, 1804, and 1820. It abolished slavery in 1846, but slaves could be redefined as "apprentices" and slavery did not totally end there until 1865; Maryland did not officially abolish slavery until November 1, 1864. Fugitive slaves on one line of the UGRR often passed from Maryland to New Jersey and then crossed the Hudson River by ferry. See Switala, *The Underground Railroad in New York and New Jersey.*
[21] Femi Lewis, "William Still," at *About Education,* http://afroamhistory.about.com/od/africanamericanwomen/a/WilliamStill.htm; Temple University Libraries, "The Live and Times of William Still." http://stillfamily.library.temple.edu/timeline/william-still.
[22] *Still's Underground Railroad* is a shortened title (Revised edition, 1872); https://books.google.com/books?id=KD9LAAAAYAAJ&pg=PA269&lpg=PA269&dq=Suspension+Bridge,+Niagara+Falls,+Methodist+church&source=bl&ots=yeGlIX_WTr&sig=l9b_b3PoX21MJYYLMKr1AbG4D9A&hl=en&sa=X&ved=0ahUKEwiguOzni9vOAhVD1B4KHSdFBDcQ6AEIPTAG#v=onepage&q=Suspension%20Bridge%2C%20Niagara%20Falls%2C%20Methodist%20church&f=false. Republished in 1879 as *The Underground Railroad;* an 1886 edition is on line in the Gutenberg collection. http://www.gutenberg.org/files/15263/15263-h/15263-h.htm. A selective Dover version has been edited with an Introduction by Ian Frederick Finseth (Mineola, NY: Dover Publications, Inc., 2007).
[23] Kate Clifford Larson, *Bound for the Promised Land. Harriet Tubman, Portrait of an American Hero* (New York, NY: Ballantine Books, 2004) xv-xvi. Larson states that the view that she conducted 300 to freedom is an exaggeration.

Harriet Tubman (1822 – 1913)
Photo by H. B. Lindsay, N.D.; Library of Congress, in the Public Domain
Image 3.4 [23b]

A third example is John P. Parker (1827—1900).[24] Parker was born a slave—his mother was African American—in Norfolk, Virginia. In Richmond, at age eight, he was sold to a doctor from Mobile, Alabama, and became a domestic servant. The doctor's sons smuggled books to him and he learned illegally to read and write. Their father, his master, encouraged him to learn the trade of iron molding. After the strong-headed Parker got into trouble and made several unsuccessful attempts to escape, the frustrated doctor put him up for sale. In 1845, Parker persuaded one of the doctor's patients, a widow named Mrs. Ryder, to buy him for $1800 plus interest on the premise that he would work to purchase his freedom. Freed eighteen months

---

[23b] In 2017 a heretofore unknown photo of the young Harriet Tubman was discovered in an old photo album once belonging to an abolitionist Quaker schoolteacher of freed slaves in Arlington, Virginia, Emily Howland. This photo was taken by Benjamin Powelson of Auburn, New York, ca. 1868 or 1869, where Tubman settled after the Civil War. It was purchased at auction by the Library of Congress and the Smithsonian National Museum of African American History and Culture. See Mark Hartsell, "Rare Photo of Harriet Tubman Preserved," Library of Congress, online.

[24] John Parker's amazing story, told to the journalist Frank Moody Gregg in the 1880s, who made notes for a proposed book on Parker, was resurrected from a Duke University archive, edited by Stuart Seely Sprague, and published in 1996 as *His Promised Land: The Autobiography of John P. Parker, Former Slave and Conductor on the Underground Railroad* (New York, NY: W. W. Norton, 1996).

later, he slowly made his way north to Jeffersonville, Indiana, then to Cincinnati, and after rescuing his family, settled in the robust Ohio River town of Ripley, which boasted many

John P. Parker (1827 – 1900)[25]
Image 3.5

abolitionists and was an important terminal in the Underground Railroad. The leader was the radical White abolitionist, the Reverend John Rankin.[26] Parker worked his trade by day, but by night slipped across the border to Kentucky and was an active UGRR conductor. Slave holders placed a $1,000 bounty on his head, which was legal under the *Fugitive Slave Act of 1850*. In his later autobiography, he claimed to have brought about 315 fugitive slaves from the slave state of Kentucky into the free state of Ohio. He recorded their names in his diary, but then destroyed it to protect everyone's safety. Parker was intelligent, ambitious, and industrious. After the war, he co-owned his own foundry and milling business. He fathered three boys and three girls, all of whom became well educated and successful in their professions.

---

[25] John P. Parker refused to have his photo taken and there is no official photo of him. Thanks to Dewey Scott, Docent at the John P. Parker House, Ripley, Ohio; see also "John P. Parker House," National Park Service Department of the Interior, http://www.nps.gov/nt/travel/underground/oh2.htm.
[26] See "John Rankin," the Ohio History Connection http://www.ohiohistorycentral.org/w/Rankin,_John?rec=319. Rankin is in the national UGRR Hall of Fame, http://www.nationalabolitionhalloffameandmuseum.org/jrankin.html. The John Rankin House was designated a National Historical Landmark in 1997. For Parker's description of Ripley and members of the UGRR there, see *His Promised Land*, Ch. 7. For an important study on the Reverend John Rankin, see Ann Hagedorn, *Beyond the River* (New York, NY: Simon and Schuster, 2004).

What Parker did was bold and dangerous, even heroic. Larry Gara described a common role of such free Blacks this way:

> Free Negroes wrote passes, gave instructions and directions, and housed fugitives in their homes, in spite of heavy penalties which befell some of them for such activity. In 1837 a Federal court in Washington, D.C., convicted a free Negro of forging a certificate of freedom [or Deed of Manumission] for one slave and a pass for another. The judge sentenced him to seven years in prison. Such severity was not uncommon.[27]

Free Blacks (Free Colored Persons) in Niagara County

The following chart gives a statistical breakdown of the population and number of Free Blacks in Niagara County.

	Population[28]	Free Blacks[29]	Slaves
1820	22,990	67	15
1830	18,482	(140?[30])	0[31]
1840	31,132	241	0
1850	42,376	317	0
1860	50,399	517	0

This chart shows that the general population as a whole much more than doubled between 1820 and 1860, and that the Free Black population in Niagara County went from 67 to 517.

---

[27] Gara, *The Liberty Line,* 54, citing Catterall, *Judicial Cases*, 2:320, 4:200; *St. Louis Daily Union*, November 2, 1846.
[28] William Pool, Editor, *Landmarks of Niagara County, New York* (Syracuse, NY: D. Mason and Co., 1897), 4; supplemented by https://en.wikipedia.org/wiki/Niagara_County,_New_York; Gazetteer of the State of New York (Albany, NY: B. D. Packard, 1824), 164.
[29] Switala, *The Underground Railroad in New York and New Jersey*, 81.
[30] This is an estimate. We know of nine free colored persons in the Town of Porter in 1830.
[31] For the abolition of slavery in New York State in 1827, see Ch. 1.

Eighteen Free Blacks in the Town of Porter, Niagara County, 1820–1865

The following statistics for 1820 to 1865 about the Town of Porter (where the Village of Youngstown is located) combine several sources: federal census data in Ancestry.com; the Census Record Booklets in the Town of Porter Historical Society Museum;[32] and information from Michelle Kratts, the Genealogist and Librarian at the Lewiston Public Library and former Niagara Falls Historian. These statistics include categories of the period—race, gender, and age—as well as the names of the person in whose house, with one exception all White, they were residing ("head of household" category). The head of household below is in bold typeface.

1820 – 0 – Colored Persons listed in the Census. No reference to any Free Colored Persons

1830 – 9 – Colored Persons listed in the Census.[33]

Simon Forte – 1 Free Colored Male (age 24 – 35)

1 Free Colored Male (age 36 – 55)

1 Free Colored Female (age 10 – 23)

Reuben H. Boughton – 1 Free Colored Female (age 24 – 35). In his household were also 4 free White males (20 – 29), 1 free White male (15 – 19), 1 free White female (20 – 29), and 1 alien.[34]

Ezekiel Jewett – 1 Free Colored Male (age 36 – 55)

1 Free Colored Female (age 10 – 23)

Elijah Boardman [Bradman] – 1 Free Colored Male (age 10 – 23)

Gideon Kelsey – 1 Free Colored Male (age 24 – 35)

1 Free Colored Female (age 24 – 35) [p. 326]

---

[32] Town of Porter Historical Society Museum, 240 Lockport Street, Youngstown, NY 14174. The census statistics refer only to those who reported.

[33] Copies of the micro-film records have many hand-written census reports that are very difficult to decipher. The small number of "Free Colored" people listed and may not be accurate. Michelle Kratts, Lewiston Public Library genealogist and the City of Niagara Falls historian, assisted in deciphering the tally marks and came up with the two people (Boughton and Jewett) who recorded three colored persons in 1830. Further digging in census data with assistance from Jean Siddall of the Town of Porter Museum produced three more colored persons (Forte, Boardman, and Kelsey).

[34] See Ch. 4 for a schooner built in Youngstown called the "R. H. Boughton" (1829).

The ferryman **John Phillips** is listed in the 1830 records.[35] But there is no reference to Free Colored People living in his household at this time. (However, see 1840.)

1840 – 5 – Colored Persons listed in the Census:

Charles Armstrong – 2 Free Colored Males, 1 (age 10 – 23) and 1 (age 24 – 35)

Charles Merchant – 1 Free Colored Female (age 10 – 23)

John Phillips – 1 Free Colored Male (age 24 – 35)

Timothy Beals – 1 Free Colored Female (age 10 – 23)

1850 – 0 – Colored Person in the Census (*Fugitive Slave Act of 1850* influence?[36])

1860 – 1 – Black Male Servant [term "Black" is used]

Nelson R. Davis (farmer and miller) family[37] – 1 Black male servant, age 50, born in Virginia. In the 1860 census, a Black person named **Austin McPherson** (written form on the electronic census was transcribed wrongly as "Austele M Pherson") was recorded as born in Virginia. He is an important link to others in the area. In the 1870 census of Lewiston, New York, McPherson was listed as a Black laborer who with his wife Maria were now living with 72-year old General Jordan Gain[e]s. Gaines was a free African American, a Black laborer, and a widower who had been married to possible abolitionist Mary McClary Gaines (original owner of Lewiston properties, including the house at 350 Second Street).[38] He was a recipient of a land grant from Gerrit Smith, and a speaker at an emancipation celebration that honored John Morrison.[39]

---

[35] For more on Phillips, see below and Ch. 6.

[36] The record that there were no slaves in the Town of Porter in 1850 might have resulted from the *Fugitive Slave Acts of 1850*, passed September 21, 1850. It was published in the preceding months and many African Americans fled to Canada. An example is Ben Hockley, whose story is reported in Ch. 9.

[37] For more on the Davis family, see Ch. 14.

[38] Gain[e]s' wife Mary McClary appears to have had a connection with the Black (or White) abolitionist network; for more on McPherson and the Gaineses, see Ch. 14.

[39] See below and Ch. 14.

1865 – 3 – A self-reporting Mulatto/Black Family, apparently permanent residents with a frame house on Main Street, Youngstown, New York (property #382 valued at $800.00) (June 30, 1865). On a map of Youngstown, this house would have been north of the Ontario House on the east side of Main Street between Lockport and Chestnut Streets.[40] Members of the family were:

William Thompson, head of household (a **barber**), age 46 [b. 1819], male (**MUL** [=Mulatto]), born in Florida.[41]

Angeline Thompson, his wife, age 20 [b. 1845], female (**BLK** [= Black]), born in Canada.

Frank Thompson, age 8/12 [8 months] (**MUL** [=Mulatto]), born in Canada.

In the Thompson household, there was also a **Dieling family of seven people** that was not listed as Black or Mulatto. Apparently, it was a White European family that boarded in the Thompson home. Individually, they were listed in the census as:

Daniel Dieling (a Prussian shoemaker) – listed as NAT, age 38

Mary Dieling – wife – [Württemberg, Germany, not Pennsylvania—listed as alien, age 35]

Caroline Dieling – daughter born in Canada, age 12

Henry Dieling – son born in Erie, age 10

Lena Dieling – daughter born in Erie, age 4

Mary Dieling – daughter born in Erie, age 2 years and 4 months

Kate Dieling – daughter born in Niagara [County], age 2 months

Perhaps there were a few more than eighteen Free Colored people since heads of households might not have wanted to officially record their number due to the haunting fear of

---

[40] There is a modified 1848 map of this area in Ch. 16.

[41] According to a letter by James Onen to the *Youngstown News* in 1908, there was a Youngstown barber named Thomas Ellis on Main Street in the early 1850s; see Ch. 10.

reprisal, especially after the *Fugitive Slave Act of 1850*. Perhaps some freed colored people, like their fugitive slave brothers and sisters, crossed over to Canada in the 1850s.

The Thompson family living on Main Street in Youngstown seems to verify that there were Free Colored people living in the Village itself, at least by the end of the Civil War.

Several bits of information are known about persons in this list.

Ferryman John Phillips, 1840: 1 Free Colored Male (age 24-35)

In the 1840 Federal Census, a free colored man age 24-35 was living in the household of John Phillips. We have more information about John Phillips.

1) John Phillips was highlighted in the 1826 New York State Law about licensing the ferry in Youngstown and ran the Youngstown Ferry for the years 1824, 1825, 1826, and 1827.[42] That same John Phillips seems to be the John Phillips listed in the 1830 Federal Census. If so, still more is known about him. In his *Survey* of Youngstown properties, Don Ames noted that John Young (1765—1840), for whom the village of Youngstown is named, sued three men in 1838, Obed Smith, *John Phillips*, and Hezekiah Scovell, and that Sheriff T. T. Roberts seized some "Goods or Chattels or Property."[43] The term "chattels" here does not refer to *human* property, that is, slaves, but *material* property. In any case, a John Phillips in the 1840 Census lists the African American living in his household as Free Colored, not a Slave.

2) In 1840, *Harry W.* Phillips applied for license to operate the Youngstown Ferry for seven years.[44] His application was co-signed by John *G.* Phillips. If the latter person was not our John Phillips, perhaps he was John Jr., brother of Harry, that is, both would have been John Phillip's sons. A license to run a profitable ferry was often perpetuated and carefully guarded in families. In short, two generations of Phillips ferrymen may be represented.

---

[42] For more on the ferryman John Phillips, see Ch. 6.
[43] Ames, *Survey*.
[44] See Chapter 6.

Charles Armstrong, Youngstown, New York
Charles Merchant, Youngstown, New York
Timothy Beals, Youngstown, New York

We consider these three together simply because we do not have more information about them or the African Americans living in their households.

Barbers and Youngstown's Mulatto Barber, William Thompson, and His Family

In the 1865 Town of Porter Federal Census, a Mulatto barber, William Thompson, and his family were living in the Town of Porter, apparently living on Main Street in Youngstown, and they had boarders.

African American barbers are a fascinating subject. Judith Wellman has written about a barber in Seneca Falls, New York. She states that according to the 1850 Federal Census there were several well-respected Blacks scattered about Seneca Falls. They were visible, had jobs, and owned property, like Youngstown's William Thompson. The most prosperous was the barber Thomas James (not the Thomas James in this book[45]). Wellman writes:

> Thomas James [of Seneca Falls] probably knew most people in town. As the local barber, he came into contact with most of the adult male population of the village. In the early 1850s, he also began to cut women's hair. In 1852, for example, Elizabeth Cady Stanton, woman's rights activist and one of James' neighbors, asked James to cut her hair short as part of her new campaign for women's health. Thomas James was also a member of the anti-slavery Wesleyan Methodist Church; by 1850 he had become a trustee.
> . . . .
> If our assumptions hold true, the [one African American] person born in Canada and the one with an unknown birthplace would most likely be fugitive slaves. It is probably no coincidence that they belonged to the same household. Thomas James, the barber, refused to tell the census taker where he had been born, although his wife, Sarah E. James, reported her birthplace as Pennsylvania, and their thirteen-year-old

---

[45] Ch. 7.

daughter, Martha, listed her birthplace as Canada. It seems likely that the James family had moved to Canada sometime before Martha's birth and had re-emigrated to the United States during the late 1830s or 1840s. Thomas James therefore stands out as the only reasonably likely identifiable self-emancipated slave in Seneca Falls in 1850. He and his wife and daughter may have been the only African American family to incorporate a fugitive.

Thomas James also stands out for other reasons. As a barber, he was the only African American listed as having a skilled job [Mills in the following quotation considers barbering to have been unskilled labor]. His family owned more than twice as much property as another Black family in the village [worth $1400]. And he was the most noticeable Black presence in local anti-slavery activities. He was the only African American to sign the anti-slavery petition sent from Seneca Falls in 1850. And he was the only local Black man to sign a petition in favor of the new [abolitionist] Free Soil Party in June, 1848. [46]

Since Wellman wrote, more research about Black barbers has appeared. In *Cutting Along the Color Line. Black Barbers and Barber Shops in America,* African American Historian Quincy T. Mills of Vassar College, who studied Black barbershops and investigated their cultural history,[47] states in an interview:

In the South, barbers were both enslaved and free Black men. There were White barbers in the North, but they were mostly immigrants, Irish and German and, later, Italian. Essentially, people associated barbering and other service work with unskilled labor, and White men positioned themselves as entitled to skilled jobs . . . Before the Civil War, most Black barbers explicitly groomed wealthy White men, like businessmen

---

[46] Judith Wellman, "This Side of the Border: Fugitives from Slavery in Three Central New York Communities," *New York History* (October 1998), 369-70.

[47] In assisting Melissa Victoria Harris-Perry [formerly Harris-Lacewell] on her first book, *Barbershops, Bibles, BET: Everyday Talk and Black Political Thought* (Princeton, NJ: Princeton University Press, 2004), Quincy T. Mills was led to research and write *Cutting Along the Color Line: Black Barbers and Barber Shops in America* (Philadelphia, PA: University of Pennsylvania Press, 2013).

and politicians. Black customers were not allowed to get haircuts in these Black-owned barbershops, mainly because White customers didn't want Black customers getting shaved next to them. That smacked too much of social equality, so barbers capitulated to the wishes of their White customers both in the North and the South. You might wonder, "Where did Black men get their hair cut?" They got haircuts on somebody's front porch, or in the yard, or in all these barbershops after hours, off the record. I wrote about the case of a fugitive slave who recorded his travels through Kentucky, where he needed a place to hide out for the night, and explicitly looked for barbershops because he knew most barbers were Black men. He found a barbershop, and he guessed the barber was Black; . . . [the barber] let him in, and immediately locked the door behind him. The fugitive's name was John Brown [not the John Brown of the Harpers Ferry attack, who was White], and he wrote that the barber said, "You can stay for the night, but you have to be gone before morning because if anyone finds you here, it will shut up my shop."

I take that to mean that if White folks found out he was harboring a fugitive slave, they wouldn't patronize his business. But if the barber was willing to open his door after hours to this enslaved person on the run, it suggests that other barbers may have opened their doors after hours for all sorts of things. There aren't enough sources to explore that in great detail, but I think it's fascinating that they hint at it.[48]

William Thompson and his family, like Seneca Falls barber Thomas James and his family, had lived in Canada. We do not know when he came to Youngstown or how long he barbered in the village, but only that he was prosperous enough to have property and was willing to fill out a census form in 1865. With respect to the antebellum 1850s and the UGRR, it certainly would be exciting if we knew more about William Thompson's story and his off-hours activities!

------

[48] The quotation is from Mills in the interview by Hunter Oatman-Stanford, "Straight Razors and Social Justice: The Empowering Evolution of Black Barbershops," *Collectors Weekly* (2014): 1-22; http://www.collectorsweekly.com/articles/the-empowering-evolution-of-Black-barbershops/.

Mills observes that White barbers in the North were mostly immigrants—Irish and German, and, later, Italian. This was because barbers in Europe were White. In other words, there would have been little or no professional stigma about northern White barbers among immigrants and perhaps—a conjecture—fewer racist attitudes about barbers. Does this possibility help to explain why a Prussian shoemaker and his German wife, presumably immigrants, and their five children were boarding in the home of a Mulatto barber?

There is no surviving information, written or oral, that free William Thompson, designated a Mulatto, his wife Angeline Thompson designated a Black, and a son Frank Thompson, designated a Mulatto, who were reported in the 1865 federal census, had been part of any Youngstown or regional UGRR network. Yet, he was a barber, and Black barbers were known to help fugitive slaves. Moreover, he was considered to be a Mulatto, which might have given him some higher status among some White customers.

If further speculation be permitted, it is worth noting that in 1886, the Reverend Thomas James (not the Seneca Falls barber) wrote in his autobiography that, "At Lockport a colored man showed me the way to the Canadian border. I crossed the Niagara at Youngstown on the ferry boat, and was free!"[49] We shall see that the Youngstown ferryman in 1821 was Elijah Hathaway, but the *Niagara Falls News* reported in 1883 that the one who "ferried" Thomas James across the Niagara River was Elijah's brother, *Olaf* Hathaway.[50] Did the colored man at Lockport have any UGRR connections in Youngstown?

Later, we point out that Nelson Davis's Black servant in 1860 was Austin McPherson who, with his wife Maria, was in 1870 living in Lewiston with Jordan Gain[e]s, the African American husband of Mary McClary Gain[e]s, deceased (1854). Mary had connections. She had been given a Warranty Deed ($1) for property from John Carter of Youngstown in 1840, and there are UGRR oral traditions about Carter. Mary's death was also reported by Frederick Douglass in his *Frederick Douglass' Paper*.[51] This suggests that she might have been an abolitionist. Was her African American husband Jordan Gain[e]s involved in the UGRR?

---

[49] James, *The Life of Rev. Thomas James, by Myself*, 6; see the longer quotation at the beginning of Ch. 1.
[50] See Chs. 6, 12. Thomas James does not identify the ferryman in his *Autobiography*.
[51] See Ch. 14.

Jordan Gaines was the speaker at the 1856 Niagara Falls gathering that celebrated the emancipation of slaves in the British West Indies in 1834. This was the same meeting at which John Morrison, a known conductor working out of the Cataract Hotel in Niagara Falls, was honored.[52]

What, then, about General Gaines' later house residents, African Americans Austin McPherson and his wife Maria? What about the free Blacks listed in the 1840 census by John Phillips, Charles Armstrong, and Charles Merchant? These links, direct and indirect, suggest the possibility that there was communication among the Free Colored people along the Lower Niagara River, and that communication possibly extended to Niagara Falls where Free Black employees of the Cataract Hotel were organized to assist fugitive slaves to freedom in Canada. None of this is certain, but UGRR networks certainly allow for the possibility—and perhaps the connection with the Thompsons.

We shall say more about these possible connections in later chapters.

Interpreting the Transnational Data and the Movement of Freedom Seekers

United States Census figures provide information that a few freed colored people were living and working in the Town of Porter, Niagara County, New York, between 1820 and 1865. The City of Lockport had larger numbers of African Americans, particularly because of jobs on the Erie Canal.[53] The City of Niagara Falls, which increasingly became a tourist destination, also had larger numbers of freed colored people working in some of the hotels, as well as a rather constant flow of freedom seekers crossing the Niagara River by ferry and, after 1855, by train to Canada at nearby Niagara City/Bellevue (Suspension Bridge Village[54]). These escapees often received help from local free African Americans.[55]

Niagara County had members of Anti-Slavery Societies and a large number of Underground Railroad supporters as part of a regional UGRR network; however, eighteen Free Blacks in the Town of Porter over a period of forty-five years is not a very large number when

---

[52] See Ch. 14.
[53] For more on Lockport and the UGGR, see Ch. 11.
[54] See Ch. 5.
[55] See the Cassey story, Ch. 12.

compared to Lockport and Niagara Falls. Perhaps there were more. One can imagine that some people did not want to officially record in the Census the number of colored people living in their community or home. On the one hand, not reporting them could have been a way to protect them from slave catchers. On the other hand, the *Fugitive Slave Act of 1850* established severe penalties for helping fugitive slaves. Marshals who did not carry out the law could be fined $1,000 (perhaps about $30,000 today[56]) and those who helped fugitive slaves by hiding or feeding them could also be fined $1,000 and jailed for six months. It is true that a number of states passed personal liberty laws that attempted to thwart implementation of the *Fugitive Slave Act of 1850*, but New York State, for all of its abolitionism and UGRR activity, was not one of them.[57] Although abolitionism was strong in western New York by the mid-1850s, perhaps it is not so surprising that in 1850, no free Blacks are recorded in the Town of Porter and in 1860, only one Black male servant is mentioned.

Where did African Americans go when they reached Canada? The Town of Niagara and Niagara (Niagara-on-the-Lake) census returns in Canada are a contrast in numbers with the Town of Porter in the United States.

---

[56] "TD Ameritrade: Official," Bureau of Labor Statistics, 1850 and 2014. http://www.in2013dollars.com/1850-dollars-in-2014?amount. Actual dollar equivalences related to the Consumer Price Index are more complex than inflation rates.

[57] Stanley W. Campbell, *The Slave Catchers*, 185. https://www.questia.com/read/104468881/the-slave-catchers-enforcement-of-the-fugitive-slave. New York had indeed passed a law that fugitive slaves should have a trial by jury in 1840, but the *Fugitive Slave Law of 1850* superseded it in theory. In *Prigg vs. Pennsylvania*, 1842, the Supreme Court ruled that Pennsylvania's 1826 personal liberty law was unconstitutional (Article IV: the fugitive slave clause). In the 1857 Dred Scott Case the Supreme Court ruled against Dred Scott's suit that he was free in a free state by claiming that Negroes were not U.S. Citizens and had no standing in the court.

Census Returns of Niagara Township and the Town of Niagara[-on-the-Lake], Canada, Including Blacks, 1842 – 1861[58]

		Black Population	Total Population	Blacks as a Percentage
1842	Township	116	2,155	
	Town	82	1,745	
	Total	**198**	3,900	5.0
1851	Township	73	2,253	
	Town	94	3,322	
	Total	**167**	5,575	3.0
1861	Township	64	2,400	
	Town	104	2,073	
	Total	**166**	4,475	3.7

The Census figures of the Canadian Town(ship) of Niagara drop somewhat from 1842 (116) to 1851 (73) and again from 1851 to 1861 (64), but increase in the Town of Niagara (Niagara-on-the-Lake) in 1851 (94) and again in 1861 (104), the total being relatively stable in 1851 (167) to 1861 (166). After 1861, there is a very significant decline in the Town of Niagara from 1861 (104) to 1871 (28) to 1881 (21) to 1891 (20) (not on the chart). The total (combined) Black population of the Township of Niagara and the Town of Niagara (Niagara-on-the-Lake) thus dropped from 166 in 1861 (3.7%) to 88 in 1871 (2.4%), to 42 in 1881 (1.2%), to 25 in 1891 (0.7%).[59] Many African Canadians moved further inland, especially to St. Catharines.[60] An influencing factor was that Niagara's economy during this time was in decline and these new citizens of British Canada needed work and the potential for jobs was shrinking. Consequently, they migrated to larger communities where they could find work, attend church, and enjoy their freedom with people who had a common background of having escaped slavery.

---

[58] See "Appendix B: Population of Niagara according to Census Records," in Power and Butler, *Slavery and Freedom in Niagara*, 77.

[59] Power and Butler, "Appendix B: Population of Niagara According to Census Records," *Slavery and Freedom in Niagara*, 77.

[60] See Ch. 8.

These figures suggest what one might expect, that many African Americans, whether free or fugitive slaves, crossed the Niagara River and became African Canadians in relatively free Canada. Some crossed at the Suspension Bridges at either Lewiston or Niagara City/Bellevue (just north of Niagara Falls), but some crossed from Youngstown to Niagara on the Youngstown Ferry or were aided by Youngstown persons with boats or by larger maritime vessels that put into port at Youngstown.[61] We document some of them in Part II of this book.

Addendum: The U. S. Military on Capturing and Returning Fugitive Slaves

The Village of Youngstown is about a mile south of Fort Niagara at the mouth of the Niagara River. One sometimes hears that the military personnel stationed at Fort Niagara would have been bound to enforce the *Fugitive Slave Act of 1850* and for this reason fugitive slaves would not have crossed at Youngstown. Does this opinion have any merit?

The question about the military is not easy to answer. According to Jerome Brubaker, the Assistant Director of Old Fort Niagara and Curator of its Archival Collections, the Fort has no artifacts or records relating to the Underground Railroad in its archive because none have been donated and the Fort has not purchased any.[62] We resort to some possibilities.

Historian Brian Leigh Dunnigan, the former Old Fort Niagara Executive Director, writes that for various reasons, troops were not always present at the Fort between 1815 and 1865.[63] Abstracting from his narrative survey, they were absent from 1826 – 1828, 1846 – 1848, 1854 – 1861, and 1863 – 1865.[64] We are most interested here in the period between the passage of *The Fugitive Slave Act of 1850* and 1865, the end of the Civil War, because, as we shall see, this was the period in which most of our sources about fugitive slaves crossing from Youngstown to Canada survive.[65]

---

[61] We shall offer evidence for these considerations in Chs. 4, 5, 6, 7, 8, 10, 11, and 13.

[62] Personal email communication from Jere Brubaker, October 21, 2014.

[63] Brian Leigh Dunnigan, *A History and Guide to Old Fort Niagara* (Youngstown, NY: Old Fort Niagara Association, 2007). Dunnigan is now Associate Director and Curator at the William L. Clements Library, Ann Arbor, Michigan. A succinct history of Fort Niagara can be accessed on the internet at http://www.oldfortniagara.org/history.

[64] Ibid.

[65] See Part II, Chs. 7 – 13.

We gain some impressions about western New York in general from an article that appeared in the Romney, Virginia, *Intelligencer*, reproduced in *The New York Times*, September 8, 1855. About eight or nine years earlier, a slave who escaped in Hardy County, Virginia, ended up in Jamestown, New York. His owner, Captain J. G. Harness, informed about March of 1855 that his Negro was in jail in Buffalo on a misdemeanor charge, sought to retrieve him. However, not a single lawyer in Buffalo would help him file the proper papers because of popular opinion. Indeed, a certain Judge Hall warned the slave owner not to pursue matters since, if he did catch him, a mob would rescue him. The Virginia newspaper commented:

> It is proper to remark here that there were no United States troops in Buffalo, else, perhaps, a foreign lawyer would have been brought on, and the mob would have been afforded an opportunity of feeling the force of bullets and bayonets. . .

> Thus we find that the people of Buffalo have in effect set at defiance the laws of the United States, have declared that they respect not the rights of property, have decided that, in no manner will they aid in carrying out the provisions of the law. The fear of the mob has made even such men as Judge Hall quail . . . If the sentiment of the people of Buffalo is a fair exponent of the sentiment of the people of the North . . . then will they force a dissolution of the Union, dire event though it may be, upon the south.[66]

That was in 1855. According to Eric Foner in *Gateway to Freedom: The Hidden History of the Underground Railroad*, this was the situation in 1861.

> In May 1861, the president's cabinet approved the decision of Benjamin F. Butler, who commanded Union forces at fortress Monroe, Virginia, *not* to return slaves who arrived at his outpost. That July, the House of Representatives adopted a resolution introduced by Owen Lovejoy, a Radical Republican from Illinois, stating that it was not "part of the duty of the soldiers of the United States to capture and return fugitive slaves." The resolution did not come before the Senate, but it indicated widespread Republican dissatisfaction with military commanders who returned runaway slaves. By

---

[66] "The Fugitive Slave Law a Dead Letter—A Case in Point," *The New York Times* (September 8, 1955), from the *Romney, Virginia, Intelligencer*. http://query.nytimes.com/mem/archive-free/pdf?res=9A0DE0DC103DE034BC4053DFBF66838E649FDE.

the end of 1861, as slaves by the hundreds, then thousands, sought refuge with the army, Lincoln declared that those who reached Union lines had become free. Early in 1862, the press reported Lincoln's view that the government had no obligation to return fugitive slaves and that in any event public opinion would not allow it to do so. That March [1862] just as federal forces were entering the Mississippi Valley, leading to a flood of slaves to the army, Congress forbade military officers from returning fugitives.

Before the war, the actions of runaway slaves had powerfully affected the national debate over slavery. Now fugitives were helping to propel the nation down the road to emancipation. . . By 1862, one historian has written, the federal government had "undertaken the work of the underground railroad."[67]

The Emancipation Proclamation was announced following the Union victory at Antietam on September 17, 1962, and became official on January 1, 1863. Thereafter, fugitive slaves were considered contraband of war and Contraband Camps were established.[68]

According to Stanley Campbell,[69] reaction to the *Fugitive Slave Law of 1850* in the North was divided between 1850 and 1854, with most Northerners considering it too harsh; there was also powerful opposition to it by abolitionists and members of anti-slavery societies, especially in New England, northern Ohio, northern Illinois, Wisconsin, and—again, note—western New York. Because of the hope of preserving the Union, the majority reluctantly accepted the law from 1851 to 1853. However, opposition to the *Fugitive Slave Law* grew stronger after 1854, in

---

[67] Eric Foner, *Gateway to Freedom: The Hidden History of the Underground Railroad* (New York, NY: W.W. Norton & Company, 2015), 223. Quoting a letter of Oliver Johnson, editor of the *National Anti-Slavery Standard*, to James Miller McKim, October 11, 1860 (note on p. 274) (italics ours).

[68] On May 9, 1863, Thomas Nast published a cartoon "Contrabands Coming into our Lines Under the Proclamation" in *Harper's Weekly*; see the cartoon at Robert C. Kennedy, "On This Day," *New York Times*, 2001. https://www.nytimes.com/learning/general/onthisday/harp/0509.html (copyrighted).

[69] Campbell, *The Slave Catchers,* 79.

part because of the passage of the Kansas-Nebraska Act (1854),[70] the widely publicized trial of Anthony Burns from Boston (1854),[71] and the Dred Scott decision in 1857.[72]

As noted, troops left Fort Niagara in 1863.[73] We may add a bit of local evidence.

The United States Congress was concerned that Britain might enter the Civil War on the side of the Confederacy, an act that would have had implications for the border with Canada, and so in 1861 a garrison was returned to the Fort for a time. Ordnance Sergeant Lewis Leffman oversaw the improvement of fortifications beginning in 1863. Leffman saw no direct military action in the Civil War, but the following story was reported in The Youngstown News section of The [*Niagara*] *Daily Gazette* of Niagara Falls, in 1883.

> The [Confederate] rebels who had fled from the south and taken their residences at Niagara just across the river in Canada, during the late war [1861-1865], had their plans all made to cross the river on a certain night and capture the post and burn it. Mr. Leffman, through a friend, was made aware of their secret machinations, and he *being alone at the fort, invited some of the citizens from the village down, armed them, loaded all the guns at the post and was prepared to give them a cordial reception with grape and canister;* but they did not appear. It is probable they learned that the fort would be defended, something they had not anticipated.[74]

Summarizing, between 1850 and 1854 it is possible that a military commander enforced the *Fugitive Slave Law of 1850* (enforcement was largely the prerogative of the officers), but there is no evidence. We think that it was unlikely. The troops at Fort Niagara left in 1854, public opinion was resisting capturing and returning fugitive slaves, and the troops did not

---

[70] *The Kansas-Nebraska Act* established "popular sovereignty," thus the right to choose whether to be a slave or non-slave state; it repealed the Missouri Compromise of 1820, which prohibited slavery in these territories.
[71] In 1853, Fugitive slave Anthony Burns was captured, tried, and found guilty in Boston. The decision provoked public protest and unrest. Subsequently, Boston sympathizers raised funds and ransomed him.
[71] Stanley W. Campbell, *The Slave Catchers,* 79.
[72] Ibid., 79. The anti-slavery meetings in Niagara County took place in 1855; see Ch. 2.
[73] Ibid., 37-45.
[74] "The Youngstown News" section of *The Daily Gazette* of Niagara Falls (New York, August 11, 1883): p. 1, col. 4 (italics ours). For more on the Leffman story, see Dennis Duling in Gretchen Duling, *et al., From the Mouth of the Lower Niagara River,* 139-140.

return until 1861. When they did return from 1861 to 1862, official national policy had changed. From 1863 to 1865, troops were gone again, and by 1865, the Civil War was over.

CHAPTER 4

Crossing the Niagara River: the Boats

Image 4.1

Slavery in Canada and New York State; Crossing the Niagara River

Upper Canada (Ontario) moved toward the emancipation of slaves with the "Simcoe Compromise" of 1793. The act did not free the slaves or their sale, or the rights of owners to track down runaway slaves, but it did end the slave trade. Some forty years later the Imperial Act of 1833, effective in 1834, stamped out slavery in virtually every country in the British Empire, which included Canada.[1] In the same period, New York State took gradual steps toward emancipation in 1799 and 1817, and finally emancipation itself on July 4, 1827.[2] However, New York slave owners could sell their slaves in southern states and avoid complete emancipation by "indenturing" them; moreover, slave owners from slave states could still enter New York State

---

[1] Power, "Simcoe and Slavery," in Power and Butler, *Slavery and Freedom in Niagara*, 26, 31. Exceptions to the 1833 law were territories possessed by the East India Company, the Island of Saint Helena, and the Island of Ceylon. Abolition of slavery took place in these areas in 1843.
[2] Blacks in New York City celebrated, but made a symbolic protest by not holding their celebratory parade until the following day, July 5, 1827.

with their slaves and stay for a period for up to nine months. This "nine months law" was repealed in 1841,[3] which was emphasized by Abolitionists and UGRR activists to visiting slaves.[4] Yet, slave catchers, kidnappers, and illegal traders continued to be active in New York State. What all this meant was that some fugitive slaves felt safe enough to settle in the free State of New York. However, the *Fugitive Slave Act of 1850*, a federal law that superseded state laws, led many African Americans in New York State, like fugitive slaves from slave states, to flee to Canada.[5]

There could be great risks to maritime captains and ferrymen who helped freedom seekers. William Still in his *The Underground Railroad* (1872) recorded the extreme case of Captain Robert Lee who in 1857 was arrested, tried, convicted, lashed, and sentenced to the Richmond Penitentiary for twenty-five years for assisting fugitive slaves to escape from Norfolk, Virginia.[6] C. H. Reed portrayed the crossing in 1872.

---

[3] *New York Laws*, 1841, CCXLVII. Discussion in Paul Finkelman, *An Imperfect Union: Slavery, Federalism, and Comity* (Union, NJ: The Lawbook Exchange, Ltd., 2000) 72, 75-76; "Slave Transit," in Peter R. Eisenstadt and Laura-Eve Moss, *The Encyclopedia of New York State* (Syracuse, NY: Syracuse University Press, 2005), 1422. https://books.google.com/books?id=tmHEm5ohoCUC&pg=PA1422&lpg=PA1422&dq=New+York+State+-+%22nine+months+law%22&source=bl&ots=MiA7R5w3wb&sig=PMLON8_8x_gQiRt1OpI3ucAfonc&hl=en&sa=X&ved=0ahUKEwjA6KOS2pvQAhVN6WMKHXQRB4AQ6AEIJDAC#v=onepage&q=New%20York%20State%20-%20%22nine%20months%20law%22&f=false.

[4] This educational strategy is brought out in the story of Cassey; see Ch. 12.

[5] For several provisions of the *Fugitive Slave Act of 1850*, see Ch. 1.

[6] William Still, *The Underground Railroad*, 111; the primary source comes from a letter by Miss G. Lewis, on which see "The Underground Railroad in Virginia. Conductors and Agents," http://racetimeplace.com/ugrr/conductors.htm, with a link to "Cap. Robert Lee," http://racetimeplace.com/ugrr/stillnarrative.htm#111.

C. H. Reed, 1872
Public Domain, New York Public Library[7]
Image 4.2

Crossing the Niagara River, the strait that flows northward from Lake Erie to Lake

Ontario, was one of the key means to reach freedom in Upper Canada. Later in this chapter we

cite Hugh Richardson, a steamer captain, who refused to help Deputy Sheriff Alexander McLeod

of Niagara, Upper Canada, transport Solomon Moseby across the Niagara River from Canada to

the United States in 1837, a case highlighted in Chapter 1. Other accounts recorded that Jacob

Green escaped to Toronto on the *Chief Justice Robinson*, captained by Richardson. The fact that

steamer captains helped fugitive slaves escape to Canada raises the question: Were any of the

known captains of the steamers that were put into Youngstown, such as the *Ontario* and the

---

[7] C. H. Reed, "Escaping from Norfolk In Capt. Lee's Skiff" (1872). Schomburg Center for Research in Black Culture, Manuscripts, Archives and Rare Books Division, Schomburg Center for Research in Black Culture, Manuscripts, Archives and Rare Books Division, The New York Public Library. "Escaping from Portsmouth, VA.; Escaping from Norfolk in Capt. Lee's skiff." New York Public Library Digital Collections. Accessed January 8, 2016. http://digitalcollections.nypl.org/items/510d47df-79a0-a3d9-e040-e00a18064a99. Also, Cassandra Newby-Alexander, *Waterways to Freedom. The Underground Journey from Hampton Road* (Norfolk, Virginia: Convention & Visitors Bureau. Norfolk: JR Norfolk, ISSUU, ND), https://issuu.com/dia1/docs/undergroundrailroad. In the account of fugitive slave "Cassey," discussed in Ch. 12 of this book, Eber Pettit wrote, "During the excitement [of the African American slave catcher diversion in Philadelphia] Cassey escaped, and before Cathcart [a slave catcher] returned with his constables she was crossing the Delaware River in a skiff" (Pettit, *Sketches*, 115).

Martha Ogden—Daniel Reed, James Van Cleve, Andrew Estes, William Vaughan—also of this stripe?[8] In later chapters, we document how Youngstown ferrymen and other individuals transported freedom seekers across the Niagara River from Youngstown to freedom in Canada (Part II).

With these UGRR activities in mind, this chapter will explore some ways for crossing the Niagara River, with particular interest in Youngstown vessels.[9]

Early Cross-River Travel on the Lower Niagara River

In the eighteenth and nineteenth centuries, travel vessels travelled freely and often across the Niagara River.[10] The earliest were Native American canoes. After the American Revolution, a few ships of the small British Navy on Lake Ontario docked at Navy Hall just below Fort George across the river from Youngstown, but most of the early cross-river vessels were *bateaux*, which were flat-bottomed boats ranging in size from eighteen to forty-eight feet that were usually pointed at both ends. Near the shore, they were driven by poles; in deeper water, they were rowed by oars. They usually required three to eight men, and could be outfitted with a mast, sail, and for military purposes, even a light canon.[11] They were used for inland transportation in both civilian and military sectors.[12]

Scows of the period were broad, small flat-bottomed boats usually with blunt ends and centerboards, that is, dropdown rudders in the middle of the boat rather than deep keels. Most

---

[8] Captain Estes turns up in the Town of Porter Federal Census records of 1830 as a White male age 40-50. In his household were also one free White female age 30-40, three free White males age 15-20, 10-15, and 0-5 respectively, and four White females, two ages 10-15 and 0-5 respectively—for a total of nine household members. This information, unfortunately, is not very helpful for activity in the UGRR.

[9] For Youngstown ferries, see Ch. 6; for the Youngstown Ferry House, see Ch. 16.

[10] For an interesting illustration of cross-river travel on the Niagara River, see the account of an excursion in 1810 of the famous politician and presidential candidate, DeWitt Clinton, at that time when he was mayor of New York City. Clinton sailed from Lewiston down the Niagara River to Fort Niagara on the brig *Ontario* (a sailing vessel with two-masts and square-rigged sails, not one of the later *Ontario* steamers). He then crossed over to Newark/Niagara in Canada (by ferry?), returned south to Queenston by carriage, and then re-crossed the river to Lewiston in the United States by ferry. See DeWitt Clinton's *Private Canal Journal*, 1810, from William W. Campbell, *Life and Writings of DeWitt Clinton* (New York, NY: Baker and Scribner, 1849). http://www.eriecanal.org/texts/Campbell/chap06-2.html#FortNiagara.

[11] See Emanuel Leutze's famous 1851 painting, "Washington Crossing the Delaware" (The Metropolitan Museum of Art), although a few details are considered to be inaccurate.

[12] "Colonial Era Bateau *Perseverance*," Lake Champlain Maritime Museum. http://www.lcmm.org/our_fleet/perseverance.htm.

often used for freight, they could operate in shallower waters and be rigged with sails (scow-schooners). So-called Durham Boats or Schenectady Boats were similar.[13]

"A View of the Boats & Manner of Navigating on the Mohawk River"
Engraving of a "Durham (Schnectedy) Boat" (with sails), 1810[14]
By Christian Schultz, 1810
Image 4.3

Such boats were common on the Lower Niagara River. In 1897, Niagara County Historian William Pool wrote:

John Gould came from New Jersey [to the Town of Porter] in 1788 as a drover. He gave some of his recollections as follows:

Col. Hunter was then in command at Fort Niagara. *Our cattle and pack horses were ferried across to Newark [Niagara] in bateaux and Schenectady boats.*

---

[13]"Durham Boats" were used at the Durham Furnace and Iron Works in Durham, Pennsylvania. See "History of The Durham Boat," Durham Historical Society, http://www.durhamhistoricalsociety.org/history2.html.
[14]Christian Schultz. *Travels on an Inland Voyage through the States of New-York, Pennsylvania, Virginia, Ohio, Kentucky, and Tennessee, and through the Territories of Indiana, Louisiana, Mississippi, and New-Orleans, Performed in the Years 1807 and 1808* (New York, NY: I. Riley, July, 1810). https://en.wikipedia.org/wiki/Durham_boat#/media/File:DurhamBoat-MohawkR.jp; http://brbl-archive.library.yale.edu/exhibitions/illustratingtraveler/customs1.htm.

Nothing then at Newark but an old ferry house and, the barracks that had been occupied by Butler's Rangers . . . We sold our cattle principally to Butler's Rangers. They [the Rangers] were located mostly at the falls, along the Four and Twelve-mile Creeks. Oxen brought as high as cows, £20.[15]

John Young, namesake of the Village of Youngstown, lived with his wife Catherine across the river in Newark/Niagara, Upper Canada. He supplied his Red Store along the Youngstown riverbank, built in 1808, with provisions from Newark.[16] The following watercolor by contemporary artist Jean Stratton imagines his store with a landing dock in front of it.

John Young's Red Store in Youngstown by Jean Stratton
(Permission from the Town of Porter Historical Society)
Image 4.4

We do not know how he transported his supplies from Niagara to the Red Store in Youngstown, but quite plausibly it was with a scow-schooner or Durham/Schenectady Boat.[17]

---

[15] Recollections of John Gould to Hunter in Pool, *Landmarks of Niagara County,* 256-57 (italics ours).

[16] Dietz, *From Flames and Four Flags*, 58, names Young's Red Store managers as Chittenden and Woodruff.[16]

[17] For an 1810 map that shows the Youngstown shoreline and possibly the Red Store, see Ch. 16.

Not many years later, on December 19, 1813, the British Army, seeking revenge for the American burning of Newark/Niagara, secretly crossed the Niagara River and landed at Five Mile Meadows three miles south of Youngstown. The Army crossed the Niagara River in *bateaux.* They marched north, captured Fort Niagara, and then headed south, burning towns and villages, including Youngstown, as far as Buffalo.

Smaller shallow-draft, flat-bottomed boats similar to scows and *bateaux* with either pointed bows and blunt or flat sterns ("Sharpies"), were used as ferry boats on the Lower Niagara River. Dramatic accounts of dangerous ferry crossings below Prospect Point at Niagara Falls portray anxious tourists in small one-man-rowed Sharpies that could carry about eight to ten people. Samuel Geil's 1853 print "View from the Ferry" illustrates the trip.

Geil's "View from the Ferry" Shows a One-man Row-boat Ferry (1851)[18]
Permission from William Bradbury, President and Chairman of the Niagara Falls Underground Railroad Heritage Area; original tinted
Image 4.5

---

[18] Samuel Geil, "View from the Ferry," in his *Niagara Falls and Vicinity* (Philadelphia, PA, 1851); also cited in Wellman, Niagara Falls Underground Railroad Heritage Area Management Plan, "Appendix C: Survey of Sites," 147. http://www.niagarafallsundergroundrailroad.org/documents/NF%20HAMP%20Report_Appendix%20C.pdf. With permission by Bill Bradbury, past Chair of the Niagara Falls Underground Railroad Committee of the Niagara Falls Underground Railroad Heritage Area Management Plan.

Underground Railroad historian Judith Wellman highlights the significance of the Niagara Falls Ferry for the UGRR:

> Many African Americans escaped to freedom on the ferry just below the Falls. We have detailed accounts of Nancy Berry, Patrick Sneed, and Martha. [African American] John Morrison, head waiter at the Cataract House [Hotel], often ferried people across the river himself.[19]

Later, we note that in 1856 or 1857 an anonymous farmer near Youngstown ferried two fugitive slaves across the Niagara River to Niagara in a "rowboat."[20]

Horse Ferries

Sail-rigged skiffs, scows, and Durham Boats had to depend on unreliable winds and the use of labor-intensive poles and oars. A solution to these drawbacks was a boat driven by horse power. Horse ferries, well known on European inland waterways, began to appear in the United States in the early nineteenth century.[21] The earlier horse ferries had a circular treadmill on which the horses walked. A striking example is the large, 63' long and 23' wide, dual-paddle "Burlington Bay Horse Ferry," discovered fifty feet deep in Burlington Bay in 1983, dating from the 1820s or 1830s (Image 4.6). Horse ferries continued for many decades, as Image 4.7 shows.

---

[19] Wellman, ibid., 142. For more on John Morrison, see Chs. 9 and 12.

[20] This Youngstown account is the main subject of Ch. 11.

[21] The key study is Kevin James Crisman and Arthur B. Cohn, *When Horses Walked on Water: Horse-Powered Ferries in Nineteenth-Century America* (Washington, D.C., and London, UK: Smithsonian Institution Press, 1998); see also Donald Shomette, "Heyday of the Horse Ferry," *National Geographic* 176/4 (1989): 548-556;"Hoofbeats Over the Water: I.N.A. Research on Horse-Powered Ferryboats," The Institute of Nautical Archaeology (INA), affiliated with the Center for Maritime Archaeology and Conservation at Texas A&M University, http://nautarch.tamu.edu/newworld/pastprojects/LChorseferry.htm.

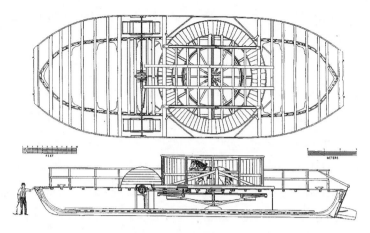

The Burlington Bay Horse Ferry Deck Construction and Inboard Profile
Ship plans by Kevin J. Crisman [22]
Image 4.6

A Sternwheel Horse Ferry with a Circular Treadmill, St. Mary's, Missouri, ca. 1900
Permission: From the collection of the Public Library of Cincinnati and Hamilton County[23]
Image 4.7

---

[22] See "Burlington Bay Horse Ferry," The United States Department of the Interior, National Park Service, Division of Historic Preservation, plans by Kevin J. Crissman, p. 29, Figure 8; see also Photo p. 61 and parallel sketch, p. 59. https://www.burlingtonvt.gov/sites/default/files/PZ/Historic/National-Register-PDFs/BurlingtonBayHorseFerry.pdf. See also Jim Kennard, "Horse Powered Ferry Boat Discovered in Lake Champlain," *Shipwreck World* (July 2, 2005), http://www.shipwreckworld.com/articles/horse-powered-ferry-boat-discovered-in-lake-champlain; http://www.shipwreckworld.com/articles/horse-powered-ferry-boat-discovered-in-lake-champlain#sthash.P42UXEiO.dpuf. More Horse Ferry images are at "Hoofbeats Over the Water."
[23] The photo is also found in John Perry, *American Ferryboats* (New York, NY: Wilford Funk, Inc., 1957). Perry claims that it was "the last ferry on the Mississippi."

J. B. Mansfield's *History of the Great Lakes*, Volume 1 (1899) records the use of a two-horse, circular-treadmill ferry on the Lower Niagara River.

> *A Horse Ferry Boat* – In 1844 the Privat Brothers at Toronto, purchased a vessel, which had been running on the Niagara river below the Falls, to ply any of those who took passage upon this vessel ever knew or cared for its name, every one calling it the "horse boat." She was 60 feet long and 23 feet wide, and was a side-wheeler. These wheels were made to revolve by two horses, which trod on a circular table, set flush with the deck in the center, and revolved upon rollers, which being connected with the shaft set the wheels in motion. The horses remained stationary on the deck, the table on which they trod revolving under them, and being furnished with ridges of wood, radiating like spokes from the center, and which the horses caught with their feet, thus setting the tables in motion. . . [24]

Mansfield does not give this horse ferry's exact location; "below the Falls" probably meant at Niagara Falls, but could have been further downstream between Lewiston and Queenston or between Youngstown and Niagara.[25]

The circular treadmill in the above horse ferry examples required a very wide boat deck and sometimes the horses became a little dizzy. A solution to these two problems was to use one or two horizontal, straight-ahead tread mills.

---

[24]J. B. Mansfield, ed., *History of the Great Lakes*, Volume I (Chicago, IL: J. H. Beers & Co., 1899) transcribed for the *Maritime History of the Great Lakes Site* by Walter Lewis and Brendon Baillod (Halton Hills, ON: Maritime History of the Great Lakes, 2003).
http://www.maritimehistoryofthegreatlakes.ca/GreatLakes/Documents/HGL/default.asp?ID=c023#, no page number; Crisman and Cohn, *When Horses Walked on Water,* 84.
[25] However, a steam-driven ferry, "The Cigar," was already operating out of Youngstown by 1834. See Ch. 6.

A Horse Boat at Empy's Ferry, Osnabruck, Ontario, 1898
James Croil, *Steam Navigation and its Relation to the Commerce of Canada and the United States,* 29[26]
Image 4.8

New York State had a very large fleet of horse ferries between 1820 and 1840. A large scow propelled by a two-horse, horizontal, straight-ahead tread-wheel was running back and forth between Lewiston and Queenston in 1831. It is represented in the lower right hand corner of an image from J. W. Orr's 1842 *Pictorial Guide to the Falls of Niagara.*[27]

---

[26] James Croil, *Steam Navigation and its Relation to the Commerce of Canada and the United States* (Montreal, Quebec: The Montreal New Company Limited, 1898), 29. Online reprint at the Open Library, Classic Book Collection (Toronto, ON: William Briggs) 29. https://archive.org/stream/cihm_02131#page/n11/mode/2up.

[27] J. W. Orr, *Pictorial Guide to the Falls of Niagara: A Manual for Visitors, Giving and Account of this Stupendous Natural Wonder; and all. The Objects of Curiosity in its Vicinity; With Every Historical Incident of Interest: and Also Full Directions for Visiting the Cataract and its Neighboring Scenes. Illustrated by Numerous Maps, Charts, and Engravings, From Original Surveys and Designs* (Buffalo, NY: Press of Salisbury and Clapp, 1842). Also, cited by Judith Wellman, "Lewiston Landing," http://niagarafallsundergroundrailroad.org/documents/25_Lewiston%20Landing.pdf. Wellman credits Karolyn Smardz Frost for finding this source. She writes that Joseph Wynn ran this ferry from Queenston to Lewiston until 1841, when Thomas Trumble took over. Job Chubbuck of Queenston, Ontario, was also the ferryman. Business for this ferry declined after construction of the [Lewiston/Queenston] Suspension Bridge in 1851, but until then, this was the only direct route across the river. Was Job Chubbuck related to Samuel Chubbuck of Youngstown? See the ferryman list, Ch. 6. Note that in the background of Orr's 1842 "Ferry at Lewiston," as Pamela Hauth, Curator for the Historical Association of Lewiston, has observed, the Brock monument on Queenston Heights looks as it did before the monument was heavily damaged by a terrorist (Benjamin Lett?) in 1840 (the monument was not re-dedicated until October 13, 1853). Orr certainly knew about the damage—he included an image of the damaged monument on the next page after the Lewiston Landing image—so he retrojected its pre-1840 condition into the "Ferry at Lewiston." The main point is that the horse ferry image in Orr belongs to the period 1824-1840, the period of the height of horse ferries on the Lower Niagara and in the same period that Samuel Chubbuck and Thomas Balmer operated a horse ferry at Youngstown, as we shall see.

FERRY AT LEWISTON.

A Two-Horse Ferry (lower right) at Lewiston, New York[28]
Permission by William Bradbury, President and Chairman of the Niagara Falls Underground
Railroad Heritage Area
Image 4.9

The Youngstown ferryman Samuel Chubbuck built large horse ferry boats in the 1820s
and 1830s and in our list of Youngstown ferrymen in Chapter 6 we include Chubbuck and
Thomas Balmer who together operated a horse ferry at Youngstown between 1828 and 1834.

Schooners

Schooners are sailboats that have from two to six masts and "gaff rigging," that is,
square-cornered sails on the foremast and the mainmast, plus one or more jibs fore with
triangular sails. The simplest is a two-mast schooner with the foremast usually shorter than the
centered mainmast (see below). In the eighteenth and early nineteenth century, there were
many schooners on the Great Lakes and the Lower Niagara; by 1830 they outnumbered all
other vessels.[29] Schooners were cheaper to run than steamers, but steamers became more
numerous after the completion of the Erie Canal in 1825, which brought new commerce to the

---

[28] Orr, *Ibid,* 183; also Wellman, *ibid.*
[29] Benjamin Louis Ford, *Lake Ontario Maritime Cultural Landscape* (Diss. Texas A&M University, August 2009), 141.
http://nautarch.tamu.edu/Theses/pdf-files/Ford-PhD2009.pdf.

Great Lakes. Yet, schooners continued in service especially because many travelers preferred their quiet, pleasant form of transportation.[30]

A Small Two-Mast Schooner with Gaff Rigging
US National Oceanic and Atmospheric Administration, Public Domain[31]
Image 4.10

A number of schooners were built at Youngstown. *The Town of Porter 1776-1976—A Bicentennial History* (1976) reports that:

> [t]here was a tremendous growth of agriculture, particularly wheat, hay, and fruit, in the Town of Porter between 1840 and 1870. A shipyard was located on the flat below what is now the Villa Apartments [1 Main Street]; some seven sailing ships were built there,

[30] "History and Development of Great Lakes Water Craft,"
http://www.mnhs.org/places/nationalregister/shipwrecks/mpdf/mpdf2.php.
For an 1850s Schooner discovered in Lake Ontario, the *C. Reeve*, see Jim Kennard, "Shipwreck Explorers Discover 1850's Schooner in Lake Ontario," *Shipwreck World* (December 14, 2009).
http://www.shipwreckworld.com/articles/shipwreck-explorers-discover-1850s-schooner-lake-ontario;
http://www.shipwreckworld.com/articles/shipwreck-explorers-discover-1850s-schooner-lake-ontario#sthash.xBzjsQlt.dpuf; also Dan Scoville and Jim Kennard, "Shipwreck Explorers Discover 1850's Schooner in Lake Ontario" (YouTube). https://www.youtube.com/watch?v=NAWEHGrAtYw.
[31] "File:Smallschooner.jpg," Wikipedia. https://en.wikipedia.org/wiki/File:Smallschooner.jpg.

mainly to haul lumber and grain to Oswego, where it was trans-shipped to Albany and New York by the Erie Canal.[32]

While the location of Youngstown ship building below the Villa Apartments is debatable (see below), seven Youngstown-built schooners are also mentioned in The *History of Niagara County, New York* (1878).[33] These numbers were probably derived from Captain James Van Cleve's beautifully hand-written, artistic manuscript containing his watercolor sketches, *Reminiscences of the Early Period of Sailing Vessels and Steamboats on Lake Ontario* (1877).[34] Van Cleve himself started working as a clerk on the first steamboat to operate on Lake Ontario, the *Ontario*, in 1826, and from there he became a captain of the steamboat *Martha Ogden* and eventually general manager of the Ontario and St. Lawrence Steamboat Company.[35] His list of vessels built at Youngstown includes the *R. H. Boughton*, 1829 ("she was the first vessel passed through the Welland Canal at its completion")[36]; the *Lewis Shickluna*, 1836; the *John Porter*, 1838; the *Star*, 1848; the *Challenge*, 1852; the *Frank Pierce*, 1853; and the *Cheney Ames*, 1873. He usually notes the owners and captains of these steamers.[37] Records in the Town of Porter

---

[32] *The Town of Porter 1776-1976— A Bicentennial History* (Porter, New York: Town of Porter, 1976), 14. If this is accurate, there was more than one place along the Youngstown shore where ships were built; see below the letter of James Onen.

[33] *History of Niagara county, New York, with illustrations Descriptive of its Scenery, Private Residences, Public Buildings, Fine Blocks, and Important Manufactories, and Portraits of Old Pioneers and Prominent Residents* (New York, NY: Sanford & Co., 1878), 121B; https://archive.org/details/cu31924100387392.

[34] James Van Cleve, *Reminiscences of the Early Period of Sailing Vessels and Steamboats on Lake Ontario with a History of the Introduction of the Propeller on the Lakes and Other Subjects with Illustrations* (Buffalo, NY: Manuscript at the Buffalo History Museum, 1877); *Early Steamboating Reminiscences From the Ontario, Martha Ogden and United States*. Oswego Palladium (Oswego, NY, April 4, 1876); *The Great Northern Route. American Lines. The Ontario and St. Lawrence Steamboat Company's Hand-Book for Travelers to Niagara Falls, Montreal and Quebec, and through Lake Champlain to Saratoga Springs. Illustrated with Maps and Numerous Engravings* (Buffalo, NY: Jewett, Thomas, & Co.; Rochester, NY: D. M. Dewey, 1852). Also, George W. Hilton, *Lake Michigan Passenger Steamers* (Ford, CA: Ford University Press, 2002), Ch. 2, n. 1 (p. 49). Thanks to Cynthia Van Ness, MLS, Director, Library and Archives, for assistance.

[35] Clarence O. Lewis, "Capt. Van Cleve, Pioneer, of Lewiston, Started Sailing Great Lakes in 1826," *Niagara Falls Gazette* (October 15, 1958); Lewiston's *Union-Sun and Journal* (October 16, 1958). Lewis' source: Erik Heyl, *Journal of the Steamship Historical Society of America* 48 (December 1953), 81-82; see further Wellman, *People and Sites*, 7. A story connects Van Cleve to the famous William Morgan Affair, see Appendix 7. The Van Cleve home still survives in Lewiston at Third and Center Streets.

[36] In the Town of Porter 1830 Federal Census, Boughton listed one free colored person in his household (see Ch. 3).

[37] Van Cleve, *Reminiscences*, 48-49. A Schooner, the *Massachusetts*, was owned in Youngstown in 1839.

Historical Museum add an eighth, also built by Shickluna, *The Two Brothers.*[38] Michael Pittavino, maritime historian at the H. Lee White Maritime Museum in Oswego, New York, has noted changes in the names of three of these schooners.[39] Of much interest for this book, the original owner of the *Challenge* was Captain Horatio N. Throop, a ship designer and captain from Pultneyville, New York, who transported "passengers" (fugitive slaves) to freedom in Canada on the 1848 steamer *Ontario.*[40]

In 1908, James Onen wrote to the *Youngstown News* that the *John Porter* schooner was built by Louis "Shickaloney," but not at the shore below the Villa apartments and not in 1838, as reported by Van Cleve, the *History of Niagara County History*, and the *Bicentennial History;*[41] rather, he claimed, it was built in 1835 "on the beach near the red store," that is, John Young's Red Store, which would have been about a block or so south, that is, near where the Youngstown Yacht Club stands today.[42] Onen's Louis Shickaloney was obviously the master shipbuilder, Louis Shickluna. Originally from Malta, Shickluna became a well-known boat builder in St. Catharines, Ontario,[43] and, as stated, had built both the *Lewis Shickluna* (1836) and the *John Porter* (1838) at Youngstown. One cannot but smile when reading Onen's comment that he was so sure that the year of the *John Porter* build was 1835 because it was in that year that Kim Kelsey's dog bit Sim Henry! However, the other sources and Michael Pittavino all give the date of the *John Porter* as 1838.

---

[38] Van Cleve himself states that Shickluna was the *ship carpenter* for the *R. H. Boughton* (p. 48), but *built* the *Shickluna* and the *John Porter* (p. 49). Records in the Town of Porter Historical Museum state that Shickluna built the *John Porter* (1836) and the *L. Shickluna* (1837), but also a third, *The Two Brothers* (1835). See also Fitch Cady, "Ship-building in Youngstown has a Long History," *The Buffalo News* (March 28, 1999).

[39] The *Challenge* was re-named the *Lamplighter* in 1856 (it carried lighthouse supplies) and the *Challenge* in 1862; the *Frank Pierce* was renamed the *General Sigal* (1862); and the *Cheney Ames* was renamed the *Grace G. Gribbie* in 1900. Thanks to Michael Pittavino for his information about boats on the Niagara River and Lake Ontario.

[40] Van Cleve, *Reminiscences*, 49. Again, see below for the Cuyler/Throop transport of fugitive slaves to Canada.

[41] *The Bicentennial History* also located the boat building activity below the Villa Apartments, 100 Main Street.

[42] The letter of James Onen, "Recollections of James Onen. Youngstown's Early Days," December 19, 1908, appeared in the *Youngstown News*, December 24, 1908; the letter is in the Youngstown Historical Society Museum; see also Vee Housman, http://www.newspaperabstracts.com/link.php?id=28591.

[43] "Remembering the Master Shipbuilder Louis Shickluna," *St. Catharines Standard*, December 11, 1914; http://www.stcatharinesstandard.ca/2014/12/07/remembering-the-master-shipbuilder-louis-shickluna; Joseph Abela, "Louis Shickluna – A Successful Singlean," *Times of Malta* (June 16, 2008). Shickluna directed the building of 140 schooners, barkentines, steamers, and other vessels. In St. Catharines near the Welland Canal a plaque commemorates him and his contribution to shipbuilding and the Canadian economy. See also Cady, "Ship-building in Youngstown."

We note two more bits of information. First, the Schooner *Governor Hunt* built in 1853 by David Rogers in Olcott, New York, was first owned by a Youngstown resident;[44] second, the *Lockport Journal* wrote that the *Auburn Daily Union*, Monday, November 19, 1860, reported the overboard drowning of young Charles Meeker of Oswego of the schooner *Carlton*, which docked at Youngstown.[45]

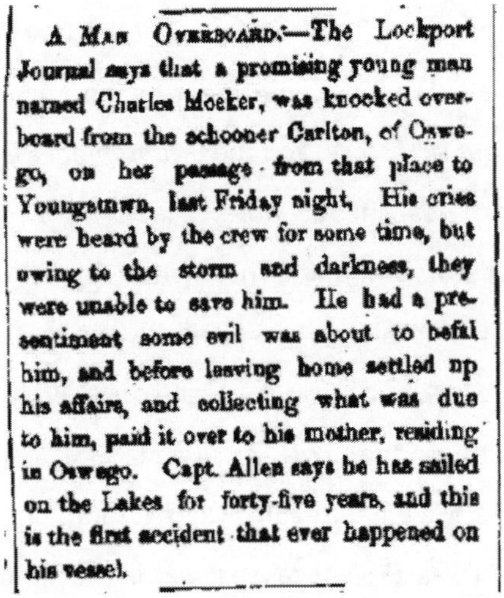
A MAN OVERBOARD.—The Lockport Journal says that a promising young man named Charles Meeker, was knocked overboard from the schooner Carlton, of Oswego, on her passage from that place to Youngstown, last Friday night. His cries were heard by the crew for some time, but owing to the storm and darkness, they were unable to save him. He had a presentiment some evil was about to befal him, and before leaving home settled up his affairs, and collecting what was due to him, paid it over to his mother, residing in Oswego. Capt. Allen says he has sailed on the Lakes for forty-five years, and this is the first accident that ever happened on his vessel.

A MAN OVERBOARD — The Lockport Journal says that a promising young man named Charles Meeker was knocked overboard from the schooner Carlton, of Oswego, on her passage from that place to Youngstown, last Friday night. His cries were heard by the crew for some time, but owning to the storm and darkness, they were unable to save him. He had a presentiment some evil was about to befall him, and before leaving home settled up his affairs, and collecting what was due him, paid it over to his mother, residing in Oswego. Capt. Allen says he has sailed on the lakes for forty-five years, and this is the first accident that ever happened on his vessel.

Newspaper Report: A Man Overboard, *Auburn Daily Union*, November 19, 1860
Fulton History[46]
Image 4.11

[44] "Governor Hunt; 1853; Schooner," Great Lakes Maritime Database. http://quod.lib.umich.edu/t/tbnms1ic/x-60238/1.

[45] The Census of 1850 records a Charles Meeker of Oswego, age 7, which would make him a "promising young man" of age 17 in 1860. In the same household were Melissa Meeker (age 37), presumably his mother.

[46] http://www.fultonhistory.com/Fulton.html; see the link to Richard Palmer, "Maritime Transcriptions."

Further documentation from Federal Census records for Oswego in 1850 shows that a seven-year old child Charles Meeker lived there. In 1860, the year of the above overboard death, he would have been seventeen, which corresponds to the report's "promising young man." Living in the same household with Charles were Melissa Meeker (age 37), perhaps his mother, the one with whom Charles settled his affairs at Oswego before his trip. Given the stormy weather and the report that "his cries were heard for some time," the tragedy was most likely an accident.

Steamboats, Steamships, Steam Ferries, and Steamboat Captains

Steamships were known in Prussia as early as 1707,[47] but they did not begin to flourish until about a century later. In North America, the Canadian *Frontenac* in 1816 was the first built, but it did not run on Lake Ontario until June 5, 1817; the first to run was the *Ontario*, built at Sackets Harbor, New York, which ran in April of 1817.[48] By the 1820s, there were four more steamers on the Niagara River Route—the *Niagara*, the *Queenston*, the *Canada*, and the *Martha Ogden*. By 1833, there were thirty to forty;[49] by 1840 more than 100![50] There were many steamboat accidents and sinkings on the Niagara River and Lake Ontario.[51]

---

[47] Croil, *Steam Navigation*, 29-30.

[48] Van Cleve, *Reminiscences*, 4, referring to the *Ontario*: "the first steamboat on the lakes." Also Croil, *Steam Navigation*, 247. Barlow Cumberland, *A Century of Sail and Steam on the Niagara River* (Toronto, ON: The Musson Book Company, 1913), Ch. 2, claims that the *Frontenac* was first also to run; however, this is disputed: "The ONTARIO. 1817. The First Steamboat on Lake Ontario Despite Cumberland's Assertions," *Maritime History of the Great Lakes*, which supports Van Cleve. http://images.maritimehistoryofthegreatlakes.ca/145/data?n=46.

[49] So the *Oswego Free Press*, December 4, 1833; *Maritime History of the Great Lakes*, http://www.MaritimeHistoryOfTheGreatLakes.ca/.

[50] "History and Development of Great Lakes Water Craft," Minnesota's Lake Superior Shipwrecks, http://www.mnhs.org/places/nationalregister/shipwrecks/mpdf/mpdf2.php.

[51] *Maritime History of the Great Lakes*, http://www.MaritimeHistoryOfTheGreatLakes.ca/. See URL extensions data?n=15 (*Chief Justice Robinson*), 16 (*Niagara*), 17 (*Cataract*), 18 (*Diamond*), 19 (*Clifton*), 20 (*Caroline*), 21 (*Baltic*), and 22 (*Queen Victoria*).

Wood Engraving of the *Ontario* (1847, departed 1848) (based on James Van Cleve)[52]
Image 4.12

The early steamboats docked at Youngstown, particularly in the summer, and ran

regular routes from Niagara River ports to ports on Lake Ontario and in the St. Lawrence River.

A Steamer Passes Fort Niagara Just North of the Village of Youngstown
James Van Cleve, "Fort Niagara," Lithograph J. P. Hall[53]
Image 4.13

---

[52] "The Steamer 'Ontario'," *Maritime History of the Great Lakes*.
http://images.maritimehistoryofthegreatlakes.ca/66320/data?n=10. The Woodcut was from the American Express
Line, but was derived from the original drawing by Captain James Van Cleve in his *Reminiscences*, 1877. See also,
http://images.maritimehistoryofthegreatlakes.ca/29846/data?n=17. This is not the 1817 *Ontario*.
[53] James Van Cleve, *The Great Northern Route,* 69. "JVC" initials are at the bottom.
http://images.maritimehistoryofthegreatlakes.ca/63722/data?n=1;
https://books.google.com/books?id=HDc9AAAAYAAJ&pg=PA147&lpg=PA147&dq=The+1848+steamboat+Ontario&
source=bl&ots=Ai78jmhFhQ&sig=-
PUeR7GHU1gipz5a88Xl1traM0k&hl=en&sa=X&ved=0CD4Q6AEwB2oVChMI47X2_fyYyQIVQ9QeCh2DuQYk#v=onep
age&q=The%201848%20steamboat%20Ontario&f=false. See also, Van Cleve's *Reminiscences*, 60.

References to Youngstown appear in newspaper advertisements and stories about travelers. We note two vessels, the early *Ontario* and the *Martha Ogden*.

The *Ontario* (1817—1831)
Based on a sketch from James Van Cleve[54]
Image 4.14

The American-built *Ontario*, the first steamer to operate on the Great Lakes, departed in April of 1817[55] and ran between Lewiston, New York, on the Niagara River and Ogdensburg, New York, on the St. Lawrence River, with main ports of call at Rochester, Oswego, Sackets Harbor, and Cape Vincent. While not always listed, Youngstown was a port of call in the summer, as the following advertisement for the American Steamboat Line of the Ontario Steamboat Company clearly shows.

---

[54] Cumberland, *A Century of Sail and Steam on the Niagara River*, 21; taken from Van Cleve, *Reminiscences*, 4; a version is also in J. R. Robertson, *Landmarks of Toronto*, 46.
[55] See Ch. 4 for the 1847 *Ontario* captained by Horatio N. Throop, who helped fugitive slaves to escape.

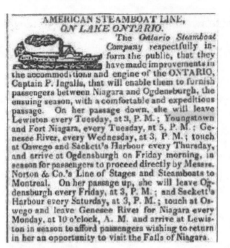

Part of an Ad in *The New York Spectator*, June 7, 1827[56]
Image 4.15

Information about the *Ontario* related to Youngstown also comes from court records about the abduction, imprisonment, and probable murder of William Morgan who was supposedly drowned by radical Masons in 1826.[57] We can summarize by quoting from Clarence O. Lewis, a former Niagara County Historian, in his article about James Van Cleve, who at the time of the Morgan Affair in 1826 was trying to land a job as purser (clerk) on the *Ontario*:

> . . . On the morning of Sept. 14, 1826 about 8:30 a.m., she [the *Ontario*] docked at Lewiston having about 30 Masons from Rochester on board. They had come to take part in the organization of a new Chapter of Royal Arch Masons in the named Benevolent Chapter. About 15 members of the Ames Chapter, Lockport, were also there and had charge of the installation ceremonies, supposed to have been held in the Lewiston Academy . . .

> After the meeting [at Lewiston, which had convened at 9 a. m.], the Rochester Masons again boarded the Ontario. James Van Cleve heard their conversation which had to do largely with the perplexing question of what should be done with Morgan [who was locked in the powder magazine at Fort Niagara]. . .

---

[56] For the rest of the ad, which mentions Youngstown's Olaf Hathaway as a local agent, see Ch. 7.
[57] For details, see Appendix 7.

THE ONTARIO docked at Youngstown and supper was served at a tavern below
the fort. . .

[Van Cleve] remained as purser on the Ontario until 1829. In 1830 he received
his commission as captain of the Martha Ogden also on Lake Ontario.[58]

The *Martha Ogden* mentioned by Clarence Lewis is another steamer that put in at
Youngstown. It was an American-built vessel constructed in 1824 and launched in 1825. The
Sackets Harbor Courier reported, "The MARTHA OGDEN [named for the wife of Thomas Ogden
of New York, one of the directors[59]] is a new boat, well found; her accommodations good; her
Captain well qualified for the command."[60] Several known captains in her record were Daniel
Reed, James Van Cleve, Andrew Estes, and William Vaughn. Van Cleve commented that "In
1826 and 1827 the Martha Ogden was on route between Youngstown and Toronto under the
command of Capt. A. Estes (margin: Andrew Estes)."[61] Barlow Cumberland added more
information about Youngstown:

On this "Martha Ogden," built at Sackets Harbor, in 1824, Captain Van Cleve, of
Lewiston, served for many years as clerk, and afterwards as captain. In a manuscript left
by him many interesting events in her history are narrated. In 1826 she ran under the
command of Captain Andrew Estes between Youngstown and York [Toronto].
Youngstown was then a port of much importance. It was the shipping place of a very
considerable hardwood timbering business, the trees being brought in from the
surrounding country. Its docks, situated close to the lake on an eddy separated from the

[58] Clarence O. Lewis, "Capt. Van Cleve, Pioneer, of Lewiston, Started Sailing Great Lakes in 1826," *Niagara Falls Gazette* (October 15, 1958); Lewis cited his source as Erik Heyl, *Journal of the Steamship Historical Society of America* 48 (December 1953) 81-82. Lewis' article also appeared in Lewiston's *Union-Sun and Journal* (October 16, 1958).

[59] *Maritime History of the Great Lakes*, http://www.MaritimeHistoryOfTheGreatLakes.ca/ commenting on the *Oswego Palladium*, December 5, 1832.

[60] *Sackets Harbor Courier*, November 15, 1832; *Oswego Free Press*, November 28, 1832; *Maritime History of the Great Lakes*, http://www.MaritimeHistoryOfTheGreatLakes.ca/;

[61] James Van Cleve, *Reminiscences*, 8, 9. See also, http://images.maritimehistoryofthegreatlakes.ca/66322/data; the *History of Niagara County, New York*, 120, repeats Van Cleve's information.

rapid flow of the river, formed an easily accessible centre for the bateaux and sailing craft which communicated with the Eastern ports on Lake Ontario.[62]

A considerable quantity of grain was also at that time raised in the district, providing material for the stone flour mill built in 1840.[63] This mill, grinding two hundred barrels per day, was in those days considered a marvel of enterprise. Though many years ago disused for such purpose it is still [in 1913] to be seen just a little above the Niagara Navigation Company's Youngstown dock.[64]

The *Martha Ogden* (launched 1824), which ran from Youngstown to York (Toronto)
1893 Sketch by W. J. Thompson; public domain, Canada[65]
Image 4.16

---

[62] A description of the shipping of timber and staves from various ports, including Youngstown, to various ports on Lake Ontario and the St. Lawrence River, probably begins with such observations by Van Cleve, *Reminiscences*, 48; see also, the notice in the *History of Niagara County,* 120.

[63] The Grist Mill (Steam Mill) at Youngstown, built by Hezekiah Smith in 1840, is noted in connection with the Davis family in Ch. 14; for a map of Youngstown and the mill's location, see Ch. 16 (No. 4).

[64] Cumberland, *Maritime History*, 28-29. See also, "History of Steam Navigation on Lake Ontario," *Oswego Commercial Times* and reprinted in the *Buffalo Morning Express*, September 16, 1847, WMHS History of Steam, at http://www.wmhs.org/history.html.

[65] Sketch of the *Martha Ogden* by W. J. Thomson in John Ross Robertson, *Landmarks of Toronto: A Collection of History Sketches of the Old Town of York from 1792 until 1833, and of Toronto from 1834 to 1895* (Toronto, ON: J. Ross Robertson, 1896), 851. Also, in Wikimedia: https://commons.wikimedia.org/wiki/Category:Drawings_of_WJ_Thompson; https://commons.wikimedia.org/wiki/File:American_Steamer_Martha_Ogden.jpg.

On June 17, 1826, an advertisement in the Toronto *Loyalist* noted that the *Martha Ogden* put in at Youngstown and that one could cross over by the Youngstown Ferry to Niagara free of cost. We have discovered that at that time the ferryman was John Phillips:[66]

> Notice. The steamboat *Martha Ogden*, Andrew Estes, master, will
> ply *between York [Toronto] and Youngstown* during the remainder of the season,
> making a daily trip from each place, Saturdays excepted, when she will
> cross but once. Hours of sailing, 6 o'clock in the morning and 3 o'clock
> in the afternoon. To accommodate the public, her hours of departure from
> each place will be changed alternately every week, of which notice will
> be regularly given. This arrangement will continue in effect, weather
> permitting, until further notice is given. *Passengers wishing to cross
> the river Niagara will be sent over in the ferry-boat free of charge.*
> Cabin passage, two dollars. Deck passage, one dollar. Agents at York,
> Messrs. M. and R. Meighan. June 13, 1826.[67]

In 1832, the *Martha Ogden* met her unfortunate end. On the night of November 12, she left Oswego for Sackets Harbor and soon encountered foul weather. According to Captain William Vaughan's description of the mishap, water in the vessel prevented the fires in the steam engine furnaces from being maintained, the engines became useless, the pumps choked, and the vessel took on more and more water. It became unmanageable and drifted onto the rocks. A brave Canadian, Mr. William Miller, courageously swam ashore, alerted the inhabitants, and a rope was attached from a tree to the boat, allowing the passengers and crew to glide safely to shore, children in a basket and adults in a sling. All were saved.[68]

---

[66] For Phillips, see Chs. 3, 6.

[67] Henry Scadding, *Toronto of Old; Collections and recollections Illustrative of the Early Settlement and Social Life of the Capital of Ontario,* Toronto, ON: Adam, Stevenson & co., 1873), online text, page 53 of 59 (italics ours). http://www.ebooksread.com/authors-eng/henry-scadding/toronto-of-old-collections-and-recollections-illustrative-of-the-early-settleme-hci/page-53-toronto-of-old-collections-and-recollections-illustrative-of-the-early-settleme-hci.shtml.

[68] William Vaughan, Oswego Free Press, November 28, 1832. Maritime History of the Great Lakes, http://www.MaritimeHistoryOfTheGreatLakes.ca/.

Niagara River Boats and the Underground Railroad

This chapter began with the tragic account of Captain Edward Lee of Norfolk, Virginia, who was tried, convicted, beaten, and imprisoned for twenty-five years for transporting fugitive slaves across the bay at Norfolk, Virginia. Recall also Horatio N. Throop [silent "h"] of Pultneyville, a hamlet east of Rochester in the Town of Williamson, Wayne County, New York, directly on Lake Ontario. Under the supervision of Throop a second *Ontario* steamer was completed in 1847[69] and he was its captain from 1848—1858. According to the 1877 *History of Wayne County, New York*, his cousin, Samuel C. Cuyler, an UGRR agent and station master at Pultneyville, whose house was an UGRR station, knew the opportunities for fugitive slaves to escape by steamboat from Pultneyville to Canada. According to the story, Cuyler would take African American freedom seekers to the dock in Pultneyville and, finding his cousin, would say, "Captain Throop, I have some 'passengers' [code language for fugitive slaves] for you." Throop would respond, "My boat runs for 'passengers.'" The fugitive slaves would thereafter board the *Ontario*. At the port of Charlotte near Rochester, a dangerous stop where there were slave catchers, the fugitives disappeared, but then reappeared when they reached Canada.[70]

There are other impressive examples of steamer captains who helped fugitive slaves. Deputy Sheriff Alexander McLeod of Niagara[-on-the-Lake] tried to return Solomon Moseby to slavery in the United States in 1837.[71] Before Moseby escaped, according to some sources,

---

[69] For the 1847 steamer *Ontario*, see above, Image: 4.12.

[70] *History of Wayne County, New York* (Philadelphia, PA: Everts, Ensign, and Everts, 1877) 195; also cited in Wellman, "Lewiston Landing," 181-92; Judith Wellman, "'Unspeakable Joy': Religion, Reform, the Underground Railroad and African American Life in the Burned-over District of Wayne County, New York," in Historical New York Research Associates, *Databases. Sites Relating to the Underground Railroad, Abolitionism, and African American Life in Wayne County, New York*. Wayne County Historian's Office Preserve (Lyons, NY: 2007--2009) 29. http://www.rootsweb.ancestry.com/~nycayuga/ugrr/phillips.html and http://www.nps.gov/subjects/ugrr/ntf_member/ntf_member_details.htm?SPFID=12731; Mary Ellen Snodgrass, "Cuyler, Samuel Cornelius (1808—1872), Cuyler, Julia Speed (1812--?)," *The Underground Railroad: An Encyclopedia of People, Places, and Operations* (New York, NY; London, UK: M. E. Sharpe, Taylor & Francis, 2008; London, UK: Routledge, 2015), https://books.google.com/books?id=RmqsBwAAQBAJ&pg=PT538&lpg=PT538&dq=HOratio+Nelson+Throop&sourc e=bl&ots=3CHvoCNyeQ&sig=qC8x4HeMhA1XvrB7hrZ_YYviVKg&hl=en&sa=X&ved=0CDUQ6AEwBGoVChMI1Z6FvNj vyAIVgT4mCh2QngB3#v=onepage&q=HOratio%20Nelson%20Throop&f=false.

[71] For a summary of the Moseby story, see Ch. 1 in this book and for the trial of Sherriff McLeod, Appendix 7 (the "*Caroline* [a steamboat] Affair"). Informative detail is found in David Murray, *Colonial Justice: Justice, Morality, and Crime in the Niagara District, 1791-1849* (Toronto, ON: University of Toronto Press, 2002), 208 (Ch. 10, 196-216, which reprints "Hands Across the Border: The Abortive Extradition of Solomon Moseby," *Canadian Review of*

Sheriff McLeod attempted to enlist steamer captains to take Moseby back to the United States via Lewiston. Hugh Richardson, who became a major figure in steam transportation on Lake Ontario, supposedly refused to help McLeod.[72] Richardson, who became captain of the luxurious steamboat *Chief Justice Robinson*, helped Jacob Green escape to Toronto.[73] In short, some steamboat captains were well-known for helping fugitive slaves escape to Canada.

The fact that steamer captains helped fugitive slaves escape to Canada raises the question: Were any of the known captains of the steamers that put into Youngstown, such as the *Ontario* and the *Martha Ogden*—Daniel Reed, James Van Cleve, Andrew Estes, William Vaughan—also of this stripe? Captain Estes turns up in the Town of Porter Federal Census records of 1830 as a white male age 40-50. In his household were also one free white female age 30-40, three free white males age 15-20, 10-15, and 0-5 respectively, and four white females, two ages 10-15 and 0-5 respectively—for a total of nine household members. This interesting information is not very helpful in answering the specific question.

Yet, there is clear evidence that some Youngstown ferrymen did indeed help fugitive slaves escape to Canada, as we shall see. Olaf Hathaway, who was working as a Youngstown agent for the American Steamboat Line on Lake Ontario in 1827, and who allowed his name to be added to the ferryman application of John Beach in 1836, was credited with having ferried the fugitive slave Thomas James from Youngstown to Niagara in 1821.[74] Most impressive, there is the autobiographical report of the African American abolitionist and fund raiser Reverend Samuel Ringgold Ward, who, with his white traveling companion, the abolitionist Reverend Hiram Wilson, witnessed a fugitive slave who had just crossed from Youngstown to Niagara on a bitterly cold January day in 1853 and was warming himself at the Niagara Ferry House stove. Ward's account includes his extensive conversation with an anonymous Youngstown ferryman.

American Studies 30/2 (2000), 187-209). The source for Richardson's involvement was Janet Carnochan (1897). The story is also cited in Wellman, "Lewiston Landing," 190.

[72] See Ch. 1 above; however, Riddell, "Slave in Upper Canada," 263, says Moseby was to go back by ferry—precisely where is not stated. Was it Youngstown?

[73] J. D. Green, *Narrative of the Life of J. D. Green, a Runaway Slave, from Kentucky. Containing an Account of His Three Escapes in 1839, 1846, and 1848* (Hudderfield, England: Henry Fielding, Pack Horse Yard, 1864), 35; http://www.docsouth.unc.edu/neh/greenjd/greenjd.html; cited also in Wellman, "Lewiston Landing," 181-92.

[74] More will be said about these persons in Chs. 6 and 14. Our evidence shows that Olafs brother Elijah was the official ferrymen in 1821.

Ward was much impressed that the wry fellow did not charge indigent fugitive slaves—as he did Ward himself![75]

Finally, there is speculation that the Youngstown Ferry House might have been an UGRR station. We shall consider this possibility in Chapter 16.

---

[75] Ward and Wilson will receive more attention in Ch. 8.

CHAPTER 5

Crossing the Niagara River: Bridges, Trains, and the Youngstown Trains

Image 5.1

The Suspension Bridges[1]

Although there was still much watercraft on the Niagara River through the 1840s and 1850s—the ferry at Youngstown was a quick and relatively economical way to get to Niagara—Underground Railroad sources from the late 1840's and 1850s also refer to the "Suspension Bridge" used by fugitive slaves to escape to Canada. By 1851, there were two suspension

---

[1] Judith Wellman, "Site of the International Suspension Bridge, 1848, 1855" at http://www.niagarafallsundergroundrailroad.org/documents/18_Site%20of%20the%20International%20Suspensio n%20Bridge.pdf; see also, "The Railway Suspension Bridge," *Bridges Over Niagara Falls: A History and Pictorial*, http://www.niagarafrontier.com/bridges.html#b2; William H. Siener and Thomas A. Chambers, "Crossing to Freedom: Harriet Tubman and John A. Roebling's Niagara Suspension Bridge," *Western New York Heritage* 13/1 (Spring 2010), 8–17 and "Harriet Tubman, the Underground Railroad, and the Bridges at Niagara Falls," *Afro-Americans in New York Life and History* 36/1 [2012]: 34-63 (*Questia* by subscription https://www.questia.com/library/journal/1G1-280967665/harriet-tubman-the-underground-railroad-and-the; Daniel L. Davis, *The Life and Times of Suspension Bridge Village*. 2nd edition (2014).

bridges across the Niagara River.[2] One was between Lewiston, New York, and Queenston, Ontario, about seven and a half miles south of Youngstown. Completed in 1851 by Edward Serrell, it carried pedestrian and vehicular traffic. This bridge was partially destroyed by a fierce storm on February 1, 1864, and thereafter unsafe and not used.[3]

James Van Cleve, "Suspension Bridge at Lewiston and Queenston" (1851—1864)[4]
Image 5.2

The second suspension bridge was located about where the current Whirlpool (Rapids) Bridge is located today, which is about three and a half miles further south (upriver) from the Lewiston-Queenston Suspension Bridge, or from the opposite direction about two miles north

---

[2] Today there are six bridges, none of them suspension bridges.

[3] Some online sources, such as the Niagara Falls Information Site, say that the destruction date was 1854 (http://www.niagarafallsinfo.com/history-item.php?entry_id=1397&current_category_id=213), but the *Niagara Falls Gazette* of February 3, 1864, reports the "Partial Destruction of The Lewiston Suspension Bridge" (http://www.bridgemeister.com/results.php?strm=but. The current arch bridge between Lewiston and Queenston opened on November 1, 1952.

[4] James Van Cleve, *The Ontario and St. Lawrence Steamboat Company Handbook for Travelers Niagara Falls, Montreal and Quebec, and Through Lake Champlain to Saratoga Springs* (Buffalo, NY: Jewett, Thomas, and Co., 1852), 57. This little travelers' guide contains many original Van Cleve Sketches. Two copies are in the Buffalo Historical Museum (1852, 1854). Thanks to Cynthia Van Ness, MLS, Library, Research, Pictures. The guide is also at https://archive.org/stream/ontariostlawrenc00ontauoft#page/56/mode/2upF; see also, Judith Wellman, "Lewiston Landing," http://www.niagarafallsundergroundrailroad.org/assets/Uploads/NF-HAMP-Report-Appendix-C-1.pdf 181-92.

(downriver) from the Falls. It opened three years earlier than the Lewiston-Queenston Suspension Bridge, on July 29, 1848. A humorous account about the dangers of crossing on this Suspension Bridge appeared in several New York papers from September 25 to 29, 1850:[5]

PERILOUS SITUATION—A gentleman informs us that a party of ladies and gentlemen visiting at Niagara Falls, hired a hack to visit the Canadian side, crossing the Suspension Bridge. While examining the Spring on the Canada shore the driver partook freely of something stronger than water and became tolerably drunk by the time the party were ready to return to the American side. In crossing the Suspension Bridge the horses got a little out of the track, owing to the carelessness of the drunken driver, and the fore and hind wheels of the carriage went off the ends of the plank, sinking to the hobs between the strands of the bridge. The inmates jumped from the carriage upon the bridge much frightened, as they might well be at even the slightest accident upon a trail bridge of wire thrown across the wild waters of Niagara, two hundred feet above in surface. The carriage and horses were safely extricated from their position, and the driver probably somewhat sobered by his fright.— *Roch. Adv.*

Newspaper Report: The Dangers of Crossing the Suspension Bridge
Image 5.3

As a result of the bridge, the community called Bellevue on the United States side grew rapidly and in 1854 it was incorporated as Niagara City. At the time it was separated from the City of Niagara Falls proper by farm land. The 1848 suspension bridge at Bellevue/Niagara City, engineered by Charles Ellet, was, like the Lewiston-Queenston bridge, a pedestrian and vehicular bridge. However, the famous bridge engineer, John A. Roebling, rebuilt it with an upper deck for rail traffic. The first locomotive, the *London*, crossed on March 8, 1855.

---

[5] E.g., the *Rochester Advocate* (September 25); the *Syracuse Standard* (September 26); Utica *Daily Observer* (September 28). Fulton History, http://www.fultonhistory.com/Fulton.html.

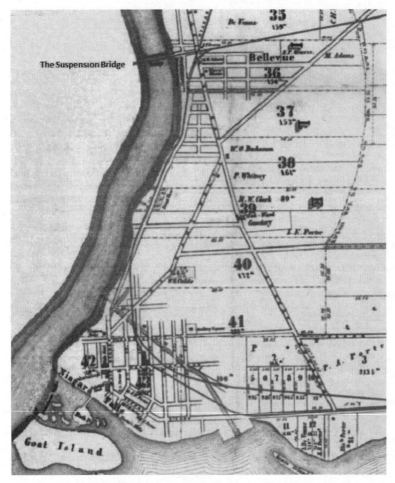

Map: Bellevue (Niagara City) and Niagara Falls, with Farmland Between
Cropped from the Tobias Witmer 1854 Map of the Town of Niagara Falls
Library of Congress[6]
Image 5.4

Another locomotive, called the *Pluto*, carried dignitaries across the following day.[7]

---

[6] Excerpt from "Map of the Town of Niagara. Drawn from Actual Surveys and Authentic Records." Tobias Witmer, Surveyor. Library of Congress. https://www.loc.gov/resource/g3804n.la002090/. One can see the names A. H. Porter, A. S. Porter, P. B. Porter, Eliz. Porter, and P. Whitney, as well as the Cataract, International, and Falls Hotels.
[7] *Schenectady Cabinet*, March 10, 1855. Fulton History. http://www.fultonhistory.com/Fulton.html. Roebling is spelled "Nobeling."

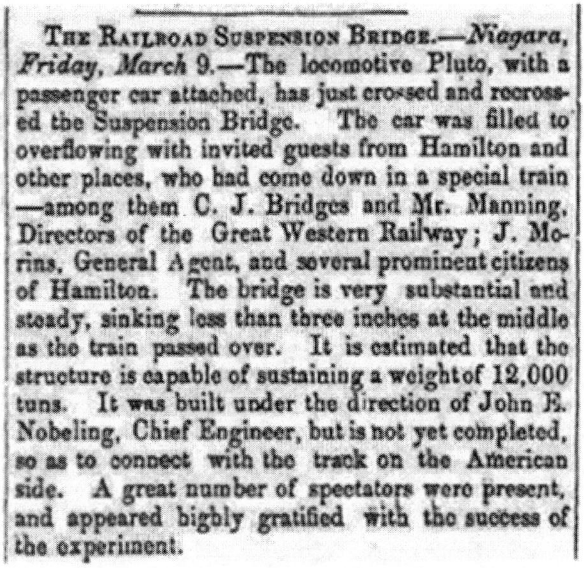

> THE RAILROAD SUSPENSION BRIDGE.—*Niagara,*
> *Friday, March* 9.—The locomotive Pluto, with a
> passenger car attached, has just crossed and recross-
> ed the Suspension Bridge. The car was filled to
> overflowing with invited guests from Hamilton and
> other places, who had come down in a special train
> —among them C. J. Bridges and Mr. Manning,
> Directors of the Great Western Railway; J. Mo-
> rins, General Agent, and several prominent citizens
> of Hamilton. The bridge is very substantial and
> steady, sinking less than three inches at the middle
> as the train passed over. It is estimated that the
> structure is capable of sustaining a weight of 12,000
> tuns. It was built under the direction of John E.
> Nobeling, Chief Engineer, but is not yet completed,
> so as to connect with the track on the American
> side. A great number of spectators were present,
> and appeared highly gratified with the success of
> the experiment.

Newspaper Report: The Locomotive *Pluto* Crosses the Suspension Bridge (1855)
Image 5.5

The bridge was officially opened to the general public ten days after the *London* crossed, March 18, 1855.[8]

Railroad companies that used the train bridge included the New York and Erie Railroad's Canandaigua and Niagara Falls extensions and The New York Central Railroad, which had consolidated other railroad lines farther east. After the Roebling train addition, it was possible to buy a ticket in New York City or Boston, or anywhere along the New York Central line in New York State, such as Albany, Syracuse, or Rochester, and travel to points in Canada via the Rail Road Suspension Bridge, which linked up with the Great Western Railway of Canada. The Roebling Suspension Bridge of 1855 was in effect an international railway bridge. A fascinating train schedule listing the distances and times between many stops can be found in *The New-York Traveller; containing Railroad, Steamboat, Canal Packet, and Stage Routes, Through the State of New York. Also, Other Information Useful to Travellers*, published already in 1845.[9]

---

[8] "Bridges Over Niagara Falls: A History and Pictorial." http://www.niagarafrontier.com/bridges.html#b2. See Daniel L. Davis, *The Life and Times of Suspension Bridge Village.* 2nd edition (2014).
[9] *The New York Traveller* (New York: J. Disturnell, July 1845).

Charles Parsons, "The Rail Road Suspension Bridge near Niagara Falls," 1855 (1855—1896)
Originally hand-colored lithograph (1857) shows lower level for carriages and foot traffic,
upper level for trains. The Falls can be seen in the background.
Public Domain, original in color [10]
Image 5.6

---

[10] Charles Parsons, "The Rail Road Suspension Bridge near Niagara Falls" (1855—1896) (New York, NY: Currier & Ives, 1857). Library of Congress Prints and Photographs Division, Washington, D. C.; color film copy transparency) cph 3b52958; http://hdl.loc.gov/loc.pnp/cph.3b52958I.D, showing the lower level for foot and carriage traffic and the upper level for railroads, as reproduced by Wellman, "Site of the International Suspension Bridge." http://www.niagarafallsundergroundrailroad.org/documents/18_Site%20of%20the%20International%20Suspensio n%20Bridge.pdf. The bridge was dismantled in 1897 to allow for the construction of the Whirlpool Rapids Bridge.

The Train Arrives in Canada: An Ad for Canada's Great Western Railway (ca. 1876)
Showing the Roebling 1855 Railroad Suspension Bridge
The Pedestrian/Vehicular Bridge is below the train level (lower right, horse and carriage;
the American and Canadian Falls are pictured in the background.
The ad is in the public domain (originally in color)
Image 5.7

A spur of the New York Central Railroad was built to Lewiston along the Niagara Gorge in 1854 and briefly extended to Youngstown in 1855 (see below).

Most important for the Underground Railroad, the new international Suspension Bridge made it possible for fugitive slaves, whether passing as free blacks or posing in the service of whites, to board a train in the east, link up with the New York Central, and travel straight across the State of New York through to Canada.[11] It became Harriet Tubman's favorite route. In 1869, Sarah Bradford offered what is now a famous account of Tubman escorting fugitive slaves

---

[11] For a list of documented slave crossings at Suspension Bridge, see Wellman, "Appendix C: Survey of Sites," 171-72

across the bridge to Canada in 1856.[12] Tubman expert Kate Clifford Larson accepts the central features of Bradford's account, although Larson describes the event a little less dramatically. As they crossed Tubman "called out to her friends to look at the great falls"; Joe Bailey, one of her escorted fugitive slaves, fearful of being recognized, "was inconsolable and would not look"; and when they reached Canada, Tubman exclaimed, "Joe, you're free!" Bailey, attracting a crowd by his joyful shouts and singing, then told Tubman that his next planned trip would be to heaven, whereupon Tubman replied, probably with a bit of humor, "You might have looked at the Falls first and then gone to Heaven afterwards!"[13] This story requires a Suspension Bridge with train traffic and from which one could see the beautiful Falls in the distance. It was the reconstructed Roebling Suspension Bridge of 1855 at Niagara City.[14]

Suspension Bridge Village[15]

The new business and commercial activity associated with the international bridge between the United States and Canada led to boom-town development. In 1854, the Hamlet of Bellevue, New York, was incorporated as the Village of Niagara City. In Theodora Vinal's words:

The new village was described by a map of Niagara Falls and Vicinity published in 1854. According to it Niagara City had a population of two thousand people; one weekly newspaper, one college for orphans; three district schools, two select schools; fifteen hotels, one bank, the terminals of five railroads, twenty-eight stores, fourteen

---

[12] Sarah H. Bradford's classic, *Scenes in the Life of Harriet Tubman* (Auburn, NY: W. J. Moses, 1869; rev. ed. *Harriet, the Moses of Her People*, 1886). Larson, *Bound for the Promised Land*, xvii, 100, says that Bradford's statement that Tubman made nineteen trips and rescued 300 fugitive slaves, often repeated in secondary literature, is an exaggeration. Actually, Tubman made about thirteen trips and rescued seventy to eighty fugitive slaves, although she gave instructions to many others. For a classic photo of Tubman, see Ch. 3.

[13] Larson, ibid., 136.

[14] Today, if one crosses at the Whirlpool Bridge, one can still see the Falls mist, but the Falls are mostly obscured by the intervening Rainbow Bridge; also, in the 1850s the Falls would have been about one hundred yards closer to the bridge (records of the erosion of the Falls began in 1842; see P. Gromosiak, *Niagara Falls Q & Q* (Meyer Enterprises/Western New York Wares Inc. 1989) 6; "Niagara Falls –Thunder Alley: Frequently Asked Questions," http://www.niagarafrontier.com/faq.html#erosion).

[15] See Daniel L. Davis, *The Life and Times of Suspension Bridge Village*. 2nd edition (2014); "Dan Davis *to* Niagara Falls History—Stories of us." https://www.facebook.com/whynotsuspensionbridge/posts/736396376465307.

mechanics' shops, two meat markets, one grist mill, one saw mill; two attorneys, two justices of the peace, and five physicians.[16]

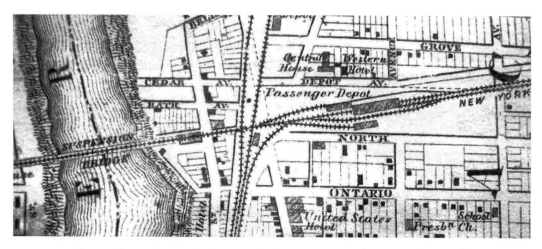

Extract from a Map of Niagara City (Suspension Bridge Village) (1860)[17]
Courtesy of the Niagara Falls Public Library
Image 5.8

Eventually there was a postal address at the Passenger Depot just up the hill from the bridge. Niagara City Stockyard statistics in 1858 were quoted by Orrin E. Dunlap in the *Niagara Gazette*, August 16, 1941:

> In 1858 there were shipped from Niagara City over the New York Central 262,375 hogs; 45,430 sheep and 24,248 cattle. Great long trains of livestock were always passing through the village casting their perfume from end to end. For six days ending May, 1, 1858 no less than 1,406 cattle, 1771 hogs, 32 horses and three dogs were shipped eastward.[18]

---

[16] Theodora Vinal, *Niagara Portage from Past to Present* (Buffalo, NY: Foster and Stewart, 1949; Henry Stewart, Inc., 1955) Niagara City Stockyards, 1858.

[17] The full map is of Niagara City, 1860. Courtesy of the Niagara Falls Public Library. Thanks to Library Director Michelle Petrazzoulo. Thanks also to Daniel L. Davis. Part of the map is reproduced at "Buffalo as an Architectual Museum," as "1855 map." http://buffaloah.com/a/nf/ntl/hist/.

[18] Orrin E. Dunlap in the *Niagara Gazette*, August 16, 1941. Cited in Daniel L. Davis, *The Life and Times of Suspension Bridge Village.* 2nd edition (2014), 39 with a different map. Also, a post in Dan Davis' Facebook, May 14, 2016.

In short, ads referring to *the* Suspension Bridge—the bridge itself—appeared in the early 1850s, but very soon the village was being called "Suspension Bridge." An advertisement from the New York *Daily Tribune* in October of 1855 refers to the route as "via Suspension Bridge, Buffalo, or Oswego. . .":[19]

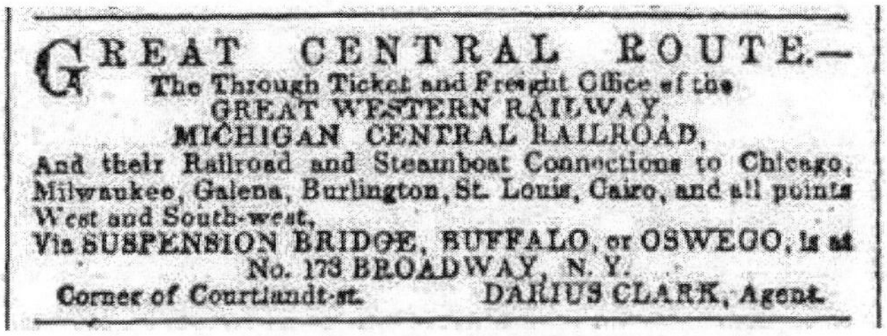
GREAT CENTRAL ROUTE.—The Through Ticket and Freight Office of the GREAT WESTERN RAILWAY, MICHIGAN CENTRAL RAILROAD, And their Railroad and Steamboat Connections to Chicago, Milwaukee, Galena, Burlington, St. Louis, Cairo, and all points West and South-west, Via SUSPENSION BRIDGE, BUFFALO, or OSWEGO, is at No. 173 BROADWAY, N. Y. Corner of Courtlandt-st. DARIUS CLARK, Agent.

An Ad For Suspension Bridge Village
Image 5.9

In Chapter 2, we listed a number of anti-slavery meetings in Niagara County in 1855, including two that took place at Youngstown. The organizer of those meetings, William J. Watkins, was also an agent for the Rochester Ladies Anti-Slavery Society. In a short note to a Mrs. Armstrong, probably an officer of the society, he told about his activity as a conductor. His statement was ambiguous: "Suspension Bridge" with no article and in a series with towns and cities could have meant the village; however, since St. Catharines and Hamilton were towns in Canada, perhaps he was referring to the bridge itself. We repeat the note here.[20]

> Mrs. Armstrong, I find upon examination, that from Dec. 15th to Aug. 9th, '57, I passed 59 fugitives to Canada, as follows. 6 to Toronto, and 53 to Suspension Bridge, St. Catharines, Hamilton, etc.
>
> Respectfully,
> Wm. J. Watkins
> P. S. Expended on behalf of the Society, $90.00. W.J.W.[21]

---

[19] *New-York Daily Tribune*, October 3, 1855. Fulton History. http://www.fultonhistory.com/Fulton.html. The name shift occurred before the railroad level was completed in 1855, e.g., in an ad in the *Daily Albany Argus* of Thursday, September 21, 1854.

[20] The VanDeusen Diary of Ch. 7 also refers to "Suspension Bridge," not *the* Suspension Bridge.

[21] Watkins letter is cited in Wellman, "Site of the International Suspension Bridge, 1848, 1855," *Niagara Falls Underground Railroad Heritage Area Management Plan Appendix C,* 171-72. This letter is archived in the

In conclusion, it was noted above that a spur of the New York Central Railroad was built to Lewiston along the Niagara Gorge in 1854 and extended to Youngstown in 1855. After discussing the Niagara River boats that docked at Youngstown in the previous chapter, we consider this railroad bed as a possible route for fugitive slaves who might have headed from Youngstown to the suspension bridges. Most importantly, documentation about two fugitive slaves who were directed to go to Suspension Bridge—probably the village—in 1855, indicates that they were diverted to Youngstown as a terminus, a most intriguing subject yet to be discussed.[22]

The Transitory Trains to Youngstown

Trains were increasingly important for the Underground Railroad by the mid-1850's, as just discussed. Two train spurs went to Youngstown in this period. Did they play a role in the UGRR? We need to look briefly at this part of the story.

It was strategically critical to connect land transportation—stage and rail lines—with water transportation—lake steamer lines (sometimes linked with ferries)—so that travelers, tourists, baggage, and cargo could easily and smoothly transfer from one to the other. The American Express Line ran steamers from Lewiston to Toronto, Rochester, Oswego, and Ogdensburg; the Canadian New Through Line ran steamers from Hamilton, to Lewiston and Queenston, various Ontario ports, Ogdensburg, and finally Montreal.[23] By 1853, the New York Central Railroad was forming contracts with Lake Erie and Lake Ontario shipping companies.[24] Two of these lines made it to Youngstown: The Buffalo and Niagara Falls Railroad Company leased to the New York Central Railroad and the Canandaigua Line.[25]

"Rochester Ladies Anti-Slavery Society and Papers 1851-1868," William L. Clements Library Manuscripts Division, University of Michigan, Ann Arbor Michigan.

[22] See Ch. 7.

[23] Cumberland, *Maritime History*, Ch. 4.

[24] Previously, a daily stage route had taken tourists from Buffalo to Niagara Falls, Lewiston, and Youngstown. See J. H. French, *Gazetteer of the State of New York: Embracing a Comprehensive View of the Geography, Geology, and General History of the State, and a Complete History and Description. Every County, City, Town, Village, and Locality. With Full Tables of Statistics* (Sold only by Subscription, 1860), 262.

[25] These two lines should not be confused with the famous Gorge Route of the late nineteenth and early twentieth centuries (1893-1935). It had a trolley line extension to and through Youngstown to Fort Niagara and to Rumsey Park and Beach, a resort area with boat and bath houses on Lake Ontario.

The Buffalo and Niagara Falls Railroad Company, formed in 1834, completed its 19-mile railroad extension from Buffalo to Niagara Falls by 1849 and, after it was leased to the New York Central Railroad in 1853, a further 6.25 mile extension to Lewiston.[26] According to Barlow Cumberland the Lewiston extension did not go all the way through the town down to the Lewiston Dock because the original plan was to extend it to the Youngstown Dock, which lay on a quiet back eddy and had the advantage of being much closer to Lake Ontario.[27] Meanwhile, a Niagara Falls and Lake Ontario Railroad company was organized in 1852.[28] The Committee consisted of Benjamin Pringle, a lawyer from Batavia, soon to be elected a United States Representative (March 5, 1853 – March 3, 1857), president; John Porter, a clerk from Youngstown, Vice-President;[29] Bradley D. Davis of Youngstown, secretary;[30] and William S. Mallory of Batavia, treasurer. The Committee raised $100,000 and eventually a track was laid on flat lands from Lewiston to Youngstown. An article from the *Niagara Falls Gazette* on January 23, 1856, expressed great anticipation about the Youngstown extension:

> . . . Youngstown is surrounded with many of the elements which go to make a flourishing country village. Porter is a rich farming town and its frontier village possesses superior facilities for reaching the eastern markets.—Added to these will ere long [before long] be the Niagara Falls and Lake Ontario Railroad which will place our neighbors in connection with all the great lines of travel east and west. The opening of this road will certainly add much to the prosperity of Youngstown and its vicinity.

---

[26] "New York Central Railroad 1853 – 1860." Old Rail History.com. http://oldrailhistory.com/index.php?option=com_content&view=article&id=211&Itemid=245 (italics ours).
[27] Cumberland, *Maritime History*, Ch. 4.
[28] Edward T. Dunn, *A History of Railroads in Western New York* (2nd ed.; Buffalo, NY: Canisius College Press, 2000) 14.
[29] "Benjamin Pringle," Wikipedia, https://en.wikipedia.org/wiki/Benjamin_Pringle.
[30] See Ch. 14.

Other sources tell a much less hopeful story. J. H. French's *New York State Gazetteer of 1860*, reported that by September 3, 1852, the Niagara Falls and Lake Ontario Line from Niagara Falls to Youngstown was "graded and rails laid, but not used."[31] If so, what happened?

The nineteenth-century *History of Niagara County* gave this vague explanation: ". . . owing to *numerous causes, too well understood to require mention in this connection*, the Niagara Falls and Lake Ontario Railroad was abandoned, and the track taken up soon after its completion."[32] William Pool was slightly more specific. About three months before the optimistic report in the *Niagara Falls Gazette* appeared he claimed that a run was actually made:

> On the 21st of October, 1855, a train was run over the line to Youngstown, and *soon afterward work on this part of the road was suspended and the track taken up*. Had the project been carried forward and the line put in operation, Youngstown would probably have been the port for the Lake Ontario steamers and would have taken much of the business which now centers at Lewiston and Niagara Falls. The portion of the road that was built was subsequently leased and is now operated by the Central Company.[33]

Pool's description implied that the project was abandoned because of insufficient funding. Perhaps one reason was the tremendous cost already incurred for laying the track from Niagara Falls to Lewiston. After noting the great expense of rock cuttings in the Niagara gorge,[34] Barlow Cumberland, in 1911, told of the one-run train and offered still more insight:

> A further extension followed when another small railway company, the *Niagara Falls and Ontario R.R.* was organized in 1852 to build a railway of 14 miles *from the Falls*

---

[31] J. H. French's *New York State Gazetteer of 1860*, 78.

[32] *History of Niagara County, N.Y.*, 340 (https://archive.org/details/cu31924100387392). Digitalized version online, 82 (italics ours).

[33] Pool, Editor, *Landmarks*, 71; repeated in Edward T. Williams, *Niagara County New York . . . A Concise Record of Her Progress and People, 1821-1921.* 2 vols. illustrated (Chicago, Il: J. H. Beers & Company, N.D. [ca. 1921]), 267-68 (italics ours).

[34] He writes of the Great Gorge Route, a trolley line that went along the Niagara River on the America side from the International Railway Terminal to Lewiston, with a trolley extension to Youngstown and the Lake Ontario beach to the east of Fort Niagara. There was a corresponding line on the Canadian side. One could take the circuit on both sides by crossing the river at the Lewiston-Queenston Suspension Bridge and at the Falls View Bridge at Niagara Falls (1897 – 1938). President William McKinley took part of this excursion on the morning of September 6, 1901. He was shot that afternoon by an assassin and died of infection on September 14.

to the shores of the Lake at Youngstown, where the steamers would be joined. Benj. Pringle, president; John Porter, vice president; Bradley D. Davis, secretary. The company, at an expense relatively much greater in those days than at the present, excavated the rock cuttings and cut the shelf in the side of the cliff upon which the New York Central Railway now runs through the Gorge, alongside the courses of the Niagara River, and the railway was graded and opened to Lewiston in 1854. *Construction was continued further to Youngstown and the track laid in 1855, but only one train was run down to the lower port. It has been said that this was necessary in order to complete the terms of the charter, and appears to have been a final effort.* The means of the company were no doubt impaired, so that shortly, afterward all further work on this extension was suspended, the track taken up, and thus in 1855 the balance of the line being leased to the New York Central, the Lewiston station had become the terminus of the railroad, where it had ever since remained. *As the transfer to the steamers was originally intended to be made at Youngstown,* there had been no need, at that time, for the station at Lewiston being constructed any nearer to the River bank.[35]

Meanwhile, in 1853 a second line, the Canandaigua and Niagara Falls line ran through Batavia to North Tonawanda and in 1854 on to the suspension bridge at Suspension Bridge Village (the Peanut Line). Local historical studies state that a spur went to Lewiston Junction where it split, one branch going into Lewiston, the other to Youngstown. A map of the railroads of New York shows that it was under construction in 1855.[36]

This seems confirmed by the Buffalo Daily Courier, March 21, 1855.:

The Niagara Falls Gazette states that the Canandaigua and Niagara Falls Railroad Co…. intend to build a large Depot at the Suspension Bridge, and that negotiations are in progress which, if successful, will ensure the early completion of the line to Youngstown.

---

[35] Cumberland, *A Century of Sail and Steam on the Niagara River*, 135 (italics ours). The Lewiston section was later extended to the Lewiston Dock along the river.
[36] "Map of the State of New York Showing its Water and Rail-Road Lines, Jan. 1855," by direction of John T. Clark, State Engineer and Surveyor. Library of Congress. https://www.loc.gov/resource/g3801p.rr002610/.

An 1855 map also implies that some track had been laid.

Map: from the Railroads of the State of New York, 1856[37]
Library of Congress, Public Domain

However, Edwin Howard briefly described this line in 1976: "The branch to Youngstown cut diagonally through the farms, down Bloody Run[38] and terminated on Water Street."[39] The following map gives one possibility for its terminus. The railroad tie, spikes, and plate from the flats below 615 Main Street (No. 4 on the map) might be from that line.

---

[37] Map of the Rail-Roads of the State of New York Prepared under the Direction of the Rail Road Commissioners, John S. Clark, William J. McAlpine, and James B. Swain. Library of Congress, https://www.loc.gov/resource/g3801p.rr002620/.

[38] "Bloody Run" was named for a bloody Iroquois attack on the routed and fleeing French soldiers who had just been defeated at the Battle of *La Belle Famille* in the Village of Youngstown on July 24, 1759.

[39] Howard, "Transportation," 16. See n. 45.

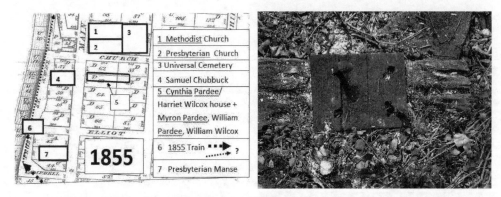

Map: Southwestern Youngstown, ca. 1855[40]
Image 5.11a

Youngstown Railroad Tie/Spikes/Plate (1855?)[41]
Image 5.11b

The train went through Bloody Run, which was (is) south of the village center.[42] However, the railroad construction changed the Bloody Run area's topography. Sara Swain, whose grandfather Isaac settled some of the property near Bloody Run—the Swain historic cobblestone house still stands—wrote that Bloody Run, also called Two Mile Run because it is two miles from the mouth of the Niagara River, or, as locals called it, simply "the Creek," was originally much wider, and that southernmost tip of five War of 1812 batteries along the Niagara had once lain at its mouth. She also noted that "Mr. Root [who lived north of the Swain house] said that when he was a boy the mouth of the Two Mile Run was wide enough for a small schooner to come in and anchor there."[43] The newer outlet of the Creek ". . . was made by the Canandaigua Railroad . . . ,"[44] and ". . . at that time [1854/1855] its mouth was filled in

---

[40] Portion of map made for H. H. Smith & the Ex. of Catherine Young by J. J. Smith, Surveyor, 1854, and filed in the Niagara County Clerk's Office under Cover 179. Modifications by Dennis Duling.

[41] No. 4 is currently 615 Main Street, a home built by Samuel Chubbuck (see Ch. 6). The home has been renovated by current owners John and Catherine Goller. Although railroad ties have been brought in to build steps down to the river, this tie has a tie plate and two spikes and is therefore likely to have dated from the 1855 train track build.

[42] The location of the Battle of *La Belle Famille* has been changed. That it took place at Bloody Run south of the Village of Youngstown center, where there has been a historical marker since 1936, was defended by Sara Swain (revised), "Appendix II. The Bloody or Two Mile Run and its Relation to Local History," *The Town of Porter 1776 – 1976*, esp. 49. The above description follows recent historical analyses by Brian Dunnigan. It is summarized in the historical marker in Constitution Park and by the new historic marker at 347 Main Street, namely, that the main battle was actually in the village center itself. There was, however, much blood spilled at Bloody Run: a small British party seeking a canon for defense before the battle was killed by the advancing French army and fleeing French troops after their defeat were killed by Native American allied with the British.

[43] Ibid., 54, 49.

[44] Ibid.

and became a part of the road bed of the railroad. . . .The turn table of the Canandaigua Railroad stood near the Letchworth barns."[45] Edwin Howard added a comment about the surviving stone bridge at Bloody Run:

> The right of way [of the railroad] is still visible in places: for years there was an open pit on the Letchworth property [a large tract across from the Swains and Roots, west of the current River Road and on the river] where a turntable for the engines was built. The only structure left is a beautiful stone bridge on the property of Theodore Booth, visible from River Road.[46]

Sara Swain also wrote of the Canandaigua line: "It ran just one train and was then sold to the New York Central."[47] On railroad maps of 1861, the track was still represented.

We may add a final point: The New York Central Railroad, which controlled the line from Niagara Falls to Lewiston and then to Youngstown, had completed its train route to the Suspension Bridge at Niagara City/Bellevue/Suspension Bridge Village and the first train, as previously stated, crossed in March of 1855. There it met the Canadian line, the Great Western Railway to Detroit, which proceeded on to Chicago and in 1856 it was extended to Toronto. The irony of the Youngstown stories is that just as the steamers were reaching the apex of their business in their important connecting links with the railroads, the railroads marked the beginning of the decline of the steamer business on the Great Lakes.[48]

We observed that the proposed railroad lines from Lewiston to Youngstown in the 1850s generated anticipation and expectation of a boom in commercial and tourist business for the village. As a result, there was a flurry of ferry applications to operate the Youngstown Ferry between 1854 and 1858, as we shall see in Chapter 6. However, the experiments with railroads to Youngstown, despite their promise, proved disappointing. The variant accounts converge on the central point: The rail lines were immediately discontinued. One can only speculate whether the railway lines north to Youngstown provided some direction for fugitive slaves who

---

[45] Ibid., 54. This was about the area of Campbell Street, Image 5.11a.
[46] Howard, "Transportation," 16. Again, at Campbell Street.
[47] Swain, 49. The one-run train stories about the Niagara and Lake Ontario Railroad and the Canandaigua Line sound suspiciously similar.
[48] Cumberland, *Maritime History*, Ch. 4.

for some unknown reason preferred, or were directed or led to cross the river at Lewiston or Suspension Bridge further south. Heading south from Youngstown, however, seems an unlikely option given the possibility of crossing by private boat or ferry at Youngstown and the greater number of slave catchers at Lewiston, Suspension Bridge, and Niagara Falls. This will be important in the instructions to Daniel and James to escape not at Suspension Bridge, but at Youngstown, in Chapter 10.

Curiously—or perhaps just what might be expected—these mid-1850s dreams and disappointments occurred precisely during the time when Harriet Tubman was active in taking fugitive slaves across the Niagara River, particularly via the new 1855 Roebling Suspension Bridge at Bellevue/Niagara City/Suspension Bridge Village. This was also the period when some of our best sources record that fugitive slaves crossed the Niagara River from Youngstown to Niagara, Canada. We are certain that some of them went by way of the Youngstown Ferry and were helped by sympathetic, anti-slavery Youngstown ferrymen, and that others were helped by individual boaters.

Ferries and ferrymen will be the main subject of the next chapter.

CHAPTER 6

Youngstown: Ferries and Ferrymen—and a Ferrywoman

Image 6.1

Ferries were an important means for freedom seekers headed north to cross rivers, and some ferrymen were active agents in helping them cross.[1] As we shall show in following chapters, it is certain from primary sources that fugitive slaves took the Youngstown Ferry across the Niagara River from Youngstown to Niagara and that some Youngstown ferry keepers were helpful.[2] That has prompted our examination of the Youngstown ferry keepers in the era of the Underground Railroad.

In pausing to think about the Youngstown Ferry, consider the insightful comment about the risks and rewards of ferry concessions in Kevin Krisman and Arthur Cohn's *When Horses Walked on Water*:

---

[1] See the ferrymen of the Nishnabotna Ferry House, Lewis, Iowa, http://www.cityoflewis.com/index.php/our-town/ferry-house.
[2] Ch. 7-13.

Ownership of a ferry concession could be a liability or an asset, depending upon the nature of the waterway, the amount of traffic, and, of course, the business acumen of the owner. Possession of rights to a heavily trafficked crossing meant full-time and highly lucrative employment for a family or a company, and these rights were jealously guarded and passed down from generation to generation. Busy ferries like these were often attended by their crews all day, and some ran on a regular, predetermined schedule.

Conversely, and more commonly, ownership of a ferry on a lightly traveled route provided only part-time employment that had to be supplemented with farming or a trade. Ferries in this category generally ran only when they were needed, which meant that travelers had to blow a horn, raise a flag, ring a bell, shout, or just patiently sit and wait until the ferry owner showed up. Indeed, some of the more marginal ferry concessions seem to have been a millstone around the neck of the proprietor, with receipts from the business barely covering the costs of building and maintenance, as well as the inconvenience of constantly being on call during daylight hours. It is hardly surprising that ferries such as these should be poorly attended and repaired.[3]

This chapter concentrates on the New York State ferrying laws and the ferrymen (one ferrywoman!) who applied for them, some of whom operated the Youngstown Ferry. The main sources are a hardly investigated treasure of applications and support/non-support petitions to "keep the ferry," that is, operate the ferry, that are tucked away in box at the Niagara Historian's Office in Lockport, New York. A discussion of the physical site of the Youngstown Ferry House is reserved for a chapter speculating about UGRR sites in Youngstown.[4]

---

[3] Kevin James Crisman and Arthur B. Cohn, *When Horses Walked on Water: Horse-Powered Ferries in Nineteenth-Century America* (Washington, D.C.; London, UK: Smithsonian Institution Press, 1998), 16.
[4] Ch.16.

Early Youngstown Ferry Licensing Laws: 1811, 1813, 1826, and 1836[5]

Early New York State ferry laws stipulated the amount of annual license fees, tolls, and length of terms for ferry operations; safety rules; maintenance regulations; and the necessity of serving the public safely and punctually.[6] New York State licensing laws for ferries in 1811, 1813, 1826, and 1836 specifically refer to Youngstown and in 1826 to Youngstown's own ferryman, John Phillips, and his heirs.

Chap. LXIV Legislative Document No. 127, 1811[7]

Ferries Across the Niagara River . . . By the 37th section of an act passed in the year 1811 (6 Web. 333) the court of common pleas of the county of Niagara was authorized "to established and regulate a ferry at ***Youngstown,*** on Niagara river, in the same manner as the courts of common pleas are authorized to establish and regulate ferries within this State by the act" of 1797."[8]

---

[5] *Index to the Session Laws of the State of New York With All Changes and Modifications Noted Under a Single Alphabet from Session of 1775 down to Session of 189* (New York and Albany, NY: Banks and Brothers, 1897) 309, 381, 379, 593; also Archie E. Baxter, *General Index of the Laws of the State of New York, 1777—1901* (Albany, NY: J. B. Lyon Company, 1902), 286.

[6] The main sources we have consulted for the Youngstown Ferry, 1810-1870, are these: The State of New York ferry and licensing laws for ferries in 1811, 1813, 1826, 1836; documents summarizing Assembly and Senate actions of the State of New York; an 1804 painting of the Canadian Ferry by Edward Walsh; Canadian maps from 1810 and 1819; Youngstown maps from 1841, 1848, 1856, 1860, and 1870; Donald B. Ames' research on deed records of property ownership in Youngstown; information about Youngstown Ferrymen's/Ferrywoman's applications, recognizances, and petitions at the Niagara County Historian's Office at Lockport, New York, and the records of the New York State Senate.

[7] *Official Index to the Unconsolidated Laws, Being the Special, Private and Local Statutes of the State of New York from February 1, 1778 to December 31, 1919* (Albany, NY: J. B. Lyon company, 1920), 494, State of New York, Ferries Authorized, Year 1811, Chapter 246, page 460; 1033.

[8] Courts of Common Pleas dealt with cases relating to unsettled debts and property matters. See more in Chs. 7 and 14; art: https://www.bl.uk/collection-items/illustration-of-the-court-of-common-pleas-westminster-hall#sthash.g1Pq80Lm.dpuf. Responding to a petition of Peter B. Porter and Augustus Porter, see Greene C. Bronson, "Report of the Attorney General, concerning the Power of the Legislature to authorize and regulate ferries." *Assembly No. 61* (January 25, 1834). Boldface ours.
https://books.google.com/books?id=bEcbAQAAIAAJ&pg=PA179&lpg=PA179&dq=1811+New+York+State+laws,+ferries,+Youngstown&source=bl&ots=J7yywBRdMn&sig=AMURyyQUNbo8a9oVlrW9mG1uG7c&hl=en&sa=X&ved=0CC8Q6AEwA2oVChMIuba6mN7FyAIVAupjCh2gHQ8e#v=onepage&q=1811%20New%20York%20State%20laws%2C%20ferries%2C%20Youngstown&f=false. The law is also listed in the *Official Index to the Unconsolidated Laws* as Legislative, Document No. 127, pages 493-94, 1033.

Chap. LXIV [1813]

An ACT Concerning Ferries (Summary_

Passed April 5, 1813.[9]

[Paraphrased, Shortened, except for No. IV]

I. Those who use ferries across bodies of water to transport "any person, or any goods, chattels or effects, for profit or hire, unless in the manner directed by this act," shall be subject to a penalty of five dollars for each offense. Fines shall be distributed, one-half to local overseers of the poor and one-half to plaintiffs.

II. The court of common pleas in each county shall grant ferry licenses to suitable persons for one year in the sum of one hundred dollars. Such persons shall keep and attend a ferry that is safe, with sufficient implements. The ferry shall run for several hours each day. The court shall set rates to be logged on file with the clerk of the county. Offences will be subject to a fine or penalty of the court not to exceed twenty-five dollars per offence, to be distributed equitably among the counties affected; the license shall cover transport of persons, goods, wares, and merchandise; it shall not affect or alter the ferry operations already granted by charter to the corporations of Albany and Hudson, or other such grants of the state, or the legal rights and privileges of other corporations; no such license shall be granted to any person who does not own or occupy the land through which the highway adjacent to the ferry shall run unless such property owners neglect to apply for a ferry license.

III. County clerks shall record every license for a charge of not more than one dollar.

---

[9] Our summary of this law is abstracted from *Laws of the State of New-York, Revised and Passed at the Thirty-Sixth Session, of the Legislature, with Marginal Notes and References* (2 vols.; Revisers William P. Van Ness and John Woodworth; Albany: C. H. Southwick & Co., 1813), Vol. II, 210-11. The law was mentioned also by Suzanne Simon Dietz, "Early New York State Legislative Session Laws Concerning the Town of Porter," *Porter's Past* 36/2 (February/March 2012): 5; *From Flames and Four Flags. The Town of Porter Yesterday and Today* (Youngstown, Suzanne Simon Dietz (BouDesigns), 2012), 33.

IV. *"And be it further enacted,* That it shall and may be lawful for the court of common pleas of Niagara county, in their sessions, to establish and regulate a ferry at **Youngstown, on [the] Niagara river.** In the same manner as the course of common pleas are authorised by this act to establish and regulate ferries within this state."[10]

Chap. 45. [1826]

AN ACT *relative to the Ferry, at Youngstown, in the County of Niagara.*

Passed February 14, 1826.

1. *BE it enacted by the People of the State of New-York, represented in Senate and Assembly,* That from and after the first day of **January next**, **John Phillips, his heirs or assigns shall be**, and thereby are hereby **authorized to keep the ferry at Youngstown** in the county of Niagara, for and during the **term of ten years**, which term will expire on the first day of January, one thousand eight hundred and thirty-seven.

2. *And be it further enacted,* That the court of common pleas, of the county of Niagara, shall . . . as they deem equitable, regulate the rates of ferriage. . . [11]

3. *And be it furter [sic] enacted*, That the said **John Phillips** . . . will at all times keep at least **two good and sufficient safe ferry boats**, for the transportation of such passengers, carriages, animals, produce, and other articles, as may be offered to be ferried across the **Niagara river, at Youngstown**, and shall at all reasonable hours, keep a sufficient number of careful and experienced men, to take charge of, and manage the said boats.

4. *And be it further enacted*, That the said **John Phillips** shall build, or cause to be built, **on or before the first day of January, one thousand eight hundred and twenty-eight, a good and sufficient boat,** so made and constructed as to be propelled either by **steam or horse power,** and of sufficient burthen and capacity to do and perform all the business of ferrying at **Youngstown** aforesaid; . . . ; and if the said

---

[10] *Laws of the State of New-York,* ibid., 11 (boldface ours).

[11] The law and the ferriage rates are recorded in *Court Minutes, Common Pleas (May 1821-Sept. 19, 1831)*, January Term 1821 (on January 2, 1827).

John Phillips shall fail faithfully and property to comply the terms and requisitions of this section, within the time therein limited, this act shall cease and be of no avail, and the said **John Phillips, his heirs and assigns**, shall forfeit all rights, privileges and immunities given, granted, or by him or them derived under and by virtue of this act. . . .[12]

Chap. 309. [1836]

AN ACT *relative to the Ferry across the Niagara river at Youngstown, in the County of Niagara.*

Passed May 12, **1836**.

The People of the State of New-York represented in Senate and Assembly, do enact as follows:

§ 1. . . a **ferry or ferries** across the **Niagara river** [*sic*] at the **village of Youngstown**, in the county of Niagara, which license or licenses shall continue in force for a term to be fixed by said court, **not exceeding ten years** for any one license. . .

§ 2. . . to transport and carry across said [Niagara] river, all such persons, cattle, horses, hogs, sheep, goods, chattels and effects, . . . for the prices, and at such several rates, as said court of common pleas shall, from time to time, prescribe and direct. . .

§ 4. The said court of common pleas shall . . . order, direct and regulate the rates of ferriage. . .

§ 5. Every such license and said rates of ferriage shall be entered in the book of minutes of said court, by the clerk thereof. . .

---

[12] *Laws of the State of New-York, Passed at the Forty-ninth Session of the Legislature, Begun and Held at the City of Albany, The Third day of January, 1826* (Albany, NY: William Gould & Co.; New-York, NY: Gould & Banks; E. Croswell, Printer, 1826), 32-33 (boldface ours). See on the Timeline 1828, John Phillips, who forfeited his license, replaced by Samuel Chubbuck.

§ 6. Any person who shall use said ferry . . . without such license, shall be deemed guilty of a misdemeanor, and on conviction thereof, shall be subject to such fine, for the use of the county of Niagara . . . not exceeding twenty-five dollars for each offence.

§ 7. The said court may examine, on oath, the applicant for such license . . . for the purpose of determining the rates of ferriage to be established.[13]

Another such law was passed in 1886.[14]

---

[13] *Laws of the State of New-York, passed at the Fifty-Ninth Session, of the Legislature, Begun and Held at the City of Albany, the Fifth Day of January, 1836* (Albany: E. Croswell, 1836), 456-57. For a reference that a report about this bill was sent to committee, see *Journal of the Assembly of the State of New York at the Fifty-Ninth Session* (Albany, New York, 1836), 152.

[14] William H. Silvernail, *Index to the Session Laws of the State of New York: With All Changes* (Albany, NY: Banks & Brothers, 1897), 593. Perhaps other laws were passed in the intervening years.

Timeline of Mainly Early Youngstown Ferries and Ferrymen

The following one-page chronological summary and the expanded outline form that follows it highlight information about Youngstown ferries and ferrymen (one ferrywoman) from 1788 to 1870. The data are primarily from handwritten applications of some fifteen ferrymen and petitions of support or opposition with citizen signatures. The documents, archived in the Niagara Country Historian's Office in Lockport, New York, are indicated by an asterisk beside the date (*). The earliest applications were called *Recognizances* and were identified by the ferryman's name and a date on the outside.[15] Who actually received the ferry license from the Niagara County Court of Pleas, how long a recipient ran the ferry, and the kind of ferries is not always clear. In 1813, New York State law ferry licenses were granted for one year, but in 1826 and 1836 for ten years. When stiff competition arose in the 1850s, petitioners wanted the term reduced to only one year. "Boats and scows" ran in 1822. In 1826, John Phillips had to promise to run a ferry propelled by either steam or horse power by January 1, 1828. Tour guidebooks show that a horse ferry was running in 1828 and 1830 and applications indicate that a horse ferry builder and his partner had a ferry license in 1829. Steam ferries were operating by 1834.

---

[15] In the early hand-written applications, the applicant promised to carry out the legal obligations of operating the ferry, which included promissory notes written to a County Judge and witnessed in the County Court of Common Pleas that the ferryman (sometimes co-signed) would pay to the State a stipulated sum if the contract was not fulfilled. The contracts were recorded by the Clerk of Court. Such documents were entered into the record of the Court of Common Pleas of Niagara County. A petitioner sometimes promised to forfeit a sum of money as a penalty for failure to meet an obligation.

Summary Timeline of Early Youngstown Ferries, Ferrymen (and a Ferrywoman)

1788   Colonel Hunter had cattle and pack horses ferried from Fort Niagara to Niagara.

1796   Captain Lemuel Cooke (1762—1839), a sergeant, operates a ferry for the Army (Fort Niagara) up to 1799.

1811   The Youngstown Ferry is authorized by the State of New York.

1813   Permission for the Court of Pleas to establish and regulate a ferry at Youngstown.

?-1814?   Robert Greensett had a license for the ferry at Youngstown.

1816   Widow Agnes Greensett petitioned to renew her one-year license for the Ferry at Youngstown.

1821   Elijah Hathaway operates the ferry (based on his 1822 recognizance/application as a renewal).

1822*   Elijah Hathaway application. Jan 2nd. *Recognizance filed Jan. 2, 1822; *Recognizance accepted.

1823*   Elijah Hathaway recognizance. Jan. 7th . *Application/recognizance, Jan. 10th. *Signed by court clerk, 11th.

1824*   John Phillips application. Recorded as granted in the Court of Common Pleas Minutes, 1821-1831.

1825*   John Phillips application on Jan. 6th for a license to "keep a ferry" **one year**. Granted by the Court.

1826   Phillips designated ferryman for **ten years, 1827-1837, if he builds a horse or steam ferry by Jan. 1, 1828.**

1826   Edward Giddins, keeper of the Fort Niagara Lighthouse, "kept the ferry." (Presumably a Fort ferry.)

1826   Free ferry passage from Youngstown to Niagara and back for passengers of the steamer *Martha Ogden*.

1827*   John Phillips' term for **ten years** begins, promising $500. However, see Phillips 1826 and Chubbuck 1829.

1828   A **"horse boat"** is operating between Youngstown and Niagara (probably Chubbuck and Balmer, 1829).

1829   Samuel L. Chubbuck, **horse ferry** builder, operates the ferry with Thomas Balmer.

1830   Davison's 1830 *Tour* Guide notes a **"horse boat"** runs between Niagara and Youngstown.

1832   Steamer *Martha Ogden* between Youngstown and Toronto with ferry connections to Niagara.

1834*   Alexander Lane operates the **first steam ferry** at Youngstown, "The Cigar."

1836   New York State Legislative Session Laws for ferry service in New York lists Youngstown.

1836*   John Beach, Sept. 13. Olaf Hathaway co-signed for $500.

1836*   Ira Race petition (see 1854*).

1838   Calvin Wilson keeps the ferry at Youngstown.

1840*   Harry W. Phillips application (co-signed by John G. Phillips [Jr.?]) for **seven years**.

1840*   Luther Wilson and Alfred P. Judd application.

1844   Between Youngstown and Niagara "a **steam ferry boat plies daily.**"

1845   **Stone Ferry House?** Remains may still exist in Constitution Park on the Niagara Gorge hillside.

1854*   John Hitchcock. Apr. 19. A petition to operate the ferry for **three years or more**. Apr. 25, 1854 filed.

1854*   John Hitchcock. A petition of support for him to be the ferryman for three years or more.

1854*   John Hitchcock. A petition of support for him to be ferrymen for three or four years or more.

1854*   John Hitchcock. A petition of support by those who have known him for three years or more.

1854*   Alexander Lane. Application submitted (see 1834). Petitioned for a license of **four years**.

1854*   Luke P. Babcock Apr. 18. Application submitted.

1854*   Apr. 11. A petition supporting Babcock; 30 signatures.

1854*   An undated petition supporting Babcock; 24 signatures.

1854*   Petition: License should be granted **only to the highest responsible bidder for one year**. 47 signatures.

1854*   Second petition: To be given to **the highest bidder for one year**; 43 signatures.

1854*   Ira Race. Application submitted. Apr. 17th. **7 years or term as the county sees fit**.

1854*   Apr. 12. Petition of support for Ira Race/**one-year** license term, 25 signatures.

1854*   Apr. 12. Petition of support for Ira Race/one-year license term, 65 signatures.

1854*   Apr. 17. Petition of support for Ira Race and one-year license term, 26 signatures.

1854*   Apr. 17. Petition of support for Ira Race and one-year license term, 54 signatures.

1855*   Dec. 15. **Transnational Petition to remove Luke P. Babcock**.

1856*   Jan. 10. **Transnational Petition to remove Luke P. Babcock**, 56 American and 8 Canadian signatures.

1858*   **Third petition to remove Luke P. Babcock** and to replace him with Ira Race "and Peter Tower."

1858*   Joel (George?) Tryon Application. March and April Applications with many signatures.

1858*   Ira Race Application for **ten years**. Apparently approved.

1860   Map. Building marked (small block) where Ferry Office would be on 1870 Map (Ferry Street).

1870   Map. "Ferry" clearly marked on Ferry Street (below houses of James P. Marshall and Mrs. Cook).

This timeline outline will now be developed in more detail.[16]

1788 **John Gould, a drover,** gave an interview stating that Colonel Hunter in command of Fort Niagara, had **cattle and pack horses ferried** across to Newark [Niagara-on-the-Lake] in *bateaux* (shallow-draft, flat-bottom boats) and Schenectady boats.[17]

1796 – 1799 Captain Lemuel Cooke (1762—1839), a sergeant in the army, operated a ferry between Youngstown and Newark (Niagara/Niagara-on-the-Lake) for the Army at Fort Niagara. He was the son of Colonel Isaac and Martha Cooke and married to Elizabeth "Betsy" (Bates); he is buried in Lewiston Cemetery beside the First Presbyterian Church of Lewiston, New York.[18] After Cooke was discharged from the army in 1799, he operated a ferry (row boats) between Lewiston and Queenston. In 1812, Cooke and his sons, Bates and Lathrop, were river guides for the Battle of Queenston Heights.[19] According to the 1820 census, Captain Cooke was living in Lewiston, New York (white, married; two sons, one 16-18, another 16-25; two daughters, one 16-25).

1799 – 1811 Fort Niagara near Youngstown is the Port of Entry and Customs House.

1811 **A ferry at Youngstown is authorized by the State of New York.**[20] In the same year, the Customs House was moved from Fort Niagara to Lewiston, New York.

1813 **Permission for the Court of Pleas to establish and regulate a ferry at Youngstown** was enacted in Chapter LXIV Laws of New York, 36th Session.[21]

---

[16] These data are not complete; hopefully, they can be supplemented in the future.

[17] O. Turner, *Pioneer History of the Holland Purchase of Western New York* (Buffalo, NY: Jewett Thomas & Co., 1849), 313; Pool, *Landmarks of Niagara County*, 256-57. For such boats, see Ch. 4. The Village of Youngstown Local Waterfront Revitalization document prepared by Thomas J. Dearing, Planning Consultant (financial assistance from the Office of Ocean and Coastal Resource Management, National Oceanic and Atmospheric Administration, provided under the coastal Zone Management Acts of 1972, U. S. Department of Commerce [1990]) II-47 states that a ferry ran in 1790. We have not confirmed this statement.

[18] This cemetery is variously called the Municipal Cemetery, the Village Cemetery, the Presbyterian Cemetery, and the Oakwood Cemetery. For Lemuel Cooke's obituary, see http://www.findagrave.com/cgi-bin/fg.cgi?page=gr&GRid=145020859.

[19] *The Lewiston Sesquicentennial, 1822—1972* says that Cooke had a third son, Isaac, and that Bates and Lathrop, along with Dr. Willard Smith, were faced with the problem of not having built a dwelling on their lands, which was alleviated by a special act in 1820 stating that the property was wetlands and therefore not suitable for dwellings. *The Lewiston Sesquicentennial, 1822—1972*, 23, 83.

[20] See above for the *Official Index to the Unconsolidated Laws* from 1778 to 1919 and the Youngstown Ferry laws at the beginning of this chapter.

?-1813 **Robert Greensitt (Greensett; Grensit)** operated an inn and tavern and had a license to operate the Youngstown Ferry; it is uncertain how far back the license went or how many times it might have been renewed. Presumably the Greensitts lost their holdings when the British burned Youngstown on December 19, 1813.[22]

1813 **December 19.** Retaliating for the American burning of Newark/Niagara in Upper Canada (Ontario) on December 10, 1813, the British re-took Fort Niagara, which they had previously occupied from 1759 to 1796, and then **burned the Youngstown settlement.**[23]

1816 **Agnes Greensitt** petitioned the New York State Senate to **renew** her (their?) ferry license. She also ran the Greensitt Inn/Tavern in 1816, 1817 and 1818, perhaps earlier.[24]

1821 **Elijah Hathaway** was the "keeper of the ferry" for at least three years (1821-1823); 1821 is implied by his application for renewal after one year in **1822** (see also **1823**). We have information about Elijah Hathaway from several sources.[25]

Elijah was the son of Alfred Hathaway of Connecticut and then Vermont (1755-1829), who was a veteran of the revolutionary War (only six months, therefore not pensioned).[26] In 1783, he married Rebecca Alford (or Alvord), whose father's first name was Olaf. They had five sons and three daughters. The second, fourth, and seventh sons were Elijah, Olaf (presumably named for his maternal grandfather; sometimes Olaff, Olif, or Oliff), and Alfred (presumably named for his paternal grandfather).

---

[21] Also in Suzanne Simon Dietz, *From Flames and Four Flags. The Town of Porter Yesterday and Today* (Youngstown, Suzanne Simon Dietz [BeauDesigns], 2012), 33.

[22] See comments on Elijah Hathaway below and more on the Greensitts in Ch. 16.

[23] See Ch. 1.

[24] See end of this chapter and Ch. 16.

[25] Thanks to Karen Noonan, who has a special interest in the Hathaways. She relies heavily on Elizabeth Starr Versailles, *Hathaway's of America* (Northampton, MA: Gazette Print. Co. 1970; Supplement, Hathaway Family Association, 1980), 185 (ref. 139) and Karen Foley, *Early Settlers of New York State: Their Ancestors* (1934—1942; reprint 2006). In addition, see the *History of Niagara County*, 335a; Pool, *Landmarks*, 260-61; *A Bicentennial History, 1776 – 1976 of the Town of Porter* (Historical Society of the Town of Porter, 1976), 9; Suzanne Simon Dietz, *From Flames & Four Flags: The Town of Porter Yesterday and Today* (Youngstown, NY: BeauDesigns, 2012); Dietz and Karen Noonan, *Early Town of Porter Residents 1800 – 1829* (Suzanne Simon Dietz, 2013); and records and notes in the Town of Porter Historical Society Museum. We have also checked the 1821-1823 hand-written applications of Elijah Hathaway for the Youngstown Ferry license and the *Court Minutes, Common Pleas (May 1821-September 19, 1831)* in the Niagara County Historian's office, 139 Niagara Street, Lockport, New York 14094. Thanks again for assistance from Catherine Emerson, Niagara County Historian; Craig E. Bacon, Deputy Historian; and Ronald F. Cary, Deputy Historian.

[26] Youngstown's Universal Cemetery has Alfred's dates as 1752-1828.

Elijah is relatively well documented in Youngstown sources. According to Holland Land Company Records in 1815, Elijah (1786—???? [probably before 1850]), locally known as "Col. Elijah Hathaway," operated the "Hathaway Tavern" in Youngstown, which was located approximately where the current Ontario House (now affectionately called "the Stone Jug"), stands, built in 1842 by Alexander Lane on the corner of Main and Lockport Streets.[27] The tavern was also an inn; a grocery store and a stable were connected to it.[28] The Hathaway Tavern and Inn were destroyed when the British army burned Youngstown on December 19, 1813.[29] After the war, Elijah Hathaway was an officially recognized "Sufferer" who made a personal property claim (loss) of $3,535.09, as well as $560.00 for four buildings destroyed (a house, the tavern/inn, store, and stable?); yet, he was "presumed not in want."[30] Elijah was listed as the Town Clerk on April 11, 1815, and April 2, 1816; recorded as an innkeeper on May 22, 1816 (had the Hathaway Inn been rebuilt?); an Inspector of Elections on May 2, 1816; and an owner of lots 28 and 31 in 1817 and 1819.[31] He was also a road "Path Master" and inspector. In the 1820 census, Elijah was still a Youngstown householder in whose household were nine other "free white" persons: one other white male 45 and over (one of his brothers, Olaf or Alfred?); one female 45 and over (Rebecca McCollum, his second wife?); one female 26 to 45 (Betsy Doran, Olaf's first wife [d. 1826]? Alfred's wife?); four males 16 to 26 (one 16-18); and two females 10 to 16. By 1830, Elijah and his family were living in Lockport.[32] He became a commissioner for the proposed Lockport and Youngstown

---

[27] See Ch. 16.

[28] See the legal requirements about inns and taverns and the discussion of "The Youngstown Ferrywoman" below.

[29] See Ch. 1.

[30] Dietz, *From Flames and Four Flags,* 7, 8; Dietz and Noonan, *Early Town of Porter Residents,* 14. Contrast the status of being "in want" on the part of Agnes Greensitt. Was Elijah Hathaway Agnes' competitor?

[31] *Book of Records of the Town of Porter*; see also Dietz, ibid., 34; Dietz and Noonan, ibid, 8.

[32] There were Quaker abolitionists in Lockport—see the comments about Lyman Spalding in Chs. 2 and 11—and Pool, *Landmarks,* mentions early settler and mill owner Otis Hathaway (76, 105, 106) and William G. Hathaway (245). Quaker Joseph C. Hathaway of Farmington, New York, near Rochester, was an UGRR agent and President of the Western New York Anti-Slavery. It is uncertain whether any of the Youngstown Hathaways were Quakers, but that seems unlikely. Pool, *Landmarks,* 265, states that Mrs. Rebecca Hathaway, Alfred Hathaway's wife and the mother of Olaf and Elijah, and their daughter, Pauline Hathaway, were active in forming the Youngstown (Porter) Society in 1823 and a burial marker in the Universal Cemetery behind the Youngstown Presbyterian Church has members of Alfred's family; see Ch. 7 for the names on the Hathaway burial marker.

Railroad Company in 1836,[33] and in that year, he and Rebecca sold their Youngstown holdings. According to the 1850 census, Elijah's wife Rebecca was a head of household with five children living in Lockport, but there is no mention of Elijah. Since we have no direct information about Elijah's death, final residence, or resting place, it is likely that he died in Lockport between 1836 and 1850.[34] Clearly, Elijah Hathaway was a man of some substance and influence.

Most important for this book, the Reverend Thomas James in his autobiography of 1886 recalled that as a fugitive slave, "I crossed the Niagara [River] at Youngstown on the ferry boat."[35] The year was probably 1821 (he claims to have been nineteen and born in 1804). The Reverend James did not identify the ferryman. However, in 1883, when he returned to Youngstown to speak at the Town of Porter (First) Presbyterian Church, the *Niagara County News*, Friday, September 21, claimed that Elijah's brother, Olaf, whose name is on a Hathaway marker in the Universal Cemetery behind the Presbyterian Church, "ferried" him across the river. However, Elijah, not Olaf, was the ferryman from 1821-1823. Perhaps Olaf made contact with his brother Elijah, or Olaf (with or without his brother's knowledge) ferried James on his own, or—this cannot be ruled out—the newspaper or its source was inaccurate, that is, perhaps it was actually Elijah, not Olaf, who ferried Thomas James across.

1822* Elijah Hathaway application. Jan 2nd. Elijah stated that he had operated the ferry for a year, that his 1821 license had nearly expired, and that he was applying for another year's license.

---

[33] Chapter 407, Laws of 1836 in the *Annual Report of the State Engineer and Surveyor of the State of New York and of the Tabulations and Deductions from the Reports of the Railroad Corporations for the Year Ending September 30, 1858* (Albany, NY: Weed, Parsons and Company, 1859), 426; see also Dietz, *ibid.*, 33.

[34] There were Quaker abolitionists in Lockport and Quaker J. C. Hathaway of Farmington is one of the prominent figures in the Daguerreotype group photo of the 1850 Fugitive Slave Law Convention at Cazenovia, New York. See Ch. 2.

[35] For details, see Ch. 7.

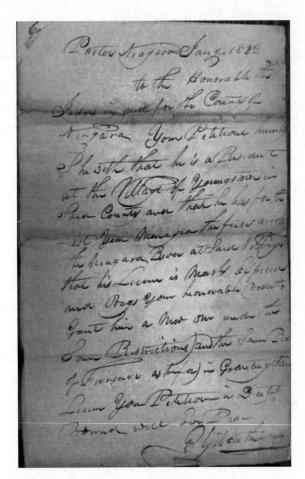

Porter Niagara Jan 2nd 1822

To the Honorable the Judge in and for the Court of Niagara. Your Petitioner humbly showeth that he is a Resident at the Village of Youngstown in said County and that **he has for the last year managed the ferry across the Niagara River** at Said Village[,] that **his term is nearly expired**[,] and begs your honorable Body to grant him a new one under the same restrictions and the same rate of tonnage as before in granting said licence (*sic*). Your Petitioner in Duty Bound will Ever Pray.

Elijah Hathaway

Elijah Hathaway Petition to Continue Operating the Youngstown Ferry, January 2, 1822
Image 6.2

1822* Elijah Hathaway Recognizance of January 2nd. Accepted by the Court of Common Pleas. Elijah promises to pay the State of New York $250 from the profits of the ferry operation and to operate it with the appropriate **boats, scows, and crews for *another* full year** (after 1821). It is accepted by the Niagara County Court of Pleas.[36]

---

[36] Elijah's license was granted in the *Court Minutes, Common Pleas (May 1821-Sept 19, 1831)*, Niagara County Historian's Office. It was recorded during the January Term, 1822. The winter rates of ferriage are given (horses, "horse creatures," man and horse, oxen, carriages, sleighs, passengers, sheep, hogs, extra property by hundred weight), with the note that ". . . they shall be reduced one half in all respects between the last day of May and the first day of October." For an example, see the rates for 1840 below.

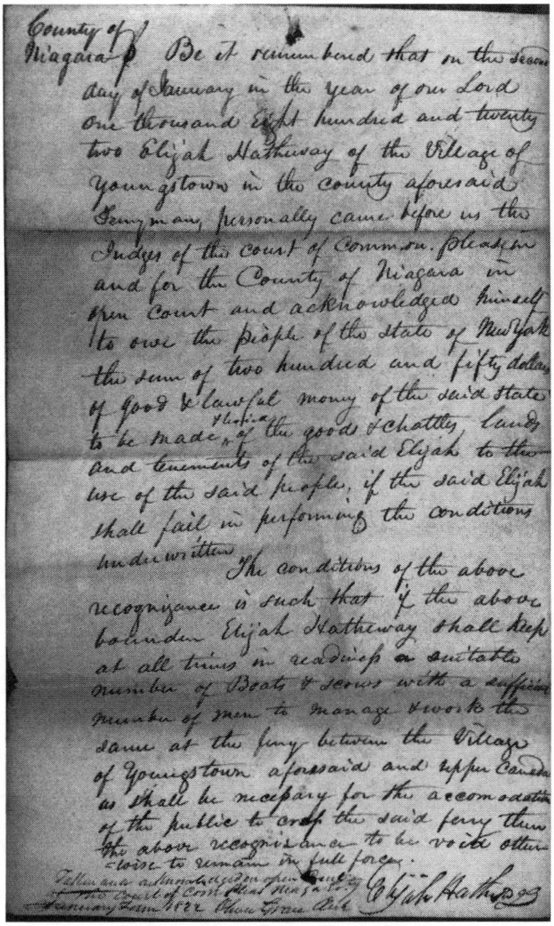

County of
Niagara   Be it remembered that on the second
day of January in the year of our Lord
one thousand eight hundred and twenty two
Elijah Hathaway of the Village of
Youngstown in the county aforesaid
Ferryman, personally came before us the
Judges of Court of Common Pleas in
and for the County of Niagara in
open court and acknowledged himself
to owe the people of the State of New York
the sum of two hundred and fifty dollars of
good & lawful money of the said state
to be made[& levied] of the goods & chattels,
lands and tenements of the said Elijah to the
use of the said people if the said Elijah
shall fail in performing the conditions
underwritten.
    The conditions of the above
recognizance is such that if the above
bounden **Elijah Hathaway** shall keep
at all times in readiness a suitable
number of **boats and scows** with a sufficient
number of **men** to manage & work the
same at the ferry between the Village of
Youngstown aforesaid and Upper Canada so
shall be necessary for the accomodation [*sic*]
of the public to cross the said ferry then the
above recognizance to be void other   -
wise to remain in full force.

Taken and acknowledged in open court
of the Court of Com Pleas Niaga' Co'ty
January Term 1822. Oliver Grace Clerk   **Elijah Hathaway**

Elijah Hathaway Recognizance to Keep the Ferry, Filed January 2, 1822
Image 6.3

1823* Elijah Hathaway Recognizance. Jan. 7th. Promises to make the ferry comfortable in the
roughest weather![37]

1823* Elijah Hathaway Application/Recognizance. Jan. 10th; signed by county court clerk 11th.

1824* John Phillips Application.[38]

1825* John Phillips Application, January 6th, license to "keep a ferry" *one year* across the
Niagara River. Recognizance promises to "keep and attend such ferry with such as so

---

[37] Elijah's license was granted in the *Court Minutes, Common Plea (May 1821-Sept 19, 1831)*, January Term 1823,
with ferriage rates.
[38] John Phillips was granted the ferry license in ibid., January Term, 1824, with ferriage rates.

many sufficient and safe boats and so many men to work the same. . ." also promising to pay $100 if in default. Gilbert W. Curtiss and Oliff Hathaway were impaneled as jurors for this term.[39] Elijah Hathaway and John Phillips were jurors in the September Term.

1825   **The steamboat *Martha Ogden*, built at Sackets Harbor in 1824, launches.** Daniel Reed, Master, leaves Lewiston for Sackets Harbor and Ogdensburg. "The MARTHA OGDEN is a new boat, well found; her accommodations good; her Captain well qualified for the command."[40] She put in at **Youngstown** (summers).

1826   **The steamboat *Martha Ogden* runs between York [Toronto] and Youngstown and back to York**, weather permitting, six days a week; Saturdays only one run, alternating hours of departure at each end. **Free ferry boat passage from Youngstown to Niagara[-on-the-Lake] and back for Passengers of the *Martha Ogden* is advertised.**[41] John Phillips must have been the ferryman. The *Martha Ogden* docked at Youngstown at the time of the Morgan Affair of 1826,[42] which was mentioned in the Morgan Trial court transcripts of 1831 (Birdseye in the following record was New York's third special counsel of 1831; the witness was Edwin Scranton).[43]

---

[39] *Court Minutes, Common Pleas*, January 5, 1825.

[40] http://www.MaritimeHistoryOfTheGreatLakes,ca/.

[41] Rochester *Album* Ad on Tuesdays, Aug 1 Aug 15, Aug 22, Aug 29, Sep 5, Sep 12, Sep 15, Sep 19, Oct 3, 1826; *Loyalist* of June 17, 1826, as recorded in Henry Scadding, *Toronto of Old; Collections and recollections Illustrative of the Early Settlement and Social Life of the Capital of Ontario,* Toronto, Adam, Stevenson & Co. Henry Scadding → Toronto of old; collections and recollections illustrative of the early settlement and social life of the capital of Ontario → online text (page 53 of 59). For the advertisement, see Ch. 4.

[42] For the Morgan Affair, see Appendix 7.

[43] Albany New York *Argus* (Sat. Mar 5, 1831); see also Clarence O. Lewis, "Early Lewiston Resident had Colorful Lake Career," *Union Sun and Journal* (October 26, 1953); cp. Clarence O. Lewis, "Capt. Van Cleve, Pioneer, of Lewiston, Started Sailing Great Lakes in 1826," *Niagara Falls Gazette* (October 15, 1958), cited in Ch. 4.

By Birdseye. The money spoken of was to be raised in Canada; or he was to have the farm: capt. Jared Darrow was the man who went with me into Canada.

Edwin Scrantom called. Now lives in Rochester; in 1826 was in Lewiston: knew Whitney, Shaw and Chubbuck: came out as one of the Rochester band to attend the installation; that night was at the Frontier House at the ball; broke up after midnight and went to Youngstown for the purpose of taking the steam boat for Canada: went in a one horse wagon: met five or six men coming up on foot: we stopped, and one of them, Mr. Chubbuck came up to the wagon, and asked me if I should return by way of Lewiston: saw one person whom I knew, James L. Barton: and heard Timothy Shaw: this was about four o'clock A. M.: about daylight; thinks it is not far from four miles this side of Lewiston where we met them: went over to York the day following: started out the day after the installation and was driven back: got into York before sundown on the 16th: remained in York over the Sabbath: went back into the country on Monday, and returned to Youngstown on Thursday, in the Martha Ogden: saw Giddins on board.

By Birdseye. The money spoken of was to be raised in Canada; or he was to have the farm: capt. Jared Darrow was the man who went with me into Canada.

Edwin Scranton called. Now lives in Rochester; in 1826 was in Lewiston: knew Whitney, Shaw and **Chubbuck;** came out as one of the Rochester band to attend the installation; that night was at the Frontier House at the ball; broke up after midnight and went to Youngstown for the purpose of taking **the steam boat for Canada;** went in a one horse wagon; met five or six men coming up on foot; we stopped, and one of them, **Mr. Chubbuck** came up to the wagon, and asked me if I should return by way of Lewiston; saw one person whom I know, James L. Barton; and heard Timothy Shaw; this was about four o'clock A. M.; about daylight; thinks it is not far from four miles this side of Lewiston where we met them; went over to **York** [Toronto] the day following; started out the day after the installation and was driven back; got into York before sundown on the 16th; remained in York over the Sabbath; went back into the country on Monday, and returned to Youngstown on Thursday, in the **Martha Ogden**; saw **Giddins** on board.

The *Martha Ogden* plies between Youngstown and York (Toronto)
Image 6.4

1826 **Edward Giddins [Giddings; Giddons]** was keeper of the lighthouse at Fort Niagara. The Fort was vacant at this time. He was also said to have "kept the ferry" ("Morgan Affair" trial testimony[44]), but precisely when is uncertain (was this ferry a military ferry?).

1826 **Ferry Law** in the New York State Legislative Session Laws for the Youngstown Ferry with service not to exceed **ten years** (quoted near the beginning of this chapter).[45]

1826 **First horse ferry on the Great Lakes.** Lester Brace and Donald Fraser were granted a five-year lease to operate a ferry service at Black Rock and installed the first horse ferry on the Great Lakes.[46]

1826 **John Phillips** was designated as the Youngstown ferryman in the 1826 Ferry Law above.[47] His license contract **required that he had to be operating a horse ferry or steam ferry on or before January 1, 1828**; otherwise, he and his heirs and assigns would

---

[44] See Appendix 7 for Chubbuck and Giddins as witnesses in the famous Morgan Affair.

[45] See the discussion above (John Phillips); Silvernail, *Index*, 381: *Laws of New York Forty-Ninth Session*, chapter 45, year 1826, and Fifty-Ninth Session, 456-57; also Dieats, *From Flames and Four Flags*, 33.

[46] On January 13, 2012, C. Andrie sent Gretchen Duling a chronological paper titled "Black Rock Ferry" that gives this information. These ferrymen petitioned to have their lease extended for nine years on March 24, 1832.

[47] John Phillips was granted the license in the *Court Minutes, Common Pleas*, January 6, 1826.

forfeit the ferry license.[48] Apparently, he did not meet the 1828 deadline and lost his license, **see 1828 and 1829.**

1827* **John Phillips** applied for **ten years,** promising **$500.** See, however, Phillips 1826; 1828. (See also, **1838** for John's Young's lawsuit against "John Phillips").

1827 **Olaf Hathaway** was working as a local Youngstown agent for the American Steamboat Line operating on Lake Ontario. **See 1821.**

1828 **First mention of the Horse Ferry (apparently run by Samuel Chubbuck and Thomas Balmer; see 1829).** An 1828 notice by Otis Wells about stage coach service and the Youngstown Coffee House indicated that the ferry operating between Youngstown and Niagara in 1828 was a "Horse Boat."[49]

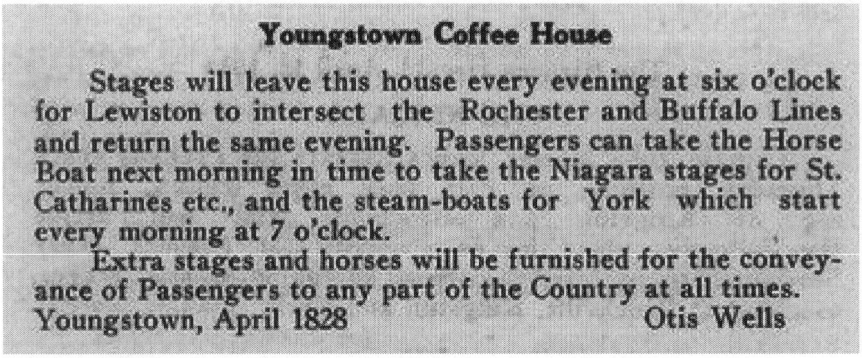

Youngstown Coffee House

Stages will leave this house every evening at six o'clock for Lewiston to intersect the Rochester and Buffalo Lines and return the same evening. Passengers can take the Horse Boat next morning in time to take the Niagara stages for St. Catharines etc., and the steam-boats for York which start every morning at 7 o'clock.

Extra stages and horses will be furnished for the conveyance of Passengers to any part of the Country at all times.
Youngstown, April 1828   Otis Wells

The Youngstown Coffee House: A Horse Boat between Youngstown and Niagara (1828)
Image 6.5

---

[48] *Laws of the State of New-York, Passed at the Forty-ninth Session of the Legislature, Begun and Held at the City of Albany, The Third day of January, 1826* (Albany, NY: William Gould & Co.; New-York, NY: Gould & Banks; E. Croswell, Printer, 1826), 32-33.

[48] In 1822 or 1824, The New York State Legislature wanted Asa Stannard at Black Rock to build a horse boat as the condition for extending his lease. He continued to use a scow rowed by four men, each with two oars, and lost his ferry lease. See Charles D. Norton, "The Old Black Rock Ferry," 91-112.

[49] This notice was cited in John Morden Crysler, *A Short History of the Township of Niagara: Touching upon Transportation, Education and Municipal Affairs from 1793 to 1893* (Niagara-on-the-Lake, Canada: The Niagara Advance, 1943), 8. Public Domain in Canada. Thanks to Karen Noonan who found this reference.

1829 Samuel L. Chubbuck (1794—1882), horse ferry builder, and Thomas Balmer operated the Youngstown Ferry (probably already in 1828).[50] Chubbuck, a son of German immigrants, was born in Vermont, moved with his family to Oneida County, New York, in 1804, and then to Lewiston in 1816, where he was a blacksmith and ran a tavern on the waterfront until 1822.[51] He was an accomplished carpenter and opened a carriage factory in Lewiston in 1823, perhaps the first in Niagara County.[52] He **built several large horse ferry boats**.[53] He moved to Youngstown in 1829 (1839?)[54] and he and Thomas Balmer were operating a horse ferry from Youngstown to Niagara[-on-the-Lake], probably already in 1828 (**see 1828**). Perhaps Chubbuck was able to do what John Phillips could not do by January 1, 1828 (according to Phillips' contract), that is, build a horse or steam ferry, and therefore Chubbuck and Balmer acquired the ferry license.[55] It was still operating in 1830, perhaps up to 1834 (**see 1834**).[56] Chubbuck was also in charge of the carpenter work at Fort Niagara when in the wake of the Canadian Rebellion of 1837/1838 the wood and earth breastworks were built (1839—1843). He was the contractor who (among other things) built the Porter (First) Presbyterian Church in 1836, dedicated in 1837. Many years later **James P. Marshall** married Chubbuck's granddaughter and Marshall also operated the Youngstown Ferry (**1870s-1880s**).[57]

---

[50] "Samuel Chubbuck, Obituary," *Niagara County News*, June 9, 1882; Bill Siddall, "Samuel Chubbuck," *Find a Grave*, added July 27, 2009, http://www.findagrave.com/cgi-bin/fg.cgi?page=gr&GRid=39961693.

[51] *Lewiston Sesquicentennial 1822—1972 in Celebration of its 150th Year of Historical Significance on the Niagara Frontier* (1972), 82; "Tavern Days," *The Brookfield Courier*, April 16, 1947

[52] Clarence L. Lewis, "Niagara County History: Carriage Era is Recalled," Town of Porter Society Museum file (an undocumented newspaper copy).

[53] "Samuel Chubbuck, Obituary" *Niagara County News* (June 9, 1882); Bill Siddall, "Samuel Chubbuck."

[54] Chubbuck built his house at 615 Main Street, across the street from 614 Main Street, the home where UGRR agent Myron J. Pardee probably lived; see Ch. 10.

[55] *The Youngstown Centennial Magazine 1854-1954*, 15.

[56] Chubbuck, age 86, claimed "I am ferryman at Youngstown," in 1880 as a witness in the murder trial of George C. Hotchkiss, *Lockport Daily Journal* (April 13, 1880).

[57] On the 1870 map, "J. P. Marshall" had the lot just north of "Mrs. Cook" above the "Ferry Ho[use]" (see above; Ch. 16).

Chubbuck built a house at 615 Main Street directly across the street from 614 Main Street where the Pardee and Wilcox families lived from about 1854 to 1868.[58] It is now a renovated Youngstown historic home.[59]

Like Giddens, Chubbuck was called in 1831 as a witness in the famous **"Morgan Affair" of 1826**. Witness Edwin Scranton testified that Chubbuck was seen that night on the road between Fort Niagara and Lewiston. On his deathbed, Chubbuck denied his participation; he was defended by his sons.[60]

Judith Wellman, drawing on Robert Foley,[61] refers to a certain *Job* Chubbuck, who lived in Canada, but was born in the United States. He, along with James Oswald, was a ferryman between Lewiston and Queenston and so was his son-in-law, Thomas McMicking. Job Chubbuck, like Samuel Chubbuck, was also a contractor/builder (Queenston's "Chubbuck Block"). In the Canadian Census Index of 1871, his residence was in the Village of Niagara. His sometime partner, Joseph Wynn (Wynne), was also the lessee of the ferry between Queenston and Lewiston. Was Job Chubbuck, builder/horse ferryman between Lewiston and Queenston, related to Samuel Chubbuck, the builder/horse ferryman between Youngstown and Niagara? Their parallel names, dates, occupations, and locations on the Niagara River are suggestive and ferrymen up and down the river usually knew each other; however, the German name Chubbuck was common and at present we have no evidence of any kinship relationship.

1829 **Thomas Balmer** operated a **horse ferry** with Samuel Chubbuck between Youngstown and Canada.[62]

1830 **Davison's 1830** *Tour Guide* **(pages 275, 279 below): a "horse boat" plied between Niagara and Youngstown.**[63]

---

[58] For more on Myron J. Pardee as an UGRR agent, and for a railroad tie and spike found behind 615 Main Street, see Chs. 10, 16 and Images 5.11b and 6.4 above.

[59] The property is now owned by John and Cathy Goller; for a likely 1855 railroad spike on the property, see Ch. 5.

[60] See the Morgan Affair court record above and details in Appendix 7.

[61] Wellman cites Robert J. Foley, "Crossing the Niagara Part I: The Ferries," *Niagara Sunday Shopping News*, Niagara Falls, Ontario, September 16, 1990.

[62] Ibid.

[63] G. M. Davison, *The Fashionable Tour: A Guide to Travellers Visiting the Middle and Northern States and the Provinces of Canada*. Fourth edition—enlarged and improved. Saratoga Springs: G. M. Davison; and by G. & C. & H. Carvill, New-York. MDCCCXXX [1830].

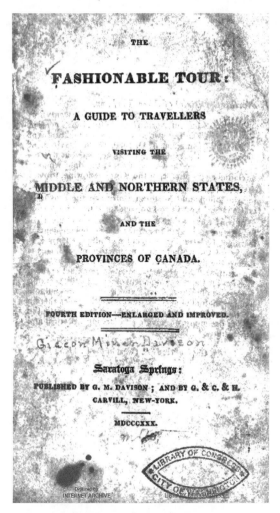

... While on the Canada shore, it is recommended to tourists to visit the Deep Cut on the Welland Canal, eight miles west of the Falls; return; proceed down the Niagara River through Queenston to Fort George or Newark [Niagara]; **cross over to Fort Niagara or Youngstown**, and proceed up the river, through Lewiston, to Manchester [Niagara Falls]. For a short excursion, there are many objects of attraction on this route, which are noticed hereafter... (p. **275**)

... Fort George, near the village [of Newark/Niagara], is the most prominent, and perhaps the only object of interest presented. It is in a state of tolerable preservation, and has generally, since the war, been occupied as a garrison by a small number of soldiers. **The river is crossed in a horse boat, to YOUNGSTOWN, containing from 40 to 50 houses, one mile north of which, and directly opposite Newark, is Fort Niagara**... (p. **279**)

Davison's 1830 *Tour Guide*: A Horse Boat between Youngstown and Niagara (1830)
Image 6.6

In 1830, the ferrymen were likely still Samuel Chubbuck and Thomas Balmer. They partnered in running their horse ferry probably until 1834, when steam ferries first appear at Youngstown. **See 1834, 1836, 1844.**

1832 The Steamer *Martha Ogden*, which ran between Youngstown and Toronto with ferry connections from Youngstown to Niagara, ran aground, but no lives were lost (see *Martha Ogden* above).

1834 **Alexander Lane* operated the first steam ferry, "The Cigar," at Youngstown** (see 1836, 1844).[64] He built a house at 545 Main Street about 1840, lived there twenty-two years,[65] and helped to build the Ontario House ("the Stone Jug") in 1842.[66]

1836 **NYS Legislative Session Laws for ferry service in New York lists Youngstown** (this law is quoted near the beginning of this chapter). The ferry license *could not exceed ten years*; ferrying without a license was considered a misdemeanor and fined by $25 for each offense. The ten-year period was challenged during the 1854-1858 competitive battles for the right to operate the Youngstown Ferry.

1836* **John Beach, Sept. 13th,** applied to run a **steam ferry or horse ferry** (see below; 1843, 1844) **for $500. Olaf Hathaway's** name was added to his application in a different hand; apparently that of the clerk A. H. Moss. As such, he became the co-signer (see above, 1827, and for Olaf's brother, ferryman **Elijah Hathaway, 1821-1823).**[67]

---

[64] Onen, "Recollections."
[65] Ames, *Survey*, Vol. 1A; Onen, "Recollections."
[66] See Ch. 13.
[67] For more details on Elijah and Olaf Hathaway, who was said to ferry fugitive slave Thomas James across the Niagara River, see Chapters 7, 14.

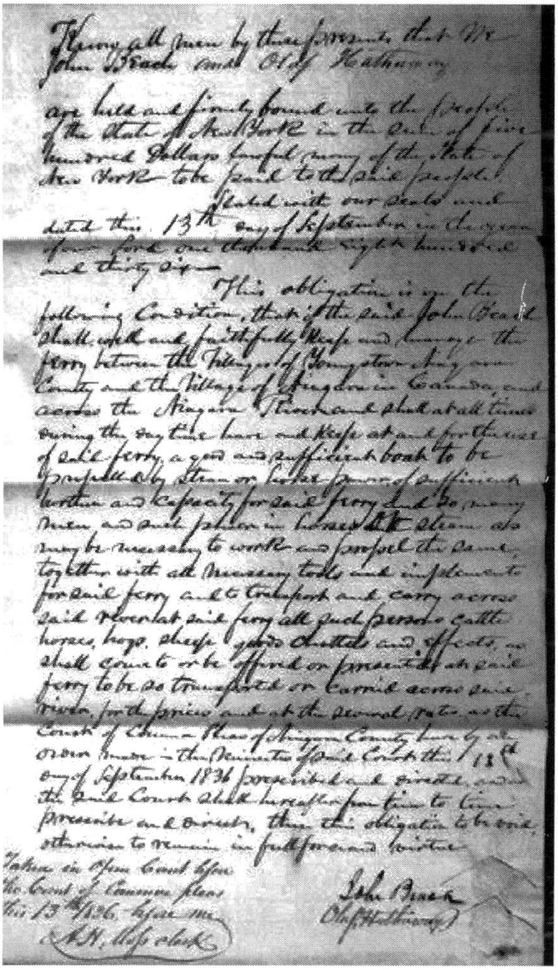

Know all men by their presents [presence] that We[,] **John Beach and Olaf Hathaway**[,] are held and family bound unto the people of the State of New York in the sum of five hundred dollars lawful money of the State of New York to be paid to the said people.

Sealed with our seals and dated the 13th day of September in the year of our Lord one thousand eight hundred and thirty six —

This obligation is on the following Condition, that if the said John Beach shall well and faithfully keep and manage the ferry between the Village of Youngstown Niagara County and the Village of Niagara in Canada, and across the Niagara River and shall at all times during the day time have and keep at and for the use of said ferry a good and sufficient boat to be propelled **by steam or horse power** of sufficient [tons] burthen and capacity for said ferry and so many men and such **power in horses and steam** as may be necessary to work and propel the same together with all necessary tools and implements for said ferry and to transport and carry across said river at said ferry all such persons, cattle, horses, hogs, sheep, goods, chattels and effects as shall come to or be offered or presented as said ferry to be so transported or carried across said river, for the prices and at the several rates as this Court of Common Pleas of Niagara County have by an order made in the Minutes of said Court this 13th day of September 1836 prescribed and directed, and in this said Court shall hereafter from time to time prescribe and direct, then this obligation to be void, otherwise to remain in full force and virtue.

Taken in open Court before
The Court of Common Pleas   **John Beach**
This 13th 1836 before me   *Olaf Hathaway*
A. H. Moss clerk

Olaf Hathaway's name added to the Petition of John Beach (1836)
Image 6.7

1836   Petition of Support for John Beach by sundry inhabitants of Niagara County to operate the ferry was reported in the State Assembly.[68]

1836*   Ira Race (1807-1899) Petition. Ira Race (1807-1899) settled in Youngstown in 1826. He was a farmer until 1833, sheriff from 1833-1836, and Justice of the Peace for forty-seven years. He held various political offices; among them Supervisor of the Town of Porter

---

[68] *Journal of the Assembly of the State of New York at the Fifty-Ninth Session* (Albany, New York, 1836), 152.

1850 – 1853, 1855, 1865-1866.[69] He shared in writing the petition to the New York State Legislature to incorporate Youngstown in 1854. **See 1854, 1858.1838.**

1838   **Calvin Wilson kept the Youngstown Ferry**. He and his wife Hanah [Hannah] owned property at 347 Main Street (NW corner of Main and Water Streets) for a year, from 1837 to 1838. Most likely their property extended down to the river.[70] He was probably the ferryman who worked in the winter months ferrying the cross-border ferry.[71]

1838   **John Young sued John Phillips** along with Obed Smith and Hezekiah Scovell (reason unknown). The 1840 Federal Census listed a "Free Colored" man living in the household of John Phillips.[72] However, see the following 1840 entry **John G. Phillips** (a son?).

1840*   **Ferry Application of Harry W. Phillips (co-signed by John G. Phillips [sons of John Phillips?])** for seven years.

1840*   **Luther Wilson[73] and Alfred P. Judd** applied for and received the ferry license. Prices:

one foot passenger six cents [pence]	0/0 .06
a horse & one person 1/6 [Shilling/pence[74]]	.18 ¼
one horse & one horse wagon two Shillings	.25
two horses and wagon three Shillings	.37 ½
cattle per head twelve & half cents	.12 ½
sheep per head six cents	.06
For every Panel or Box of food there Amt.	.03
For all other things not enumerated above	
half the amount of Ferriage which	

---

[69] Pool, *Landmarks*, Ch. XV.

[70] Ames, *Survey*, Vol. 1A.

[71] For his role in the famous "*Caroline* Affair" [1837], see Appendix 7.

[72] See Ch. 3; above the 1826 ferry law.

[73] Luther Wilson and his brother Reuben were namesakes of the Village of Wilson, New York. Luther was a surveyor, grist mill owner, land owner, merchant, teacher, Methodist lay leader, philanthropist, Village President, and Supervisor (1843-1845; 1855-1856); see "Celebrating the 100th Anniversary of the Village of Wilson, New York," https://archive.org/stream/WilsonCentennial18581958Booklet/Wilson%20Centennial%201858-1958%20Booklet_djvu.txt; Pool, *Landmarks*, XVIII, 302-215.

[74] The slash / in slanted form was derived from an elongated "S," originally an abbreviation for a gold Roman coin, the *solidus*, and adopted to abbreviate the British shilling, which was equivalent to 12 pence (cents). 1/6 would be one shilling and six pence. Equivalences in modern dollars and cents can be based on several variables and are almost impossible to determine, but horses and cattle were about twice a much as humans. See Chs. 8, 10.

John Beach **[see 1836]** by his license heretofore granted
had a right to receive for ferriage. . .

1844 **The Daily Steamboat Ferry plied between Youngstown and Niagara** (see 1834 and
1836). The following advertisement appeared in the *Niagara Democrat*, Wednesday,
April 24, 1844:

> **Village lots for Sale—(Lands of the late John Young, deceased)**—At the Village
> of Youngstown, Niagara Co., N. Y., which is pleasantly located on the Niagara
> River, one mile from the mouth, and from Fort Niagara at the head of Lake
> Ontario. Directly opposite Youngstown is Niagara, in Canada, overlooked by the
> heights of Youngstown.
>
> Youngstown is on a commanding elevation of land with a climate healthy,
> and water excellent, growing in wealth, population, and commercial importance.
> It has a fine view of the lake and Victoria's dominions. **Between Youngstown and
> Niagara a steam ferry boat plies daily. It [Youngstown] has a good harbor for
> vessels of any capacity. Steamboats during the summer months run daily
> between the place [Youngstown] and Toronto and Hamilton in Canada, and
> Oswego, N. Y.** As a place for business for men of enterprise or capital, it offers
> flattering advantages; and as a country residence for men of leisure, taste, or
> wealth, it is second to few on any of our western rivers or lakes.
>
> Lots of all sizes, from small or large business lots to building lots of 3, 5,
> or 10 acres, can be had at fair prices, and a long credit given for most of the
> purchase money. Inquire of Alexander Lane, Youngstown; John Fulton, Niagara—
> November 25, 1843."[75]

---

[75] *Niagara Democrat* (published in Lockport), April 24, 1844 (bold face ours). The sentences are quoted from an ad
in the *Niagara Democrat* by Mrs. Daniel Wilson in "Not So Long Ago," *Youngstown Centennial. Youngstown 1854—
1954,* 41, 43, 45. The ad's Alexander Lane completed building the Ontario House in 1842, on which see, Chs. 7 and
16.

1845 **Youngstown Ferry House made of stone** may have existed.[76]

1848 **Charles Ellet's Suspension Bridge** between Niagara City (Bellevue), New York, and Niagara Falls, Ontario, was completed. It was able to carry foot and buggy traffic across the Niagara River. The site was below the Whirlpool Rapids (near today's Whirlpool Rapids Bridge). Until this date, the only way to get from bank to bank was by boat.[77]

1851 **First Queenston-Lewiston Suspension Bridge completed.** It was destroyed by wind in 1864, resulting in resumption of ferryboat service between Lewiston and Queenston. Meanwhile, ferries are still important to get from Youngstown to Niagara.

1854 **April 18. Youngstown incorporated as a village.** Both **Luke P. Babcock** and **Ira Race**, competitors for the ferry operation, participated in preparing the petition to incorporate the Village of Youngstown. See **1854, Luke P. Babcock** and **Ira Race [see also Ira Race 1836]**.

1854 **Railroads to Youngstown**. Competition for the ferry license became especially sharp between 1854 and 1858, in lieu of the two railroads to Youngstown.[78]

1854* **(April 19). John Hitchcock.** A petition that John Hitchcock be granted a license to operate the ferry for the terms of **three years or more**. First signature was Josiah Tryon; also signed by D. Pomroy, J. Pomroy. Outside: April 25, 1854.**[79]**

1854?* John Hitchcock. A petition of support to be the ferryman **for three years or more** (among signers: Josiah Tryon).

1854?* John Hitchcock. A petition to support him as ferrymen for **three or four years or more**.

1854?* John Hitchcock. A short petition of support by those who have known him for **three years or more**, that he owned a boat, and that he often crossed the river in rough weather.

1854* **Alexander Lane Application Submitted** April 18th. Lane was a former ferryman (**See 1834)**. Petitioned for four years.

---

[76] For detail on the Ferry House, see Ch. 16 and the notes on 1860 and 1870 below.
[77] See Chs. 4, 5.
[78] See Ch. 5.
[79] See Samuel Ringgold Ward in Ch. 8.

1854* **Luke P. Babcock Application submitted** April 18th.[80] According to Donald Ames'
Historical and Family Survey, Luke bought 627 Main Street (south of Samuel Chubbuck's
house at 615) from Samuel M. Chubbuck. In the 1850 Federal Census, Luke Babcock was
a 54-year-old (b. 1796) carpenter from Connecticut living in the household of tavern
keeper **Robert McKnight**, age 41, born in Ireland. In the same dwelling, lived nineteen
people. This might have been the Ontario House since McKnight owned it from 1851 to
1856. **See 1836 and 1854, Ira Race.**

1854* **Apr. 11. A petition of thirty signatures supporting Babcock.**

1854* **An undated petition of twenty-four signatures supporting Babcock; it included** UGRR
agent **Myron J. Pardee** and his hardware business partner **E. P. Pomroy.**[81]

1854* **An undated petition of twenty-four signatures supported Babcock.**
Apparently approved; however, see the 1855 and 1858 petitions for his removal.

1854* **A petition that the ferry license be granted only to the highest responsible bidder and
only for one year, and the proceeds go to Town of Porter schools.**[82] It had 47
signatures.

---

[80] Pool, *Landmarks*, 263.
[81] E. P. Pomroy was the business partner in the 1854 *Pardee and Pomroy* hardware business in the Davis Brick
Block on Main Street; we think that his partner Myron J. Pardee was an UGRR agent; see Ch. 10.
[82] Ibid., again, E. P. Pomroy's signature is important historical evidence.

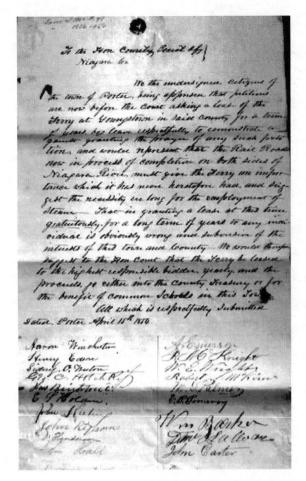

To the Hon. County Court Of
Niagara Co.

We the undersigned citizens of the Town of Porter, being apprisen that petitions are now before the court asking a lease of the Ferry at Youngstown in said county for a term of years by leave respectfully to remonstrate against granting the prayer of any such petition, and would represent that the Rail Road now in process of completion on both sides of Niagara River, must give the Ferry an importance which it had never heretofore had, and suggest the necessity be long for the employment of steam-- That in granting a lease at this time gratuitously for a long term of years to any individual is obviously wrong and subversive of the interests of this town and County. We would therefore suggest to the Hon. Court that **the Ferry be leased to the highest responsible bidder yearly** and the proceeds go either into the County Treasury for the benefit of common schools in this Town.

All which is respectfully submitted
Dated Porter April 15th 1854

A Petition to Limit the Ferry License to the Highest Bidder for One Year (1854)
Figure 6.8

[NOTE: on this page are the signatures of **E. P. Pomroy** of *Pardee & Pomroy*[83] and **John Carter,**[84] **and further down, Lewis Leffman,**[85] **George Swain**, and **William Swain.**]

1854* **A second petition** was attached, that those who signed a previous petition agreed to the highest bidder/one year petition; it had 43 signatures.

---

[83] For E. P. Pomroy, see Ch. 10.
[84] For John Carter, see Ch. 14.
[85] For Lewis Leffman, see the Addendum, Ch. 3.

1854* **Ira Race Application Submitted. Apr. 17th.** He had a previous application, **1836.** "Ten years" was crossed out and above the line was added "7 years," but then additionally "or such other term as the county shall see fit to grant." **See 1836** for information about Ira Race.

1854* **April 12th. Petition of support for Ira Race and one-year license term,** 25 signatures.

1854* **April 12th. Petition of support for Ira Race and one-year license term,** 65 signatures.

1854* **April 17th. Petition of support for Ira Race and one-year license term,** 26 signatures.

1854* **April 17th. Petition of support for Ira Race and one-year license term,** 54 signatures.

1855* **December 15th. Transnational (!) Petition to Remove Luke P. Babcock** eight months after his application filed to be a Ferry Keeper. Initial signature is **Joseph L. Fowler.**

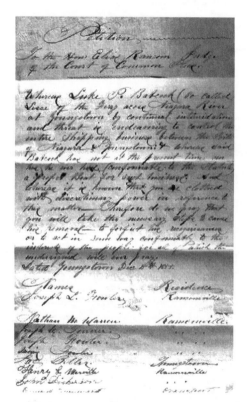

Petition - - - - - - - - - - - -

To the Hon. Elias Ransom Judge
Of the Court of Common Pleas
———
Whereas   Luke P. Babcock (so called)   Lesse [sic] of the Ferry across Niagara River at Youngstown by continual intimidation and threat is endeavoring to control the entire shipping business between the Ports of Niagara & Youngstown: & whereas said Babcock has not at the present time nor has he had (conformable to the statute) a proper Boat for such business: And whereas it is known that you are clothed with discretionary power in reference to this matter – Therefore do we pray that you will take the necessary steps to cause his removal – to forfeit his recognizances (sic) or act in some conformably to the interests of the people - for all of which the undersigned [**See 1856**] will ever pray.
Dated Youngstown Dec 15th 1855

[Signatures follow]

A Transnational Petition to Remove Luke P. Babcock, December 15, 1855
Figure 6.9

1855 **"Niagara Falls" Suspension Bridge** at Bellevue/Niagara City, redesigned by John Roebling with an upper deck for train traffic, opens on March 8. Train travel from New York City to the bridge with a connection to the Great Western Railway in Canada allowed another possibility for fugitive slaves to cross the Niagara River.[86]

1856* **Jan. 10th. Petition.** Fifty-six American and eight Canadian signatures were added to 1855 petition to remove Luke P. Babcock; then 64 more American signatures were added, for a total of 170 signatures from 1854 to 1856!

1858* **Another transnational petition to Remove Luke P. Babcock** and to replace him with Ira Race; "and Peter Tower" (Town Supervisor 1879) was inserted [co-signer?]).

1858* **Joel (George?) Tryon Application.** March and April applications with many signatures.

1858* **Ira Race** application for ten years. **Apparently approved**.

1860 **The schooner *Carlton*** docked at Youngstown.[87]

1860 **Youngstown Ferry House** was probably marked (box) where Ferry Street should be.

1870 **Youngstown Ferry House.** The 1870 street, house, and property map of Youngstown[88] has a box marked "Ferry Ho[use]" on the edge of the Niagara River shore jutting into the water in the vicinity of what is now called Constitution Park at 333 Main Street across the street from Falkner Park. In 1870, the Ferry House was clearly indicated below the house of "Mrs. [Maria Greensitt] Cook," daughter of Robert and Agnes Greensitt, a ferryman (ca. 18??-1815?) and a ferrywoman (1815 or 1816).[89] The lot immediately north belonged to James P. Marshall, who also operated the ferry;[90] he was married to the granddaughter of Samuel Chubbuck.

The material above contains information about ferry laws related to Youngstown, Youngstown Ferry House(s), more than a dozen ferrymen and a ferrywoman, and the various kinds of ferries used between Youngstown and Niagara—scows, horse ferries, and steam ferries

---

[86] See Chs. 5 and 10 for more on "the Suspension Bridge." In 1897, this International Suspension Bridge was replaced by the Whirlpool Rapids Bridge, also with two decks. For Harriet Tubman, see Ch. 3.

[87] *Auburn Daily Union*, Monday, November 19, 1860.

[88] "Approximate date of map 1870" on the map itself.

[89] For detailed discussion of the Greensitts and the Ferry House, see Ch. 16.

[90] *History of Niagara County*, 340a.

between 1815 and 1870. This documentation is informative not only as a general background about ferries and ferrypersons, but in knowing more about transportation to freedom in Canada and some of those who were operating the Youngstown Ferry at the time fugitive slaves crossed from Youngstown to Niagara. Anticipating the following chapters, the following chart correlates fugitive slaves who crossed with dates and ferrymen:

Fugitive Slave Crossing	Date	Ferryman
Olaf (Elijah?) Hathaway ferried fugitive slave Thomas James	1821	Elijah Hathaway
A fugitive slave ferried in winter witnessed by Samuel R. Ward	1853	John Hitchcock?
Ben Hockley's attempt to raft cross the river on an old gate	1853	John Hitchcock?
Father and son fugitive slaves sent to Youngstown's "Mr. Pardee"	1855	Luke P. Babcock
Two fugitive slaves "rowed" across Niagara by a farmer	1856/7	Luke P. Babcock
"Col. P____" fakes Cassey's escape to the Youngstown Ferry	1861	Ira Race
Eleven fugitives land at King's Landing (from Youngstown?)	ca. 1863	Ira Race

Five of the persons who applied for the ferry license also owned Youngstown inns or taverns in the period of the Underground Railroad.

Ferryman	Owned Inn/Tavern	
Elijah Hathaway	Hathaway House prior to 1812; burned by British in 1813; rebuilt by 1816?	? years
Robert Greensitt	Inn/Tavern and Ferry; burned by British in 1813	? years
Agnes Greensitt	Inn/Tavern 1815?-1818?	? years
Luther Wilson	Ontario House 2/9/41 – 4/9/41	3 months
Alexander Lane	Ontario House 4/9/1841 – 5/9/1848 and 7/5/1850 – 5/7/1851	8 years

It should be stated that we know of nothing remotely comparable to the courageous African American hotel workers at Niagara Falls, New York, who helped fugitive slaves escape cross the Niagara River, but the correlation of ferrymen and inn and tavern owners in

Youngstown is worth mentioning, especially since it is known that some ferry houses were stations on the Underground Railroad and have been so officially recognized.[91]

The Youngstown Ferrywoman

Was there really a Youngstown ferrywoman? If the criterion is possession of an official Youngstown Ferry license, the answer is absolutely "yes!" Her story deserves to be told.

First, a few preliminary comments are in order.

Before the War of 1812, Youngstown was a very small settlement indeed. On an 1810 Canadian map of Fort George and the Town of Niagara there were only seven boxes (buildings) on the Youngstown shore.[92] Niagara County Historian Catherine Emerson confirms this picture by quoting from a letter of Colonel Simon Larned to Colonel Walbach in 1814, that Youngstown was "an inconsiderable settlement . . . of about 6 or 8 houses."[93] Similarly, William Pool concluded that "[o]nly a very small settlement was gathered at Youngstown at the time of the devastation of the frontier by the British in 1813."[94] Pool also wrote that according to a New York State law passed in 1801, an inn and tavern keeper "shall keep in his house at least two spare beds for guests, with good and sufficient sheeting and covering" and "good and sufficient stabling," including enough hay (even in winter) and grain for four horses and other stock.[95] In relation to Youngstown Karen Noonan forwarded to us a public announcement from the *Niagara Sentinel* of 1823 titled simply "S. G. Williams," which advertised "accommodation of

---

[91] See further, Ch. 16.

[92] See Ch. 16.

[93] Catherine Emerson, "An Industrious and Worthy Woman. The Chronicle of Betsy/Mary Doyle and her Husband Andrew," *Old Fort Niagara* (November/December, 2011). Her source is in n. 24: "Letter from Colonel Simon Larned, Greenbush Cantonment, April 5, 1814 to Colonel Walbach, Adjutant General, from National Archives, " Letters received from the Office of the Adj. General 1805 – 1812, retrieved from www.footnote.come/image/273003125. Horatio Gates Spafford, *A Gazetteer of the State of New York*, H. C. Southwich, Albany, NY, 1813, p. 334.

[94] Pool, *Landmarks*, 260.

[95] See "An Act to Lay a Duty on Strong Liquors and for Regulating Inns and Taverns," Passed 7th April, 1801, In *Laws of the State of New York Published by Authority* (Albany, NY: Charles R. and George Webster, 1802), Chapter 164, No. IX, p. 488 and No. XI, 495-96. https://books.google.com/books?id=voNZAAAAYAAJ&pg=PA488&lpg=PA488&dq=New+York+State+law+concerning+inns+and+taverns+-+beds+and+horses&source=bl&ots=DZZWIABTYo&sig=WcsVZTJzKZK06o1_rC1lfC-gE04&hl=en&sa=X&ved=0ahUKEwip3eGRjrTNAhVHOSYKHXKJAQQQ6AEIIzAB#v=onepage&q=New%20York%20State%20law%20concerning%20inns%20and%20taverns%20-%20beds%20and%20horses&f=false. "Phillips and Williams" might have been John Phillips and S. G. Williams."S. G. Williams," the *Niagara Sentinel*, September 26, 1823.

travelers" in Youngstown. Williams' tavern promised a commanding view of the river, the lake, Fort Niagara, and the Town of Niagara in Canada; liquors that were guaranteed to be first rate and prices that were competitive; and an expensive stable and shed, with horses "carefully attended."[96] In short, at least one Youngstown inn and tavern owner was attempting to meet state regulations.

Between 1810 and 1830, Youngstown grew from seven buildings to about forty or fifty.[97] Yet, it appears to have had a rather large number of taverns. The 1878 *History of Niagara County* noted these tavern owners in this period: Elijah Hathaway, Robert Campbell, Andrew Brady, Wright Miles, John McBride, James Cato, and "Phillips and Williams"— presumably John Phillips (see above, 1826) and Stephen G. Williams (the inn ad above; see also below).[98] The "Records of Recognizances[99] for Inn Keepers AD 1816" in the *Book of Records of the Town of Porter*[100] lists five inn keepers on May 18: Elijah Hathaway, Andrew Brady, Agnes Greensitt, John McBride, and James Cato.

---

[96] "S. G. Williams," *Niagara Sentinel*, September 26, 1823. Thanks to Karen Noonan for forwarding this article.
[97] See the comment in Davison's 1830 *Tour Guide* above, Image 6.6.
[98] *The History of Niagara County, New York*, 339; the list is repeated in Suzanne Simon Dietz and Karen Noonan, "Town of Porter 1800- 1829" (map) (BeauDesigns)."Phillips" was probably John Phillips, a ferryman from 1824 to 1827 (see ferryman chronology above); "S. L. Williams" in the 1840 federal Census was probably a mis-transcription of "S. G. Williams" (the "L" was simply a curved line and could have been a "G").
[99] This term is defined above in connection with petitions for a license to operate the Youngstown Ferry.
[100] It is in the Niagara County Historian's Office, Lockport, New York, photocopy in the Porter Town History Museum.

Inn Keepers in the *Book of Records of the Town of Porter*, May 22, 1816[101]
(Elijah Hathaway, Andrew Brady, Agnes Greensitt, John McBride, James Cato)
Image 6.10

Inn keepers Campbell, Miles, and "Phillips and Williams" who were mentioned in the *History of Niagara County* are missing from the *Book of Records*, but four are the same: Hatheway [*sic*], Brady, McBride, and Cato. Most important here, a new name appears: Agnes Greensitt, the only woman on the list.[102]

Robert Greensitt is not in the above lists of inn keepers, but historian William Pool wrote in 1897: "Robert Grensit [Greensitt] kept the first tavern in this town on the site of Youngstown, and the house was conducted by his widow after his death."[103] The date of Robert Greensitt's death is uncertain (1813, 1814, or 1815?), but Agnes was certainly a widow by 1816 (see below). Earlier, the 1810 Federal Census listed "R. Greenset" as living in the Town of Cambria, which at the time (until 1812) included the Town or Porter, therefore the Village of Youngstown.[104] In his household were seven free white persons: one male 26-44 (Robert), one female 45 and over, one male and one female 16-25, and 5 children under 16, that is, 2 males and 3 females. Presumably the female over 45 was Agnes Greensitt. We also know that on March 12, 1812, Robert bought a large tract of land from John Young (discussion below).[105]

---

[101] *Book of Records of the Town of Porter* archived in the Niagara County Historian's Office, Lockport, New York.
[102] Dietz observed that "'Elijah Hatheway (sic), Agnes Grineensitt (sic), [and] Daniel Kelly" were recorded as "recognition of innkeepers in the town in 1817" (Dietz, *From Flames and Four Flags*, 34). Agnes' name on May 22, 1816, was spelled "Greensitt"; also, the term "recognition"—"recognized" in the original source—probably meant the "Recognizances" in the source heading, which implied an obligation to fulfill requirements, as in the ferry applications.
[103] Pool, *Landmarks*, 260 (italics ours).
[104] Dietz and Noonan, *Early Town of Porter Residents*, 3.
[105] See 1841 map; Donald Ames, "Youngstown, A Village Steeped in History," who reproduces the top half of the map.

Suzanne Simon Dietz cites an 1827 treasury audit about properties lost during the War of 1812, which shows that the "Greensitt buildings" consisted of "a log house, a stable, a carpenter shop, and a storehouse" (they did not meet standards for occupation by the military during the War of 1812).[106] Nonetheless, in 1822 the widow Agnes Greensitt was listed among the "Sufferers" of the war, that is, those who made a claim for property destroyed by the British, which in Youngstown would have been December 19, 1813. "Mrs. Agnes Greensitt, her husband dead, house and furniture destroyed, presumed to be in want (thought to be in Ontario County with her children)."[107] Agnes was partially compensated. Her loan request was for $1,000, but she received only $600, and it had by then accrued $63.00 interest. The 1827 federal report shows that "Greensitt's Robert administratrix" had filed a personal property claim (loss) for $2,502.50 and a buildings claim for $1,850.00. The government estimated the latter's value was only $1,585 and she was authorized to receive ("vouched") for only $1,250.00.[108] Another source about Agnes listed her as "Greensitt, Agnes/Mrs. Anna – Youngstown, husband died, received $80 in relief."[109]

Agnes Greensitt is also listed in the "Town of Porter Minutes" in the *Book of Records of the Town of Porter*. The town was divided into seventeen road work districts, each marked by boundaries, each administered by a "Path Master," with lists of those who oversaw the road work in their district. Here is the record for District 2, the heart of Youngstown, probably 1821:[110]

---

[106] Dietz, *From Flames and Four Flags*, 6; the source is a *Letter from the Third Auditor of the Treasury. A Report of his Proceeding in Relation to Payment for Property Lost, Captured or Destroyed while in Service of the United States* (Washington, DC: Gales and Seaton, 1827).

[107] Dietz, Ibid. 7, n. 2. The source is the "Report of the Committee on the Petition of the Niagara Sufferers" related to an Act of the New York State Assembly of January 29, 1822. It listed loans that were due on February 13, 1822.

[108] Ibid., 8.

[109] Ibid., 9.

[110] "Town of Porter Minutes" in the *Book of Records of the Town of Porter.* For the other sixteen districts (without the names), see ibid., 36; Dietz and Noonan, *Early Town of Porter Residents 1800 – 1829*, 26-27. The year 1821 is an inference from the following year, 1822; however, the previous year was 1817, so it might be any year 1818-1821.

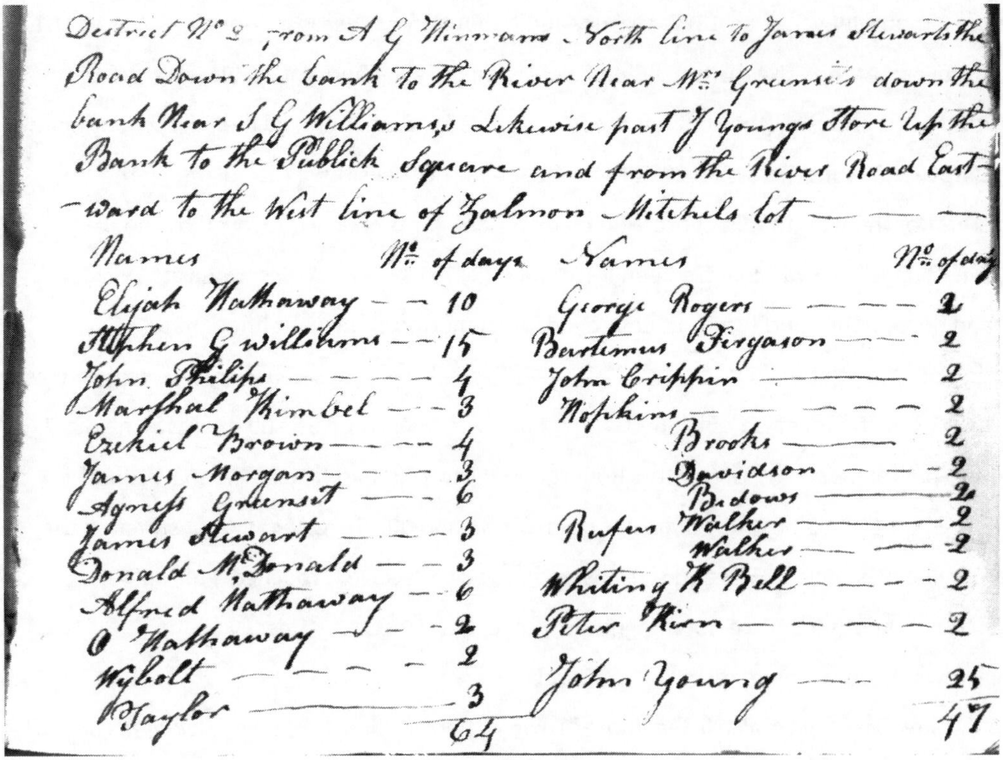

**District 2 (1821?) in the *Book of Records of the Town of Porter*
Image 6.11**

A transcription reads:

District 2, from A. G. Hinman's north line to James Stewart's Road down **the bank to the river near Mrs. Greensitt's**, [and] down the bank near S. G. Williams. Likewise part [past?] of Young's store up the bank to the Publick Square and from the River Road eastward to the west line of Salmon Mitchel's lot.

Names	No. of days	Names	No. of Days
Elijah Hathaway	10	George Rogers	2
Stephen G. Williams	15	Bartimus Firgason	2
John Philips	4	John Crippin	2
Marshal Kimbel	3	Hopkins	2

Ezekiel Brown	4	Brooks[111]	2
James Morgan	3	Davidson	2
Agnes Greensit (*sic*)	6	Bidows	2
James Stewart	3	Rufus Walker	2
Donald McDonald	3	Walker	2
Alfred Hathaway	6	Whiting K Bell	2
O Hathaway	2	Peter Kirn	2
Wybolt	2	John Young	25
Taylor	3		
	64		

Transcription: Youngstown District 2 in the *Book of Records of the Town of Porter*
Image 6.12

District 2 included familiar names: John Young (namesake of Youngstown); brothers Alfred Hathaway, O[laf] Hathaway (ferried a fugitive slave), and Elijah Hathaway (ferryman and inn keeper) (see Chapter 7); John "Philips" (*sic*; ferryman; see above); Stephen G. Williams (inn keeper, just mentioned). Most importantly here, there is a woman supervisor, Agnes "Greensit," six days. She and James Stewart were for several days responsible for "James Stewart's Road down the bank to the river near Mrs. Greensitt's," a property that will be examined more closely later in this book. Was this the road near the Greensitt property that became State Street (Chapter 16)? In 1822 and 1823, John Young, Alfred Hathaway, "Olif" Hathaway, Elijah Hathaway, James Stewart, and John Phillips are again on the list for "Road Work," but the name of the woman Agnes "Greensit" is gone.

In short, Agnes Greensitt was a Sufferer of the War of 1812, who lost property and was "in want," but who received some government compensation; a widow by 1816; an inn keeper who was running an inn; and one listed for road work for District 2, the Youngstown district in 1821. The location was "down the bank" near her property.[112]

---

[111] The reason for the indentations are not clear. Did the recording secretary not know first names? That theory does not explain Wybolt, Taylor, or Hopkins, who also do not have first names.
[112] See the Greensitt property map, Ch. 16, Image 16.9.

How was Agnes Greensitt related to operation of the Youngstown Ferry?

Robert Greensitt, Agnes' husband, was not only an inn keeper, but also had a license to keep the Youngstown Ferry. Similarly, as Agnes Greensitt continued to manage the Greensitt Inn after Robert's death, so she was also granted a license to operate the Youngstown Ferry after Robert's death. A woman who operated both a tavern and a ferry, like a man, was not without precedent. In a section on "Female Inn Keepers" in his study *Colonial Americans at Work*, Herbert Applebaum writes:

> In many cases, taverns were located near ferries and innkeepers were appointed to run the ferry. In 1715, the North Carolina Council appointed Annie Wilson to keep "a good and sufficient ferry" over the Periquimans River. In 1756, a court in Beaufort County, North Carolina, appointed Elizabeth Hill to keep a ferry from her dwelling across the river to Richard Ellgoods's plantation.[113]

The 1813 New York State Ferry Law required that, if possible, ferry keepers should own the property of the road to the ferry landing site. Our clearest evidence for the Youngstown Ferry House is from an 1870 map, or by inference, an 1860 map, and from a possible Ferry House nearby dated possibly to the 1840s.[114] That site was below the Greensitt property and, as just noted, Agnes Greensitt was responsible for road work there (State Street?), probably in 1821. It is therefore striking that there is a surviving record of Agnes' license to operate the Youngstown Ferry, that is, an 1816 report of the New York State Senate that records her petition to renew her ferry license.

> The petition of Agnes Greensett, widow of Robert Greensett deceased, setting forth, that the said Robert in his life time, obtained a grant to keep a ferry between Youngstown and the Canada shore, that since his death she has kept the said ferry one year, under a license of the court of common pleas of Niagara county, and praying that the legislature may authorize a licence [*sic*] to be granted for her for such length of time, in such manner and under such restrictions and regulations, as may be deemed most

---

[113] Herbert Applebaum, *Colonial Americans at Work* (Lanham, MD; New York, NY; London, UK: University Press of America, Inc., 1996), 255-56.

[114] See the discussion of the Youngstown Ferry House, Ch. 16.

proper in order to keep a safe and convenient ferry at Youngstown, was read, and refered [sic] to a select committee, consisting of Mr. R. Smith, Mr. Prendergast and Mr. Ganson.[115]

Clearly, the widow Greensitt had possessed a Youngstown Ferry license for at least one year, a license officially granted by the Court of Common Pleas of Niagara County, perhaps for the year 1816, but perhaps 1815 or, less likely, even earlier (according to the 1813 law licenses were limited to one year; had she renewed before?). Agnes wanted to extend her license, but she was not petitioning the County Court of Common Pleas at Lockport, as was legal and customary, but rather the New York State Senate in Albany. Again, she was petitioning for *an extension of the license that had already been granted at least once for one year*. Her request was submitted to a Senate select committee which reported back:

Mr. R. Smith, from the select committee, to whom was referred the petition of Agnes Grensett [sic], reported, that the object of the petitioner is to obtain an extension of the license, by which she is permitted to keep a ferry across the Niagara river at Youngstown.

The reason assigned for that measure is, that the ferry cannot be kept as it should be, without incurring considerable expense in boats, repairs and attendance; and that after all, her right is secured but for one year, after which time another may obtain the ferry, and her boats and property in them may be sacrificed.

It is true that the ferry is put upon that footing, and the fortune of any application must rest upon that contingency, according to the present law.

---

[115] *Journal of the Senate of the State of New York: at their Fortieth Session, Begun and held at the Capitol, the City of Albany, the Fifth Day of November, 1816* (Albany, NY: J. Buel, 1816), 138. The description accords with state ferry laws. If she kept the ferry for one year after Robert's death, did Robert die in 1815?

If it is the object of the law to secure rights to their possessors, the enquiry follows, whether the individual who would keep a ferry should have his licence [*sic*] secured by a longer term than one year. The committee are aware that this ferry cannot be kept without considerable expense in boats and implements. But while it admits the possibility that the petitioner may be unduly dispossessed of it, and may consequently sustain an injury, it sees the power of granting the licence [*sic*] delegated to a court, which must be supposed to be too intelligent not to discern the claims of every applicant, and too impartial to bestow its favors on the undeserving.

The committee will further observe, that a suggestion is advanced through the medium of a friend to the petitioner, that a competitor has formerly attempted to wrest the ferry from her, and that improper instruments were employed for that purpose, and that the real right of the petitioner was endangered thereby. It is known by one member of this committee that this suggestion is founded on fact.

But the committee are of [the] opinion, that it is rather the duty of the court to guard the rights of applicants, than for the legislature to adopt any new principles in relation to them.

Resolved, That the house do concur with the committee, in their said report.

Resolved, That the petitioner have leave to withdraw her said petition.[116]

The widow Greensitt, who must have supported her family by running a new tavern and the ferry, received a hearing and even the sympathy of the Senate committee and Senate itself, but not much more. They recognized that her husband and she had received a previous ferry license and even that a competitor had "formerly attempted to wrest the ferry from her, and that improper instruments were employed for that purpose, and that the real right of the petitioner was endangered thereby."[117] However, they also recognized that she needed to invest a considerable amount of money in boats, equipment, repairs, and men to operate it (as

---

[116] Ibid.

[117] Who was the anonymous competitor? We do not know. Could it have been Elijah Hathaway, who, like Agnes Greensitt, was operating a hotel in 1816 and 1817 and was running the ferry by 1821? See below, *The Town of Porter Book of Records*.

a Sufferer, she, unlike Elijah Hathaway, the ferry keeper from 1821-1823, was "in want" after the war[118]). The committee's response, accepted by the Senate, was to fall back on the state ferry law. The decision was that the Niagara County Court of Pleas at Lockport should resolve the problem. We do not know what the Court of Pleas in Lockport actually decided, but she was a woman "in want," and despite our knowledge of other known ferry women, the judge and all the known licensed ferry keepers on the Niagara River were men.

Let us now indulge in a bit of historical imagination by comparing Agnes Greensitt to Youngstown's most famous heroic woman, Betsy Doyle.[119]

Andrew Doyle, Betsy Doyle's husband, was born in St. Davids, Ontario, and therefore a British Canadian, but in 1810 he enlisted in a United States artillery unit stationed at Fort Niagara. Since military wives were allowed to live with military husbands, perhaps she lived with him at the fort, perhaps serving as a matron doing drudge work. However, Andrew was captured at the Battle of Queenston Heights on October 13, 1812, was sent to York, then Kingston, and then Montreal. Because of his British heritage, Doyle was one of twenty-three or so prisoners considered to be British traitors and used as an example to be tried for treason. He was shipped to England where Doyle suffered in imprisonment, but was eventually released after the war, returned to the United States in 1815, married in 1819, received a pension, and died in Canada.

What happened to Betsy and Agnes?

Consider first Betsy. After Andrew was captured in October of 1812, Betsy and her children might have continued to live at the Fort, but because her husband was no longer there,

---

[118] We have wondered whether the soon-to-be ferryman Elijah Hathaway was her unjust, unnamed competitor, but there is no evidence for that, and his brother Olaf was certainly remembered as having had a sterling character (see Ch. 7).

[119] Our major source for Betsy Doyle is Catherine Emerson, "An Industrious and Worthy Woman. The Chronicle of Betsy/Mary Doyle and her Husband Andrew," *Old Fort Niagara* (November/December, 2011); see also "War of 1812 Heroine: Betsy Doyle," which also honors Niagara County Historian Catherine Emerson's research on Betsy, http://www.nyusd1812.org/our-ancestors/betsy-doyle.html; J. Maloni, "Maziarz announces War of 1812 Heroine Betsy Doyle awarded Women of Distinction," Lewiston-Porter Sentinel (Mar 16, 2012), http://www.wnypapers.com/news/article/current/2012/03/16/105821/maziarz-announces-war-of-1812-heroine-betsy-doyle-awarded-women-of-distinction; "Autumn 1812: Betsy Doyle Helps Operate a Cannon to Defend Fort Niagara," National Park Service, https://www.nps.gov/articles/betsy-doyle.htm.

she might also have moved to Youngstown.[120] If so, she no doubt would have known (Robert and?) Agnes Greensitt since at the time, as noted previously, Youngstown was a tiny frontier settlement of only a few houses. In that case, she, like Agnes Greensitt, would have heard bombardments of Fort Niagara by the British on November 21, 1813. However, perhaps she was still at the Fort. Either way, Betsy ended up carrying hot shot for the six-pound cannon that was strategically positioned on the "French Castle" roof. For this heroic act, she is justifiably famous.

How did Betsy escape? That is unknown, but if she was living in Youngstown rather than at the Fort, she would have more easily escaped with her children. After a hard 310-mile trek, a journey of nearly four months, she ended up in Greenbush Cantonment, an army post near Albany, New York.[121] There she became a nurse and laundress for six years, sometimes without military pay. She became ill and died in 1819, probably, due to her wages, without the aid she so desperately needed.[122]

Agnes Greensitt, meanwhile, was either helping to run (again, her husband's exact date of death is uncertain), or perhaps running by herself, the Greensitt Inn and Tavern, probably located at the top of the bluff facing the Niagara River across from British Newark/Niagara, not far from the ferry landing below. If Robert was away or already deceased, she might have also been operating the Youngstown Ferry. If so, she would have been left alone with her five children. Whatever the case, on December 19, 1813, the British took Fort Niagara forcefully by surprise and then headed south. They burned Youngstown, including her tavern and the other buildings on the Greensitt property. Perhaps the Greensitt ferry boat and equipment were confiscated, damaged, or destroyed; they were not specifically mentioned in her Sufferer's report.[123]

---

[120] Emerson, "An Industrious and Worthy Woman": "It has not yet been determined whether Betsy's house was in the Fort proper, which extended much further south than present, or if she lived on the edge of the fort in Youngstown."

[121] A "cantonment," related etymologically to the Swiss district called a "canton," was a military encampment for a long period of time—longer than temporary encampments such as those that moved forward at times of advances and backward at times of retreats.

[122] Ibid.

[123] In escaping the British, Betsy Doyle and her children walked over three hundred miles east to the East Greenbush Cantonment, a journey of nearly four months. Although she did not always receive military pay, she

Agnes escaped with her five children. She journeyed to Batavia and then went on to Ontario County. Whereas Betsy never returned to Youngstown, Agnes clearly did. The *Town of Porter Book of Records* for 1816 and 1817 continued to list "Agnes Greensett" among "Records of Recognizance's for Inn Keepers"; she also applied for renewal of her ferry license in 1816; she was responsible for maintaining a road near the Greensitt property in 1821; and, as we have seen, her descendants inherited that property.[124]

Betsy and Agnes were amazing women who took up the roles of their husbands and in this regard a further comment is appropriate. An influential study by social historian Lauren Thatcher Ulrich describes colonial and frontier American working class women who took up their husbands' occupations and social roles when their husbands were not present for some reason, such as men at war, men at sea, men deceased. Ulrich calls them "deputy husbands."[125] Certainly, these two heroic Youngstown women, Betsy Doyle and Agnes Greensitt, fit the role of Ulrich's "deputy husbands." They assumed traditional male roles, survived in wartime, escaped, and attempted to put their lives back together in the post-war period.[126]

---

became a nurse and laundress for six years. She became ill and died in 1819, probably without the aid she so desperately needed.

[124] For more on the Greensitt property in relation to Youngstown's Ferry House, see Ch. 16.

[125] Lauren Thatcher Ulrich, *Good Wives: Images and Reality in the LIves of Women in the Northern New England, 1650-1750* (New York, NY: Alfred A. Knopf, 1982), 34-35. "Social role" is a major category of analysis in the social sciences and Ulrich uses the language "role performance."

[126] As noted (n. 119), the main source for Betsy Doyle is the Niagara County Historian, Kate Emerson, who is her champion. Led by Emerson, Betsy Doyle has been inducted into New York State's Women of Distinction and a Betsy Doyle historical marker was dedicated in Youngstown's Falkner Park on March 22, 2014. Gretchen Duling was an organizer for the December 19, 1813, commemoration of the burning of Youngstown. See "The War of 1812," http://www.oldfortniagara.org/history.

PART II
Seven Accounts

Part I attempted to set the stage for understanding Youngstown's strategic location and role in the Underground Railroad. It included an introduction to slavery, sketches of Anti-Slavery Societies including meetings at Youngstown; nineteenth-century census data for Niagara County; the problems and solutions of crossing inland waterways in the United States; watercraft and trains at Youngstown; and New York State ferry laws with a timeline of Youngstown's ferrymen, including a ferrywoman.

Part II, the heart of the book, is derived from primary and supporting sources. We have ordered them according to the likely chronology of the events they describe.

Chapter 7: ex-fugitive slave Thomas James' autobiographical account (1886) about a Youngstown citizen who ferried him to Canada (1821); **Chapter 8**: Samuel Ringgold Ward's autobiographical account (1855) about a fugitive slave who crossed from Youngstown and warmed himself at the Niagara Ferry House (1853); **Chapter 9:** letters and newspaper evidence about Ben Hockley, a fugitive slave who failed in his attempt to cross at Youngstown on an old gate, but was miraculously rescued by a steamer (1853); **Chapter 10:** John VanDeusen's diary entry about fugitive slaves, Daniel (father) and James (son), who were sent from Newark, New York, to meet a Youngstown agent—"Mr. Pardee" (1855); **Chapter 11**: Thomas Birnmore's letter to Wilbur Siebert recalling two slaves he hid in his room at the *Lockport Daily Journal*, who were sent to Youngstown and ferried across the Niagara River by an anonymous Youngstown farmer (1856 or 1857); **Chapter 12**: UGRR Conductor Eber Pettit's interview about an 1861 carriage race from Niagara Falls to the Youngstown Ferry as a diversion, allowing a fugitive slave Cassey to escape from Niagara Falls to the Lockport area; and **Chapter 13**: a soldier later recalls that eleven fugitive slaves who landed at the King's Wharf (Navy Hall Wharf) below Fort George next to Niagara[-on-the-Lake], Ontario, no doubt via the Youngstown Ferry (ca. 1862).

These seven accounts reveal that the Village of Youngstown on the Niagara River was an Underground Railroad crossing point to Canada and that some Youngstown citizens participated in helping fugitive slaves cross to freedom and were part of the UGRR network.

CHAPTER 7

Youngstown's Olaf Hathaway Ferried Fugitive Slave Thomas James to Niagara, Canada, 1821

Image 7.1

Thomas James and Olaf Hathaway

In 1883, this statement appeared in the *Niagara County News*, Friday, September 21:

Rev. Thos. James (colored) of Rochester preached in the [Youngstown] Presbyterian Church Sunday evening [September 16, 1883] to a full house, comprising the congregations of that church and the M.E. church. Rev. James is an old man, being now in his 80th year, and was one of the first Anti-Slavery lecturers of the country, for which he was mobbed at LeRoy and other places. He was born in slavery, but fled from his captors when quite a young man, and crossed the river [Lower Niagara] in his flight sixty-three years ago [1821] at this place [Youngstown]. *Olaf Hathaway, an old resident of this place long since dead* [1840], *ferried him across.* He [Thomas James] afterwards returned and resided several months in this locality.[1] At the close of the service a collection was taken up for his benefit and about $7 realized. He lectured in the Presbyterian Church at Lewiston Tuesday evening.[2]

The Reverend Thomas James Photo (1804-1891)
Photo: Find a Grave (Mt. Hope Cemetery, Rochester, New York)[3]
Image 7.2

---

[1] In his *Autobiography*, James says that in this period he chopped wood for John Rich.

[2] *Niagara County News,* Youngstown, NY, Sept. 21, 1883, 4:3 (italics ours). This statement was also reported to members of the Town of Porter Historical Society by Vee L. Housman in 2001, http://newsfeed.rootsweb.com/th/read/NYNIAGAR/2001-09/1000862274; it is also cited by Wellman, "Site of the Ferry Landing at Youngstown," Wellman, Judith. "Site of the Ferry Landing at Youngstown," *Survey of Sites, Appendix C,* 177-81. http://www.niagarafallsundergroundrailroad.org/assets/Uploads/NF-HAMP-Report-Appendix-C-1.pd.; "UGRR SITES." http://www.niagarafallsundergroundrailroad.org/.

[3] "Find a Grave." http://www.findagrave.com/cgi-bin/fg.cgi?page=gr&GRid=23570464. This photo has not been otherwise confirmed, but the handwritten Register of Interments, Mt. Hope Cemetery, Rochester, NY, has Thomas James, age 91 (!), died of pneumonia, buried on April 2, 1892 (!), residing on Tremont St., Section NW[7]Pt 3671/2 (R 8-1). He could not have been 91 if he was born in 1804, but his chronology is sometimes uncertain, see n. 6. Perhaps his supposed age, 91 was related to the year of his death , 1891. http://www.lib.rochester.edu/IN/RBSCP/Databases/IMAGES/MtHope/disc1/00000987.pdf.

The Reverend Thomas James Burial Marker, Mt. Hope Cemetery, Rochester, New York
Photo: Find a Grave
Image 7.3

The following excerpts are taken from the *Life of Rev. Thomas James, by Himself.*[4] It should be noted that in this noteworthy and revealing document, the conditions of slavery and the many consequences African Americans had to face, even after being freed, are described. We have quoted, judiciously we hope, more than the usual amount of primary source material. Thomas James's last words, we believe, are especially relevant in today's world of the Twenty-First Century (see p. 413).

Excerpts from *Life of Rev. Thomas James, by Himself,* 1886[5]

[No changes in spelling or punctuation from the original text have been made. The pages used within the source are numbered.]

---

[4] Selections from Thomas James, *Life of Rev. Thomas James, by Himself* (Rochester, NY: Post Express Printing Company, 1886), 5-23.
[5] For an initial excerpt from Thomas James' *Autobiography*, see Ch. 1.

TO THE READER.

The story of my life is a simple one, perhaps hardly worth the telling. I have written it in answer to many and oft repeated requests on the part of my friends for a relation of its incidents, and to them I dedicate this little volume.

THE AUTHOR

[Page 5] Rochester, Feb. 15, 1886. I was born a slave at Canajoharie, this state [New York], in the year 1804.[6] I was the third of four children, and we were all the property of Asa Kimball,[7] who, when I was in the eighth year of my age, sold my mother, brother and elder sister to purchasers from Smithtown, a village not far distant from Amsterdam in the same part of the state. My mother refused to go and ran into the garret [small attic room] to seek a hiding place. She was pursued, caught, tied hand and foot and delivered to her new owner. I caught my last sight of my mother as they rode off with her. My elder brother and sister were taken away at the same time. I never saw either my mother or sister again. Long years afterwards my brother and I were reunited, and he died in this city [Rochester] a little over a year ago. From him I learned that my mother died about the year 1846 in the place to which she had been taken. My brother also informed me that he and his sister were separated soon after their transfer to a Smithport [Tennessee] master, and that he never heard of her subsequent fate. Of my father I never had any personal knowledge, and, indeed, never heard anything. My other sister, the youngest member of the family, died when I was yet a youth.

While I was still in the seventeenth year of my age [1821], Master Kimball was killed in a runaway accident; and at the administrator's sale I was sold with the rest of the property, my new master being Cromwell Bartlett of the same neighborhood. As I remember, my first master was a well-to-do but rough farmer, a skeptic in religious matters, but of better heart than address; for he treated me well. He owned several farms and my work was that of a farmhand. My new master had owned me but a few

---

[6] A slave often did not know the exact year or day of his or her birth; nonetheless, we have placed possible dates in brackets in his narrative and suggested them in our commentary. See n. 3.

[7] Judith Wellman places the farm of Asa Kimball, Thomas James' first master, near Buel, a hamlet in the Town of Canajoharie, New York, forty-one miles east of Utica. Kimball settled in this Mohawk Valley region about 1800 and had several farms (email attachment 11/13/16).

[Page 6] months [late 1821 to March 1822?] when he sold me, or rather traded me, to George H. Hess, a wealthy farmer of the vicinity of Fort Plain [New York].[8] I was bartered in exchange for a yoke of steers, a colt and some additional property, the nature and amount of which I have now forgotten. I remained with Master Hess from March until June of the same year [1822?], when I ran away. My master had worked me hard, and at last undertook to whip me. This led me to seek escape from slavery. I arose in the night, and taking the then newly staked line of the Erie Canal for my route, traveled along it westward until, about a week later, I reached the village of Lockport [New York]. No one had stopped me in my flight. Men were at work digging the new canal at many points, but they never troubled themselves even to question me. I slept in barns at night and begged food at farmers' houses along my route. At Lockport a colored man showed me the way to the Canadian border. *I crossed the Niagara [River] at Youngstown on the ferry boat, and was free!*[9]

Once on free soil, I began to look about for work, and found it at a point called Deep Cut on the Welland Canal, which they were then digging.[10] I found the laborers a rough lot and soon had a mind to leave them. After three months had passed, I supposed it safe to return to the American side, and acting on the idea I crossed the [Niagara] river. *A farmer named Rich, residing near Youngstown, engaged me as a wood chopper.*[11] In the spring I made my way to Rochesterville [New York village from 1817–1834, which became the city of Rochester, New York] and found a home with Lawyer Talbert. The chores about his place were left to me, and I performed the same service for Orlando Hastings. I was then nineteen years of age [1823?]. As a slave I had never been inside of a school or a church, and I knew nothing of letters or religion. The wish to

---

[8] Judith Wellman, "Town of Minden, Hessville Homes and Cemetery," notes that George H. Hess (1773-1840) was married to Maria Elizabeth Yordan in 1793, that the couple had eight children, and that their daughter Catherine, second oldest, was married to Cromwell K. Barlett, the second owner of "Tom" (email attachment 11/13/16).

[9] Italics ours. The ferry license from 1821-1823 was possessed by Elijah Hathaway, brother of Olaf Hathaway. See Chs. 6, 14, 16, and below.

[10] James' memory chronology—he appears to refer to 1822-1823—is difficult to coordinate with the construction of the Deep Cut, November 30, 1824 (ground-breaking ceremony)—November 26, 1829. See "The Old Welland Canal Fields Guide." http://oldwellandcanals.wikidot.com/the-deep-cut; http://www.tbhs.ca/hughes/tunnel.html.

[11] Italics ours. The *Niagara County News*, September 21, 1883 (above) reports that "he returned and resided in this vicinity [Youngstown] several months [Fall 1822-Spring 1823]." This fits his comment that he was age nineteen.

learn awoke in me almost from the moment I set foot in the place, and I soon obtained an excellent chance to carry the wish into effect. After the opening of the Erie Canal, [1825] I obtained work in the warehouse of the Hudson and Erie line and found a home with its manager, Mr. Pliny Allen Wheeler. I was taught to read by Mr. Freeman, who had opened a Sunday school of his own for colored youths, on West Main Street, or Buffalo Street as it was then called. But my self-education advanced fastest in the warehouse during the long winter and spring months when the canal was closed and my only work consisted of chores about the place and at my employer's residence. The clerks helped me whenever I needed help in my studies. Soon I had learning enough to be placed in charge of the freight business of the warehouse, with full direction over the lading of boats. I became a member of the African Methodist Episcopal Society in 1823, when the church was on Ely Street, and my studies soon took the direction of **[p. 7]** preparation for the ministry.

In 1828 I taught a school for colored children on Favor Street, and I began holding meetings at the same time. In the following year I first formally commenced preaching, and in 1830 I bought as a site for a religious edifice the lot now occupied by Zion's church. In the meantime the Ely street society had ceased to exist, its death having been hastened by internal quarrels and by dishonesty among its trustees. On the lot already mentioned, I built a small church edifice, which was afterwards displaced by a larger one, the latter finally giving way to the present structure on the same site. I was ordained as a minister in May, 1833, by Bishop Rush. I had been called Tom as a slave and they called me Jim at the warehouse. I put both together when I reached manhood and was ordained as Rev. Thomas James. . . **[p. 8]** . . . At Palmyra [New York] I found no hall or church in which I could speak. Indeed, the place was then a mere hamlet and could boast of but half a dozen dwellings. My tour embraced nearly every village in this and adjoining counties, and the treatment given me varied with the kind of people I happened to find in the budding settlements of the time. In the same fall [1835] I attended the first Anti-Slavery State Convention at Utica [New York; see pp. 36-37].

In 1835 I left Rochester to form a colored church at Syracuse . . . I was stationed nearly three years at Syracuse, and was then transferred to Ithaca, where a little colored religious society already existed. I bought a site for a church edifice for them, and saw it built during the two years of my stay in the village. Thence I was sent to Sag Harbor, Long Island, [New York] and, finally, to New Bedford, Massachusetts. . .

It was at New Bedford that I first saw Fred. Douglass. He was then, so to speak, right out of slavery, but had already begun to talk in public, though *not before White people*. He had been given authority to act as an exhorter by the church before my coming, and I some time afterwards licensed him to preach. *He was then a member of my church.*[12]

[pp. 9 and 10 omitted]

[Page 11] One of the earliest cases in which I became interested as a laborer in the Anti-Slavery cause was that of the Emstead [Amistad] captives. The slaver Emstead was a Spanish vessel which left the African coast in 1836 with a cargo of captive Blacks. When four days out the slaves rose, and, coming on deck, threw overboard all but two of the officers and crew. The two they saved to navigate the vessel; but instead of taking the vessel back to the coast they had just left, as they were directed by the Blacks, the two sailors attempted to make the American main, and the vessel finally drifted ashore near Point Judith, on Long Island Sound. The Spanish minister demanded the surrender of the Blacks to his government. They were taken off the ship and sent to Connecticut

---

[12] Italics and boldface not in original. On Fredrick Douglas, see pp. 35-36 above.

for trial. Arthur Tappan[13] and Richard Johnson interested themselves in the captives, and succeeded in postponing their trial for two and a half years. Two young men were meanwhile engaged to instruct the captives, and when their trial at last came, they were able to give evidence which set them free. They testified that they had been enticed on board of the slaver in small parties for the ostensible purpose of trade, and had then been thrown into the hold and chained. There were nearly one hundred of the captives, and on their release we tried hard but vainly to persuade them to stay in this country. I escorted them on shipboard when they were about to sail from New York for their native land.

[Pages 12–15 omitted]

[p. 16] I returned to Rochester in 1856, and took charge of the colored church in this city. In 1862 I received an appointment from the American Missionary Society to labor among the colored people of Tennessee and Louisiana, but I never reached either of these states. I left Rochester. . .

[Pages 17–20 omitted]

[p. 21] Many a sad scene I witnessed at my camp of colored refugees in Louisville [Kentucky]. There was the mother bereaved of her children, who had been sold and sent farther south lest they should escape in the general rush for the federal lines and freedom; children, orphaned in fact if not in name, for separation from parents among the colored people in those days left no hope of reunion this side [of] the grave; wives forever parted from their husbands, and husbands who might never hope to catch again the bright-eye and the welcoming smile of the helpmates whose hearts God and nature

---

[13] Brothers Arthur and Lewis Tappan were Congregationalist Calvinists, successful businessmen, and abolitionists who had helped William Lloyd Garrison found the New England Anti-Slavery Society, the American Anti-Slavery Society in 1833, abolitionist Oberlin College in 1935 (which boasts a Tappan Square and a Tappan Hall), and the American and Foreign Anti-Slavery Society in 1840. They supported the defense of the Amistad African slaves in 1839-1840 and the Underground Railroad. See Lewis Tappan, *The Life of Arthur Tappan* (New York, NY: Hurd and Houghton, 1870).

had joined to theirs. Such recollections come fresh to me when with trembling voice I sing the old familiar song of Anti-Slavery days:

> Oh deep was the anguish of the slave mother's heart
>
> When called from her darling forever to part;
>
> So grieved that lone mother, that heart-broken mother
>
> In sorrow and woe.
>
> The child was borne off to a far distant clime
>
> While the mother was left in anguish to pine;
>
> But reason departed and she sank broken-hearted
>
> In sorrow and woe. . .

[p. 22] In June, 1868, I was elected general superintendent and missionary agent by the General Conference of the African Methodist Episcopal Congregation [Washington D.C.].

My last charge was the pastorate of the African Methodist Episcopal Church at Lockport [New York]. Between three and four years ago both my eyes became affected by cataracts, and I now grope my way in almost complete blindness . . . My home is again in the city of Rochester, where I began my life work. In 1829 I married in this city a free colored girl, and by her had four children, two of whom are now married and living at the West. My first wife died in 1841. Sixteen years ago [1870] I married again. My wife was a slave, freed by Sherman at the capture of Atlanta and sent north . . . She is the companion of my old age. . .

[p. 23] . . . I sing the old "Liberty Minstrel" songs, which carry me back to the days when the conscience of the North was first awakened to the iniquities of slavery. Blessed be God that I have lived to see the liberation and the enfranchisement of the people of my color and blood!

The Rev. Thomas James concludes his 1886 book by asking and answering a question:

[p. 23] You ask me what change for the better has taken place in the condition of the colored people of this locality in my day. I answer that the Anti-Slavery agitation developed an active and generous sympathy for the free colored man of the North, as well as for his brother in bondage. We felt the good effect of that sympathy and the aid and encouragement which accompanied it. But now, that the end of the Anti-Slavery agitation has been fully accomplished, our White friends are inclined to leave us to our own resources, overlooking the fact that social prejudices still close the trades against our youth, and that we are again as isolated as in the days before the wrongs of our race touched the heart of the American people. After breathing for so considerable a period an atmosphere surcharged with sympathy for our race, we feel the more keenly the cold current of neglect which seems to have chilled against us even the enlightened and religious classes of the communities among which we live, but of which we cannot call ourselves a part.[14]

Thomas James' Obituary, 1891

(*Holly* [New York] *Standard*, April 30, 1891)

Rev. Thomas James

Rev. Thomas James, the colored preacher who died in Rochester April 18, was one of the best known colored men in this section of the state. He has visited most of the villages near Rochester, selling his autobiography and has from time to time preached in many Western New York churches while going about soliciting aid for some church enterprise in which he was interested.

---

[14] *Life of Rev. Thomas James, by Himself* (Rochester, NY: Post Express, 1886), 23. Electronic version funded by the National Endowment for the Humanities. http://docsouth.unc.edu/neh/jamesth/jamesth.html.

He was born a slave in Canajoharie, N. Y., in 1804. His parents were sold when he was eight years old and he never saw them again. He was sold to a farmer for a yoke of oxen and made his escape traveling along the line of the Erie Canal then being dug to Lockport, *and from there to Youngstown,*[15] *where he crossed to Canada* and found work on the Welland canal then also being dug.

Subsequently he returned to Rochester. He was a preacher in Lockport several years. In 1837 he ordained Fred Douglass, who had then recently been released from slavery. Many of our readers can scarcely believe that New York was a slave state within the memory of some now living.[16]

The Farmer John Rich and the Fugitive Slave Thomas James

We cite two sources for John Rich, Thomas James's autobiography and the Federal Census records of 1830. James's autobiographical comment reads: "After three months [from my crossing to Canada from Youngstown] had passed, I supposed it safe to return to the American side, and acting on the idea I recrossed the river. *A farmer named Rich, residing near Youngstown, engaged me as a wood chopper.*"[17] The U. S. Census of 1830, indicates that John Rich was the head of a household of nine White persons, that is, one male between ages 50 and

---

[15] Italics ours.

[16] *Holly Standard*, April 30, 1891 (italics ours). Again, Thomas James's precise chronology is not always easy to determine. The *Niagara County News* of Friday, September 21, 1883, reports that he was "in his 80th year" when he spoke the previous Sunday, September 16, 1883, at the Presbyterian Church. Presumably that means that he was age 79 and would have been born before September 21, 1804. That can fit his obituary that he was born in 1804. However, this date is not easy to coordinate with the comment in his *Autobiography* that he was 17 years old when he was sold to Cromwell Bartlett, then a few months later to George H. Hess with whom he stayed "from March until June of the same year" (Spring of 1822?), then escaped to Lockport, went to Youngstown, crossed the river, found work on the "Deep Cut of the Welland Canal," and was back in Rochester at age 19 (September 21, 1823—September 21, 1824?). It is unlikely that it took him two years to get to the canal and then return to Rochester at age 19, and still work on the "Deep Cut" of the Welland Canal, which did not begin until November of 1824 (see Alan Hughes, "Merrit's Survey and the Tunnel to Nowhere," Thorold and Beaverdams Historical Society, http://www.tbhs.ca/hughes/tunnel.html; http://oldwellandcanals.wikidot.com/the-deep-cut). One must remember again that birth dates of fugitive slaves are often imprecise and that James was drawing on memory and the sequence of events more than sixty years later. He seems to be rather accurate for ages seventeen to nineteen (1821-1823) otherwise.

[17] James, *Life of Rev. Thomas James, by Himself*, 6 (our italics). http://www.math.buffalo.edu/~sww/0history/thomas.james.narrative.html .

60, one female between 30 and 40, one male between 20 and 30, one female between 15 and 20, and five children between the ages of 5 and 10, that is, 4 boys and 1 girl.[18]

This information about John Rich is brief, but potentially informative for the UGRR in several ways: 1) after some freedom seekers arrived in Canada they continued to cross the Niagara River back and forth when they had jobs or wanted to continue their involvement in the UGRR (examples: Harriet Tubman and Cassey); 2) local ferryman were not just involved in ferrying freedom seekers, but also must have gotten to know African Americans who took the Youngstown Ferry back and forth from Youngstown to Niagara; 3) some local White citizens of Youngstown must have been aware of these crossings and even ridden the ferry with African Americans; and 4) it is plausible that African Americans were occasionally seen in the tiny village of Youngstown; we have cited some free African Americans in Niagara County and in 1865 a Black family, that is, a Mulatto barber and his family, that lived in the village.[19]

Olaf Hathaway

We note again three sources about Thomas James. His obituary says that he crossed to Canada from Youngstown; his *Autobiography* says that he took the Youngstown Ferry to Canada; and the *Niagara County News* of September 21, 1883, reported that the one who "ferried" the fugitive slave Thomas James across the Niagara River to freedom was Youngstown's Olaf Hathaway. What can be said about Olaf Hathaway?[20]

---

[18] Federal Census, Town of Porter, 1830, 324, John Rich was a "head of family," a "Free *White*," and a "male."

[19] See Chs. 3, 14.

[20] Thanks to Karen Noonan, who has a special interest in Olaf Hathaway. In addition to local sources, she relies heavily on Elizabeth Starr Versailles, *Hathaway's of America* (Northampton, MA: Gazette Print. Co. 1970; Supplement, Hathaway Family Association, 1980), 185 (ref. 139) and Karen Foley, *Early Settlers of New York State: Their Ancestors* (1934—1942; reprint 2006). Gretchen and Dennis have consulted *History of Niagara County*, 335a; Pool, *Landmarks*, 260-61; *A Bicentennial History, 1776 – 1976 of the Town of Porter* (Historical Society of the Town of Porter, 1976), 9; Suzanne Simon Dietz, *From Flames & Four Flags The Town of Porter Yesterday and Today* (Youngstown, NY: BeauDesigns, 2012); Dietz and Karen Noonan, *Early Town of Porter Residents 1800 – 1829* (Suzanne Simon Dietz, 2013); records and notes in the Town of Porter Historical Society Museum; and ferryman applications in the Niagara Country Historian's Office, with thanks to Catherine Emerson, Historian; Craig E. Bacon, Deputy Historian, and Ronald F. Cary, Deputy Historian.

We have already given some basic information about Olaf's family.[21] Olaf was Elijah's younger brother. Former Town of Porter Historian Vee Housman's transcription of the *Book of Records of the Town of Porter, 1815—1823* listed other Hathaways as Alfred Hathaway, 1821-1822; Alfred Sr., 1823; Alfred Jr. 1823; Elijah 1815-1823; E. [?] 1815; and O. [?] 1821, Olef 1822, and Olif 1823—different spellings of Olaf.[22] The Universal Cemetery behind the Presbyterian Church (corner of Main and Church Streets) has a marker inscribed with the following six names: Alfred D. Hathaway (1752—1828), Olaf's father; Rebecca Hathaway (1760—1850), Olaf's mother; Olaf Hathaway (1790—1840); Betsy Doran Hathaway (1802—1826), Olaf's first wife; Adaline B. Richards Hathaway (1806—1883), Olaf's second wife; and Adaline M. Hathaway, died June 7, 1832, aged 10 months, who must have been the daughter of Olaf and his second wife, Adaline B. Hathaway. Note the year and day of Betsy Doran Hathaway's death: March 17, 1826. That was the exact year and day that the first of Olaf's two daughters, also named Betsy, was born. Secondary sources sometimes claim that she was the daughter of Olaf's second wife, Adaline B. Richards Hathaway,[23] but the death of the mother and birth of the baby girl on the same day, plus the name "Betsy D." for the baby girl make it virtually certain that her mother was Betsy Doran Hathaway who died in childbirth. Note that Olaf's daughter Betsy D. Hathaway would have been aged 24 in 1850, and that is exactly what we find in the Federal Census of 1850.

---

[21] See Chs. 6 and 14 for more information about the Hathaways, especially Elijah Hathaway.

[22] See also Dietz and Noonan, *Early Town of Porter Residents,* 22. Housman's transcription is from the *Book of Records of the town of Porter* at the Office of the Niagara County Historian in Lockport. Spellings in these records vary—"Olaf," "Olef," "Olif," "Oliff." Another spelling was "Olaff" (see below). A hand-written genealogical study of the Hathaways in the Town of Porter Museum by Town of Porter Town Historian Vee Hausman (deceased) tries to sort out the Hathaways by suggesting that Elijah and Mary Hathaway's first son was "Alfred" and a second son, Alfred's brother, was called "Oliff." However, in her marginal notes, Hausman raises the question whether Elijah's *brother* was "Alfred," and whether *Alfred* Sr. was the father of Alfred Jr. and Olaf. An article, *"DAR Traces Another Son of the American Revolution,"* in *The Buffalo News,* June 20, 1981, claims that "Albert J. Hathaway," whose grave site is in the Universal Cemetery, built the Hathaway Inn and that *"Albert's"* brother was *"Isaac."* Yet, the current Universal Cemetery Hathaway grave marker beside which is the 1981 DAR identifying marker related to the *Buffalo News* article (visible in the grave marker photo below), actually has, as stated in other sources, the name "Alfred," not "Albert"!

[22] Donald C. Shaw and June P. Zintz, compilers, "Niagara County Purchasers Under Land Contracts in 1835," *Western New York Genealogical Society Journal,* 3/4 (March 1977): 161.

[23] Pool, *Landmarks*, 30.

The three brothers Elijah, "Oliff," and Alfred Jr. were all heads of households in the Federal Census of 1830. As noted, Elijah was residing in Lockport by 1830, but Alfred and Oliff were still in the Town of Porter where the Village of Youngstown is located. In Oliff's household was one Free White male aged 30-40 (Olaf would have been about 39), one Free White female aged 20-30 (Adeline would have been 24), one free White female aged 10-15, as well as one free White male and one free White female under the age of 5.

We know a little about Olaf from land records. In 1835, he had a land contract with the Holland Land Company to purchase land in Township 15, Range 9, a six-square mile parcel east of Youngstown.[24] We do not know if the contract was fulfilled. Also, Donald Ames' *Survey* states that Olaf "occupied [rented?] Lot 9" in the Village of Youngstown itself on June 10, 1833, and Ames adds that one should "see [the] map."[25] On the 1841 Lot 1 Mile Reserve map of Youngstown commissioned by Catherine Young, J. P. Haines shows that Lot 9 on Main Street was 520 Main Street, the next lot south of Lot 8 at 500 Main Street, the latter on the corner of Main and Hinman Streets. It appears that Olaf was in the process of purchasing 520 Main Street, but, again, there is no information about whether the contract was fulfilled. John Porter bought the lot in 1839 and Olaf died in 1840. That same lot was purchased in 1845 by Olaf's son-in-law Osborn Canfield, a farmer and husband of Olaf's daughter "Betsy D." In 1849, Bradley D. Davis bought it. He also inherited his father Jason Davis's Lot 8, or 500 Main Street, after his mother Martha died in 1864, at which time he also came into possession of the lots behind them on Second Street.[26] So it was that these lots fell to the Davis and Haskell families.[27] As noted, the 1830 Federal Census mentions Olaf, his second wife Adeline, a female aged 10-15, and a boy and a girl each under 5 years of age, but we cannot track exactly where they lived or whether Olaf actually owned the properties in or east of Youngstown.[28]

---

[24] Ibid.

[25] Ames, *Survey*, Vol. 3. Also, he appears to have had land transactions for Lot 21 of the Holland Land Company in 1837, which would have been outside the village; see the *Western New York Genealogical Society Journal* 3/4 (March 1977).

[26] 1870 map.

[27] See Ch. 14.

[28] Ibid.

We have discovered what Olaf might have done for a living at least part of his life. Recall that the American Steamboat Line on Lake Ontario run by the Ontario Steamboat Company advertised the steamship *Ontario* (1817-1831) and listed local agents who were in charge of freight and passenger tickets. In Chapter 4, we reproduced part of the ad from Rochester's *New York Spectator*, June 7, 1827. Here we give the full ad, which shows that the agent for the American Steamboat Line at Youngstown at that time was Olaf Hathaway.

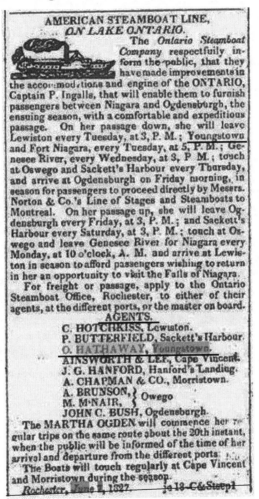

Rochester's *New York Spectator*, June 7, 1827 (Olaf Hathaway, Youngstown Agent)
Image 7.4

This advertisement—there are others like it in other newspapers[29]—adds to the information about Olaf's familiarity with the Niagara River. This possibility is reinforced by his name being added to John Beach's application for the Youngstown Ferry license in 1836 by the Clerk of Court proxy and his commitment thereto of $500.[30] Interestingly, Olaf Hathaway was associated with John Beach also in the following court evidence.

Court minutes of the Court of Common Pleas in Lockport mention Olaf and his brother Elijah a number of times.[31] In several cases, Olaf was the defendant. For example, in 1829 he was ordered to pay the Plaintiffs damages of $125.00 if in a forthcoming final judgment he could not show just cause why the damages should not be paid (*nisi*).[32] In another example "Olaff"—along with John Beach—was summoned to appear in court to face Plaintiff Nathan Ryan and others. Note the X.

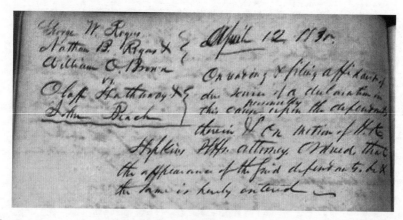

Affidavit Summoning Olaf Hathaway to the Court of Common Pleas, April 12, 1830
Image 7.5

---

[29] E.g., *The American, for the Country*, New York (June 1, 1827); *Albany Evening Journal*, Tuesday, Jun 15, 1830.
[30] See Ch. 6.
[31] *Court Minutes Common Pleas (May 1821-Sept. 19, 1831)*. See Ch. 6.
[32] Ibid., May 5, 1829.

Transcription by Dennis Duling:

George W. Rogers, Nathan B. Ryan**X**, and William O. Brown vs. Olaff Hathaway**X** & John Beach

April 12. 1830

On reading and filing affidavit of due [*illegible*] of a declaration in this cause∧^personally

upon the defendants therein. On motion of H. K. Hopkins Ptffs. [Plaintiffs'] Attorney, ordered, that the appearance of the said defendants (an **X** [by] the name) is hereby entered—

In sum, Olaf was the brother of a documented ferryman who ferried from 1821-1823; he himself was an agent for the Ontario Steamship Company in 1827; he was named along with John Beach in an affidavit in 1830; and he co-signed for $500 in the application of John Beach to be the ferryman in 1836. We have no evidence that he himself was a regularly operating ferryman, but these activities and family relationships certainly put him in position to have "ferried" Thomas James across the Niagara River in 1821—unless his ferryman brother Elijah was the actual ferryman and the 1883 *Niagara Falls Gazette* report some fifty-two years after the event was somehow in error.[33] Yet, there is a report that Olaf was a man of high moral character and great bravery, one who risked his life for others on the Niagara River. William Pool described Olaf Hathaway's upstanding character in 1897[34] and Karen Noonan has found its literary source, Olaf's obituary in the *Niagara Democrat and Lockport Balance* of 1840.

---

[33] Thomas James spoke at the Porter (First) Presbyterian Church in 1883, approximately fifty-two years after the event. He does not give the name of the ferryman in his *Autobiography*, but only that he was "ferried." Olaf was a member of the Presbyterian Church at Youngstown and his name is on the Hathaway grave marker (we do not have the date of the marker). The marker does not mention Elijah, who had moved to Ransomville. One might imagine that people in the congregation *thought* that Olaf was the ferryman and told that to the *Niagara Falls Gazette* reporter, when it was really Elijah the ferryman who ferried James across. However, there is no evidence for this speculation. Olaf knew the river and undoubtedly had access to (sometimes ran?) the Youngstown Ferry, and the surviving information about Olaf's brave and noble character fits the news report that it was Olaf. However, as noted in Ch. 6, Mrs. Rebecca Hathaway, Alfred Hathaway's wife and the mother of Olaf and Elijah, and their daughter Pauline Hathaway helped to form the Youngstown (Porter) Society in 1823 and the burial marker in the Universal Cemetery behind the Youngstown Presbyterian Church has members of Alfred's family.
[34] William Pool, ed., *Landmarks,* Part III, "Family Sketches," 30. https://archive.org/stream/landmarksofniaga00pool/landmarksofniaga00pool_djvu.txt (last accessed June 24, 2015). Reprint (London, UK: Forgotten Books, 2013) 577, http://www.forgottenbooks.com/readbook_text/Landmarks_of_Niagara_County_New_York_1000895084/577

At Youngstown, on Friday last Oliff Hathaway, aged 49 years. The deceased was in many respects one of the most remarkable men in Western New York. To a powerful frame he united a daring intrepid and generous spirit, which often led him to risk his life when the lives of others have been in jeopardy. In the winter season when the navigation of the Niagara has been obstructed by ice and boats have been in danger of being borne out into the lake, to the certain destruction of those on board, he has on many occasions gone out on floating ice and rescued them at the peril of his life. Whenever his fellow men were in danger, he was always near at hand to afford them relief; whenever the oppressed ask[ed] for assistance he was always prompt to furnish it. In all the relations of like he was an exemplary man and the community in which he lived all long regret his loss.[35]

The comments about helping his "fellow men . . . in danger" and his continual furnishing assistance to "the oppressed" are striking. They add to information about his knowledge of the Niagara River. Most of all, they are consistent with the report that he ferried the fugitive slave Thomas James to freedom.

Betsy D. Hathaway Canfield

We end with a note about Olaf's and Betsy Doran Hathaway's daughter, Betsy D. Hathaway Canfield, who might have been the ultimate source of the description of Olaf's sterling character in both his obituary and in Pool's *Landmarks*. According to Pool, she received her early education in Youngstown, but left at age seventeen to live in Willoughby, Ohio, for two years (to visit Hathaway relatives?). Upon her return in 1845, she married Osborn Canfield, a successful farmer, carpenter, businessman, and property owner in Youngstown.[36] If Betsy was the source of Olaf's obituary, did she know that her father had assisted the freedom seeker Thomas James to reach Canada? Did others of the oppressed he helped—fugitive slaves— receive such assistance along the way? Was Betsy herself sympathetic to their plight? Perhaps.

---

[35] *Niagara Democrat and Lockport Balance*, 5/24 (Wednesday February 5, 1840) page 3, column 2.
[36] Pool, *Landmarks* , 30.

Olaf Hathaway died in 1840. In the Federal Census of that year his brother Alfred Jr. and his wife Adeline are heads of households. In the 1850 Census, his daughter Betsy D. Canfield, age 24, was listed as the wife of the successful farmer, carpenter, property owner, and businessman, Osborn Canfield.

We return to the main point, that according to the *Niagara County News*, Friday, September 21, 1883, Olaf Hathaway was reported to have "ferried" fugitive slave Thomas James across the Niagara River to freedom in Canada.

Hathaway Grave Marker in the Universal Cemetery (Youngstown)
behind the Youngstown (First) Presbyterian Church
"Olaf Hathaway died Feb. 1, 1840 aged 50 years"
Photo by Karen Noonan
Image 7.6

CHAPTER 8

Samuel Ringgold Ward, a Youngstown Ferryman, and a Fugitive Slave, 1853

Image 8.1

Samuel Ringgold Ward was born in slavery in Maryland on October 17, 1817.[1] Three years later his family escaped with him to New Jersey,[2] and in 1826 his family moved to New York City in the free state of New York. He received a general education that furthered his interest in studying the Bible in an African Free School. After graduating, he worked as a teacher in African American schools and developed an acute interest in abolition. In his early 20's he married Emily E. Reynolds and in 1839 he was licensed to preach as a Congregational minister by the New York Congregational (General) Association. At the same time, he was

---

[1] Samuel Ringgold Ward, *Autobiography of a Fugitive Negro: his Anti-Slavery Labours in the United States, Canada and England* (London: John Snow, 35, Paternoster Row, 1855); Ronald K. Burke, *Studies in African American History and Culture* (ed. Graham Hodges; New York, NY, and London, UK: Garland Publishing, Inc., 1995); "Ward, Samuel Ringgold," *Dictionary of Canadian Biography* IX (1861-1870).
http://www.biographi.ca/en/bio/ward_samuel_ringgold_9E.html.

[2] New Jersey was not a free state. It had passed a gradual emancipation law in 1804, but it did not formally abolish slavery until 1846, and even then there was a loophole called "apprentices for life." New Jersey finally eliminated slavery in 1864. See Switala, "New Jersey—The Backdrop," in *Underground Railroad in New York and New Jersey*.

The Reverend Samuel Ringgold Ward (1817—1866)
Public Domain[3]
Image 8.2

---

[3] Photo in Ward, *Autobiography of a Fugitive Slave*. Schomburg Center for Research in Black Culture, Manuscripts, Archives and Rare Books Division, The New York Public Library. "Samuel Ringgold Ward." New York Public Library Digital Collections, http://digitalcollections.nypl.org/items/510d47db-bc20-a3d9-e040-e00a18064a99.

assigned to be a traveling agent for the first American Anti-Slavery Society and soon afterwards he became an agent for the New York Anti-Slavery Society. His first pastorate in 1841 was in a White Congregational Church in South Butler, Wayne County, New York. Donna D. Burdick, Smithfield Town Historian, has assembled evidence that Ward also lived in Peterboro, New York, in 1840 and 1841,[4] and that abolitionist Gerrit Smith of Peterboro called Ward his neighbor.[5] She has found a deed dated September 1, 1846, recorded September 8, 1846, showing that Gerrit Smith deeded one-third of a single Peterboro property to Ward and two other persons, H. H. Garnet and Syracuse UGRR activist Germain Wesley Loguen,[6] each also receiving one-third.[7]

---

[4] 1840 NYS Census, Madison Co., Town of Smithfield, 175: Samuel R. Ward - 1 Male under 10, 1 Male 24-36, 1 Female under 10, 1 Female 24-36 , all listed under "Free Colored persons"; Letter of Ward to *The Friend of Man* (January 22, 1841; published February 9, 1841); Ward, "Labors of Rev. Hiram Wilson," *The Colored American* (March 31, 1841). He signs the article "S. R. Ward, Peterboro, Feb. 25th, 1841."

[5] Letter of Gerrit Smith to Gen. John H. Cooke (December 11, 1840): "One of my neighbors is the Reverend Samuel Ringgold Ward." For more on Gerrit Smith, see Chs. 2, 9, 10, 14.

[6] Jermain Wesley Loguen (1814—1872)—he added the "n" to his last name—was an ex-slave who in 1834 escaped from the Logue family to Canada, returned to the United States, became a Methodist Episcopal preacher, landed in Rochester (1837), and then in Syracuse (1841). He was married to Caroline Storum of Busti, New York, in 1840 and they had five children. Loguen became a well-known abolitionist, lecturer, and UGRR conductor. He was probably involved (with abolitionist John Thomas?) in the writing of *The Rev. J. W. Loguen, as a Slave and as a Freeman* (Syracuse, N. Y.: J. G. K. Truair & Co., 1859) at http://docsouth.unc.edu/neh/loguen/loguen.html. Like Samuel Ringgold Ward, he was given property by Gerrit Smith and was involved in the "Jerry Rescue" at Syracuse (see below). For a summary based on several sources by Jenn Williamson, see "J. W. Loguen (Jermain Wesley), 1814-1872," at *Documenting the South*, http://docsouth.unc.edu/neh/loguen/summary.html. He has been entered into the National Abolition Hall of Fame and Museum, http://www.nationalabolitionhalloffameandmuseum.org/jloguen.html. See the Jack Watson story in Ch. 15.

[7] Thanks to Donna D. Burdick, Smithfield Town Historian. She observes that the deed date, September 1, 1846, was the same date that Gerrit Smith granted 120,000 acres of land to African Americans, each about forty acres, in the Black colony of "Timbuctoo" near North Elba, New York (near Lake Placid) in order to get them out of the poverty of cities and to give them property that, if successfully cultivated, would be worth $250, the legal requirement for Blacks to vote in New York State at the time. For more on Smith's grants of property (averaging about forty acres each), see Chs. 2, 14.

Recorded the 8th day of November 1847 at 12. o'clock at noon —

Wm. A. Holmes Dep. Clk.

This Indenture, made the first day of September one thousand eight hundred and forty six Between Gerrit Smith of Peterboro State of New York of the first part and Samuel R. Ward Preacher of the Gospel of Cortland village Cortland County State aforesaid of the second part Witnesseth, that the said party of the first part in consideration of One dollar, and of his desire to have all Share in the means of subsistence and happiness which a bountiful God has provided for all, has granted sold and quit claimed to the said party of the second part his heirs and assigns forever All that parcel of lands in the county of Madison and State aforesaid being an undivided one third part (the other parts are this day conveyed to H. N. Garrett and J. N. Logan of the following premises in the village of Peterboro aforesaid bounded north by the Green street 73 feet (73), thence East by the premises owned & occupied by Hiram Holden South by a line parallel to the north line and distant therefrom five chains west by the premises owned and occupied by Nehemiah Huntington — On the premises is a two Story white house now occupied by Duplessis Nash — with the appurtenances and all the estate title and interest of the said party of the first part In Witness whereof the said party of the first part has hereunto set his hand and seal the day and year first above written Gerrit Smith (L.S.) Sealed & delivered in presence of — State of New York Madison County &c On the first day of September 1846. Gerrit Smith to me well known, and by me Known to be the individual described in who executed the within deed came before me and acknowledged that he had executed the same E. Holmes Judge Co. Courts & Counsellor Sup. Court. —

Recorded the 8th day of November 1847 at 1. o'clock P. M.

Wm. A. Holmes Dep. Clk.

Deed Transferring Peterboro Property: Gerrit Smith to Samuel Ringgold Ward, 1846
Image 8.3a

Here is Donna Burdick's transcription:[8]

Recorded the 8th day of November 1847 at 12. o'clock at noon --.

Wm. A. Holmes, Dep. Clk.

This Indenture, made the first day of September one thousand eight hundred and forty six. Between Gerrit Smith of Peterboro, State of New York, of the first part and Samuel R. Ward, Preacher of the Gospel of Cortland Village, Cortland County, State aforesaid of the second part. Witnesseth that the said party of the first part in consideration of One dollar, and of his desire to have all share in the means of subsistence and happiness which a bountiful God has provided for all, has granted, sold and quit claimed to the said party of the second part, his heirs and assigns forever. All that parcel of land in the county of Madison and State aforesaid being an undivided one third part (the other parts are this day conveyed to H. H. Garnet and J. W. Loguen) of the following premises in the village of Peterboro aforesaid, bounded north by the Green 73 feet (73) thereon, east by the premises owned and occupied by Hiram Hadden, south by a line parallel to the north line and distant therefrom five chains, west by the premises owned and occupied by Nehemiah Huntington. On the premises is a two story White house now occupied by Duplissus Nash — with the appurtenances and all the estate, title and interest of the said party of the first part. In Witness whereof the said party of the first part has hereunto set his hand and seal the day and year first above written. Gerrit Smith (L. S.) sealed & delivered in presence of State of New York, Madison County ss [namely]. On the first day of September 1846, Gerrit Smith to me well known, and by me known to be the individual described in & who executed the written deed came before me and acknowledge that he had executed the same. E. Holmes Judge Co. Courts & Counsellor Sup. Court.

Recorded the 8th day of November 1847 at 1 o'clock P. M.

Wm. A. Holmes, Dep. Clk.

Transcription of Deed Transferring Peterboro Property to Samuel Ringgold Ward, 1846
Image 8.3b

Meanwhile, in 1843 Ward began to have medical problems with his tonsils, which made it difficult for him to continue his public speaking and preaching. He left his pastorate and went

---

[8] Thanks again to Donna D. Burdick, Smithfield Town Historian, email (email October 13, 2016). We added the recording date and clerk on the top line from the original. Burdick notes that Ringgold Ward and his wife Emily E. Ward, now of Syracuse, sold the property to James Barnett on August 25, 1851 (recorded August 26, 1851). The two-story house was then occupied by Timothy Stow. The new deed also states that in a private examination Emily Ward acknowledged that she "executed the conveyance freely without any fear or compulsion of her husband," a common legal practice at that time. Finally, by comparing this deed with others, she thinks that the letters after Madison County are "ss" and that they mean "to wit," "namely."

to Geneva, New York, to study medicine under the guidance of Doctors Williams and Bell. After he improved, he returned to the church and became pastor of the Congregational Church in Cortland Village, New York, from 1846 to 1851. In 1846, he was also vice-president of the abolitionist American Missionary Association[9] and in this period he became increasingly involved in politics because of his strong conviction that slavery had to end.

Other abolitionists became aware of Ward's talents. At the Free-Soil Convention of 1848 in Buffalo, New York, Frederick Douglass wrote:

> Mr. Ward especially attracted attention at that convention. As an orator and thinker he was vastly superior, I thought, to any of us, and being perfectly Black and of unmixed African descent, the splendors of his intellect went directly to the glory of race. In depth of thought, fluency of speech, readiness of wit, logical exactness, and general intelligence, Samuel R. Ward has left no successor among the colored men among us...[10]

In 1851, Ward and his family left Cortland and moved to Syracuse. That autumn the city was alive with visitors to the New York State Convention of the anti-slavery Liberty Party. On October 1st, the gathered Convention was disrupted with the announcement that William ("Jerry") Henry, an ex-slave cooper (barrel maker) in Syracuse, had been arrested by federal marshals under the terms of the *Fugitive Slave Act of 1850*. Participants at the convention stormed out of the meeting and rushed to assist Jerry. They converged on the building where he was being held and were able to get him out to the street; he got as far as the Erie Canal, but was recaptured and this time jailed at the Police Justice offices at the Townsend Block (now the Arcade building). A Vigilance Committee of twenty-seven persons, seven of them African Americans, was formed to rescue Jerry. Ward was one of them.[11] That evening a crowd of about 2,500 gathered outside the police station at the time for Jerry's arraignment and forced its way into the building. Although a few shots were fired, the huge crowd overwhelmed the marshals and carried Jerry away, somewhat injured, to safe places in Syracuse. He was then

---

[9] For more on the American Home Missionary Society and the north-south Baptist split over slavery, see Ch. 10.
[10] *The Life and Times of Frederick Douglass, Written by Himself* (3rd rev. ed.; Boston, MA: De Wolfe & Fiske Co., 1892 (first edition, 1855; reprint Mineola, N.Y.: Dover Publications, Inc., 2003), 198-99.
[11] Another was Jermain Wesley Loguen who, like Ward, was gifted one-third of a Peterboro property by Gerrit Smith, as noted in the above deed. See n. 6 for brief autobiographical information.

taken to Oswego by wagon and was soon crossing over Lake Ontario to freedom in Kingston, Canada. After the famous "Jerry Rescue," nineteen Federal indictments were handed down.[12] Ward, a member of the Vigilance Committee that planned the rescue, avoided prosecution by immediately fleeing to Canada.[13]

In Canada, Ward started a newspaper, *The Provincial Freeman*, and worked for the Anti-Slavery Society of Canada, which paid his passage to Britain to attend the British and Foreign Anti-Slavery Society Convention in April 1853. Afterward, he toured Britain giving lectures to raise funds for the work of the Anti-Slavery Society of Canada. Ward was well accepted by the British and quite successful in fund-raising. It was also a fortunate time for Ward to be in England because of serendipitous connections with Harriet Beecher Stowe. In 1852, Stowe published *Uncle Tom's Cabin* based on the life of Black Canadian abolitionist Reverend Josiah Henson. The book triggered tremendous attention and interest in the anti-slavery movement. In 1853, she was a guest in England and Ward had the good fortune to be staying three weeks in May at the "Surrey Chapel Parsonage." At that time, Mrs. Stowe's influential husband, the Reverend Dr. Calvin E. Stowe, and her gifted brother, the Reverend Charles Beecher, were also boarding there.

---

[12] "The Laboratory of Abolitionism, Libel, and Treason: Syracuse and the Underground Railroad." A Special Exhibition at Syracuse University. http://library.syr.edu/digital/exhibits/u/undergroundrr/case3.htm. The site includes several letters from the Special Collections Research Center at Syracuse University Library (see further, below), including a letter of J. M. Clappe, the brawny ironworker who led the crowd in the rescue, to Gerrit Smith on January 3, 1852; a speech of the Rev. Samuel J. May appealing to the "higher law" against the Fugitive Slave Law, 1851; and a letter from Frederick Douglass to Gerrit Smith, November 6, 1852.

[13] Jayhme A. Sokolow, "The Jerry McHenry Rescue and the Growth of Northern Antislavery Sentiment during the 1850s," *Journal of American Studies* 16/3 (Dec. 1982): 440 (427-45). JSTOR. Online at http://www3.gettysburg.edu/~jrudy/history/Jerry%20Rescue/Processing/The%20Jerry%20McHenry%20Rescue%20and%20the%20Growth%20of%20Northern%20Antislavery%20Sentiment%20-%20Jayme%20Sokolow.pdf. Another member of the Vigilance Committee who fled to Canada was the prominent ex-slave Germain Wesley Loguen, who had settled in Syracuse. For a brief sketch, see above.

Ward's successful trip and speaking engagements throughout Britain generated funds for the Anti-Slavery Society of Canada's work to support fugitive slaves in Canada; it is also said that they enabled Ward's semi-retirement in Jamaica in 1855. There he farmed and served a small Baptist church until 1860. He died in St. George Parish in Jamaica in 1866.[14]

The following account is an excerpt from Samuel Ringgold Ward's *Autobiography of a Fugitive Slave: His Anti-Slavery Labours in the United States, Canada and England* (1855). It describes a fugitive slave who had crossed the Niagara River from Youngstown to Niagara by means of the Youngstown Ferry on a cold winter day, January 11, 1853. The fugitive was warming himself at the Niagara Ferry Office stove.[15] The account also mentions Ward's travelling companion, a White abolitionist, the Reverend Hiram Wilson. Ward and Wilson were crossing from Niagara to Youngstown, the opposite direction, on the Youngstown Ferry. Here is Ward's account, with sentences showing the ferryman's involvement in helping fugitive slaves escape to Canada.

. . . Another [freedom seeker] was so unfortunate as to be obliged to travel in the winter. I met him at a ferry on the Niagara River, [as I was] crossing from Niagara, on the British side, to Youngstown, on the New York side. It was a bitterly cold day, the 11th of January, 1853. Crossing the river, it was so cold that icicles were formed upon my clothes, as the waves dashed the water into the ferry boat. It was difficult for the Rev. H. Wilson and myself—we travelled together—to keep ourselves warm while driving; and my horses, at a most rapid rate, travelled twelve miles almost without sweating. That day, this poor fellow crossed that ferry [from Youngstown to Niagara] with nothing upon his person but cotton clothing, and an oilcloth topcoat. *Liberty was before him, and for it he could defy the frost.* I had observed him, when I was in the office of the ferry, sitting not *at,* but *all around,* the stove; for he literally *surrounded and covered it* with his

---

[14] Editors of the *Encyclopedia Britannica*, "Samuel Ringgold Ward. American Abolitionist." http://www.britannica.com/biography/Samuel-Ringgold-Ward.

[15] Ward, *Autobiography*, 173-175. This would have been about three months before his trip to England to attend the British on a Foreign Anti-Slavery Society in April.

Winter's Cold Niagara River between Youngstown and Niagara-on-the-Lake near the Mouth of Lake Ontario
Photo by Dennis Duling
Image 8.4

shivering legs and arms and trunk. And what delighted me was, everybody in the office seemed quite content that he should occupy what he had discovered and appropriated. I yielded my share without a word of complaint. There was not much of the stove, and we all let him enjoy what there was of it.

The ferryman was a bit of a wag—a noble, generous Yankee; who, when kind, like the Irish, are the most humane of men. Upon asking the fare of the ferry, I was told it was a shilling.

Said I, "Must I pay now, or when I get on the other side?"

"Now, I guess if you please."

"But suppose I go to the bottom, I lose the value of my shilling," I expostulated.

"So shall I lose mine, if you go to the bottom without paying in advance," was his cool reply.

I submitted, of course. When partly across, he said to me, "Stranger, you saw that 'ere Black man near the stove in the [Niagara] office, didn't you?"

"Yes, I saw him, very near it, all around it—all over it, for that matter."

"Wall . . . if you can do anything for him, I would thank you, for he is really in need. He is a fugitive. I just now brought him across [from Youngstown]. I am sure he has nothing, for he had but four pence to pay his ferry."

"But you charged me a shilling, and made me pay in advance."

"Yes, but I tell you what; when a darky comes to this ferry from slavery, I guess he'll get across, shilling or no shilling, money or no money."

Knowing as I did that a Yankee's—a good Yankee's—guess is equal to any other man's oath, I could but believe him. He further told me, that sometimes, when they had money, fugitives would give him five shillings for putting them across the ferry which divided what they call Egypt from Canaan. In one case a fugitive insisted upon his taking twenty-four times the regular fare. Upon the ferryman's refusing, the Negro conquered by saying, "Keep it, then, as a fund to pay the ferriage [fare paid for a ferry passage] of fugitives who cannot pay for themselves."[16]

Samuel Ringgold Ward wrote this passage with deep compassion for a freezing, probably exhausted, fugitive slave who had just arrived in Canada. He recalled the experience dramatically. It is precisely the kind of impression favorable to memory's recall, and it must have moved him deeply as he related his impressions not only of the slave, but of the kind response of the people waiting and allowing him more than his share of the warmth of the stove in the Ferryman's office.

While relating his ferry crossing on the Niagara River to Youngstown, Ward shifted to a description of his light-hearted exchange with a droll, humorous, but "noble, generous" ferryman. He did not give the ferryman's name. Unfortunately, we are not certain of the ferryman in 1853, but, you will recall, there was great competition for the job in 1854 and probably it was one of those. One possibility was John Hitchcock who received several petitions

---

[16] *Ibid.*, 174-175 (italics ours). Equivalences in current coinage is difficult to determine, but since a shilling was twelve pence, the fugitive had only one-third of the fare and was in any case charged nothing; see Chs. 6, 10. Egypt and Canaan represented slavery and freedom in the Promised Land, respectively.

of support,[17] one of them claiming that he, Hitchcock, was known to brave the foul Niagara River weather.[18]

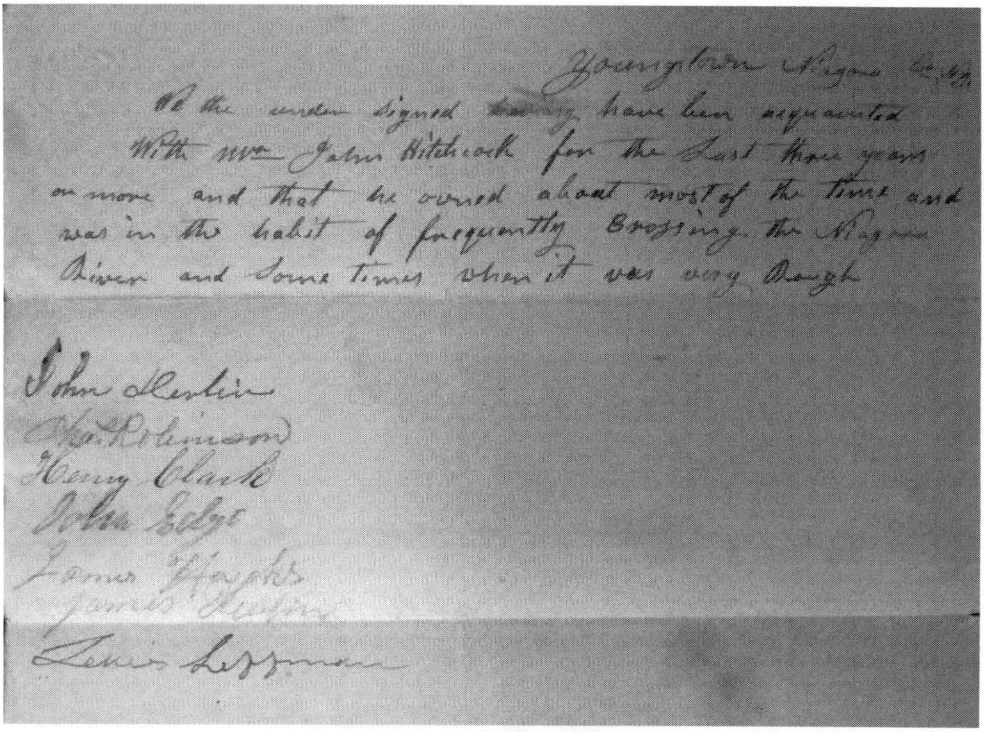

From a Petition of Support for John Hitchcock, 1854
Image 8.5

Here is a transcription:

> Youngstown Niagara C̲o̲., N. Y.
>
> We the under signed ~~having~~ have been acquainted
>
> with Mr. John Hitchcock for the last three years
>
> or more and that he owned a boat most of the time and
>
> was in the habit of frequently crossing the Niagara
>
> River and sometimes when it was very rough.

---

[17] See John Hitchcock in Ch. 6.

[18] The last signature on the petition is that of Lewis Leffman; see the Addendum in Ch. 3 for Leffman's account of his defense of Fort Niagara during the Civil War (1863).

Hiram Wilson (1803 – 1864)

A reader of Samuel Ringgold Ward's *Autobiography* could easily pass over the single reference to his travelling companion, "the Rev. H. Wilson," as he described the bitterly cold, icy Niagara River crossing on January 11, 1853. Here, again, is the statement: "It was difficult for the Rev. H. Wilson and myself—we travelled together—to keep ourselves warm while driving; and my horses, at a most rapid rate, travelled twelve miles almost without sweating." This comment implies that Ward (or a driver?) was driving a buggy or carriage twelve miles, a distance that most likely referred to the St. Catharines-to-Niagara leg of the trip, which is twelve miles.

Who was "the Rev. H. Wilson"? He was Hiram Wilson (1803-1864), a White Congregationalist minister, missionary, abolitionist, and fund raiser in Upper Canada.[19]

There is no known photo of Hiram Wilson (1803-1864)
Image 8.6

---

[19] "Hiram Wilson Papers," Oberlin College Archives; "Hiram Wilson," https://en.wikipedia.org/wiki/Hiran_Wilson; "Hiram Wilson Biography (September 25, 1803 - April 16, 1864)," http://www.uwo.ca/huron/promisedland/wilson/Biography.html; "Hiram Wilson," http://www.oberlin.edu/external/EOG/LaneDebates/RebelBios/HiramWilson.html; Switala, *Underground Railroad*, 142. Switala, 142 calls Wilson a "White minister" who appears "frequently in escape stories from the Niagara-Buffalo area of New York."

Wilson was born on September 25, 1803, in Ackworth, New Hampshire. He attended the Oneida Institute of Science and Industry in Whitestown, New York, in Oneida County,[20] a ministerial training school that emphasized intellectual, moral, and physical education, but combined it with manual labor ("industry"). During the 1830s, the anti-slavery movement was rapidly growing in New York State and the Oneida Institute is often said to have been the nation's first fully integrated college. Theodore Dwight Weld was a student there, but he led several students to transfer to Lane Presbyterian Seminary in Cincinnati, which also emphasized manual labor. Lane's president was the prominent theologian and abolitionist, Lyman Beecher, among whose prominent children was Harriet Beecher Stowe. The increasingly radical Weld, a student leader, organized debates about abolition—the "Lane Debates."[21] Hiram Wilson also transferred from Oneida to Lane at this time and joined the abolitionist group. In 1835, they, along with three members of the administration and some faculty, left Lane for the newly formed, interracial, Oberlin Seminary at Oberlin, Ohio, near Cleveland, whose president was the famous evangelist, Charles G. Finney. In 1836, the students in this group became the Seminary's first graduating class. It included Hiram Wilson.

That same year President Finney financed Hiram Wilson to go to Upper Canada and observe the condition of thousands of transplanted African Americans, most of them former fugitive slaves from the United States. Wilson discovered that they were experiencing discrimination and poverty and that they needed education and vocational skills. The next Spring, Wilson returned to Canada as a representative of the American Anti-Slavery Society.[22] He was a White missionary, but he joined together with a Black ex-slave Josiah Henson, reputedly the prototype of "Uncle Tom" in *Uncle Tom's Cabin*.[23] At the time, Henson was seeking to fulfill his dream of building a school with a strong manual labor emphasis for African

---

[20] Utica, the county seat of Oneida County, was the center of anti-slavery in Upstate New York. Jan De Amicis, "The Utica Freedom Trail Walking Tour: A Proposed Trail of Abolitionist and Underground Railroad Sites." Utica Center for Small City and Rural Studies.
https://www.utica.edu/academic/institutes/ucsc/doc/Utica%20Walking%20Tour%202%20Oct%202013.pdf

[21] For more on Weld and the Anti-Slavery Society, see Ch. 2.

[22] Ibid. for comments about the anti-slavery societies.

[23] In his *An Autobiography of the Rev. Josiah Henson* (Christian Age Office, 1876; Boston: B. B. Russell & Co. Princeton, NJ, 1879), Henson advertized himself as "Uncle Tom"; Harriet Beecher Stowe wrote a short Preface; Appendix A in Henson's book contains a brief biography of her. See also William H. Pease and Jan H. Pease, "Henson, Josiah," *Dictionary of Canadian Biography* 11 (1881-1890).
http://www.biographi.ca/en/bio/henson_josiah_11E.html.

American children. Wilson's education at Oneida and Lane made him an apt partner. In his *Autobiography,* Henson claimed that Wilson was his "faithful friend," that the two cooperated for almost thirty years, and that Wilson "took an interest in our people" and "continued his important labors of love in our behalf."[24] Wilson's humanitarian and philanthropic Quaker friend, James C. Fuller of Skaneateles, New York, raised a substantial sum of money in England for Henson and Wilson. In 1838, the two organized a convention in London, Upper Canada, to carry out Henson's plan. They, plus an anonymous person (Fuller?), formed a committee that purchased 200 acres of forested land at the town of Dawn on the Sydenham River in southwestern Upper Canada in 1841. There they established the British-American Institute around which a largely Black community grew up, and which was dedicated to general, theological, and vocational education and training. It became known as the Dawn Settlement. Wilson attracted other donors, including the abolitionist and philanthropist Gerrit Smith of Peterboro, New York. Henson was its patriarch and spokesman and he sat on the executive committee. However, White men were the official administrative heads, and Wilson served in that capacity from 1842-1847.

---

[24] Henson, ibid., 72.

The Dawn Settlement Marker near Dresden in Chatham-Kent County, Ontario
29251 Uncle Tom's Road, Dresden, Ontario, Canada N0P 1M0
Figure © Ontario Heritage Trust (formerly Ontario Heritage Foundation)
Used with permission from Steven Cook, Site Manager
Image 8.7

In 1843, Hiram Wilson attended the World Anti-Slavery Convention in England. Samuel Ringgold Ward also attended; perhaps they met there. Afterwards, Wilson raised more money in England for the Dawn Settlement. However, by 1847 the Settlement was in temporary financial difficulty and being accused of mismanagement. Mourning his wife's death in 1848, Wilson left (he eventually married again and had five children). Wilson established a number of schools in Canada. In 1849, he set up an ex-fugitive slave haven and school in St. Catharines, which became an UGRR refuge for fugitives, including Harriet Tubman and those she rescued.[25] Wilson also wrote letters to William Still about fugitive slaves whom Still had helped in Philadelphia and who later arrived safely at Wilson's haven in St. Catharines.[26]

---

[25] "Ross, Harriet (originally named Araminta) (Tubman; Davis)." *Dictionary of Canadian Biography*. http://www.biographi.ca/en/bio/ross_harriet_14E.html.
[26] E.g., Still, *Underground Railroad* (1872 edition), 263, 264-65, 406.

In 1855, Benjamin Drew penned the following tribute to Wilson:

I have seen the negro—the fugitive slave, wearied with his thousand miles of travelling by night, without suitable shelter meanwhile for rest by day, who had trodden the roughest and most unfrequented ways, fearing, with too much cause, an enemy in every human being who had crossed his path; I have seen such arrive at Mr. Wilson's, bringing with him the subdued look, the air of sufferance, the furtive glance bespeaking dread, and deprecating punishment; I have seen such waited on by Mr. and Mrs. Wilson, fed and clothed, and cheered, and cared for. Such ministrations give a title to true greatness, a title recognized by Divine wisdom, and deriving its authority from revelation itself: "Whosoever would be great among you, let him be your minister."[27]

William Lloyd Garrison recorded Wilson's obituary in *The Liberator* on May 13, 1864.

In sum, the paths of African American Samuel Ringgold Ward and a White European American minister Hiram Wilson crossed and they had a mutual interest in helping the fugitive slaves who settled in Upper Canada. It is not surprising that the Reverend Hiram Wilson was the traveling companion of the Reverend Samuel Ringgold Ward when the two crossed the Niagara River on the Youngstown Ferry that bitterly cold day in January of 1853. Together they witnessed a fugitive slave who had just crossed from the opposite direction and was warming himself at the stove in the Niagara Ferry Office. Samuel Ringgold's autobiographical account of that day is the best memory source we have of a lively, engaging, yet compassionate Youngstown ferryman who helped fugitive slaves cross from Youngstown to freedom in Canada.

---

[27] Benjamin Drew, *The Refugee; or a North-Side View of Slavery, St. Catharines. The Refugee, or the Narratives of Fugitive Slaves in Canada Related by Themselves, with an Account of the History and Condition of the Colored Population of Upper Canada* (Boston, MA: John P. Jewett and Company; Cleveland, OH: Jewett, Proctor and Worthington; New York: Sheldon, Lamport and Blakeman; London: Trübner and Co., 1856), 18. http://docsouth.unc.edu/neh/drew/drew.html.

CHAPTER 9

The Ben Hockley Saga, 1853

Image 9.1

Newspaper reports about Ben Hockley centered on a fugitive slave's brave attempt to escape to freedom to Canada in 1853 by using an old gate as a raft to traverse the swift Niagara River, from either Lewiston or Youngstown. Hockley failed to reach the opposite shore and according to the reports he drifted twelve miles out in Lake Ontario where he was miraculously rescued by the *Chief Justice Robinson* steamer on its way to Toronto.

The accounts about Ben Hockley are not about the Underground Railroad and Youngstown's role in it, but they tell the dramatic story about an African American who is being hunted down in the wake of the *Fugitive Slave Act of 1850*. We make the case in this chapter that Hockley's attempted launch was more likely from Youngstown than from Lewiston.

ASLEEP ON THE RAFT.

"Asleep on the Raft" (E. W. Kemble)[1]
(Sketch by E. W. Kemble in *Adventures of Huckleberry Finn*, 1885. Public Domain)
Image 9.2

There are three major sources for the Ben Hockley saga: newspaper accounts, letters, and census data.

Fifteen Newspaper Reports

In two different articles, UGRR historian Judith Wellman examined eight newspaper reports about the Hockley story.[2] She attributed the discovery of all eight to Christopher

---

[1] E. W. Kemble, "Asleep on the Raft," in Mark Twain, *Adventures of Huckleberry Finn* (New York, NY: Charles W. Webster & Co., 1885), Ch. XV, 118. The sketch was taken from the Gutenberg Project of free, public domain e-books online, http://www.gutenberg.org/; http://www.gutenberg.org/files/76/76-h/76-h.htm.

[2] Wellman, "Larry Gara's Liberty Line in Oswego County, New York, 1838—1854: A New Look at the Legend," *Afro-Americans in New York Life and History* (January 31, 2001) https://www.questia.com/read/1P3-494776751/larry-gara-s-liberty-line-in-oswego-county-n., n. 18, cited four reports: *North American* (a semi-weekly from Toronto (August 5, 1853); the *Mail* of Niagara, Canada (August 10, 1853); the Weekly *North American* of Toronto (August 11, 1853); and *National Anti-Slavery Standard* (August 20, 1853). One of these four, the *Mail* quoted a fifth, the Toronto *Patriot* (August 4, 1853). She quoted and relied on the *Mail* version in "Lewiston Landing," her *Niagara Falls Underground Railroad Heritage Area Management Plan, Appendix C: Survey of Sites Relating to the Underground Railroad, Abolitionism, and African American Life in Niagara Falls and Surrounding Area, 1820—1880* (April 2013), 191, http://www.niagarafallsundergroundrailroad.org/assets/Uploads/NF-HAMP-Report-Appendix-C-1.pdf. In a note on that page (n. 21), she added three more sources: the St. Catharines *Journal* (August 11, 1853), *The Liberator* (August 19, 1853), and the Norwalk *Reflector* (August 30, 1853 [our date for this version is August 16, 1853]). See also her *Niagara Falls Underground Railroad Heritage Area Management Plan, Appendix C: Survey of*

Densmore, formerly the archivist at the State University of New York, Buffalo, and currently (2017) curator of the Friends Historical Library at Swarthmore College. Wellman centered on the Niagara *Mail* which located the Hockley launch at Lewiston. However, in a footnote she also noted that the *North American* located Hockley's launch at Youngstown, a possibility that led us to a quest for reports.[3] One of her eight, the Niagara *Mail*, quoted another, a ninth, the Toronto *Patriot*. Recently, Densmore discovered still another, a tenth, report that was skeptical of the whole incident. With the assistance of librarians and local historians, we have tracked down these reports and have found five more, for a total of fifteen.

The earliest sources for the Ben Hockley story are the Toronto *Patriot*, the *Mail's* explicitly stated source, and the Toronto *Leader*. Both were published on August 4, 1853, the day after Hockley's reported escape attempt and rescue. The *Patriot* placed the escape attempt at Lewiston; the *Leader* placed it at Youngstown. The other versions edited the earliest accounts and added commentary; they illustrate the speedy dissemination of mid-nineteenth century, post-telegraph news; the growth of stories in partisan and sensationalist newspaper interpreters of the day; and the frequent comparison of Ben's attempted river escape in 1853 to the fictional Eliza's river escape in Harriet Beecher Stowe's best-selling novel, *Uncle Tom's Cabin*, published the previous year.

The Lewiston Version

1) Toronto *Patriot*, Thursday, August 4, 1853.
2) *Rome Daily Sentinel*, Rome, NY, Tuesday, August 9, 1853 (copied Toronto *Patriot*).
3) Niagara *Mail*, Wednesday, August 10, 1853 (copied *Patriot*; added commentary).
4) *Frederick Douglass's Paper*, Friday, August 12, 1853 (mostly copied the *Patriot*).
5) *National Anti-Slavery Standard*, Saturday, August 20, 1853 (copied Douglass).

Here is the earliest Lewiston version from the Toronto *Patriot* of August 4, 1853.

Sites Relating to the Underground Railroad, Abolitionism, and African American Life in Niagara Falls and Surrounding Area, 1820—1880. http://www.niagarafallsundergroundrailroad.org/assets/Uploads/NF-HAMP-Report-Appendix-C-1.pdf; Underground Railroad Heritage Area, "UGRR SITES." http://www.niagarafallsundergroundrailroad.org/,
[3] Wellman, "Lewiston Landing", 191, n. 21.

REMARKABLE INCIDENT— ESCAPE OF A SLAVE.

The steamer 'Chief Justice Robinson,' on her way from Lewiston to Toronto yesterday morning, at about 10 o'clock, and about twelve miles from Niagara, picked up a colored man floating on a raft made of a gate. He gave his name as Ben Hockley, and stated that he had been a slave in Tenessee, from whence he had made his escape. At Oswego, he heard that some men from the south were in pursuit of him, upon which he made his way to Lewiston. Arrived there, he was afraid to apply for passage on any of the steamboats for fear of being detained or given up to his pursuers, but made a bold stroke for life and freedom by launching himself upon the gate, hoping by this means to make his way over to the Canada side. He found the current, however, too strong for him, and drifted out into the lake, till picked up by the 'Chief Justice,' as above stated. He is a man of above 50 years of age.

"Remarkable Incident—Escape of a Slave." *Toronto Patriot*,
Thursday, August 4, 1853[4]
Image 9.3

This earliest and simplest Lewiston version in the Toronto *Patriot* states that "a colored man" named "Ben Hockley," who had been a slave in Tennessee, had escaped, and had come to Oswego, New York, heard that he was being pursued by "men from the south." He somehow "made his way" to Lewiston and, afraid to take a steamer, procured a gate and sought to raft himself across the Niagara River to Canada; however, the strong river current caused him to drift out into Lake Ontario. "Floating" about twelve miles from shore, he was picked up by a steamer, the *Chief Justice Robinson*,[5] as it headed to Toronto; the time of the rescue was about 10:00 A.M. The account concludes that Ben was more than fifty years old.

---

[4] Thanks to the Toronto Public Library for scanning and emailing the *Patriot* version.
[5] The anti-slavery Captain Richardson associated with the escape of Solomon Moseby story (Ch. 1) captained the *Chief Justice Robinson* only until 1851. The vessel was sold in 1850 and Richardson became the harbor master at

The *Rome Daily Sentinel* copied the Toronto *Patriot verbatim*, except for spelling his name "Hockly."[6] The Niagara *Mail*, most often cited for this story, also copied the *Patriot* version exactly, including the "Hockley" spelling, but it added a dramatic, sympathetic commentary:

> The above incident is worthy of a place in "Uncle Tom's Cabin"—and yet is but a
> sample of the many hardships which these poor creatures have to encounter in freeing
> themselves from the "House of Bondage"[7]—as "by night they travelled and by day they
> hid" to reach our Free shores. 'Twas not a week ago, we saw a poor fellow just got over
> the river, he was in his Plantation dress, torn, and travel-stained with the dust of every
> mile between this and Tennessee. Hot spirit of liberty how lightly he trod Canadian
> earth!—his countenance fairly shone with happiness. He had been but a *chattle* [sic]
> before, now he felt himself to be a man. We sympathized with his delight—but who that
> had never been a Slave could sound the depths of his joy as he said, "Thank the Lor'!
> Masre [Master] I am a free man now, thank God!" Yes, thank God! There is one land in
> North America, where the poor fugitive is *safe* from the blood hounds that bay up to the
> river's bank, but *no further*—where the vile informer spies to no purpose, and the
> hireling Marshal with the fugitive slave law in his land, stops short, and returns *nuila
> bona* [legal language: "without the goods," that is, without the slave as property], as he
> looks across the frontier and marks the line that bounds his jurisdiction—to him and his
> errand, a wall of impossible fire—and ever may it be so. [8]

Toronto. A direct connection between Richardson and Hockley in 1853 is unlikely; see Scadding, *Toronto of Old*,
http://www.maritimehistoryofthegreatlakes.ca/documents/scadding/default.asp?ID=c004; Ch. 4.
[6] Thanks to Donna Burdick, Smithfield Town Historian, for emailing the *Rome Daily Sentinel* version.
[7] Exodus 20:2:" I am the LORD thy God, which have brought thee out of the land of Egypt, out of the house of
bondage. . ." (King James Version, 1611, the normative Protestant translation in the nineteenth century); the New
Revised Standard Version of 1989 has in place of the "house of bondage" the "house of slavery."
[8] Thanks to Sandra Enskat, Special Collections, St. Catharines Public Library, for emailing the Niagara *Mail* report.
Part of it was quoted by Nancy Butler, "Starting Anew," 72-73; see Ch. 1 in this book.

The commentary on the *Patriot* version in the [Niagara] *Mail* a week after the event claimed that the story was "worthy of a place in the best-seller *Uncle Tom's Cabin*" (1852). It included the account of the miraculous escape of the fugitive slave Eliza and her baby daughter

"The Mother's Struggle"[9]
(Eliza's Courageous Crossing the Ohio River)
(Illustration by Hammatt Billings for *Uncle Tom's Cabin*, 1853, Headpiece, Chapter 7,
used by permission)
Image 9.4

---

[9] This illustration was rendered by Hammatt Billings for *Uncle Tom's Cabin; or, Life among the Lowly*, by Harriet Beecher Stowe (Illustrated Edition. Original Designs by Billings; Engraved by Baker and Smith; Boston, MA: John P. Jewett and Company, 1853), Ch. 7, used by permission. It is from the Clifton Waller Barrett Collection, University of Virginia. http://utc.iath.virginia.edu/uncletom/illustra/53illf.html. It was one of 117 new Billings illustrations added in the 1853 printing, which appeared just before Christmas in 1852. See further, "Chapter VII. Comment by Jo-Ann Morgan." Interpretation of Hammatt Billings' "The Mother's Struggle." *Uncle Tom's Cabin* in the *National Era*. The Harriet Beecher Stowe Center, https://nationalera.wordpress.com/further-reading/chapter-7-comment-by-jo-ann-morgan/.

across the Ohio River from Kentucky, a slave state, to Ohio, a free state.[10] The parallel between the fugitive slave Eliza's crossing while floating on a melting block of ice on the Ohio River and fugitive slave Ben Hockley's failed crossing while floating on an old gate on the Niagara River was clearly implied and was repeated in several newspaper stories. The *Mail* commentary expanded with other colorful details: the "poor creature's"/"poor fugitive's" shabby plantation clothing; his trials in escaping from the "House of Bondage" in Tennessee; his being pursued by the "blood hounds" and betrayed by the "vile informers"—"by night they travelled and by day they hid"; his reaching the Niagara River border where the marshal could not cross the "wall of fire" and had to turn back empty handed (*nuila bona*); and the escaped fugitive's happy, shining countenance and joyful praise of the Lord upon reaching the Canadian earth—the land of freedom where he was no longer chattel and felt himself finally to be a man. The interpreter noted that although the Canadians realized that they could not really know the slave's trials, they truly sympathized.

The succinct *Patriot/Rome Daily Sentinel/Mail* version of the initial report was paraphrased in the *Frederick Douglass Paper* of August 12, 1853, a week and a day later, but the original clearly shone through and the commentary was different. The name was "Hockly" as in the *Rome Daily Sentinel*. The added paraphrases and the final correspondent's commentary are underlined below.

> **DARING ATTEMPT AND SUCCESSFUL ESCAPE OF A SLAVE – ANOTHER BOLD STROKE FOR FREEDOM. –** A friend at Toronto has just told us that as the steamer *Chief Justice Robinson* was on her way from Lewiston to Toronto, about twelve miles from Niagara, on Wednesday last, about 10 o'clock in the morning, the passengers saw a colored man floating on a raft made of a gate. He was immediately picked up and taken aboard. He gave his name as BEN HOCKLY; [he] stated that he had been a slave in Tennessee and had made his escape to Oswego. While there, he chanced to hear that some men from the south were in pursuit of him; so he fled to Lewiston. – When he arrived there he was

---

[10] In Ch. 8, we noted the association of Samuel Ringgold Ward with Josiah Henson, the supposed prototype of Uncle Tom in Stowe's influential novel, as well as Ward's stay of several weeks in Surrey Chapel Parsonage in England where Stowe's husband, the Reverend Dr. Calvin E. Stowe, and brother, the Reverend Charles Beecher, were also boarding.

afraid to apply for a passage on any of the <u>steamboats</u>, for fear of being captured. <u>In this</u> <u>emergency, he resolved to make</u> a bold stroke for freedom; <u>so he lashed</u> himself <u>to a</u> gate, <u>and</u> launched <u>forth upon the Niagara River, in hopes that he should</u> make his way to the Canada <u>shore. In this, however, he was mistaken; the force of</u> the current was too strong for him and drifted him out into the lake. <u>He was providentially rescued by the</u> <u>British steamer</u>, as above stated, *"and carried into the Ladies' Saloon."*

One correspondent adds, "There were Yankees on board, who seemed as if they could have hidden themselves behind the looking glass, or have sunk into an augur-hole when they saw their crushed victim *floating on a gate*, and thus making for the land of freedom; but all England [*sic*] ladies and gentlemen seemed to weep and yet rejoice to see *such a bold stroke for freedom.*" – J. G.[11]

The *Frederick Douglass Paper* added details and updating: 1) "yesterday morning" became "Wednesday last" (another week had elapsed); 2) the steamer passengers were the first to see the colored man; 3) Ben's name was spelled "H-o-c-k-l-y" (no "e"); 4) Ben *overheard* that he was being pursued and "fled" to Lewiston; 5) his fear of being "detained or given up to his pursuers" was changed to his being "captured in this emergency"; 6) the "Niagara River" was explicit; 7) the second mention of the "Chief Justice" was omitted; and 8) "50 years of age" was omitted. The correspondent's commentary made two additional points: 1) Ben was put in the "Ladies Saloon" (seagoing vessels of the day, including lake steamers, often had such lounges for relaxation and tea[12]); 2) the English ladies and gentlemen wept and were joyful about the rescue, but the Yankees were embarrassed and wanted to disappear -- clearly a judgment on not only the slave law, but also the Americans. Finally, the *Frederick Douglass*

---

[11] "Daring Attempt and Successful Escape of a Slave—Another Bold Stroke for Freedom," *Frederick Douglass Paper*, August 12, 1853, *Accessible Archives, African American Newspapers*. http://www.accessible.com/accessible/docButton?AAWhat=builtPage&AAWhere=FREDERICKDOUGLASSPAPER.18 530812_001.image&AABeanName=toc1&AACheck=5.82.8.2.2&AANextPage=/printBuiltImagePage.jsp; transcription at http://www.accessible.com/accessible/print?AADocList=1&AADocStyle=&AAStyleFile=&AABeanName=toc1&AAN extPage=/printFullDocFromXML.jsp&AACheck=35.1.1.2.1 (last accessed December 9, 2015).
[12] A "Ladies Saloon" was in the *Mary Powell* and the Martha's Vineyard steamer. See "History and Development of Great Lakes Water Craft," Minnesota's Lake Superior Shipwrecks, http://www.mnhs.org/places/nationalregister/shipwrecks/mpdf/mpdf2.php.

Paper attributed the story to a "friend." Was he the journalist commentator of the *Patriot* who signed the piece "J. G."?

This version was copied in the *National Anti-Slavery Standard* eight days later, August 20, 1853.[13]

The Youngstown Version

1) *The* [Toronto] *Daily Leader,* Thursday, August 4, 1853.
2) Toronto *North American,* Friday, August 5, 1853 (semi-weekly; developed *Leader*).
3) Toronto *North American*, Friday, August 11, 1853 (copied semi-weekly *North American*).
4) St. Catharines *Journal*, August 11, 1853 (copied Toronto *North American*).
5) Boston *Evening Transcript*, August 12, 1853 (refers to *Leader*).
6) Sandusky (Ohio) *Democratic Mirror* (short version, date not known).
7) Norwalk (Ohio) *Experiment*, Tuesday, August 16, 1853 (copied the Sandusky *Mirror*).
8) Norwalk (Ohio) *Reflector*, August 16, 1853 (copied the Sandusky *Democratic Mirror*?).
9) *The Kalida Venture*, August 19, 1853 (copied Toronto *Leader* [C. W.])
10) Boston *The Liberator*, Friday, August 19, 1853 (copied the *Leader)*.

The report in the Toronto *Leader* was published on a "Thursday"—the same day as the *Patriot*—and referred to a "case [that] occurred yesterday," or Wednesday, August 3, 1853.[14]

---

[13] Wellman, *Niagara Falls Underground Railroad Heritage Area*,
http://www.niagarafallsundergroundrailroad.org/assets/Uploads/Featured-Story-1853-Daring-Attempt.pdf
and http://www.niagarafallsundergroundrailroad.org/history-and-documents/historical-documents/daring-attempt-and-successful-escape-of-a-slave/.
[14] For the August 3, 1853, day of the week, see http://www.onedayhistory.com/day-of-week/1853-august-3/.

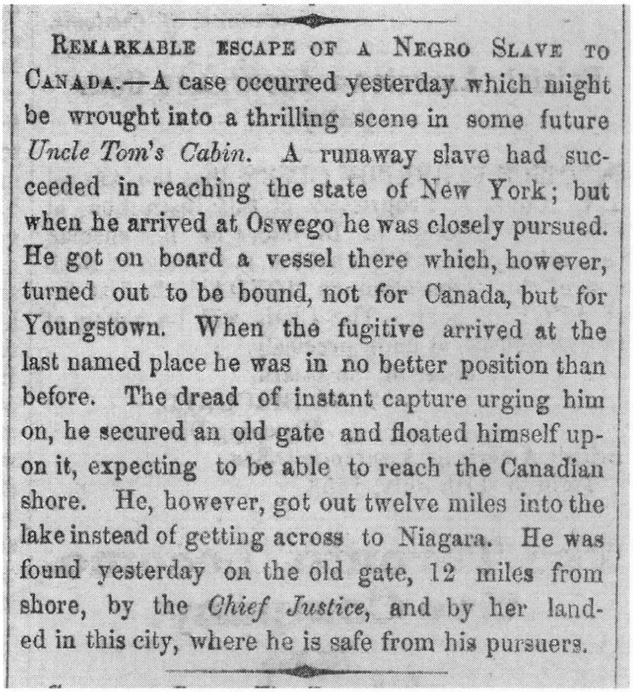

> REMARKABLE ESCAPE OF A NEGRO SLAVE TO CANADA.—A case occurred yesterday which might be wrought into a thrilling scene in some future *Uncle Tom's Cabin*. A runaway slave had succeeded in reaching the state of New York; but when he arrived at Oswego he was closely pursued. He got on board a vessel there which, however, turned out to be bound, not for Canada, but for Youngstown. When the fugitive arrived at the last named place he was in no better position than before. The dread of instant capture urging him on, he secured an old gate and floated himself upon it, expecting to be able to reach the Canadian shore. He, however, got out twelve miles into the lake instead of getting across to Niagara. He was found yesterday on the old gate, 12 miles from shore, by the *Chief Justice*, and by her landed in this city, where he is safe from his pursuers.

"Remarkable Escape of a Negro Slave to Canada." [Toronto] *Daily Leader*,
Thursday, August 4, 1853[15]
Image 9.5

The earliest and simplest Youngstown version in the *Leader* reports that an unnamed "runaway slave" from another state[16] came "closely pursued" to Oswego, New York, and there *boarded a steamer* expecting that it would take him to Niagara[-on-the-Lake] on the Canadian shore; instead, however, it docked at *Youngstown.* He disembarked but, fearing his capture, procured an old gate and attempted to use it as a raft to float directly across the river to Niagara. However, he drifted out into Lake Ontario where he was picked up twelve miles from

---

[15] Thanks to the Toronto Public Library for scanning and emailing the *Leader* version.

[16] As noted above, census reports disagree on Ben Hockley's birth place and it is difficult to know exactly when he was a slave. The *Patriot* newspaper version says that he was being pursued by slave catchers from Tennessee. Had he been sold to a master in Tennessee before escaping to either Sackets Harbor (by 1840) or Oswego (1841? [see below]). Was he captured and sent to Tennessee between 1850 and 1853? The accounts of his departure from Oswego in the Edwards-to-Smith letters of 1850 (see below) and the escape saga of 1853 under discussion suggest a more recent escape and pursuit, whatever his Virginia and Tennessee associations might have been.

the shore by the steamer *Chief Justice* [*Robinson*] bound for Toronto. He arrived safely in Canada. The first sentence states that the event would fit "a thrilling scene in some future *Uncle Tom's Cabin*."

The *Daily Leader* version was copied word-for-word in *The Kalida Venture*[17] and in William Lloyd Garrison's *Liberator*.[18] The semi-weekly *North American* and its interpretation was then copied in the Toronto weekly *North American*[19] and the St. Catharines *Journal*.[20] In this version, the report has a different heading and a *lead-in* commentary that expands on the *Leader's* initial clause, "a thrilling scene in some future *Uncle Tom's Cabin*," specifically mentioning Eliza. This version's additions are underlined:

[17] *The Kalida venture*, August 19, 1853, http://chroniclingamerica.loc.gov/lccn/sn85038078/1853-08-19/ed-1/seq-1/#date1=1853&index=0&rows=20&words=bachelor+unfortunate&searchType=basic&sequence=0&state=Ohio&date2=1854&proxtext=unfortunate+%2B+bachelor&y=12&x=6&dateFilterType=yearRange&page=1.
[18] *The Liberator*, August 19, 1853. http://fair-use.org/the-liberator/1853/08/19/the-liberator-23-33.pdf.
[19] *The North American*, August 5, 1853. https://news.google.com/newspapers?nid=_OXeSy2IsFwC&dat=18530805&printsec=frontpage&hl=en.
[20] Thanks to Sandra Enskat, Special Collections, St. Catharines Public Library, for emailing the St. Catharines *Journal*, August 11, 1853.

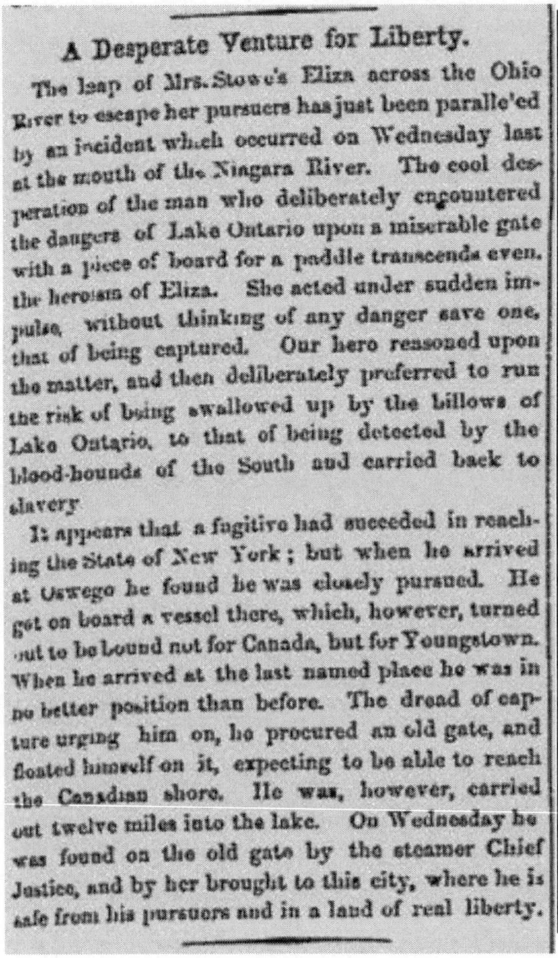

A Desperate Venture for Liberty.

The leap of Mrs. Stowe's Eliza across the Ohio River to escape her pursuers has just been paralle'ed by an incident which occurred on Wednesday last at the mouth of the Niagara River. The cool desperation of the man who deliberately encountered the dangers of Lake Ontario upon a miserable gate with a piece of board for a paddle transcends even the heroism of Eliza. She acted under sudden impulse, without thinking of any danger save one, that of being captured. Our hero reasoned upon the matter, and then deliberately preferred to run the risk of being swallowed up by the billows of Lake Ontario, to that of being detected by the blood-hounds of the South and carried back to slavery.

It appears that a fugitive had succeeded in reaching the State of New York; but when he arrived at Oswego he found he was closely pursued. He got on board a vessel there, which, however, turned out to be bound not for Canada, but for Youngstown. When he arrived at the last named place he was in no better position than before. The dread of capture urging him on, he procured an old gate, and floated himself on it, expecting to be able to reach the Canadian shore. He was, however, carried out twelve miles into the lake. On Wednesday he was found on the old gate by the steamer Chief Justice, and by her brought to this city, where he is safe from his pursuers and in a land of real liberty.

A Desperate Venture for Liberty.

The leap of Ms. Stowe's Eliza across the Ohio River to escape her pursuers has just been paralle'ed by an incident which occurred on Wednesday last at the mouth of the Niagara River. The cool desperation of the man who deliberately encountered the dangers of Lake Ontario upon a miserable gate with a piece of board for a paddle transcends even the heroism of Eliza. She acted under sudden impulse, without thinking of any danger save one, that of being captured. Our hero reasoned upon the matter, and then deliberately preferred to run the risk of being swallowed up by the billows of Lake Ontario to that of being detected by the blood-hounds of the South and carried back to slavery.

It appears that a fugitive had succeeded in reaching the State of New York; but when he arrived at Oswego he found he was closely pursued. He got on board a vessel there, which, however, turned out to be bound not for Canada, but for Youngstown. When he arrived at the last place he was in no better position than before. The dread of capture urging him on, he procured an old gate, and floated himself on it, expecting to be able to reach the Canadian shore. He was, however, carried out twelve miles into the lake. On Wednesday he was found on the old gate by the Steamer Chief Justice, and by her brought to this city, where he is safe from his pursuers and in a land of real liberty.

"A Desperate Venture for Liberty," *North American*, August 5, 1853
Image 9.6

Again, the main story (second paragraph) is the same as the *Leader*, except that the title, "Remarkable Escape of a Negro Slave to Canada," is changed to "A Desperate Venture for Liberty"; the *Leader's* sentence referring to the event as "yesterday" is changed to "Wednesday last," another day having lapsed and the first sentence reference to *Uncle Tom's Cabin* is much expanded (underlined above). The commentary says that "our hero's" heroism is greater than "the leap of Mrs. Stowe's Eliza [on the ice] across the Ohio River to escape her pursuers." Furthermore, the Youngstown location of the attempted crossing is more explicit as the mouth of Lake Ontario, that is, the Niagara River between Youngstown and Niagara. The fugitive is pursued by the "blood-hounds of the South"; the gate is "miserable"; the fugitive "reasons" his strategy and finds a "piece of board for a paddle" to cross the river; he is a man of "cool desperation" who knows that he runs "the risk of being swallowed up by the billows of lake [sic] Ontario"; Canada is "a land of liberty," as implied by the title. Recall that these heightened heroic themes were quite typical of North American newspaper reporting.[21]

There are three shorter versions that also give the location as Youngstown. They are found in Ohio newspapers, namely, the Sandusky *Mirror*[22]; the Norwalk *Experiment*, August 16, 1853 (copied from the Sandusky *Mirror*); and the Norwalk, Ohio *Reflector*, also August 16, 1853 (same as *Reflector*; presumably also from the Sandusky *Mirror*). Here is the Norwalk *Experiment*:

> A Fugitive Slave was taken up in Lake Ontario, twelve miles off Youngstown, where he had floated on an old gate. His dread of pursuit and capture led him to attempt this precarious change of reaching the Canadian shore. He fell into hands that landed him safe in Toronto on the 4th ins.—[Sandusky Mirror, N.D.]

These ten versions located the attempted crossing of Ben Hockley at Youngstown, New York. They are likely built on the Toronto *Leader*. They state that Hockley's miscalculated steamer trip from Oswego mistakenly landed him in Youngstown and that is where he attempted to cross. The core account is always the same; the longer versions embellished the story with heroic themes, especially from *Uncle Tom's Cabin*. In contrast to the *Patriot* versions, the negative comments about the Americans are not nearly as sharp.

---

[21] See Larry Gara, *The Liberty Line*.
[22] The Sandusky *Democratic Mirror* ceased publication in 1853. See http://chroniclingamerica.loc.gov/lccn/sn84028061/holdings/.

The Boston Skeptic's Version

The Boston *Evening Transcript* of August 12, 1853, recently discovered by Christopher Densmore (2016), notes the Toronto *Leader* version and locates the gate launch in Youngstown. However, it is unique; it doubts the core story's validity!

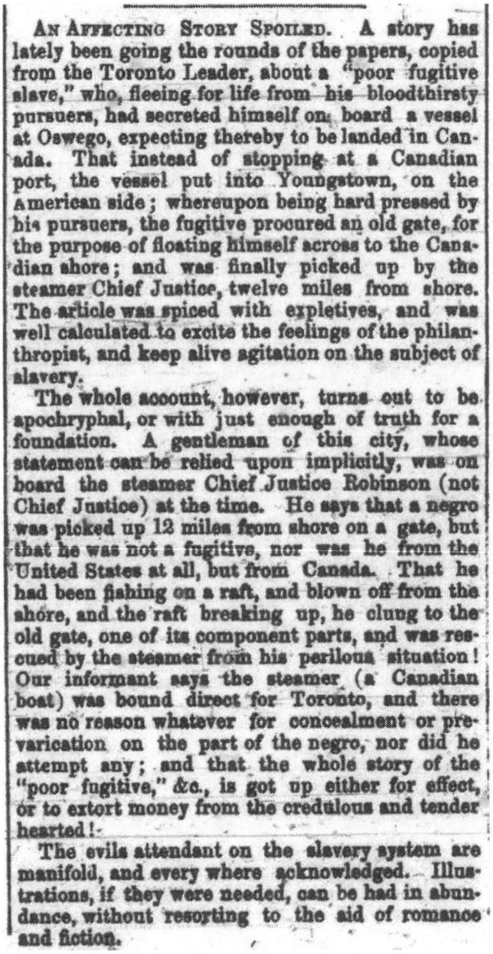

AN AFFECTING STORY SPOILED. A story has lately been going the rounds of the papers, copied from the Toronto Leader, about a "poor fugitive slave," who, fleeing for life from his bloodthirsty pursuers, had secreted himself on board a vessel at Oswego, expecting thereby to be landed in Canada. That instead of stopping at a Canadian port, the vessel put into Youngstown, on the American side; whereupon being hard pressed by his pursuers, the fugitive procured an old gate, for the purpose of floating himself across to the Canadian shore; and was finally picked up by the steamer Chief Justice, twelve miles from shore. The article was spiced with expletives, and was well calculated to excite the feelings of the philanthropist, and keep alive agitation on the subject of slavery.

The whole account, however, turns out to be apochryphal, or with just enough of truth for a foundation. A gentleman of this city, whose statement can be relied upon implicitly, was on board the steamer Chief Justice Robinson (not Chief Justice) at the time. He says that a negro was picked up 12 miles from shore on a gate, but that he was not a fugitive, nor was he from the United States at all, but from Canada. That he had been fishing on a raft, and blown off from the shore, and the raft breaking up, he clung to the old gate, one of its component parts, and was rescued by the steamer from his perilous situation! Our informant says the steamer (a Canadian boat) was bound direct for Toronto, and there was no reason whatever for concealment or prevarication on the part of the negro, nor did he attempt any; and that the whole story of the "poor fugitive," &c., is got up either for effect, or to extort money from the credulous and tender hearted!

The evils attendant on the slavery system are manifold, and every where acknowledged. Illustrations, if they were needed, can be had in abundance, without resorting to the aid of romance and fiction.

Boston *Evening Transcript*, August 12, 1853[23]
Archives, Boston Public Library
Image 9.7

---

[23] Thanks to Christopher Densmore, curator of the Friends Historical Library at Swarthmore College, for finding this version and sending it to us. Thanks also to the Boston Public Library's Karen S. Shafts, Assistant Keeper of Prints, Print Department; Sean Casey, Rare Books and Manuscripts; and Henry Scannell, Curator of Newspapers and Microtext for forwarding a clean photocopy.

The reporter credits the Toronto *Leader*'s Youngstown version as the originating point of various versions. He refers to the "poor fugitive slave" (this expression sounds more like the "poor creature" in the Lewiston version of the Niagara *Mail*, which copied the *Patriot*) and added a commentary. He states that the source of his exposé is an anonymous eyewitness aboard the *Chief Justice Robinson*, who is identified only by his status, "a gentleman of this city [Boston]," as well as his implied honesty, "whose statement can be relied upon implicitly. . ." The appeal to an anonymous source is understandable, but it is unsatisfactory and requires trusting not only the source's credibility, but the reporter's, as well. The reporter's witness claims that the "negro" was a Canadian fisherman who had been fishing off a raft, part of which was a gate, blown off course. Finally, the reporter granted some slight possibility for the credibility of the core story, but he concluded by debunking the whole as a dramatic attempt to play on the sympathies—and the wallets—of naïve and innocent readers.

We shall comment on this version later; first, we cite more information about Ben Hockley.

Ben Hockley's Earlier and Later Life: Census Data and the Gerrit Smith Archive

There are two important primary sources that help to fill in parts of Ben Hockley's life. The first consists of Federal Census records from 1840, 1850, 1860, 1865, and 1870, plus New York State Census records from 1855. The second is the Gerrit Smith Archive in the Special Collections Research Center (SCRC) at Syracuse University which contains letters from Smith's land agent, friend, and fellow abolitionist, John B. Edwards of Oswego, and Smith's own Register of land transactions. From these sources, we construct a few more details.[24]

---

[24] Noted in Ch. 2 is a standard biography of Gerrit Smith, Norman K. Dann, *Practical Dreamer*.

1840	Name	Gender	Free slave	Color	Age/ Birth-date	Birth-place	Living At:	Value of Real Est. Owned	Read & write	Pro-fess./ trade
	Benjamin Hockley	male	free	colored	24-35	---	Sackets Harbor	---	---	---
		female	free	colored	24-35	---	Sackets Harbor	---	---	--
		female	free	colored	Under 10	---	Sackets Harbor	----	----	
1850	Benj Hawkly	male	----	B**	45	[N. Y.] "	Oswego	$600	----	Cook
	Susan Hawkly	female	----	"	34	"	Oswego		----	
	Henry Hawkly	male	----	"	2	"	Oswego		----	
1853	**Escape to**	**Toronto**	**in Aug**							
1855 NY June	Benj Hawkly	M	Relat. To Head (married)	B or M /	50	**Virginia**	years lived @ Oswego 14	$600 (owner of land) / (yes)	Can vote / (yes)	Cook
	Susan "	F	Wife (married)	/	37	**Lewis [NY]**	14			Wash woman
	Henry "	M	Child	/	8	**Oswego [county]**	8			
	George "	"	"		4	**Canada**	---	Alien		
	Susan Carpenter	F	Help (married)		29	**Oswego [county]**				
1860	Benj Hockley	male	----	B	50 1810	**N. Y.**	Detroit	----	no	laborer
	Susan Hockley	female	----	B	48 1812	do (= ditto)	Detroit	----	----	
	Henry Hockley	male	----	B	13 1847	do	Detroit	----	In school	
	George Hockley	male	----	B	10 1851?	**Canada***	Detroit	----	In school	
1870	Benjamin Hawkley	male	----	black	58 1812	**Virginia**	Detroit	----	no	laborer
	Susan Hockley	female	----	black	57 1812	New York	Detroit	----	----	Keeping house
	Henry Hockley	male	----	----	23 1847	"	Detroit	----	----	Cook on a boat
	George Hockley	male	----	----	20 1851?	**Canada***	Detroit	----	----	laborer

*In 1870, Benjamin "Hawkley" is listed as a "father of a foreign born child" and Susan as "mother of foreign born child" (George Hawkley was born in Canada). **B = black; M = mulatto

Census Data Chart for Ben Hockley

Dennis Duling

Image 9.8

According to the 1855 New York State Census and the 1870 Federal Census, "Benj Hawkly" (1870: "Benjamin Hawkley") was born in the State of Virginia—a slave state. However, in the Federal Census of 1850 and 1860 his birthplace was listed as the State of New York. One possible explanation for the discrepancy is that in the months before the 1850 Federal Census taker filled out Hockley's form on August 7, 1850, there were discussions in Congress about a fugitive slave law reported in the news media. The *Fugitive Slave Act of 1850* was passed a little over five weeks later, on September 18, 1850. The late Spring and early Summer would have been a period of high anxiety for African Americans and this is confirmed for Hockley by two of the three letters from John Edwards to Gerrit Smith. These two letters, one in 1851, the other in 1852, claim that Ben had fled Oswego for Canada (we note the key passages later). A similar point about Ben could be made about the 1860 census, not long before the Civil War. Finally, census data shows that Ben was probably in Canada about 1851—a point to which we shall return. In 1850 and 1860, Ben claimed birth in a free state, New York, but Virginia was the more likely place of his birth.

When was Ben born? The Census report of 1840 states his age as between 24 to 35; in 1850 as age 45; and in 1855 (New York State Census) as age 50. If we combine these sources, a birth date of about 1805 appears, which is close to, but not exactly the same as, the Toronto *Patriot* newspaper report that he was over 50 in 1853. However, the 1860 Federal Census also says he was 50; and the 1870 Federal Census says he was just 58! In short, he could have been born any time between 1805 and 1812. As noted in connection with Thomas James, exact birth dates of fugitive slaves are, as in this case, often difficult to establish.

Whatever Ben's precise birth state and age, the 1840 Census listed "Benjamin Hockley" as a Free Colored male—recall the New York State manumission laws of 1827 and 1841[25]— between the ages of 24 to 35 living in Sackets Harbor, New York. At that time, he was married to a Free Colored female—the 1855 New York State Census says that his wife was from Lewis, New York—between the ages of 24 and 35. In 1840, there was also in their household a Free Colored female child under the age of ten, perhaps their daughter. However, we never hear of her again, even in the census data.

---

[25] For a brief history of slavery in New York State, see Ch. 1; the 1827 and 1841 laws are noted in Chs. 1, 4.

Deducing from the 1855 New York State Census records, Hockley and his wife Susan had been living in Oswego already fourteen years which, if accurate, indicates that they would have moved from Sackets Harbor to Oswego about 1841. The first son of Ben and Susan, Henry, was born about 1847 (he was eight years old in the 1855 State Census, thirteen in the 1860 Federal Census, and twenty-three in the 1870 Federal Census); their second son, four years younger, was born in Canada in 1851.

Why Canada? This requires digging deeper into Ben's Oswego period.

One of Gerrit Smith's philanthropic/abolitionist projects was the "sale" of farmland for $1.00 to African Americans. A dramatic example is "Timbuctoo" in the Adirondacks of New York, whereby Smith granted 120,000 acres of land to African Americans, that is, some 3,000 deeds averaging forty acres each.[26] However, not all of Smith's land transactions with African Americans were gifts. An example is his land deal with Ben Hockley at Oswego, New York.

John B. Edwards, Smith's friend, was an anti-slavery abolitionist and UGRR champion who did much of the local UGGR organization work in Oswego, but he was also Smith's Oswego land agent and broker[27] who periodically reported to Smith by letter about the status of Smith's properties. The Gerrit Smith archive at Syracuse University's Special Collections Research Center (SCRC) preserves some of Smith letters and his land transaction data (Volume 88) and in three letters Edwards mentioned Ben Hockley. Each letter began with Edwards' customary inside address "Oswego" and the date on the upper right corner and on the next line on the left his customary greeting "Mr Gerrit Smith" and "Dear Sir." Each concluded with his customary,

---

[26] See Ch. 2 for a summary of Gerrit Smith's philanthropy, Ch. 8 for his gift to Samuel Ringgold Ward, Ch. 11 for his land deal with Myron J. Pardee of Palmyra (then of Youngstown), and Ch. 14 for his land deals in Lewiston, New York.

[27] For Edwards activities, see Charles M. Snyder, "The Antislavery Movement in the Oswego Area," Eighteenth Publication of the Oswego County Historical Society, Oswego County (Oswego, NY: Paladium-Times, Inc., 1955 [February 15], 4, 7-12, http://ochs.nnyln.org/ochs-issues/ochs-issue-1955.pdf.

"Respectfully your friend" and signature "J. B. Edwards." Here are the extracts from the three letters that mention Hockley, the last as a photocopy.[28]

<dl>
Oct 12, 1850: "....Benj Hockley is now pretty content to remain here." (p. 2).

Feb'y 1, 1851: "B. Hockley has gone to Canada. He was afraid of the Fugitive Law – He thought likely he might return in the Spring & wish[ed] to retain his house & Lot..." (p. 2).

Feb'y 13, 1852
</dl>

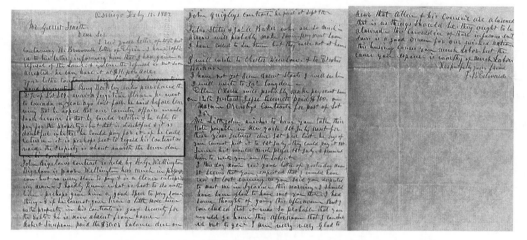

Letter of John B. Edwards to Gerrit Smith, February 13, 1852
Image 9.9

---

[28] The second letter, dated "Feb'y 1, 1851," also contains the important quotation about Myron J. Pardee's debt to Garrit Smith described in Ch. 10.

Feb'y 13, 1852, page 1:

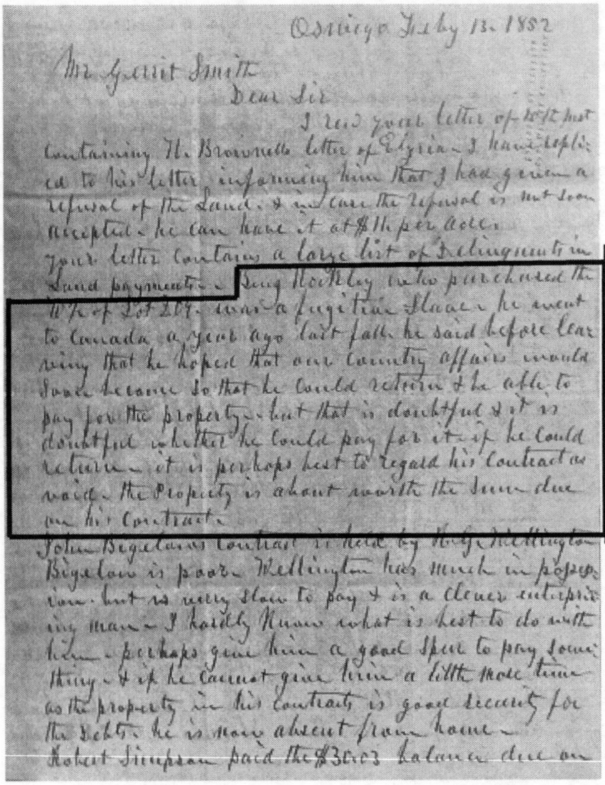

Oswego Feby 13. 1852

Mr Gerrit Smith

Dear Sir

I recd your letter of 10th inst containing H. Brownell's letter of Elyria - I have replied to his letter informing him that I had given a refusal of the land - & in case the refusal is not soon accepted - he can have it at $11 per acre

Your letter contains a large list of delinquents in land payments - Benj Hockley who purchased the N ½ of Lot 209 - was a fugitive slave - he went to Canada a year ago last fall he said before leaving that he hoped that our country affairs would soon become so that he could return & be able to pay for the property - but that is doubtful & it is doubtful whether he could pay for it if he could return - it is perhaps best to regard his contract as void - the property is about worth the sum due on his contract.

John Bigelow's contract is held by Hugh Wellington - Bigelow is poor - Wellington has much in possession - but is very slow to pay & is a clever enterprising man - I hardly know what is best to do with him - perhaps give him a good spur to pay something - & if he cannot give him a little more time as the property in his contracts is good security for the debts - he is now absent from home -

Robert Simpson paid the $30.03 balance due on

"Benj Hockley who purchased the N ½ of Lot 209 was a fugitive slave. He went to Canada a year ago last fall. He said before leaving that he hoped that our country affairs would soon become so that he could return & be able to pay for the property – but that is doubtful & it is doubtful whether he could pay for it if he could return. It is perhaps best to regard his contract as void. The property is about worth the sum due on his contract."

Extract from Page 1 of the Letter of John B. Edwards to Gerrit Smith, February 13, 1852
Image 9.10

These three Edwards letters show that the fugitive slave "Benj Hockley" had purchased "a lot and a house," apparently by land contract, from wealthy abolitionist Gerrit Smith (Edwards Letter, February 1, 1851), which was located in Oswego, New York, at "**the N ½ of Lot 209**. . ." (Edwards Letter, February 13, 1852). Judith Wellman's research team results in Oswego County, written by Wellman in *Survey of Historic Sites Relating to the UGRR, Abolitionism, and African American Life in Oswego County*, was the basis for a site map in *The Underground Railroad in Oswego County. A Driving Tour. Oswego Country Freedom Trail*, a brochure put together by the Oswego County Freedom Trail Commission and Committee chaired by former

Oswego County Historian, Barbara Dix.[29] Site Number 10 on the map, titled "Site of the Ben and Susan Hockley House," is at 19 East Sixth Street. However, beside Number

**19 East Sixth Street Today,
Oswego, New York (built 1890)**
Photo by Dennis Duling
Image 9.11

10 is a black dot, which indicates that the historical Hockley house is no longer there. Justin White, the current Oswego County Historian, confirms that the location of the Hockley House was on East Sixth Street between Seneca and Schuyler Streets. Although White has been unable to find any deed or mortgage from Hockley's time in the Historian's Office, current real estate ads give the Property Legal Description as **B 51, L 209** 016-013-000: **L 209**. Block 51, Lot 209, turns out to be an old Property Legal Description that still exists in documents in

the Oswego County Real Property Office and in the Oswego City Assessor's Office.[30] Therefore, **B 51, L 209** is Lot 209, the lot to which Edwards referred in his letter of February 13, 1852. Today, a modest three-bedroom home exists at this address. Oswego real estate advertisements say that it was built in 1890, and that date is on the deed. In short, the lot was the lot Hockley was purchasing from Smith, but the current house dates from a later time.[31]

---

[29] Research on Ben Hockley was initially done by Judith Wellman's research team, which Wellman put together in "Survey of Historic Sites Relating to the UGRR, Abolitionism, and African American Life in Oswego County," originally on the SUNY Oswego website, but no longer available.

[30] This identification is confirmed by officials in these offices.

[31] The Driving Tour UGRR map is online at http://visitoswegocounty.com/wp-content/uploads/UGRR.pdf. Real Estate information for "19 E 6th St." is at Redfin. https://www.redfin.com/NY/Oswego/19-E-6th-St-13126/home/72363652. The email from Oswego County Historian Justin White to Gretchen Duling that confirms the street location of Hockley's lot was on November 11, 2015. The Oswego County Office reports by telephone that the additional 016-013-000 number and the 1890 build date of the current house are on the deed and that the additional number was an old tax assessment number.

The 1850 Census included the information that "Benj Hawkly," a black man aged 45 born in New York State and living in Oswego, worked as a cook and owned property valued at $600. If that figure referred to the agreement with Gerrit Smith, Hockley was in the process of paying installments to Smith for a lot and house, although legally the property was still owned by Smith (a land contract). This arrangement appears to have been the case since it corresponds with comments in Edward's third letter to Smith, February 13, 1852, which states that Hockley had *not yet* paid for the property. Note that the first letter, October 12, 1850, states that Hockley was "pretty content to remain here" (in Oswego). However, fewer than five months later, as stated in Edwards's second letter on February 1, 1851, Hockley had fled to Canada because he was afraid of the *Fugitive Slave Act of 1850*. We have also seen that his second son, George, was born in Canada. Yet, Hockley hoped to return in the Spring—presumably the Spring of 1851—and also hoped to keep his lot and house, that is, presumably, to continue his contractual payments. These sequences seem to suggest that there was a time lag between what Hockley thought and did and Edward's reporting it to Smith. In the third letter, February 13, 1852, Edwards says that Hockley departed "a year ago last fall," that is, the fall of 1850, presumably not long after the first letter, because of the *Fugitive Slave Act* of September 18. However, by early 1852 Edwards was becoming skeptical about whether Hockley would ever return and pay off his lot and house. He wrote, "It is perhaps best to regard his contract as void." He then states its value was the same as the original contract, which, if we use the 1850 Federal and the 1855 State Censuses, was $600. Obviously, Hockley was not—or was not yet—a recipient of one of Gerrit Smith's land grants.

In the 1840 Census, Hockley claimed that he was a Free Colored man; however, the letters of John Edwards indicate that he left Oswego for Canada in 1850 because of the *Fugitive Slave Act* and that he feared being captured as a "fugitive slave," which is precisely what John B. Edwards called him. What really happened to him after he left Oswego in late 1850? What happened to his wife Susan and his son Henry?

Recall that the Toronto *Patriot* of August 1853 reported that Hockley claimed he had been a slave in the slave state of Tennessee[32]—some newspaper reports speak of his having been hunted by "men from the south" or by "blood-hounds of the south"—but that he had escaped and was now being pursued. Did these reports imply a *recent* capture and escape?[33] Did he make it to Canada when he left Oswego in 1850? According to the censuses of 1855, 1860, and 1870, his second son George was born in Canada, probably in 1851, four years after Henry. However one constructs the chronology, it is certain that at least his wife Susan was in Canada in 1851!

In short, although we cannot track Ben's movements precisely between the Fall of 1850 and August of 1853, a likely scenario is that he went to Canada with his wife Susan and son Henry, that George was born there, that presumably he came back to Oswego, New York, since in 1853 we find him attempting to escape to Canada from Oswego once again![34]

The Case for Youngstown

Let us return to the Ben Hockley escape attempt in 1853. The above information— newspaper reports, census data, letters, and a Register—begs for some further historical reflection.

Judith Wellman originally highlighted the Niagara (Ontario) *Mail*'s version (without the dramatic commentary), which was reported in the *Mail* to have to come from the Toronto *Patriot*, now known to have been on August 4, 1953.[35] This version—there are at least four other examples—accents Lewiston and therefore has no miscalculated steamer ride from

---

[32] Tennessee. Senator James Murray Mason of Tennessee, who believed that slavery was necessary to preserve the economy and culture of the South, drafted the *Fugitive Slave Act of 1850*; see "Mason, James Murray. 1911 *Encyclopædia Britannica*, Vol 17," https://en.wikisource.org/wiki/1911_Encyclop%C3%A6dia_Britannica/Mason,_James_Murray.

[33] Again, Hockley was likely born in Virginia.

[34] See the ideological interpretations of nineteenth century American newspapers in "American Newspapers, 1800—1860: City Newspapers" (University Library, University of Illinois at Urbana-Champaign). http://www.library.illinois.edu/hpnl/guides/newspapers/american/1800-1860/city.html.

[35] Wellman, "25. Lewiston Landing," 191; http://www.niagarafallsundergroundrailroad.org/assets/Uploads/NF-HAMP-Report-Appendix-C-1.pdf; http://www.niagarafallsundergroundrailroad.org/. "UGRR SITES."

Oswego to Youngstown, as cited in the *Leader* version and its descendants. The *Mail's* slightly greater detail includes the identification of the fugitive slave as "Ben Hockley," a very critical point. Wellman was not alone in highlighting the Niagara *Mail* and Lewiston.[36] Yet, in a footnote she also noted that the *North American* (August 5, 1853) cited Youngstown as an alternative account and in recent personal discussion she is willing not to rule it out as a possibility.[37]

It was her footnote on the *North American* that led us to collect and analyze fifteen versions and we think that a very good case can be made for Youngstown. First, the Toronto *Leader* rivals the *Patriot* in terms of early date—one day after the Lake Ontario rescue on August 3, 1853. One might argue that the quantity of newspapers we have assembled is greater for Youngstown, which is true, but Textual Critics know that quantity is less important than determining the originating story and tracking the lineage of its descendants.[38] Second, we have seen that Youngstown, which has a slow-flowing eddy and docks and was closer to Lake Ontario's other ports,[39] was a port of call, especially in the summer, and that steamers ran regularly scheduled "packets" (cargo, passengers, and mail) between Youngstown and "Little York" or Toronto. This was fully documented in Chapter 5. It was also a stop on other routes:

> The line of steamers which plied between Ogdensburg and Lewiston, in former years, touched at Youngstown, which was an important landing. These steamers will be remembered by the older residents of the village. They were the "Ontario," the "Cataract," the "New York" and the "Northerner." They began to run about 1845, and the business was continued until sometime in 1856 or 1857.[40]

---

[36] E.g., Mary Ellen Snodgrass, *The Underground Railroad: An Encyclopedia of People, Places, and Operations* (M. E. Sharpe, Taylor & Rancis, 2008; Routledge, 2015), 270.

[37] Wellman, "Lewiston Landing," note 21 says of the *North American* version: Ben Hockley "arrived at Youngstown, not Lewiston." Her note has led us to track these sources. In a discussion at a conference on the UGRR in Niagara-on-the-Lake, she was open to the possibility of Youngstown.

[38] In thousands of ancient manuscript variants, counting manuscripts is much less important than determining the "archetype" (beginning of the family tree) and tracking descent lineages (who copied whom).

[39] *History of Niagara County*, 121.

[40] *History of Niagara County*, 340.

To this list we added the earlier steamers, the *Martha Ogden* and the early *Ontario* in the 1820s and 1830s. Third, consultation with contemporary boaters on the Niagara River and Lake Ontario reveal that it would have been much easier for a raft to reach the Canadian shore from Lewiston than from Youngstown. It is a full seven miles downstream from Lewiston to the mouth of the river at Lake Ontario while Youngstown is less than a mile. The longer distance would have given a rafter more time and opportunity to reach the opposite shore, especially if the rafter had a paddle; indeed, at certain points the current causes floating objects to drift toward the Canadian shore. Fourth, the river at Youngstown has a back eddy that would initially cause a raft to flow in the opposite direction, upstream. This eddy can hinder crossing the river (modern kayakers have no problem if it is a calm day). Fifth, and more importantly, once one gets into the main current of the river it is swifter between Youngstown and Niagara than it is at points in the seven-mile trip between Lewiston and the mouth of the river. Sixth, the river is not only swift—two to three feet per second—but also very wide between Youngstown and Niagara.

In short, distance, river width, and currents make it much more difficult to raft across the Niagara River from Youngstown than from Lewiston, and therefore more likely that an attempted crossing that failed was launched at Youngstown. Finally, in reporting the story it would have been easy to substitute Lewiston for Youngstown; Lewiston was larger and more important as a steamship port and better known in Canada. Calling Youngstown "Lewiston" on the part of non-locals persists until this day.

Given the higher credibility of the historicity of the core story, the silence on how Hockley got to Lewiston in the Lewiston version, and the greater difficulty of crossing the Niagara River on a gate/raft at Youngstown, we judge that the probability lies with the Youngstown version of Hockley's attempted escape.

CHAPTER 10

A Young Fugitive Slave James and his Father Daniel Sent to UGRR Agent "Mr. Pardee" of Youngstown, 1855

Image 10.1

In his 1982 *History of the Presbyterian Church, Newark, New York, 1825-1980*, Robert Hoeltzel recorded an account of a small group of Newark Presbyterian churchmen who gave money and directions to a young slave boy to go with his father, who was waiting at the Newark Depot, to Youngstown, New York.[1] Hoeltzel's primary source was a Diary of one of those churchmen, John P. VanDeusen.[2]

---

[1] Hoeltzel, Robert L. *A History of the Presbyterian Church, Newark, New York, 1825-1980* (Lyons, NY: Wilprint, 1982), 50. Mr. Hoeltzel is now deceased.

[2] The Diary is mentioned in a paragraph by Judith Wellman (with credit to Marjory Allen Perez), "Site of the Ferry Landing at Youngstown," *Niagara Falls Underground Railroad Heritage Area Management Plan Appendix C: Survey of Sites Relating to the Underground Railroad, Abolitionism, and African American Life in NiagaraFalls and Surrounding Area, 1820-1880* (New York Historical Research Associates, 2012) http://www.niagarafallsundergroundrailroad.org/documents/24_Site%20of%20the%20Ferry%20Landing%20at%2

We visited Newark, New York. There the office administrator of the Park Presbyterian Church helped Gretchen to locate four of the VanDeusen Diaries in the Newark-Arcadia Historical Society Museum.[3] The Diary entry of February 16, 1855, provides further evidence that there was an Underground Railroad network operating in the Western New York region. It says that fugitive slaves should be sent to a certain "Mr. Pardee" at Youngstown, New York. Pardee had lived in Palmyra, not far from Newark, but had since migrated to Youngstown. Robert Hoeltzel had transcribed the VanDeusen Diary entry, but Gretchen re-transcribed it, attempting to stay as close as possible to the way that VanDuesen wrote, including his style and punctuation.[4] We present it momentarily, but first offer some background information.

Newark, New York, and the Park Presbyterian Church

The Erie Canal at Newark, New York	A Canal Boat at Newark, New York

Photos by Dennis Duling
Images 10.2a & 10.2b

Newark, New York, is about thirty-eight miles southeast of Rochester, a few miles from Lyons and Palmyra, both of which are mentioned in the VanDeusen Diary entry. The town is situated on the Erie Canal, which opened in 1825, and it was also a stop on the New York

---

0Youngstown.pdf. John P. VanDeusen is described as "John P. Van Deusen [*sic*] of Palmyra, New York"; at the time of the *Diary*, he was John P. VanDeusen of Lockville, New York, a section of Newark, New York. See Appendix 3.
[3] Other VanDeusen diaries seem to exist, but they have not been given to the Newark-Arcadia Historical Society Museum in Newark, New York.
[4] John P. VanDeusen, Diary, 1855, in the Newark-Arcadia Historical Society Museum, transcribed by Gretchen Duling, Oct. 22, 2014. See biographical comments later and Appendix 6 for more about VanDeusen.

Central Railroad, which by May 1, 1853, had consolidated other railroads that included the Rochester, Lockport, and Niagara Falls Railroad (the Falls Road Railroad).[5] When we decided to see the Diary for ourselves, Gretchen telephoned the administrative assistant of Newark's Park Presbyterian Church, Bethany Comella, and discussed the purpose of our visit. Ms. Comella was very enthusiastic. We arrived some days later and met her and the pastor, the Reverend Kirk Baker. Both were intrigued about the Diary and went searching in the church's archives for more information. They made an astonishing discovery: an 1850 flier announcing a meeting at the church ("the Presbyterian Meeting House") to hear the testimony of a fugitive slave, David Green Wheelbanks, who was scheduled to lecture and discuss the controversial *Fugitive Slave Act of 1850* at the church on November 9, 1850. The law had only recently been signed by President Millard Fillmore. Fugitive slave Wheelbanks' appearance in this manner was clearly a courageous act at this time.

For us, the Broadside find was especially important since it not only contributed to information about the lecturing activities of the David Green Wheelbanks, but it also reinforced our growing understanding of anti-slavery sympathies of some members of the Newark Presbyterian Meeting House.[6]

---

[5] The New York Central Railroad consolidated many previously existing railway companies, each with its own history; see Wikipedia, "Category: Predecessors of the New York Central Railroad," https://en.wikipedia.org/wiki/Category:Predecessors_of_the_New_York_Central_Railroad. See the end of Ch. 5, "The Transitory Trains to Youngstown."

[6] David Green Wheelbanks is a documented anti-slavery lecturer; see, for example, Tanya Warren, Compiler, Historical New York Research Associates, "Freedom Seekers, Abolitionists, and Underground Railroad Helpers, Cayuga County, New York," http://www.cayugacounty.us/portals/0/history/ugrr/report/pdf/consolidated.pdf.

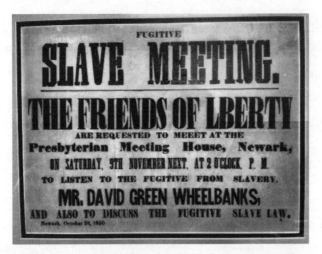

Broadside of the David Green Wheelbanks Lecture and Fugitive Slave Law Discussion
(Courtesy of the Administrative Commission of the Park Presbyterian Church, 2014)
Image 10.3

The Current Park Presbyterian Church, Newark, New York
Photo by Dennis Duling
Image 10.4

Ms. Bethany Comella helped Gretchen to make contact with Christopher Davis, curator of the nearby Newark-Arcadia Historical Society Museum, which had four of the VanDeusen diaries.[7] We are grateful to the Park Presbyterian Church for its cooperation and to Christopher Davis, the director of the Newark-Arcadia Historical Society Museum, who was very helpful and has since sent us more information about John P. VanDeusen.

John P. VanDeusen and the *VanDeusen Diary* Entry, February 16, 1855

**John P. VanDeusen
in 1905, at 84 years of age[8]
Image 10.5**

---

[7] For the Newark-Arcadia Historical Society and Museum, see http://newarkarcadiamuseum.org/. More diaries exist but they have not yet been given to the Museum.
[8] Thanks to Christopher Davis, Museum Director of the Newark-Arcadia Historical Society Museum.

In 1931, John P. VanDeusen's daughter, Anna S. VanDeusen, wrote a history of the VanDeusen family that included a section on the life of her father, which we now summarize.[9]

John P. VanDeusen was born on March 24, 1821, in Pittstown, New York. His father was Lucas VanDeusen, a tanner, and his mother was Minerva (Porter) VanDeusen. John was the oldest of eight children, only four of whom survived to adulthood. Lucas eventually moved with his family to Newark where he engaged in several unskilled occupations. The adult John married Anna M. Lay and the couple had five children. John was a farmer who also took up teaching. He was also an active member of the Newark Presbyterian Meeting House, which became Park Presbyterian Church, and the Temperance Movement. He also engaged in local and national politics. Anna died in 1906 and John in 1910.

The VanDeusen Diary entry of February 16, 1855, is of significance because it suggests that a certain "Mr. Pardee" of Youngstown, formerly of Palmyra, became an agent—at Youngstown. In other words, as we shall see, a network cluster in the Newark-Lyons-Palmyra area was probably linked with another in the Youngstown area.

6A VanDeusen Diary in the Newark-Arcadia Historical Society Museum
Displayed on top is the February 1855 entry (see below)
Photo by Gretchen Duling
Image 10.6

---

[9] A letter from Christopher Davis, ibid., to Gretchen Duling, dated December 19, 2014, includes an Introduction to the diaries by Robert L. Hoeltzel, Arcadia Town Historian (deceased), and the "Life of John P. VanDeusen" by VanDeusen's daughter, Anna S. VanDeusen (1931).

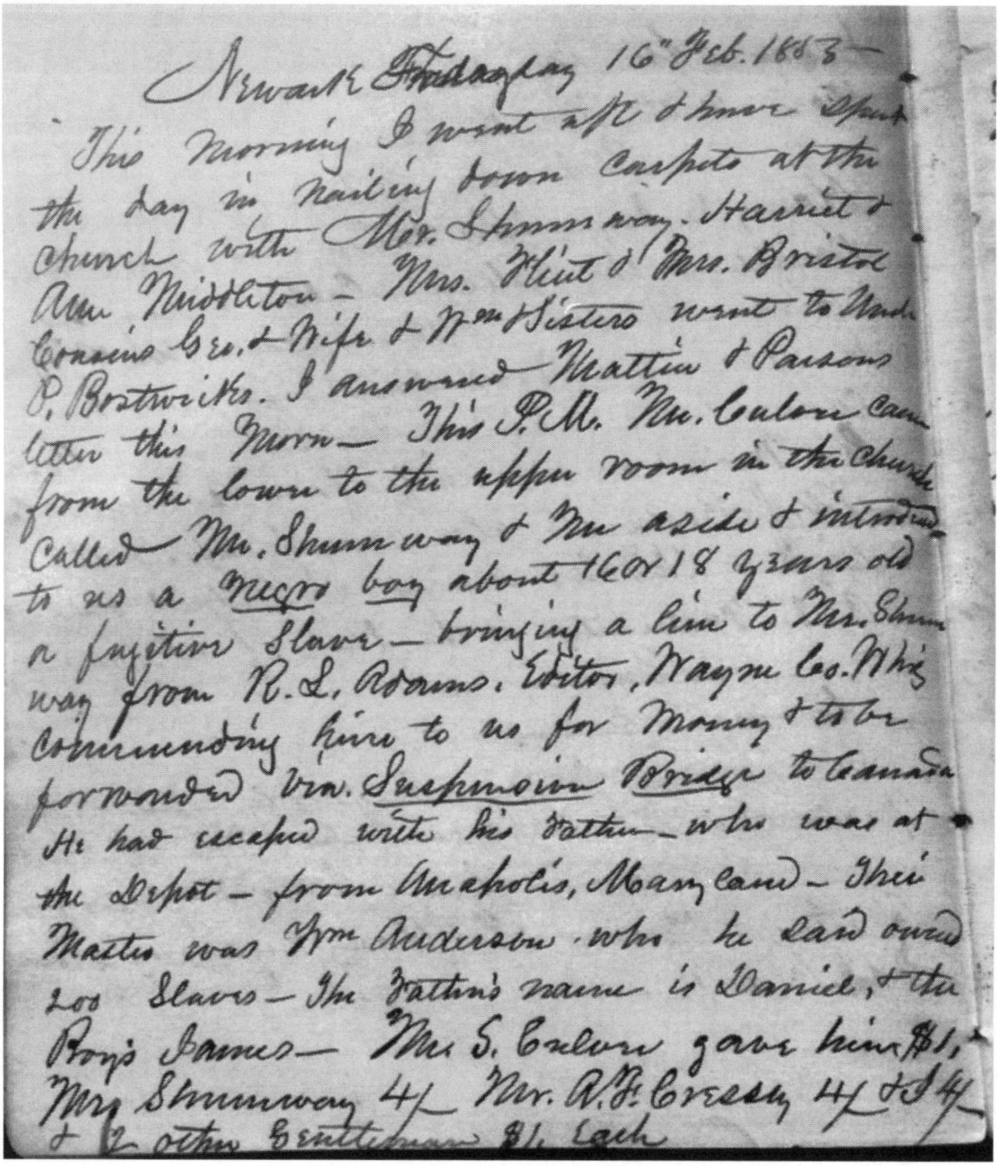

The VanDeusen Diary of Friday, February 16, 1855
Image 10.7

Gretchen Duling's transcription of Friday, February 16, 1855:

[Page 1]

Newark, Friday, 16th Feb. 1855.

This morning I went out to spend the day in nailing down carpets at church [the Presbyterian Meeting House (Park Presbyterian Church] with [the pastor] Mr. Shumway . . . [in preparation for the dedication on March 8th of the rebuilt church building which had damage by fire]. . . This P.M. Mr. Culver came from the lower to the upper room in the church. [He] called Mr. Shumway and me aside to introduce us [to] a Negro boy about 16 or 18 years old a fugitive Slave −bring[ing] a line [brief letter, note] to Mr. Schumway from R. L. Adams, Editor, *Wayne Co. Whig*[10] commending him to us for money & to be forwarded via Suspension Bridge to Canada. He had escaped with his father who was at the Depot [the New York Central Railroad, which ran through Arcadia?] − from Annapolis, Maryland [Maryland was a slave state] − Their Master was Wm. Anderson who he said owned 200 slaves − The Father's name is Daniel and the Boy's name James. Mr. S. Culver gave him $1, Mr. A. F. Cressy gave him 4/ [Shillings], and I 4/ [Shillings], & 2 other Gentlemen $1 each [$4.50].[11]

---

[10] *The Palmyra Whig* was moved to Lyons, New York, in 1839 and renamed the *Wayne County Whig* (it was renamed again as the *Wayne County Republican* in 1855). Rodney L. Adams, a printer, built up the paper and was its successful editor from 1852 to 1859. See George W. Cowles, Assisted by H. P. Smith and Others, *Landmarks of Wayne County, New York, Illustrated* (Syracuse, NY: D. Mason & Company, Publishers, 1895), 136.

[11] The slash / in slanted form was derived from an elongated "S," originally an abbreviation for the gold Roman coin, the *solidus*, and retained for the shilling. The shilling was worth 12 pence (pennies) (see Chs. 6, 8). Robert L. Hoeltzel, *Hometown History, Village of Newark, Town of Arcadia* (Newark, NY: G. McCellan of Arcadia Historical Society, 2000), tries to be precise: four shillings = 50 cents; therefore, $4.50 was collected, equivalent at that time to a little more two day's pay for a semi-skilled workman, or if $1.00 then is about $30.00 today, almost $135.00.

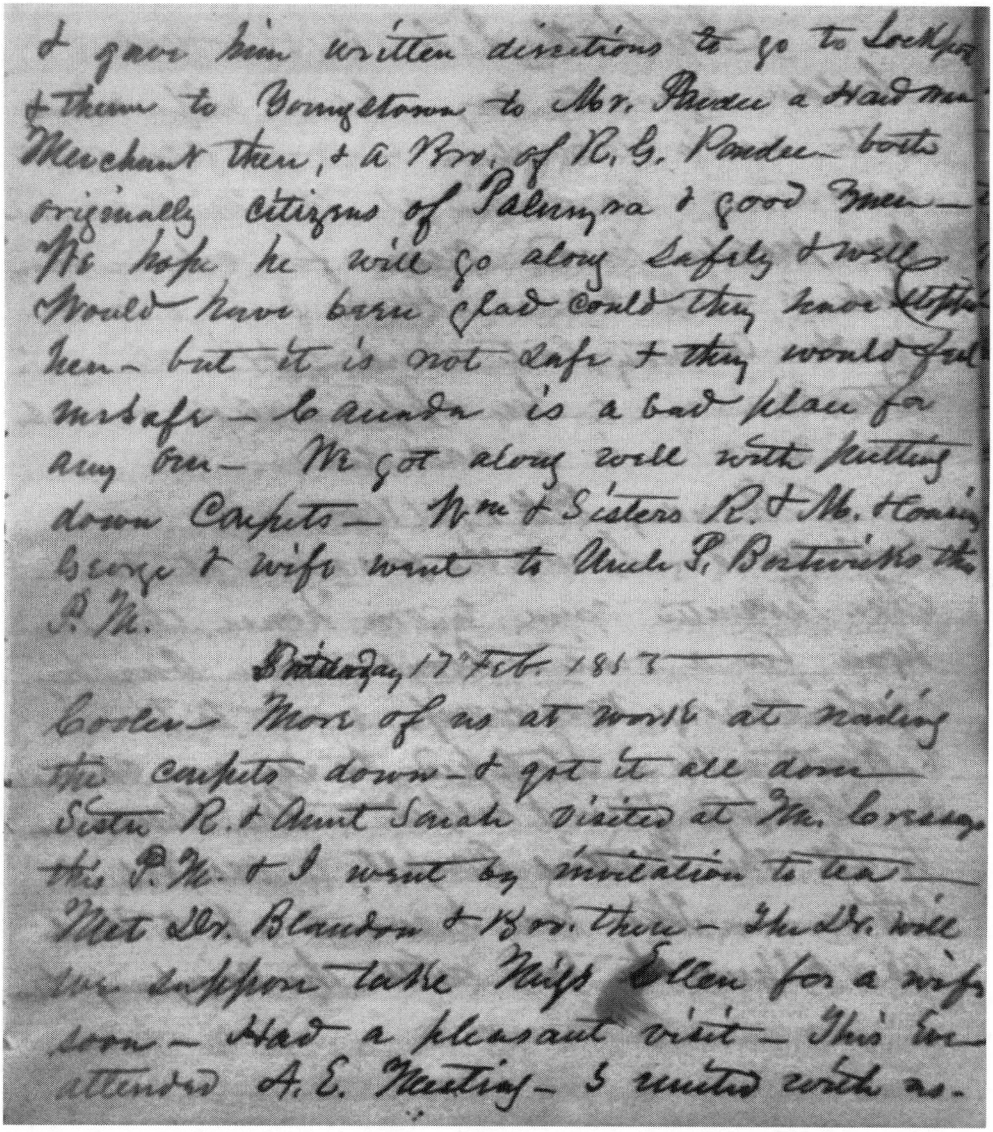

& gave him written directions to go to Lockport
& thence to Youngstown to Mr. Pardee a Hardware
Merchant there, & a Bro. of R. G. Pardee — both
originally citizens of Palmyra & good men —
We hope he will go along safely & well —
Would have been glad could they have kept
him — but it is not safe & they would feel
unsafe — Canada is a bad place for
any One — We got along well with putting
down Carpets — Wm & Sisters R. & M. & Cousin
George & wife went to Uncle P. Bostwicks this
P. M.

Saturday, 17 Feb. 1855 ———
Cooler — Most of us at work at nailing
the carpets down — & got it all done —
Sister R. & Aunt Sarah visited at Mr. Creasings
this P. M. & I went by invitation to tea —
Met Dr. Blaudou & Bro. there — The Dr. will
we suppose take Miss Ellen for a wife
soon — Had a pleasant visit — This Eve.
attended A. E. Meeting — I united with us.

The VanDeusen Diary of February 16, 1855 (Continued)
Photo by Gretchen Duling
Image 10.8

[Page 2; first half of page]

I gave him written directions to go to Lockport & then to Youngstown to Mr. Pardee a Hardware Merchant there, & Bro. of R. G. Pardee both originally citizens of Palmyra & good men_ We hope he will go along safely & we would have been glad could they have stopped here _ but it is not safe + they would feel unsafe _ Canada is [not][12] a bad place for any one _ We got along well with putting down carpets . . .

We need to interpret the Diary entry.

The Reverend George R. H. Shumway and
the Lyons, Palmyra, and Newark UGRR Network

The Rev. George R. H. Shumway[13]
Photo in Hoeltzel, *Hometown History*, 1
Image 10.9

The pastor "Mr. Shumway" in the VanDeusen Diary entry was the Reverend George Randall Howe Shumway, born in Oxford, New York. He was a graduate of the Auburn Theological Seminary in Auburn, New York, in 1834. Many Auburn Seminary faculty and students were abolitionists and in that year they formed one of the first anti-slavery societies in New York State. Two years later they published anti-slavery resolutions in the New York State Anti-Slavery Society publication called *The Friend of Man*. They also collected signatures for anti-slavery petitions they generated and sent them to Congress, a well-known strategy of *The Friend of Man*.

Shumway graduated from Auburn in 1834, the year after the American Anti-Slavery Society was formed.[14] His first pastorate was at the Western Presbyterian Church (The

---

[12] Surely, VanDeusen did not mean to say that Canada is a "bad" place in the context of sending fugitive slaves there; he must have accidently written "bad" instead of "good" (his script for the term "good" occurs five lines earlier, and this is simply not the same word). Hoeltzel seems to have handled the problem by not printing this sentence and replacing it with ". . . . ." (p. 50). We have chosen instead to insert "not" in brackets.

[13] Shumway became the moderator of the Geneva Presbytery in 1849 and of the Lyons Presbytery in 1862; he was also the Stated Clerk (the main ongoing office) from 1844-1969.

Presbyterian Meeting House) in Palmyra, New York, from 1835 to 1842. In 1835, the New York Anti-Slavery Society was organized at the home of famous abolitionist Gerrit Smith and his wife Ann Smith in Peterboro, New York.[15] In the following year, 1836, the year of the Auburn Resolutions, Shumway became involved in organizing the abolitionist movement in Palmyra.

Shumway's abolitionist sympathies can be documented in more detail. On October 3, 1836, abolitionist agent W. C. Rogers paid Shumway a visit. He reported in *The Friend of Man*, "I find our friends [in Palmyra] firm & in excellent spirits . . . [The Reverend Shumway] is fully engaged in the work . . . [and he] . . . thinks it important that a course of lectures by Bro. [Theodore] Weld[16] be given this winter. In *this* place I found a host; men of nerve indeed. Truly gratifying was it to witness their spirit."[17] Ten days later, on Thursday, October 13, the new Palmyra Anti-Slavery Society, a coalition of mainly Quakers and Presbyterians with some Methodists and perhaps some Baptists, met in the Presbyterian Meeting House and listened to a lecture by John Thomas of the Society of Friends. It was Shumway who summarized the Palmyra meeting in a short letter published in the abolitionist weekly, *The Friend of Man*, in November of 1836.[18]

---

[14] See Ch. 2.

[15] Ibid.

[16] For Theodore Weld's image and influence, see Chs. 2 and 8.

[17] *Friend of Man*, October 3, 1836; quoted by Judith Wellman, "'Unspeakable Joy': Religion, Reform, the Underground Railroad and African American Life in the Burned-Over District of Wayne County, New York," in Historical New York Research Associates, *Databases. Sites Relating to the Underground Railroad, Abolitionism, and African American Life in Wayne County, New York* (Lyons, NY: Wayne County Historian's Office, 2007--2009), 16.

[18] George R. H. Shumway, letter of October 17, 1836, to *The Friend of Man* (November 3, 1836).

> Palmyra, (Wayne Co.) Oct. 17th, 1836.
>
> To the Editor of the Friend of Man.
>
> DEAR SIR :—On Thursday evening of last week, there was a meeting of the Palmyra Anti-Slavery Society in the Lecture Room of the Presbyterian Meeting House in the village.
>
> An interesting address on slavery and the means for its removal, was delivered by John Thomas, of the Society of Friends. A delegation was then appointed to attend the meeting occurring in your city this week, and a contribution made to the funds of your Society. The cause is advancing. We were in no way molested. There is, in truth, in P. too much good sense—too much love of order, liberty and religion to countenance the shameless misrule and riotous movements which have given an unenviable notoriety to Boston, Troy, Cincinatti, &c.
>
> We wish you God speed. Be encouraged—truth and mercy—the Bible and its Divine Author are with you— and with you are the prayers and alms of thousands.
>
> Yours, truly,
>
> G. R. H. SHUMWAY.

Shumway Report of a Palmyra Anti-Slavery Meeting, October 13, 1836
Image 10.10

Shumway reported that a delegation from Palmyra would be attending a forthcoming Western New York Anti-Slavery Meeting (1838) and that the Palmyra branch had collected a contribution for the Society. A little more than a year later, December 1, 1837, another meeting of the Palmyra Anti-Slavery Society at Palmyra's Western Presbyterian Church (the Presbyterian Meeting House) took place and Shumway served as a member of its Executive Committee.

Three weeks later, on December 20, 1837, a group of Palmyra women met at the Shumway home to organize a Female Anti-Slavery Society in the Town of Palmyra, and Mrs. Emily Shumway was one of its five Managers.[19] In a statement about their formation,

---

[19] *The Friend of Man*, Vol. 2, No. 37 (February 1838).

. . . [I]t was concluded in view of the demoralizing influence of American slavery upon its unhappy victims as also upon the community generally where it exists—and the necessity of moral effort to remove this odious system from the common country, and to ameliorate the condition of our degraded sisters who are daily exposed to the torturing lash of the cruel driver, and every indignity that the vilest passions of man can conceive—to form ourselves into a society for the more effectual promotion of our purpose.[20]

There followed a Preamble that quoted the anti-ethnic, anti-slavery, gender inclusive statement of St. Paul in Galatians 3:28 (King James Version), "there is neither Jew nor Greek, there is neither bond nor free, there is neither male nor female, for ye are all one in Christ Jesus." The Preamble continued by saying ". . . slavery as it exists in the United States is a sin of the most revolting character in the sight of God. . ."[21]

In 1838, the Anti-Slavery Convention for Western New York met at the Bethel Church in Rochester on January 10, 11, and 12. Among the representatives from Palmyra was the Reverend George R. H. Shumway, who was on the Committee to Prepare Business for the meeting, for which he prepared a lengthy report that was adopted. It began:

1st. Resolved, That we esteem slavery incompatible, with all the principles of a representative government, contradictory to the solemn declaration of our independence, subversive of all the principles of our free institutions, hostile to peace and unity of feeling between the South and the North, corrupting and debasing in its nature, with a blot upon the nation, a war upon humanity and a sin against God, necessarily involving, if persisted in, both slaveholders and slaves in utter ruin.[22]

---

[20] *The Friend of Man,* ibid.
[21] Ibid. Slavery was also considered to be a sin in the 1833 American Anti-Slavery Society's Declaration written by William Lloyd Garrison.
[22] *The Friend of Man,* Volume 2, Number 33, January 31, 1838. Online at Cornell University. http://fom.library.cornell.edu/cgi-bin/cornell-fom?a=d&d=TFOM18380131.2.2&srpos=3&e=-------en-20--1--txt-txIN-Shumway-----#. Samuel C. Cuyler was the representative from Pultneyville; see Ch. 4 in this book.

Women who attended the meeting, some from Palmyra, held an Anti-Slavery Fair that raised funds and they contributed them to the Western New York Anti-Slavery Society and the Underground Railroad.[23]

It is clear that in Palmyra the Shumways were on the ground floor of the anti-slavery movement and were involved in the formation and development of Anti-Slavery Societies not only in Palmyra, but in Western New York at large.

After an interim Stated Supply position from 1842-1844 at a Patterson, New Jersey Presbyterian Church, Shumway became minister of the Newark Presbyterian Society (the Park Presbyterian Church), only nine miles from Palmyra. He was the pastor there twenty-five years, from 1844 to 1869. Given his Auburn Theological Seminary background and his role as an established anti-slavery activist at Palmyra, it is not surprising that he became a central figure in a local anti-slavery network at Newark, which might well have centered in the liberal New School Park Presbyterian Church.[24] In historian Robert L. Hoeltzel's terms,

> The rev. George R. H. Shumway was noted through the area as an ardent abolishionist [sic] during the years preceeding [sic] the Civil War, and an outspoken Union partisan during the war. . . The entry in John P. VanDeusen's diary for February 16, 1855 (while the new church building was being readied for occupancy) suggests that the rev. Mr. Shumway may have had a regular part in the 'Underground Railroad'.[25]

In short, the leading abolitionist in Newark was surely Rev. George R. H. Shumway, Pastor of Newark's Presbyterian Church from 1844 to 1869.

---

[23] *Friend of Man*, Vol. 3, No. 33 (January 31, 1838); *The Friend of Man* online at Cornell University; cited in Wellman, "'Unspeakable Joy'," 15.

[24] Old School Presbyterians were doctrinally orthodox Calvinists who rejected revivalism and congregation-centered government (like the Congregationalists), both of which were acceptable to New School Presbyterians. These differences led to schism among Presbyterians that began in 1837. Some New School Presbyterians merged with the Calvinistic Congregationalists.

[25] Hoeltzel, *Hometown History*, 39, 50

According to the VanDeusen Diary, the young fugitive slave James and his father Daniel had escaped from slavery under a master, a certain William Anderson of Annapolis, Maryland, with 200 slaves. Curiously, a slave house, one of possibly six, has survived on a plantation once

A Slave House on the Antebellum Plantation "Grassland"
of William Anderson, Annapolis Junction, Anne Arundel County, Maryland
About twenty-five yards from the main house, built ca. 1853
Permission: The Grassland Foundation, Inc., Marvin H. Anderson, President
Photo by Donna Ware, Surveyor, 1984
Image 10.11

belonging to a certain William Anderson of Annapolis *Junction*, Maryland, although it is hardly likely that this plantation had 200 slaves (see Figure 10.11).[26] In any case, when James arrived at

---

[26] This slave house, one of possibly six such houses (one of the surviving buildings) on William Anderson's plantation, "Grassland," was built sometime in 1852-1854 (the main house, 1853). It is made of brick noggin, but covered with weather boards. In 1984, the plantation was nominated for the National Register of Historic Places by Donna Ware, who took the photo (https://mht.maryland.gov/secure/medusa/PDF/Anne%20Arundel/AA-94.pdf). Anderson's journal or diary, including descriptions of the buildings, has been given to the Maryland Historical Society by his great grandson, John Bowie, Jr. See Cora Woodward (Anderson) DuLaney, *Extract of Diary or Farm Journal of William Anderson of "Grassland" 1853 to 1875 and Certain Related Documents*, 1965 (Footnotes prepared in 1987-1988 by Marvin H. Anderson). For a social historical description of slave houses, including this one, see George W. McDaniel, *Hearth & Home: Preserving a People's Culture* (American Civilization. Philadelphia, PA: Temple University Press, 1982); also, McDaniel, "Housing," in Randall M Miller and John David Smith *Dictionary of Afro-American Slavery, Updated, with a New Introduction and Bibliography* (Westport, CN; London, UK: Praeger,

the Presbyterian Church in Newark, he was taken to the Reverend Mr. Shumway and VanDeusen by Mr. Culver. James carried a letter for Shumway from Rodney L. Adams, a printer and editor of the *Wayne Co. Whig* in nearby Lyons, New York.[27] Adams asked that money be given to the fugitive slaves Daniel and James. Shumway and five lay churchmen of the Newark (Park) Presbyterian Church are mentioned, three by name: the just noted Stephen Culver, a retired lawyer/civil engineer and architect for the new Newark church, also Sunday School Superintendent (1844—1858); Albert Franklin Cressy, a grocer and pew holder; and John P. VanDeusen, the author of the Diary.[28] They and two unnamed men each gave the freedom seekers money totaling about $4.50, or over $100 today (2016). The Diary gives no indication that these lay leaders were surprised at the appearance of the African American freedom seekers, nor was there any indication that the Reverend Shumway hesitated in presenting James to them. Indeed, wrote VanDeusen, they would have been happy to have had the freedom seekers remain in Newark (where?), but they realized that it was not safe there, which seems to have betrayed their knowledge of slave catchers in the Newark area. Clearly, a regional network of the UGRR was involved.

"Mr. Pardee"

Despite R. L. Adams' instruction to send Daniel and James to Suspension Bridge (Village), the VanDeusen Diary states "I [John P. VanDeusen] gave him [fugitive slave James] written directions to go to Lockport & then to Youngstown to Mr. Pardee a Hardware Merchant there, & Bro. of R. G. Pardee both originally citizens of Palmyra & good men."

1997), 341-46. Grassland, privately owned in 1984, was turned over to the Grassland Foundation in 1987 (see http://www.grasslandfoundation.com/, including photos). A special thanks to Marvin H. Anderson, President, The Grassland Foundation, Inc., who thinks that his great uncle's plantation with six or fewer houses hardly had 200 slaves. We agree. Did James exaggerate? Did VanDeusen misunderstand? Was this a different Wm. Anderson?
[27] See n. 10 above.
[28] The 1850 census lists Stephen Culver (age 38) as a lawyer with a physician, Orrin A. Lovejoy (age 29), and Clarissa A. Lovejoy in his household, and Albert F. Cressey (age 55) with Anne Cressey (age 51) and Martha Cressey (age 12) in his household. Further information is given by Hoeltzel, *Presbyterian Church*, 42-45. For a possible ex-slave's house at Niagara-on-the-lake, see Ch. 1.

Who was Mr. Pardee of Youngstown?

VanDeusen's Diary described the Pardee brothers as "good men" and "Mr. Pardee" as a respectable Youngstown hardware merchant. His comment about Mr. Pardee's business is confirmed in a letter of James Onen to the *Youngstown News* in 1908. Onen had been a resident of Youngstown, but had left for Michigan in August of 1854, the year before the VanDeusen Diary entry. The Onen letter was published online in 2006 by Vee Housman (posthumously), a former Town of Porter Historian (deceased 2005), who introduced Onen's letter like this:

> . . . [On December 19, 1908, a letter was written] to the editor of *The Youngstown News* . . . by James Onen who was born around 1834 in New York State, the son of Dennis and Catherine (Welch) Onen who were both born in Ireland. James lived in Youngstown until 1854 when he moved west to Michigan. The rest of his family continued to live in Youngstown until they died. They're all buried in the Catholic Cemetery on Oak Street in Youngstown. This local Onen family is still remembered here as boat builders and mariners.[29]

Onen's own Introduction to his 1908 letter to the *Youngstown News* indicated his main purpose: to correct some of historian William Pool's information that had been used as a source in a previous *Youngstown News* editorial on Youngstown's past. Included in Onen's letter are these memories:

> The Davis brick block was built previous to 1854.[30] I left Youngstown August 2, 1854, and prior to the time I left the dear old place, *Pardee & Pomroy* were engaged in the hardware business in the room where Miss [Catherine] Kelly is now located [1908].

---

[29] Notice of Vee Housman, Town of Porter historian, N.D., about James Onen, "'Recollections of James Onen. Youngstown's Early Days,' *The Youngstown News* (December 24)," 1908)
http://www.newspaperabstracts.com/link.php?action=detail&id=28591.
http://archiver.rootsweb.ancestry.com/th/read/NY-OLD-NEWS/2006-09/1157310292 (added Sep 3, 2006). One of the more recent ferries from Youngstown to Niagara-on-the-Lake was the *Anna F. Onen* (there was more than one *Anna F. Onen*). See the Time-Line History of the Youngstown Ferry, Ferrymen, Riverboats, and Bridges in Chapter 6 of this book.

[30] The much cited date for the Davis Brick Building in Pool, *Landmarks*, is 1855; Onen, "Recollections," claims, however, that the Davis Brick Building was there when he left in 1854. This date is also implied in an article in the *Niagara Falls Gazette* quoted below. The bricks were from the brickyard of John Carter; see Chs. 14, 16.

The B[radley] D. Davis store was in the rear room now occupied by the express company. Charlotte Colman kept a millinery store where Thomas Ellis had his barber shop. Charlotte was the first woman I ever saw dressed in bloomers.[31]

Miss Catherine Kelly's Youngstown Store in the 409 (Haskell) Building (date unknown)
Courtesy: Town of Porter Historical Society
Image 10.12

---

[31] Onen, "Recollections"; see also Judith Wellman in the Underground Railroad Heritage Area Commission, *People and Sites Relating to the Underground Railroad, Abolitionism, and African American Life, 1820-1880* (Historical New York Research Associates, Inc. for edr. Companies and the Niagara Falls), 65. Onen's letter was cited in connection with boat building at Youngstown in Ch. 4. Bloomers, a bold, audacious fashion statement by feminists in the late 1840s/early 1850s, were loose, healthier, knee-length dresses with pantaloons that allowed women freedom (literally and symbolically) in public. They were named after Amelia Bloomer, a woman's rights and temperance advocate, who attended the first women's rights convention in Seneca Falls, New York, in 1848, and was the driving force behind *The Lily*, the first woman's newspaper. http://www.findagrave.com/cgi-bin/fg.cgi?page=gr&GRid=2529. Perhaps Charlotte Colman was a feminist who was advertising her bloomers!

In an article on Youngstown in the *Niagara Falls Gazette*, January 23, 1856, there is more information about the hardware store of *Pardee & Pomeroy* (Pomroy is also spelled with an "e"[32]) located in the Davis Brick Block:

> . . . We found, on visiting our [Youngstown] neighbors one day last week that the hand of improvement had been busy. During the last year Messrs. J. Davis & Co. have erected a very fine block of stores. The building is three stories in height from the street, with one or two stories in the basement on the declivity of the bank. The building is constructed of brick with iron fronts, and presents a very pleasant appearance. One story is occupied by Messrs. J. Davis & co. as a general dry goods, grocery and crockery store. They appear to be doing, as they have for many years past, a heavy business. Another store [*sic*; story?] is occupied by *Messrs. Pardee & Pomeroy as a hardware store. We were altogether surprised to find that business conducted on so extensive a scale. These gentlemen have been in the business there two years, and if we are not greatly mistaken in appearances they are justly deserving the support of all that region of country. Their stock is large, of sufficient variety, and, from the trade they are receiving, is probably sold as cheap as elsewhere.* Another and the smallest store is occupied by Miss Wilson as a millinery establishment.[33]

The key point is that Onen's letter and the Niagara Falls report included references to the Youngstown hardware business, *Pardee & Pom[e]roy*, located in the front of the Davis Brick Block at 409 Main Street since 1854,[34] and the latter lauded the business acumen of "these gentlemen." Was the hardware merchant of *Pardee & Pom[e]roy* the same VanDeusen's hardware merchant "Mr. Pardee," to whom fugitive slaves Daniel and James were to report? The answer is "yes."

---

[32] The spelling with an "e" in the article will be significant for census information about the Pomeroy residence in Lancaster, New York (see below).

[33] "Youngstown," *Niagara Falls Gazette* (January 23, 1856) 2:4 (italics ours). For a photo of the Davis Brick Block, see Ch. 16.

[34] www.newspaperabstracts.com/link.php?action=detail&id=28591. For more about the Davis family and the Davis Brick Block, see Chs. 14, 16.

The Pardees and the Wilcoxes; The Gerrit Smith Connection

Intimate networks are composed of family and friends ("strong ties"), not casual acquaintances, friends of friends, or more distant, sometimes unknown, contacts, or friends of friends of friends ("weak ties").[35] There were strong ties between the Pardees and the Wilcoxes. VanDeusen wrote that the hardware merchants "Mr. Pardee" and his brother, "R. G. Pardee," were "good men" who hailed from Palmyra, New York. A check of the 1850 census records show that at that time in Palmyra there lived a white male Myron J. Pardee (age 26) living with a white female, Cynthia A. Pardee (age 21, his wife), and an infant male, William W. Pardee (age 0, their son). Four other residents lived in that household, a white male William Wilcox (age 61), a white female Harriet N. Wilcox (age 16: daughter? niece?), a white male Asa Curth (age 18), and a white female Julia Nobles (age 17). Living in the same household was probably not the only link between the Pardees and the Wilcoxes. It is very likely that the Pardee boy, **W**illiam **W**. Pardee, was named after **W**illiam **W**ilcox. The Pardees and Wilcoxes were either relatives or very close friends.

There is an interesting connection between Myron Pardee with the famed abolitionist Gerrit Smith (1797-1874) of Peterboro, New York. In the previous chapter, we noted that the Gerrit Smith archive at Syracuse University's Research Center (SCRC) preserves some letters to Smith, including three letters from his Oswego friend and agent, John B. Edwards, about Ben Hockley, and his land transaction Register (Volume 88).[36] Also preserved is a letter from Edwards about a Smith contract with Myron J. Pardee! Smith had lent Pardee money, apparently to buy a lot and a house in Palmyra, and Pardee was paying off his loan in installments. Here is Edward's letter to Gerrit Smith dated July 1, 1851.

---

[35] For comments on social network analysis (SNA), see Preface and Appendix 1 to this book.
[36] See Ch. 9. For Smith's philanthropy, see also Chs. 2, 8, 14.

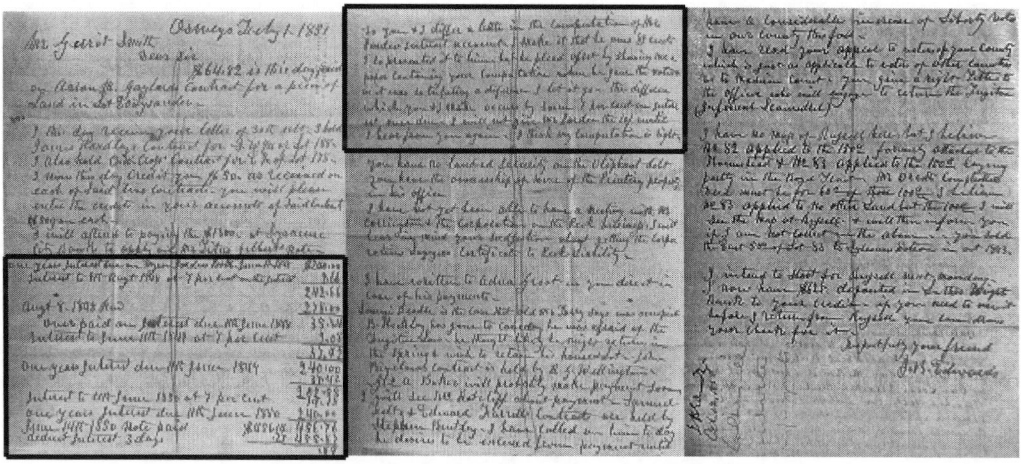

Letter of John B. Edwards to Gerrit Smith, July 1, 1851
Permission from the Syracuse University Library Archives, Syracuse, New York
Photo by Dennis Duling
Image 10.13

Here is part of the section about Myron Pardee (zooming in on the bottom, left box, page 1):

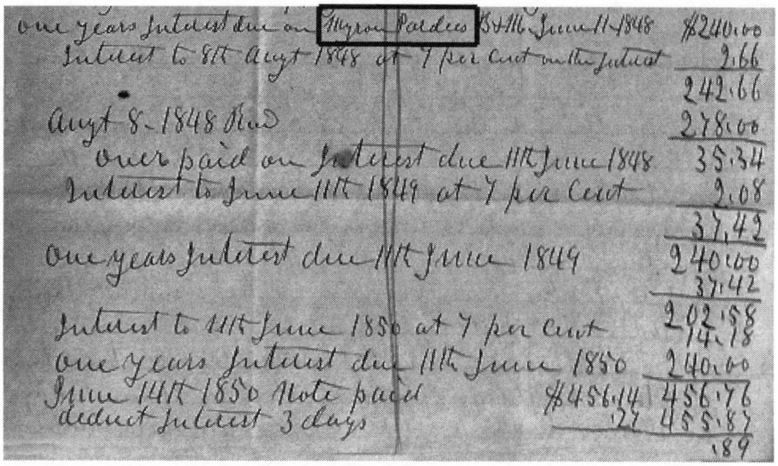

Extract A of Letter of John B. Edwards to Gerrit Smith, July 1, 1851
Photo by Dennis Duling
Image 10.14

Transcriptions by Dennis Duling:

One year's interest due on **Myron Pardee's** B & M[37] June 11, 1848		$240.00
Interest to 8th Aug[us]t 1848 at 7 per cent on the interest		2.66
		242.66
Aug[us]t 8 – 1848 Ru- [unknown term]		278.00
Over paid on interest due 11th June 1848		35.34
Interest to June 1850 at 7 per cent		2.08
		37.42
One year's [sic] interest due 11th June 1849		240.00
		37.42
		202.58
Interest to 11th June 1850 at 7 per cent		14.18
One year's [sic] interest due 11th June 1850		240.00
June 14th 1850 note paid	$456.14	456.76
deduct interest 3 days	.27	455.87
		.89

Here is the rest of the section about Myron Pardee (zooming in on the top of page 2):

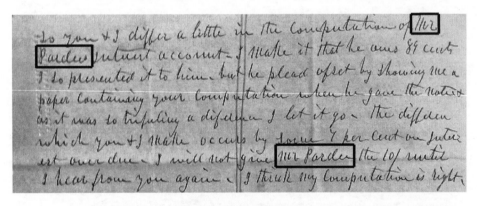

Extract B of Letter of John B. Edwards to Gerrit Smith, July 1, 1851
Photo by Dennis Duling
Image 10.15

Transcription:

> So you & I differ a little in the computation of **Mr
> Pardee[']s** interest account – I make it that he owes 89 cents.
> I so presented it to him, but he plead upset by showing me a
> paper containing your computation when he gave the notes &
> as it was so trifuling [sic] a difference I let it go. The difference
> which you and I make occurs by some 7 per cent on inter-
> est over due. I will not give **Mr Pardee** the 10/[38] until

---

[37] Bill or Balance and Mortgage?

I hear from you again. I think my computation is right.
[Edwards' other notes on property transactions follow]

Myron Pardee was paying back his debt (a mortgage?) to Gerrit Smith at $240 per year plus interest and penalties for late payments. The letter contains information covering three years (1848, 1849, and 1850) and seems to indicate that Myron paid off the note. However, he believed that Gerrit Smith had made a computation error and Edwards agreed, thus Edward's clarification and explanation to Smith.

This Edwards-to-Smith letter reinforces the census data of 1850, that Myron Pardee was living in Palmyra, and perhaps more, that he was, as VanDeusen said, a "good man," that is, he was paying off a debt plus interest and penalties, perhaps on his purchase of property and house in Palmyra.

There is still more information about Myron J. Pardee. The expectation that the Lewiston-Youngstown Railroad lines would bring business to Youngstown led to a major competition for the license to operate the Youngstown Ferry between 1854 and 1858.[39] One of the ferry petitioners in 1854 was Luke P. Babcock, who lived at 600 Main Street (on the corner of Main and Church Streets, immediately north of 614 Main Street, our proposed home for the Pardees and the Wilcoxes). Two of the persons who signed a petition to support Luke Babcock's 1854 Youngstown Ferry application were—*one directly under the other*—"M. J. Pardee" and "E. P. Pomroy"—*Pardee and Pomroy!*[40]

---

[38] Monetary equivalences across time and from the British to the American systems in various geographical areas are complex and difficult to calculate. / abbreviates the shilling (= 12 pence) and there were 20 shillings to the British pound (120 pence). 10/ was about a half a pound, and that was about a week's pay for a semi-skilled laborer. Some calculations state that $1 was about $30-35.00 in 2016 value.

[39] See Ch. 6.

[40] This petition is among the hand-written petitions of support to the Niagara County Court of Pleas for Luke P. Babcock's application for a license to keep the Youngstown Ferry (Niagara County Historian's Office at Lockport, New York, Niagara County).

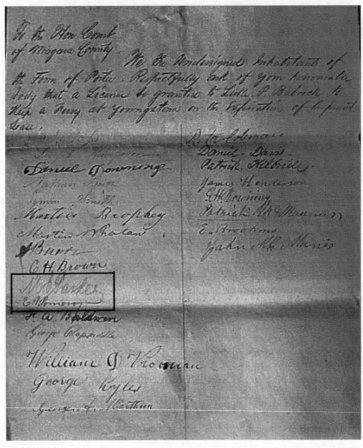

M. J. Pardee and E. P. Pomroy[41] Sign Luke Babcock's 1854 Ferry Petition
Image 10.16

E. P. Pomroy presumably had second thoughts about supporting Babcock. He signed another petition, this one stating that "the ferry license be granted only to the highest responsible bidder and only for one year, and the proceeds go to Town of Porter schools."[42]

To return to the main point: Who was the VanDeusen Diary's "Mr. Pardee," the "good man" and hardware merchant to whom the fugitive slaves Daniel and James at Newark were sent at Youngstown, and what more can be said about his link to the Underground Railroad?

---

[41] "Pomroy" is sometimes spelled "Pomeroy." See the 1870 Census below.
[42] See Ch. 6.

The answer to the first part is that "Mr. Pardee" was Myron J. Pardee, a hardware merchant and "good man" who emigrated from Palmyra to Youngstown with his family and the Wilcoxes sometime between 1850 and 1854. Evidence for his presence in Youngstown by 1854 comes from James Onen's statements about the hardware store *Pardee & Pomroy*; the signatures of M. J. Pardee and E. P. Pomroy on an 1854 petition supporting Luke P. Babcock's application to be ferryman;[43] an 1856 *Niagara Falls Gazette* news article about *Pardee & Pomeroy's* business success; the purchase of Youngstown properties from Thomas and Elizabeth Brighton, including Lots 114, 141, and 142 by William Wilcox; and a house at 614 Main Street by Cynthia Pardee and Harriet Wilcox in 1854, the house and properties then sold in 1868.[44]

Did the Wilcoxes think that the lots would be valuable because they were close to the new Lewiston-to-Youngstown train extensions?[45] That would have possibly been the case for the later railway/trolley line through Youngstown to Lake Ontario, the Lewiston Youngstown Frontier Railway (the Old Fort Route) of 1895 to 1935 that came into the village on Third Street past the William Wilcox properties (lots 114, 141, 142).[46] However, the two trains in the 1850s came into the village along the Niagara River.[47]

Wilcox lost his properties in 1868 "by foreclosure to [Levi] Parsons thru Myron J. Pardee,"[48] that is, Myron Pardee appears to have been William's real estate agent. Again, that was the year that Cynthia A. Pardee and Harriet N. Wilcox sold their property at 614 Main

---

[43] Ibid.

[44] For the Brighton-to-Pardee/Wilcox house transaction, see Ames, *Historical and Family Survey of 'The Old Village', Youngstown, N.Y. Third Street 1992* (Vol. 2). The Brighton-to-Wilcox lot numbers are based on Jesse P. Haines, Surveyor, "Map of the Village of Youngstown in Niagara County," previously surveyed by Ezekiel Brown for John and Catherine ("Caty") Young. In the Federal Census of 1880, Thomas Brighton of Youngstown was born in Ireland "about" 1820; in the New York State Census of 1875, he was 53, born in Ireland, thus about 1820/21. He died in 1906. Early maps of Youngstown show some of Brighton's and Brown's property holdings. See also the *Married Women's Property Act of 1848* in New York State mentioned in Ch. 14.

[45] See Ch. 5.

[46] See the 1936 map of Youngstown and the wall mural in the Youngstown Historical Museum; J. Maloni, "22-foot Mural of Lewiston Youngstown Frontier Railway to be Unveiled Sept. 19 [2011]," *Niagara Frontier Publications* [*Niagara Wheatfield Tribune, Island Dispatch, Lewiston-Porter Sentinel*] (September 6, 2011). http://www.wnypapers.com/news/article/current/2011/09/06/103605/22-foot-mural-of-lewiston-youngstown-frontier-railway-to-be-unveiled-sept.-19.

[47] Currently, residents of Main Street claim ruins of the train on their properties. See the photo of a railroad tie and spike in Ch. 5. However, other evidence suggests the train stopped at a Campbell Street "turn around."

[48] Ames, Survey; On the 1870 Youngstown map, L. Parsons owns the lot just west of Lot 114 and Second Street.

Street to Jonas W. Brown. In short, the Pardees and Wilcoxes of Palmyra in 1850 were the same Pardees and Wilcoxes who migrated to Youngstown by 1854; two of them—the women—had their names together on property in Youngstown between 1854 and 1868 and William Wilcox owned lots on Elliot Street between Second and Third streets in the same period. It is likely that, as in Palmyra, they were all living in the same household at 614 Main Street (see Chapter 16 for a photo of the current house).

There can be no doubt: VanDeusen's Mr. Pardee, the good man and hardware merchant from Palmyra, New York, was Myron J. Pardee in the Palmyra Federal Census of 1850; the Myron J. Pardee who paid off his house debt to Gerrit Smith in 1851; the Pardee of Youngstown hardware merchants *Pardee & Pomroy* in 1854; the Myron Pardee whose spouse co-signed for a home at 614 Main Street in 1854; and the M. J. Pardee who with E. J. Pomroy signed Luke Babcock's ferry petition of 1854. He was the Youngstown UGRR contact/agent to whom VanDeusen sent Daniel and James from Newark in 1855!

What about "Mr. Pardee's" brother "R. G. Pardee," the other "good man" mentioned in the VanDeusen Diary? R. G. Pardee does not appear in the above records.[49] Where was he? We do not know, but perhaps still in Palmyra. We found a "Pardee, Richard G." of Palmyra, N.Y. listed as one of the "Directors for Life" in *The Twenty-Third Report of the American Home Missionary Society* of 1849.[50] The American Home Missionary Society was a Baptist missionary society that by this time was an abolitionist-leaning society; indeed, it was the very center of the so-called Georgia Test Case earlier in 1844, a major event in the Baptist church schism over slavery.[51] This schism is worth a brief digression since it might help clarify the views of R. G. Pardee—and perhaps his brother, Myron.

The Georgia State Baptist Convention recommended to the Baptist Home Board of the Missionary Society that Elder James E. Reeve should be accepted as a missionary candidate.

---

[49] There was a white male Richard G. Pardee (age 20-29) in the Seneca Falls 1840 census and in the same household a white female (20-29, presumably his wife), two younger white males (age 15-19, under 5), and one white female (10-14). In the Palmyra 1850 census, there is a Richard **S.** Pardee (age 38), a Rebecca C. Pardee (age 35), and a Ward C. Pardee (age 13).

[50] *The Twenty Third Report of the American Home Missionary* Society (New York: William Osborn, 1849), 119, 123.

[51] Some members of the American Home Missionary Society, disappointed that it did not take a stronger stand against slavery, formed the American Missionary Association in 1846. Black Abolitionist Samuel Ringgold Ward was its vice-president that year. For more on Ward, see Ch. 8.

However, Reeve was a slave owner in Alabama and for that reason the Home Mission Board rejected him. Southern Baptists in slave states responded to the snub with the *Alabama Resolutions* (1844) according to which they threatened to withdraw financial support to the General Baptist Convention and Missionary Society unless their proposed candidates for the mission field were accepted—slave owners or not. The Reeve candidacy was clearly a trial balloon about slavery by pro-slavery southern Baptists. The Home Mission Board did not bend. It persisted in denying Reeve's candidacy. It maintained that in thirty years no slave owner had ever applied, that Baptist missionaries did not travel with servants, that therefore their missionaries could not take slaves into the mission field, and that the Society would never approve any arrangement that implied approval of slavery. This anti-slavery stance contributed to the withdrawal from the General Baptist Convention by Baptists from nine southern states. They formed their own counter-convention, the now familiar Southern Baptist Convention. After the Civil War, the Home Missionary Society together with freed slaves continued to carry forward its anti-slavery convictions by sponsoring Negro colleges and universities in the South.[52]

This brief digression into Baptist Church history does not prove that R. G. Pardee, the other good man of Palmyra, was ever in Youngstown—but it does suggest that he had strong abolitionist sympathies.

What happened to the Pardees, the Wilcoxes, and E. P. Pom(e)roy? We have no information about the Wilcoxes after 1868. That same year a certain Myron J. Pardee was living in Buffalo, but it is not likely that he was our Myron J. Pardee.[53] Much more promising is the 1870 Federal Census which shows that a Myron J. Pardee was living in Lancaster, Erie County, New York. The 1850 Palmyra Federal Census noted above recorded that Myron was 26 in 1850; in the 1870 Federal Census, twenty years later, Myron J. Pardee of Lancaster was 46. The name and the age match perfectly. Moreover, in his household was Cynthia Pardee, his spouse, who in the 1850 Census was 21, and in 1870, twenty years later, age 41, again a perfect name and

---

[52] At this writing, there are 106 such institutions. For a current list of the 106 HBCU colleges, see "List of Historically Black Colleges and Universities,"
https://en.wikipedia.org/wiki/List_of_historically_black_colleges_and_universities.
[53] See E. A. Thomas, *Buffalo City Directory* (Buffalo, NY: Franklin Steam Printing House, 1868), 369. This Myron Pardee seems to have had a business at 57 Exchange Street and was living at 369 Michigan Avenue.

age match. They were certainly Palmyra's and Youngstown's couple, Myron and Cynthia Pardee. Their presumed son, William W. Pardee, who in 1870 would have been in his 20s, is not listed, but a John Pardee, age 16, is listed and is "attending school." He was probably William W.'s younger brother.[54]

We have no more secure information about Myron's business partner, E. P. Pom(e)roy, but we offer an intriguing possibility. The 1870 Federal Census records that in the house next to that of Myron and Cynthia Pardee in Lancaster lived a certain Elizabeth Pomeroy, which is how Pomroy was spelled in the *Niagara Falls Gazette* article about the successful *Pardee & Pomroy* hardware business in Youngstown in 1856. Census takers and others did not always spell names the same way, as we have seen.[55] Born in New York, Elizabeth Pomeroy was 56 years old and owned real estate valued at $3,057. In her household were a white female born in New York, Lydia Pomeroy, age 32, a seamstress; a white female born in New York, Julia Pomeroy, age 23, also a seamstress; a white male born in New York, Perry Pomeroy, age 20, who "works on a farm"; and a white female born in New York, Mary L. Pomeroy, age 14, who was attending school. Given Onen's reference to *Pardee & Pomroy*, spelled *Pardee & Pomeroy* in the *Niagara Falls Gazette*, a Pomeroy family living next to the Myron J. and Cynthia Pardee family in Lancaster seems to be more than mere coincidence, and perhaps here we have found E. P. Pom[e]roy's wife, ex-wife, or widow, Elizabeth.

We return to the main point. According to the VanDeusen Diary, freedom seekers Daniel and James were directed to make contact with "Mr. Pardee," a "good man" and a hardware merchant originally from Palmyra, but in 1854 a resident of Youngstown. He was Myron J. Pardee, whose brother was R. (Richard) G. Pardee, another good man with at least abolitionist sympathies. In Youngstown, Myron was an UGRR agent.

---

[54] United States Federal Census for Lancaster, Erie County, New York, June 23, 1870, Roll M593, p. 391A.
[55] Recall that there were several Census spellings of "Ben Hockley" and that Onen spelled "Shickluna" as "Shickaluny."

Suspension Bridge Village or Youngstown?

According to the VanDeusen Diary, the Lyons newspaper editor, R. L. Adams, requested in a letter to Newark's Reverend George Shumway that James and his father be forwarded "via Suspension Bridge to Canada." However, as noted previously, VanDeusen's Diary says that VanDeusen gave James "written directions to go to Lockport & then to Youngstown." How should this be interpreted?

In 1855, there were two suspension-bridge crossings on the Lower Niagara to Canada,[56] the Lewiston/Queenston Bridge of 1851, known as the Upper Suspension Bridge, and the Bellevue/Niagara City Suspension Bridge.[57] If Daniel and James went to the Lewiston/Queenston bridge by travelling *through* Youngstown, they could have rendezvoused with Mr. Pardee, and he could have sent, or conducted, them to Lewiston. From the perspective of distance Lewiston would certainly have been a more likely option than Bellevue/Niagara City/Suspension Bridge Village since it was closer to Youngstown, about 7.5 miles. In February and March of 1855, the fugitive slaves could have followed a railroad bed of one of the Youngstown trains south.[58]

A second option was that they went on to the Suspension Bridge further south at Suspension Bridge Village. Note that the Diary does not say *the* Suspension Bridge, whether it be the 1848, 1851, or 1855 bridge, but simply *via* Suspension Bridge, that is, presumably, Suspension Bridge *Village*, which sometimes had that meaning even before the train opened in 1855. If this was the meaning they could have gone either through Youngstown or taken the New York Central Railroad from Newark through Lockport directly to Suspension Bridge Village. However, in this case it is unlikely that they crossed by train because, although the 1848 Suspension Bridge at Bellevue was closed during the early railroad tier construction and reopened by 1854, the VanDeusen Diary entry of February 16, 1855, was written a month before the official public opening of the Roebling train level addition on March 18, 1855. It is unlikely that Daniel and James took more than a whole month to travel from Newark to Suspension Bridge Village. If this were their option, they would have taken the pedestrian level.

---

[56] See Ch. 5.
[57] *History of Niagara County,* 257, 269.
[58] See Ch. 5.

These two options, however, are apparently moot. Lyon's instruction to go "via Suspension Bridge" was apparently abandoned. The VanDeusen Diary says that VanDeusen gave James written instructions to go to Lockport (how?) and then to *Youngstown* on to see "Mr. Pardee," and the form of VanDeusen's statement implies Youngstown was the crossing point *instead of* Suspension Bridge Village. The Reverend Shumway, whose first pastorate was in Palmyra just nine miles from Newark, might well have been personally acquainted with the good man and hardware merchant named Mr. Pardee, originally from Palmyra. Probably VanDeusen also knew him. Did they also know about his business contact with the abolitionist Gerrit Smith and that he was the brother of an abolitionist-leaning R. G. Pardee? In any case, fugitive slaves Daniel and James were sent to Myron J. Pardee at Youngstown.

In short, the most plausible reconstruction is that a local UGRR network in the Lyons-Palmyra-Newark region was connected to the local Lockport network which was connected to Youngstown by a contact—we think, an agent—"Mr. Pardee," that is, Myron J. Pardee, who with his family and the Wilcoxes had migrated from Palmyra to Youngstown by 1854. He was known to VanDeusen and the Reverend Shumway, who had been an active abolitionist in Palmyra. If VanDeusen's instructions about James were carried out, it is very likely that the fugitive slaves were either ferried across the Niagara River by a Youngstown ferryman—by our reconstruction it could probably have been John Hitchcock or the controversial Luke P. Babcock, whose petition Myron Pardee and E. P. Pomroy initially signed—or, alternatively, by some anonymous individual boater such as John Carter.[59]

In Chapters 14 and 16, we speculate about the Davis Family who owned the building called the Davis Brick Block where the *Pardee & Pomroy* hardware business was located and about the probable home of the Pardee and Wilcox families, 614 Main Street. For now, however, we turn to another primary source, this one underpinning the VanDeusen Diary connection between the Lockport network and Youngstown. That is the Thomas Birnmore Letter.

---

[59] See Ch. 12.

The Lyons, Newark, Palmyra, and Youngstown Connection, 1855

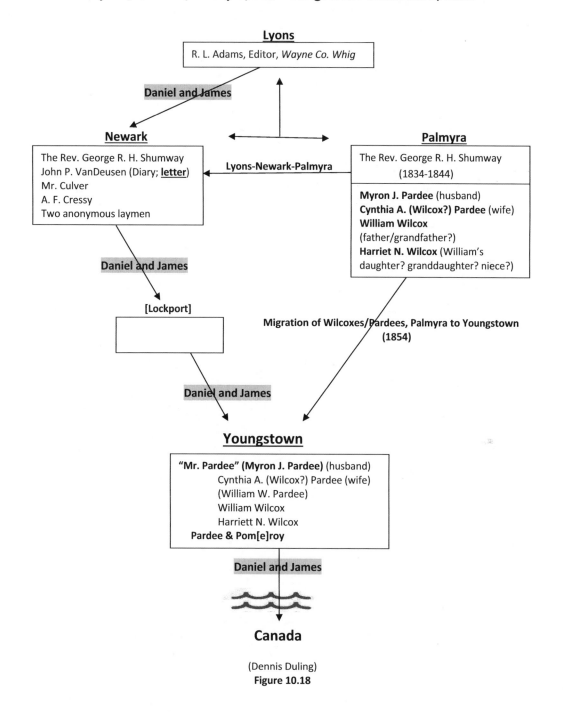

Lyons

R. L. Adams, Editor, *Wayne Co. Whig*

Daniel and James

Newark

The Rev. George R. H. Shumway
John P. VanDeusen (Diary; **letter**)
Mr. Culver
A. F. Cressy
Two anonymous laymen

Lyons-Newark-Palmyra

Palmyra

The Rev. George R. H. Shumway
(1834-1844)

Myron J. Pardee (husband)
Cynthia A. (Wilcox?) Pardee (wife)
William Wilcox
(father/grandfather?)
Harriet N. Wilcox (William's
daughter? granddaughter? niece?)

Daniel and James

[Lockport]

Migration of Wilcoxes/Pardees, Palmyra to Youngstown
(1854)

Daniel and James

Youngstown

"Mr. Pardee" (Myron J. Pardee) (husband)
Cynthia A. (Wilcox?) Pardee (wife)
(William W. Pardee)
William Wilcox
Harriett N. Wilcox
Pardee & Pom[e]roy

Daniel and James

Canada

(Dennis Duling)
Figure 10.18

CHAPTER 11

Two Fugitive Slaves Sent from Lockport are Rowed to Canada by a Youngstown Farmer, 1856 or 1857

Image 11.1

John P. VanDeusen of Newark, New York, directed fugitive slave James and his father Daniel to go to Youngstown through Lockport. There is further information about the Underground Railroad connection between Lockport and Youngstown in the Thomas Birnmore Letter of 1896. First, we offer a little information about the local Lockport UGRR network.

Lockport and the Underground Railroad

Judith Wellman writes:

> Early settlement by Quakers made Lockport a center of both Underground Railroad activities and African American settlement. Quakers such as Darius Comstock, supervisor of work on the Erie Canal in the early 1820s; Lyman Spalding, mill owner; Isaac Smith, Lockport's first doctor, and his wife Ednah Smith; and Moses Richardson, publisher of the *Lockport Daily Journal*, made Lockport a strong abolitionist anchor. Sites relating to both these European Americans and to the two hundred African Americans who lived in Lockport by 1855 and afterward, including well known freedom seeker George Goines and entrepreneur Adam Mossell, need further documentation.[1]

Much more could be discussed about abolitionists, agents, and conductors at Lockport, as well as the many Lockport freedom seekers who are included in Judith Wellman's Database and Survey of Sites.[2] We cannot discuss them here, but note as an example Lyman Spalding.[3]

Lyman Spalding was a prominent banker, manufacturer, and real estate investor in the Lockport area, but had become a Quaker, a Mason, an editor (with Thomas B. Barnum) of the anti-Calvinistic, anti-sectarian faith-without-works newspaper *Plain Truth*, and an editor of the newspaper titled *Priestcraft Exposed and Primitive Christianity Defended* (1828-1830), which sought to distinguish between true, primitive-based Christianity and sectarian revivalism. Spalding's Rationalist ideology in the last newspaper is described by Kathleen Riley: "*Priestcraft Exposed* consistently claimed to be an advocate of the cause of freedom, in keeping with the spirit of rational religion and liberal principles—as opposed to proselytizing 'priests' [money-grubbing evangelists] who sought to impose their interpretation of religion on the

---

[1] Wellman, "Survey of Sites," 19. http://www.niagarafallsundergroundrailroad.org/assets/Uploads/NF-HAMP-Report-Appendix-C-1.pdf.

[2] Ibid. On Spalding, see Chs. 2 and 6.

[3] "Guide to the Lyman A. Spalding Papers, 1811-1864," Collection Number 522, Division of Rare and Manuscript Collections Cornell University Library, http://rmc.library.cornell.edu/EAD/htmldocs/RMM00522.html.

community."[4] Most important, like most Quakers by this time, Spalding was a strongly anti-slavery advocate. He recorded the formation of the Niagara County Antislavery Society in his Journal.[4b]

Lyman Spalding is mentioned in the Thomas Binmore/Birnmore letter. First, however, we note how the letter came to be written.

The J. W. Davis Letter to Wilbur Siebert

In 1896, the prominent historian of the Underground Railroad, Professor Wilbur H. Siebert of Ohio State University, wrote an article about the Underground Railroad that appeared in the *American History Review*. In a footnote, he stated that he would respond to anyone who would send him UGRR information.[5] His intent was to gather reliable data for his forthcoming book *The Underground Railroad from Slavery to Freedom: A Comprehensive History*, published in 1898.[6] Not long after the request appeared, Siebert received a note from J. W. Davis (place of origin unknown) who suggested that Siebert write to a certain Thomas "Binmore" of Montreal, Quebec, Canada, for information. Siebert did. Both the Davis letter (undated; had to be 1896) and the one who responded as Thomas "Birnmore" (1896) are archived in the Siebert Collection of the Archives/Library of the Ohio History Connection (originally the Ohio State Archaeological and Historical Society) in Columbus, Ohio.[7]

---

[4] Kathleen Riley, *Lockport. Historic Jewel of the Erie Canal* (Charleston, SC: Arcadia Publishing, 2005), 59. Some Eighteenth Century Enlightenment Rationalists explained gospel miracle stories as propaganda of ambitious, self-serving priests.

[4b] See above, Ch.2, p. 44.

[5] Wilbur H. Siebert, "Light on the Underground Railroad," *The American Historical Review* 1/3 (1896) 455 (455-63) [JSTOR at http://www.jstor.org by subscription]. Siebert gave his address as "W. H. Siebert, 40 Shepard Street, Cambridge, Mass." For Siebert, who is quoted several times in this book, see Preface and Appendix 5.

[6] Wilbur H. Siebert, *The Underground Railroad from Slavery to Freedom: A Comprehensive History* (New York, NY, and London, England: The Macmillan Co., 1898; reprint Mineola, NY: Dover Publications, 2006). See comments about Siebert and his book in our Preface.

[7] The Davis letter (1896) about Binmore and Siebert's letter to Binmore (1896) are both in the Siebert Collection of Archives/Library of the Ohio History Connection (originally the Ohio State Archaeological and Historical Society) at 800 E. 17th Ave., Columbus Ohio, 43211. They are Nos. 243, 582, 1541, 4847. They are digitalized in "Ohio Memory. A Collaborative Project of The Ohio Historical Connection and the State Library of Ohio" and will eventually be available without a membership fee. Thanks to Lily Birkhimer.

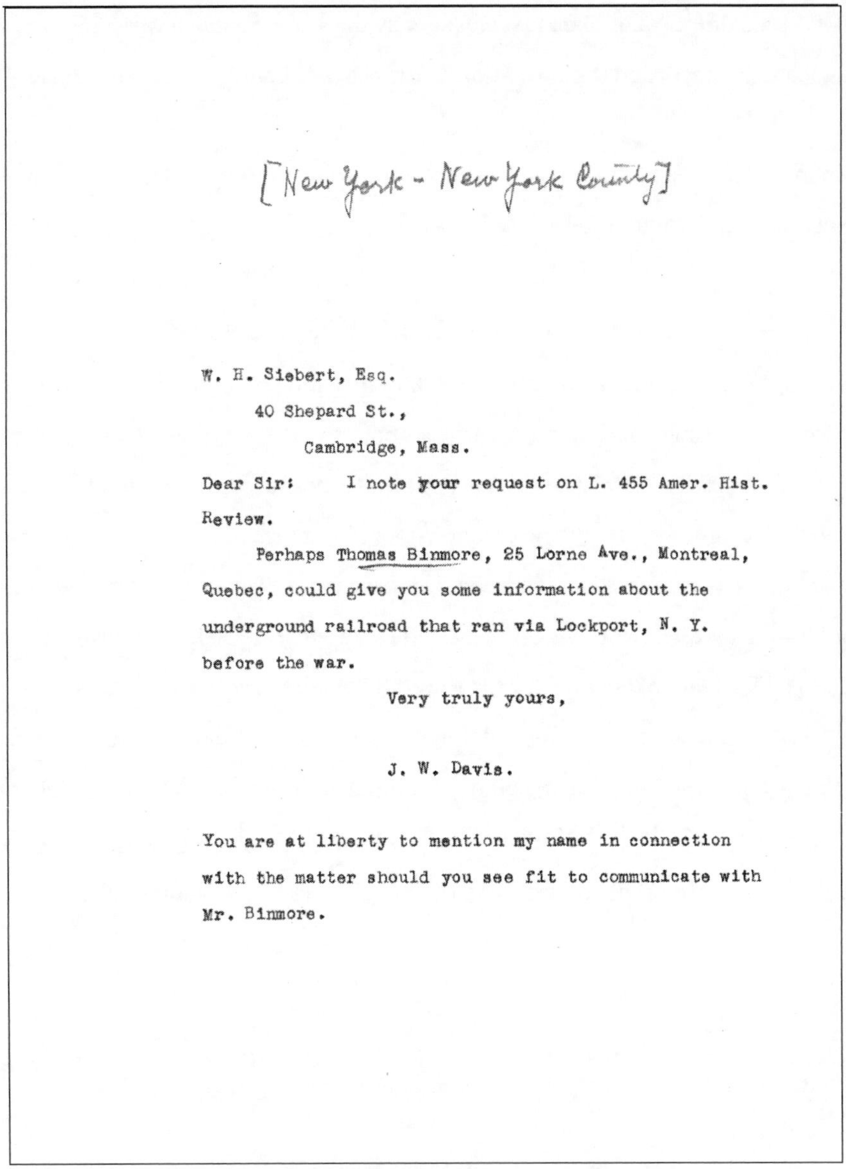

[New York - New York County]

W. H. Siebert, Esq.

40 Shepard St.,

Cambridge, Mass.

Dear Sir: I note your request on L. 455 Amer. Hist.
Review.

Perhaps Thomas Binmore, 25 Lorne Ave., Montreal,
Quebec, could give you some information about the
underground railroad that ran via Lockport, N. Y.
before the war.

Very truly yours,

J. W. Davis.

You are at liberty to mention my name in connection
with the matter should you see fit to communicate with
Mr. Binmore.

J. W. Davis Letter to Wilbur H. Siebert
Image 11.2

Siebert's Questionnaire and Note to Thomas Binmore

Siebert made the contact. He sent Binmore his printed INQUIRY CONCERNING THE "UNDERGROUND RAILROAD," a formal, printed questionnaire with seven questions about the UGRR, writing in by hand the period 1840 to 1860 and signing it.[8]

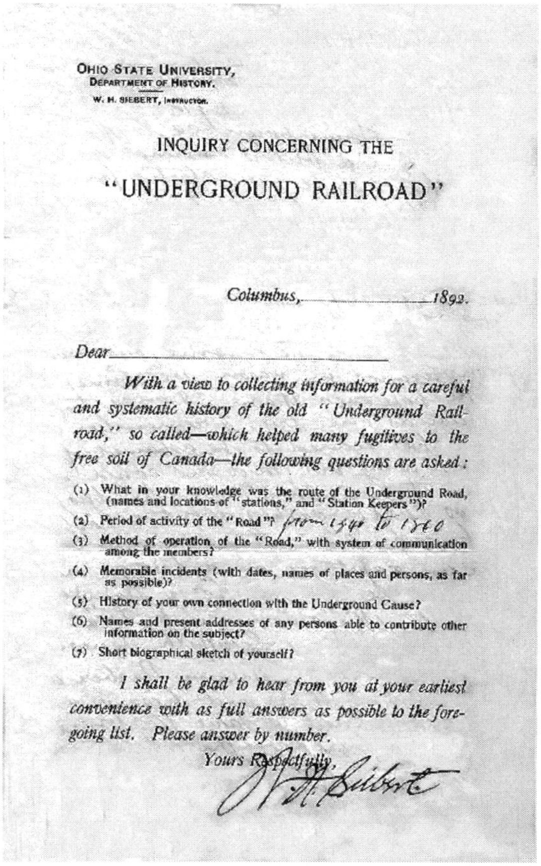

The Siebert Questionnaire and Note to Thomas Binmore
Image 11.3

The "Inquiry" contained the following questions:

1) What in your knowledge was the route of the Underground Road (names and locations of "stations" and "Station Keepers")?

---

[8] The questionnaire is VMF156 in the Siebert Collection.

2) Period of activity of the "Road"? [handwritten insertion: from 1840 to 1860]

3) Method of operation of "the Road," with system of communication among the members?

4) Memorable incidents (with dates, names of places and persons as far as possible.)

5) History of your own connection with the Underground Cause?

6) Names and present addresses of persons able to contribute other information on the subject?

7) Short biographical sketch of yourself.

The Three-Page Response of Thomas Birnmore to the Siebert Questionnaire

Professor Siebert received answers to the seven questions of his "Inquiry," but the respondent's name in the surviving, typewritten copy, was spelled with an "r," "Birnmore."

[New York: Niagara County]

28 Lorne Ave.,

Montreal, Canada,

27 April, 1896.

Mr. W. H. Siebert,

40 Shepard St.,

Boston, Mass.

Dear Sir:-

In reply to your letter of the 14th inst. I
would say: Generally That my knowledge was very limited,
and for a very short time. You may readily imagine
that under the Fugitive Slave Law, the less one knew
the better, and moreover it is so long ago that I have
forgotten many details.

First   I was in Lockport, N.Y. as an employee of the
Lockport Daily Journal about 1856 and 1857, and
occupied an isolated room at the back of the office
for a bedroom. Those whom I remember as movers in
the matter were Lyman Spaulling (Miller and Banker)
and M. C. Richardson (Editor of said paper) and were
probably "Station Keepers." There were others whom I
have forgotten.

A. The Thomas Birnmore Response to Wilbur H. Siebert
Image 11.4a

One night, they knowing me to be a young Englishman, asked me if I would take charge of a fugitive for the night, and I did so.

Second   My connection only lasted during the years 1856 and 1857, as I then returned to Canada.

Third   I cannot answer further than that I was given to understand that no one knew the Station further off than the next each way. The fugitive (always singly excepting in one case where two young men came together) always arrived at dusk, with some credential which I believe was given to Mr. Spaulding, who gave them directions for the next and last Station.

Fourth   We were much afraid of certain people whom would have informed against us, and have tried to return the slaves. The only two fugitives that made any impression on my mind were the two mentioned as being together, to whom I gave up my bed, who would not go in a waggon, [sic] as they were afraid they might be returned, yet slept peacefully locked up in my bedroom, whilst I walked around the town because I was afraid to go to a house for fear of exciting suspicion. Several times afterwards I also did the same thing. These men came from some point in Erie County, and diverged from the direct road because the slave hunters were at Niagara Falls and Lewiston. We sent them to a farmer

B. The Thomas Birnmore Response to Wilbur H. Siebert
Image 11.4b

near Youngstown, N. Y., who took them over in a row
boat to Niagara, Ontario.[x] Our boast was that we
never lost a man. Sometimes they started early in
the morning on foot, I taking them in that case until
they could make no mistake in the road. I understand
that the men were to go to St. Thomas, Ontario, when
in Canada.

Fifth   You have it above.

Sixth   They are all dead.

Seventh Of no interest to any one outside of my own
     family.

Extra.   There was a slave found in Lockport a few years
    previous to 1856. Some people attempted to arrest him.
    Daniel Price, Chauncey Morton and others armed them-
    selves to prevent the arrest, but it was not necessary
because the man was smuggled off whilst the hunters were
preparing to get him. (Chauncey Morton was a cousin of
Governor Morton.)

                    Yours truly,

                    Thos. Birnmore

P.S.   Please send me a circular when publishing your book.

[x]   At the mouth of Niagara River.

C. The Thomas Birnmore Response to Wilbur H. Siebert
Image 11.4c

A Closer Look at the Siebert and Birnmore Letters

A few general comments about the letters are in order.

Both letters are now archived in the Siebert Collection at the Ohio History Connection in Columbus, Ohio. Both are in typewritten form and both have penciled-in editorial additions and changes. The editing of the Lewis Letter has "Thomas Binmore" underlined and a handwritten heading in brackets, "New York – New York County." A bracketed heading also occurs on the second letter, but with this typewritten form: "New York – Niagara County."

We made contact with the Ohio History Connection. Lily Birkhimer, who had emailed the letters to us and forwarded our queries to the Curator of the Siebert archive, John Haas. He and his staff then researched the Siebert Collection for us. In an email, he wrote,

> The collection includes over 80 boxes, but as far as we can tell there is only one box of original hand written (and some typed) letters . . . It appears Siebert's secretaries or students typed the letters out for ease of research; just a guess. The letters in the one original box were all marked with a small stamp: "Copied"! And those letters show up in the many volumes of the state underground railroad section of the collection.

As a further clarification of the volumes, Haas wrote, "The volumes . . . were and are bound, but were not sent to a printer. They, or Siebert and his students, put the typed transcriptions into state and county order and had those typewriter sheets bound into volumes."[9] Some Siebert materials were related to Indiana and Jeannie Regan-Dinius, Director of Special Initiatives, Indiana Division of Historic Preservation and Archaeology, wrote to Dennis Duling and agreed about the typed letters:

> From what we have in Indiana, we have a combination of re-typed letters (I assume by secretaries) and some hand-written letters (we had assumed they are original to the person, but no proof of that). Spelling at this time is still fluid and then with transcription and typos, we just stress for people not to stress too much about spelling.[10]

---

[9] Emails dated November 15 and November 16, 2016. Thanks again to Lily Birkhimer of the Ohio History Connection, who forwarded the letters to us.
[10] Email of Tuesday, November 22, 2016.

There are other questions about the letters. If the letters are transcriptions was his name Binmore or Birnmore? Without the (handwritten?) original letter, that is impossible to answer. We call him "Thomas Birnmore," the spelling now preserved in the surviving, typed, presumably transcribed, letter itself.

Also, the transcriptions contain penciled-in spelling and grammatical changes. First, the *Lockport Daily Journal* is underlined by hand. Second, several minor spelling changes have been corrected by hand. Third, there is a closing of the space in the left margin and a crossing out of misspelled words. Fourth, whether correct or not, Lyman Spalding's name is spelled *"Spauling,"* which, curiously, Siebert perpetuated in his Appendix E. It has been corrected in pencil by hand, initially—incorrectly—by inserting a "d" *before* the "l," resulting in "Spaudling." Obviously, the corrector meant to put the "d" *after* the "l," since the name is spelled as "Spalding" later in the letter and that is the usual spelling. Someone has also corrected grammar in the letter ("whom" to "who"). Finally, Siebert added the name "W. H. Childs" to "Binmore," "Spauling" (*sic*), and "M. C. Richardson" in his book's Appendix E.

More important than the variations and corrections is the fact that the Birnmore Letter is a major source for Youngstown as a crossing site on the Underground Railroad. We can track Birnmore's response to Siebert by seeing how he answers Siebert's seven questions.

Birnmore stated that in Lockport he was "a young Englishman" from Canada. He recalled that about 1856 and 1857 (his uncertainty), while employed by the *Lockport Daily Journal*, he was asked by Lyman Spalding, a "Miller and Banker," and M. C. Richardson, the editor of the *Lockport Daily Journal*, "probably [UGRR] Station keepers"—he forgot the names of others[11]—to hide a fugitive slave. Thereafter, from time to time he would hide individual fugitive slaves in his room at the back newspaper office of the *Journal*. He recalled that the fugitive slave "always arrived at dusk" with some identifying credential that, he believed, was given to Mr. "Spaulding." In Chapters 1 and 3, we mentioned the deeds of manumission carried by freed slaves and in Chapter 10, we noted the letter written by the editor of the Wayne Co. *Whig*, R. L. Adams, introducing the father/son fugitive slaves Daniel and James to the Newark Presbyterians. The Birnmore Letter mentions something analogous to the latter.

Birnmore also wrote that no one else but Spalding knew the "Station further off than the next each way," that is, Spalding knew more than the previous station and the following station; Birnmore also wrote, however, that Spalding would give the fugitive directions for the "next *and last* Station." Did he mean two stations, Youngstown and one before Youngstown or just Youngstown? Birnmore also emphasized that the two fugitive slaves had been diverted from some place in Erie County and, to avoid the many slave catchers at Niagara Falls and Lewiston, they were not sent down the "direct road" to Niagara Falls—presumably to the Suspension Bridge—*but rather to Youngstown*. Despite his comment that no one knew the previous and next stations but Spalding, Birnmore seems in this case to have known "the (next and?) last Station"—*Youngstown*. In other words, either Youngstown was the next *and* last station, or another station lay somewhere *between* Lockport and Youngstown, such as Warrens Corners, as suggested by an article about fugitive slave Charles Brown, or some site in the Ransomville area.[12]

The fugitive slaves were not sent from Lockport to Suspension Bridge, as R. L. Adams of Lyons had directed Daniel and James. They were sent to Youngstown, the "last Station." Were they sent to a more specific site in Youngstown, perhaps the Ontario House or, more likely, the Davis Brick Building where the hardware merchants *Pardee & Pomroy* were located or the residence of the agent Myron J. Pardee? Birnmore did not mention these details; perhaps he did not know them or did not remember them. He did remember and report that "a farmer

---

[11] Again, Spalding, Richardson, and Childs are listed with "Binmore" in Siebert's Appendix E. Wellman has noted others (see the previous quotation) and the autobiography of Thomas James mentions a conductor four miles from Lockport, "Dennis W___," on whom see Ch. 9 in this book.

[12] For site speculations, see Chs. 15, 16.

near Youngstown . . . took them over [across the Niagara River] in a row boat," possibly in a *bateau*-like boat.[13] Who was the farmer? Was he the farmer/builder/brick yard owner John Carter who lived just outside the village, who loved boating, and for whom there are UGGR oral traditions?[14] Was he Nelson Davis who had a black servant in his home, Austin McPherson, who was later living with "General" Jordan Gaines in Lewiston, who had UGRR connections in Niagara Falls?[15] Was he John Rich who had employed fugitive slave Thomas James as a wood chopper many years earlier?[16] We say more about them later.[17]

Summarizing, Thomas Birnmore in a letter to UGRR historian Wilbur Siebert, in reference to the UGRR network in Lockport, New York, in 1856 or 1857, cited the Lockport conductors Lyman Spalding and M. C. Richardson and a safe hiding place—Birnmore's own room—in the offices of the *Lockport Daily Journal*. It was an apparent UGRR station. Birnmore recalled that he himself had hidden fugitive slaves in his room there and from Lockport they were directed by Lyman Spalding to "the next and last Station," ultimately, whether next or next and last, Youngstown. There a farmer rowed them across the Niagara River to freedom in Canada! Who was that anonymous farmer? John Carter? Nelson Davis? John Rich? We do not know, but they are reasonable candidates. In any case, Spalding apparently knew of an agent in Youngstown, which suggests the possibility that other fugitive slaves—some hidden by Birnmore—were sent there and ferried across the river as well. How many will most likely never be known.

---

[13] See Ch. 4.

[14] See Ch. 14 for oral traditions about John Carter's love of boating on the Niagara River and his transporting of fugitive slaves across the Niagara River. Also, he sold property to Mary McClary Gaines, probably an abolitionist.

[15] See Ch. 14 for speculations about the Davis Brick Block and 614 Main Street, as well as extended person network of Myron Pardee, Nelson Davis, Austin McPherson, Jordan Gaines, Mary McClary Gaines, and John Carter, plus links to the Lewiston and Niagara Falls networks.

[16] Thomas James, *Life of Rev. Thomas James, by Himself*, 6.

[17] See Ch. 14.

CHAPTER 12

A Race to the Youngstown Ferry as a Diversion to Help Cassey Escape from Slave Catchers, ca. 1860/1861

Image 12.1

Eber M. Pettit, UGRR Conductor and Interviewer

The story of Cassey is told by Eber M. Petitt (1802—1885), an Underground Railroad agent and conductor in the villages of Fredonia, Cordova, and Versailles in Chautauqua County, Western New York. In 1868, he published his reminiscences of his interviews with fugitive slaves for a weekly called the *Fredonia Censor* of Fredonia, New York. Pettit used pseudonyms and signed his articles as simply "Conductor" because he wished to protect the identity of those involved in the Underground Railroad, including himself. In 1879, however, he published them separately under his own name as *Sketches in the History of the Underground Railroad*.[1] He did

---

[1] Eber M. Pettit, *Sketches in the History of the Underground Railroad* (Westfield, NY: Chautauqua Region Press, 1879, Introduction by W. McKinstry); reprinted with an Introduction with Notes by Paul Leone (Westfield, New York, Chautauqua Region Press, 1999), Chapter XVI, 146-47. The 1879 version can be found online at https://archive.org/details/sketchesinhistory00pett. Pettit's accounts are derived mainly from his interviews of

so at the urging of the editor of the *Censor*, Willard McKinstry, who also edited and introduced his book.

Paul Leone, the editor of a 1999 reprint of *Sketches*, rightly describes Pettit's accounts, especially the discourses in them, as literary and imaginative.[2] Nonetheless, he also notes that when they are compared to William Still's generally trustworthy *The Underground Railroad: A Record*, Pettit's accounts of the UGRR and UGRR routes to the Niagara River are generally accurate.[3] In relation to Niagara County, Pettit gives further evidence that crossings of the Niagara River were made not only at the Suspension Bridges north of Niagara Falls, but also via ferries at Lewiston and Youngstown.[4]

Pettit's dramatic, engaging version of the escape of a female slave named "Cassey" in 1860 or 1861 appears in Chapter XVI of his *Sketches*.[5] The story assumes that Youngstown was a known Niagara River crossing on the Underground Railroad. Here we quote the Youngstown-related section of Pettit's Cassey drama.[6]

---

fugitive slaves; his study is dedicated to Frederick Douglass. For many details, see Wendy Straight, "Eber M. Pettit, the Underground Railroad, and the Fredonia Baptist Church" (December 2009),
http://www.rootsweb.ancestry.com/~nychauta/CHURCH/FredoniaBapt/Straight-EberMPettit.pdf.
[2] Leone, ibid., ix-xi.
[3] Leone, ibid., x: "the works share a remarkable similarity." For William Still, see Ch. 1 of this book.
[4] Pettit, *Sketches*, Chapter XVI; Leone, ibid., 146. For further comment, see the Pettit obituary in Appendix 4.
[5] The usually suggested date of 1861 derives from a comment late in the story that Cassey was hiding with "Jimmy" near Lockport when "the rebels fired on our flag," that is, Fort Sumter, April 12, 1861. It is accepted by Judith Wellman, see, e.g., "Site of the Home of Peter A. Porter, Elizabeth Porter, and Josephine Porter," in "Appendix C: Survey of Sites," 89.
http://www.niagarafallsundergroundrailroad.org/documents/NF%20HAMP%20Report_Appendix%20C.pdf. The alternative, 1860, is argued by Paul Leone who in his Notes to the 1999 reprint of Pettit's *Sketches* reasons that ". . . the Irishman Jimmy's mention of Lincoln and the 'other nagur' [p. 120]" refers to Lincoln's dark-complexioned running mate prior to the 1860 election, that is, Hannibal Hamlin of Maine, who was sometimes stigmatized as a "mulatto," a factor used by Lincoln's political opponents to ridicule him (Pettit, *Sketches*, 1999 edition, 146-47).
[6] The text is quoted from the 1879 version online of Pettit, *Sketches*, Ch. XVI, 113-21.
https://archive.org/details/sketchesinhistory00pett. The online 1879 edition is contributed by the Johns Hopkins University Sheridan Libraries and is "not in copyright."

The Cassey Story in Eber Pettit, *Sketches*[7]

[p. 113] Cassey was a slave in Baltimore; her master's name was Claggett. She had been assured by those who knew, that she was about to be sold to a man who was making up a coffle [a train of slaves fastened together] for the markets in Louisiana or Texas. None but slaves can imagine the terror felt in view of such a prospect. Cassey fled like a frightened bird, and succeeded in reaching a place of safety near Haddonfield, N.J., where she obtained service in a respectable family. She was industrious, steady and honest, and her cheerful, obliging manners secured her many friends, yet a sadness was ever present on her countenance, for she had left in Baltimore a child, little more than a year old. Her master had not been unusually severe, but she had experienced and witnessed enough of slavery to dread it for her child, and she therefore determined to make a desperate effort to save her little one from the liability of being sold and treated like a mere brute. The kind Quaker people among whom she had [p. 114] found a home tried to dissuade her from attempting so hazardous an enterprise, deeming it not only dangerous, but well nigh hopeless; but the mother's heart yearned for her babe and she finally decided to try to save it at all hazards.

She went to Baltimore and proceeded directly to the house of a colored family, old friends of hers, in whom she could safely confide. To her great joy, she found that they approved her plan and were ready to assist her. Arrangements were soon made to convey the child to a place about twenty miles from Baltimore, where it would be well taken care of until the mother could safely take it to New Jersey.[8]

Before she could leave the city her master was informed that she was there and sent constables in pursuit of her, but her friends were apprized of it in season to give her warning, and her own courage and ingenuity were adequate to the emergency. She

---

[7] Pettit, Ibid., 113-21 (selections).
[8] Maryland did not officially abolish slavery until November 1, 1864; New Jersey abolished slavery in 1846, but slaves could be redefined as "apprentices" and slavery did not totally end there until 1865; see above, n. 155.

disguised herself in sailor's clothes and walked boldly to the Philadelphia boat. There she walked up and down the deck smoking a cigar, occasionally passing and re-passing the constables who had been sent to take her. The constables left the boat after waiting till it was about to start; they were watching for a colored woman to come on board answering to her description.

Like Cassey, Anna Maria Weems (ca. 1840?-?) Escaped as a Man in 1855
Blackpast.org; Public Domain[9]
Image 12.2

The boat brought her safely to Philadelphia, and she soon reached her friends in Haddonfield [N. J.],[10] who rejoiced over the history of her escape and the success of her enterprise. A few weeks after she went to the place where her child had been left, and succeeded in bringing it away in safety.

For a short time her happiness seemed to be complete; but she soon began to be harassed with fears that her master would succeed in finding them and take them

---

[9] http://www.blackpast.org/aah/weems-anna-maria-1840#sthash.IXWWJbFJ.dpuf.
Like Cassey, and with the aid of Quakers, Anna Maria Weems, escaped in 1855 from Montgomery County, Maryland, to Washington D.C., and from there, dressed as Dr. Ellwood Harvey's carriage driver, "Joe Wright," on to visit William Still in Philadelphia (see Ch. 3). Then she went to Sarah Tappan, Lewis Tappan's wife, in New York City (see Chs. 2, 7) and then, accompanied by the Reverend Amos Freeman, Pastor of Brooklyn's Siloam Presbyterian Church, by train to the Dawn Settlement in Ontario (on which, see Ch. 8).
[10] Haddonfield, N.J, is across the Delaware River, about ten miles SE of Philadelphia.

both back to slavery. At length she resolved to go to **[p. 115]** Philadelphia, which was not far distant, and get the advice of Benjamin Harrison, a Quaker who was ever ready to aid fugitives from slavery. He advised her to leave her child in the care of a family living quite remote from public travel, where it would be entirely safe, and go herself farther north. Acting upon friend Harrison's advice, she had placed her child in the care of the family that he recommended and returned to Philadelphia, intending to start north in a day or two; but, passing along the street in which her friend lived, she met Cathcart, the speculator to whom she had been sold. Hurrying forward, she reached the door of her friend in time to go in before he could get hold of her. Harrison saw the chase and locked his doors. Cathcart placed men about the house to watch while he went for constables and a warrant. It was evening, and the offices being closed, he was slow in obtaining his papers; meanwhile, in passing through his kitchen, Harrison saw that two of his domestics seemed very merry over some project they had on foot, and he watched their movements. One of them put on an old cloak and a dilapidated bonnet, and opening the front door looked up and down the street; and rushing out she turned a corner and ran with all her might. The watchers saw it all, sprang from their hiding places and overtook her. She screamed and called for the police, who soon arrived and took all parties into custody. During the excitement Cassey escaped, and before Cathcart returned with his constables she was crossing the Delaware River in a skiff.[11] She was so terribly frightened by this adventure that she determined not to stop again short of Canada. Having saved her earnings, she was able to travel by steamboat and canal packet [small boats carrying mail, passengers, and goods], and soon arrived in Canada and found friends in a home at Lundy's Lane, near Niagara Falls [Ontario].

[p. 116] Cassey's boy was a fine, active little fellow, and she determined to earn money to buy his freedom, for, being a very capable woman, she commanded high wages. The agent of the U.G.R.R., at Niagara Falls [New York], was a wealthy gentleman, living some two miles back from the river, where he had an excellent farm, a fine mansion, splendid stock and superb horses. All the negro servants at the Falls were in

---

[11] See "Escaping from Norfolk in Capt. Lee's Skiff" near the beginning of Ch. 4.

the secret service of the institution [the U.G.R.R.], and not a few of the white citizens were friendly toward it. When Cassey had been in Canada three or four years our agent above mentioned applied to her to engage in his service, and as he would pay her much higher wages then she could obtain in Canada, she, supposing that all danger had passed, came over on the Suspension Bridge and went to work for him. She never went into the village except to go occasionally to meeting on Sunday. One Sunday, as she passed out of the church, she saw a man standing near the door, sharply scanning the features of every colored person that came out. Her eyes met his and they recognized each other, but she managed to get away in the crowd and he lost sight of her.

The facilities offered by the fugitive slave law for capturing runaway slaves had made it a profitable business, and Cathcart had bought "running" a large lot of fugitives expecting to make a good speculation if he could capture even one in ten of them. He had come on to the Falls, rightly guessing that some of them would be about there, and he was at the church door in pursuit of his regular business. One of the shrewdest men, either white or black, that lived in that village, was Ben Jackson, a free Negro. Ben was a servant in the hotel where Cathcart was stopping, and he had already, as was his custom, taken pains to talk with other colored servants in Cathcart's presence about the slaves running away **[p. 117]** and coming here to work for almost nothing, saying, "We 'spectable niggers can't get anything to do half the time, and we get dreful little when we get a place. They ought to be tuck back where they belong." Cathcart went directly to Ben, and taking him aside, he described Cassey, told where he saw her, and inquired if Ben knew her. "Yes," said Ben, "I knows her. She lives over to Lundy's Lane. She comes over on the Suspension Bridge sometimes to Methodist meeting." Cathcart had already engaged a score of shaggy Democrats to start at his bidding, and he sent two of them without delay to watch the bridge, and others were sent to *all the crossing places between Tonawanda and Youngstown,*[12] the gate-keeper at the bridge having told him that no such person had crossed over to Canada that day.

---

[12] Italics ours.

Ben lost no time in sending word to Cassey and to Col. P___, with whom she lived, telling them how he had misled the slave hunter. As soon as it was dark a trusty conductor started with Cassey towards Lockport, and Col. P___ had his fleetest team harnessed to a closed carriage, standing in his barn ready to start at a moment's warning.

Cathcart came back from the bridge, and calling the landlord aside, told him that he had seen one of the slaves that he was looking for; he also related what Ben had said to him. "Well," said the landlord, "Ben is a trusty fellow generally, but you ought to know better than to confide in any negro on business relating to fugitives." "But I heard him saying that the runaway niggers were working for low wages and ought to be sent back." "Ben said that," replied the landlord, "when he knew you would hear it. Did the woman recognize you?" "I think she did," said Cathcart. "Then," said the landlord, "no time is to be lost. She has no doubt **[p. 118]** gone to Col. P____. He has wealth and influence, and whatever you do with him must be done legally. You have the law and the strongest party in the State on your side, while he knows just how much or how little the law can do for you. He has at his command means for hiding and running off these people that no one has yet found out. *They call it the Underground Railroad. They must go underground or by balloon, for once in his hands they are never seen again this side of the river.*"

The President had not been so careless of the interests of his slaveholding friends who visit the Falls as to leave them without the means of reclaiming their fugitive servants. A Commissioner and Marshals were located there, so that Cathcart, although it was Sunday evening, had his papers in the Marshal's hands as soon as possible, and he, with his deputies, were by ten o'clock, p. m., approaching Col. P____'s place by different roads. Meanwhile, the Colonel had his spies out, and he was on the front seat of his carriage, with his driver, in his barn.

When the Marshal drew near, a signal was given, the barn door opened suddenly, and the Colonel, with the fastest team in Niagara County, dashed out and down the road toward Lewiston. The Marshal was coming on that road and tried to stop him, but he passed on and was followed by the officers who tried to get ahead. The Colonel tantalized them by allowing them to come alongside, but to get by or to stop him was out of the question. *Thus he led them all the way to the ferry at Youngstown, having passed Lewiston without stopping. At Youngstown he allowed them to drive past him, but before the Marshal could get to him he turned about and started back toward home, the officers still keeping in sight of him until he drove into his barn.*[13] When he stopped the officers were close by, and rushing up to both sides of the carriage, were astonished to find no person inside of it, the Colonel having been careful to allow them to keep near enough to know positively that no person had left the carriage since it started. "Come into the house, gentlemen, and have some refreshments," said the Colonel. "Bill, rub down their horses, they are a fine team, and have tried the bottom of my grays. I thought you would give it up at Lewiston, but as you decided to go on I thought if any team in this county could show better bottom for a long drive than mine, I should like to know it." By this time the Marshal had made up his mind that there was no game there, and he drove on without waiting for Bill to groom his horses or to hold any conversation with the Colonel. . .

[**pp. 119-121.** *The Pettit account continues with how Cassey had meanwhile been secretly conducted to a station near Lockport managed by an Irish Conductor, Dennis W___, who convinced his Irish friend Jimmy to hide Cassey for a few days. See the summary comment on Dennis W___ below.*]

---

[13] *Ibid.*

[p. 121] She had been at Jimmy's place when the rebels fired on our flag, after which Cassey went back and found her boy, and as fugitives were not safe in New Jersey she decided to remain with her Quaker friends.

If Pettit was correct, Col. P___ must have believed that racing to the Youngstown Ferry would fool the Niagara Falls slave catchers about Cassey's attempted escape. This supposition is clear in two passages. "Cathcart [the slave catcher] had already engaged a score of shaggy Democrats to start at his bidding, and he sent two of them without delay to watch the bridge, and *others were sent to all the crossing places between Tonawanda and Youngstown*. . ." "[Col. P____] . . . led them all the way *to the ferry at Youngstown*, having passed Lewiston without stopping.[14] *At Youngstown* he allowed them to drive past him, but before the Marshal could get to him he turned about and started back toward home, the officers still keeping in sight of him until he drove into his barn." These passages could also imply that Youngstown ferrymen would accommodate, even help, fugitive slaves, as in the account related by Samuel Ringgold Ward.[15]

Again, although Pettit's account is literary and imaginative, it is generally considered to be accurate with regard to UGGR routes. If so, the Cassey story is at least supporting evidence of the Youngstown Ferry's connection with the Underground Railroad.

To add to this point, we take a closer look at much discussed conductors who were involved in the plot to deceive the slave catchers, Col. P_____, "Ben Jackson," and "Dennis W. ___." They were part of a Niagara Falls Underground Railroad network most likely centered in the Cataract Hotel.

---

[14] See Carl J. Constantino, *History of the Underground Railroad Along the Niagara Frontier* (Master's Thesis; Lewiston, New York: Niagara University History Department, 1947), 52-56.
[15] See Ch. 8.

The Niagara Falls-Lockport Network
1. "Col. P _____"

The first name to be identified in Eber Pettit's story is "Col. P___." Christopher Densmore, followed by Judith Wellman, has suggested two possible options for his identity: Colonel Peter Augustus Porter (1827—1864) and General Parkhurst Whitney (1784—1862).[16]

A. Colonel Peter Augustus Porter; the Peter A. and Matilda Porter Home

Colonel Peter Augustus Porter, the first option, came from one of Niagara Falls' most eminent families. Peter Augustus Porter's uncle, Augustus S. Porter, was the first judge in Niagara Falls—he was often called "Judge Porter"—and many places were named for him, including the Town of Porter where the Village of Youngstown is located. Peter's father, Peter Buel Porter, also had a distinguished career. A graduate of Yale, he became a lawyer, a hawkish member of the United States House of Representatives (1809-1813), a Major-General of the New York State militia during the War of 1812, a New York Secretary of State (1815-1816), a Commissioner to carry out the Treaty of Ghent (1816), and a United States Secretary of War under John Quincy Adams (1828-1829). The Porter brothers were wealthy and powerful. In 1764, a mile-wide strip of land on both sides of the Niagara River from Lake Erie to Lake Ontario had been deeded from the Iroquois to the British in reparations for those killed in the "Devil's Hole Massacre" in 1763, and the Mile Strip on the eastern side became the New York State Mile Reserve sold off at auction in 1805. The Porter brothers bought sections of the Mile Strip. They were determined to develop it and were active in buying and developing land, especially in Niagara Falls. (John Young bought Lots 1 and 2 of the Mile Strip, which became the heart of Youngstown).

---

[16] Christopher Densmore's "Underground Railroad Agents in Western New York," Revised, March 2000, includes "[Col.] P___." http://library.buffalo.edu/archives/exhibits/old/urr/PDFs/agents.pdf;
see also, *True Wesleyan* (NY), August 14, 1850: 1847c.; *Niagara Falls Gazette*, August 25, 1883; Judith Wellman, "Jackson," in "People and Sites."

Peter Augustus Porter, Peter Buel Porter's son, was also well on the way to a distinguished career, but his life was cut short. He graduated from Harvard (1845); studied at Heidelberg, Berlin, and Breslau (1846—1849); graduated from Harvard Law School (1857); and was briefly a member of the New York State Assembly (1862). He declined an appointment as Secretary of State, choosing rather to enter the Union Army. He was appointed a colonel of the 129th New York State Volunteers on July 7, 1862, and was tragically killed in action while leading a charge at the bloody Battle of Cold Harbor on June 3, 1864. In the city of Niagara Falls, Peter Augustus Porter was—and still is—an honored Civil War hero.

Peter A. Porter can be contrasted with his uncle and father on at least one major point: His uncle, Judge Augustus Porter, like most wealthy aristocrats of the day, had been a slave owner and his distinguished father, Peter B. Porter, had helped his brother-in-law and friend, the slave owner David Castleman, pursue Solomon Moseby in Canada—not as a fugitive slave, but as a horse thief, which under Canadian law meant that he was a felon and, if convicted, could be extradited back to slavery in the United States.[17] In contrast, Colonel Porter—if he was Col. P____—was a conductor and perhaps also a station master in the Underground Railroad.[18]

Colonel Porter is one option for Col. P____. The influential Porter brothers, Peter's uncle and father, built beautiful homes not far from the Falls[19] and in the late 1850s, Peter and his second wife Josephine Matilda Morris (1831—1892) did the same. Living with them were George W. Hawley and his spouse Caroline E. Hawley, but more importantly, Peter's sister Elizabeth Porter, an elegant, well-educated, and widely-travelled woman, who—this is

---

[17] For Moseby's escape at Niagara, Canada, in 1837, see Ch. 1; for steamer Captain Hugh Richardson's refusal to help return Moseby to the United States, see Ch. 4.

[18] If Pettit was correct that Cassey attended a Methodist Church meetings on Sundays, could it have been the Falls Street Methodist Church (1849-1864), a short distance from Peter and Matilda Porter's (Col____?) home? African Americans sometimes worshipped at White Churches, although they were normally segregated.

[19] Ibid. See Judith Wellman, "Site of the Augustus Porter House," http://www.niagarafallsundergroundrailroad.org/underground-railroad-sites/site-of-the-augustus-porter-house/ "Site of the Peter Buell Porter House," http://www.niagarafallsundergroundrailroad.org/underground-railroad-sites/site-of-the-peter-buell-porter-house/..

significant for Colonel Porter's possible activity—was a well-known and ardent abolitionist.[20] It is thought that she was able to find jobs for free African Americans and freedom seekers, possibly through the Niagara Falls hotel owner Alva Gluck.[21] It is therefore very possible that the Colonel Peter A. and Matilda Porter Home was a station on the Underground Railroad.

The escape of Cassey is an important piece of evidence about Youngstown and the UGRR. In Pettit's account, it was nighttime. Col. P____ diverted Cathcart and his slave catchers by harnessing his fastest steeds and driving a carriage, supposedly containing Cassey, from Niagara Falls to the Youngstown Ferry, whereupon he turned around and went back to his home in Niagara Falls. Meanwhile, Cassey was being spirited off with a conductor to rendezvous with "Dennis W___" four miles outside Lockport.

B. Parkhurst Whitney, the Cataract House Hotel, and the Whitney-Trott House

One wrinkle in identifying Col. P.___ with Colonel Peter A. Porter is that according to Pettit's account of the Cassey story the farm of Col. P.___ was "two miles back from the river." We cannot be sure whether this location was actual or fictional, but if it has any merit, it does not correspond well with the site of Colonel Porter's mansion and barn, which was very near the Niagara River in the city of Niagara Falls. The "two miles" reference fits a little better—but not much—the location of Parkhurst and Celinda Whitney's home, which was located about where the old Niagara Falls Public Library exists today (the Carnegie Library at Main Street and Ashland, not the modern Earl W. Bridges Library). While it was not two miles back from the

---

[20] Judith Wellman, "Site of the Home of Peter A. Porter, Elizabeth Porter, and Josephine Porter," http://www.niagarafallsundergroundrailroad.org/underground-railroad-sites/site-of-the-home-of-peter-a-porter-elizabeth-porter-and-josephine-porter/. This site, until recently, was the site of the Fallside Conference Center. The Center has been partly demolished, partly reconstructed with a new 192-room DoubleTree Hilton hotel by the Merani Hotel Group, now open (January, 2017); see https://www.facebook.com/meranihotelgroup/; https://www.facebook.com/doubletreeniagarafalls/; http://doubletree3.hilton.com/en/hotels/new-york/doubletree-by-hilton-hotel-niagara-falls-new-york-IAGBADT/index.html.

[21] Alva Gluck owned the Spencer House and the International Hotel; both hotels also employed African Americans; both burned (1892; 1918); see *Souvenir History of Niagara County, New York* (The Pioneer Association of Niagara County, 1902), 191; also "Gluck" in Judith Wellman, "Database," at "Niagara Falls Underground Railroad Heritage Area," http://www.niagarafallsundergroundrailroad.org/assets/Uploads/Niagara-Falls-Underground-Railroad-Project-Database.pdf.

river, it was certainly closer to the 1855 Suspension Bridge used by Cassey to come from Lundy's Lane to Col. P___'s home. To consider this option, a little information about the Cataract Hotel, owned by Parkhurst Whitney, his sons, and others will be helpful.

Recall that the 1827 law that abolished slavery in New York State contained a provision that allowed slave owners from slave states or territories to bring their slaves with them into the state for as long as nine months, but that on May 25, 1841, that provision of the law was repealed. Henceforth, slaves brought into the state by their masters were in the eyes of the State free.[22] Abolitionists and those active in the UGRR did not hesitate to inform slaves in transit of their legal status in New York State. The Cataract Hotel, located just above the Falls, had a policy of hiring well-trained, free African Americans cooks and waiters. The 1850 census, taken in September not long before the *Fugitive Slave Act of 1850* was passed, shows that at least 64%, perhaps as many as 80%, of the Cataract Hotel staff had been born in slave states, a much higher percentage than in the Town of Niagara as a whole (50%). In the census of 1860, the year of (or before) the Cassey escape, the census shows about 53.3% of Cataract employees were African American, which was about equal to sixty workers. (The nearby International Hotel employed fifty-two African Americans). Not surprisingly, it was rumored that the Cataract Hotel was an Underground Railroad station and its employees were agents and conductors.[23] In short, these data suggest that Parkhurst Whitney encouraged the activities of the UGRR.

---

[22] See Ch. 4.

[23] This data (and more data) comes from the section "African American Waiters and Cooks" in Judith Wellman's article "Site of the Cataract House,"UGRR SITES, http://www.niagarafallsundergroundrailroad.org/underground-railroad-sites/site-of-the-cataract-house/.

The Cataract House (Hotel), 1842
J. H. Orr, Pictorial Guide *to the Falls of Niagara: A Manual for Visitors*, 55[24]
Image 12.3

The anti-slavery reputation of the Cataract Hotel is illustrated in *The Times-Pecayune* newspaper of New Orleans already in 1841, which was emphasized by Lewiston librarian and genealogist and former Niagara Falls Historian, Michelle Kratts.[25] In the longer report, Mr. James C. Evans of 10 Charles Street, New Orleans, wrote that he and his family, accompanied by their favorite servant girl, were making a trip to New York City and, having decided to stop over at Niagara Falls, they registered at the Cataract House of P. Whitney & Sons. While they were out viewing the Falls, their slave girl took care of their children. Upon their return to the hotel, the slave girl was sent to the kitchen to get milk for the infant. When she did not return within the expected time, Evans tried to find her. He learned that she had in his words "been taken"

---

[24] J. H. Orr, *Pictorial Guide to the Falls of Niagara: A Manual for Visitors* (Buffalo, NY: Salisbury and Clapp, 1842), 55, http://purple.niagara.edu/library/nfguides/or51-64.pdf.

[25] *The Times-Pecayune*, Wednesday, August 4, 1841, page 2, http://www.newspapers.com/newspage/25527127/. Michelle Kratts, "Bringing Lost Souls Home: John Morrison, a Hero of Niagara," part of her Oakwood Cemetery, Niagara Falls, Series "Hearts of War Part One: The War of 1812 at Oakwood Cemetery" at Kratt's Corner (Tuesday March 26, 2013), http://myoakwoodcemetery.com/kratts-korner/2013/3/26/bringing-lost-souls-home-john-morrison-a-hero-of-niagara.html. Our extract is a little longer than Kratt's extract.

across the river to Canada. Convinced that she had been abducted against her will, he and some of his friends the following day learned that she was in Niagara[-on-the-Lake] and went to look for her. He wrote that when he and three companions arrived, they were surrounded by large numbers of Negroes who would not permit him to speak to her in order to determine whether she desired to return with them. The African Canadians also claimed that nothing had happened at the Cataract House in Niagara Falls, New York. Although Evans admitted that he had no proof that the Cataract Hotel workers were really involved, he wrote the following in *The Times-Pecayune*:

> The proprietors of the Cataract House keep in their employ, as servants, a set of free Negroes, many of whom have wives and relatives in Canada, and they have an organized plan of taking off all slaves that come to the house. The Messrs. Whitney keep these fellows in their employ, knowing them to be engaged in this business; therefore, it behooves all southern people travelling north to avoid the 'Cataract House' at the falls of Niagara. The 'Eagle Hotel,' kept by C. B. Griffin & Co. is the house which should be patronized by all persons from the south. The proprietors are not abolitionists, and they employ no free Negroes; all their servants are white.[26]

General Parkhurst Whitney operated the Cataract Hotel from 1825 to 1845. When he retired to his farm in 1845, the management of the hotel was taken over by his son Solon Whitney, his son-in-law James Trott (who had been in charge of the employees), and Dexter Jerauld. James Trott and his wife, Celinda Whitney, Parkhurst's daughter, moved in with Parkhurst and his wife, also named Celinda Whitney, in 1849. The hotel's reputation in relation to the UGRR later fostered a local Niagara Falls legend that tunnels under the Parkhurst-Trott house led to the barn and the Niagara River; however, Judith Wellman states that these legends appear to date from mid-twentieth century. Nonetheless, she also writes: "[T]he actions of the Whitney-Trott families . . . offer compelling if circumstantial evidence of their support for the Underground Railroad."[27]

---

[26] Ibid.

[27] Wellman, "Site of the Whitney-Trott House," http://www.niagarafallsundergroundrailroad.org/underground-railroad-sites/site-of-the-whitney-trott-house/.

Parkhurst Whitney is a reasonable alternative for Col. P___, especially given the reputation of the Cataract Hotel. A problem with this identification is that Whitney was remembered as a general, not a colonel. In some respects, then, Colonel **P**eter Augustus **P**orter—note the double "P"—no doubt influenced by his abolitionist sister Elizabeth, remains a viable candidate for Col. P___.

2. "Ben Jackson" and the Cataract House, Niagara Falls

A second name in Eber M. Pettit's story about Cassey is "Ben Jackson." He is portrayed as a shrewd, Free African American working in one of the hotels in Niagara Falls. His main role in the story is helping Cassey to escape from the slave hunter Cathcart by offering him false information and then warning Cassey and her employer, Col. P___, that she was in danger of being captured. As a diversion to fool Cathcart, Col. P.___ had his carriage hitched up to his fleet-footed horses and drove it empty at night to the Youngstown Ferry, slowly enough to allow the pursuing Marshall and his officers to visibly stay within range. Then Col. P.___ turned around and drove his carriage back to his barn. The officers, upon arriving and learning that the carriage was empty, realized the ruse and did not respond to Col. P___'s offer to care for their horses and imbibe in refreshment at his home, but went on their way. Meanwhile, Cassey—led by an anonymous conductor—escaped to meet up with an Irish agent four miles from Lockport, a certain "Dennis W___."[28]

Who was "Ben Jackson"? No one knows for certain, but Christopher Densmore cautiously speculated that Eber Pettit might have used this name as a pseudonym for John Morrison or Daniel Crosby, or one of the other African American hotel workers/agents in Niagara Falls.[29] Using false names was not unusual; abolitionists and activists in the UGRR often kept participants' names secret.[30]

---

[28] Eber M. Pettit, *Sketches,* 86-88; Constantino, History *of the Underground Railroad Along the Niagara Frontier*, 52.

[29] Christopher Densmore, "Fugitive Slave Cases in Niagara County: A Glimpse into the Underground Railroad" (Niagara County Historical Society, Lockport, NY, Feb. 24, 2000).

[30] Pettit called himself simply "Conductor" when he first published his book in 1868.

Consider, first, John Morrison, about whom more is known. Morrison was, by 1859, the head waiter at the Niagara Falls' Cataract House, which could fit the description of Ben Jackson. He was listed in the 1850 census as a Free African American, forty years old. He was known for his part in an attempted, but failed, rescue of a female slave from the Niagara Falls Eagle Hotel in 1847 and he apparently suffered an injury while working at the Cataract House that year. As noted previously in connection with the Niagara Falls Ferry at Prospect Point,[31] he "often ferried people [fugitive slaves] across the river himself."[32] This point is clearly made in an account by Robert Clemens Smedley about the visit to the Cataract Hotel of Rachael Smith, daughter of the Quaker abolitionist Joseph Smith (not the Mormon) of Pennsylvania.

In October 1859, Joseph's daughter Rachel visited Niagara Falls, and registered at the Cataract House. The head waiter, John Morrison, seeing her name and residence upon the book, approached her one day and politely made apology for intruding himself; but said he would like to ask if she knew a man named Joseph Smith in Pennsylvania. She replied that he was her father. He continued, "I would like to tell you about the poor fugitives I ferry across the river. Many of them tell me that the first place they came to in Pennsylvania was Joseph Smith's. I frequently see them when I visit my parents at Lundy's Lane. Many of them have nice little homes and are doing well." He ferried some across the river during two of the nights she was there.[33]

---

[31] See Ch. 4.

[32] Wellman, "Site of the Ferry Landing," Appendix C, http://www.niagarafallsunderground·ailroad.org/assets/Uploads/NF-HAMP-Report-Appendix-C-1.pdf, 142 or http://www.niagarafallsundergroundrailroad.org/assets/Uploads/01-The-Site-of-the-Ferry-Landing.pdf \.

[33] Robert Clemens Smedley, *History of the Underground Railroad in Chester and the Neighboring Counties of Pennsylvania* (Lancaster, PA: John A. Herstand, 1883), 231-32 (227-32), https://archive.org/stream/historyundergro00smedgoog#page/n10/mode/2up. See Wellman, "Site of the Cataract House," in *Appendix C. Survey of Sites*, 48-79, http://www.niagarafallsundergroundrailroad.org/assets/Uploads/NF-HAMP-Report-Appendix-C-1.pdf. Thanks to Michelle Kratts for finding this reference. See her "Bringing Lost Souls Home."

Smedley's story is supported by another document. Michelle Kratts writes, "We found the actual reference to this encounter in the Cataract Register. Rachael Smith was indeed a guest at the Cataract House in October of 1859. This is where Rachel signed her name and where Morrison noted that she may be connected to the Underground Railroad (*Courtesy: Niagara Falls Public Library*)."[34]

There is more information about John Morrison. In 1856, his friends honored him with a beautiful gold-headed cane at the annual celebration of emancipation in the British West Indies (August 1, 1834), which was part of the move toward emancipation in the British Empire.[35]

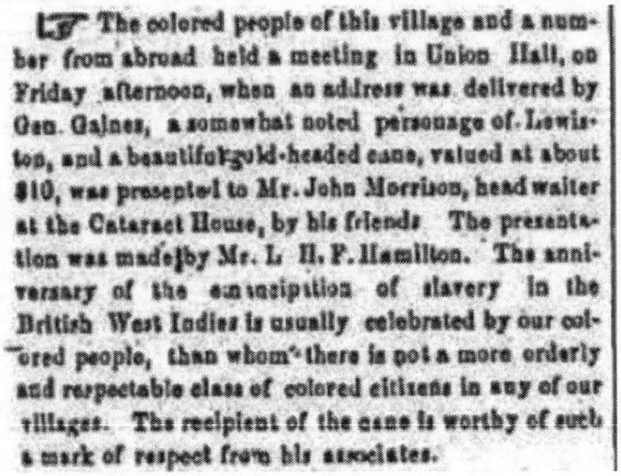

The colored people of this village and a number from abroad held a meeting in Union Hall, on Friday afternoon, when an address was delivered by Gen. Gaines, a somewhat noted personage of Lewiston, and a beautiful gold-headed cane, valued at about $10, was presented to Mr. John Morrison, head waiter at the Cataract House, by his friends. The presentation was made by Mr. L. H. P. Hamilton. The anniversary of the emancipation of slavery in the British West Indies is usually celebrated by our colored people, than whom there is not a more orderly and respectable class of colored citizens in any of our villages. The recipient of the cane is worthy of such a mark of respect from his associates.

Newspaper Clipping Honoring John Morrison, *Niagara Falls Gazette*, August 5, 1856
Image 12.4

---

[34] Kratts, ibid.; Wellman, ibid., 77-78. For Parkhurst Whitney's employment of African Americans in the Cataract Hotel (including a possible picture of John Morrison!), see Wellman, "Site of the Cataract House," *Survey of Sites,* 48-79, http://www.niagarafallsundergroundrailroad.org/assets/Uploads/NF-HAMP-Report-Appendix-C-1.pdf (image on p. 66).
http://www.niagarafallsundergroundrailroad.org/documents/02_Site%20of%20the%20Cataract%20House.pdf.
[35] The Newspaper clipping from August of 1856 is found in Kratts, "Bringing Lost Souls Home."
http://myoakwoodcemetery.com/kratts-korner/2013/3/26/bringing-lost-souls-home-john-morrison-a-hero-of-niagara.html. For more on the emancipation in the British Empire and Canada, see Chs. 1, 2 and for Morrison Ch. 2 and Michelle Kratts, "Bringing Lost Souls Home: John Morrison, a Hero of Niagara" in "Hearts of War Part One: The War of 1812 at Oakwood Cemetery," Oakwood Cemetery, Niagara Falls, Series. Online at Kratt's Corner, March, 26, 2013, http://myoakwoodcemetery.com/kratts-korner/.

This honor hints at Morrison's brave, risky activity in the Underground Railroad. Also, the apparent connection between John Morrison and Jordan Gaines is tantalizing. We shall say more about General Gaines in relation to Austin McPherson and Gerrit Smith.[36]

The nearby International Hotel in Niagara Falls employed fifty-two African Americans, one of whom was its steward Daniel R. Crosby, another candidate for Ben Jackson.[37] Crosby was the son of a Kentucky fugitive slave who settled in Toronto. He worked at the Cataract Hotel and then advanced as the head waiter at the International Hotel from 1853 to the 1870s. Unfortunately, less is known about him.

3. "Dennis W_____," near Lockport, New York

A third name in Pettit's account of Cassey was the Irish conductor called "Dennis W ___," an "active and industrious man" and member of the abolitionist Liberty Party. He was said to have lived four miles outside of Lockport on a farm between the Erie Canal and Ridge Road.[38] Col. P___ apparently sent freedom seekers to Dennis W___ when dangers arose at the Niagara River. The most direct route from Niagara Falls to Lockport by land was Lockport Road coming to the town on its southwest side. The conductor who brought Cassey to Dennis W___ told him that he should not keep Cassey at the latter's station because he, Dennis, was suspected of having a connection to the UGRR. In responding to this warning, Dennis took her to a remote house on his farm where his Irish friend "Jimmy" was living. It is well known that many Irish immigrant laborers were resentful about competition for jobs by Free Blacks and, according to Pettit, Jimmy had to be convinced that it was absolutely necessary to hide and keep an African American woman safe. Dennis first explained her plight. The friend's response was extremely negative. His outburst was based on what he had heard at a Democrats' meeting in Lockport.

---

[36] See Chs. 2, 11, 14 for more on Gerrit Smith and the Gaines property.

[37] Christopher Densmore, "Fugitive Slave Cases in Niagara County. A Glimpse into the Underground Railroad," Niagara County Historical Society (Lockport, NY: February 24, 2000).

[38] Pettit's account about Dennis W ____ does not focus on Youngstown, but on Lockport after Cassey's arrival there, and is for the sake of brevity omitted from the Cassey story extract above. Dennis W___ is found in Pettit, *Sketches*, 119-21. [38] Christopher Densmore's "Underground Railroad Agents in Western New York," Revised, March 2000, includes "Dennis W___," http://library.buffalo.edu/archives/exhibits/old/urr/PDFs/agents.pdf.

When Jimmy calmed down, Dennis W ___ told him about an African American woman who had taken care of him in Boston [Massachusetts] when he first came from Ireland. He was sick, needed to be cared for, and had no money. Dennis did not know she was an African American until he was well, came into the light, and saw her for the first time. She told him her name was "Margaret" and she had a gentleman son, Samuel R. [Ringgold] Ward who was well educated (recall Ward's autobiographical account of crossing the Niagara River at Youngstown).[39] Being kindhearted, she gave him money to launch him on his way. With deep gratitude for her help, Dennis vowed to himself that he would always help African Americans whenever he could. Margaret Ward had saved his life.

Jimmy was touched by Dennis W___'s story and so agreed to hide Cassey for a few days.

Pettit ended his Cassey story by writing that while Cassey was at Jimmy's, the rebels fired on Fort Sumter (April 12, 1861).[40] This significant event, which started the Civil War, meant that Cassey could go back and get her son near Philadelphia. While in New Jersey she made a decision to stay with her Quaker friends. Otherwise, perhaps Dennis W ___ would have brought her or sent her from Lockport to the Youngstown Ferry to cross back into Canada.

No one knows the identity of Dennis W___ at this point. A remote possibility is the well-known conductor Thomas Root of Pekin, not too far from Lockport.[41]

In short, Pettit's engaging drama of fugitive slave Cassey's escape from slave catchers in Niagara Falls in 1860 or 1861 assumes that the Youngstown Ferry was a well-known means to cross the Niagara River to freedom in Canada. It was an important site on the Underground Railroad.

---

[39] See Ch. 8. Was this identity an "imaginative" flourish by Pettit?
[40] Pettit, *Sketches*, http://www.civilwar.org/battlefields/fort-sumter.html (Last accessed July 31; as noted above this statement is used by some scholars to date the account (n. 5).
[41] See Ch. 15.

CHAPTER 13

Eleven Fugitive Slaves, ca. 1861/1862

Image 13.1

Eleven Fugitive Slaves Arrive at King's Wharf, ca. 1862

In her book *History of Niagara* published in 1914, Canadian historian Janet Carnochan recorded a fugitive slave account based on what a sergeant remembered while he was living at Navy Hall as a boy. Navy Hall is located below Fort George on the Canadian side of the Niagara River and just below it is King's Wharf on the water. Navy Hall and its wharf have a long history. Maps as early as 1810 locate a wharf in front of Navy Hall, not far from the ferry house.[1] The wharf was originally intended as landing for the shuttle between Fort George and Fort Niagara, which never materialized. The original Navy Hall and wharf were destroyed by the

---

[1] See the 1810 map at the beginning of Ch. 16.

Americans in the War of 1812. They were rebuilt after the war. Both are adjacent to the Niagara-on-the-Lake.[2] In his book about the area, Richard Merritt writes:

> ...[T]he [rebuilt] Navy Hall site is nearly 250 years old. The Navy Hall wharf, now a popular perch for amateur fishermen and the occasional mooring site for commercial marine enterprises, has been a naval and public dock for a similar period. In recognition of its rich and colourful past, Navy Hall was designated a National Historic Site in 1969.[3]

King's Wharf is directly across the Niagara River from Youngstown. In 1914, the soldier who spoke to Carnochan vividly recalled the arrival of eleven freedom seekers at King's Wharf about fifty years earlier. In 1993, Niagara Historian Nancy Butler, quoting Carnochan's account of 1914, added that "...on reaching Niagara [Canada] the [eleven] fugitives' relief at arriving safely and their joy at attaining liberty at long last must have impressed the local residents..."[4] Here is Carnochan's version of the soldier's story as quoted by Butler:

> A pathetic little story was told lately by a sergeant in the Volunteer Camp here: "I was a little boy living in the Red Barracks (Navy Hall) about 50 years ago, my father being a soldier, and I saw one day a party of eleven black people land at King's Wharf. They were all escaped slaves, men, woman and children, and their action in landing was indelibly impressed on my memory. I shall never forget how they all knelt down, and kissing the ground, fervently thanked God, the tears streaming from their faces, that they were now in a free country.[5]

---

[2] 1810 and 1819 maps of the Niagara River and shorelines are in Ch. 16; discussion of the ferrymen is in Ch. 6.

[3] Richard D. Merritt, *On Common Ground. The Ongoing Story of the Commons in Niagara-on-the-Lake* (2012), Ch. 5, "Navy Hall."

[4] Power and Butler (with Joy Ormsby), *Slavery and Freedom in Niagara*, 48-49.

[5] Janet Carnochan, *History of Niagara* (Toronto, ON: William Briggs, 1914; reprint Belleville, ON: Mika Publishing, 1973), 205-206.
https://books.google.com/books?id=lRY1AQAAMAAJ&printsec=frontcover&dq=Janet+Carnochan,+History+of+Niagara&hl=en&sa=X&ved=0CB0Q6AEwAGoVChMIiqO8qYyTxglVSn6SCh068QA1#v=onepage&q=Janet%20Carnochan%2C%20History%20of%20Niagara&f=false (last accessed July 27, 2015); Power and Butler, *ibid.*

Present-day (2016) King's Wharf, Niagara-on-the-Lake, Ontario, upgraded in 1977
[Wharf in the foreground; note the fisherman]
Fort George at Niagara-on-the-Lake, Ontario, is in the Background
Photo 0964 by Glenn Clark: Spring 2014 [6]
Image 13.2

Human memories are subject to error ("false memories"). Yet, the soldier's reminiscence—at least the core of it—is worthy of consideration as a historical occurrence. A boy who saw such a large group of Black freedom seekers arriving at King's Wharf, a very unusual experience, is of the type that is not likely to have been forgotten. Indeed, the soldier *claimed* that the event was indelibly imprinted in his memory. It was obviously a positive memory. He had probably retrieved and recounted it before and so it would have been reinforced in his long-term memory.[7]

King's Wharf is directly across the Niagara River from Youngstown, which suggests the probability that the group had been ferried across the river by a Youngstown ferryman. The time, "about 50 years ago," is not exact; if adjusted backward a couple of years, the arrival of the fugitive eleven slaves would have been about 1861-1863, that is, during the period when

---

[6] This is part of the view, a little farther away, from the Duling home in Youngstown.
[7] A. Jansari and A. J. Parkin, "Things that Go Bump in Your Life: Explaining the Reminiscence Bump in Autobiographical Memory," *Psychology and Aging* 1 (1996) 85–91. Research on autobiographical memories of older adults indicates that they more easily recall first-time events that occurred in childhood or adolescence (the "reminiscence bump").

the federal law to return fugitive slaves to the South was still legally in effect, although it was being challenged in the North. Perhaps it was shortly before or not long after Abraham Lincoln's "Emancipation Proclamation" on January 1, 1863, or at least before June 18, 1864, when the *Fugitive Slave Act of 1850* was repealed by an Act of Congress. The ferryman in this period was probably Youngstown's Ira Race (1807-1899), whose 1858 petition to operate the Youngstown Ferry for ten years was apparently approved. Race, you will recall, was a farmer, then sheriff, and at this time Justice of the Peace. Earlier, he had helped write the petition to incorporate Youngstown in 1854.[8]

The story of the joyful celebration of the eleven freedom seekers upon reaching Canada is similar to other such accounts. Unfortunately, we do not know anything more specific about these eleven.

Currently, the site of the historic King's Wharf provides a place for resting, fishing, and observing the beautiful Niagara River, Fort Niagara, and the Youngstown bluff in New York.

---

[8] Pool, *Landmarks*, Ch. XV; for Ira Race as a ferryman, see Ch. 6 (**1836**; **1854**; **1858**).

PART III
Speculations

The six chapters of Part I laid the foundation for Youngstown's role in the Underground Railroad. The seven chapters of Part II focused on seven accounts about those who crossed the Niagara River to Canada by the Youngstown Ferry or with the aid of an individual Youngstown boater, plus an attempt of a freedom seeker to cross on a raft.

Part III has three chapters that are progressively more speculative. Indeed, some readers might want to exclude them since they do not have the kind of primary and secondary evidence contained in Part II. We have decided to include them as a set of possibilities worthy of consideration.

Chapter 14 contains intriguing possibilities based on an already established regional UGRR network. Written and oral sources feature men and women who have some documentable network connections with each other, but whose UGRR involvement in some cases is probable, in others only possible. Chapter 15 documents possible UGRR locations near Youngstown with stories from newspapers and oral traditions. Chapter 16 speculates about UGRR physical sites in Youngstown itself. They are possibilities related to the persons already discussed in this book.

CHAPTER 14

Extended Networks:
The Davis and Haskell Families, Austin McPherson, John Carter, Jordan and Mary McClary Gaines

Image 14.1

An entry in the 1855 John P. VanDeusen Diary mentions an UGRR agent "Mr. Pardee," a hardware merchant, from Palmyra who by 1854 was a hardware merchant in Youngstown.[1] Other sources show that he was Myron J. Pardee, a partner with E. P. Pomroy at *Pardee & Pomroy*; that his family shared a household with the Wilcoxes in Palmyra, and probably also in Youngstown, since both families owned property in Youngstown and the Pardee and Wilcox women owned 614 Main Street together.

The *Pardee and Pomroy* hardware business was located in a front section of the Davis Brick Block, owned by Bradley Davis at 409 Main Street, at least since 1849. The building was

---

[1] See Ch. 10.

strategically located at the top of the bluff, or Niagara Gorge, overlooking the Niagara River.[2] The 1860 Federal Census records that a Black servant in the house of Nelson R. Davis, Bradley's brother, was Austin McPherson. In 1870, McPherson was living in the Lewiston home of Jordan Gaines at 350 (North) Second Street. This property had originally belonged to Youngstown's John Carter who deeded it to Jordan's wife Mary McClary Gaines. It is striking that Mary's death in November of 1854 was recorded in *Frederick Douglass' Paper* of January of 1855, as noted in Chapter 12. Moreover, in 1856 Jordan Gaines was the guest speaker at a Niagara Falls emancipation celebration at which UGRR conductor John Morrison was honored. All these associations raise the question whether the Davis family itself was involved in the UGRR network.

The Davis and Haskell Families

Jason Davis, the brother of Gordon Davis, an early settler in Youngstown in 1823, came with his two sons Bradley ("B. D.") and Nelson R. Davis from New Hampshire to Lewiston, New York, where they lived for one year about 1830. After going back to New Hampshire, they returned to the area and settled in Youngstown in 1835. They set up a general store that included groceries, dry goods, hardware, leather goods, and other basic necessities of the times.[3] In 1842, Jason bought property from Hezekiah Smith on the southwest corner of Main and Lockport Streets, diagonally across from the Ontario House, and moved his business there. He extended his property south in 1849.[4] By 1854, the Davis Brick Block had been built there by Jason's son Bradley. The *Pardee & Pomroy* hardware store was in the front part of the building by 1854.

In 1853, Jason Davis purchased 500 Main Street on the corner of Main and Hinman Streets. A large, corner lot home was built there between 1853 and 1856, the year that Jason died. An 1860 resident map places Mrs. Davis, Jason's wife Martha, there. Martha Davis lived

---

[2] See Chs. 15, 16.

[3] Onen, "Recollections."

[4] Pool, *Landmarks*, says that the Davis Brick Block was built in 1855; however, Onen, ibid., says that it was there when he left in 1854 and an article in the *Niagara Falls Gazette* of 1856 states that the business had been there two years. Onen also states that in 1854 Bradley Davis's store was in the back of the building and that *Pardee and Pomroy* was in the front.

out her days at 500 Main Street until she reportedly died "from excitement" because of a destructive fire in the Davis Brick Block in 1863.[5] Their son Bradley inherited the property and by 1860 he also owned the abutting lot just south of 500 Main Street at 520 Main Street. His name is also on maps of the back lots behind the houses on Second Street. Bradley moved Pickwick Hall, a cultural and social gathering center, from Main Street to the corner lot behind 500 Main Street, 505 Second Street.[6] This new arrangement is represented by an image found in the *History of Niagara County* (1878).

**Residence and Property of Bradley D. Davis (formerly of Jason Davis),
the Corner of Hinman (carriage) and Main (right corner) Streets, 500 Main Street, c. 1878**
(the current home is closer to the corner)
History of Niagara County, 340
Image 14.2

The 1870 map shows that 520 Main Street just to the south (Lot 9), which at one time Olaf Hathaway supposedly "occupied," also has an impressive house built by B.D. When he and his wife (also named Martha) died in 1882, their daughter Estella and her husband, A. H. Dutton, inherited the corner house along with other properties, including farm lands, while their daughter Elvira and her husband Nelson D. Haskell inherited the house at 520 Main Street, the huge red barn behind it, the Grist Mill, the 409 Building and other properties. So, it was that

---

[5] According to the *Niagara Falls Gazette* (April 22, 1863) a fire destroyed stores and hotels from the Davis Brick Block to Hinman Street on the west side, or river side, of Main Street.
[6] 505 Second Street is now (2016) an apartment building in disrepair.

the imposing Davis Brick Block at 409 Main Street became the N. D. Haskell Building and the 520 house became the Davis/Haskell property. The barn is still called the "Haskell Barn."

The Davis/Haskell Home, 520 Main Street, built c. 1877
Photo by Karen Noonan
Image 14.3a

The Red "Haskell Barn" behind the Davis/Haskell Home
Photo by Dennis Duling
Image 14.3b

Again, do the Davis family and homes have anything to do with the Underground Railroad? We can only speculate. If Onen's 1854 letter was accurate, Bradley Davis had built the Davis Brick Block by 1854 and we know that *Pardee & Pomroy* had their hardware business in the front section. Onen's dating seems to be confirmed by an article in the 1856 *Niagara Falls Gazette* that *Pardee & Pom[e]roy*, established two years earlier, was a quite successful business. An advertisement by what was called "Davis and Co." that same year shows that Bradley Davis had a store selling diversified household products in his building. He undoubtedly rented or leased to *Pardee and Pom[e]roy*. Was he aware of agent Myron J. Pardee's connections with the Underground Railroad in 1855?

We know less about Jason Davis's other son, Nelson R. Davis, but in the 1860 Federal Census, he gave his occupation as "farmer" and he was also listed at the bottom of the Youngstown 1860 map as a farmer on land south of the village proper. On that same map his wife, Mrs. N. R. Davis, had properties on the north end of Main Street in the village, one about where the present-day Constitution Park is located (where the old State Street came up the hill).[7] Also in the 1860 Federal Census, Nelson Davis listed thirteen people living on his farm in addition to himself. Most significantly, as noted, he reported that he had one Black male "servant" named Austin McPherson, who a decade later was living in Lewiston in the household of Jordan Gaines at 350 (North) Second Street.[8]

We are speculating here that there might have been family and friend network ties between the Davis family and others involved in the UGGR. Bradley Davis owned the Davis Brick Block where the UGRR agent Myron J. Pardee shared a hardware business with E. P. Pomroy. Ten years later, Nelson Davis's African American servant Austin McPherson, who was born in Virginia, was living in Lewiston in the residence of African American "General" Jordan Gaines, who was also from Virginia. Jordan Gaines' wife, the original owner of the Lewiston property, was most likely an abolitionist.[9] At the very least, Davis and perhaps other family members might have ignored and remained silent about the involvement of the people living or working for their family and in their community. One must always remember that in small villages such as Youngstown, people knew each other from churches, socialized with each other at numerous occasions, and joined together for management of the village and the school. Religion, social relationships, and economics interacted. Would the activities of Myron J. Pardee whose

---

[7] See Chs. 6 and 16.
[8] See the section on Jordan and Mary McClary Gaines of Lewiston below.
[9] Ibid.

business was in the Davis Brick Block, have gone totally unnoticed by Jason Davis and his sons Nelson and Bradley?

Mention of Austin McPherson as the Black servant of Nelson Davis in Youngstown and as a house resident of Jordan Gaines in Lewiston leads to further exploration of the network ties between Youngstown and Lewiston. We note again that there were links between the African Americans Jordan Gaines and the Niagara Falls Cataract House (Hotel) workers, particularly the UGRR conductor John Morrison, and between Mary McClary Gaines and the famous Frederick Douglass (see further, below). These ties are related to the Underground Railroad. Let us explore a little further.

Austin McPherson

Austin McPherson, a Free African American, was listed in the 1860 Federal Census as Nelson Davis' fifty-year old Black servant. He was living with thirteen other people on Nelson R. Davis's farm south of the center of Youngstown. In the 1870 Census, ten years later, this same Austin McPherson was listed as a "Black male day laborer," age 56 (!), in the house of a "Black male day laborer," 72-year-old General Jordan Gaines, in Lewiston, New York. Both were born in Virginia. Also living there was a "B[lack]" female named "Maria," age 52, who was keeping house. These three resided at 350 (North) Second Street, Lewiston, New York, on a property that John Carter of Youngstown sold to Jordan's wife, Mary McClary Gaines, in 1840. Again, Mary, who died in 1854, was likely an abolitionist and perhaps involved with the UGRR.[10] This connection is all the more intriguing when we learn a little more about John Carter, Mary McClary Gaines, and Jordan Gaines.

---

[10] See the email interchange between Michelle Kratts and Judith Wellman quoted above.

John Carter: Lewiston and Youngstown, New York

There were at least six John Carters living in Western New York, three in Niagara County, one each in Wilson, Newfane, and Youngstown.[11] Youngstown's John Carter was a prosperous mason, a farmer, and a builder who ran a brickyard. He was born in Tooley Park, Leicestershire, England, on November 1, 1814. Both of John's parents died in England. He and an uncle immigrated to America in 1823. John came to Buffalo in 1832, purchased property in Lewiston, and finally settled in Youngstown in 1840. It may be relevant that he had spent some time traveling in the southern slave states. At age twenty-seven, on September 30, 1841, he married a Canadian milliner, Mary Ann Clyde, who was born in New Brunswick, Canada on Oct. 12, 1821. They apparently had seven children.[12] Mary Ann died on June 21, 1897, at the age of 75. John continued farming at 110 Lake Street (locally known today as "the Carter Farm," but no longer in the Carter family) until he died at the age of 91 in 1905. Mary Ann and John are buried in Oakland Rural Cemetery, just outside of Youngstown on Route 18F (Lake Road).

---

[11] Gretchen Duling has developed the John Carter materials; thanks also to Karen Noonan. The main sources for the Youngstown Carters are the Carter Family Folder, Town of Porter Historical Society Museum Family Genealogical Files; personal communication from a family member, Deborah Carter Fox; Pool, *Landmarks*, 302; and Virginia Howard, "John Carter, Noted Pioneer, Youngstown Area Builder," *Niagara Falls Gazette* (September 28, 1953): 20. Pool also mentioned a John Carter who was a Town of Wilson Supervisor (1833-1842); he was possibly John *B.* Carter in the Federal Census data of 1830, 1860, and 1870; he was born in 1818, married Maria, and fathered four children. John Carter of Newfane is found in the census data of 1840 and 1850; in 1850 he and his wife Maria are 33 and have three children. There was also a John Carter in Eden and two more in Buffalo.
[12] Pool, *Landmarks*, ibid., cites ten children; Howard, ibid., discusses six children. Thanks to Debora Fox, Carter's great, great, great granddaughter, for listing seven children.

John Carter (1814-1905)
Courtesy: The Town of Porter Historical Museum, Youngstown, New York
(touched up by D. Duling)
Image 14.4

Youngstown's John Carter was a prominent Youngstown citizen. He was one of several

men who incorporated themselves to form the Episcopal parish, which they named St. John's

Episcopal Church in 1868. After the cornerstone of St. John's was laid in 1878 (on land donated

by Ordnance Sergeant Lewis Leffman[13]), Carter and Benjamin Root, owner of the Ontario House

at that time, became wardens. Carter was also a trustee of—indeed built—the Methodist

Episcopal Church and held the mortgage on the Methodist Church building for a period while it

was closed (1869-1876).[14] Census data between 1860 and 1880 show that he had several

occupational designations: in 1860 a Master Brick Layer, in 1865 a mason, in 1875 a farmer, and

---

[13] Donald E. Locker, *Lewis Leffman: Ordnance Sergeant United States Army*. Occasional Contributions No. 22
(Lockport, NY: Niagara County Historical Society Inc., 1974); Dennis Duling in *From the Mouth*, 137—140. Leffman
asked that his name be remembered three times a year in St. John's church services. In the church are a "Leffman
pew" photo and dedication plaque. For Lewis Leffman, his family, and Fort Niagara, see the end of Ch. 3.
[14] Pool, *Landmarks*, 266.

in 1880 a Master Brick Layer again. As mentioned, he owned a brickyard—his bricks were used for the Davis Brick Block—and he is still remembered for building many buildings and other structures in the area, including the retaining wall around Fort Niagara, the Pillars Mansion on River Road south of the Village center, the Cadet School at Stella Niagara (the mother house of the Franciscan nuns), the Quade, Smithson, and Baker homes outside of Youngstown, and, of course, the beautiful brick Carter homestead.[15] There is a story that John walked each day from his home in Youngstown to Lewiston where he built the spectacular Lewiston Manor (now Hennepin Hall), with its magnificent chimneys and fireplaces.[16]

John Carter Farmstead House, built ca. 1858
New York State Historic *Register* and the National Historic *Register*
Photo by: Dennis Duling
Image 14.5

More important there are reports that connect John Carter with the Underground Railroad. In 1953, Virginia Howard wrote that Carter owned a boat and was often on the Niagara River. She made the following claim without citing sources: "The boat of John Carter

---

[15] Virginia Howard, "John Carter, Noted Pioneer, Youngstown Area Builder," Niagara Falls Gazette (September 28, 1953): 20.
[16] *Lewiston Sesquicentennial 1822—1972*, 93.

was reputedly used many times in helping runaway slaves to escape pursuit and cross the river to the harboring shores of Canada. This was probably part of the system of the 'underground' route to help slaves gain their freedom."[17] Lewiston Librarian and Genealogist Michelle Kratts found a typed single-spaced page titled, "History of 350 N. Second Street, Lewiston, New York."[18] This undated document contains the comment that Carter "was known to have spent a lot of time in his boat on the Niagara River" and was "an active abolitionist in the Underground Railway." Kratts herself notes: "John Carter, who owned the area's first brickyard, was also a builder and worked on many of the structures in the area. It was believed that he also had a boat which he used to take runaways across the river".[19] Do these reports stem from earlier oral traditions?

If these reports have at least a kernel of truth, they are quite suggestive for Carter's role in the Underground Railroad network, including a link with Lewiston as a property owner.

Jordan and Mary McClary Gaines [Gains], Lewiston, New York

In the Federal Census of 1840 there are nine Free Colored people living together in the household of "Jourden Gains" in Lewiston, New York: a male 36 through 54 (according to the 1860 Federal Census Jordan was a 61-year old Mulatto, or 41 in 1840) and a female in the age category 36 through 54; a male 24 through 35; a male 20 through 23; and a female 10 through 23. These five persons were presumably Jordan, his wife Mary,[20] their sons Robert and Joseph, and their daughter Melinda. However, there were four others—two boys and two girls—all under the age of 10. Were they grandchildren? Perhaps one was Richard Gains who in the 1860 Federal Census was age 17 and according to the 1865 New York State Census age 23. Also living with Gaines at that time was Harrison Carter, age 42.[21] Neither Richard Gains nor Harrison Carter was reported in 1870 when Austin McPherson and Maria were living with Jordan Gaines.

---

[17] Howard, "John Carter." She does not give the source of Carter's abolitionist connections.
[18] For further comment about this document, see below on Jordan and Mary Gaines.
[19] Michelle Kratts, Lewiston Librarian and Genealogist; see also her comments in Gretchen Duling, *et al.*, *From the Mouth of the Lower Niagara*, 21.
[20] The census assumes that Mary McClary Gaines was Black; see below for the possibility that she might have been White. Or was she just light-skinned or "Mulatto"?
[21] We have no information about Harrison Carter, specifically whether he had any connection to John Carter.

We need to learn more about Jordan and Mary and their possible links to Youngstown's John Carter and to the UGGR.

In 1837, John Carter purchased a village block in Lewiston from the State of New York (Carter block, left box on the map). It was the third block from the Niagara River and lay between Second Street and Third Street. It was bounded on the north by Mohawk Street and on the south by Oneida

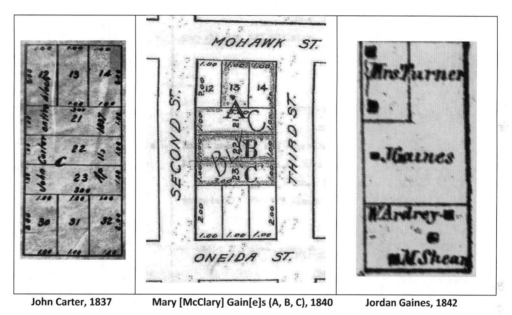

| John Carter, 1837 | Mary [McClary] Gain[e]s (A, B, C), 1840 | Jordan Gaines, 1842 |

Maps: John Carter's Block and the Mary and Jordan Gaines Parcels in Lewiston, New York[22]
Image 14.6

Street. The block was subdivided into nine parcels or lots: three N-S lots on the north side (12, 13, 14), three N-S lots on the south side (30, 31, 32), and three E-W lots in the middle (21, 22, 23). In 1840, the year that John Carter settled in Youngstown, he sold Parcels A, B, and C to a "Mary Gains," a transaction that is recorded in the property's 1840 Warranty Deed which has

---

[22] Thanks to Historical Association of Lewiston Museum Curator Pamela Hauth for her help in locating maps.

the "Grantee" of the three middle properties as "Mary GAINES." The same transaction is also in the Deeds Index of Niagara County for the year 1846 as the Warranty Deed to "Mary Gains."[23]

	WARRANTY DEED.
No. 3	Dated Oct. 27th, 1840
John Carter	Ack'd Nov. 1st, 1844 and Recorded Nov. 2nd, 1846
to	in Liber 39 of Deeds at Page 189.
Mary Gains.	Cons. $1.00 and conveys
	parcels "A" "B" "C" above

Warranty Deed: John Carter to Mary Gains, 1840
Image 14.7

Note that on the 1840 map (the middle map) Parcel A (21, 22, 23) extends into two more lots (Lots 13, 14). The total transfer seems to have been five lots. Note also that these five lots are shaded together as a single unit and that the letters "B L K C" are written in the section, perhaps designating Block C for taxation purposes. The earliest tax record in 1842 attributes these five lots to Mary's husband, "JGaines," that is, Jordan Gaines. This might have been because the Married Women's Property Laws Act of New York was not passed until 1848. Before that law, a woman lost her rights to control or acquire property she had previously bought before marriage, or inherited after marriage (if not from her husband), and she was not permitted to make contracts, keep her own wages or rents, *transfer or sell properties*, or engage in a lawsuit.[24] The John Carter-to-Mary Gaines was a property transaction. In 1842, was Mary's husband's name used for the five lots for legal and tax purposes? In any case, as we shall see, descendants of Mary claimed the property. Finally, we note that the 1840 census records that four children were living with Jordan and Mary Gaines: two males (Robert and Joseph?) and two females under age 10 (was one Melinda?).

---

[23] This is correct; Michelle Kratts sent us the deed history of the property. See also, Kratts in Gretchen Duling, *et al.*, *From the Mouth of the Lower Niagara River*, 21.
[24] See "Married Women's Property Laws." Library of Congress, https://memory.loc.gov/ammem/awhhtml/awlaw3/property_law.html.

Mary Gaines died in 1854. Her husband Jordan continued to live in the small house on Parcel A (Carter Lot 21), which became 350 North Second Street, possibly built about 1850.[25] In the 1865 New York State Census Harrison Carter (?), age 42, and Richard Gaines, age 23 (born in 1842), were also living with Gaines, who was then 66. In the 1870 Federal Census, Austin MacPherson and Maria were living at 350 Second Street with Jordan Gaines, now age 76.

Remodeled Home of Mary McClary Gains and Jordan Gains [Gaines], built ca. 1850
350 North Second Street, Lewiston, New York
Photo by Dennis Duling
Image 14.8

The later history of the properties sheds a little more light on Mary McClary Gaines and her husband Jordan. The properties—at least Parcels A (21), B (22), and C (23)—were passed on to their sons Robert R. Gaines and his wife Mary, Joseph M. Gaines and his wife (--?), their daughter Melinda R. Brazier and her husband Henry Brazier, names found in the census of 1840 above, and, finally, in 1887 to John Fleming, as indicated by an Affidavit of 1930.[26] The death certificate of Melinda R. Brazier forwarded to us by Michelle Kratts states that Melinda was born in Lewiston, New York, April 5, 1836, and died December 17, 1926, age 91, while residing

[25] Ibid. Michelle Kratts discovered a typed history of 350 Main Street noted above, but its source and date are uncertain.
[26] Ibid.

in the Home for Aged and Infirm in Hamilton, Wentworth County, Ontario. The certificate records that Melinda was Colored, that her father was Jordan Gaines, and that her mother's maiden name was Mary McClary, born in Lexington, Kentucky. One might reasonably conclude that Mary McClary Gaines was also colored, which would be consistent with the 1840 Federal Census: "Jourden Gains," a Free Colored male (in 1860 he was listed as Mulatto) in Lewiston, age 36-54, is living with a *Free Colored female*, age 36-54. However, an Affidavit of John Fleming's daughter, Mary E. MacCollum, claims that she received 350 (North) Second Street from her father. It notes the three Gaines children and their spouses and it raises interesting questions about race. It states:

> . . . that said Robert R. Gaines, Joseph H. Gaines, and Melinda R. Brazier were the children and all the heirs at law of *Mary Gaines who was the wife of a negro* well known locally as "General Gaines" who survived his said wife, resided with his family on one of the above mentioned lots [Lot A?], died prior to the giving of the aforesaid quit claim deeds by his children in 1887 and was well known to deponent; and that the surname of said family was often spelled "Gains" instead of "Gaines."[27]

Mary was described as "the wife of a negro." This could imply that Fleming's daughter believed that Mary was White. If she actually was, it suggests a so-called mixed marriage between Jordan Gaines and Mary McClary, presumably some time before 1836, the birth year of Melinda.[28] Other possibilities are that Mary was a light-skinned Mulatto or passed as White.[29] In any case, the claim is that the two Gaines men and Melinda Brazier were property heirs of Mary Gaines, the original owner of the property.

---

[27] Affidavit dated December 14, 1939, in the record of deeds for 350 North Second Street.

[28] Contemporary people might think that "mixed marriages" are mostly recent. However, census data about marriages between African American men and White women between 1850 and 1865 were more common than they were before attitudes were influenced by Jim Crow laws and the Ku Klux Klan in the South; they were also more common in the North than in the South. See Aaron Gullickson, "Black/White Interracial Marriage Trends, 1850—2000," *Journal of Family History* 31/3 (July 2006), 299-301, Figure 4 (289-312). Curiously, in the Census of 1870 Jordan Gaines is listed as "White"; given the other evidence about him, this was hardly likely.

[29] For the many historical and contemporary complexities and complications of passing relative to definition of terms, social identity, social role, unconscious racial identity, the one-drop rule, Jim Crow contexts, the law, and judgments of others, see Randall Kennedy, "Racial Passing," *Ohio State Law Journal* 62:1145 (2001): 1-29. Online at http://moritzlaw.osu.edu/students/groups/oslj/files/2012/03/62.3.kennedy.pdf.

This discussion of the Gaines family and heirs seems like a diversion. However, consider first the connection between John Carter and Mary "Gains." According to the Birnmore Letter, the subject of Chapter 8, two fugitive slaves were rowed across the Niagara River at Youngstown by an anonymous farmer. John Carter was listed as a farmer in the 1875 census and there were oral traditions that he was active in transporting fugitive slaves across the Niagara River from Youngstown to Canada. In short, if the oral traditions have any kernel of truth, the link between John Carter and Mary McClary Gaines might have extended beyond a transfer of Lewiston property to involvement in the UGRR.

We come to an important point: Mary McClary Gaines' death in 1854 was reported in *Frederick Douglass' Paper* dated January 12, 1855. It stated: "DIED. Lewiston, on the 14th Nov. last, Mrs. MARY GAINS, died at age 55 years."[30] When Michelle Kratts came across this reference in *Frederick Douglass' Paper* she raised the question to Judith Wellman about whether Mary McClary Gaines might have had a role in the abolitionist movement. Wellman responded, "It would certainly imply that she was part of the Black (or White) abolitionist network, active enough to have come to Douglass's attention."[31] Kratts later expanded:

> The Gains . . . family is one of the earliest recorded African American families in
> Lewiston and one of the most curious. Jordan Gains, who initially shows up in the 1840
> census with nine "free colored" individuals living in his household, may be the first
> African American landholder in Lewiston . . . well, actually, his wife Mary McClary.[32]
> Although the census lists Jordan as the head of the household, the ownership of his
> property was actually claimed by Mary. A Warranty Deed dated October 27, 1840,
> reveals a land transaction transferring Parcels "A," "B," and "C" from John Carter to
> Mary Gains. Interestingly, there is an oral tradition that links John Carter with the
> Underground Railroad. John Carter, who owned the area's first brickyard, was also a
> builder and worked on many of the structures in the area. It was believed that he also
> had a boat which he used to take runaways across the river. Perhaps there was a

---

[30] *Frederick Douglass' Paper*, January 12, 1855, in African American Newspapers, Accessible Archives.
[31] Email communication from Judith Wellman to Michelle Kratts.
[32] Michelle Kratts naturally assumed with good reason (the 1840 census) that Mary was African American; we have suggested that this is a little uncertain since she was called "the wife of a negro" in a later Affidavit.

particular reason John Carter released his land in Lewiston to Mary Gains for $1 in 1840.[33] The present owners of the property and a local historian believe that the Gains family may have been key members of the Underground Railroad network in Lewiston.[34]

There are other network links that should be noted, particularly between Jordan Gaines and John Morrison on the one hand and the famous abolitionist Gerrit Smith on the other hand.

According to the *Niagara Falls Gazette* in 1856, General Gaines, as he was called, was the guest speaker at Niagara Falls' Union Hall for the annual celebration of the emancipation of slaves in the British West Indies on August 1, 1834. The year 1834 was also the effective emancipation date in the British Empire noted in Chapters 1 and 12. This was the very same celebration at which John Morrison, head waiter of the Cataract House (Hotel) in Niagara Falls, was honored by his friends with the gift of a beautiful gold-headed cane, a gift surely given to him—at least in part—for his role as an active and courageous conductor in the Underground Railroad. Recall that Morrison himself had courageously rowed fugitive slaves across the Niagara River at Prospect Point below the Falls and that he was a plausible option for the identity of Ben Jackson who in Eber Pettit's story helped Cassey to escape the slave catchers at Niagara Falls.[35] All this suggests an intriguing connection: General Gaines was the guest speaker at the Niagara Falls emancipation celebration that honored a heroic Underground Railroad conductor. Recall again that *Frederick Douglass' Paper* recorded Mary McClary Gaines' death in 1855, suggesting that she was likely an abolitionist involved in a (Black/White?) UGRR network. The Upper Suspension Bridge crossed between Lewiston and Queenston. Was Jordan Gaines (like his wife Mary?) also active in the UGRR?

---

[33] A Warranty Deed of $1 does not specify the actual price of the transaction.
[34] Michelle Kratts in Gretchen Duling, *et al.*, *From the Mouth of the Lower Niagara River*, 21. In the discussion of John Carter above, Kratts's discovery of a typed history of 350 Main Street in Lewiston was noted; it mentions Carter's boat and possible connection with the UGRR; so do other reports about John Carter.
[35] See Ch. 12.

Another striking link existed between Jordan Gaines and the wealthy abolitionist and UGRR financier Gerrit Smith. Recall that Smith lent money to Youngstown's UGRR agent Myron J. Pardee[36] and to fugitive slave Ben Hockley to buy property in Oswego.[37] The Syracuse University's Special Collections Research Center (SCRC) archive, which contains the Edwards-to-Smith letters (Volume 88), also houses Smith's *Register*, a thick book containing many of his land transactions. In the back of the *Register*, there are 122 pages described as "Distribution of lands to colored men, begun in 1846." This includes Smith's grants of some 120,000 acres, about forty acres each, to some 3,000 persons.[38] The *Register* was organized by New York counties, one of which was titled "Niagara." On the Niagara County page, we discovered as the last entry that Smith gave forty acres to Jordan Gaines ("Jedan Gaines") of Lewiston in 1847. The small, clearer writing was apparently inserted by Smith's clerk, but the heading with date, location, and amount in larger, less legible writing apparently was by Smith.[39]

---

[36] Ch. 7.

[37] Ch. 9.

[38] A 3 x 5-inch card tucked in the *Register* is engraved with the heading "Homestead, Peterboro, New York." It states that the land grants enabled Colored men to vote. This is so if the land could be developed worth $250. However, the card appears to be incorrect on two counts. It says that Smith gave away 3,000 acres; he actually gave away 120,000 acres to 3,000 colored men. It says that the small writing is that of Smith and the large writing that of his clerk, but the reverse is more likely. See the following note.

[39] That the larger, poorer writing was from Smith is the judgment of Norman K. Dann, Smith's biographer, in personal conversation at Peterboro and by email. For Dann's discussion of Smith's clerks, some of whom were land agents in other cities, see his *Practical Dreamer*, 298-301.

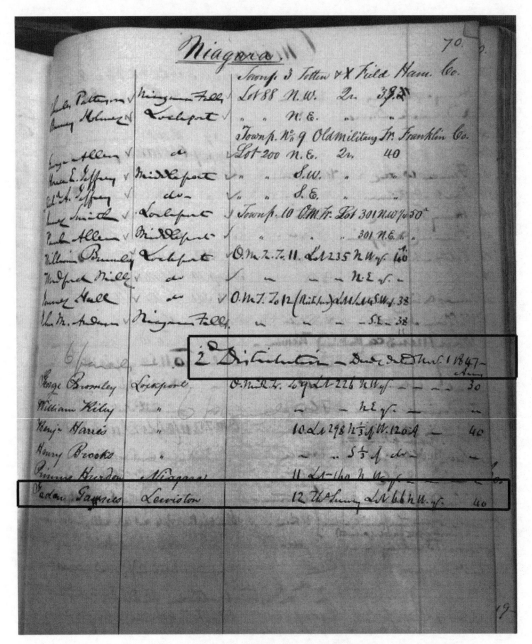

***Register* of Gerrit Smith's Land Transactions, Including One to "Jedan Gaines"**
Courtesy of the Special Collections Research Center (SCRC) at Syracuse University Libraries Archive
Gerrit Smith Papers Housed on Site
Photo by Dennis Duling
Image 14.9

A transcription of Smith's heading (the first box) is "**2nd Distribution – Deeds dated Nov. 1, 1847**—and the word under 1847 is surely "**Acres,**" with acreage amounts in the columns below it. The sixth column entry below the heading reads:

"*Jedan Gaines* | *Lewiston* | *12 USSurvey* | *Lot 6.6 NW*.q. | *40*."

The mark after "**NW.**" could be taken as "of" or the square root symbol $\sqrt{}$, but is much more likely a cursive "q.," a deduction based on "$2\imath$," on the same page (above right) in the more artistic, cursive script, apparently the clerk's. If so, "**NW q.**" refers to the location of Jordan Gaines's grant, the "NW quarter."[40] This probably corresponds to a division by "quarters" in the United States Survey System.[41]

All this suggests that in 1847 "Jedan Gaines" received forty acres, probably in the very northwest section of the Town(ship) of Lewiston. In addition, he inherited five lots in 1854 from his deceased spouse Mary McClary Gaines in the Village of Lewiston. On one lot (parcel "A") was a house at 350 Second Street. In New York, in 1847, there was still a requirement of property ownership worth at least $250 for African American males to vote (it had been removed for White males in 1821). If Smith gave some 120,000 acres in approximately forty-acre parcels to about 3,000 African American men at Timbuctoo in New York, he was also giving them the right to vote *if* they developed the rather poor acreage so that it was worth $250.00.[42] We should add that Smith helped to organize the Liberty Party in New York which held its first convention in 1840 and included women—the first Women's Rights Convention was in 1848 at Seneca Falls—and African Americans, including a few African American women. Much of this

---

[40] Ibid.

[41] Using vertical and horizontal axes, the United States survey system divides large blocks of land into squares within squares. Each large block contains sixteen six-mile squares, or "townships." Each township contains thirty-six one-mile square "sections," which are numbered from 1 to 36 horizontally from right to left, or east to west, beginning in the northeast corner. Each of these mile-square "sections" is further subdivided into four quarters—northeast, northwest, southeast, and southwest, each quarter containing 160 acres, which are subdivided into four quarters of forty acres each (these can be subdivided further into halves, quarters, or even smaller lots).

[42] The law that land worth $250 was required for Black males to vote in 1847 was abolished in 1870.

party was absorbed by the Free Soil Party in 1848.[43] That year, and again in 1852, a radical, uncompromisingly abolitionist remnant of the Liberty Party formed by Smith, the National or True Liberty Party, nominated him for the presidency of the United States, and so did the Industrial Congress in 1848 and the Land Reformers in 1856. He did not win, but he was elected to the United States House of Representatives as an Independent in 1852. He resigned on August 7, 1854.

Summary

We have come full circle. In 1855, John P. VanDeusen recorded in his Diary at Newark, New York, that he recommended that Daniel and James make contact with a certain "Mr. Pardee," a hardware merchant and good man. We gave strong evidence that he was Myron J. Pardee, who migrated with family and friends from Palmyra to Youngstown, and whose brother, R. G. Pardee, was a lifelong officer in an abolitionist missionary society. Several sources show that by 1854, Pardee and his business partner, E. P. Pom[e]roy, were running a successful hardware business, *Pardee & Pomroy*, in the Davis Brick Block owned by Bradley G. Davis, whose brother was Nelson R. Davis. Nelson Davis's Black servant in Youngstown in 1860 was Austin McPherson. Ten years later, Austin and his companion/wife Maria were living in the home of 72-year old Jordan Gaines at 350 (North) Second Street in Lewiston. This property was part of a block that had been purchased in 1837 by John Carter of Youngstown, who is remembered in some late sources as a boater who transported fugitive slaves across the Niagara River. In 1840, Carter transferred three middle parcels of his block (21, 22, 23 = "A," "B," "C") to Jordan Gaines' wife, "Mary Gains," "A," "B," and "C," recorded in a Warranty Deed in 1840, re-recorded in 1846. The little house where Jordan, Austin, and Maria were living, 350 (North) Second Street, was built on parcel "A." Mary's death in 1854 was cited in *Frederick Douglass' Paper* in 1855, suggesting that she might have been part of a Black or White abolitionist network. Her husband Jordan seems to have inherited Mary's lots (Carter parcels 21, 22, 23) and came into possession of two more (13, 14). In addition, Jordan owned forty

---

[43] The Free Soil Party argued that the states won in the Mexican-American War (1846 – 1848)—California, Utah, Nevada, New Mexico, and Arizona—should enter the union as free states, not slave states.

acres of land, probably in the northwestern corner of the Town of Lewiston (outside the Village). They were apparently gifted to him by the famous abolitionist and land magnate Gerrit Smith, who had owned property in the Village of Lewiston. In 1856, General Jordan Gaines, as he was known, was the speaker at an emancipation ceremony in Niagara Falls that additionally honored John Morrison, an Underground Railroad conductor operating out of the Cataract House in Niagara Falls and known for ferrying fugitive slaves across the Niagara River at Prospect Point. He is a strong candidate for Eber Pettit's pseudonymous "Ben Jackson," who was credited with helping Cassey to escape while "Col. P___" created a diversion by racing his empty carriage from Niagara Falls to the Youngstown Ferry and back. One wonders whether, given all the links associated with 350 (North) Second Street, Lewiston, it was also a station on the Underground Railroad.

These connections suggest the possibility that the Youngstown contact "Mr. Pardee" in the VanDeusen Diary, the co-owner of a hardware business in the Davis Brick Block, might have had UGRR links not only with the Lyons-Palmyra-Newark and Lockport networks, but also the Lewiston and Niagara Falls networks. A forerunner of this UGRR activity was Olaf Hathaway. In other words, there is circumstantial network evidence reinforcing primary sources that Youngstown, particularly because of its ferry across the Niagara River to Canada, was part of a larger, regional UGRR network.

CHAPTER 15

More Niagara County UGRR Network Possibilities

Image 15.1

In Chapter 2, we noted a series of Anti-Slavery meetings in May, June, and August of 1855 at locations in Niagara and Orleans Counties. They included in their regional sequence Olcott, Wilson, Ransomville, Youngstown, Lewiston, Pekin, and Lockport. In Chapter 10, we observed that according to the VanDeusen Diary young fugitive slave James and his father Daniel were probably sent from Lyons, New York, to Newark, then to Lockport, then on to "Mr. Pardee" in Youngstown. In Chapter 11, we learned from the Birnmore Letter that fugitive slaves from Erie County were hidden in a back room at the *Lockport Daily Journal* office before being forwarded to a farmer at Youngstown who rowed them across the Niagara River. Birnmore's letter recalled two Lockport conductors, Lyman Spalding and M. C. Richardson, and they are listed with Binmore (Birnmore) and W. H. Childs in Wilbur Siebert's list of Lockport conductors in Appendix E of his *The Underground Railroad*. Chapter 12 portrays Cassey's escape to a conductor near Lockport, "Dennis W____" (as well as his friend Jimmy) with the help of "Col. P___'s" dramatic, but empty, carriage race to the Youngstown Ferry, a deception that links the Niagara Falls network centered in the Cataract Hotel and conductor "Ben Jackson" with both

Lockport and Youngstown. The biography of Thomas James discussed in Chapter 7 mentions one UGRR route, the Erie Canal construction across New York State, which went from Albany to Buffalo and included Syracuse, Rochester, and Lockport.[1] The New York Central train line in the 1850s followed a parallel route, but split with one branch going to Buffalo, the other to the Suspension Bridge at Bellevue/Niagara City/Suspension Bridge Village near Niagara Falls. There was also a Lewiston spur and, for a brief moment, New York Central and Canandaigua extensions to Youngstown.

These networks and the links within and between them raise questions about not only the social network links, but also the spatial network: stations, depots, safe houses, barns, churches, secret rooms—and the distances between them. There is often a great deal of difficulty in documenting the authenticity of Underground Railroad physical sites such as these and many would not pass the criteria of the Wellman Scale.[2] In short, the underlying ground in this chapter is less stable and for some historians, the evidence is insufficient to support them as part of the Underground Railroad. Yet, some information is known and it is worthwhile to explore the possibilities and speculate about them. Perhaps more concrete evidence will eventually come to light.

---

[1] Historic maps at "The Erie Canal," http://www.eriecanal.org/maps.html.
[2] See Preface and Ch. 17 for the Wellman Scale.

Distances to Youngstown from Outlying Sites

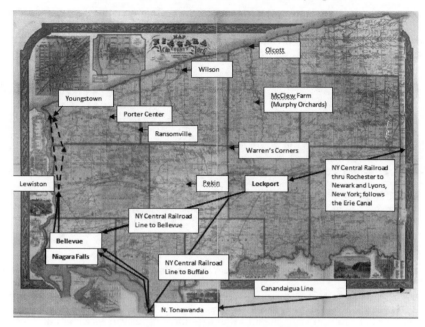

Historic Map of Niagara County, 1850
Public Domain, Library of Congress
Sites added by Dennis Duling
https://www.loc.gov/resource/g3803n.la000522/
Image 15.2

If we could zoom in on the above 1850 map online we would see more clearly many rivers, streams, towns, villages, and the route of the New York Central Railroad (consolidated in 1853). Barring that, we have inserted some key locations. Here are the approximate distances in miles to Youngstown:

1.	147	Syracuse	8.	18	Warrens Corners
2.	100	Newark	9.	13	Niagara Falls
3.	73	Rochester	10.	13	Wilson
4.	27	Buffalo	11.	12	Pekin
5.	22	Lockport	12.	7	Ransomville
6.	18	Olcott	13.	7	Lewiston
7.	18	Burt (McClew Farm)	14.	5	Porter Center

Distances in Miles to Youngstown
Image 15.3

More distant locations have been discussed in previous chapters; in this chapter, the emphasis will be on other sites in Niagara County apart from Lewiston and Niagara Falls, discussed in the previous chapter. It is important to remember that UGRR stations were usually only a few miles apart.

Charles H. (and Libby) McClew and the McClew Farmstead (Murphy Orchards)

Eighteen miles east of Youngstown it is possible to head north from Lockport via Eighteen Mile Creek about eleven miles and arrive at Burt, New York, in the Town of Newfane. This location is just a mile and a half south of Olcott, which is on the shore of Lake Ontario. A short distance west from Eighteen Mile Creek in Burt is little Hopkins Creek, which runs through the old McClew Farmstead.

There are oral traditions that former owners Charles H. McClew and his wife Libby McClew were UGRR conductors and station masters. Certainly, the McClew Farmstead was well located between Rochester and the Niagara River region. Under the McClew barn is a trap-door cellar accessible through a narrow entrance large enough for one person to descend by a ladder. The chamber below is L-shaped, about 12 by 15 feet. In recent years, its floor is covered with black decaying material and its walls marked by crumbling white plaster. Not so long ago there were on the floor smashed shards, shoe fragments, rusty eating utensils, parts of leather gloves, and pieces of tar paper. An article in the *Smithsonian Magazine* of 1996 called it "a cultural archaeologist's mother lode."[3] The underground chamber, sometimes called a secret room, has enhanced the oral tradition that under the barn was an UGRR hiding place and that the McClew farmstead was an UGRR station.

---

[3] Donavan Webster, "Traveling the Long Road to Freedom, One Step at a Time," *Smithsonian Magazine* 27/7 (October 1996): 48-50. http://www.smithsonianmag.com/ist/?next=/history/traveling-the-long-road-to-freedom-one-step-at-a-time-1-43841138/; the article features Anthony Cohen's journey by foot and rail tracing the route of a fugitive slave along the Erie Canal to Murphy Orchards, the Niagara River, and Canada. Online at http://iipdigital.usembassy.gov/st/english/texttrans/2005/06/20050606101156pssnikwad3.773135e-02.html#ixzz3oZ5VmeDk.

**Hopkins Creek on the
McClew Farm,
Burt, New York**
Courtesy of Murphy
Orchards
Photo by Dennis Duling
Image 15.4a

**Looking Down through the Trapdoor into a Cellar
Room under the McClew Barn**
McClew Education and Interpretative Center, Inc., of
Murphy Orchards in Burt, New York, Town of Newfane
Courtesy of Murphy Orchards
Photo by Dennis Duling
Image 15.4b

Literary evidence that the McClew Farm was an UGRR station has not yet surfaced, however, and the room has never been archaeologically surveyed and excavated in any formal way. Nonetheless, the farmstead, called Murphy Orchards under the leadership of Carol Murphy (deceased), has become The McClew Educational Interpretive Center, Inc., at 2402 McClew Road, Burt, New York. The farm frequently receives busloads of school children and the old house serves lunch and tea for guests and tourists. The farm has also become a local historic landmark of the Town of Newfane and a member of, and local Interpretive Center for, the New York State Underground Railroad Heritage Trail. The National Parks Service Underground Railroad Network to Freedom recognizes its educational program.

Charles Brown of Warren's Corners

About ten miles southwest of the McClew Farm is the hamlet of Warrens Corners, which lies at the intersection of Route 93 (Town Line Road) from the South and Route 104 (Ridge Road), which runs from Wrights Corners (East) to Lewiston (West). Heading toward Lewiston, Routes 93 and 104 run concurrently for about three and a half miles where, at the hamlet of Molyneaux Corners, 93 (North Ridge Road) diverges from 104 (Ridge Road) and heads to Youngstown (in Youngstown, Route 93 is Lockport Road). Still another road comes into Warrens Corners, Stone Road, which comes from the Southeast about six and a half miles from Lockport (Stone Road becomes Old Niagara Road before it enters Lockport). In the 1850s, Stone Road was "Lockport and Warren Corners Plank Road." According to a Lockport *Journal* article of June 20, 1854, cited in the *Anti-Slavery Bugle* of Salem, Ohio, on August 12, 1854, a fugitive slave named Charles Brown was living on the edge of Warrens Corners on Lockport and Warren Corners Plank Road in a house on Mr. Mighells' farm next to David Carlton's place.[4] Here is the article:

> SLAVE-HUNTERS IN THE EMPIRE STATE-- The following letter is from the Lockport (N.Y.) *Journal*:[5] Warrens Corners, Niagara Co., June 20, 1854: Southern bloodhounds and slave catchers are abroad! Our remarkably quiet neighborhood has this day been thrown into great excitement from the appearance and suspicious deportment of some strangers. Charles Brown, a colored man, who has resided in our midst more than two years, and who has won the respect of all who made his acquaintance, was, at an early hour this morning, rather surprised by the appearance of his master's nephew from Kentucky. Two gentlemen had been making strange maneuvers in the neighborhood by

---

[4] Thanks to Mr. and Mrs. Herman Erbacher of Warrens Corners for initial clarification of the area (confusing to outsiders) and to Brooke Morse, Cambria Town Historian, for further information about the roads and sources for the area. She noted that the Brown and Mighell families are in the Lockport census data of 1850, 1855 (state), and 1860. For the roads, see "Map of Niagara County, New York (1852),"
https://www.loc.gov/resource/g3803n.la000522/
and former Niagara County Historian, Clarence O. Lewis, "Early County Plank Roads Entered Through Toll Gates," Lockport *Union-Sun and Journal* (July 23, 1851),
http://fultonhistory.com/Newspaper%2018/Lockport%20NY%20Union%20Sun%20Journal/Lockport%20NY%20Uni on%20Sun%20Journal%201953/Lockport%20NY%20Union%20Sun%20Journal%201953%20-%202828.pdf.
[5] Thomas Birnmore hid fugitive slaves in his room at the Lockport *Journal* office in 1856 or 1857; for this account, see Ch. 11.

the residence of Brown on the Lockport and Warren Plank Road, going toward Lockport. They stopped nearly in front of Mr. David Carlton's then wheeled around and drove up the lane to Brown's house. One of them went back to Mr. Carlton's and inquired for Mr. Mighells (on whose farm Brown lives): the other remained in the carriage looking directly through the door of Brown's house, watching apparently for some one. The one in quest of Mr. Mighells pretended to want to rent his farm for the ensuing year. Brown saw him, recognized him. It was the nephew of his old master! Brown fled to the woods *with the avowed intention of crossing the Niagara River*. We have not heard from him yet to-night, but *we hope that he has kept clear of the river, as all the crossings are undoubtedly watched. It probably was the plan of the hunters to start him from his place and trap him there.* But we know that others are on the alert, and that the fugitive will not be captured without a struggle.[6]

Despite warnings cited in the newspaper (to throw off slave catchers?), Brown intended to head west and cross the Niagara River. Was he, like two fugitive slaves at nearby Lockport a couple of years later, sent to Youngstown to avoid the dangers of Lewiston or Niagara Falls, both towns more populated with slave catchers? We do not know. If he was, he might have been back at Warrens Corners by 1855 since he and Mighells are in the 1855 State and 1860 Federal Census.

---

[6] Cited in Wellman, "People and Sites Relating to the Underground Railroad, Abolitionism, and African American Life, 1820-1880 Niagara Falls and Niagara County," with the comment that the Brown house was likely a safe house (italics ours). On Warrens Corners, see Pool, *Landmarks of Niagara County, New York,* Ch. VIII (Town of Cambria), 247-48.

Thomas Root, Pekin, New York[7]

Following the roads from Warrens Corners southwest (Ridge Road [Route 104], or Townline Road [Route 429] or Warren Plank Road to Lower Mountain Road [425] and Townline Road [429], one comes to Pekin, New York, a distance of about nine miles, where Thomas Root lived.

Thomas Root was born in 1817 in Onondaga, New York. The following year his family moved to Pekin, New York, eight miles west of Lockport. The oldest of seven children, he had to take charge of his siblings at age fourteen when his father died. Root was able to overcome poverty and hardships enough to get an education and to begin teaching school at age seventeen. Because he developed a talent for the law and business, people sought his advice and counsel. He married Martha B. Orton and the couple had five children.

Root remained a farmer, but he was remembered as being a man of sterling character, an active Methodist, and committed to public service. He was the Town of Cambria Supervisor twice and a justice of the peace for more than forty years. Already an abolitionist by the young age of twenty-one, he debated against slavery, became involved in organizing the anti-slavery movement in his region, for some years was a member of the anti-slavery Republican Party in Niagara County, and in 1853 joined other leaders in Niagara County to help nominate persons to office who would seek to repeal the *Fugitive Slave Law of 1850*. Here are a few words from his obituary of 1903:

> He intensely hated all oppression of the poor or helpless. This characteristic carried him into the anti-slavery movement . . . [H]e led the anti-slavery movement in his town (nearby Cambria) so effectually that when it crystallized into the Republican Party organization, Cambria became the banner anti-slavery town of Niagara county.

---

[7] Pool, *Landmarks*, Part III (Family Sketches), 134-35; "Obit—Thomas Root of Pekin, NY, 1903," probably from *The Lockport Union Sun and Journal*, between 5 and 10 June, 1903, http://boards.ancestry.com/surnames.root/843/mb.ashx; Brooke Genter, Cambria Town Historian, "The Underground Railroad in Pekin," http://www.townofcambria.com/content/docs/Underground%20newsletter%20Historian.pdf

His place was a station on the underground railroad and he frequently assisted fugitives toward freedom in Canada. Each winter for several years, with a neighbor, Marvin Roberts, he got together a sleigh load of provisions and distributed it among the colony of fugitives at St. Catharines, Ont. So far was his thought from the present southern idea of the disgrace of eating with a negro, that any poor fugitive applying for his aid was seated at his table for meals and treated with the same courtesy that the most wealthy or cultured guest would have received. No one was ever discriminated against his house because of poverty or condition.[8]

In 1992, the Castellani Art Museum at Niagara University honored Thomas and Martha Root's home at 3106 Upper Mountain Road with an Underground Railroad sculpture.[9]

The Ransomville Connection

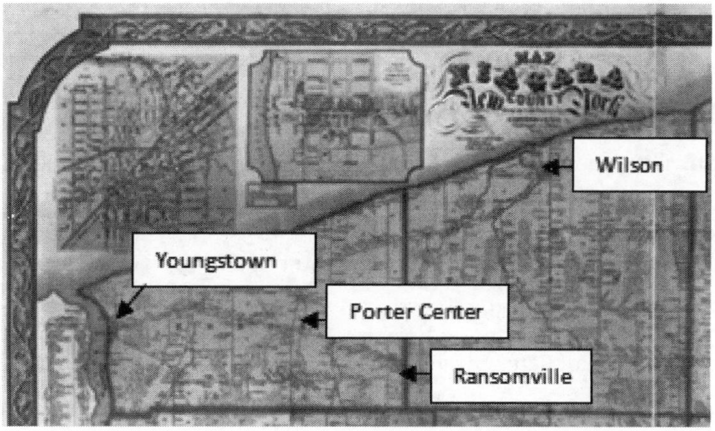

From the Historic Map of Niagara County, 1850
Public Domain, Library of Congress
Sites added by Dennis Duling
https://www.loc.gov/resource/g3803n.la000522/
Image 15.5

---

[8] "Obit.," ibid.; Genter, ibid. For St. Catharines and fugitive slaves, see Ch. 8.
[9] Genter, ibid.

One could travel northwest from Pekin to Ransomville, New York. Another option would be to head west from Warrens Corners on North Ridge Road (Youngstown-Lockport Road, Route 93) to the Hamlet of Ransomville, New York, which is only seven miles east of Youngstown. There is some speculation that along the way the North Ridge Methodist Church [c. 1848] near the intersection of Route 425 was also an UGGR stop, but no evidence is known at the church itself. Here are some traditions about Ransomville.

The Elbridge Gary Harris House

The granddaughter of Elbridge Gary Harris, Miss Adelaide Harris, is reported to have stated in a *Niagara Falls Gazette* article of May 19, 1954: "Grandfather [Elbridge Gary] Harris was a strong abolitionist and acted as a Ransomville agent for the Underground Railroad. He frequently concealed run-away slaves in his house [cellar] until they could be safely transported across the river to Canada."[10]

At the recommendation of a local Ransomville historian, Ms. Millie Hillman, who was one of the originators of the Ransomville Historical Room, Gretchen was directed to Ms. Ruth Gates, a retired Ransomville teacher, now living in Florida. Ms. Gates had researched the history of Ransomville, especially the UGRR, in order to present it to her students studying their local history. In a telephone conversation with Gretchen, Ms. Gates agreed with the content in the *Niagara Gazette* article given by the granddaughter of Elbridge Gary Harris.

This led to some further exploration.

On the eastern side of Ransomville on the north side of Lockport Road (Route 93) there is a large grey house trimmed in white (once also a store). It was renovated in 2014, but its

---

[10] Reported in an article titled "Beaver Dam in Creek Was Problem For Early Settlers of Ransomville Who Came by Covered Wagon Trails," *Niagara Falls Gazette*, May 19, 1954, 19. The statement appears to be a direct quotation from the granddaughter, Miss Adelaide Harris, who is mentioned in the article, but it is not so indicated by quotation marks.
http://fultonhistory.com/newspaper%208/Niagara%20Falls%20NY%20Gazette/Niagara%20Falls%20NY%20Gazette%201954%20May-Jun%20Grayscale/Niagara%20Falls%20NY%20Gazette%201954%20May-Jun%20Grayscale%20-%200099.pdf.

Renovated Harris House on Youngstown-Lockport Road in Ransomville, New York
Photo by Dennis Duling
Image 15.6

architecture helps to indicate its vintage. The original house was built by Elbridge Gary Harris about 1850. His Ransomville store [house] remained for over a century in one family and his granddaughter, Miss Adelaide Harris, reported to the *Niagara Falls Gazette* of 1954 that her grandfather's house was a station on the Underground Railroad.[11] Currently, we have no further information about the house.

The Gilbert W. Curtiss Ransomville House (Hotel)

Gideon Curtiss settled in Ransomville about 1817 and built a log tavern.[12] In the 1820s, his brother Captain Gilbert W. Curtiss arrived. Captain Curtiss made a home for himself and, after returning to Connecticut to get his bride, returned in 1825 and opened a second log tavern. Captain Curtis was also a grain farmer. His son Warren A. Curtiss added poultry to the farm and it became one of the largest poultry farms in the country by the early Twentieth Century. The Curtiss brothers and their descendants are remembered as some of the hamlet's most prominent settlers.

---

[11] Ibid.
[12] Pool, *Landmarks*, Ch. XVI, 258.

In 1840, Captain Curtiss built a new, larger, and more comfortable hotel/tavern to replace his small log tavern. He named it the Ransomville House. William Pool in his *Landmarks* stated that it is traditionally believed to have been a stop-over on the Underground Railroad.[13] Judith Wellman found this oral tradition worth including in her data base, but noted cautiously, "It is *believed* that during the Civil War it was a stop-over on the UGRR."[14]

Hotel and Warehouse of the Curtiss Brothers in Ransomville, New York, 1878[15]
Image 15.7

The Ransomville Wesleyan Methodist Church, ca. 1855

John Wesley, the father of Methodism, was strongly opposed to slavery. His American follower, the ascetic-minded Francis Asbury, encouraged Methodist preachers to work for emancipation. Correspondingly, the Methodist Episcopal Church in the late Eighteenth Century was strongly anti-slavery. However, in the early Nineteenth Century the official position of the denomination, led by prominent bishops such as Bishop Elijah Hedding of the New England Conference, softened, became more neutral, and some leaders opposed abolitionism as too radical, believing that a strong pro-slavery Methodism would lead to a split in the church denomination. It eventually did.[16] Meanwhile, in 1834 the first Methodist anti-slavery society

---

[13] Ibid., 263, 264, 266.

[14] *North Tonawanda News*, 1975. Judith Wellman, "People and Sites Relating to the Underground Railroad, Abolitionism, and African American Life, 1820-1880, Niagara Falls and Niagara County," 64 (italics ours). http://www.niagarafallsundergroundrailroad.org/assets/Uploads/Niagara-Falls-Underground-Railroad-Project-Database.pdf.

[15] *History of Niagara County, New York*, 346; see 333.

[16] Fred J. Hood, "Methodist Bishops and Abolitionism," *Border States On-Line* maintained by Harold D. Tallant, Department of History, Georgetown College (Middle Tennessee State University, 1973, 2000),

was formed in New York City. On November 8, 1842, three prominent, active abolitionist Methodists who believed that slavery was a sin and that the denomination was betraying its anti-slavery heritage—Orange Scott, LaRoy Sunderland, and Jotham Horton—announced in New England that they were withdrawing from the Methodist Episcopal Church. Others followed. In February of 1843, a separatist Wesleyan Anti-Slavery Convention was held in Andover, Massachusetts, where on May 31, 1843, twenty-one anti-slavery resolutions were passed. Then delegates came to Utica, New York, and formed the Wesleyan Methodist Connection of America, which advocated anti-slavery—and anti-episcopal—principles. Many Wesleyan pastors became UGRR conductors and many Wesleyan churches became UGRR stations.[17] Not surprisingly, the southern Methodists separated from the northern Methodists that very same year. ". . . [I]t came to be said of the Wesleyans, as of the Quakers, that almost every neighborhood where a few of them lived there was likely to be a station of the Secret Road to Canada."[18]

A series of anti-slavery meetings took place in Niagara and Orleans Counties in 1855.[19] Two of those meetings were held at Ransomville, one on Saturday, June 2, another on Monday, August 27.[20] Where did they meet? If it was not the Ransomville House, perhaps it was the Ransomville Wesleyan Methodist Church.[21]

---

https://www.google.com/#q=Fred+J.+Hood%2C+%E2%80%9CMethodist+Bishops+and+Abolitionism%2C%E2%80%809D+.

[17] "Anti-Slavery Roots. The Wesleyan Church." https://www.wesleyan.org/229/antislavery-roots. Orange Scott became the editor of *The True Wesleyan*. See also, the Reverend O. Scott, *The Ground of Secession from the M. E. Church, or Book for the Times: Being an Examination of Her Connections with Slavery, and also her Form of Government. Revised and Corrected. To Which is added Wesley Upon Slavery* (New York, NY: C. Prindle, 1848), https://spider.georgetowncollege.edu/htallant/border/bs1/hood.htm.

[18] Wilber Siebert, *The Underground Railroad from Slavery to Freedom*, 95.

[19] See Ch. 2,

[20] *Frederick Douglass' Paper*, May 4, 1855; *Frederick Douglass' Paper*, July 27, 1855; see also the *North Tonawanda News* 1975. Youngstown was also on the circuit; see above, Ch. 3.

[21] The Ransomville Wesleyan Methodist Church is no longer active. The building has other uses.

Once the Wesleyan **Methodist Church, Ransomville, New York, originally ca. 1855**
3653 Ransomville Road, Ransomville, New York
Now an Apartment Building [2017]. A door was behind the steps.
Google Earth photo
Image 15.8

The Reverend Glezen Fillmore and Fillmore Chapel

Another possibility for an Underground Railroad station was the original Fillmore

Chapel, situated at the intersection of Dickersonville and Youngstown-Wilson Roads, a little

west of Ransomville about 6.5 miles east of Youngstown. To gain perspective, a little history of

its namesake, the influential Reverend Glezen Fillmore, is instructive.

Glezen Fillmore was born December 22, 1789, in Bennington, Vermont, and married

Lovina (dubbed "Aunt Vina") in 1809.[22] The couple adopted three children and made their

---

[22] Sanford Hunt, "Discourse of Memorial of Rev. Glezen Fillmore," Delivered in the Grace Methodist Episcopal Church, Buffalo, New York (February 14, 1875); "Dr. and Mrs. Fillmore," in Hunt, *History of the Methodist Episcopal Church in Buffalo from its Origin to the Close of 1892* (Buffalo, NY: H. H. Otis & Sons, 1893): 104-11; Mary Jane Haight-Eckert, "Rev Glezen Fillmore", https://open.bu.edu/bitstream/handle/2144/556/Hunt%2c%20S.%20Discourse%20on%20Memorial%20of%20Rev .%20Glezen%20FIllmore.pdf?sequence=1. Find a Grave, http://www.findagrave.com/cgi-bin/fg.cgi?page=gr&GRid=22291683. Records in the Grant County Archives, Grant County, Indiana, Data of Personal Interviews and other Authentic Sources of Local Information, 1912, Volume 2, 740 and 808. For more information about Rev. Fillmore see, "Rev. Glezen Fillmore" in *Ladies' Repository* 21/6 (1861): 366-67, http://quod.lib.umich.edu/cgi/t/text/pageviewer-idx?c=moajrnl;cc=moajrnl;rgn=full%20text;idno=acg2248.1-21.006;didno=acg2248.1-21.006;view=image;seq=0396;node=acg2248.1-21.006%3A23. New York Erie County Census 1855, 1865, 1875; 1850. John W. Percy, "Pioneer Preacher Glezen Fillmore. A 200-year Heritage on the Niagara Frontier," *Western New York Heritage* 11/4 (Winter 2009): 56-63.

home in Clarence, New York.[23] He was licensed to preach in 1809, and, after his father withdrew his opposition to his chosen profession, he became a full member of the Genesee (Western New York Methodist) Conference in 1818.

As a Methodist circuit rider, Glezen Fillmore was often away from home. For a time, the center of his circuit was Black Rock and Buffalo. He built the first Methodist church in Buffalo in 1818 and became the Presiding Elder of the Erie District, which extended from Lake Ontario to Meadville, Pennsylvania. He is reported to have had very successful ministries in the Pittsburgh Conference, the Rochester area, and the Lockport area. He was deeply committed to his churches, which included East Porter, Youngstown, and Wilson. It is reported that he never missed a church service, a church meeting, and meetings of the Genesee Conference, to which he committed himself for fifty-six years. Tales abound about his rugged frontier life, for example, his travels through inclement weather, and his loyal horse "Jack." Physically, Fillmore was a very large man, about 300 pounds; it was said that ". . . his rotundity of body would fill almost any pulpit, and the rotundity of his voice developed by long practice in preaching at camp-meetings would fill any church!"[24] His last post was Rochester. On January 26, 1875, he died in Clarence, New York, where he is buried.

---

[23] Sanford Hunt, *History of the Methodist Episcopal Church in Buffalo from its Origin to the Close of 1892* (Buffalo, NY: H. H. Otis & Sons, 1893): 108-11.

[24] An excerpt from a letter to Rev. Charles Andrew Lawrence from Mr. G. Everell McLaury (November 19, 1908) in the Eden, Erie County, New York Methodist Episcopal Church 95th Anniversary Booklet (1813—1908).

Glezen Fillmore (1789—1875)[25]
Image 15.9

Our first question is: Did Glezen Fillmore have abolitionist sympathies?

An answer to this question requires digging.[26] The Genesee (Western New York) Methodist Conference Records show that Fillmore held important leadership positions for almost a half a century;[27] it also includes information about slavery discussions and votes. One possible indication of Fillmore's views is that two years after abolitionist Wesleyan Methodists in Lockport separated from the Methodist Episcopal body in 1833, Glezen gave the sermon for the dedication of their new church building, June 13, 1835.

There are other hints of his views. At the twenty-eighth Genesee Conference (a regional, or annual conference) in Perry, New York, in September 1837, the Methodist Bishop Hedding gave a key address. Hedding rejected the institution and system of slavery, but he advocated a

---

[25] The photo is also Frontispiece in Hunt, *History of the Methodist Episcopal Church*; Percy, "Pioneer Preacher Glezen Fillmore," 56; and "Genesee Annual Conference of the Methodist Episcopal Church," Conference Archives, 140. https://archive.org/details/cu31924029471152.

[26] Francis W. Conable, *History of the Genesee Annual Conference, from its Organization by Bishops Asbury and McKendree, from its Organization by Bishops Asbury and McKendree in 1810 to the Year 1884 by the Rev. F. W. Conable* (2nd ed.; New York, NY: Phillips & Hung, 1885), 140, https://archive.org/details/cu31924029471152; http://archive.org/stream/cu31924029471152/cu31924029471152_djvu.txt.

[27] Ibid.

unity-minded, compromising version of the Bible's Golden Rule, that fair-minded, slave-owning brothers in the South should be treated as you would want yourself to be treated. Meanwhile, outside the official Conference gathering, zealous Wesleyan Methodists Orange Scott and George Storrs from the New England Conference were giving anti-slavery addresses to large crowds of preachers and onlookers. The Conference itself responded by forming a Methodist Preachers' Anti-Slavery Society. When the Conference met the following year in Elmira, the anti-slavery group was twice disrupted by mobs. The Conference reacted by passing a resolution against mob action and appointed a Committee of Five to draw up a statement about slavery for a Conference vote. Glezen Fillmore was appointed to the committee. Its report affirmed that there was no reason not to publish official Conference sentiments about slavery and reaffirmed the traditional Methodist stance that slavery is a "great evil" in the moral sense. It stated, ". . . as to the foreign traffic in human beings, . . . the buying and selling of men, women, and children with an intention either to originate or perpetuate their enslavement, is a violation of the disciplinary interdict [a prohibition]. . ." However, it did not directly address the civil and political status of slavery and stated that because slavery was a national political problem, it should not be discussed on the Sabbath and that itinerant preachers must not neglect their usual ministerial responsibilities to gain public attention on slavery; neither should they influence others against their brethren or "those who are over us in the Lord" (presumably the bishops), and particularly that they should not put their brethren's names, statements, or activities in the press.[28] When Bishop Hedding attempted to soften the Committee of Five statement with his Golden Rule Argument, the abolitionist faction objected and Hedding's even more moderate view was omitted from the Committee report.[29] Hedding accepted it. The report was adopted unanimously and Hedding ordered it published. It is possible that Fillmore spread this moderate Conference position in the churches of his Western

---

[28] *History of the Genesee Annual Conference,* 407-410.

[29] Charles Elliott, *History of the Great Secession from the Methodist Episcopal Church in the Year* 1845, Eventuating in the Organization of the New Church, Entitled the "Methodist Episcopal Church, South" (Cincinnati, OH: Schwarmstedt & Poe, 1855), 335, https://books.google.com/books?id=bB0RAAAAIAAJ&pg=PR14&lpg=PR14&dq=Genesee+Conference:+Bishop+Hedding's+addresses+on+slavery&source=bl&ots=DYZm_YUV1t&sig=XpXVThZYG8Pfly9DFcdoGYKqKWw&hl=en&sa=X&ved=0ahUKEwjQlLD869nJAhXLXh4KHUgTD7YQ6AEIHDAA#v=onepage&q=GeneseeGenesee%20Conference%3A%20Bishop%20Hedding's%20addresses%20on%20slavery&f=false; https://archive.org/stream/schisminmethodis00norw/schisminmethodis00norw_djvu.txt.

New York circuit (presumably not on the Sabbath!). Fillmore was important in these deliberations and in 1840 he was appointed to present a report on slavery to the General (national) Conference.[30]

The next General Conference (a meeting of the combined Annual Conferences every four years) began on May 1, 1844 in New York City. By now, the slavery conflict in the denomination had become intense; indeed, the Conference, which would have normally lasted a few days, continued for a record six weeks! The igniting spark was what to do about a prominent bishop, James O. Andrew of Georgia. Bishop Andrew reported that he had promised to protect a slave woman who asked him to care for her until she turned nineteen, at which time she would either go to the free colony of Liberia,[31] or be set free, but then she changed her mind and decided to remain with him, which under Georgia law meant that she was his slave. He stated that he had also inherited a male slave from his first wife, although he allowed him to leave when he could take care of himself, if he wished. His second wife, however, retained her slaves whom she had inherited from her late husband, although Bishop Andrew reported that he would not claim ownership and affirmed that he had never sold or bought slaves.[32] Debates about Bishop Andrew ensued for a full twelve days! Should he resign temporarily? Should he resign permanently? Should he be deposed? New England Conference

---

[30] *Journal of the General Conference* of the Methodist Episcopal Church (New York, NY: G. Lane& C. B. Tippett, 1844), 27,
https://books.google.com/books?id=OHURAAAAIAAJ&pg=PA27&lpg=PA27&dq=Slavery+The+Committee+of+Five+i n+the+Genesee+Conference&source=bl&ots=CXCRvlhexD&sig=42sxZgcKJqbBVB7P_SagY82hmhg&hl=en&sa=X&ve d=0ahUKEwjPhtau8tnJAhUF7R4KHQsxC7oQ6AEIHDAA#v=onepage&q=Slavery%20The%20Committee%20of%20Fiv e%20in%20the%20Genesee%20Conference&f=false.

[31] Ex-slaves and free blacks in the United States and West Indies could migrate to the free colony of Liberia in West Africa, a United States protectorate founded in 1820/1821. This alternative was encouraged by *The Society for the Colonization of Free People of Color of America*, or *American Colonization Society* (ACS), founded in 1816. The motives of the formation of the society—pro-slavery or anti-slavery—have been much debated. See "History of Liberia: A Timeline," Library of Congress, https://www.loc.gov/collections/maps-of-liberia-1830-to-1870/articles-and-essays/history-of-liberia/; Douglas R. Egerton and Judith Mulcahy, "American Colonization Society," in Paul Finkelman, editor-in-chief, *Encyclopedia of African American History: 1619-1895 From the Colonial Period to the Age of Frederick Douglass* (Oxford, England: Oxford University Press, 2006), 55-59.

[32] Phillip Stone, "How the Methodist Church split in the 1840s," *SC United Methodist Advocate* (February, 2013); reprinted in Wofford College. History Document and Photos from the Archives.
http://blogs.wofford.edu/from_the_archives/2013/01/30/how-the-methodist-church-split-in-the-1840s/.

members refused to compromise their anti-slavery position and after more debates about due process, the General Conference voted 111 - 69 that Bishop Andrew should resign.

A Committee of Nine was then appointed, one from each of the nine regional conferences (both north and south), to draft the terms of separation, should secession unfortunately occur. Glezen Fillmore was appointed to represent the Genesee Conference. As a consequence, Fillmore helped to frame the document that, if agreed upon by the Annual Conferences of the slave states in the South, would ultimately become the foundation for the "Great Separation" in Methodism. It required that if the slave states wanted to secede, they should be united, and it included complicated issues about the equitable distributions of church properties in the South. The burden was put upon the Annual Conferences to decide whether the separation would be violent or amicable. The southern Conferences agreed to the document, seceded amicably, and formed a parallel denomination, the Methodist Episcopal Church South, at Louisville, Kentucky in 1845.

Committee members made statements to the 1844 General Conference. Here is a description of Glezen's statement by the official historian of the Conference, Charles Elliott:

Mr. G. Fillmore, one of the committee, explained the labors of the committee. The design of God in raising up the Methodists was to spread Scriptural holiness through the land. The brethren from the south feared they could not do this under existing circumstances. The north said if they yielded any of the ground they had taken, they should throw impediments in their own path in carrying out the same object. Methodism, as the child of providence, adjusts herself to the circumstances of the case. The resolutions do not say that the south must go, shall go, will go, or that anybody wants them to go; but simply make provision for such a contingency. He [Fillmore] did not think there was a man among them who would dare to lay his head upon his pillow if he held from his southern brethren one cent of their common funds.[33]

---

[33]Charles Elliott, *History of the Great Secession from the Methodist Episcopal Church in the Year 1845, Eventuating in the Organization of the New Church, Entitled the* "Methodist Episcopal Church, South" (Cincinnati, OH: Schwarmstedt & Poe, 1855), 335.
https://books.google.com/books?id=bB0RAAAAIAAJ&pg=PR14&lpg=PR14&dq=Genesee+Conference:+Bishop+Hedding's+addresses+on+slavery&source=bl&ots=DYZm_YUV1t&sig=XpXVThZYG8Pfly9DFcdoGYKqKWw&hl=en&sa=X

We have briefly entered this complicated issue in Methodism to gain some sort of footing about Fillmore's position on slavery. As a member of the Genesee (Western New York) Conference Committee of Five he seems to have taken a moderate anti-slavery position. As a member of the General Conference's Committee of Nine he helped to formulate the basis for the division of the denomination into the northern and southern churches. In the heat of the slavery controversy, Fillmore seems to have held a moderate, not radical, anti-slavery position.

In conclusion, it is necessary to mention that Glezen Fillmore was a cousin of President Millard Fillmore, who signed into national law the *Compromise of 1850*, of which the *Fugitive Slave Act of 1850* was a part.

The University of Virginia's Miller Center on American Presidents summarizes:

Millard Fillmore - 07/09/1850: President Zachary Taylor dies suddenly of cholera at the age of 55 . . . Vice President Millard Fillmore is slated to assume the duties of the presidency. **July 09, 1850.**

[Millard] Fillmore personally opposed slavery but signed the Fugitive Slave Law [September 18, 1850] for two reasons. First, he believed the South would secede if its demands, including a fugitive slave law, were not met. Second, Fillmore believed he could use the Compromise to unite the Whig Party behind a single national platform. Fillmore, a Whig from New York, tried to press other Northern Whigs to support the Compromise and the Fugitive Slave Law. He worked to prevent Northern Whigs who opposed the Fugitive Slave Law from winning elections and used his patronage powers to appoint Pro-Fugitive Slave Law political allies to federal office.

&ved=0ahUKEwjQlLD869nJAhXLXh4KHUgTD7YQ6AEIHDAA#v=onepage&q=GeneseeGenesee%20Conference%3A%20Bishop%20Hedding's%20addresses%20on%20slavery&f=false.

While Fillmore's support for the *Compromise of 1850* helped stall the Southern secessionist movement, his efforts to unite the Whigs behind the Compromise failed, in large part because of the Fugitive Slave Law. Antislavery Whigs, who thought the law unjust, refused to support Fillmore for President in 1852. The Fugitive Slave Law, moreover, only deepened existing, and eventually fatal, divides within the Whig Party over slavery.[34]

Slavery Historian Paul Finkelman in his recent book on Millard Fillmore is not so generous. He roundly condemns both Fillmore's character and motives, stating that,

> . . . on the central issues of the age his vision was myopic and his legacy is worse . . . He signed and aggressively—indeed fanatically—implemented the Fugitive Slave Act of 1850, which was arguably the most oppressive law in American history. . . In the end, Fillmore was always on the wrong side of the great moral and political issues of the age: immigration, religious toleration, equality, and most of all, slavery.[35]

What might Glezen Fillmore have thought about his cousin Millard's decision in 1850? Frank Hayward Severance in *Old Trails on the Niagara Frontier* (1899) offered his opinion. Severance first recounted the dramatic story of a fugitive slave from western Kentucky, Jack Watson, whose sister Nannie had been abused and beaten to death in 1856 by their master, also named "Watson." Concerned for his life and in his self-defense, Jack killed his master, fled, and was pursued by slave catchers and dogs. With anti-slavery support, he eventually found himself hiding in the garret (a small loft) of the Methodist Church in Wesleyville, Pennsylvania, near Erie. The story goes that one night during a revival meeting in the church, the worshippers

---

[34] "Millard Fillmore. Key Events" at American President, The Miller Center at the University of Virginia. http://millercenter.org/president/fillmore/key-events.

[35] Paul Finkelman, *Millard Fillmore. President of the United States of America, 1850—1853* (New York, NY: Henry Holt and Company, 2011), 137.

down below were overcome by emotion—and so was Jack, who began shouting from above, "Glory, glory, amen! Hallelujah!" and similar ecstatic utterances. Reports said that some worshippers below were convinced that they heard the angel Gabriel! Others, knowing Jack was hiding above, feared he would be found and endanger them. Fortunately, he was not discovered. He moved on to meet his friend, the well known ex-slave Baptist preacher and abolitionist Jarm W. Logue of Syracuse, New York.[36] After telling this story, Severance continued by taking up a reported meeting between Glezen and Millard Fillmore:

> . . . Rev. Glezen Fillmore, a famous pioneer of the Methodist Episcopal Church in Buffalo and for more than half a century an honored member of the Genesee Conference was engaged in *raising funds for the Freedmen's Aid Society*. One day his cousin, the late ex-President Millard Fillmore, rode out from Buffalo to visit him. During the conversation the venerable preacher related the story of [freedom seeker Jack] Watson's escape as Watson himself had told it *while at Fillmore's Underground Railroad depot*. The former President was strongly touched by the story, and at its close he drew a check for fifty dollars for the Freedmen. "Thank you, thank you," said the good parson. "I was praying that the Lord would open your heart to give ten dollars, and here are fifty."[37]

Millard Fillmore's decision to sign the *Fugitive Slave Act of 1850* is condemned by historians as one of the worst, most tragic decisions in presidential history. Severance agreed: "No passage in American history displays more acrimony than this."[38] However, Glezen Fillmore's record was not the same. His moderate anti-slavery stance in trying to solve the Great Separation in the Methodist church included Wesley's and the denomination's early anti-slavery stance. It contained no exceptions for slave-owners held by more conservative church leaders. He helped formulate the terms of the anticipated separation between the northern

---

[36] "Jarm W. Logue" was Jermain Wesley Loguen (1814—1872). Like Samuel Ringgold Ward, he was given property by Gerrit Smith and was involved in the "Jerry Rescue" at Syracuse; for a brief biographical statement, see Ch. 8.

[37] Frank Hayward Severance, *Old Trails on the Niagara Frontier,* 268-269 (italics ours). In a footnote, p. 268, Severance states that he heard the account from Mr. Frank Henry, wrote it out, and published it in the Erie *Gazette* in 1880.

[38] Ibid., 269.

and southern Methodists. If Severance's anecdote has any historical merit, Glezen Fillmore also had an Underground Railroad Depot (station) somewhere outside of Buffalo and attempted to raise money for freedmen (and freedwomen) during the Civil War and the Reconstruction Era.[39]

We add that Glezen Fillmore was a Republican (the party of Abraham Lincoln) who strongly believed in preserving the Union and that he sent three sons to its defense in the Civil War.

Fillmore Chapel, East Porter, New York

Our second question is: Could the original Fillmore Chapel have been an UGRR depot or station?

Fillmore Chapel is situated in the northeastern part of the Town of Porter (East Porter) about 6.5 miles east of Youngstown at the intersection of Dickersonville and Youngstown-Wilson Roads. Circuit riders helped to form the original congregation there in 1821 at the home of George Ash, who became the first local pastor.[40] (Glezen Fillmore was Superintendent of the Erie District at the time). The first Methodist Episcopal Church building was built there in 1852; the current building was built about 1916. The following description at the congregation's 150th anniversary in 1971 refers to the naming of the Chapel:

Serving our church on the cutting edge of the new western frontier called forth men of great stamina and conviction. One of the most outstanding of these was The Reverend Glezen Fillmore (cousin of President Millard Fillmore) [who] was Superintendent of the Erie District (1821-1824) at the time when the East Porter Class was formed, an office for which he served again for three years in 1835. He also served as Superintendent of the Niagara District on two occasions: 1843-1845; and 1854-1857.

---

[39] The Freedmen's Aid Society—"freedmen" referring to freed slaves (including female slaves)—was founded in 1861 (1866?) by the American Missionary Association (AMA), an interdenominational society financed by northern Congregationalists, Presbyterians, and Methodists, to provide housing for teachers sent from the North to educate freedmen/freedwomen and their children, especially in the South. For the strong Methodist involvement, see "Freedmen's Aid Society Methodist Episcopal Church History," http://drbronsontours.com/bronsonfreedmensaidsocietymethodistepiscopalchurchhistory.html.
[40] A bulletin celebrating the church's 150th anniversary in 1971. Data collected during the Ransomville, NY, Sesquicentennial Celebration in 1967 and submitted to the Ransomville Library Local History area by Mr. and Mrs. Harry Figura and the Rev. Ann Cole, who forwarded it to Gretchen in an e-mail on March 9, 2015.

It is little wonder so appropriate a name as Fillmore Chapel should have been given to this building at its dedication in 1852.[41]

In the previous quotation, Frank Severance referred to Fillmore's Underground Railroad depot. If this comment has any merit, was he referring to the first Fillmore Chapel? Possibly, but there is no certainty. As noted, there were traditions and reports of UGRR safe houses and conductors in nearby Ransomville. Also, Olcott, Wilson, and Ransomville each hosted two Anti-Slavery meetings in 1855, as did Youngstown, which had an agent, Myron Pardee.[42] Led by Glezen Fillmore, some early members of the Fillmore Chapel might well have believed in the abolition of slavery and aided fugitives in the UGRR, as, for example, did some members of the Methodist Episcopal Church in Wesleyville, Pennsylvania, and almost certainly the Wesleyan Methodists in nearby Ransomville. Let us say just a little more.

Gretchen's curiosity about the Fillmore Chapel led her to make an appointment to discuss its history with the minister, the Reverend Anne Cole, newly appointed at the time, in November of 2011. The Reverend Cole said that the church still has members who are descendants of the original families. At that time, she had no new information to confirm or contradict Gretchen's question whether Fillmore Chapel might have been part of a regional Underground Railroad network. The pastor suggested that Gretchen look into the Genesee Conference Archives where she might find some leads, and this approach has been taken above in tracking the Reverend Glezen Fillmore.[43]

The present chapel is situated between Ransomville and Youngstown at a fairly isolated country crossroads that today is surrounded by a large span of farm fields and a few farm houses. We have made a case for UGRR activity in Youngstown and offered some traditions about Ransomville. The open, isolated setting of the earlier chapel would have been conducive for its functioning as an UGRR safe house between Ransomville and Youngstown—in this case,

---

[41] Ibid.

[42] See Chs. 2, 10 in this book.

[43] For more on the Genesee Conference Minutes Regarding Anti-Slavery (1837-1876) and the Reverend Gleason Fillmore's Involvement (1849, 1850, 1854, 1861, 1862 to 1865), see the Genesee Conference Minutes Beginning in 1837. Conference Archives: http://www.unyumc.org/pages/detail/1015.

a safe church or place of refuge, perhaps like the Wesleyville church that hid Jack Watson near Erie. If so, the possibility, perhaps even the likelihood, exists that the old Fillmore Chapel was a safe house as part of a regional network.

Glezen Fillmore's sentiments, Severance's comments about Fillmore's fund-raising for freedmen and his chapel depot—again, Severance does not give the location—and Fillmore Chapel's strategic location are at least consistent with the possibility that fugitive slaves could have been dropped off there or arrived on foot at night for rest, food, and directions on where to proceed next in order to cross the Niagara River a few miles down the road at Youngstown. This possibility is, of course, speculative.

Current Fillmore Chapel Building, built ca. 1916
United Methodist Church
2523 Youngstown-Wilson Road, Ransomville, NY
Original Chapel, built ca. 1852
Photo by Gretchen Duling
Image 15.10

CHAPTER 16

Youngstown Underground Railroad Site Possibilities

Image 16.1

Chapter 14 contains speculations about some known networks, census data, and oral traditions, particularly connecting Youngstown, Lewiston, and Niagara Falls. Chapter 15 contains speculations about sites east of Youngstown such as Warrens Corners, Burt, Pekin, and the locations closer to Youngstown, particularly Ransomville and Porter Center. UGRR scholars stress the great difficulty of documenting the authenticity of physical sites in the Underground Railroad, such as secret tunnels and secret rooms, despite the claims sometimes made for such sites. We would not defend the certainty of the physical sites discussed in this chapter as UGRR sites, either, but we think that they are worth imagining as possibilities, and some look more promising than others. We title the chapter simply: "Youngstown Underground Railroad Site *Possibilities*."

After reconstructing a Youngstown map on which there are numbers we will refer to in the chapter, we take up possible sites, beginning with the most to the least likely.

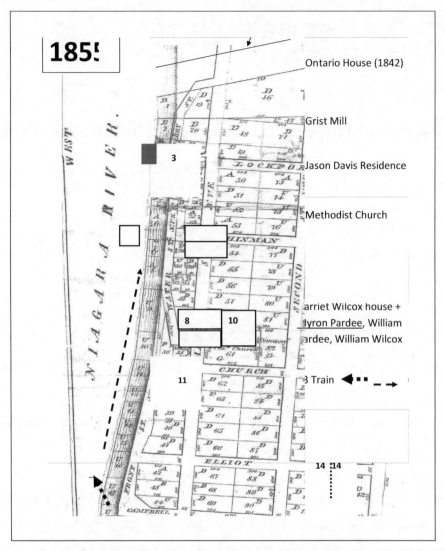

185!

- Ontario House (1842)
- Grist Mill
- Jason Davis Residence
- Methodist Church
- arriet Wilcox house + Myron Pardee, William ardee, William Wilcox
- 3 Train

Map of the Village of Part of Youngstown Created for 1855 (D. Duling)
Created from the 1848 "Map of the Village of Youngstown in Niagara County" and
Search/Survey maps
325 Main Street (1847) and 333 Main Street (1848)[1]
Image 16.2

[1] Modifications of the 1848 map for 1855 include cropping, the addition of State Street, the Ferry House (on 1870 map, implied on 1860 map), key sites, and the key site legend. The 1848 map, Jesse Haines, Surveyor, is in the map collection of the Town of Porter Historical Society Museum. Modifications are by Dennis Duling. For related maps, see Ch. 6. The turntable for the Canandaigua line (13; heavy dashes) was reportedly near Campbell Street.

The Youngstown Ferry House (Map, No. 1)

The most likely—and most exciting—possibility for an Underground Railroad connection is a surviving structure that might well have been the Youngstown Ferry House.

Ferry houses and their functions varied considerably. Some were the homes of ferrymen; some included a waiting room and ticket office; some had overnight sleeping quarters for travelers, or were connected to, or not far from, inns and taverns; some were rather comfortable inns; some, however, were very modest: "Here one Con. O'Niel was the ferryman at a very early day, living by 'the black rock,' in a hut, which was at once his ferry house, and home."[2] It must be added: some, such as the small Nishnabotna Ferry House in Lewis, Iowa,[3] are historically recognized stations on the Underground Road.

What sort of Ferry House was at Youngstown? Did it have any connection with the Underground Railroad? No contemporary sketch of the Youngstown Ferry House exists, but there is some information.

Consider first the early ferry houses at Niagara and Youngstown. In 1788, John Gould recalled that there was "[n]othing then at Newark [Niagara (-on-the-Lake)] but an old ferry house and the barracks that had been occupied by Butler's Rangers."[4] John Young's Red Store on the Youngstown side of the river was open by 1808 and supplies from Niagara where Young lived were probably transported across the river to the Red Store to be unloaded at a store dock.[5] An 1810 map shows that there was a second building on the Youngstown shore. This could have been a ferry house. Recall that a New York State ferry law was passed in 1811 and that in 1813 a New York State law highlighted the Youngstown Ferry.[6] An image of the Niagara Ferry House is found in Edward Walsh's earlier 1804 painting.

---

[2] In Charles D. Norton, "The Old Black Rock Ferry," 1863 (Publications of the Buffalo Historical Society, 1879): 91-112; transcribed from the original by Walter Lewis (Halton Hills, ON, Canada: Maritime History of the Great Lakes, 2003), http://www.maritimehistoryofthegreatlakes.ca/documents/BlackRockFerry/default.asp?ID=c1.

[3] The Nishnabotna Ferry House, Lewis, Iowa, http://www.cityoflewis.com/index.php/our-town/ferry-house.

[4] Recollections of John Gould to Hunter in Pool, *Landmarks of Niagara County,* 256-57. Fort George, begun in 1796 after the British finally left Fort Niagara under the Jay Treaty, was not completed until 1802.

[5] See Ch. 4, Image 4.4, for an artist Jean Stratton's imaginative rendition of John Young's Red Store—with a dock.

[6] See Ch. 6; seven Youngstown structures in 1810 is about right. See below, the six-to-eight structures in 1813.

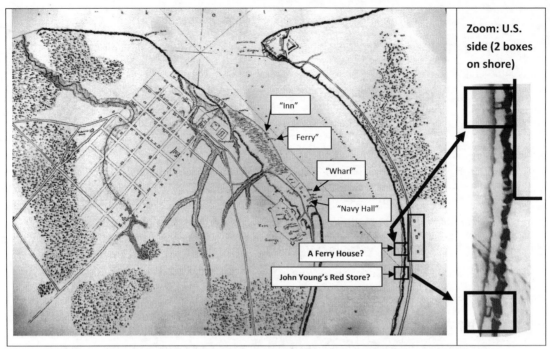

1810 Map of Niagara, Fort George, Inn, and Ferry
Two Buildings (Boxes) on the U.S. Shore, Five (One box) on the Bluff Above
© Library and National Archives Canada. Used by Permission[7]
Image 16.3

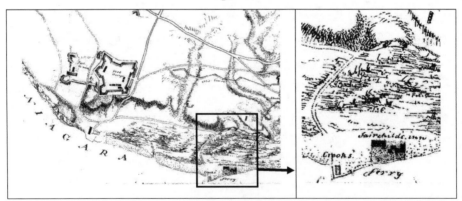

An 1819 Map of the Military Reserve of Fort George; Crooks' Ferry, Fairchild's Inn
© Library and Archives Canada. Used by Permission[8]
Images 16.4a & 4b

---

[7] No. V Upper Canada Plan of Niagara. November 20, 1810 by A. Gray. Cartographer Reference Number NMC – 19551. Permission: Library and National Archives Canada.
[8] An 1819 Map of the Military Reserve of Fort George. Reference Number NMC – 22531. Permission: Library and National Archives Canada.

Edward Walsh, *A View of Fort George, Navy Hall and New Niagara*
Taken from the Un. States Fort of Old Niagara, 1804 (originally watercolor)
© William L. Clements Library, University of Michigan. Used by Permission.[9]
Image 16.5

Blowup from the Walsh 1804 Painting: *Ferry Landing, Ferry House, and Inn*
Extracted and Enlarged by Dennis Duling
Left: Ferry Landing and Ferry House; far right: Inn (as so marked on 1810, 1819 maps)
Image 16.6

[9] Edward Walsh, "A View of Fort George, Navy Hall and New Niagara, taken from the "Un. States' Fort of Old Niagara," watercolor, 1804, from *Sketches from Nature made in Upper Canada in the Years 1803, 1804 and 1805* by E. Walsh, M.D., 49th Regiment. William L. Clements Library, University of Michigan. Thanks to Associate Director and Curator of Maps Brian Dunnigan; Curatorial Assistant and Reading Room Supervisor, Jayne Ptolemy. The town was called "Newark" between 1792 and 1798. It officially reverted to its earlier name "Niagara" in 1798, but was sometimes still called "Newark." Thanks to James Reynolds of Niagara-on-the-Lake for help in tracking down both the maps and the Walsh painting, and to Sarah Kaufman of the Niagara Historical Society and Museum, who gave us specific information on several maps and directed us to the Library and Archives of Canada.

In this example, the inn was separate from the Ferry House and Ferry Landing. In an 1870 sketch by F. H. Granger, the tavern is close to, if not connected to, the ferry house.

F. H. Granger Sketch: "Newark Ferry House, Navy Hall, Tavern, 1870"
Courtesy of the Niagara Historical Society & Museum[10]
Image 16.7

In short, there are early images of ferry houses on the Canadian side of the Niagara River and the possibility that there was a Youngstown Ferry Landing or House on an 1810 map.

The earliest map of the Village of Youngstown we have consulted dates from 1841.[11] Jesse Haines, the surveyor/cartographer, designated the street along the Niagara River between State Street and Water Street as "Ferry Street" (the upper part of it is below, left, Figure 16.8a). Haines' similar Map of the Village of Youngstown in Niagara County seven years later, 1848, has the same identification. Although Ferry Street disappears from an 1860 map (part of it is below, middle, Figure 16.8b); there is nevertheless a black square indicating a building about where one would expect the Ferry House to have been. The square is *near*—but not directly on—the shore; it is below the house of "Mrs. Cook."[12] On the 1870 map (part of it is below, far right, 16.8c), the "Ferry Ho[use]" at that location is clearly designated on the shoreline, indeed extends out into the river, which suggests also a Ferry Landing or loading/unloading dock, analogous to that in the 1804 Walsh painting. Again, it is below the house of "Mrs. Cook," and the house of "J. P. Marshall" is next door to the north.

[10] Thanks to Sarah Maloney Kaufman, Managing Director of the Niagara Historical Society and Museum in Niagara-on-the-Lake, Ontario.
[11] This map was commissioned for Catherine Young, the widow of Youngstown's namesake John Young. "Caty" Young died in 1840, about three months after John, so might never have seen the map.
[12] "Mrs. Cook" was Maria Greensitt Cook, a daughter of Robert and Agnes Greensitt (see below).

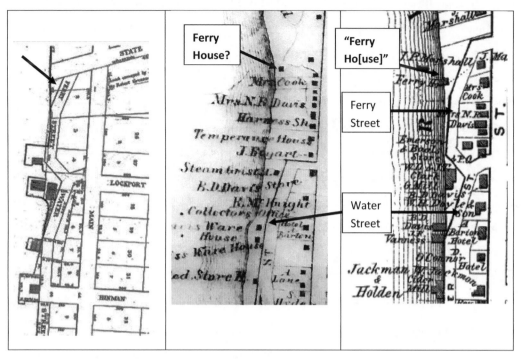

Haines' 1841 (and 1848) Map[13] 1860 Map[14] 1870 Building/Name Map[15]

Maps: Youngstown 1841, 1860, and 1870

Images 16.8a, 8b, & 8c

We cannot be absolutely certain that a Youngstown Ferry House existed earlier than 1860, but it is very likely. First, in addition to Canadian analogies and maps just noted, Youngstown was granted the right to operate a ferry by the State of New York in 1811 and ferry laws refer specifically to the Youngstown Ferry in 1813, 1826, and 1836.[16] Second, the 1813 law states that "no such [ferry] license shall be granted to any person who does not own or occupy the land through which the highway adjacent to the ferry shall run unless such property owners

---

[13] Town of Porter Historical Museum on Lockport Street. The 1841 and 1848 maps do not show buildings; the 1841 version does have docks. A Ferry House first appears in the 1860 and 1870 maps.

[14] Town of Porter Historical Museum. The 1860 map shows a building (arrow) on what *would be* Ferry Street if the cartographer had included it. Thanks to Associate Historian Ron Cary for forwarding the 1860 map to us from the Niagara County Historian's Office in Lockport.

[15] The 1870 map is available at the Town of Porter Historical Museum and graces the walls of some homes and businesses. It has the Ferry House clearly marked.

[16] See Ch. 6.

neglect to apply for a ferry license"[17] and Robert Greensitt's tract of land, bought from John and Catherine Young on March 16, 1812 (recorded on various deeds and on the 1841 map), had waterfront property on which the "Ferry Ho[use]" of the 1870 map is marked. Third, both Robert, who died before 1816,[18] and his wife Agnes who inherited his land and property, operated the ferry.[19] Fourth, at the death of Agnes Greensitt (ca. 1830?[20]) five Greensitt children each inherited 1/5 of the property. Subsequent property exchanges are complex, but Robert's and Agnes' daughter Maria (Greensitt) Cook's one-fifth was a little over half of Lot 2 on the 1841 map (number 2, sideways = Lot 333 on the 1848 map [Lot 19 on the 1841 map]).[21] Its owner's name on the 1870 map that marks the "Ferry House" was "Mrs. Cook." She was Robert and Agnes Greensitt's daughter Maria G. Cook. Fifth, the fugitive slave Thomas James was reported as "ferried" by Olaf Hathaway from Youngstown to Niagara in 1821 and Olaf's brother, Elijah Hathaway, was running the ferry that year, but from where?[22] Sixth, Haines, still the cartographer in 1870, placed the "Ferry Ho[use]" directly on the riverbank, but, as we shall soon see, there was nearby a stone structure on the hillside.

Today, the land owned by ferry operators Robert and Agnes Greensitt which was passed on in the family to Maria G. Greensitt Cook—the same land where the "Ferry House" existed—corresponds with 333 Main Street, the location of Constitution Park.[23]

---

[17] There is room for further research on ferrymen who owned property along the river; certainly, they included the Greensitts, perhaps Elijah Hathaway (a Town of Porter map shows that he had property there in 1834), Samuel Chubbuck, and Chubbuck's son-in-law, James P. Marshall.

[18] Ames, *Survey*, on 330 Main Street, Falkner Park: "No will was found for Robert Greensit (*sic*) nor the date of his death."

[19] See the special section about the ferrywoman, Ch. 6. Ownership of the land near the ferry would correspond to the 1813 law.

[20] The Greensitt children/heirs seem to have received and sold these properties and parts of them between 1831 and 1835; Alfred Seth Cook, Maria's husband, seems to have acquired the most. See Ames, "Falkner Park (Youngstown 330)," *Survey* (1992).

[21] Maria G. (Greensitt) Cook named her son *Greensitt*—his grandfather's and mother's last name—and he eventually inherited this portion.

[22] See Ch. 7.

[23] Ibid. The smaller portion of Lot 2 on the 1841 map just north of it is 330 Main Street. On the 1870 map, the latter was owned by J. P. Marshall, attested also by a Surrogate Court notice in the *Lockport Journal* (October 15, 1903). Marshall married Samuel Chubbuck's granddaughter and he also operated the Youngstown Ferry (1870s-1880s).

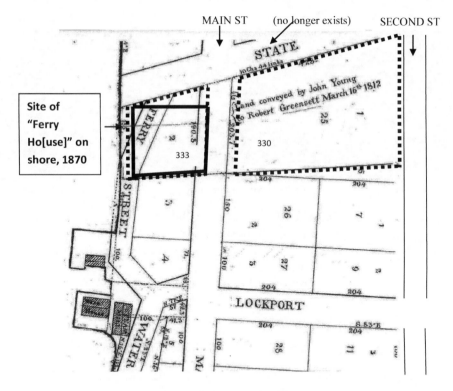

1841 Map (Modified by D. Duling):
Greensitt Purchase, Constitution Park (2 = 333 Main), Falkner Park (25 = 330 Main)
R. Greensitt 1812 (...); 333 Main Street (—) = Mrs. Cook, 1870 = Constitution Park
Image 16.9

Today, the park has an upper level above the hill on Main Street and a lower level that descends down the hill to the north end of Ferry Street next to the North Dock. There is a public stairway from the upper level down the bank to the lower level. About halfway up (or down) the stairs on the hillside is a square stone structure that supports a platform from which tourists and other observers can have a grand view of the Niagara River and Canada. On a 1908 map this structure was not a platform, but a stone building, and on deed surveys from 1986 it was called a "stucco building."[24]

---

[24] A vague photo of the house marked "Hover Craft" exists in the Town of Porter Historical Society Museum.

| Upper Level: 333 Main | Stairs down to Platform | Stairs up to Platform |

Constitution Park and the Platform
(Water Lot 1/North Dock & River in background)
Left, middle photos: Dennis Duling; Right photo, "Village of Youngstown LWRP Monitoring Report of June 2012"[25]
Images 16.10a, 10b, & 10c

What was the stucco building originally? Here is a proposal.

In 1988, Brian Dunnigan, then Executive Director of Fort Niagara,[26] and Mrs. Peggy Hanson of Youngstown, asked John H. Conlin, President of the Landmark Society of the Niagara Frontier, to examine the building. On April 29, 1988, Conlin wrote a letter to Ms. Claire Ross of the New York State Office of Parks, Recreation and Historic Preservation in Albany, and copied it to Ms. Dorothy Rolling, the then Niagara County Historian, and Mrs. Hanson. In it Conlin reported the results of his examination. Part of Conlin's typewritten letter reads:

> The building is a small stone two-story gable roof building approx. 16' square. It is built into the embankment of the Niagara River and the ridge of its roof is well below the upper ground level. It has been heavily stuccoed and the stucco has been painted brown. It also has a modern one-story addition at the front of the lower level and at the rear of the upper level . . . [the front addition is gone; an earlier front door is visible].
>
> The facade of the building faces the river and the Canadian shore. From the building one has a clear view of the entire shoreline sweep of the river to its mouth and Lake Ontario with Fort Niagara visible at this intersection. The gable façade of this

---

[25] http://www.dos.ny.gov/opd/programs/WFRevitalization/LWRP_Monitoring/YoungstownMonitoringReport.pdf.
[26] At the time, Dunnigan was Executive Director of (Old) Fort Niagara; today, he is an Associate Director and Curator of Maps at the William L. Clements Library (see note on the 1804 Walsh painting above).

building is located nearly opposite the Canadian Fort George.[27] Its location is also very near or on the first mile mark of the State Reservation line.[28] Fort Niagara's original garrison ground ended at the one mile line of the State Reservation [earlier State Street]. Brian Dunnigan looked at it [the house] and did not relate it to any military use of known history.[29] *The building is rumored to be the first tavern in Youngstown. However if it were to be a stopping place for travelers, they would most likely have been travelers that were crossing the river. The building is also rumored to be a stop on the underground railway. Of course all such rumors are taken with a grain of salt, yet ought not to be excluded from consideration.[30]*

. . . .

[M]y inspection concluded that the building *dates at least to c 1845* . . . [Three regularly spaced second story windows] "are *pre-1850* . . . The jambs also have case iron window clutch stops of a type *dating to mid-century.* The door on a small closet at the rear of the second floor has cast iron hinges (5 section) and the door itself is a beaded wide board batton door. This appears to have been *in place since c. 1845.*"

. . . .

There is a very narrow stair up the interior south wall which may be original. The upper level was at one time all one room without even an attic . . . The lath used is not split lath but is an early type of small dimension sawn lath which I have found *used contemporaneously with split lath prior to 1850* . . . [italics added]

---

[27] Sightlines to Fort George can be a little deceptive; we live north of the location in question, but we look directly at Fort George, too! Today trees obscure the old house/platform view of Fort Niagara and the coastguard station.
[28] This line marked the northern boundary of the John Young property, a portion of which was bought by Robert Greensitt, March 16, 1812. It was approximately where State Street was and is now the north side of Falkner Park.
[29] There is a historical marker on the upper level for the Salt Battery which dates from the War of 1812 period. For the location of five batteries along the Niagara River at Youngstown, see Benson J. Lossing, *The Pictorial Field-Book of the War of 1812; or, Illustrations, by Pen and Pencil, of the History, Biography, Scenery, Relics, and Traditions of the Last War for American Independence* (New York, NY: Harper & Brothers, 1868), 599.
[30] For accounts of the Youngstown freedom seeker crossings, some by ferry, see Chs. 7-13.

Conlin noted that the planner of the proposed Youngstown park (Constitution Park) suggested that the building be removed "if it is not of historic value." Clearly, Conlin thought that *it was.*

My opinion is that this building whether it *dates to only c. 1845 or to even earlier* has multiple historic significance. It is located where there was a ferry to the Canadian side. *It may have been the ferryman's house and as such almost certainly would have been a stopping place for travelers waiting for their trip across the river, sometimes overnight.* Since this ferry was one of the very few points of regular crossing along the Niagara River international boundary *it almost certainly would have been a crossing place at the final destination of the underground railway.* As a piece of vernacular architecture it seems to be unique as a type in the area. It is the only such stone building I know of built into the embankment of the Niagara River, a very historical river and river [*sic*] bank.

I further feel that the building represents an excellent opportunity for the Village to create something distinctive and recognizably historic in their park area, making it a focus of the rick [*sic*; rich] riverside history of the area. This would require removing the modern additions and perhaps even restoring it to its mid-century appearance. There is any case much more to be learned about the building.

Please see what you can do to insure that this information is not lost.[31] [italics added]

Although Conlin's proposal that the restored house could become a historic centerpiece for Constitution Park was never fully executed, most of the heavy stone structure, which had had several uses, was saved. It became the foundation for the platform noted above.

Dennis Duling made email contact with Conlin who on July 3, 2016, came to Youngstown and reexamined the house. Here is his evaluation (email, date inserted):

---

[31] Letter of John H. Conlin, President of the Landmark Society of the Niagara Frontier to Ms. Claire Ross of the New York State Office of Parks, Recreation and Historic Preservation in Albany (copied to Mrs. Hanson and Ms. Dorothy Rolling, Niagara County Historian). We thank Karen Noonan for drawing our attention to this important letter.

Dear Mr. Duling,   Monday, July 4, 2016

I have inspected the site in the Youngstown Park [July 3]. Good news. The building has essentially survived.

The viewing platform covers a story and a half of the stone house that I reported on in 1988. The elevation facing the river has stone infill in a window and two doorways of the lower story. Above this the lower half of an upper story window has also been filled in. The design which completely seals off the interior is a good solution to preserving the site. *The view from the platform is the view that would have been available to the upper story of the house.* The stone used as infill probably comes from what was removed from the upper story. (Of course the concrete block attaching the building to the cliff [at the back] is not very old.)

It is a pleasant park and it is wonderful that there is easy public access to the viewing platform.

Glad to be of help,

John Conlin

Meanwhile, Karen Noonan, who had been studying Youngstown houses, inquired about the building and with the help of Jean Siddall, the Curator at the Town of Porter Historical Museum, came up with sixteen photos of the house in the period of demolition. Here are two.

Constitution Park: The Stone Building (A Ferry House?) Embedded in the Hillside
Images 16.11a & 11b

Dennis Duling observed from the photos that the building appeared to be much wider across the front than it was deep and that a 1986 survey of area marked the frontage of the stone building as twenty-six feet and seven inches (26'7"), therefore not sixteen feet (16'), as in Conlin's description. On July 13, Dennis measured the building. Its depth was sixteen feet (on the right, south side), but the frontage was almost twenty-seven feet, as in the 1986 property survey. He asked John Conlin to clarify further and received another email (date inserted):

Hello Dennis,   July 14, 2016

. . . I can clarify that in my original inspection of the edifice [1988], I was trying to identify the *very oldest part* of a building that had been altered through the years.

I was able at that time to make observation of the interior wall and ceiling materials and of the joisting [horizontal supporting beams between foundations, walls, or beams that support a floor or ceiling] and concluded that the oldest part of that entire structure was approx. 16"x16" square.

The elevation facing the river has been extended a couple of times, however the south wall close to the stairway is 16 feet and is probably a surviving original dimension.

Some expansion may have taken place quite early on in the history of the building.

The whole stone base of the platform is probably within your special period of interest.

Hope this helps,

John [italics added]

Dennis had measured the window as the same width as the door, but the second window on the far right was narrower. In a still more recent email, John Conlin explained that the window to the right of the door on the ground level (approximately in the center, below the middle window on the second story) was once a door. These observations suggest that the addition extending the building from sixteen to twenty-seven feet wide was on the left (north) side, that the original door was made into a window, and that a new door the size of the original one was built. Perhaps the second story and its three balanced windows were added at this time.

The photos of the Constitution Park stone building above (16.11a, 16.11b), as well as those below (16.12a, 16.12b) were taken during the partial demolition. They confirm Conlin's view that the reconstruction preserved the bottom part of the upper story, that is, it included the bottom sections of the windows, the half frames of which were filled in and survived as part of the foundation of the contemporary platform. In the right photo, the top of the eventual platform foundation wall will be located at the level where the middle worker is sitting, again about half way down the old window frames. In front of him is a narrow wall which is approximately where the original outside wall was on the story below. In the left photo, the original 16' by 16' building is suggested by broken lines. The sixteen-feet, ground-level, square structure was extended to the north (to the left in the left photo; to the right in the right photo) by almost eleven feet; the original door became a window; a new door was built (the same width); and a second story with three balanced windows was added.

Constitution Park 1988: The Stone Building (A Ferry House?) Embedded in the Hillside
Looking East   Looking West
Images 16.12a & 12b

The real question is: Was the 16' x 16' original building a simple Ferry House at the time of the UGRR, as Conlin suggests it might have been?

An apparent problem is that, as far as we are aware, the only *clearly* marked "Ferry Ho[use]" location in the nineteenth century is on the 1870 map and that structure was directly on the river's edge and extending into the river, suggesting a landing or dock. That structure does not correlate well with the location of the stone house some yards back from the river, partly up the bluff. However, the black mark on the 1860 map, which represents a building, is not directly on the shoreline. We suggest three major possibilities:

1. The house on the hillside is not the "Ferry Ho[use]" on the 1870 map because it is not on the shore. From maps we have consulted, the hillside house first appears later on a 1908 Youngstown map.[32] The floor plan of the expanded stone house is clearly outlined on 1980s property surveys and the above reconstruction shows an expanded building with a new door. One might conclude that the original building was built after 1870 and before 1908 and then expanded. If this option is chosen, Conlin's expert judgment that the original hillside house dates before 1850 would have to be rejected and its possible importance for the Underground Railroad would disappear.

2. The hillside house was the same structure as that marked "Ferry Ho[use]" on the 1870 map. The most obvious problem is, again, that the 1870 cartographer, who was very precise about locations and building footprints, placed the "Ferry Ho[use]" directly on the shore and half of it jutted out into the river. The stone building, however, is several yards back from the waterline, about a third of the way up the Constitution Park hill. To correlate the riverside and hillside locations, it might be suggested that the river was wider and higher and that Ferry Street—if it actually angled up toward Main Street about thirty degrees and met State Street as the old maps (since Haines) suggest—went *behind* the house (not impossible, but very hard to imagine today). It might be supposed that the shoreline changed over time, partly as a result of the destructive power of ice jams on the river (1844, 1883, 1909, 1936, 1955).[33] This wider,

---

[32] This map is a special example of early Youngstown in *A Historical Look at Youngstown and the Town of Porter New York. Newspaper Articles written by Donald B. Ames, Village Historian*, Introduction and p. 5. It shows the Grist Mill and this building as stone buildings.

[33] Suggested by Karen Noonan.

deeper river hypothesis, however, has an obvious difficulty: If the current hillside house was also at the river's edge, Ferry Street (and presumably Water Street further south, including part of the Grist Mill and John Young's store) would have been under water. This option allows for Conlin's judgment, but this last difficulty seems insurmountable.

3. The hillside house was indeed a stone Ferry House built before 1850 (originally 16' x 16') and subsequently expanded (16' by 27'). In this regard, Karen Noonan has observed that two other stone structures in Youngstown, the Grist (Steam) Mill of 1840 and the Ontario House of 1842, were built in this same period. Gretchen Duling suggested that perhaps an original wooden frame or clapboard Ferry House was destroyed by fire (1813?) and rebuilt of stone; that was the case with the rebuilding of the burned Hathaway Inn as the Ontario House. In any case, the stone hillside house could have functioned as a modest ferryman's quarters at times and perhaps also a small overnight room for travelers awaiting the next day's ferry. If the width was expanded to twenty-seven feet and a second story added fairly early, its functionality would have been improved. A possible analogy is the Canadian shoreline Ferry House with a dock in Walsh's 1804 painting, which was not far from an inn (recall that inn keepers often operated the ferries). This option could be easily correlated with Conlin's analysis about the 1840's date of the original square building, its expansion (he suggests possibly fairly early), and his suggestion that it might have functioned as an overnight inn for travelers, indeed perhaps freedom seekers.

Option one is not impossible, but not preferable since it abandons an expert's careful dating of the hillside house and its internal fixtures. Option two is hardly likely for topographical reasons. Option three, although it is not easy to correlate all the maps with dating, is the most likely and we prefer it. This option opens the possibility that there were two Youngstown Ferry Houses, and that one of them has survived on the hillside. If so, perhaps we do have something like an image of a Youngstown Ferry House. Could some earlier, wooden version of the Ferry House have existed at the time of Robert and Agnes Greensitt, who bought the property from

John Young back in 1812? Is it represented on the 1810 Canadian map? The Greensitts each had a license to operate the ferry and the hillside house would have been on the Greensitt property. If this possibility seems to be a stretch, it is less problematic from the period of the Underground Railroad, given Conlin's dating of the stone house. The stone building and perhaps also the shoreline structure could have had some utility for some of the ferrymen who helped fugitive slaves in the 1850's. Since freedom seekers crossed at Youngstown and were helped by some ferrymen, did it also function as an overnight haven for fugitive slaves before they crossed the river to freedom? Possibly.

The Davis Brick Block (Map, No. 2)

In Chapter 12, we speculated that the Davis family might have had knowledge of the UGRR: "Mr. Pardee" of *Pardee and Pomroy*, the contact person for fugitives Daniel and James, had a business located in the David Brick Block by 1854 and Nelson Davis had a Black servant, Austin McPherson, who later lived with General Jordan Gaines in Lewiston.

In the middle of the nineteenth century, the Davis Brick Block at 409 Main Street, diagonally across the street from the Ontario House, was the most imposing building in Youngstown. It was built of bricks from John Carter's brickyard, which had been established about 1850.[34] Jason Davis bought waterfront property and built there a wharf and a storehouse. He also purchased the stone Grist (Steam) Mill (Map, No. 4), built by Hezekiah Smith in 1840, and he and his son Bradley D. Davis rebuilt it after it was damaged by fire in 1853. Later "B. D.'s" daughter Elvira married Nelson Davis Haskell in 1879,[35] and in the 1890s, the signs on the building read "N. D. Haskell," as photos show. Water Street begins alongside the north side of the Davis Brick Block (409 Main Street) building and goes down the hill to the river where it meets Ferry Street at the Grist Mill.

---

[34] See Ch. 14 for oral traditions about Carter's involvement in the UGRR; for the Carter bricks, see Dietz, *From Flames and Four Flags*, 58.

[35] For this leading family see the genealogical Records in the Town of Porter Museum researched by Karen Noonan and Gretchen Duling.

N. D. HASKELL
Grist Mill
Niagara River
Canada
Water Street, top of hill
Main Street
Lockport Street
1890's

Front of the Davis Brick Block ("N. D. Haskell" Building), 409 Main Street, 1890's
Courtesy of the Town of Porter Historical Museum
Image 16.13

A second photo marked "1890's" shows the waterfront from the Niagara River side (looking [north] east). The back side also has a sign reading "N. D. Haskell."

Eldorado Hotel (1880s -1930s [torn down])
Ferry Street
Grist Mill (upper level later replaced by condos, lower by RCR Yachts, Inc., maintenance)
"N. D. Haskell" Building = Davis Brick Block (sign: "N. D. Haskell")
Water Street

Niagara River Waterfront, ca. 1890
Left to Right: Eldorado Hotel; Grist Mill; Haskell Building
Courtesy of the Town of Porter Historical Museum
Modifications by Dennis Duling
Image 16.14

409 Main St. Building/ Apartments (Davis Brick Block)

Condos

RCR Yachts Maintenance (Stone bottom of the old Grist Mill)

Ferry Street

Water Street

YYC facility

Youngstown Yacht Club

The Youngstown Waterfront Today[36]
Image 16.15

The possible location of the old Ferry House (1855 Map, No. 1) is out of range to the left. The park where John Young's Red Store once stood is out of range to the right; today (2017), a boat launch, the new Niagara Jet Adventures Company, and a marina/condo are there.

At Newark, New York, in 1855 John P. VanDeusen wrote in his Diary the following comment: "I gave him [the fugitive slave James] written directions to go [with his father Daniel] to Lockport & then to Youngstown to Mr. Pardee a Hardware Merchant there, & Bro. of R. G. Pardee both originally citizens of Palmyra & good men." According to several sources the hardware business *Pardee & Pomroy* was located in the front section of the Davis Brick Block by 1854[37] and, as we have established, "Mr. Pardee" of *Pardee & Pomroy* was Myron J. Pardee.[38] Were they linked to the ferrymen who ferried fugitive slaves across the river in the 1850s and 1860s? Did Daniel and James connect with Myron J. Pardee at *Pardee & Pomroy* in the Davis Brick Block (subsequently the "N. D. Haskell" Building)? Did Daniel and James cross by the

---

[36] Youngstown Heritage Tours and Tourism, originally in color.
http://youngstownnyhttc.wix.com/youngstownnyhttc#!North Dock/zoom/mainPage/image1a59.
[37] See Ch. 14.
[38] See Ch. 10.

Youngstown Ferry or with the help of some unknown farmer/boater, such as John Carter? All these are possibilities.

The Ontario House, 358 Main St. (Main and Lockport Streets), ca. 1842 (Map, No. 3)

To reiterate, early nineteenth-century maps above show that State Street, which no longer exists, came down the bank from Main Street and ended at Ferry Street along the Niagara River. A small square already on the 1860 Youngstown map might have represented the Ferry House (Map, No. 1), possibly the stone house discussed above. However, a "Ferry Ho[use]" as clearly marked did not appear until the 1870 map and that ferry house extended out into the Niagara River.

Today, Ferry Street along the river is a narrow, right-of-way road that does not carry regular street traffic. Its north end is at the lower level of Constitution Park and the current Village North Dock. Along the street there is space for Youngstown Yacht Club (YYC) yacht and boat storage, especially in the winter, and occasional parking. Its south end is at Water Street, which comes down the hill from Main Street (map, No. 3). At the intersection is what remains of the Grist (Steam) Mill of 1840 (Map, No. 4; burned 1851; repaired by the Davis family). Today, the bottom story of the Grist Mill is used as a maintenance building by RCR Yachts, Inc.; the top half was destroyed by a storm. In its place are condos overlooking the river. After coming down the hill, Water Street continues south as a one-way street for one block along the river. In the mid-19th century, warehouse wharves were along Water Street (Map, No. 5). Today, the Youngstown Yacht Club (formed in 1931), the Village South Dock, and the village park (where John Young's Red Store once stood), a boat launch, the new Niagara Adventures Jet Boat Company, and a marina/condo are there. Water Street once continued to meet Front Street (the road narrows on the above map), which continued south as far as Campbell Street (south of Map, No. 12). Today, Front Street is also gone (presumably eroded away; the shoreline is absent on the 1860 map, but reappears on the 1870 map!). Water Street re-ascends up the hill to Main Street approximately across from the Methodist Church (Map, No. 8).

Returning to the beginning of Water Street at the top of the bluff there is the 409 Main Street Building, which was once called the Davis Brick Block (Map, No. 3), built by 1854. Diagonally across from Main Street is the Ontario House or "The Stone Jug" (Map, No. 2, 358 Main Street), built in 1842. The question is: Was the Ontario House across from the Davis Brick Block (Map, No. 2) in any way a site for helping fugitive slaves escape across the river?

Olaf Hathaway's brother, Colonel Elijah Hathaway, a ferryman from 1821 to 1823 (or longer), built and owned the forerunner of the Ontario House, the old Hathaway Tavern/Inn, which was burned by the British on December 19, 1813. Elijah's brother was Olaf Hathaway, who in 1827 was an agent for the Ontario Steamboat Company. He was reported to have ferried the fugitive slave Thomas James across the river in 1821.[39] There is a long-time gap between Elijah's and Olaf's activity in the early 1820s, the construction of the Ontario House in 1842, and the building of the Davis Brick Block in 1854, that is, between Olaf's ferrying a fugitive slave across the river and the fugitive slave contacts and other crossings in the 1850s and early 1860s. We have no information about employees in the Ontario House in any way comparable to UGRR-supported African American hotel workers in Niagara Falls. Yet, the location of the Ontario House was just across the street from the Davis Brick Block overlooking the Niagara River and both buildings were not far from what was the likely spot of the Ferry House (Map, No. 1). This certainly gives some cause for speculation.

---

[39] See Chapter 7.

Ontario House or "The Stone Jug" (1890s?), built ca. 1842
Courtesy of the Town of Porter Museum
Image 16.16

The Pardee/Wilcox House, 614 Main Street (Map, No. 11)

Myron J. Pardee and his wife Cynthia A. Pardee had a young son, William W. Pardee. In Palmyra, the three lived in the same house as William Wilcox and the young Harriet N. Wilcox, along with Asa Curth and Julia Nobles. The Pardees and the Wilcoxes were probably relatives, or at least intimate friends, since, not only did they live in the same house in Palmyra (and probably Youngstown), but the boy William W. Pardee was most likely named after William Wilcox. Myron's brother "R. G." was almost certainly Richard G. Pardee of Palmyra listed in 1849 as a "Director for Life" in the American Home Missionary Society, an abolitionist society. The Pardees and the Wilcoxes migrated to Youngstown in 1854. There, Myron Pardee and E. P. Pomroy opened their hardware store in the Davis Brick Block.[40]

Myron's wife Cynthia A. Pardee and Harriet N. Wilcox purchased property together from Thomas and Elizabeth Brighton at 614 Main Street (Map, No. 11 on the 1855 map) on October 4, 1854.[41] On October 23, Harriet became Mrs. Harriet N. (John) Hart (survey below). The

---

[40] See Ch. 10.

[41] According to the Federal Census of 1880 Thomas Brighton of Youngstown was born in Ireland about 1820; in the New York State Census of 1875, he was 53, born in Ireland, again about 1820/21. He died in 1906. Early maps of Youngstown show some of Brighton's and Brown's property holdings.

Brightons also sold property to William Wilcox: Lot 114 on the corner of Second and Elliot streets and the nearby Lots 141 on Elliot Street and 142 at Third and Elliot streets (Map, No. 14 on the 1855 map above).[42] On June 29, 1868, fourteen years after their purchase of 614 Main Street, Cynthia Pardee and Harriet Hart sold the property to Jonas W. Brown. That same year William Wilcox sold his Youngstown properties by foreclosure. His broker was Myron Pardee. The current occupant of 614 Main Street, Mrs. Patricia Phillips, provided us with Jesse P. Haines' survey, also noted in Donald Ames' survey book: [43]

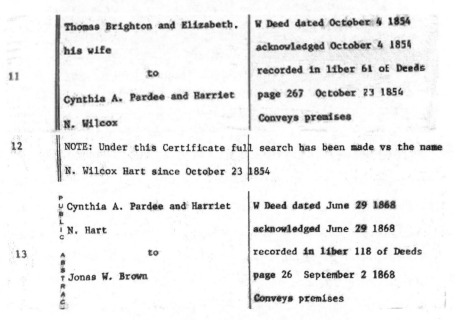

Jesse P. Haines' Survey A: 614 Main Street
Image 16.17

---

[42] The lot numbers are based on Jesse P. Haines, Surveyor, "Map of the Village of Youngstown in Niagara County," previously surveyed by Ezekiel Brown for John and Catherine Young.

[43] In Mrs. Phillips Survey: "From the map of the village of Youngstown, Niagara County, N.Y. made by Jesse P. Haines in the year 1848 filed in Niagara County Clerk's Office March 3, 1890 in Cover #171 in Book 1 of Maps page 28, now in Book 8 of Microfilmed at page 784 [Part of Lot 2 Mile Reserve]." Ames, *Historical and Family Survey of 'The Old Village', Youngstown, N.Y. Third Street 1992* (Vol. 2).

There had been legal problems about the property at the death of John and Catherine Young in 1840, but according to a deed of 1842 and the earlier Haines 1848 survey (left, below), the property included "Parcel B." The deed of 1868 shows that Cynthia A. Pardee and Harriet N. (Wilcox) Hart sold it to Jonas W. Brown, whose name is on the 1870 map as "J. Brown." The map shows that there was clearly a structure on the lot—apparently, a house.

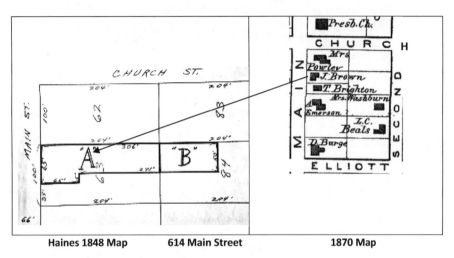

Haines 1848 Map   614 Main Street   1870 Map

Jesse P. Haines' Survey B: 614 Main Street; 1870 Map
Image 16.18

The current, quaint house according to Donald Ames was built (as a replacement or renovation?) in 1927, but the historic marker on the house says 1840.[44]

---

[44] The current occupant, Mrs. Patricia Phillips, thinks that the current house was at one time a barn; possibly, but the 1870 map by Jesse P. Haines attempts to replicate carefully the footprint of houses, and it, plus the name, suggests that J. Brown's structure at this time was probably a house.

Current House at 614 Main Street, built ca. 1927[45]
Photo: Gretchen Duling
Image 16.19

We return to the key question: Where did fugitive slaves Daniel and James rendezvous with their Youngstown contact "Mr. Pardee"? If not at *Pardee & Pomroy* in the Davis Brick Block at 409 Main Street, perhaps a couple of blocks south in a house listed under the name of Myron J. Pardee's wife Cynthia A. Pardee and (relative? friend?) Harriet N. (Wilcox) Hart from 1854 to 1868. If so, did the earlier structure at 614 Main Street ever function as an UGRR safe house?

The Sealed Room in the Old John F. Clapsaddle (Clapsattle) Cellar (East of the Village, Not on the Map)

Several members of the Clapsaddle family owned land east of the Village of Youngstown in the hamlets of Porter Center and Tryonville (slightly north). William Pool wrote in *Landmarks*, "William and John Clapsaddle came into the town in 1816, John locating on Lot 9. He built the first saw mill and grist mill about the year 1817, and kept an early tavern at what is now Tryonville."[46] On an 1875 map of Porter, it is possible to locate the properties of W. [William]

---

[45] The deed in 1920 had a mortgage of $1,000; the deed in 1927 jumped to $4,000; Ames, *Survey*, states "Built-C-1890 [1890, not 1890], 1927."
[46] Pool, *Landmarks*, 258.

Clappsaddle, Mrs. M. Clappsaddle, J. [John F.] Clapsaddle, and G. Clappsaddle.[47] Former Town of Porter historian Vee Housman wrote that John Clapsaddle married Mary L. Quade on October 18, 1854.[48] According to the current Town of Porter Historian, Suzanne Simon Dietz, "[John] Clapsaddle had 100 acres on Lot 9 and was a commissioner of 'The Lockport and Youngstown Rail-Road Company.'"[49]

A notice in the *Niagara Falls Gazette* of 1964 written by Clarence O. Lewis, the Niagara County Historian from 1950—1968, quotes a letter from Mrs. Andrew M. Smith that refers to the house of "J. F. Clapsattle," that is, John F. Clapsaddle. Mrs. Smith's letter raises the question whether a sealed-off room in their old J. F. Clapsattle house on Braley Road (Porter Center), judged too large to be a root cellar and in the wrong location for a cistern, was a hiding place on the Underground Railroad.

OLD COUNTY COMMUNITIES LOCATED by Clarence O. Lewis

. . . a letter came to me on January 22, 1964, in which Mrs. Andrew M. Smith, presently of the Lake Road, Town of Porter, but formerly living in a brick house more than 100 years old, probably built by J. F. Clapsattle (that being the name on the 1852 map.).[50] . . . The old Clapsattle brick house Mrs. Smith (once an owner of this house) describes as follows:

When we first came to Youngstown, we purchased the former Clapsattle home on the Brayley Road. In the course of remodeling this place, we became rather involved in the history of the area. We found that the brick used in the house had been made in John Carter's brick works on the Lake Road, and that he had used molds which were much larger than any other obtainable brick. In the

---

[47] Map of Porter Township, Olcott, Youngstown P.O., Tyronville, Ransomville, Fort Niagara. From Niagara and Orleans County 1875 (New York, NY: D. G. Beers & Co., 1875).

[48] Housman, *Town of Porter's Past, Newsletter of the Town of Porter Historical Society* 22/2 (October, 1998).

[49] Dietz, *From Flames and Four Flags*, 27, 33.

[50] This must refer to John F. Clapsaddle. According to Dietz, *From Flames and Four Flags*, Clapsaddle had 100 acres on Lot 9 (p. 27) and was a commissioner of "The Lockport and Youngstown Rail-Road Company," (p. 33). Vee Housman in *Town of Porter's Past, Newsletter of the Town of Porter Historical Society* 22/2 (October 1998) wrote that John Clapsaddle married Mary L. Quade on October 18, 1854.
http://www.rootsweb.ancestry.com/~nyniagar/extras/portnews98.htm.

cellar, we discovered a large sealed area excavated under the wing of the main part of the house. This could not have been a cistern because of its location and was much too large for a root cellar of those times. We wondered if the house had been a link in the underground [railroad] of pre-Civil War days.[51]

Mrs. Smith's suggestion is not made on the basis of written or oral tradition, but on the basis of the room's unusual size and distinctive location.

The John Carter Farmstead
(North of the Village Center [Route 18F], Not on the Map)

In Chapter 12, the connection was made between John Carter, who sold five Lewiston lots to Mary McClary Gaines, whose death was mentioned in *Frederick Douglas' Paper*. A further connection was made between Nelson Davis's Black servant, Austin McPherson, who later lived in Lewiston with Mary McClary Gaines' widower, Jordan Gaines, who himself was a speaker at a Niagara Falls emancipation celebration that honored UGRR conductor John Morrison in 1856. No further connection between Carter and Mary McClary Gaines and John Carter was established. Yet, the possibility was offered that Carter, a farmer and mason who loved to boat on the Niagara River, was the anonymous farmer who rowed to freedom in Canada the two fugitive slaves who spent the night in Thomas Birnmore's room at the back of the *Lockport Daily Journal*. If the suggestion has any merit—there are some traditions about Carter's involvement in the Underground Railroad—so does the possibility that they stayed overnight somewhere on the John Carter Farmstead. The connection hangs on a very thin thread, but is worth some speculation.[52]

---

[51] Clarence O. Lewis, "Old County Communities Located," *Niagara Falls Gazette* (February 5, 1964): 8 (italics ours).
[52] For a photo of the John Carter Farm, see Ch. 14.

The Porter Presbyterian Church of Youngstown, New York, 1837 (Map, No. 9)

Quakers, Baptists, Methodists, and Presbyterians in the North were among those religious denominations that counted among their members abolitionists and Underground Railroad activists.[53] As noted in Chapter 2, William J. Watkins, the Rochester abolitionist, scheduled Anti-Slavery meetings in Youngstown, New York, on Monday, June 4, 1855,[54] and (supposedly with [the support of?] Frederick Douglass) on Tuesday, August 28, 1855.[55] The location of these meetings is unknown. Perhaps it was The Presbyterian Church of the Town of Porter, now The First Presbyterian Church of Youngstown, first organized in 1823 (Map, No. 9).[56] Recall that the contractor who built the church building was ferryman and horse boat builder Samuel L. Chubbuck, who lived at 615 Main Street across the street from Pardee/Wilcox house at 614 Main Street (Map, No. 11). This church is the site where the Reverend Thomas James, formerly a fugitive slave who crossed the Niagara River at Youngstown in 1821, gave his talk in late 1883.[57] There, he told attendees, mainly Presbyterians and Methodists, about his experiences as a slave. Again, the *Niagara Falls News* (September 21, 1883, 4:30) reported that he had been ferried to Canada by Olaf Hathaway, a church member whose name appears on the Hathaway gravestone in the Universal Cemetery behind the Presbyterian Church.

---

[53] Among Presbyterian Ministers, note especially the Rev. John Rankin of Ripley, Ohio. Rankin is in the national UGRR Hall of Fame and the John Rankin House has been designated a National Historical Landmark. See Ch. 3.
[54] *Frederick Douglass' Paper*, May 4, 1855.
[55] Ibid., July 27, 1855.
[56] Edwin L. Howard and Virginia M. Howard, *The History of Youngstown, New York* Occasional Contributions of the Youngstown Historical Society No. 5 (Lockport, NY: Niagara County Historical Society, 1951; revised and reissued by the Town of Porter Historical Society, ed. Marjorie L. Stratton (Youngstown, NY, 2007),7, state that the organizers were Mr. and Mrs. Bartol, Mr. Kelly, Mrs. Lutts, Mrs. McCormick, Mrs. Rebecca Hathaway and her daughter Pauline, and Judge Ashbel G. Hinman, all members of the First Presbyterian Society of the Town of Porter.
[57] The Presbyterian Minister at that time was the English-born John Reid, who most likely would have lived in the Presbyterian manse at 715 Main Street. See "The Roll Call of Ministers" of the first 25 years of the church in *The 175th Anniversary Booklet of the First Presbyterian Church Society of Youngstown, New York* (1998), 15.

It is very unfortunate that the records of the Presbyterian Church of the Town of Porter in Youngstown were burned in a fire at the Session Clerk's home (date unknown). We have no evidence that other church members apart from Olaf Hathaway were involved in the UGRR.[58]

Porter (First) Presbyterian Church of Youngstown, New York
Photo from the 175th Anniversary Booklet (1978)   (100 Church Street corner of Main Street)
Courtesy: Rev. Dr. Rex Stewart (2014)   Photo by Karen Noonan (2014)
Images 16.20a & 20b

First Methodist Episcopal Church, built ca. 1854 (Map No. 8)

The church building of Youngstown's First Methodist Episcopal Church, organized in 1852 with twenty members, was completed by John Carter in 1854 at 560 Main Street. On the 1855 map, it is just north (Map, No. 8) of the current Presbyterian Church (Map, No. 9). The Methodist parsonage (called Hinman House) at one time stood between the two church buildings.

In 1869, services ceased in the Youngstown Methodist church building. It was put up for auction and purchased by John Carter.[59] Services were renewed in 1872 when the Methodist Conference merged the Youngstown congregation with the Porter Center congregation. That

---

[58] Research in the national archives of the Presbyterian Church in Philadelphia might possibly turn up more information.
[59] For John Carter and the oral tradition that he ferried fugitive slaves across the Niagara River, see Ch. 14.

merger fell apart in 1876, so Carter deeded the building back to the Youngstown congregation, which continued services again in 1877.[60] This was the congregation that met with the Presbyterians in the Presbyterian Church in 1883 to hear the Reverend Thomas James, an ex-fugitive slave, speak.

The building did not survive as a Methodist church building and eventually it was turned into apartments. In 2003, it was purchased by the First Presbyterian Church.

Formerly, the First Methodist (Epis.) Church of Youngstown, New York, built ca. 1854
560 Main Street—Currently an Apartment Building
Photo by Gretchen Duling
Image 16.21

We are unaware of any records about members of this congregation being activists in the UGRR. Recall, however, that some members of Methodist churches in general were involved in the UGRR. Examples discussed previously are the Methodist Church in Wesleyville, Pennsylvania; the Methodist Church's involvement in the Anti-Slavery American Missionary Society; the abolitionist Wesleyan Methodist churches; and perhaps the Fillmore Chapel just east of Youngstown.[61]

---

[60] Pool, *Landmarks*, 266.
[61] See Ch. 15.

233 Main Street (Map, No. 16)

At the edge of the Niagara Gorge, north of the old State Street (no longer exists) about where the Main Street Grill exists today is 233 Main Street (Map, No. 16 on the 1855 map). Immediately north of it today is a paper street, that is, an official Village of Youngstown lot, once called Niagara Street (no longer exists).[62] On this vacant lot the public can walk to the top of the Niagara Gorge (the bluff) and look out on the grand vista of the mouth of the Niagara River where it empties into Lake Ontario, as well as Fort George and Niagara-on-the-Lake, Canada, directly on the opposite shore.

In 1995, Gretchen Duling had a discussion with Cora Gushee, the Town of Porter Historian (deceased in 2006 at age 103), about the cottage at 230 Main Street across the street from 233 Main Street. In raising the possibility that the cottage might have had UGRR connections, Cora paused thoughtfully, pointed across the street to 233 Main Street, and said that there had been a secret room in that house. Asked about how she acquired that information, Cora responded that she had heard about it through elderly people who told her that as children they had played in this room and that they were aware of why it existed. Note also that a cobblestone tunnel next to a gully alongside the no-longer existent Niagara Street immediately to the north was discovered by employees of the Youngstown Department of Public Works in the mid-1950s. Danny Schissler, a former employee of the DPW (deceased), documented much recent history of Youngstown by video and informed Gretchen that the cobblestone tunnel was turned into a storm drain.

As far as we know, there is no further information to support Cora Gushee's comment, but her oral report and the tunnel suggest at least the possibility of UGRR activities on North Main Street in the Old Village of Youngstown.

---

[62] J. P. Haines, "Map of Part of the Village of Youngstown" for William Clark and S. B. Piper, 1845; filed in Niagara County Clerk's Office February 24, 1851; in Microfilm Map Book 8, p. 776.

233 Main Street
Photo by Gretchen Duling 1995
Image 16.22

230 Main Street, c. 1840/1850 (Map, No. 15)

The just-mentioned discussion and interview Gretchen Duling had with Cora Gushee in 1995 took place at 230 Main Street, on which at the time there was a small, historic cottage on the corner of Main and William Streets. It was directly across the street from 233 Main Street. The cottage had a cobblestone cellar with two openings that had been sealed. The larger opening faced Main Street. The other side opening was on the north wall. There is no written or oral history connecting this cottage with the UGRR, but it is interesting that the cottage's sealed openings would have provided access to the just-mentioned tunnel across Main Street, so we included it as a possibility in this book.

As an aside, the little cottage's original front rooms and its barn behind the house had additional history as part of the Rum Run (bootlegging) between Youngstown and Canada during the Prohibition Era (1920—1933).

230 Main Street at Main and William Streets

Original House (ca. 1840/1850) in 1995   Renovated 1998; razed in 2015
Photo by Gretchen Duling   Photo by Dennis Duling
Images 16.23a & 23b

In summary, the locations in this chapter are speculative. Most promising are the two places of the Youngstown Ferry House along the Niagara River. After that, the location where Daniel and James met "Mr. Pardee," that is, *Pardee & Pomroy* in the Davis Brick Block at 409 Main Street or the Pardee/Wilcox House at 614 Main Street. The other sites are increasingly less defensible, but remain as interesting possibilities.

PART IV
Evaluations and Conclusions

Evaluations and conclusions place the Youngstown Underground Railroad Network Database on the Wellman Scale, evaluates the items, and draws conclusions about the importance of Youngstown for the Underground Railroad.

CHAPTER 17

Summary, Evaluations, and Conclusions:
The Youngstown Underground Railroad Network Database and the Wellman Scale

Image 17.1

Historical Sources

The value of historical information is normally based on the value of the historical sources in which the information is found. The most valuable sources are *primary* sources—authentic sources generally from the time and place of the person or event. They are more valuable than *secondary* sources, such as later historians' accounts of persons, places, and events. Both kinds of sources are more valuable than opinions and speculations without evidence.

Part I of this book (Chapters 1-6) contains primary sources, such as documented Anti-Slavery Society records, census data, and information about watercraft on the Great Lakes.

However, these chapters are more general and depend heavily on some secondary sources such as histories of slavery, of the Underground Railroad, of land and water transportation on the Great Lakes and the Lower Niagara River.

Part I sets the stage for Part II: fugitive slave crossings to Canada (Chapters 7-13). These chapters are based mainly on primary sources, mostly written, and are the heart of the book. Let us take a quick review.

Chapter 7 takes up Olaf Hathaway's act of ferrying fugitive slave Thomas James across the Niagara River from Youngstown to Canada about 1821, which was reported in the *Niagara County News* in 1883, not long after James' return to Youngstown as the Reverend Thomas James to speak at the Porter (First) Presbyterian Church (of Youngstown). In his 1886 autobiography, James offered details about following the Erie Canal under construction to Lockport, his crossing by the Youngstown Ferry to Canada to work on the Welland Canal, and his return to Youngstown to chop wood for a Youngstown farmer, John Rich. Since Olaf Hathaway's brother Elijah Hathaway was operating the Youngstown Ferry in 1821, perhaps he was also involved in the escape.

Chapter 8 highlights a Youngstown Ferry episode in Samuel Ringgold Ward's autobiography. Ward records that in 1853 he and his traveling companion, the Reverend Hiram Wilson, both of whom had been active among ex-slave immigrants to Upper Canada, were traveling (apparently) from the St. Catharines area and were crossing on the Youngstown Ferry from Niagara to Youngstown on a raw January day. They had just witnessed a fugitive slave warming himself by the stove in the Niagara, Canada, Ferry House. Ward included in his account his interchange with, and impressions of, the gritty Youngstown ferryman who told them how he helped fugitive slaves escape to Niagara and did not charge those who were poor.

Chapter 9 recounts the saga of Ben Hockley's attempted escape to Canada on an old gate on August 3, 1853, a story recorded in fifteen varying newspaper reports within a month of the event. We have attempted to reconstruct the newspaper lineage and have concluded that the Youngstown version, rather than the Lewiston version, was more likely historical. More information about Hockley has been found in census data from 1840 to 1870 and in three letters from to Gerrit Smith from his abolitionist land agent and friend, John Edwards of Oswego, about Hockley's purchase of property in Oswego.

Chapter 10 is dependent primarily on one of the John VanDeusen Diaries written in the same year as the persons, sites, and events it records, 1855. He tells of Presbyterian churchmen in Newark, New York, who gave money to a fugitive slave, James (and his father Daniel waiting at the depot), who had come from Lyons, New York, with instructions to go to Suspension Bridge. VanDeusen, however, instructed them to meet with a hardware merchant named "Mr. Pardee" at Youngstown. More facts about "Mr. Pardee," have been generated from census data from Palmyra (1850) and Lancaster (1870), New York; petitions of and for ferrymen (1854); property deeds and surveys in Youngstown researched by Donald B. Ames (1992); and a letter (1854) and a newspaper article (1856) about *Pardee & Pom[e]roy*, the Youngstown hardware store. A reasonable conclusion is that Mr. Pardee was Myron J. Pardee—a local Youngstown UGRR agent.

Chapter 11 takes up a late nineteenth century exchange between the UGRR historian Wilbur H. Siebert and Thomas Birnmore. In a footnote to his article in the *American Historical Review* of 1896, Siebert asked those with information about the Underground Railroad to send it to him. J. W. Davis responded by suggesting that he contact a certain Thomas "Binmore" of Montreal, Canada. Siebert sent Binmore his standard seven-question questionnaire, which he signed and on which he had scribbled a time frame limitation, 1840-1860. A point-by-point response from Thomas Birnmore—spelled with an "r"—survives in a typed transcription. Birnmore detailed experiences that occurred at Lockport in 1856 or 1857 when he was a young English reporter who on a number of occasions had hidden fugitive slaves in his living quarters at the back of the *Lockport Daily Journal* office. Birnmore was careful to inform Siebert about what he remembered, which included Lockport conductors, the Lockport station, his own risky involvement, and most important, two fugitive slaves who were sent to a Youngstown farmer who rowed them across the Niagara River to freedom in Canada.

Chapter 12 takes up the dramatic story about the fugitive slave Cassey in 1860 or 1861, recorded by Eber Pettit, an UGRR agent and conductor in Chautauqua County, Western New York. Pettit had written important UGRR newspaper articles in the *Fredonia Censor* (1868) about his personal interviews of fugitive slaves and their experiences and these became the basis of a book (1879). Pettit's accounts, especially the dialogues, are literary and imaginative, but they are oral history composed by one who was directly involved in the UGRR and experts have judged that within them are nuggets of UGRR history, particularly the routes to the Niagara River. The Cassey account tells of the nighttime deception of the slave catcher Cathcart and his cronies by a certain "Col. P___," who tricked them by driving his carriage, supposedly containing fugitive slave Cassey, from Niagara Falls to the Youngstown Ferry and back as they were in hot pursuit by the Marshall and his officers. Meanwhile, Cassey escaped to the area of Lockport, New York.

Chapter 13 tells the story of eleven fugitive slaves who in the early 1860s landed at King's Wharf below Fort George and Navy Hall at Niagara, Canada, directly across the Niagara River from Youngstown, presumably by ferry. The story, derived from the memory of a Canadian sergeant who witnessed the dramatic event some fifty years earlier, appeared in a historical study by Canadian historian Janet Carnochan in 1914.

For those who like visual representations, here is a simplified sociogram that attempts to summarize the connected persons and sites in the UGRR network behind these accounts.

A UGRR Regional Network Related to Youngstown: A Sociogram/Model

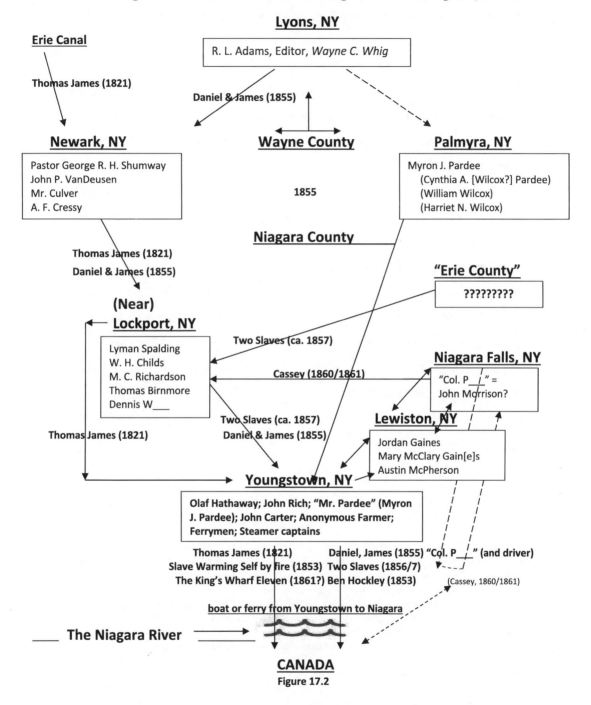

CANADA

Figure 17.2

Part III (Chapters 14 – 16) consists of three chapters that do not have the kind of primary evidence found in Part II, but they contain social relationships, connections, or links—both strong and weak ties—that are possible. Chapter 14 takes up persons in the network of those in Part II, some of whom lived in Lewiston and Niagara Falls. Chapter 15 speculates about possible UGRR persons and sites in Niagara County east of Youngstown, some of which have been previously reported as important for the UGRR, but not connected with Youngstown. Chapter 16 returns to Youngstown and suggests possible stations and safe houses, and most importantly the possible ferry houses in Youngstown. This material is also speculative.

In Part IV—this chapter—we attempt to evaluate the UGRR data about Youngstown on the well-known source and historical improbability/probability scale developed by Judith Wellman (see Preface).[1] The scale has two dimensions: value of *sources* and value of *the* historical content in these sources. They generally reinforce each other, but not always. Valued sources do not always contain historical information. For example, census data from 1790 to 1865 is very important primary source material for supplementary information about participants, that is, gender and race—Slaves, Free White males, Free White females, Free Colored persons, Black, Mulattos, and by 1860 Chinese and taxed Indians[2]—but these data offer nothing specific about the UGRR.

---

[1] See the summary "How Do we Separate Fact from Fiction in Underground Railroad Sites," in "Uncovering the Underground Railroad in the Finger Lakes," http://www.co.seneca.ny.us/wp-content/uploads/2015/02/Uncovering-UGRR-in-Finger-Lakes.pdf;
for an application, see Tanya Lee Warren, Compiler, *Freedom Seekers, Abolitionists, and Underground Railroad Helpers,* Cayuga County, New York. Historical New York Research Associates.
http://www.cayugacounty.us/portals/0/history/ugrr/report/pdf/consolidated.pdfhttp://www.cayugacounty.us/portals/0/history/ugrr/report/pdf/consolidated.pdf. For an introduction, Underground Railroad Free Press at http://www.urrfreepress.com/#Scale; also, Judith Wellman, "Oral Traditions and Beyond: A Guide to Documenting the Underground Railroad." Unpublished manuscript, August 18, 2015.
[2] "Measuring Race and Ethnicity Across the Decades: 1790–2010," United State Census Bureau. Online at http://www.census.gov/population/race/data/MREAD_1790_2010.html.

Sources, Data, and the Wellman Historical Improbability/Probability Scale

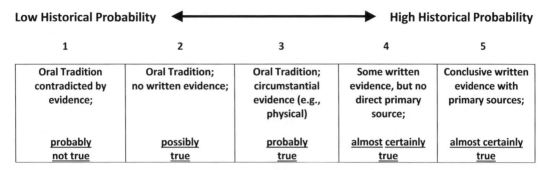

Low Historical Probability ⟵⟶ **High Historical Probability**

1	2	3	4	5
Oral Tradition contradicted by evidence; probably not true	Oral Tradition; no written evidence; possibly true	Oral Tradition; circumstantial evidence (e.g., physical) probably true	Some written evidence, but no direct primary source; almost certainly true	Conclusive written evidence with primary sources; almost certainly true

Wellman Scale
Figure 17.3

  In the grid below, abbreviations about the status of persons based on limited themes indicated by abbreviations is found in Column 2, STATUS. Our judgment about sources and the data contained in them based on the Wellman Scale is found in Column 6, "SCALE." These two columns have vertical arrows above them and vertical titles. As one expects, the best data rely on mainly primary sources in Chapters 7 – 13; they receive the highest evaluation. Our database is very inclusive, larger than the actual crossing accounts. As in all historical reconstruction, our judgments contain varying degrees of subjectivity.

The Youngstown Network Database
Figure 17.4

Legend

Wellman's Abbreviations:

A	=Abolitionist
AA	=African American
FS	=Freedom Seeker
W	=White

Dulings' Additional Abbreviations:

FB	=Free Black
FF	=Family/Friends ("Strong") Ties
S/SH	=Station; Safe House
Ag/C	=Agent/Conductor
Spec	=Speculation
——	=Network Clusters

⬜ **Village of Youngstown**   *** = cited elsewhere in the chart**

PERSONS & SITES DATA BASE	STATUS	DATE	LOCATION: NEW YORK STATE or ONTARIO	SOURCES	W. SCALE	MISSCELLANEOUS INFORMATION	BOOK CHAP
Lyons, Palmyra, Newark							
1. R. L. Adams	W A Ag	1855	Lyons, NY	VanDeusen Diary 1855	5	*Wayne Co. Whig* newspaper editor who sent ***Rev. Shumway** at Newark a letter of introduction for **FSs *Daniel** and ***James**, asking for them to be given money and to be shown the way to the Suspension Bridge.	10
2. Park Presbyterian Ch.	S/SH?	1855	Newark, NY	VanDeusen Diary 1855; Hoeltzel, *History Presby. Church; Newark*	4	Sponsored anti-slavery lectures, one by David Green Wheelbanks (1850). Perhaps a station; not safe for **FSs** to stay in Newark in 1855.	10
3. Rev. George H.R. Shumway	W A Ag/C	1855	Palmyra, NY> Newark, NY	VanDeusen Diary 1855; Census 1840, 1850, 1860; Hoeltzel, *History Presby. Church; History ... of Newark...*	5	Presbyterian minister; graduate of Auburn Theological Seminary; Anti-Slavery Movement organizer/promoter at Palmyra 1834-42; New Jersey 1842-1844; minister and leader of Anti-Slavery Movement at Newark 1844-1865; urged lectures be given by Theodore Weld.	10
4. Mrs. Emily Shumway	W A	1855	Newark, NY	*History of Wayne Co.*	5	George Shumway's spouse. Helped organize, officer of, Ladies Anti-Slavery Society at Palmyra.	10
5. John P. VanDeusen	W A	1855	Newark, NY	VanDeusen Diary 1855; Anna S. VanDeusen, "Life of John P. VanDeusen" (C. Davis email>G. Duling)	5	Presby. layman at Park Presby. Church; Diary author; instructions for **FS** James to go to Lockport, Youngstown & Suspension Bridge; gave $ to **FS** James.	10

PERSONS & SITES DATA BASE	STATUS	DATE	LOCATION: NEW YORK STATE or ONTARIO	SOURCES	W. SCALE	MISSCELLANEOUS INFORMATION	BOOK CHAP
6. Albert F. Cressy	W FF A	1855	Newark, NY	VanDeusen Diary 1855	4	Pres. Layman; grocer; gave money to **FS** James.	10
7. Stephen Culver	W FF A	1855	Newark, NY	VanDeusen Diary 1855	4	Pres. Layman; lawyer/civil engineer/architect. Gave money to **FS** James.	10
8. 2 Anonymous Men	W FF A	1855	Newark, NY	VanDeusen Diary 1855	4	Pres. Laymen; gave money to **FS** James.	10
9. R. G. Pardee	W FF A	1849 1855	Palmyra, NY	VanDeusen Diary 1855; *23rd Rpt, Amer. Home Missionary Society* 1849; ferrymen petitions	5	A "good man," brother of "Mr. Pardee" (***Myron J. Pardee**); a "Director for Life" of the abolitionist Home Mission Society of the Baptist Convention.	1, 10
10a.*"Mr. Pardee" (Myron J. Pardee) [* = cited elsewhere]	W FF A Ag/C	184?-?; 1854-1868	Palmyra, NY> Youngstown, NY (>Lancaster, NY)	VanDeusen Diary 1855; 1850 & 1870 Censuses; Ames *Survey* 1992; J. Onen's letter to the *Youngstown News*, 1908;	5	A "good man" from Palmyra = ***Myron J. Pardee**; loan from ***Gerrit Smith**; Cynthia A. Pardee (wife?) and William W. Pardee (son?); William Wilcox and Harriet Wilcox lived in same household. Pardees and Wilcoxes migrated, Palmyra to Youngstown; a hard-ware merchant at Youngstown by 1854; Cynthia and Harriet bought 614 Main Street; William Wilcox owned Lot 114 Second St. and Lots 141, 142 Elliot St.; ***Myron** was William Wilcox's real estate agent; ***Myron** was a UGRR agent for ***Daniel**, ***James**.	10, 14, 16
11a.* Daniel (father)	FS	1855	Lyons, NY>Newark, NY; Youngstown, NY>Niagara, ON	VanDeusen Diary 1855	5	**FS** father: Lyons> Newark> Lockport>Youngstown. Helped by agent ***Myron J. Pardee** to cross to Canada from Youngstown.	10, 14, 16
12a.* James (son)	FS	1855	Lyons, NY>Newark, NY; Youngstown, NY>Niagara, ON	VanDeusen Diary 1855	5	**FS** son: Lyons> Newark>Lockport> Youngstown. Helped by agent ***Myron J. Pardee** to cross to Canada from Youngstown.	10, 14, 16
Youngstown							
10b.* Myron J. Pardee (="Mr. Pardee")	W Ag/C	1854-68	Palmyra, NY>Youngstown, NY (>Lancaster, NY)	VanDeusen Diary 1855; 1850 & 1870 Censuses; Ames *Survey* 1992; Onen's 1908 letter to *Youngstown News*; ferrymen's petitions	5	See 10a data. Hardware merchant, *Pardee & Pomroy* in ***Davis Brick Block**, 409 Main Street, Youngstown. Wife Cynthia A. Pardee co-owned 614 Main Street. Myron and partner E. P. Pomroy signed 1854 ferrymen's petitions.	10, 14, 16

PERSONS & SITES DATA BASE	STATUS	DATE	LOCATION: NEW YORK STATE or ONTARIO	SOURCES	W. SCALE	MISSCELLANEOUS INFORMATION	BOOK CHAP
11b.* Daniel=11a	FS	1855	Lyons, NY>Newark, NY>Youngstown, NY>Newark, ON	VanDeusen Diary 1855	5	See 11a. data. Newark to Lockport to "Mr. Pardee" at Youngstown.	10
12b.* James=12a	FS	1855	Lyons, NY>Newark, NY>Youngstown, NY>Newark, ON	VanDeusen Diary 1855	5	See 11a data. Newark to Lockport to "Mr. Pardee" at Youngstown.	10
13.*"Davis Brick Block" (409 Main Street)	Spec: S/SH?	1855	Youngstown, NY	Ames Survey 1992; Onen's 1908 letter to *Youngstown News*	?	Site of *Pardee & Pomroy* hardware. *Myron J. Pardee, co-owner, was an UGRR agent; was the store ever used for S/SH?	10, 16
14. 614 Main Street	S/SH?	1855	Youngstown, NY	Ames Survey 1992; Phillips deed and survey	?	House of Cynthia Pardee and Harriet Wilcox (1854-1868); other Pardees & Wilcoxes lived with them. Was the house a S/SH?	10, 16
15. Bradley D. Davis	W FF?	1849	Youngstown, NY	Ames Survey 1992	?	Rebuilt Davis Brick Block (409 Main Street) 1854; knowledge of agent *Myron Pardee?	10, 14, 16

Lockport

PERSONS & SITES DATA BASE	STATUS	DATE	LOCATION: NEW YORK STATE or ONTARIO	SOURCES	W. SCALE	MISSCELLANEOUS INFORMATION	BOOK CHAP
16. Thomas Birnmore (Thomas Binmore)	W Ag/C	1856/57	Lockport, NY	J. W. Davis letter to Wilbur Siebert 1896; **Birnmore Letter to Wilbur Siebert 1896**; Siebert, *UGRR: From Slavery to Freedom*, Appendix E, 1898	5	Lockport Agent; Englishman from Canada; wrote about his role in hiding fugitive slaves in his room (a **station**) at the *Lockport Daily Journal*; mentions Lockport conductors and the directions of 2 **FS's** to go to Youngstown to be rowed across the Niagara River to Niagara, Ontario.	11
17. J. W. Davis	W FF?	1856/57	Lockport, NY	J. W. Davis letter to Wilbur Siebert 1896	5	Responded to Wilbur Siebert's request in journal for UGRR information; gave name "Thos. Binmore" (Birnmore) of Montreal.	11
18. Lyman Spalding	W A C	1856/57	Lockport, NY	Birnmore Letter to Wilbur Siebert 1896; Siebert, *UGRR; From Slavery to Freedom*, Appendix E, 1898	5	Banker, manufacturer, real estate investor, Quaker; Mason; Lockport conductor and "Station Keeper"; gave **FS**s directions to next station. "Station Keeper"	11
19. M. C. Richardson	W A C	1856/57	Lockport, NY	Birnmore Letter to Wilbur Siebert 1896; Siebert, *UGRR; From Slavery to Freedom*, Appendix E, 1898.	5	Lockport Conductor; called "Station Keeper."	11
20.* Dennis W __	W, A Ag/C	1860	Lockport, NY	Pettit, *Sketches*	5	Hid **FS** *Cassey near Lockport. Station Keeper; enlisted friend Jimmy to hide Cassey	12

PERSONS & SITES DATA BASE	STATUS	DATE	LOCATION: NEW YORK STATE or ONTARIO	SOURCES	W.S.C.A.L.E	MISSCELLANEOUS INFORMATION	BOOK CHAP
21a.*2 Fugitive Slaves	FS, FS	1856/57	Lockport, NY	Birnmore Letter to Wilbur Siebert 1896	5	Came from Erie County and hid in *Thomas Birnmore's room at the *Lockport Daily Journal*; were sent to Youngstown and from there were rowed to Niagara, On., Canada by an anonymous farmer (see No. 22).	11
Youngstown							
21b*. 2 Fugitive Slaves	FS, FS	1856/57	Youngstown, NY	Birnmore Letter to Wilbur Siebert 1896	5	See 20a. Were rowed across the Niagara River from Youngstown to Niagara, Canada by an anonymous farmer (see 21a; 22).	11
22. Unknown, anonymous Farmer		1856/57	Youngstown, NY	Birnmore Letter to Wilbur Siebert 1896	5	(= *Nelson R. Davis? *J. Carter? *John Rich?). Rowed 2 FSs from Youngstown to Niagara, On., Canada.	11
23a. *Austin McPherson	FB	1860	Youngstown, NY	1860 Fed Census	5	"Laborer"; from Virginia; was a "black servant" of farmer *Nelson R. Davis in 1860. See 23b.	3, 11, 12, 14
Lewiston							
23b. *Austin McPherson	FB	1870	350 Second Street, Lewiston, NY	1870 Fed Census	5	Black "Servant" of Youngstown's *Nelson R. Davis in 1860; from Virginia; in 1870 lived with wife *Maria in the Lewiston home of *Jordan Gaines, 350 Second Street.	3, 11, 14
24. *Maria McPherson	FB	1870	350 N. Second Street, Lewiston, NY	1870 Fed Census	5	Lewiston wife of *Austin McPherson, 350 Second Street.	14
25. *Gen. Jordan Gaines	FB Ag/C	1840-1870; 1856	350 Second Street, Lewiston, NY	1840, 1860, 1870 Fed Censuses; *Gerrit Smith's *Register* of gifted FS properties; *Niag. Falls Gazette* 1856; 350 N. Second St. one pager; Lewiston property maps.	5	"Laborer"; from Virginia; speaker in Niagara Falls (1856) honoring *John Morrison; husband of *Mary McClary Gaines; inherited her house at 350 N. Second Street in Lewiston (1854); was deeded 40 acres in the Town of Lewiston by wealthy Abolitionist *Gerrit Smith in 1847.	3, 14
26. Mary McClary Gaines	W? Ag/C?	1840 1854	350 Second Street, Lewiston, NY	1840 census; *Frederick Douglass' Paper*; *Warranty Deed* for 350 N. Second Street;1939 Affidavit; 350 N. Second Street one pager.	5	Death notice in *Frederick Douglass' Paper* (1854) suggests probable Abolitionist; purchased *350 Second St., Lewiston from *John Carter of Youngstown; wife of *Gen. Jordan Gaines; in 1840 census she is Colored; 1939 Affidavit transaction for 350 N. Second St. might imply she was White.	3, 14

PERSONS & SITES DATA BASE	STATUS	DATE	LOCATION: NEW YORK STATE or ONTARIO	SOURCES	W.SCALE	MISSCELLANEOUS INFORMATION	BOOK CHAP
Niagara Falls							
27. Cataract House (Hotel)	A S/SH?	1841-1860	Niagara Falls, NY	*The Times-Pecayune*, August 4, 1841; 1850 Census; Wellman, "Cataract Hotel."	5	Most employees were ex-slaves; some agents or conductors; hotel developed reputation as abolitionist. Owned by ***Parkhurst Whitney** and sons.	4, 12
28. *"Ben Jackson"	FB	1860 or 1861	Niagara Falls, NY	Pettit, *Sketches*.	5	Hotel employee (pseudonym for ***John Morrison** or ***Daniel Crosby**?); informed ***Cassey** that she was being pursued by slave catcher Cathcart.	12, 14
29. *Cassey	FS	1860	Niagara Falls, NY Lundy's Lane, ON Near Lockport, NY	Pettit, *Sketches*	5	A former slave in Baltimore; disguised self as sailor to get to Philadelphia; escaped to Lundy's Lane, Canada; came back to Niagara Falls to work for *"**Col. P___**"; pursued by Cathcart; informed by ***Ben Jackson** and escaped to "***Dennis W___**" at a site near Lockport.	12, 14
30. *"Col. P___"	W C A	1860 or 1861	Niagara Falls, NY > Youngstown>Niagara Falls, NY	Pettit, *Sketches*	5	Drove horse & carriage from Niagara Falls, NY, to the Youngstown Ferry as a decoy for *Cassey's escape to Lockport area. A pseudonym that probably referred to ***Col. Peter A. Porter,** but perhaps ***Gen. Parkhurst Whitney.**	12, 14
31. Peter A. Porter Home	Spec S/SH?	1860	Niagara Falls, NY	Sources: see Wellman, "...Home of Peter A. Porter... "*Sites*, Appendix C.	3	Possible UGRR station.	12
32. Parkhurst Whitney Home	S/SH? Spec	1860 or 1861	Niagara Falls, NY	Sources: see Wellman, "...Whitney-Trott House," *Sites*	3	Possible UGRR station or safe house.	12
Youngstown							
33. Youngstown Ferry		1811-1886	Youngstown, NY	NY State ferry licensing law 1813, 1826, 1836, 1886; *Ontario & Martha Ogden* schedules; Pettit, *Sketches*; Samuel R. Ward *Autobiography*; Youngstown 1870 map; newspapers ads	5	Ferry and ferrymen Samuel Chubbuck, Calvin Wilson, John Phillips; ***Col. P___** diversion to Youngstown Ferry; ***Samuel R. Ward**'s story of the ***FS** warming himself by the Niagara, ON, stove and his travel on Youngstown Ferry; Ferryman ***John Phillips**;	1, 4, 5, 6, 7, 8, 9, 10, 12, 13, 14, 16

PERSONS & SITES DATA BASE	STATUS	DATE	LOCATION: NEW YORK STATE or ONTARIO	SOURCES	W.SCALE	MISSCELLANEOUS INFORMATION	BOOK CHAP
34. Youngstown Ferry Houses		1845; 1853 1856/57, 1860, 1870	Youngstown, NY	Ferry licenses; 1845? Hillside House; 1860, 1870 maps; ferrying laws, No. 33	3	Site of **FS** and **FB** crossings to Niagara and back. ***Samuel Ringgold Ward; *11 freedom seekers?; *Daniel and James; *2 fugitive slaves?**	4, 6, 8, 10, 12, 13, 16
35. Olaf Hathaway	W Ag/C?	1821-1840	Youngstown, NY	*New York Spectator* June 7, 1827; *Albany Evening Journal*, June 15, 1830; *American for the Country* June 1, 1827; Universal Cemetery headstones; Ames Survey 1992; *Niagara Democrat & Lockport Balance* February 5, 1840.	5	Youngstown baggage and ticket agent for the Ontario Steamboat Company; and J. Young Co.; Holland Land contracts; "ferried" **FS *Thomas James** to Niagara, ON; "a daring intrepid and generous spirit, which often led him to risk his life when the lives of others have been in jeopardy," and always furnished assistance to "the oppressed." Brother was ***Elijah Hathaway**. Buried in the Universal Cemetery, Youngstown.	4, 6, 7, 14, 16
36. *(Rev.) Thomas James	FS	1820 or 1821	Youngstown, NY Welland Canal, ON	*Niagara County News*, Friday, September 21, 1883; *Life of Rev. Thomas James, by Himself* (1886); obit. *Holly Standard*, April 30, 1891.	5	**FS** of Master Kimball, Cromwell Bartlett, George H. Hess; escaped; followed Erie Canal being dug to Lockport; "colored man" showed him way to Youngstown; took Youngstown Ferry to Canada; worked on Welland Canal; returned to near Youngstown and worked for ***John Rich**, a farmer; then to Rochester, Long Island, Massachusetts, Rochester. Was ordained as Methodist minister 1833; ordained Fred Douglass. Spoke at Youngstown Presbyterian Church 1883.	1, 4, 6, 7, 10, 14, 15
37a. *Anonymous freedom seeker	FS	1853	Youngstown, NY Niagara, ON	***S. R. Ward**, *Autobiography of a Fugitive Slave...*	5	A freezing **FS** crossed by the Youngstown Ferry; warming self by the Niagara Ferry Office stove.	8
38a. *Rev. Samuel Ringgold Ward	B A	1853	Youngstown, NY	***S. R. Ward**, *Autobiography of a Fugitive Slave...*	5	Ex-Slave from Maryland; joined American Anti-Slavery Society 1839; as member of Liberty Party in the 1840s he was nominated to be a candidate for Vice-President of the United States. Famous anti-slavery orator. Crossed to Youngstown with the Rev. H. Wilson in January 1853; witnessed a freezing **FS** hugging the Niagara Ferry Office stove. See 37a, b.	8

PERSONS & SITES DATA BASE	STATUS	DATE	LOCATION: NEW YORK STATE or ONTARIO	SOURCES	W. S C A L E	MISSCELLANEOUS INFORMATION	BOOK CHAP
39a. (Rev.) Hiram Wilson	W A	1853	Youngstown, NY	*S. R. Ward, *Autobiography of a Fugitive Slave...*	5	White abolitionist minister, fund raiser; educated at abolitionist Oneida; also, Lane, Oberlin seminaries; partnered with ex-slave Josiah Henson to found the Dawn Institute for fugitive slaves in Ontario. He and *S. Ringgold Ward crossed from Niagara to Youngstown in 1853. See 37a, 38b.	8
40a.* 11 Freedom Seekers	A FSs	ca. 1862	Youngstown, NY; Niagara, On	Carnochan, *Hist. of Niagara*, 1914.	4	Presumably ferried from Youngstown to King's Wharf.	13
Ontario							
37b. *Anonymous freedom seeker	FS	1853	Youngstown, NY Niagara, ON	*S. R. Ward, *Autobiography ...*	5	A freezing **FS** crossed by the Youngstown Ferry;	8
38b. *Rev. Samuel Ringgold Ward	A FB	1853	Youngstown, NY	Ward, *Autobio. of a Fugitive Slave...*	5	See 37a, b.	8
39b. *H. Wilson	W, A	1853	Youngs.; ON	*Ward, Autobio.	5	See 39a.	
40b.* 11 freedom seekers	FS	ca. 1862	Youngstown, NY Niagara, On	Ca. 1860-1863	4	11 **FS's** arrive at King's Wharf, Niagara, ON	13
41. *King's Wharf			Niagara, ON		4	Location of arrival of 11 **FS's** (46a).	13
42. *Chloe Cooley	slave	1793	Queenston, ON Lewiston, NY	Report of the of the Upper Canada Executive Council, Navy Hall, March 21, 1793 recorded in William R. Riddell, "Slave in Upper Canada," *Journal of Criminal Law and Criminology* 14/2, Article 6 (1923) 253-54	5	Slave sold by Canadian master to American master and forcefully taken from Queenston across the Niagara River to Lewiston, energizing Lt. Gov. John Graves Simcoe to pass the 1793 Slave Law.	1
43. Solomon Moseby	FB/FS	1837	Niagara, ON	Sir Charles Moss, Chief Justice of Ontario in Riddell, "Slave in Upper Canada," 263	5	In Niagara accused of stealing his American master's horse; former owner David Castleman, brother-in-law of *Peter B. Porter, helped to arrange his deportation; attempt deport him to. U.S. via Ferry, but rescued by African Canadians.	1, 4

PERSONS & SITES DATA BASE	STATUS	DATE	LOCATION: NEW YORK STATE or ONTARIO	SOURCES	W. SCALE	MISSCELLANEOUS INFORMATION	BOOK CHAP
Town of Porter & Youngstown							
44. Col. Elijah Hathaway	W	1815; 1821-1823; 1834	Youngstown, NY	Tn. of Porter Hist. Society Museum Records of Oaths; Holland Land Co. Records; Foley, *Early Settlers of New York State*; Versailles, *Hathaway's of America*; Hist. of Niagara County 335a; Pool, *Landmarks*, 260-61; Dietz, *From Flames and Four Flags*; Dietz and Noonan, *Early Town of Porter Residents, 1800-1829*; Ferry applications, Niag. Co. Hist. Society; Census 1820, 1830.	?	Owned Hathaway Tavern/Inn; War of 1812 "Sufferer"; ferryman 1821-1823 when his brother *Olaf ferried *Thomas James to Canada; Path master and inspector of elections; commissioner for the proposed Lockport and Youngstown Railroad Company in 1836.	6, 7, 14
45. Betsy D. (Hathaway) Canfield	W FF	1845	Youngstown, NY	Youngstown's Universal Cemetery; Ames Survey 1992	?	Daughter of *Olaf Hathaway; wife of Osborn Canfield; source of Olaf's obituary?	7
46. Hathaway Tavern/Inn	Spec	1813; 1816?	Youngstown, NY	*NY Spectator*, June 7, 1827	?	Owned by ferryman *Elijah Hathaway, Olaf's brother; burned down by British Dec. 19, 1813; site of future *Ontario House (1842).	16
47. *Ontario House	Spec	1842-	Youngstown, NY		?	Location not far from Youngstown Ferry. Successor to Hathaway Inn.	14, 16
48. *John Phillips	W	1825-1828 (1827?); 1836 1840	Youngstown, NY	1826, 1836 NY Ferry Laws; 1840 Census Ferrymen file, Lockport Historian's Office;	5	Ran ferry 1825-1827; Youngstown 1836 ferry license referred to Phillips. 1 FB male living in his household (1840 census).	3, 6

PERSONS & SITES DATA BASE	STATUS	DATE	LOCATION: NEW YORK STATE or ONTARIO	SOURCES	W. S C A L E	MISSCELLANEOUS INFORMATION	BOOK CHAP
49. *John Carter	W Ag/C?		Youngstown, NY	Oral tradition?; Carter Family Folder, Tn. of Porter Historical Society Museum Family Genealo-gical Files; Debby Carter Fox; Virginia Howard, "John Carter…" *Niagara Falls Gazette* Sept. 28, 1953, 20; Pool, *Landmarks*, Pt III; Lewiston maps.	2	Mason/ farmer/boater; owned brick yard; built many noted brick buildings and structures in Youngstown and Lewiston; oral traditions are that he rowed **FSs** from Youngstown to Niagara, perhaps the 2 **FSs** sent from Lockport to Youngstown, 1856-57. Sold Lewiston property to probable abolitionist ***Mary McClary Gaines** in 1840 (including 350 Second Street); inherited by her husband ***Jordan Gaines** (connected to ***John Morrison**).	11, 14
50. John Carter Farm	Spec		Youngstown, NY	Oral tradition?	2	See No. 49.	11, 14, 16
51. *John Rich	W Ag/C?	ca. 1823; 1856-1857	Youngstown, NY	Thomas James, *Autobiography*; 1830 Census	5	Farmer; hired **FS *Thomas James** to chop wood when James returned to the U.S. Might have rowed to Canada the ***2 FSs** sent from Lockport to Youngstown.	7, 11
52. Simon Forte	W	1830	Porter, NY	1830 Census	5	3 **FBs** in household.	3
53. Reuben H. Boughton	W	1830	Porter, NY	1830 Census	5	1 **FB** in household.	3
54. Ezekiel Jewett	W	1830	Porter, NY	1830 Census	5	2 **FBs** blacks in household.	3
55. Elijah Boardman	W	1830	Porter, NY	1830 Census	5	1 **FB** in household.	3
56. Gideon Kelsey	W	1830	Porter, NY	1830 Census	5	2 **FBs** in household.	3
57. Charles Armstrong		1840	Porter, NY	1840 Census	5	2 **FBs** in household.	3
58. Charles Merchant	W	1840	Porter, NY	1840 Census	5	1 **FB** in household.	3
59. Timothy Beals	W	1840	Porter, NY	1840 Census	5	1 **FB** in household.	3
60. Nelson R. Davis	W	1860	Porter, NY	1860 Census	5	Prosperous farmer; brother of Bradley D. Davis; 1 **FB** servant ***Austin McPherson in household.**	3, 11, 14
61. William Thompson	FB	1865	Youngstown, NY	1865 Census	5	Self-reported Mulatto; barber; born in Florida; only **FB** family with property in Youngstown (Main Street).	3
62. Angeline Thompson	FB	1865	Youngstown, NY	1865 Census	5	**William Thompson**'s "black" wife born in Canada. Only **FB** family with property in Youngstown.	3
63. Frank Thompson	FB	1865	Youngstown, NY	1865 Census	5	**Thompson**s' son; born in Canada; "Mulatto."	3

PERSONS & SITES DATA BASE	STATUS	DATE	LOCATION: NEW YORK STATE or ONTARIO	SOURCES	W. SCALE	MISSCELLANEOUS INFORMATION	BOOK CHAP
64. *Benjamin Hockley	FB FS	1853	Youngstown, NY	15 newspaper articles; 3 letters *John B. Edwards to *Gerrit Smith (1851, 1852, 1853); censuses: 1840, 1850, 1855 (State), 1860, 1870; Butler in *Slavery and Freedom*, 72; Wellman, *NF UGRR Heritage*; *Database*	4	b. in Virginia; at Sackets Harbor (1840); Oswego (1841-1855+?); was purchasing lot & house from *Gerrit Smith; he, wife, and son escaped to Canada; 2nd son born in Canada; returned to Oswego; took steamer to Youngstown (1853) and tried to paddle to Niagara on old gate; caught in Niagara River current; picked up by *Chief Justice Robinson* 12 miles out in Lake Ontario; back in Oswego w. family 1855; in Detroit 1860 and 1870.	9
65. Paper Street (formerly Niagara Street)	Spec		Youngstown, NY		?	cobblestone tunnel to Niagara River, beside 233 Main Street	16
66. 233 Main Street	Spec SH?		Youngstown, NY		?	Possible secret room?; house beside paper street, No. 66.	16
67. 230 Main Street	Spec	1850?	Youngstown, NY		?	Cobblestone basement w. 2 sealed openings across from 233 and 235 Main Street.	16
68. Presbyterian Church	Spec	1855 1883	Youngstown, NY		?	Main and Church Streets. Built by *Samuel Chubbuck. Site of *Thos. James lecture in 1883. Site of Anti-slavery meetings, 1855?; cf. Ch. 2.	7, 16
69. Methodist Epis. Church	Spec	1855	Youngstown, NY		?	Built 1854; North of Presbyterian Church; possible site of Anti-slavery meetings in 1855?; cf. Ch. 2.	7, 16
70. Elbridge Gary Harris	W A Ag/C		Ransomville, NY	Adelaide Harris, granddaughter; interview report in *Niagara Falls Gazette*, May 19, 1954.	4	"Grandfather [Elbridge Gary] Harris was a strong abolitionist and acted as a Ransomville agent for the Underground Railroad."	15
71. E. G. Harris House	S/SH		Ransomville, NY	Adelaide Harris, granddaughter, May 19, '54 *Niag. Falls Gazette*	3	"He frequently concealed run-away slaves in his house until they could be safely transported across the river to Canada."	15
72. Gilbert W. Curtiss	W Ag/C		Ransomville, NY	Traditional belief; Pool, *Landmarks*, 263, 264, 266.	4	Possible agent or conductor?	15
73. Curtiss Hotel	SH?		Ransomville, NY	Traditional belief; Pool, *Landmarks*, 263, 264, 266; Wellman data.	3	Traditional Belief: "a stop-over on the Underground Railroad." UGRR Station; site of Anti-Slavery Meeting?	15
74. Wesleyan Meth. Church	Spec		Ransomville, NY		?	Wesleyans abolitionist; Anti-Slavery Meetings in 1855?	15
75. Glezen Fillmore	W Spec	b. 1789- d. 1875	East Porter, NY Youngstown, NY		?	Methodist itinerant minister; abolitionist sympathies?	15

PERSONS & SITES DATA BASE	STATUS	DATE	LOCATION: NEW YORK STATE or ONTARIO	SOURCES	W. SCALE	MISSCELLANEOUS INFORMATION	BOOK CHAP
76. Fillmore Chapel	Spec		East Porter, NY		?	A Methodist church strategically located east of Youngstown.	15
77. John Clapsaddle	W spec		East Porter, NY		?	Next entry.	15
78. "Clapsaddle House"	Spec		Braley Road, East Porter, NY	Mrs. Andrew M. Smith, farm owner, in letter to C. O. Lewis, *Niagara Falls Gazette*, 1964	?	Sealed off and wrongly placed basement room in purchased Braley Road house.	15

Misc. Orleans and Niagara Counties

PERSONS & SITES DATA BASE	STATUS	DATE	LOCATION: NEW YORK STATE or ONTARIO	SOURCES	W. SCALE	MISSCELLANEOUS INFORMATION	BOOK CHAP
79. Lemuel Pratt	W A	1855	North Ridgeway, NY, Orleans County	Obit.: Died, in Somerset, New York, September 16, 1856. . . pioneer in . . . the Anti-Slavery cause." Listed in Wellman Database	5	North Ridgeway, Orleans Co; Active churchman and deacon; temperance and anti-slavery movements; organized anti-slavery meetings for Watson (and Frederick Douglass) that included Youngstown.	2
80. Charles Brown	FS	1854	Warrens Corners, Town of Cambria, Niagara County	Lockport, *Journal*; *Anti-slavery Bugle* of Salem, Ohio, August 12, 1854	5	Highly respected "colored man" was living on Mr. Mighells' farm at Warrens Corners; escaped into the woods from two slave catchers, one of them his master's nephew; sympathetic article hopes he will avoid the Niagara River since slave catchers are at all crossings.	15
81. Charles H. McClew	W A? Ag/C?		Burt, NY, Town of Newfane, Niagara County	Local tradition	3	Farmer. Local tradition of involvement in UGRR.	15
82. Libby McClew, wife	W Ag/C?		Burt, NY, Town of Newfane	Local tradition	3	Charles McClew's wife.	15
83. McClew Farm	Spec		McClew Road, Burt, NY, Town of Newfane, Niagara County	Local tradition; Donavan Webster, "Traveling the Long Road to Freedom, One Step at a Time," *Smithsonian Magazine* 27/7 (October 1996) 48-50.	3	Room under barn; farm is an official UGRR education center.	15

PERSONS & SITES DATA BASE	STATUS	DATE	LOCATION: NEW YORK STATE or ONTARIO	SOURCES	W. SCALE	MISSCELLANEOUS INFORMATION	BOOK CHAP
84. Thomas Root	W A Ag/C	1848-1863	Pekin, NY, Towns of Cambria and Lewiston, Niagara County	"Obit—Thomas Root of Pekin, NY, 1903," *The Lockport Union Sun and Journal* between 5 and 10 June 1903? Pool, *Landmarks*, Part III, 134-35. Brooke Genter, "The Underground Railroad in Pekin."	5	Compassionate, anti-discriminatory farmer, Methodist, town supervisor, justice of the peace, and anti-slavery activist; fugitive slave conductor; distributed food to former slaves in Canada; his and Martha Root's home at 3106 Upper Mountain Road an UGRR station.	15
85. Martha Root	S/SH	1848-1863	Pekin, NY	See No. **85.**	5	Spouse of Thomas Root; UGRR station in their house at 3106 Upper Mountain Road.	15
86. Root House	S/SH	1848-1863	Pekin, NY			UGRR station at 3106 Upper Mountain Road.	
87. *Gerrit Smith	W A Ag/C		Peterboro, NY		5	Famous wealthy abolitionist and UGRR conductor who gave 120,000 acres to African Americans in the Adirondacks, as well as to others, including ***Gen. Jordan Gaines** and ***Samuel Ringgold Ward**. Loan to ***Myron J. Pardee**; sold property to ***Ben Hockley** in Oswego. Smith's Peterboro home was an UGRR station. His Oswego friend and land agent was ***John B. Edwards**.	1, 8, 9, 14, 16
88. *John B. Edwards	W A Ag/C		Oswego, NY	3 letters to ***Gerrit Smith**; C. M. Snyder, "The Antislavery Movement in the Oswego Area," (Oswego, NY: Paladium-Times, Inc., 1955 [February 15]), 4, 7-12	5	Friend and abolitionist agent of ***Gerrit Smith** at Oswego, NY. Wrote letters about ***Ben Hockley** transaction to Smith and ***Myron J. Pardee**.	7, 9

Summary

Our focus in this book has been to document as accurately as possible Youngstown's involvement in a regional Underground Railroad network. We have included information about Ransomville and other sites in the Town of Porter, as well as persons and sites in the larger network, especially in Niagara County, as they were linked with Youngstown.[3] These have been indicated in the discussions and two sociograms (Chapter 10; above) and summarized in the above database chart. Relying heavily on primary sources and using the Wellman Scale we have attempted to make judgments about the *seventy-nine items in the chart (eighty-eight items numbered minus nine duplications marked by a and b)*.

Our results include the following points:

1) There are both written and oral sources showing that UGRR fugitive slaves/freedom seekers crossed the Niagara River at Youngstown. Physical evidence of sites—stations, safe houses—in Youngstown is speculative (Chapter 14). However, it cannot be doubted that the Youngstown Ferry was involved in transporting fugitive slaves. The Niagara Ferry in Canada is mentioned in 1788 and existed on maps by 1810; legal documents for the Youngstown Ferry existed as early as 1811. Evidence of Youngstown licensed ferrymen has survived from as early as about 1820 and Ferry Street was on Youngstown maps in 1841. This means that there are strong possibilities for Ferry House sites along the Niagara River in Youngstown and the strongest possibility is one or perhaps two Youngstown Ferry Houses. A hypothetical case can be made for other stations, for example, the workplace and home of Myron J. Pardee, that is, the Davis Brick Block where *Pardee & Pomroy* hardware was located and, we think, the probable home of the Pardees and Wilcoxes at 614 Main Street from 1854 – 1868. It is possible to speculate about several other locations, for example, the Carter Farm and the Youngstown Methodist and Presbyterian Churches.

---

[3] For Social Network Theory (SNA) see Preface; Appendix 1.

2) Information about schooner construction at Youngstown survives and watercraft on the Niagara River and Lake Ontario, including schooners and steamers, docked from time to time at Youngstown. Some captains of such vessels are known to have been willing to transport fugitive slaves to Canada.

3) There is also information about local shipping agents at the ports on the Niagara River and Lake Ontario. One of those agents was Olaf Hathaway, who is recorded as having ferried fugitive slave Thomas James to Niagara about 1821. His brother Elijah was a ferryman from 1821 to 1823 and it is plausible to think that Elijah was also involved.

4) There also exists reliable information, including documented laws, about the Youngstown Ferry, including a horse ferry, starting in the early Nineteenth Century, and undeniable evidence that Youngstown ferrymen—and perhaps also our Youngstown ferrywoman—helped fugitive slaves escape to Canada. In addition to the Hathaways, the gritty, compassionate, Youngstown ferryman in the autobiography of abolitionist Samuel Ringgold Ward is instructive.

5) There is primary source documentation that fugitive slaves went to, or were sent to, Youngstown from other locations, particularly through the Lyons/Palmyra/Newark and Lockport local networks, but also from Niagara Falls. They were either rowed across the Niagara River to Canada by individuals—Olaf (and/or Elijah) Hathaway, but possibly also John Carter, about whom there are local stories, or John Rich, who hired Thomas James, or Nelson R. Davis, who had an African American "servant," Austin McPherson—or were ferried across on the official Youngstown Ferry, suggested by the autobiography of Thomas James and confirmed particularly by the account of Samuel Ringgold Ward.

6) Census records show that there were a number of Free Blacks living in the Town of Porter during the Underground Railroad Era, and by 1865 a Mulatto barber and his family in the Village of Youngstown. It is likely that from time to time there was communication among them (for example, Nelson Davis's servant Austin McPherson was living with Jordan Gaines of Lewiston in 1870, and Gaines had connections with the Niagara Falls abolitionist/conductor John Morrison in 1856) and sympathetic (White?) abolitionists, perhaps Jordan's wife, Mary McClary Gaines, of Lewiston.

7) Records of anti-slavery meetings reveal that in 1855 such meetings were held in Youngstown.

Five primary sources— the Diary of John P. VanDeusen, the Birnmore Letter, the personal interview of Cassey by Eber Pettit, and two autobiographical accounts by Ministers Samuel Ringgold Ward and Thomas James—explicitly mention or imply that Youngstown was a crossing place on the Underground Railroad. There is also an eyewitness memory account of a Navy Hall Sergeant about eleven fugitive slaves landing at King's Wharf, presumably from Youngstown, in the early 1860s. These sources also show that some members of the village were part of a larger UGRR network and that there were persons such as Olaf Hathaway and Myron J. Pardee, along with anonymous Youngstown ferrymen and other Youngstown persons who had boats on the Niagara River and participated in helping fugitive slaves. The Cassey story underlines the importance of the crossing site, as well. Readers may or may not agree with our judgments on the Wellman Scale, but there is no doubt: The cumulative weight of evidence provides indisputable proof that Youngstown on the Lower Niagara River was part of the Underground Railroad network and that some of its citizens, especially ferrymen, from time to time played an important role. Indeed, it is very possible that these surviving accounts are the tip of the iceberg.

The Underground Railroad was secretive, but there is clear information about the role of Youngstown and surrounding villages in the local and regional Underground network. More research needs to be done and will undoubtedly turn up further information. We encourage others to take up this challenge.

******

The Reverand Thomas James, whose comments opened Chapter 1, concluded his autobiography, at this writing more than 130 years old, by answering a question of great contemporary relevance, especially given racial relations in 21st Century. We cite it again:

You ask me what change for the better has taken place in the condition of the colored people of this locality in my day. I answer that the Anti-Slavery agitation developed an active and generous sympathy for the free colored man of the North, as well as for his brother in bondage. We felt the good effect of that sympathy and the aid and encouragement which accompanied it. But now, that the end of the Anti-Slavery agitation has been fully accomplished, our White friends are inclined to leave us to our own resources, overlooking the fact that social prejudices still close the trades against our youth, and that we are again as isolated as in the days before the wrongs of our race touched the heart of the American people. After breathing for so considerable a period an atmosphere surcharged with sympathy for our race, we feel the more keenly the cold current of neglect which seems to have chilled against us even the enlightened and religious classes of the communities among which we live, but of which we cannot call ourselves a part.[4]

"A final river to cross"

is a concrete reality of the past,

but it is

also a metaphor:

There are still more rivers to cross.

---

[4] Thomas James, *Life of Rev. Thomas James, by Himself* (Rochester, NY: Post Express Printing Company, 1886), 23.

PART V:
Appendices, Bibliography, and Index

APPENDIX 1:

Social Networks and Social Network Analysis

This book is an attempt to gain a stronger impression of local and regional Underground Railroad networks related to Youngstown. As stated in the Preface, the academic field called Social Network Analysis (SNA) gathers contemporary data and often uses graphs, logarithms, and software programs to analyze social networks. Historians cannot electronically generate new information from the past and analyze it with the mathematical sophistication of SNA, but they can construct network sociograms that are heuristic models, that is, visual diagrams that simplify complex information and aid in explanation and understanding.[1]

Social Network Analysis is not new;[2] however, boosted in the 1950s by British anthropologist John A. Barnes,[3] it has grown exponentially in recent years. In his instructive handbook on SNA, contemporary specialist Charles Kadushin, a sociologist very interested in the humanities, including history, offers a simple definition: ". . . [a] network is simply a set of relations between objects which could be people, organizations, nations, items found in a Google search, brain cells or electrical transformers. . . . [W]e are concerned with *social* networks, and what passes through these networks—friendship, love, money, power, ideas, and even disease."[4]

SNA has a number of concepts and a specialized jargon. Networks can be formal and tight, as in corporate relationships, or they can be informal and loose, as in UGRR networks. They can be based on close family and friends ("strong ties"), such as the Reverend Rankin and

---

[1] Such models in the humanities are heuristic. See Duling, "Paul's Aegean Network: The Strength of Strong Ties"; "The Jesus Movement and Social Network Analysis," pp. 301-32 in Bruce J. Malina, Wolfgang Stegemann, and Gerd Theissen, editors, *The Social Setting of Jesus and the Gospels* (Minneapolis, MN: Fortress Press, 2002) (published also in German and Italian translation).

[2] Linton C. Freeman, *The Development of Social Network Analysis. A Study in the Sociology of Science* (Vancouver, BC: Empirical Press, 2004).

[3] John A. Barnes, "Class and Committee in a Norwegian Island Parish," *Human Relations* 7 (1954): 39-58.

[4] Charles Kadushin, *Understanding Social Networks. Theories, Concepts, and Findings* (Oxford, UK: University Press, 2012), 3–4.

his wife and sons at Ripley, Ohio, or distant acquaintances ("weak ties"), such as John VanDeusen in Newark and Myron J. Pardee in Youngstown. Sub-networks or network "clusters" have a leader, such as the Reverend George Shumway in Newark or John Morrison in Niagara Falls. There are one or more go-betweens ("brokers")—agents and conductors—that link sub-networks to other sub-networks to form a larger, overarching or umbrella network. It is possible to collect information about these relationships and to create graphs or grids—matrices of persons or places—showing varieties of connections, such as persons between Newark, Lockport, Lewiston, and Youngstown. The direction or "flow"— "what passes through these networks"—can be one direction from "superiors" such as a station master to "inferiors" in the network; back and forth (reciprocal) from equals to equals, such as agents to agents or slaves to slaves; or even between opponents/enemies ("network polarization"), for example: Morrison to Cathcart. What passes through these networks is critical: information, the next station, food, shelter, clothing, monetary support, and, indeed, fugitive slaves themselves. After collecting and analyzing the information it is possible to construct "sociograms." Normally, they are diagrams with dots representing persons or groups or places and lines between them with arrows indicating the direction or flow and social distance. Shorter lines represent close relationships ("strong ties"); longer lines represent more distant relationships ("weak ties"); intersecting lines indicate overlaps and multiple relationships; and so on.[5]

---

[5] In 1929, Frigyes Karinthy wrote a play called *Chains* which held that everyone is connected to everyone else through acquaintance ties of no more than six degrees. His idea was popularized in a play (1990) and a movie (1993) by John Guare, each titled *Six Degrees of Separation*; it also morphed into a parlor game, "Six Degrees of Kevin Bacon." See further Stanley Milgram, "The Small World Problem," *Psychology Today* 1 (1967): 61–67, who theorized that the acquaintance chains averaged 5.2 intermediaries.

Here is a simplified sociogram that links two local UGRR networks.

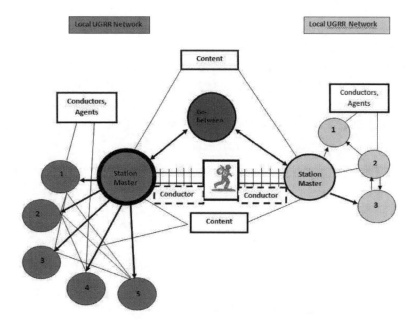

A Simplified Sociogram Linking Two Local Networks
Dennis C. Duling
Image 18.1

APPENDIX 2:

Timeline of Owners of the Ontario House Property, 1842—Present
358 Main Street   Youngstown, New York

Original Time-line prepared by Donald Brigham Ames,

Historical and Family Survey of "The Old Village," Youngstown, N. Y., 1992

Additional information taken from an article (no date) by Donald Ames, deceased Youngstown Historian.

This information was also on the cover of a past Ontario House menu.

Adaptations and Additions by Gretchen A. Duling, Ph.D., in 2017

Legend:

** **Early Youngstown Ferrymen = 3**

 * **Women Owners or Managers of the hotel, restaurant, and bar = 10**

1. The State of New York   Land purchased by John Young from New York State in 1811.

2. **Elijah Hathaway   Built prior to 1812, burned by British in 1813 (rebuilt by 1816?)

3. Reuben Wilson   10/5/1833 – 2/9/1841   = 8 years

4. **Luther Wilson   2/9/1841 – 4/9/1841   = 3 months

5. **Alexander Lane   4/9/1841 – 5/9/1848   = 7 years

6. Thomas Phillips   5/9/1848 – 12/28/1848   = 7 months

7. William Decatur   12/28/1848 – 7/5/1851   = 1 year

8. **Alexander Lane   7/5/1850 – 5/7/1851   = 1 year

9. Robert McKnight   5/6/1851 – 11/12/1866   = 15 years   He died in 1866.

    McKnight may have built the 50-foot-long wooden addition.

10. *Mary J. Root   11/12/1866 – 3/16/1881   = 15+ years

    McKnight's wife and daughter Mary Root ran the hotel.

11. Thomas Brighton   3/16/1881 – 1/8/1890   = 9 years

    Brighton tried to sell out in 1887 using the follow advertising:

    "The well known Ontario House, four-story stone, with two-story

Wing and basement containing 47 rooms, electric bells in part of the rooms, three good cisterns, one well, large icehouse, commodious stables and sheds. It overlooks Niagara River and Lake. (Note: This was before the El Dorado Hotel was built in 1891).

12. Timothy J. Murphy   1/8/1890 – 4/24/1913   = 23 years

Became owner in 1913 and put up the first sign. *The Niagara Journal* reported in 1892. ". . . Murphy has erected a fine new barn. It will accommodate 25 horses, 40 tons of hay and has two water tanks with a capacity of 40 barrels each." Note: Many older residents tell of riding or driving into the village for school and leaving their horses there.

13. *Hattie Murphy   4/24/1913 – 9/18/1914   = 1.5 years

Timothy Murphy died in 1913 and his widow, Hattie, sold the hotel to George Monahan who was followed by Anna Kutskillis.

14. George F. Monahan   9/18/1914 – 8/3/1921   = 7 years

15. *Anna Kutskillis   8/3/1921 – 12/28/1925   = 4 years

16. Leo & Jerome Bergey   12/28/1925 – 12/10/1928   = 3 years

Leo and Jerome Bergey owned it for 3 years before returning it to Kutskillis.

17. John Kutskillis   12/10/1928 – 9/16/1931   = 3 years

18. *Karolina Sciera   9/16/1931 – 9/4/1938   = 7 years

Karolina was deeded the property.

A long period of extended family ownership began.

19. *Wanda Kapinos   10/15/1938 – 4/8/1943   = 5 years

Karolina died in 1938 and left the property to her two daughters, Wanda Kapinos and Caroline Holody.

20. *Caroline Holody   4/8/1943 – 6/20/1987   = 43 years

Caroline was deeded the property in 1943.

21. *Rennie F. Sikoski
   *Olga Matthews
   *Eugenia Wojcik (sisters)   9/15/1987 – 11/17/2015   = 28 years

Following Caroline's death in 1987, her three daughters, Rennie,

Silkoski, Olga Matthews, and Eugenia Wojcik were joint owners until 1991 when Eugenia became sole owner. Her family moved into the hotel with her grandmother when she was young. The family renovated the building and installed a new electrical system and a better heating unit. Michael Holody (husband of deceased Caroline) had all the stonework pointed up and the old wooden porch rebuilt of stone as it is today. The Ontario House was granted the first liquor license in New York State. Eugenia, her husband (deceased), and sons Eddie, Andrew, and Martin Wojcik ran the hotel and "Stone Jug" until they sold it in 2015. It was in the ownership of this extended family from 1931 to 2015 = nearly 75 years!

22. Michael &

  *Barbara Costello became owners on 11/17/2015. Renovations are in process. Their son, Peter Costello, operates the bar and dining areas.

APPENDIX 3:

Excerpts from *The Fugitive Slave Act of 1850*[6]

BE IT enacted by the Senate and House of Representatives of the United States of America in Congress assembled, That the persons who have been, or may hereafter be, appointed **commissioners**, . . . Who . . . are authorized to exercise the powers that any justice of the peace, or other magistrate of any of the United States, may exercise in respect to offenders for any crime or offense against the United States, by arresting, imprisoning, or bailing . . .

SEC. 2. And be it further enacted, That the Superior Court of each organized Territory of the United States shall have the same power to appoint **commissioners** to take acknowledgments of **bail and affidavits**, and to take **depositions of witnesses** in civil cases, which is now possessed by the Circuit Court of the United States; . . .

SEC. 5. And be it further enacted, That it shall be the **duty of all marshals and deputy marshals to obey and execute all warrants and precepts** issued under the provisions of this act, when to them directed; and should **any marshal or deputy marshal refuse to receive such warrant, or other process, when tendered, or to use all proper means diligently to execute the same, he shall, on conviction thereof, be fined in the sum of one thousand dollars**, to the use of such claimant, on the motion of such claimant, by the Circuit or District Court for the district of such marshal; and after arrest of such fugitive, by such marshal or his deputy, or **whilst at any time in his custody under the provisions of this act, should such fugitive escape, whether with or without the assent of such marshal or his deputy, such marshal shall be liable, on his official bond, to be prosecuted for the benefit of such claimant, for the full value of the service or labor of said fugitive in the State, Territory, or District whence he escaped**: . . . the said commissioners, . . . [are] hereby authorized and empowered, within their counties respectively, to appoint, in writing under their hands, any **one or more suitable persons**, from time to time,

---

[6] *Amy Ridenaur's National Center.* http://www.nationalcenter.org/index.html.

to execute all such warrants . . . ; . . . to ensure a faithful observance of the clause of **the Constitution** referred to, in conformity with the provisions of this act; and **all good citizens are hereby commanded to aid and assist** in the prompt and efficient execution of this law, whenever their services may be required, as aforesaid, for that purpose; and said warrants shall run, and be executed by said officers, anywhere in the State within which they are issued.

SEC. 6 . . . **In no trial or hearing under this act shall the testimony of such alleged fugitive be admitted in evidence**; and the certificates in this and the first [fourth] section mentioned, shall be conclusive of the right of the person or persons in whose favor granted, to **remove such fugitive to the State or Territory from which he escaped**, and shall prevent all molestation of such person or persons by any process issued by any court, judge, magistrate, or other person whomsoever.

SEC. 7. And be it further enacted, That any person who shall knowingly and willingly obstruct, hinder, or prevent such claimant, his agent or attorney, or any person or persons lawfully assisting him, her, or them, from arresting such a fugitive from service or labor, either with or without process as aforesaid, or shall rescue, or **attempt to rescue**, such fugitive from service or labor, from the custody of such claimant, his or her agent or attorney, or other person or persons lawfully assisting as aforesaid, when so arrested, pursuant to the authority herein given and declared; or shall **aid, abet, or assist such person** so owing service or labor as aforesaid, . . . ; or shall harbor or conceal such fugitive, so as to prevent the discovery and arrest of such person, after notice or knowledge of the fact that such person was a fugitive from service or labor as aforesaid, shall, for either of said offences, **be subject to a fine not exceeding one thousand dollars, and imprisonment not exceeding six months**, ...

Sec. 8 . . . in all cases where the proceedings are before a commissioner, he shall be entitled to a **fee of ten dollars** in full for his services in each case, upon the delivery of the said certificate to the claimant, his agent or attorney; or **a fee of five dollars** in cases where the proof shall not, in the opinion of such commissioner, warrant such certificate and delivery, inclusive of all services incident to such arrest and examination, to be paid, in either case, by the claimant, his or her agent or attorney. . .

SEC. 9 . . . it shall be the duty of the officer making the arrest to retain such fugitive in his custody, and to remove him to the State whence he fled, and there to deliver him to said claimant, his agent, or attorney. And to this end, the officer aforesaid is hereby authorized and required **to employ so many persons as he may deem necessary to overcome such force**, and to retain them in his service so long as circumstances may require. The said **officer and his assistants, while so employed, to receive the same compensation, and to be allowed the same expenses, as are now allowed by law for transportation of criminals,** to be certified by the judge of the district within which the arrest is made, and paid out of the treasury of the United States.

Approved, September 18, 1850

APPENDIX 4:

Eber M. Pettit Obituary

Obituary

A NOTED PHILANTHROPIST.
Death of Dr. Eber M. Pettit[7]

Dr. E. M. Pettit died in this village May 18, 1885, at the age of 83 years.

A painful sense of bereavement pervaded our village on Wednesday evening, as the news rapidly spread from house to house of the death of Dr. Pettit. It was so sudden, and took all by surprise. And yet everyone seemed to say in thought or word, as the news was broken to them, blessed are the pure in heart. He had suffered from slight hoarseness for a few days, but was in the village on Monday, going about our streets with his usual elastic step, pleasantly greeting his friends and enjoying the social intercourse which was so inspiring with one of his genial nature. He expressed regret at not being able to enjoy a social gathering on Saturday at the house of a septuagenarian friend. It did not then seem possible that he was so near the shore from which he was soon to pass to the other side. But an All Wise Providence had numbered his days without the usual premonitions attending such a departure. In the afternoon of Wednesday, his hoarseness became more serious, his inability to throw off secretions increased, till finally the death struggle terminated in the early evening hour, and he was peacefully at rest.

Dr. Eber M. Pettit was born in Pompey, Onondaga Co., May 5, 1802. He had just passed his 83d birthday when the summons [death] came. At an early day he came to Fredonia with his

---

[7] *The Fredonia Censor*, May 20, 1885.

father, Dr. James Pettit. When still a young man he went to Versailles [NY], to engage in business, where he lived for many years.

More than sixty years ago he became a prominent agent and conductor on the *Underground Railroad*. Many a fleeing fugitive from slavery has found an asylum and safe conduct to liberty through his instrumentality. On one of the four principal lines with which he was connected, many fugitives were aided when on their way to Canada, numbering on all lines in the thousands. His position was often attended with peril. The Fugitive Slave Act of 1850 imposed a fine of $1,000 for selling or giving away a meal of victuals to one of these fugitives. Some of the noblest and purest men in the country suffered these severe penalties, though he has often said that if the law had been enforced against him, he would have been made bankrupt many times over.

About five or six years after the war [1861-1865], when his commission in this service of humanity had expired by virtue of the *Emancipation Proclamation* [1863], the company broken up and the stock divided among the passengers he was importuned to write out the history of some of these most remarkable escapes. The history of The *Underground Railroad* was written in a series of numbers for the *Fredonia Censor*. They were charmingly written, and attracted much attention. Some years later, in 1879, the sketches were published in a small volume, and many copies distributed among his friends, who will keep them as choice memorials of his philanthropy and self-sacrificing nature.

He also took a deep interest in the welfare of the Indians, on the border of whose reservation he resided for many years. He was their trusted counselor and friend, and aided to procure the necessary legislation for the protection of the reservation and the preservation of their rights. He was the projector of the Reservation school and the Superintendent over twenty years. He chose for teachers those who took an interest in their welfare and progress. . . . In every work of philanthropy when he had opportunity, his heart and hand were engaged with heartfelt earnestness. In this he was no respecter of persons. In his benevolent work his best services were rendered without regard to distinctions of race or color. His kind heart and hand were ever open to the needs of humanity. No one, we venture to say, in the large circle of acquaintances, ever knew a nobler or more unselfish man. In his unostentatious charities to the poor, he was most exemplary. Very often the recipients were unaware who was the giver. Early in life he became a member of the Baptist Church, to which he was fervently devoted, and yet with a liberality that recognized the image of the Master under all circumstances, in all walks of life, without regard to creed or denominational name.

There was an integrity of principle manifested through all his long and useful life. He dared to do right though he should stand alone with all the world against him. He would be true to his conscientious convictions though the heavens should fall. He was a firm believer in the higher law. His life was one of faith and trust, and his death that of the righteous and to their reward he has gone.

The fleeing fugitive from slavery, the red man whose cause he championed, the poor who received aid from his bountiful hand, the philanthropist in whose circle he was such a conspicuous example, the Christian who has respect to the recompense of reward in life beyond, will all enshrine the memory in their inner hearts, and will mourn his departure with heartfelt grief, and yet will rejoice that the great Giver of all good has vouchsafed to them a friend. A large concourse of people attended the funeral at the Baptist Church last Saturday afternoon. The pastor Rev. Dr. Palmer, a friend of many years, paid a worthy tribute to the good man so suddenly removed from our midst.

APPENDIX 5:

Excerpts from Wilbur H. Siebert's

The Underground Railroad from Slavery to Freedom:

A Comprehensive History **(1898)**

- **Relative Anonymity and Obscurity of Actors in the Underground Railroad:**

  "In general the participants in the underground operations were quiet persons, little known outside of the localities where they lived, and were therefore members of a class that historians find it exceedingly difficult to bring within their field of view" (Chapter 1, p. 2).

- **His thoughts about the growth of the UGRR:**

  "With the growth of a thing so unfavorable as was the Underground Railroad, local conditions must have (had) a great deal to do. The characteristics of small and scattered localities and even of isolated families, are of the first importance in the consideration of a movement such as this. These little communities were in general the elements out of which the underground system built itself up. The sources of the convictions and confidences that knitted these communities together in defiance of what they considered unjust law can only be learned by the study of local conditions . . . The western portions of New York . . . are dotted over with communities where negroes learned the meaning of Yankee hospitality" (Chapter 2, pp. 30 – 31).

- **The arrival of Freedom Seekers in Buffalo, NY:**

  "In western New York fugitives began to arrive from the neighboring parts of Pennsylvania and Ohio between 1835 and 1840, if not earlier. Professor Edward Orton [in his conversation with Professor Siebert at Ohio State University, Columbus, Ohio in 1893] recalls that in 1838, soon after his father moved to Buffalo, two sleigh-loads of negroes from the Western Reserve were brought to the house in the night-time and Mr. Frederick Nicholson, of Warsaw, New York, states that the underground work in his vicinity began in 1840. From this time on there was apparently no cessation of fugitives into Canada at Black Rock, Buffalo and other points" (see *Sketches in the History of the Underground Railroad*, by Eber M. Pettit, 1879) (Chapter 2, pp. 35-36).

- **Summarizing his research on the expansion of the UGRR:**

"We may summarize our findings in regard to the expansion of the Underground Railroad, then, by saying that it had grown into a wide-spread "institution" before the year 1840, and in several states it had existed in previous decades. This statement coincides with the findings of Dr. Samuel G. Howe in Canada, while on tour of investigation in 1863. He reports that the arrivals of runaway slaves in the provinces, at first rare, increased early in the century; that some of the fugitives, rejoicing in the personal freedom they had gained and banishing all fear of the perils they must endure, went stealthily back to their former homes and brought away their wives and children" (Chapter 2, p. 43).

- **UGRR Secret Ways for Communication (Code Language; Hidden Transcripts):**

"Much of the communication relating to fugitive slaves was had in guarded language. Special signals, whispered conversations, passwords, messages couched in figurative phrases were the common modes of conveying information about underground passengers, or about parties in pursuit of fugitives. These modes of communication constituted what abolitionists knew as the 'grape-vine telegraph.' The signals employed were of various kinds and were local in usage. The 'hoot-owl' signal was used along the Ohio River . . . Different neighborhoods had their peculiar combinations of knocks or raps to be made upon the door or window of a station when fugitives were awaiting admission. The answer to an inquiry, 'Who's there?' the reply was, 'A friend with friends'" (Chapter 3, p. 56).

- **Informal Organization of the UGRR:**

  "It is quite apparent that the Underground Railroad was not a formal organization with officers of different ranks, a regular membership, and a treasury from which to meet expenses. A terminology, it is true, sprang up in connection with the work of the Road, and one hears of station-keepers, agents, conductors, and even presidents of the Underground Railroad; but these titles were figurative terms, borrowed with other expressions from the convenient vocabulary of steam railways; and while they were useful among abolitionists to save circumlocution they commended themselves to the friends of the slave by helping to mystify the minds of the public. The need of organization was not felt except in a few localities" (Chapter 3, p. 67).

- **One Purpose for the Vigilance Committees was Financial:**

  "The Vigilance Committee of Philadelphia defrayed the travelling expenses of many refugees in sending some to New York City, some to Elmira and a few to Canada . . . Frederick Douglass, who kept a station at Rochester, New York, received contributions of money to pay the railroad (The New York Central Railroad from Rochester west to Canada) fares of the fugitives he forwarded to Canada and to give them a little more for pressing necessities" (Fragment of a letter from which Mr. Still quotes Mr. Douglass; Chapter 3, pp. 78, 80).

- **Emancipators' Devotion Despite Danger:**

  "Considering the kind of labor performed and the danger involved, one is impressed with the unselfish devotion to principle of these emancipators. There was for them, of course, no outward honor, no material recompense, but instead such contumely and seeming disgrace as can now be scarcely comprehended . . . they were rich in courage, and their hospitality was equal to all emergencies" (Chapter 4, p. 87).

- **The Scottish Covenanters and the Wesleyan Methodists:**

  "It is a fact worthy of record in this connection that the teachings of the two sects, the Scotch Covenanters and the Wesleyan Methodists, did not exclude the negro from the bonds of

Christian brotherhood, and where churches of either denomination existed the Road was likely to be found in active operation" (Chapter 2, p. 32).

- **Siebert sums up his book with this statement:**

"In view of all this it is safe to say that the Underground Railroad was one of the greatest forces which brought on the Civil War, and thus destroyed slavery" (Chapter 11, p. 358).

Siebert's Appendix E: A Catalogue of Names of Practical Emancipators:

In Siebert's book the names of those that belonged to this class of practical emancipationists, (he) catalogued 3,211. Of interest to us personally: Gallia County, Ohio (p. 421), where Gretchen Duling grew up along the Ohio River, had 45 names; Coshocton, Ohio (p. 419), where Dennis Duling grew up had 14 names; and Niagara County, New York, had 4 listed (p. 415). They were: Thomas "Binmore," W. H. Childs, M. C. Richardson, and Lyman "Spaulding." Monroe County, New York, had the most for New York State: 46 (p. 414). Among those listed in Monroe was Frederick Douglass. His name means that black and white emancipationists were catalogued together (Chapter 4, p. 87; Appendix E, pp. 403-439).

APPENDIX 6:

John P. VanDeusen

Permission to use provided by Christopher Davis, Museum Director of the Newark-Arcadia Historical Society and Museum, December 2014. http://newarkarcadiamuseum.org/.

A. "Life of John P. VanDeusen" by his Daughter Anna S. VanDeusen (1911)

John Porter VanDeusen was born on March 24, 1821, in Pittstown, Rensselaer County, New York. He was the oldest of the eight children of Lucas VanDeusen and Minerva (Porter) VanDeusen to live to maturity. Four other children died in infancy. Lucas VanDeusen was a native of Kinderhook, Columbia County, New York and was a direct descendent of Abraham Pietersen VanDeusen who emigrated from Haarlem, Holland, to New Amsterdam (now New York City) about 1636. Minerva Porter was a native of Middleborough, Massachusetts, and was of English descent.

About 1829 or '30, Lucas VanDeusen, a tanner by trade, having suffered business reverses, decided to move his family westward, perhaps as far as Michigan Territory. En route, however, they stopped in the Newark, New York, area to visit Minerva's two sisters who had married men named Bostwick and who were residing here. Liking the area, they went no further west. The family rented a house in the Marbletown area. Lucas supported his family from his garden and by working as a shoemaker, going from house to house.

In 1835, the family purchased a 40-acre farm in what is now the village of Newark. It extended from South Main Street west to Military Brook, and from what is now West Maple Avenue nearly to High Street. The farm house still stands, 616 Mason Street.

After about six months, the farm was sold at a good profit and the family moved to Vienna (now Phelps) where a farm was purchased and the family lived for seven years. In 1845, Lucas VanDeusen traded his Ontario County farm for one on the Blue Cut Road, east of the village of Lockville (Arcadia/East Newark). The farm house is still standing, 6653 Blue Cut Road. Here the family was living during the time John kept his Diary, and remained for many years.

John VanDeusen, being in less than rugged health, was unsuited to farming, so, while still living on the Vienna farm, began teaching in the district school. In 1840, he left home going first to Ohio, and then to Kentucky where he taught school for a while. When his health failed, he returned home, but soon moved to the state of Georgia where he taught school in Macon and in Milledgeville for several years.

In 1848, having returned to his parents' farm, John rented a room in Lyons where he opened a daguerreotype[8] studio, walking the four and a half miles from home to Lyons daily. He kept at this trade about three years.

About 1851, he began a business he had long considered—the making of shingles by cutting the wood at a different way of the grain, by which method he believed the shingles would last longer. His shop was located beside the Erie Canal in Newark, on the north side of what is now West Union Street, west of the end of Scott Street. He worked at this trade intermittently for many years, interrupting the work by a term of school teaching north of Clyde, and by buying grain and produce in Michigan, Iowa, and Illinois, as mentioned in the diary material.

In 1861, he moved his shingle-making business to a location on what is now East Union Street, abutting the Erie Canal, just east of the end of Colton Avenue. After some years, he went into the fruit-evaporating business in the same building. He continued in this business until he retired.

On May 22, 1862, John VanDeusen married Anna M. Lay, a native of Westerlo, Albany County, New York, one of the nine children of Robert and Cornelia (Hamilton) Lay. The Lay family long occupied the home built by Captain Joseph Miller, founder of the village of Newark, and long considered Newark's oldest house. Robert Lay was proprietor of a general store in Newark and occasionally taught school. Anna Lay taught in the elementary grades in the Newark Union School before her marriage. Five children were born to John and Anna. Robert L. (1864-1942) was a farmer in Newark all his life and became the father of three daughters. Emma (1866-1872) died at six years of age. Anna S. (1869-1945) taught in the Lyons Union School for 35 years, lived in Lyons and never married. Clinton S. (1871-1945) graduated from

---

[8] Daguerreotype: "An early photograph produced on silver or a silver-covered copper plate; also: the process of producing such photographs." http://www.merriam-webster.com/dictionary/daguerreotype.

Cornell University and became head of the Manual Training Department of Kent State College, Kent, Ohio. He married and had two sons and a daughter. Ella M. (1876-1941) graduated from Bradley Polytechnic Institute and was supervisor of music and drawing in the public schools of Sayville, L. I. [Long Island], and never married.

John and Anna first set up housekeeping in a house, no longer standing, on East Miller Street, just east of the former Northern Central R. R. station. Shortly after, they moved to a house on East Avenue, Newark, where they lived the remainder of their married life. The house is no longer standing, but was opposite the end of Grant Street.

John VanDeusen was long interested in the work of the Presbyterian Church in Newark; in the Temperance Movement; and in both local and national politics. Both he and his wife taught Sunday school for many years. (It is known that Anna was a member of the Presbyterian Church Choir in the 1890s.) In 1867, he was elected a Deacon in the church and remained so until his death, 43 years later.

Anna (Lay) VanDeusen died April 26, 1906, at 68 years of age. Although he was seventeen years older than his wife, and had never been in robust health, John P. VanDeusen outlived his wife by four years, dying May 1, 1910 at the age of 89 years. He is buried in Newark Cemetery, together with five generations of his family.

B. Comments on VanDeusen's Diaries by Historian Robert L. Hoeltzel

Four of VanDeusen's diaries—there are more—are housed in the Newark-Arcadia Historical Museum of Newark, New York. Robert L. Hoeltzel (deceased), former Arcadia Town Historian, offers the following commentary on the diaries and the above biographical sketch of John P. VanDeusen by his daughter, Anna VanDeusen.

Miss VanDeusen also mentioned her father's diary-keeping. During the time he conducted a daguerreotype studio in Lyons (ca.1848-51). "[A]s the new business was not very rushing, he decided that he had the time, and began to keep a diary. This he continued about fourteen years. He did this, he said, because he wanted to check on his progress in his religious life, and he liked to record certain events and later refresh his memory of them by looking over what he had written." She added the comment, "these books (diaries) . . . contained valuable information of the current events of the Villages of Newark and Lyons during those years." Only five books, covering the period 1855-61 (with some omissions during this period) which came into my possession some years ago, are known to exist.[9] These books are in a very fragile condition. They are currently held in the Newark-Arcadia Historical Museum in Newark, New York.

In an attempt to make the contents of these diaries more accessible, R. L. H. took a few liberties. He deleted most of the entries made by Mr. VanDeusen during the time he spent outside Wayne County, mostly in Illinois, Iowa and Michigan, as that material would seem to be of limited interest to those unfamiliar with the areas. All other material he copied without deletions. The very few additions he made for clarification are enclosed in brackets [ ]. Although Mr. VanDeusen spent several years as a school teacher, he was somewhat careless in his diary-entries in his use of punctuation and capitalization. For example, it was customary for him to use a dash – in place of a comma or period, although he did use some commas and periods. For ease in reading R. L. H. substituted the proper punctuation for the dashes. He often started words with what appear to be capital letters, whether or not proper usage required capitalization. Some sentences, on the other hand, were started with small letters. Because of the quaintness of these and certain spelling errors, R.L. H. copied the material as written.

Only a few avid students of local history will find this material of interest, but as one who enjoys such reading, I greatly regret the loss of the additional diaries.

---

[9] Christopher Davis, Museum Director of the Newark-Arcadia Historical Society and Museum, thinks that there are more diaries, primarily because of the numbering scheme of the four in the museum.

APPENDIX 7:

**Ferrymen Edward Giddin[g]s, Samuel Chubbuck, and Calvin Wilson;
the Morgan Affair (1826) and the *Caroline* Affair (1837/1838)**

The "Morgan Affair"

To understand the first two ferrymen, Edward Giddin[g]s and Samuel Chubbuck a brief background comment needs to be made about the famous William Morgan Affair.

In August of 1826, William Morgan, perhaps a rejected and disillusioned Mason, announced at Batavia, New York, that he would be revealing Masonic secrets in a forthcoming book titled *Illustrations of Masonry by One of the Fraternity Who Has Devoted Thirty Years to the Subject*. He was backed by John Davids, Russell Dyer, and a printer named David C. Miller.[10]

Revealing Masonic secrets was absolutely forbidden by the Masons, some of whom were very powerful, high-level politicians. On September 10th there was an attempt to burn down the office of the printer David Miller. Then, Morgan was jailed in Canandaigua on a charge (trumped up?) of stealing a shirt and cravat (a scarf-like forerunner of the tie) at a tavern. The charge was dismissed for lack of evidence and Morgan was released, but then immediately rearrested for owing $2.69 as a debt to an innkeeper. On September 12th this debt was paid by Laton Lawson; then, the jailor's wife was persuaded to release Morgan. However, as he left the jail he was abducted by several radical Masons (including Lawson!) and, according to the jailor's wife's later testimony, he was shouting "Murder!" in the struggle.

The rest of the story varies according to different court witnesses, chroniclers, and historians. The core of the story is that Morgan was thrown into a carriage by four men, spirited

---

[10] Morgan, William. *Illustrations of Masonry by One of the Fraternity Who Has Devoted Thirty Years to the Subject*. http://www.sacred-texts.com/mas/morgan/morg04.htm. Revised and corrected by George R. Crafts as *The Mysteries of Freemasonry. All the Degrees of the Order Conferred in a Master's Lodge.* Project Gutenberg eBook, http://www.gutenberg.org/files/18136/18136-h/18136-h.htm

off in the night, ultimately to Fort Niagara, where he was "detained" in the Fort's powder magazine. A plot to send him to the "care" of Canadian Masons was rejected by the Canadians, whereupon he was allegedly shackled and weighted, taken by boat out to the mouth of the Niagara River, and dropped overboard. Ironically, Morgan's *Illustrations* was almost immediately published. One passage suggests the fate of anyone who revealed Masonic secrets: execution and the body thrown into the sea.[11] A body that was believed by Morgan's wife to have been her husband was washed up on the Lake Ontario shore, but it was never proved to everyone's satisfaction that it was actually Morgan.

Records show that fifty-four Masons were indicted, fifteen separate trials occurred, and ten Masons, including Eli Bruce, the Niagara County Sheriff, were convicted, with varying, although rather short, sentences. Whatever the precise facts of the case, the Morgan Affair became a national and prolonged scandal. As a result, the powerful Freemasons faced a backlash; indeed, an Anti-Masonic Party grew strong enough to hold a presidential convention in 1832. The controversy raged into the 1840s and beyond.[12]

What of Youngstown ferrymen? Two of them, Edward Giddin[g]s and Samuel Chubbuck, were summoned.

1. Edward Giddin[g]s

Edward Giddins [sometimes spelled Giddings or Giddons] was keeper of the lighthouse at Fort Niagara and a ferryman (apparently at the Fort) sometime in the 1820s. He was a Mason called to testify about what happened to Morgan at Fort Niagara in 1826. Here is one

---

[11] Morgan, revised and corrected by George R. Crafts, *The Mysteries of Freemasonry,* under the heading "CEREMONIES OF THE ADMISSION AND INITIATION OF A CANDIDATE IN THE FIRST DEGREE OFFREEMASONRY," 8-9 (= Morgan, *The Illustrations,* 1827, 21-22): [pg. 8] "BINDING MYSELF UNDER NO LESS PENALTY THAN TO HAVE MY THROAT CUT ACROSS, MY TONGUE TORN OUT BY THE ROOTS, AND MY BODY BURIED IN THE ROUGH SANDS OF THE SEA AT LOW WATER MARK,*WHERE THE TIDE EBBS AND FLOWS IN TWENTY-FOUR HOURS*: so help me God, and keep me steadfast in the true performance of the same" [italics ours].

[12] William Preston Vaughn, "The Morgan Affair and Its Consequences," Ch. 1 of his *The Anti-Masonic Party in the United States 1826-1843* (Lexington, KY: University Press of Kentucky, 1983; paperback 2009); "William Morgan Digital Library," http://olivercowdery.com/morganhome/morgtxt.htm; "The Story of William Morgan," *The Times,* Centennial Edition (Batavia, New York, 1918), fultonhistory,com; Erik McKinley Erikson and J. Hugo Tatch, *The Builder Magazine* 12/9 (1926) under the heading "THE MYSTERY STILL UNSOLVED", http://www.phoenixmasonry.org/the_builder_1926_september.htm.

description of Giddin's testimony from the *Batavia Times Centennial Edition* of 1918.

Story of The Ferryman[13]

Edward Giddins, on being called, testified that in September, 1826, he lived at Fort Niagara, and kept the ferry; was called up the night of September 12th by a man who said he had the perjured scoundrel who had revealed the secrets of Masonry, that he was bound, hoodwinked and under guard.

> [I] went over the river with a party who wanted to deliver the prisoner to the Masons of Canada, for them to do with him as they thought proper. Morgan was sitting on a piece of timber when I went out of the [Lighthouse Keeper's] house; he had a handkerchief over his eyes; he was then led to the boat by two men, one hold of each arm; [he] appeared to be very weak. Two of the men got out of the boat and went up to the town (Niagara). I was told to wait until they returned. They were gone two hours. They were not ready to receive Morgan and we went back and put him again in the magazine. Morgan cried murder a good many times, and said: "I am determined not to be bled by that doctor." The men threatened him and Morgan halloed and made more noise. They told him to choose in what mode he would be put to death; he said "that of a soldier; shoot me." Col. King, who is now dead, had this conversation with him. They told Morgan if he would behave himself and make no noise he should be taken care of, and he put in a better business than he was ever in. [There follows a description of the magazine and "Giddin[g]'s" testimony about Col. King].

2. Samuel L. Chubbuck

Samuel Chubbuck and Thomas Balmer operated a horse ferry at Youngstown in 1829 (probably 1828) and Chubbuck continued until 1834. Chubbuck built boats, including large

---

[13] From the Batavia NY *Times* (1918), 14, transcribed as written; see "The Morgan Affair," a section of "History of Old Fort Niagara" at http://www.oldfortniagara.org/history.

horse ferries.[14] Like Giddens, he was implicated in the disappearance of Morgan and had to testify.

Samuel Chubbuck had joined the Masons while he was living in Lewiston and had attained the degree of Royal Arch Mason. In 1831, he and four other men were charged with Morgan's death and tried by a jury in Lockport. They were reported to have been seen walking from Youngstown to Lewiston about 3:00 A.M. on September 13, 1826, the early morning (night) after Morgan disappeared.[15] However, they were acquitted on insufficient evidence.

Eventually, conflicting "confessions" about Morgan's death surfaced. R. H. Hill reported that he had slit Morgan's throat; he was discharged as being insane. Avery Allyn said in an 1829 affidavit that Richard Howard had publically confessed at a New York Masonic meeting that he was one of the murderers. According to John L. Emery in a pamphlet in 1849, Henry L. Valance confessed that Morgan had weights attached to his body and was taken by three men in boat and dropped overboard in the Niagara River. Thurlow Weed reported in several newspaper articles and an autobiography that John Whitney on his death bed had confessed that Morgan was taken first to Canada, and that five Masons, one of them Whitney himself, left a Masonic meeting at Lewiston, went to the fort, put Morgan in a boat, and threw him into the Niagara River. One of the five, he said, was Samuel Chubbuck. Weed made a famous statement about the body that washed ashore, that it "was a good enough Morgan until after the election." Finally, there were reports about what Chubbuck himself said shortly before his death on June 4, 1881, namely, that on the night of September 24, 1826, he, John Whitney, and Colonel William King, had dropped a weighted "parcel" into the Niagara River—Morgan's body.[16]

Samuel Chubbuck died at Youngstown in June of 1881. The *Utica Morning and Daily Gazette* of Utica, New York, December 4, 1882, reported in a dispatch to the Philadelphia *Press* from Allentown, Pennsylvania, that one of Samuel Chubbuck's two sons living in Allentown, Charles Chubbuck, claimed that his father had never commented on the affair publically, but rather had consistently told his family that the Masons had nothing to do with the

---

[14] "Samuel Chubbuck, Obituary"; Siddall, "Samuel Chubbuck"; Virginia Howard wrote, "Samuel Chubbuck's Ferry Carried Horses at Youngstown in 1830s," but we do not have this source.

[15] The trial transcript from the newspaper *Argus* of 1826 about the steamer *Martha Ogden* mentions Chubbuck; see Ch. 6.

[16] Erikson and Tatch, "THE MYSTERY STILL UNSOLVED."

disappearance of Morgan. To Charles Chubbuck's mind, Edward Giddin[g]s, the lighthouse keeper at Fort Niagara, who claimed that Morgan was confined at the Fort, was an atheist whose testimony was excluded (that had been common); that the washed-up body on Lake Ontario was not that of Morgan, but of Timothy Monroe; and that "it would have been better for the country had [Thurlow] Weed disappeared at the same time Morgan did."[17]

Given the conflicting testimonies, a further comment about Morgan's disappearance is in order. *The Builder Magazine*, a Masonic publication, detailed the 1826 Morgan Affair and concluded: "Thus it is evident that the disappearance of Morgan remains yet to be explained, and the probability is that his ultimate fate will always remain an unsolved mystery."[18] Perhaps. However, in 1983 William Preston Vaughn (1933—2014), a professor at University of North Texas, an historian of the Masons, and—this is significant—a very active Mason himself, held a very different position:

> This writer agrees with New York's third special counsel of 1831, Victory
> Birdseye, that Morgan was probably murdered by misguided Masons who, when the
> Canadian deal fell apart, panicked and decided that by getting rid of the author, they
> would somehow prevent publication of *The Illustrations.* To their chagrin, not only did
> the book appear, duly advertised, in mid-December, but within a year, Morgan's
> abduction and alleged murder had produced a violent moral crusade against Masonry
> and an incipient political party as well. . .[19]

The "Caroline *Affair*"

Information about Calvin Wilson, the Youngstown ferryman who owned and kept the Youngstown Ferry in 1838, comes primarily from his testimony in the trial of Alexander McLeod, accused of murder in the famous "*Caroline* Affair" of 1837. Again, a little background is necessary.[20]

---

[17] *Utica Morning and Daily Gazette*

[18] Ibid.

[19] Vaughn, *The Anti-Masonic Party in the United States 1826-1843, 5; see also "William Morgan - Revenge of the Freemasons," at "Murder by Gaslight," http://www.murderbygaslight.com/2009/12/william-morgan-revenge-of-freemasons.html.*

[20] The trial transcripts also have information about Youngstown's Seth Hinman.

The *"Caroline* Affair" was a major event in the Upper Canada (Ontario) Rebellion of 1837-1838, often called "the Mackenzie Rebellion." William Lyon Mackenzie, a high-ranking Scottish-born Canadian politician was critical of upper class British rule in Upper Canada. He attracted followers who wished to set up a less elitist, more democratic republic on the model of the Americans. Mackenzie was expelled from Parliament. Unrest grew and he lost his bid for a seat in Parliament in 1836. In 1837, the Mackenzie faction rebelled. The insurrection was quickly put down, but some remaining rebels took refuge on Navy Island, located in the Upper Niagara River on the Canadian side, but near the northern tip of Grand Island, New York, on the American side.[21] The plan was to invade the Canadian mainland, aided by sympathetic American volunteers. Rumors spread that a little steamboat ferry, the *Caroline*, owned by Buffalonian William Wells, was supplying the rebels with food and weapons. On December 29, 1837, a British flotilla of five boats with about two hundred men attacked the *Caroline* which at the time was docked at Port Schlosser *near* Navy Island, but also on the American side of the river in New York. They captured the boat, killed at least one (Amos Durfee), perhaps others, and chased off the crew and others, torched the boat, and set it adrift in the rapids. What was left of the burning boat went over Niagara Falls. Interpreted by many Americans as a British invasion of the United States, the incident, much embellished in the press, caused a national furor. Mackenzie moved to the United States, was initially jailed, but upon his release, continued his political involvement, at first in Rochester and New York City, then Canada.[22]

---

[21] For its location, see www.soto.on.ca/national-historic-sites-of-southern-ontario/navy-island.html.

[22] "William Lyon Mackenzie," *Dictionary of Canadian Biography*
http://www.biographi.ca/en/bio/mackenzie_william_lyon_9E.html. The United States government took the Upper Canada Rebellion seriously enough to re-fortify Fort Niagara and direct its canons toward Canada, as noted in the discussion of Lewis Leffman at the end of Ch. 3.

Destruction of the American Steamboat *Caroline*
Library of Congress; public domain
Image 18.2

Alexander McLeod, a Scottish Canadian was for a time a sheriff in Niagara [on-the-Lake] in Upper Canada (Ontario), thus also a British subject. In 1840, he was put on trial in Utica, New York, for the murder of an African American, Amos Durfee, in the raid on the *Caroline* at Port Schlosser. According to trial transcripts,[23] McLeod bragged about his part in the affair in January of 1838 and to prove it he displayed blood on his sword at Davis's tavern in Niagara, a boast that was repeated in Buffalo. However, trial witnesses did not support McLeod's story and by 1840 he had an alibi. It was also determined at the trial that if the men were following orders,

---

[23] *The Trial of Alexander McLeod for the Murder of Amos Durfee. Gould's Stenographic Reporter; Published Monthly in the City of Washington, and Devoted to the Recording of Important Trials, or Treason, Murder, Highway Robbery, Mail Robbery, Conspiracy, Riot, Arson, Burglary, Seduction, Etc., also Miscellaneous Speeches.* Vol. 14, (1841); Marcus T. C. Gould, assisted by H. Fowler, *The Trial of Alexander McLeod, for the Murder of Amos Durfee, at the Burning and Destruction of the Steamboat Caroline, by the Canadians, December 29th, 1837* (New York, NY: Gould, Banks & Co., 1841); John D. Lawson, "The Trial of Alexander McLeod for the Burning of the Steamboat *Caroline*, and the Murder of Amos Durfee, Utica, New York, 1841," *American State Trials: A Collection of the Important and Interesting Criminal Trials which have taken place in the United States, from the Beginning of our Government to the Present Day* (St Louis, MO: F. H. Thomas Law Book Co., 1917) 88 (Vol. 7, 61—416). See also "British-American Diplomacy: the *Caroline* Case" in the Yale Law School's *Avalon Project: Documents in Law, History, and Diplomacy*" ,http://avalon.law.yale.edu/19th_century/br-1842d.asp. McLeod was the sheriff in the famous Solomon Moseby incident, Ch. 1.

perhaps those who gave the orders—the British command—should be punished. McLeod was acquitted.

3. Calvin Wilson

In 1841, Calvin Wilson from Wilson, New York, owner and "keeper of the ferry" at Youngstown in 1838,[24] was summoned to testify at the McLeod trial in 1840. According to trial transcripts of October 4, he admitted that he knew Alexander McLeod and reported that he had seen him with several others at a pub ("public house") in Niagara [-on-the-Lake] between January 5 and 15, 1838, a few days after the raid. He admitted that he was sympathetic with the rebels and had given them about $200, and that after the *Caroline* Affair had entertained them at his house. However, under cross-examination, he refused to incriminate himself, a "poor man" with a family, by saying that he was not directly involved with groups opposed to the government of Canada or a member of any secret society (other than the Masons). He also denied that he had entertained Benjamin Lett, the rebel who, inspired by Mackenzie, is usually believed to have blown up and heavily damaged the Brock Monument on Queenston Heights about five and a half months earlier, on April 17, 1840.[25] Wilson also testified that McLeod had claimed that three, four, or perhaps five were killed in the *Caroline* attack and for sure attested that a "damn Yankee" or "damn rebel" was shot on the wharf.[26] One known victim was Amos Durfee, an African American who was a sailor on the *Caroline*. He was murdered "execution style" with a pistol.[27]

---

[24] *The Trial of Alexander McLeod*, 73, 75.
[25] See Ch. 4.
[26] *The Trial of Alexander McLeod,* 73-75.
[27] Ibid., 17-19 for the Indictment of McLeod and others from Niagara County, which describes Durfee's death.

The Body of an African-American, Amos Durfee, killed at Port Schlosser in the *Caroline* Affair of 1837, as illustrated in 1885.
This work is in the public domain in the United States
Image 18.3

APPENDIX 8:

Three Amendments to the United States Constitution[28]

Amendment XIII.   December 6, 1865   (Abolition of Slavery)

> **Section 1:** Neither slavery nor involuntary servitude, except as a punishment for crime whereof the party shall have been duly convicted, shall exist within the United States, or any place subject to their jurisdiction.

> **Section 2:** Congress shall have power to enforce this article by appropriate legislation.

Amendment XV.   February 3, 1870   (Voting Rights, African-American Men)

> **Section 1:** The right of citizens of the United States to vote shall not be denied or abridged by the United States or by any State on account of race, color, or previous condition of servitude.

> **Section 2:** The Congress shall have power to enforce this article by appropriate legislation.

Amendment XIX.   August 18, 1920   (Voting Rights for all Women, including African-American Women)

> The right of citizens of the United States to vote shall not be denied or abridged by the United States or by any State on account of sex (gender).

---

[28] *The United States Constitution and Related Documents (*Korea: Post Miniatures by Graphic Image, 2007) 57, 61, 64.

BIBLIOGRAPHY

Abela, Joseph. "Louis Shickluna – A Successful Senglean." *Times of Malta.* June 16, 2008.

"Abolition of Slavery Timeline." *Wikipedia.* https://en.wikipedia.org/wiki/Abolition_of_slavery_timeline.

"Abolitionist Movement." *History.* www.history.com/topics/abolitionist-movement.

A Century of Population Growth in the United States, From the First Census of the United States to the Twelfth (1790-1900). Washington, D.C.: Government Printing Office, 1909, Ch. XIX, pp. 132-34. https://www2.census.gov/prod2/decennial/documents/00165897ch14.pdf .

"An Act to Lay a Duty on Strong Liquors and for Regulating Inns and Taverns," Passed 7th April, 1801. In *Laws of the State of New York Published by Authority.* Albany, NY: Charles R. and George Webster, 1802. https://books.google.com/books?id=voNZAAAAYAAJ&pg=PA488&lpg=PA488&dq=New+York+State+law+concerning+inns+and+taverns+-+beds+and+horses&source=bl&ots=DZZWIABTYo&sig=WcsVZTJzKZK06o1_rC1lfC-gE04&hl=en&sa=X&ved=0ahUKEwip3eGRjrTNAhVHOSYKHXKJAQQQ6AEIIzAB#v=onepage&q=New%20York%20State%20law%20concerning%20inns%20and%20taverns%20-%20beds%20and%20horses&f=false.

Ahrens, Edward D. *The Devil's Hole Massacre—A True Story.* Sanborn, New York: Rissa Productions, 2004.

Affidavit. MacCollum, Mary E., descendant of Jordan and Mary McClary Gaines. Affidavit of for 350 Second Street, Lewiston, December 14, 1939.

"African American Newspapers Collection." Accessible Archives. African American Newspapers. http://www.accessible-archives.com/2011/02/african-american-newspapers/. Membership required.

The African Americans. Many Rivers to Cross. Six-hour documentary. With Henry Lewis Gates, Jr. PBS Television Series, 2013. A Film by Kundhardt McGee Productions, Inkwell Films, and THIRTEEN Productions. LLC in association with Ark Media. First four episodes are on YouTube and the whole can be purchased. http://www.pbs.org/wnet/african-americans-many-rivers-to-cross/. Website No longer active.

Album (Rochester, New York). Multiple dates, 1826.

Albany Evening Journal, 15, 1830.

American Anti-Slavery Almanac 1840. Boston Public Library. https://archive.org/details/americanantislav1840chil.

"American Anti-Slavery Society." Editors of the *Encyclopedia Britannica.* http://www.britannica.com/EBchecked/topic/19269/American-AntiSlavery-Society.

American, The, for the Country, New York, June 1, 1827.

"American Newspapers, 1800—1860: City Newspapers." University Library, University of Illinois at Urbana-Champaign. http://www.library.illinois.edu/hpnl/guides/newspapers/american/1800-1860/city.html.

Ames, Donald Brighton. A Historical and Family Survey of 'The Old Village,' Youngstown, N.Y. Third Street 1992. Vol. 1A (Fascicle collection).

Ames, Donald Brighton. *Historical and Family Survey of the "Old Village" of Youngstown, New York.* 8 vols. Plastic comb bound. Youngstown, NY: Town of Porter Historical Society Museum, 1992. Bound edition at the Niagara County Historian's Office, Lockport, New York.

Andrews, William L. *To Tell a Free Story*. Chicago, IL: University of Illinois Press, 1986.

Andrie, C. "Black Rock Ferry." Unpublished Paper. January 13, 2012.

Annual Report of the State Engineer and Surveyor of the State of New York and of the Tabulations and Deductions from the Reports of the Railroad Corporations for the Year Ending September 30, 1858. Albany, NY: Weed, Parsons and Company, 1859.

Anonymous. "Rev. Glezen Fillmore." *Ladies' Repository* 21/6 (1861): 366-67.

Anonymous. "Anti-Slavery Roots. The Wesleyan Church." https://www.wesleyan.org/229/antislavery-roots.

Anonymous. "Dr. and Mrs. Fillmore." Sections on "Discourse of Memorial of Rev. Glezen Fillmore." Delivered in the Grace Methodist Episcopal Church, Buffalo, New York, February 14, 1875. In Sanford Hunt, *History of the Methodist Episcopal Church in Buffalo from its Origin to the Close of 1892*. Buffalo, NY: H. H. Otis & Sons, 1893.

Anonymous. "Freedmen's Aid Society Methodist Episcopal Church History." http://drbronsontours.com/bronsonfreedmensaidsocietymethodistepiscopalchurchhistory.html.

Anonymous. "Samuel Chubbuck, Obituary." *Niagara County News*, June 9, 1882.

"Anti-Slavery Meetings in Niagara and Orleans Counties." *Frederick Douglass' Paper*. Accessible Archives. African American Newspapers. http://www.accessible-archives.com/collections/african-american-newspapers/.

"Anti-Slavery Roots. The Wesleyan Church." https://www.wesleyan.org/229/antislavery-roots.

Argus (Albany, New York), March 5, 1831.

"Asleep on a Raft." A sketch by E. W. Kemble in Mark Twain, *Adventures of Huckleberry Finn* (New York, NY: Charles W. Webster & Co., 1885) Ch. XV, 118, in the Gutenberg Project of free, public domain e-books online, http://www.gutenberg.org/; http://www.gutenberg.org/files/76/76-h/76-h.htm.

Auburn Daily Union, November 19, 1860.

"August 3rd 1853 Day of the Week." http://www.onedayhistory.com/day-of-week/1853-august-3/.

Aug, Lisa. *Beyond the Falls: A Modern History of the Lower Niagara River.* Niagara Falls, NY: Niagara Books, 1992.

Bail, Raymond. *The Underground Railroad*. New York, NY: Houghton Mifflin Company, 1995. (Youth).

Barnes, John A. "Class and Committee in a Norwegian Island Parish." *Human Relations* 7 (1954): 39-58.

Baxter, Archie E. *General Index of the Laws of the State of New York, 1777—1901*. Albany, NY: J. B. Lyon Company, 1902.

"Benjamin Pringle." *Wikipedia*. https://en.wikipedia.org/wiki/Benjamin_Pringle.

Berry, Daina Ramey. *The Price for Their Pound of Flesh. The Value of the Enslaved, from Womb to Grave, in the Building of a Nation.* Boston, MA: Beacon Press, 2017.

Besecker, Aaron. "Construction of New Niagara Falls Hotel to Start in November." News Niagara, *News Niagara Reporter* (October 22, 2014). http://www.buffalonews.com/city-region/niagara-falls/construction-of-new-niagara-falls-hotel-to-start-in-november-20141022

Bial, Raymond. *The Underground Railroad*. Boston, MA: Houghton Mifflin Company, 1995.

Bibb, Henry. *Narrative of the Life and Adventures of Henry Bibb, an American Slave, Written by Himself.* New York, NY: Published by the Author, 1849.

Blackson, Charles L. *The Underground Railroad. First-Person Narratives of Escapes to Freedom in the North.* New York, NY: Prentice Hall Press, 1987.

Blight, David W., editor. *Passages to Freedom: The Underground Railroad in History and Memory*. Washington, D. C.: Smithsonian Books in Association with the National Underground Railroad Freedom Center, 2004.

Blockson, Charles L. *Hippocrene Guide to The Underground Railroad*. New York, NY: Hippocrene Books, 1994.

Bordewich, Fergus M. *Bound for Canaan: The Epic Story of the Underground Railroad, America's First Civil Rights Movement.* New York, NY: Amistad, 2005; New York, NY: HarperCollins, 2006.

Bordewich, Fergus M. *The First Congress: How James Madison, George Washington, and a Group of Extraordinary Men Invented the Government.* New York, NY: Simon & Schuster, 2016.

Bradford, Sarah H. *Scenes in the Life of Harriet Tubman*. Auburn, NY: W. J. Moses [Printer], 1869; revised as *Harriet, the Moses of Her People*. New York, NY: Geo. R. Lockwood and Son, 1886.

Breyfogle, William. *Make Free: The Story of the UGRR*. New York, NY: J. B. Lippincott, 1958.

"British-American Diplomacy: the Caroline Case." *Avalon Project: Documents in Law, History, and Diplomacy*. Yale Law School. http://avalon.law.yale.edu/19th_century/br-1842d.asp.

"Broadsides, Leaflets, and Pamphlets from America and Europe." In "An American Time Capsule: Three Centuries of Broadsides and Other Painted Ephemera." Portfolio 248, Folder 1, Library of Congress. http://memory.loc.gov/cgi-bin/query/h?ammem/rbpebib:@field(NUMBER+@band(rbpe+24800100)).

Brubaker, Jerome. Old Fort Niagara Assistant Director and Curator. October 21, 2014. Personal email communication with Gretchen Duling.

Burton, Lauren Elizabeth. Evaluating the National Underground Railroad Network to Freedom Program of the National Park Service. M.A. Thesis. Philadelphia, PA: University of Pennsylvania, 2014.

Butler, Nancy. "Starting Anew: The Black Community of Early Niagara." Pp. 41-73 in Michael Power and Nancy Butler (with Joy Ormsby). *Slavery and Freedom in Niagara*. Niagara-on-the-Lake, ON: The Niagara Historical Society, 1993.

Cady, Fitch. "Ship-building in Youngstown has a Long History." *The Buffalo News* (March 28, 1999).

Calarco, Tom, et al. *Places of the Underground Railroad. A Geographical Guide.* Santa Barbara, CA: ABC-CLIO, LLC, 2011.

Calarco, Tom. *The Search for the Underground Railroad in Upstate New York*. Charleston, SC: The History Press, 2014.

Campbell, Stanley W. *The Slave Catchers: Enforcement of the Fugitive Slave Law, 1850-1860.* Chapel Hill, NC: The University of North Carolina Press, 1970. https://www.questia.com/read/104469009/the-slave-catchers-enforcement-of-the-fugitive-slave.

"Cap. Robert Lee." Excerpts from William Still's *The Underground Railroad*. http://racetimeplace.com/ugrr/stillnarrative.htm#111

Carnochan, Janet. *History of Niagara*. Toronto, ON: William Briggs, 1914; republished Belleville, ON: Mika Publishing, 1973.

"Category: Predecessors of the New York Central Railroad." *Wikipedia*. https://en.wikipedia.org/wiki/Category:Predecessors_of_the_New_York_Central_Railroad.

"Caution, Colored People of Boston." Broadside. Rare Books and Manuscripts Department, Boston Public Library in Boston, Massachusetts. http://chnm.gmu.edu/lostmuseum/lm/307/.

"Chapter VII. Comment by Jo-Ann Morgan." Interpretation of Hammatt Billings' "The Mother's Struggle." *Uncle Tom's Cabin* in the *National Era*. The Harriet Beecher Stowe Center. https://nationalera.wordpress.com/further-reading/chapter-7-comment-by-jo-ann-morgan/.

Clinton, DeWitt. *Private Canal Journal*, 1810. In William W. Campbell, *Life and Writings of DeWitt Clinton*. New York, NY: Baker and Scribner, 1849. http://www.eriecanal.org/texts/Campbell/chap06-2.html#FortNiagara.

"Conductors and Agents." The Underground Railroad in Virginia. http://racetimeplace.com/ugrr/conductors.htm.

Constantino, Carl J. *History of the Underground Railroad along the Niagara Frontier*. M.A. Thesis Niagara University. Lewiston, NY: Niagara University History Department, 1947.

"Constitution and Slavery, The." Constitutional Rights Foundation. http://www.crf-usa.org/black-history-month/the-constitution-and-slavery.

Copeland, Peter F. *The Story of the Underground Railroad*. Mineola, NY: Dover Publications, Inc., 2000. (Multi-Age).

Court Minutes [Niagara County Court of] Common Pleas (May 1821-Sept. 19, 1831). Book 1. Niagara County Historian's Office, Niagara Street, Lockport, NY.

Cowles, George W. Assisted by H. P. Smith and Others. *Landmarks of Wayne County, New York, Illustrated.* Syracuse, New York: D. Mason & Company, Publishers, 1895.

Crisman, Kevin James, and Arthur B. Cohn. *When Horses Walked on Water: Horse-Powered Ferries in Nineteenth-Century America*. Washington, D.C.; London, UK: Smithsonian Institution Press, 1998.

Croil, James. *Steam Navigation and its Relation to the Commerce of Canada and the United States*. Montreal, QC: The Montreal New Company Limited, 1898. Online reprint at the Open Library, Classic Book Collection. Toronto, ON: William Briggs. https://archive.org/stream/cihm02131#page/n11/mode/2up.

Cumberland, Barlow. *A Century of Sail and Steam on the Niagara River*. Toronto, ON: The Musson Book Company, 1913.

Daily Albany Argus, September 21, 1854.

Daily Gazette (Niagara), August 11, 1883.

Daley, James, editor. *Great Speeches by African Americans: Frederick Douglas, Sojourner Truth, Dr. Martin Luther King, Jr., Barack Obama, and Others*. Mineola, NY: Dover Publications, 2006.

"Dan Davis *to* Niagara Falls History—Stories of Us" [Suspension Bridge]. https://www.facebook.com/whynotsuspensionbridge/posts/736396376465307

Dann, Norman K. *Practical Dreamer. Gerrit Smith and the crusade for Social Reform*. Hamilton, NY: Log Cabin Books, 2009.

Dann, Norman K. *When We Get to Heaven. Runaway slaves on the Road to Peterboro*. Hamilton, NY: Log Cabin Books, 2008.

Dann, Norman K. *Whatever It Takes. The Antislavery Movement and the Tactics of Gerrit Smith*. Hamilton, NY: Log Cabin Books, 2011.

Davis, Christopher Davis (Museum Director of the Newark- Arcadia Historical Society and Museum). To Gretchen Duling, December 19, 2014. Contains Robert L. Hoeltzel, "Introduction, John P. VanDeusen."

Davis, Daniel L. *The Life and Times of Suspension Bridge Village*. 2nd edition. 2014.

Davis, Daniel L. Suspension Bridge Historian. Interview with Dennis Duling.

Davis, Dernoral. "A Contested Presence: Free Blacks in Antebellum Mississippi, 1820–1860." Mississippi Historical Now. Mississippi Historical Society. http://mshistorynow.mdah.state.ms.us/articles/45/a-contested-presence-free-blacks-in-antebellum-mississippi-18201860.

Davison, G. M. *The Fashionable Tour: A Guide to Travellers Visiting the Middle and Northern States and the Provinces of Canada*. 4th edition. Saratoga Springs, NY: G. M. Davison; New York, NY: G. & C. & H. Carvill, 1830.

"Declaration and Constitutions of the American Anti-Slavery Society, The." New York, NY: Anti-Slavery Society, 1835. http://scua.library.umass.edu/digital/antislavery/016.pdf.

Deed of Gerrit Smith. Peterboro Land Granted to Samuel Ringgold Ward and Two Others. Forwarded by Donna D. Burdick, Smithfield Town Historian.

Democratic Mirror (Sandusky, Ohio), 1853. No exact date.

Densmore, Christopher. "American Anti-Slavery Society Branches in Western New York, 1837—1838." State University of New York at Buffalo ("U.B."), University Archives, an archive titled "Reform, Religion and the Underground Railroad in Western New York," derived from the *Daily Commercial Advertiser* (Buffalo, New York), July 13, 1835. http://library.buffalo.edu/archives/exhibits/old/urr/PDFs/ASS-WNY.pdf.

Densmore, Christopher. "Fugitive Slave Cases in Niagara County. A Glimpse into the Underground Railroad." Niagara County Historical Society. Lockport, NY: February 24, 2000.

Densmore, Christopher. "Underground Railroad Agents in Western New York." Revised, March 2000. http://library.buffalo.edu/archives/exhibits/old/urr/PDFs/agents.pdf.

Dietz, Suzanne Simon. "Early New York State Legislative Session Laws Concerning the Town of Porter." *Porter's Past* 36/2 (February/March 2012): 5.

Dietz, Suzanne Simon, and Karen Noonan. *Early Town of Porter Residents 1800-1829*. Youngstown, NY: BeauDesigns, 2013. Includes separate map.

Dietz, Suzanne Simon. *From Flames & Four Flags. The Town of Porter Yesterday* and *Today.* Youngstown, NY: BeauDesigns, 2012.

Dietz, Suzanne Simon. "History of Porter." Town of Porter. Niagara County. http://townofporter.net/history-of-porter.

Dietz, Suzanne Simon. *Lewiston's Underground Railroad: In a Series of Johnnie's Adventures.* Youngstown, NY: BeauDesigns, 2013. (Elementary K-4).

Dietz, Suzanne Simon. *Porter Images of America.* Mount Pleasant, SC: Arcadia Publishing Co., 2005.

Dollarhide, William. *New York. State Censuses and Substitutes.* Foreword by Gordon L. Remington. North Salt Lake, UT: Heritage Creations. Genealogical Publishing Co., Inc., 2005.

Douglass, Frederick. *Narrative of the Life of Frederick Douglas an American Slave.* Frederick Douglass, 1854; Mineola, NY: Dover Publications, Inc., Dover Books, 2006.

Douglass, Frederick. *The Life and Times of Frederick Douglass, Written by Himself.* 3rd revised edition; Boston, MA: De Wolfe & Fiske Co., 1892. First unexpanded edition, 1845; reprint Mineola, N.Y.: Dover Publications, Inc., 2003.

Drew, Benjamin. *The Refugee; or a North-Side View of Slavery, St. Catharines. The Refugee, or the Narratives of Fugitive Slaves in Canada Related by Themselves, with an Account of the History and Condition of the Colored Population of Upper Canada.* Boston, MA: John P. Jewett and Company; Cleveland, OH: Jewett, Proctor and Worthington; New York: Sheldon, Lamport and Blakeman; London: Trübner and Co., 1856. http://docsouth.unc.edu/neh/drew/drew.html.

Duling, Dennis C. *A Marginal Scribe. Studies in Matthew in Social-Scientific Perspective.* Matrix 7. Cascade Books. Eugene, OR: Wipf and Stock Publishers, 2014.

Duling, Dennis C., "Introduction" (with James Reynolds); "Peace, the 1837-1838 Rebellions, and the Civil War"; "Lewis and Elizabeth Leffman and Their Daughter Sarah"; "World War II: Another War"; "The Lake Ontario Ordnance Works and (Chemical) Waste Management"; "The Story of William Suitor, Youngstown's Rocket Propelled James Bond"; "Youngstown's NFL Connection: From Splash to Dash"; "Bibliography." In Gretchen Duling, *et al. From the Mouth of the Lower Niagara River: Stories of Four Historic Communities.* Goulah Design Group. Youngstown, NY, 2012.

Duling, Dennis C. "Memory, Collective Memory, Orality, and the Gospels." *HTS Teologiese Studies/Theological Studies* 67/1 (2011): 103-113. The A.G. van Aarde *Festschrift* online at http://www.hts.org.za/index.php/HTS/article/view/915/1496 Art. #915, 11 pages. DOI: 10.4102/hts.v67i1.915.

Duling, Dennis C. "Problems and Possibilities of Social Network Analysis from a Social-Scientific Critical Perspective: Paul's Aegean Recruitment Communities." Keynote Address of the combined meeting of the International Social Context Group and the NordForsk-Network. Helsinki-Järvenpää, Finland, June 18, 2012. Revised for the Annual Meeting of the Society of Biblical Literature, Chicago, Illinois, 2012.

Duling, Dennis C. "Social Memory and Commemoration of the Death of 'the Lord': Paul's Response to Banquet Factions at Corinth." Pp. 289-310. *Memory and Identity in Ancient Judaism and Early Christianity. A Conversation with Barry Schwartz. Semeia* Study Series. Edited by Tom Thatcher. Atlanta, GA: Society of Biblical Literature Press, 2014; Schwartz response, Pp. 332–33.

Duling, Dennis C. "The Jesus Movement and Network Analysis." *Biblical Theology Bulletin* 29/4 (1999) 156-75; *Biblical Theology Bulletin* 10/1 (2000) 3-14. Pp. 301-32 in Bruce J. Malina, Wolfgang Stegemann, and Gerd Theissen, eds. *The Social Setting of Jesus and the Gospels.* Minneapolis, MN: Fortress Press, 2002. German: "Die Jesusbewegung und die Networkanalyse." Pp. 134-57 in Bruce J. Malina, Wolfgang Stegemann, and Gerd Theissen editors, *Jesus in neuen Konteksten.* Stuttgart: Kohlhammer, 2002; Italian: "Movimento di Gesù e Analisi delle reti sociali." Pp. 180-202 in *Il nuovo Gesù storico. Paideia.* A cura di Wolfgang Stegemann, Bruce J. Malina, and Gerd Theissen. Introduzione allo studio della Bibbia, Supplementi n. 28. Religione e teologia. Brescia.

Duling, Gretchen A. *Adopting Joe: A Black Vietnamese Child.* Rutland, VT: Charles E. Tuttle Company, 1977.

Duling, Gretchen A. *A Legacy of Mutual Trust: The Diary (June 1944 – May 1946) and Letters (1944 – 2005) of Otto Herboth, World War II German Prisoner of War Interned at Fort Niagara*, New York. Youngstown, New York: Old Fort Niagara Association, Inc., 2009.

Duling, Gretchen A., Dennis C. Duling, Karen Noonan, and Toby Jewett. "Youngstown, New York, U.S.A." Pp. 123-62 in Gretchen A. Duling, Dennis Duling, Karen Noonan, Toby Jewett, James Reynolds, James Smith, Linda Fritz, Michelle Kratts, and Teresa Sharp Donaldson. *From the Mouth of the Lower Niagara River: Stories of Four Historic Communities, Commemorating 200 Years of Peace on the Border*. Niagara Greenway Approved Projected funded by the Niagara County Host Community Independent Publication. Buffalo, NY: Goulah Design Group, 2012.

Duling, Gretchen A., et al. *From the Mouth of the Lower Niagara River: Stories of Four Historic Communities, Commemorating 200 Years of Peace on the Border*. Niagara Greenway Approved Projected funded by the Niagara County Host Community Independent Publication. Buffalo, NY: Goulah Design Group, 2012.

Duling, Gretchen A. *The Journey of the French Coat: Adventures in the Wilds from Fort Niagara to the Our House Tavern* (Gallipolis, Ohio). Youngstown, New York, NY: Gretchen A. Duling, 2013.

Duling, Gretchen A. *Voices from The Recitation Bench: Oral Life Histories of Rural One-Room School House Retired Career Teachers from Southeastern Ohio*. Lewiston, NY: Edwin Mellen Press, 1997.

Dunlap, Orrin. *Niagara Gazette*, August 16, 1941.

Dunn, Edward T. *A History of Railroads in Western New York*. 2nd ed. Buffalo, NY: Canisius College Press, 2000.

Dunnigan, Brian Leigh. *A History and Guide to Old Fort Niagara*. Revised and expanded edition. Youngstown, NY: Old Fort Niagara Association, Inc., 2007.

Edwards, John B. To Gerrit Smith, February 1, 1851.

Edwards, John B. To Gerrit Smith, February 13, 1852.

Edwards, John B. To Gerrit Smith, October 12, 1850.

Egerton, Douglas R., and Judith Mulcahy. "American Colonization Society." Pp. 55-59 in Paul Finkelman, editor-in-chief, *Encyclopedia of African American History: 1619-1895 From the Colonial Period to the Age of Frederick Douglass*. Oxford, England: Oxford University Press, 2006.

"Elial Todd Foote." 1800s Antislavery Activists. http://ugrr.orbitist.com/content/foote.

Elliott, Charles. *History of the Great Secession from the Methodist Episcopal Church in the Year 1845, Eventuating in the Organization of the New Church, Entitled the "Methodist Episcopal Church, South."* Cincinnati, OH: Schwarmstedt & Poe, 1855. https://archive.org/details/historyofgreatse00elli; https://books.google.com/books?id=bB0RAAAAIAAJ&pg=PR14&lpg=PR14&dq=Genesee+Conference:+Bishop+Hedding's+addresses+on+slavery&source=bl&ots=DYZm_YUV1t&sig=XpXVThZYG8PfIy9DFcdoGYKqKWw&hl=en&sa=X&ved=0ahUKEwjQlLD869nJAhXLXh4KHUgTD7YQ6AEIHDAA#v=onepage&q=GeneseeGenesee%20Conference%3A%20Bishop%20Hedding's%20addresses%20on%20slavery&f=false.

Emerson, Catherine. "An Industrious and Worthy Woman. The Chronicle of Betsy/Mary Doyle and her Husband Andrew." *Old Fort Niagara* (November/December 2011). See "War of 1812." See Maloni, J.

Ericson, Erik McKinley, and J. Hugo Tatch. "The Mystery Still Unsolved." *The Builder Magazine* 12/9 (1926). http://www.phoenixmasonry.org/the_builder_1926_september.htm.

Evening Transcript (Boston, Massachusetts), August 12, 1853.

"Expansion Bridge 1855 Map." Mary Ann and Bill Rolland Collection. *History – National Hotel. Buffalo as an Architectural Museum*. http://buffaloah.com/a/nf/ntl/hist/map.JPG.

Experience Heritage Tours & Tourism in Youngstown, American History Happened in Youngstown. Youngstown, New York. Sponsored by the Youngstown Heritage Tours and Tourism Committee and a grant from the Niagara Falls National Heritage Area. Available at the Town of Porter Historical Society Museum, Youngstown, New York. Researched and written by Gretchen A. Duling and Karen Noonan. 2013.

Experiment (Norwalk, Ohio), August 16, 1853.

"Exploring a Common Past. Researching and Interpreting the Underground Railroad. Part 2: Using Primary Sources: the Historians' Toolbox." National Park Service. https://www.nps.gov/parkhistory/online_books/ugrr/exugrr3.htm.

"File:Smallschooner.jpg." *Wikipedia*. https://en.wikipedia.org/wiki/File:Smallschooner.jpg.

Finkelman, Paul. *An Imperfect Union. Slavery, Federalism, and Comity*. Studies in Legal History. Chapel Hill, NC: The University of North Carolina Press, 1981.

Finkelman, Paul. *Millard Fillmore*. New York, NY: Times Books, Henry Holt and Company, 2011.

Finkelman, Paul. "Slave Transit." Pp. 1422 in Peter R. Eisenstadt and laura-Eve Moss, *The Encyclopedia of New York State*. Syracuse, NY: Syracuse University Press, 2005. https://books.google.com/books?id=tmHEm5ohoCUC&pg=PA1422&lpg=PA1422&dq=New+York+State+-+%22nine+months+law%22&source=bl&ots=MiA7R5w3wb&sig=PMLON8_8x_gQiRt1OpI3ucAfonc&hl=en&sa=X&ved=0ahUKEwjA6KOS2pvQAhVN6WMKHXQRB4AQ6AEIJDAC#v=onepage&q=New%20York%20State%20-%20%22nine%20months%20law%22&f=false.

Foley, Robert J. "Crossing the Niagara Part I: The Ferries." *Niagara Sunday Shopping News*, Niagara Falls, Ontario, September 16, 1990.

Foner, Eric. *Gateway to Freedom: The Hidden History of the Underground Railroad*. New York, NY: W.W. Norton & Company, 2015.

Foote, E. T. *Antislavery Scrapbook*. The New York Chautauqua County Historical Society. N.D.

Ford, Benjamin Louis. *Lake Ontario Maritime Cultural Landscape*. Dissertation Texas A&M University, August 2009. http://nautarch.tamu.edu/Theses/pdf-files/Ford-PhD2009.pdf.

Forrester, Glenn C. *Niagara Falls and the Glacier*. Hicksville, NY: Exposition Press, 1976.

Frazier, Patricia. "Niagara's Negroes Kept Vigil at Jail." *Niagara Advance, Historical Issue* (1976). Quotes a letter of Oliver Johnson, editor of the *National Anti-Slavery Standard*, to James Miller McKim, October 11, 1860.

Frederick Douglass's Paper, August 12, 1853; January 12, 1855. May 4, 1855; July 27, 1855.

Freeman, Linton C. *The Development of Social Network Analysis. A Study in the Sociology of Science*. Vancouver, BC: Empirical Press, 2004.

French, J. H. *Gazetteer of the State of New York: Embracing a Comprehensive View of the Geography, Geology, and General History of the State, and a Complete History and Description. Every County, City, Town, Village, and Locality. With Full Tables of Statistics Sold only by Subscription*, 1860.

Friend of Man, October 3, 1836; January 31, 1838; Vol. 2, February 1838.

Fritz, Jean. *Brady*. New York: Puffin Books, 1960. (Youth).

Fritz, Linda, with Susan Allen, Helena Copeland, Maureen Ott, and Paulette Peggs. "Queenston." Pp. 45-78 in Gretchen A. Duling, *et al.*, *From the Mouth of the Lower Niagara River: Stories of Four Historic Communities, Commemorating 200 Years of Peace on the Border*. Niagara Greenway Approved Projected funded by the Niagara County Host Community Independent Publication. Buffalo, NY: Goulah Design Group, 2012.

From the Mouth of the Lower Niagara River: Stories of Four Historic Communities, Commemorating 200 Years of Peace on our Border. Available at Historical Association of Lewiston, Lewiston, NY; Town of Porter Historical Society Museum, Youngstown, NY; Niagara Historical Society and Museum, Niagara-on-the-Lake, ON, Canada. Researched and written by: Gretchen A. Duling, Dennis C. Duling, Karen Noonan, Teresa Sharpe Richardson, Michelle Kratts, James Reynolds and Linda Fritz. 2012.

Frost, Karolyn Smardz, and Veta Smith Tucker. *A Fluid Frontier. Slavery, Resistance, and the Underground railroad in the Detroit River Borderland*. Foreword by David W. Blight. Detroit, MI: Wayne State University Press, 2016.

"Fugitive Slave Meeting. The Friends of Lberty[*sic*]." Broadside. Administrative Commission, Park Presbyterian Church, Newark, NY. Discussion with David Green Wheelbanks.

Fulton History.com. http://www.fultonhistory.com/Fulton.html.

Gaines, Wesley John. *The Negro and the White Man*. Philadelphia, PA: A. M. E. Publishing House, 1897.

Gates, Henry Louis, Jr. "100 Amazing Facts about the Negro." *The African Americans. Many Rivers to Cross*. http://www.pbs.org/wnet/african-americans-many-rivers-to-cross/history/who-really-ran-the-underground-railroad/.

Gara, Larry. *The Liberty Line: The Legend of the Underground Railroad*. Lexington, KY: The University of Kentucky Press, 1961. Reprint 1996.

"Garrison and Douglass: Friendship and Estrangement." *Pilgrim Pathways. Notes for a Diaspora People*. https://pilgrimpathways.wordpress.com/2010/07/29/garrison-and-douglass-friendship-and-estrangement/.

Geil, Samuel. *Niagara Falls and Vicinity*. Philadelphia, PA: S. Geil and J. L. Delp, 1853.

Gellman, David N. *Emancipating New York: The Politics of Slavery and Freedom, 1777—1827. Antislavery, Abolition, and the Atlantic World*. Baton Rouge, LA: Louisiana State University Press, 2006.

"Gerrit Smith Estate National Historic Landmark, Peterboro, New York, The." http://www.gerritsmith.org/.

Goller, Catherine. 615 Main Street, Youngstown, New York. Interview with Dennis Duling.

Gould, Marcus T. C., assisted by H. Fowler. *The Trial of Alexander McLeod, for the Murder of Amos Durfee, at the Burning and Destruction of the Steamboat Caroline, by the Canadians, December 29th, 1837*. New York, NY: Gould, Banks & Co., 1841.

"Governor Hung; 1853; Schooner." Great Lakes Maritime Database. http://quod.lib.umich.edu/t/tbnms1ic/x-60238/1.

Granger, F. H. "Newark Ferry House, Navy Hall, Tavern, 1870." Painting. Niagara Historical Society & Museum, Niagara-on-the-Lake, Ontario, Canada. Sarah Maloney Kaufman, Managing Director.

"'Great Cazenovia Fugitive Slave Law Convention' August 21 and 22, 1850, The." Daniel H. Weiskotten argues that Theodore Weld is in the photo. http://www.rootsweb.ancestry.com/~nyccazen/Shorts/1850Convention.html. Photo taken by Ezra Greenleaf Weld. See Humphreys, *Agitate! Agitate! Agitate!* The negative original is in the Madison County Historical Society (Heritage No. 19, 1994); the reverse with the correct positioning is in the Getty Museum.

Green, J. D. *Narrative of the Life of J. D. Green, a Runaway Slave, from Kentucky. Containing an Account of His Three Escapes in 1839, 1846, and 1848. Hudderfield, England:* Henry Fielding, Pack Horse Yard, 1864. http://www.docsouth.unc.edu/neh/greenjd/greenjd.html.

Greenwood, Barbara. *The Last Safe House*. New York, New York: Scholastic, 1998. (Youth).

Griffler, Keith, P. *Front Line of Freedom*. Lexington, KY: University Press of Kentucky, 2004.

Guare, John. *Six Degrees of Separation*. A play. 1990.

"Guide to the Lyman A. Spalding Papers, 1811-1864." Collection Number 522, Division of Rare and Manuscript Collections. Cornell University Library. http://rmc.library.cornell.edu/EAD/htmldocs/RMM00522.html.

Gullickson, Aaron. "Black/White Interracial Marriage Trends, 1850—2000." *Journal of Family History* 31/3 (July 2006): 299-301.

Hagedorn, Ann. *Beyond the River: The Untold Story of the Heroes of the Underground Railroad*. New York, NY: Simon & Schuster, 2002.

Haight-Eckert, Mary Jane. "Rev Glezen Fillmore." *Find a Grave*. http://www.findagrave.com/cgi-bin/fg.cgi?page=gr&GRid=22291683.

Haines, Jesse. Surveyor and Cartographer. Made many maps of Youngstown.

Harper's Weekly, May 9, 1863. Thomas Nast cartoon "Contrabands Coming into our Lines Under the Proclamation." In Robert C. Kennedy, "On This Day," *New York Times*, 2001. https://www.nytimes.com/learning/general/onthisday/harp/0509.html.

Harris-Perry [formerly Harris-Lacewell], Melissa Victoria. *Barbershops, Bibles, BET: Everyday Talk and Black Political Thought*. Princeton, NJ: Princeton University Press, 2004.

Hartsell, Mark. "Rare Photo of Harriet Tubman Preserved." Library of Congress. https://medium.com/@librarycongress/a-new-view-of-harriet-tubman-e1f468d31e68

Hendrick, George, and Willene Hendrick. *Fleeing for Freedom*. Chicago, IL: Ivan R. Dee, 2004.

"Henry and Mary Bibb, Publishers of the Voice of the Fugitive Newspaper." The Harriet Tubman Institute for Research on Africa and Its Diasporas. http://tubman.info.yorku.ca/educational-resources/breaking-the-chains/toronto/henry-and-mary-bibb/.

Henry, Natasha L. *Emancipation Day: Celebrating Freedom in Canada*. Toronto, ON: National Heritage Books, 2010.

Hilton, George W. *Lake Michigan Passenger Steamers*. Ford, CA: Ford University Press, 2002.

"Hiram Wilson Biography (September 25, 1803 - April 16, 1864)." Hiram Wilson Project Website. http://www.uwo.ca/huron/promisedland/wilson/Biography.html.

"Hiram Wilson Papers, 1835-1856." Oberlin College Archives. http://www.oberlinlibstaff.com/archon/?p=collections/controlcard&id=277.

"Hiram Wilson." Oberlin College. http://www.oberlin.edu/external/EOG/LaneDebates/RebelBios/HiramWilson.html.

"Hiram Wilson." *Wikipedia*. https://en.wikipedia.org/wiki/Hiram_Wilson.

"History. 1790 Overview." United States Census Bureau. https://www.census.gov/history/www/through_the_decades/overview/1790.html

"History and Development of Great Lakes Water Craft." Minnesota's Lake Superior Shipwrecks. http://www.mnhs.org/places/nationalregister/shipwrecks/mpdf/mpdf2.php

Historical Society of the Town of Porter. *The Town of Porter, 1776-1976. A Bicentennial History*. Youngstown, NY: Historical Society of the Town of Porter, 1976.

History of Niagara County, N. Y., with Illustrations Descriptive of its Scenery, Private Residences, Public Buildings, Fine Blocks, and Important Manufactories, and Portraits of Old Pioneers and Prominent Residents. New York, NY: Sanford and Company, 1878. https://archive.org/details/cu31924100387392.

History of the Genesee Annual Conference, from its Organization by Bishops Asbury and McKendree, from its Organization by Bishops Asbury and McKendree in 1810 to the Year 1884 by the Rev. F. W. Conable. 2nd ed. New York, NY: Phillips & Hung, 1885.

"History of Old Fort Niagara." Old Fort Niagara. http://www.oldfortniagara.org/history.

"History of Steam navigation on Lake Ontario." *Oswego Commercial Times*; reprinted in the *Buffalo Morning Express*, September 16, 1847; WMHS History of Steam. http://www.wmhs.org/history.html.

"History of the Durham Boat." Durham Historical Society. http://www.durhamhistoricalsociety.org/history2.html http://archive.org/stream/cu31924029471152/cu31924029471152_djvu.txt.

History of Wayne County, New York. Philadelphia, PA: Everts, Ensign, and Everts, 1877.

Hoeltzel, Robert L. *Hometown History, Village of Newark, Town of Arcadia*. Newark, NY: G. McCellan of Arcadia Historical Society, 2000.

Hoeltzel, Robert L. *A History of the Presbyterian Church, Newark, New York, 1825-1980*. Lyons, NY: Wilprint, Inc., 1982.

Hoeltzel, Robert L. "Introduction, John P. VanDeusen." In a letter of Christopher Davis (Museum Director of the Newark-Arcadia Historical Society and Museum) to Gretchen *on History. Magazine of the American Historical Association*. https://www.historians.org/publications-and-directories/perspectives-on-history/march-2013/the-frailty-of-historical-truth.

Holly Standard, April 30, 1891.

Hood, Fred J. "Methodist Bishops and Abolitionism." *Border States On-Line* maintained by Harold D. Tallant, Department of History, Georgetown College. Middle Tennessee State University, 1973, 2000. https://www.google.com/#q=Fred+J.+Hood%2C+%E2%80%9CMethodist+Bishops+and+Abolitionism%2C%E2%80%9D.

"Hoofbeats Over the Water: I.N.A. Research on Horse-Powered Ferryboats." The Institute of Nautical Archaeology (I.N.A.), affiliated with the Center for Maritime Archaeology and Conservation at Texas A&M University. http://nautarch.tamu.edu/newworld/pastprojects/LChorseferry.htm.

Hopkins, Brian, and Robin J. Wilson. "The Truth About Königsberg." https://www.maa.org/sites/default/files/pdf/upload_library/22/Polya/hopkins.pdf.

Howard, Edwin L., and Virginia M. Howard. *The History of Youngstown, New York.* Occasional Contributions of the Youngstown Historical Society No. 5. Lockport, NY: Niagara County Historical Society, 1951; revised and reissued by the Town of Porter Historical Society, ed. Marjorie L. Stratton, Youngstown, NY, 2007.

Howard, Edwin L. "Transportation in Porter, 1840–1910." P. 16 in *The Town of Porter 1776 – 1976. A Bicentennial History.* The Local History Sub-Committee of the Bicentennial Commission of the Town of Porter, 1976.

Howard, Edwin L., and Virginia M. Howard. "The History of Youngstown." *The Youngstown Centennial Magazine 1854-1954.*

Howard, Virginia. "John Carter, Noted Pioneer & Youngstown Area Builder." *Niagara Gazette*, Sept. 28, 1953. http://images.maritimehistoryofthegreatlakes.ca/63722/data?n=1; https://books.google.com/books?id=HDc9AAAAYAAJ&pg=PA147&lpg=PA147&dq=The+1848+steamboat+Ontario&source=bl&ots=Ai78jmhFhQ&sig=-PUeR7GHU1gipz5a88Xl1traM0k&hl=en&sa=X&ved=0CD4Q6AEwB2oVChMI47X2_fyYyQIVQ9QeCh2DuQYk#v=onepage&q=The%201848%20steamboat%20Ontario&f=false.

Hughes, Alan. "Merrit's Survey and the Tunnel to Nowhere [Welland Canal]." Thorold and Beaverdams Historical Society. http://www.tbhs.ca/hughes/tunnel.html.

Humphreys, Hugh. *Agitate! Agitate! Agitate! The Great Fugitive Slave Law Convention and its Rare Daguerreotype.* Madison County Heritage, 1994.

Hunt, Sanford. "Discourse of Memorial of Rev. Glezen Fillmore." Delivered in the Grace Methodist Episcopal Church, Buffalo, New York. February 14, 1875. Pp. 104-11 in Hunt, *History of the Methodist Episcopal Church in Buffalo from its Origin to the Close of 1892.* Buffalo, NY: H. H. Otis & Sons, 1893.

"Illustrations of the Anti-Slavery Society Almanac of 1840." Library of Congress, Portfolio 248, Folder 1 as part of "Broadsides, Leaflets, and Pamphlets from America and Europe. Online at "An American Time Capsule: Three Centuries of Broadsides and Other Painted Ephemera." http://memory.loc.gov/cgi-bin/query/h?ammem/rbpebib:@field(NUMBER+@band(rbpe+24800100)).

Index to the Session Laws of the State of New York with All Changes and Modifications Noted Under a Single Alphabet from Session of 1775 down to Session of 1897. Edited by William H. Silvernail. New York and Albany, NY: Banks and Brothers, 1897.

James, Thomas. *Life of Rev. Thomas James, by Himself.* Rochester, NY: Post Express Printing Company, 1886. Online at http://www.math.buffalo.edu/~sww/0history/thomas.james.narrative.html.

Jansari, A., and A. J. Parkin. "Things that go Bump in Your Life: Explaining the Reminiscence Bump in Autobiographical Memory." *Psychology and Aging* 11 (1996): 85–91.

"Jerry Rescue and its Aftermath, The." The Laboratory of Abolitionism, Libel, and Treason: Syracuse and the Underground Railroad. A Special Exhibition at Syracuse University. http://library.syr.edu/digital/exhibits/u/undergroundrr/case3.htm.

Johnson, J. F., editor. *Proceedings of the General Anti-Slavery Convention, Called by the Committee of the British and Foreign Anti-Slavery Society, and Held in London from Tuesday June 13th to Tuesday June 20th, 1843.* British and Foreign Anti-Slavery Society, N.D.

Johnson, Oliver. Editor of the *National Anti-Slavery Standard*. To James Miller McKim, October 11, 1860. Quoted by Foner, *Gateway to Freedom*, 274.

"John P. Parker, Conductor, on the Underground Railroad." History Matters. The U.S. Survey Course on the Web. http://historymatters.gmu.edu/d/6232/.

"John P. Parker House." Aboard the Underground Railroad. National Park Service. U.S. Department of the Interior. https://www.nps.gov/nr/travel/Underground/oh2.htm.

Journal of the General Conference of the Methodist Episcopal Church. New York, NY: G. Lane & C. B. Tippett, 1844. https://books.google.com/books?id=OHURAAAAIAAJ&pg=PA27&lpg=PA27&dq=Slavery+The+Committee+ of+Five+in+the+Genesee+Conference&source=bl&ots=CXCRvlhexD&sig=42sxZgcKJqbBVB7P_SagY82hmhg &hl=en&sa=X&ved=0ahUKEwjPhtau8tnJAhUF7R4KHQsxC7oQ6AEIHDAA#v=onepage&q=Slavery%20The% 20Committee%20of%20Five%20in%20the%20Genesee%20Conference&f=false.

Journal (St. Catharines, Ontario), August 11, 1853.

Kadushin, Charles. Understanding Social Networks. Theories, Concepts, and Findings. Oxford, UK: University Press, 2012.

Kalida Venture, The (Boston, Massachusetts), August 19, 1853.

Karinthy, Frigyes. *Chains*. A play. 1929.

Kennard, Jim. "Shipwreck Explorers Discover 1850's Schooner in Lake Ontario." *Shipwreck World* (December 14, 2009). http://www.shipwreckworld.com/articles/shipwreck-explorers-discover-1850s-schooner-lake-ontario.

Kennard, Jim. "Horse Powered Ferry Boat Discovered in Lake Champlain." *Shipwreck World* (July 2, 2005). http://www.shipwreckworld.com/articles/horse-powered-ferry-boat-discovered-in-lake-champlain.

Kent, James. *Commentaries on American Law*. Vol. 2. Boston, MA: Little, Brown and Company, 1860. https://books.google.com/books?id=169XAAAAcAAJ&pg=PA295&lpg=PA295&dq=every+negro,+mulatto, +or+mustee,+within+the+state,+born+before+the+4th+of+July,+1799&source=bl&ots=HMD4TUb6KG&sig =j4KTVIz1ZV_soG7xGmxeCdMK4wo&hl=en&sa=X&ved=0CCIQ6AEwAmoVChMI2qv70djHyAlVWNljCh0c5Q pF#v=onepage&q=every%20negro%2C%20mulatto%2C%20or%20mustee%2C%20within%20the%20state %2C%20born%20before%20the%204th%20of%20July%2C%201799&f=false.

Kratts, Michelle, and Teresa Sharp. "Lewiston, New York, U.S.A." Pp. 5-45 in Gretchen A. Duling, et al. From the Mouth of the Lower Niagara River: Stories of Four Historic Communities, Commemorating 200 Years of Peace on the Border. Niagara Greenway Approved Projected funded by the Niagara County Host Community Independent Publication. Buffalo, NY: Goulah Design Group, 2012.

Kratts, Michelle. "Bringing Lost Souls Home: John Morrison, a Hero of Niagara." In "Hearts of War Part One: The War of 1812 at Oakwood Cemetery." Oakwood Cemetery, Niagara Falls, Series. Online at Kratt's Corner, March 26, 2013. http://myoakwoodcemetery.com/kratts-korner/.

Kratts, Michelle. Lewiston Public Library Genealogist and former City of Niagara Falls Historian. Interviews with Gretchen and Dennis Duling.

Land Contract. Gerrit Smith to Ben Hockley, February 3, 1847.

Larson, Kate Clifford. *Bound for the Promised Land. Harriet Tubman, Portrait of an American Hero*. New York, NY: Ballantine Books, 2004.

Laws of the State of New -York, Passed at the Fifty-Ninth Session, of the Legislature, Begun and Held at the City of Albany, the Fifth Day of January, 1836. Albany, NY: E. Croswell, 1836.

Laws of the State of New-York, Passed at the Forty-ninth Session of the Legislature, Begun and Held at the City of Albany, The Third day of January, 1826. Albany, NY: William Gould & Co.; New-York, NY: Gould & Banks; E. Croswell, Printer, 1826.

Laws of the State of New-York, Revised and Passed at the Thirty-Sixth Session, of the Legislature, with Marginal Notes and References, Vol. 2. 2 vols. Revisers William P. Van Ness and John Woodworth. Albany: C. H. Southwick & Co., 1813.

Lawson, John D. *American State Trials: A Collection of the Important and Interesting Criminal Trials which have Taken Place in the United States, from the Beginning of Government to the Present Day*. Volume 7, No. 8: 61—416. St Louis, MO: F. H. Thomas Law Book Co., 1917.

Lawson, John D. "The Trial of Alexander McLeod for the Burning of the Steamboat *Caroline*, and the Murder of Amos Durfee, Utica, New York, 1841." *American State Trials: A collection of the Important and Interesting Criminal Trials which have taken place in the United States, from the beginning of our Government to the Present Day*. Vol. 7, 61—416. St Louis, MO: F. H. Thomas Law Book Co., 1917.

Lester, S. J. (Cora Woodward [Anderson] DuLaney). *Extract of Diary or Farm Journal of William Anderson of "Grassland" 1853 to 1875 and Certain Related Document*, 1965. Footnotes prepared in 1987-1988 by Marvin H. Anderson.

Lewis, Clarence O. "Capt. Van Cleve, Pioneer, of Lewiston, Started Sailing Great Lakes in 1826." *Niagara Falls Gazette*. October 15, 1958; reprinted in Lewiston's *Union-Sun and Journal*. October 16, 1958.

Lewis, Clarence O. "Early County Plank Roads Entered Through Toll Gates," Lockport *Union-Sun and Journal* (July 23, 1851). http://fultonhistory.com/Newspaper%2018/Lockport%20NY%20Union%20Sun%20Journal/Lockport%20NY%20Union%20Sun%20Journal%201953/Lockport%20NY%20Union%20Sun%20Journal%201953%20-%202828.pdf.Lewis, Clarence O. "Early Lewiston Resident had Colorful Lake Career." *Union Sun and Journal*. October 26, 1953.

Lewis, Clarence O. "Niagara County History: Carriage Era is Recalled." Town of Porter Society Museum file. An undocumented newspaper copy.

Lewis, Clarence O. "Old County Communities Located." *Niagara Falls Gazette*. February 5, 1964.

Lewis, Harold T. *Yet with A Steady Beat: The African American Struggle for Recognition in the Episcopal Church*. Valley Forge, PA: Trinity Press International. 1996.

Lewis, Miss G. "The Underground Railroad in Virginia. Conductors and Agents." National Humanities Center. Toolbox Library: Primary Sources in U.S. History and Literature. *Register's office Lib no. 2 of manumissions page 62 - / W F Slocum Register*. Quoted by William Still, *The Underground Railroad*, 111. http://nationalhumanitiescenter.org/pds/maai/identity/text2/text2read.htm;

Lewiston Sesquicentennial 1822—1972 in Celebration of its 150th Year of Historical Significance on the Niagara Frontier, The. Lewiston, NY: 1972.

Liberator, The. An abolitionist weekly edited and published by William Lloyd Garrison, 1831-1865. http://www.accessible-archives.com/collections/the-liberator/. Also http://fair-use.org/the-liberator/; http://www.theliberatorfiles.com/.

Locker, Donald E. *Lewis Leffman: Ordnance Sergeant, United States Army*. Lockport, NY: Occasional Collections of the Niagara County Historical Society 22, 1974.

Loguen, Jemain Wesley (with John Thomas?). *The Rev. J. W. Loguen, as a Slave and as a Freeman*. Syracuse, N.Y.: J.G.K. Truair & Co., 1859. Copyright: University of North Carolina at Chapel Hill (1999). Online: http://docsouth.unc.edu/neh/loguen/loguen.html.

Lossing, Benson J. *The Pictorial Field-Book of the War of 1812; or, Illustrations, by Pen and Pencil, of the History, Biography, Scenery, Relics, and Traditions of the Last War for American Independence*. New York, NY: Harper & Brothers, 1868.

Lowenthal, David. "The Frailty of Historical Truth: Learning Why Historians Inevitably Err." *Perspectives on History. Magazine of the American Historical Association*. March, 2013. https://www.historians.org/publications-and-directories/perspectives-on-history/march-2013/the-frailty-of-historical-truth.

Lowenthal, David. *The Past is a Foreign Country*. Cambridge, UK: Cambridge University Press, 1985; revised 2015.

Maloni, J. "22-foot Mural of Lewiston Youngstown Frontier Railway to be Unveiled Sept. 19 [2011]." *Niagara Frontier Publications. Niagara Wheatfield Tribune, Island Dispatch, Lewiston-Porter Sentinel*. September 6, 2011. http://www.wnypapers.com/news/article/current/2011/09/06/103605/22-foot-mural-of-lewiston-youngstown-frontier-railway-to-be-unveiled-sept.-19.

Mansfield J. B., editor. *History of the Great Lakes*. Volume 1. Chicago, IL: J. H. Beers & Co., 1899. Transcribed for the *Maritime History of the Great Lakes Site* by Walter Lewis and Brendon Baillod. Halton Hills, ON: Maritime History of the Great Lakes, 2003.

Manumission certificate for a slave named George, signed by Radcliffe and Riker, New York City, 24 April 1817. Permission of the New York Public Library, Slavery and Abolition Collection, Thomas Lisanti, Manager, Permissions and Reproduction Services. For other examples of Deeds of Manumission from several states, see the New York Heritage Digital Collections, Slavery Collection. http://cdm16694.contentdm.oclc.org/cdm/search/searchterm/manumission.

"Map of Niagara County, New York (1852)". https://www.loc.gov/resource/g3803n.la000522/

Maritime History of the Great Lakes. http://www.maritimehistoryofthegreatlakes.ca/.

"Married Women's Property Laws." Library of Congress.
https://memory.loc.gov/ammem/awhhtml/awlaw3/property_law.html.

"Mary Ann Shadd [Cary]." Blackpast.org. http://www.blackpast.org/gah/cary-mary-ann-shadd-1823-1893#sthash.2JQFdMdh.dpuf.

"Mason, James Murray. 1911 *Encyclopædia Britannica*, Vol. 17."
https://en.wikisource.org/wiki/1911_Encyclop%C3%A6dia_Britannica/Mason,_James_Murray.

Maloni, J. "Maziarz Announces War of 1812 Heroine Betsy Doyle awarded Women of Distinction [Catherine Emerson]." *Lewiston-Porter Sentinel*. Mar 16, 2012,
http://www.wnypapers.com/news/article/current/2012/03/16/105821/maziarz-announces-war-of-1812-heroine-betsy-doyle-awarded-women-of-distinction.

McDaniel, George W. *Hearth & Home: Preserving a People's Culture*. American Civilization. Philadelphia: Temple University Press, 1982.

McDaniel, George W. "Housing." Pp. 341-46 in Randall M. Miller and John David Smith, *Dictionary of Afro-American Slavery, Updated, with a New Introduction and Bibliography.* Westport, CN; London, UK: Praeger, 1997.

McLaury, G. Everell. To Rev. Charles Andrew Lawrence, November 19, 1908. In the Eden, Erie County, New York Methodist Episcopal Church 95th Anniversary Booklet. 1813—1908.

McManus, Edgar J. *A History of Negro Slavery in New York*. Forward by Richard B. Morris; Syracuse, NY: Syracuse University Press, 1966.

Merritt, Richard D. *On Common Ground. The Ongoing Story of the Commons in Niagara-on-the-Lake.* Toronto, ON: Dundurn, 2012.

Milgram, Stanley. "The Small World Problem." *Psychology Today* 1 (1967): 61–67.

"Millard Fillmore. Key Events." The Miller Center at the University of Virginia.
http://millercenter.org/president/fillmore/key-events.

Miller, Connie A. *Frederick Douglas, American Hero. An International Icon of the Nineteenth Century*. Xlibris Corporation, 2008.

Mills, Quincy T. *Cutting Along the Color Line: Black Barbers and Barber Shops in America*. Philadelphia, PA: University of Pennsylvania Press, 2013.

Mills, Quncy T. "Straight Razors and Social Justice: The Empowering Evolution of Black Barbershops." Interview with Hunter Oatman-Stanford. *Collectors Weekly* (2014): 1-22.
http://www.collectorsweekly.com/articles/the-empowering-evolution-of-black-barbershops/.

Moments from the Past and Beyond. 175th Anniversary Booklet of the First Presbyterian Church Society of Youngstown, NY, The. 1998.

"The Morgan Affair." A section of "History of Old Fort Niagara." http://www.oldfortniagara.org/history.

Morgan, William. Illustrations of Masonry by One of the Fraternity Who Has Devoted Thirty Years to the Subject. http://www.sacred-texts.com/mas/morgan/morg04.htm. Revised and corrected by George R. Crafts as The Mysteries of Freemasonry. All the Degrees of the Order Conferred in a Master's Lodge. Project Gutenberg e-book. http://www.gutenberg.org/files/18136/18136-h/18136-h.htm.

Murphy, Carol L. *A Brief History of the Underground Railroad in Niagara County New York.* The McClew Interpretive Center, Inc. at Murphy Orchards, 2402 McClew Road, Burt, NY 14028. Made possible by a grant from the Niagara Council of the Arts. Produced by Mark Beckstein of White Bird Video Productions, © 2001.

Murray, David. "Hands Across the Border: The Abortive Extradition of Solomon Moseby." *Canadian Review of American Studies* 30/2 (2000) 187-209. Reprinted in *Colonial Justice: Justice, Morality, and Crime in the Niagara District, 1791-1849*. Toronto, ON: University of Toronto Press, 2002. Chapter 10, 196-216.

Murray, David. *Colonial Justice: Justice, Morality, and Crime in the Niagara District, 1791-1849*. Toronto, ON: University of Toronto Press, 2002.

"Muskingum River Underground Railroad Corridor." Remarkable Ohio. Ohio History Connection. Ohio Historical Society Markers, Roscoe Village. http://www.remarkableohio.org/index.php?/category/229.

Myers, John L. "The Beginning of Anti-Slavery Agencies in New York State, 1833-1836." *New York History* 43/2 (April 1962): 149-181.

http://www.maritimehistoryofthegreatlakes.ca/GreatLakes/Documents/HGL/default.asp?ID=c023#.

"National Abolition Hall of Fame and Museum. Gerrit Smith (1797-1874)." http://www.nationalabolitionhalloffameandmuseum.org/gsmith.html.

National Anti-Slavery Standard, August 20, 1853.

National Park Service. "Autumn 1812: Betsy Doyle Helps Operate a Cannon to Defend Fort Niagara." https://www.nps.gov/articles/betsy-doyle.htm.

National Underground Railroad Network to Freedom. *Discovering the Underground Railroad: Junior Ranger Activity Book*. Atlanta, Georgia: National Park Service Southeast Region. No publication date. (Parents; teachers; ages 5-6 complete 3 activities; ages 7-10 complete 6 activities and ages 10 and older complete 10 activities. For further information: http://www.nps.gov/ugrr.

Newby-Alexander, Cassandra. *Waterways to Freedom. The Underground Journey from Hampton Roads*. Norfolk, Virginia: Convention & Visitors Bureau. Norfolk, Virginia: JR Norfolk, ND.

Newman, Marc. "Slavery and Insurrections in the Colonial Province of New York." *Social Education* 59/3 (1995): 125-29. http://www.socialstudies.org/sites/default/files/publications/se/5903/590301.html.

"New York Central Railroad 1853–1860." Old Rail History.com. http://oldrailhistory.com/index.php?option=com_content&view=article&id=211&Itemid=245.

New-York Daily Tribune, October 3, 1855.

New York Laws, 1841, CCXLVII.

"New York Slave Laws: Colonial Period." http://law2.umkc.edu/faculty/projects/ftrials/negroplot/slavelaws.html.

New York Spectator, The, June 7, 1827.

New York Spectator (Rochester, New York), June 7, 1827.

New York Times, June 15, 1884; May 25, 1885.

New York Traveller, The; Containing Railroad, Steamboat, Canal Packet, and Stage Routes, Throughout the State of New-York, Also, Other Information Useful to Travellers. New York, NY: J. Disturnell, 1845.

Niagara County News, June 9, 1882; September 21, 1883.

Niagara Democrat and Lockport Balance, February 5, 1840.

Niagara Falls Gazette, August 25, 1883.

Niagara Democrat, April 24, 1844.

Niagara Democrat (Lockport), April 24, 1844.

Niagara Gazette, 1986. Permission from Illustrator, Andrew Skish, *Niagara Co. Underground Railroad Conductors*, Niagara Falls, New York.

Niagara Mail (Niagara[on-the-Lake], Ontario), Wednesday, August 10, 1853.

"Nishnabotna Ferry House." City of Lewiston, Cass County, Iowa. Cass County Mormon Trails Association. http://www.cityoflewis.com/index.php/our-town/ferry-house.

Noonan, Karen. Emails with Gretchen and Dennis Duling.

North American (Toronto, Ontario), Friday, August 5, 1853 (semi-weekly).

North American (Toronto, Ontario), August 11, 1853.

Norton, Charles D. "The Old Black Rock Ferry." 1863. Publications of the Buffalo Historical Society, 1879, 91-112. Transcribed from the original by Walter Lewis (Haltom Hills, ON: Maritime History of the Great Lakes, 2003). http://www.maritimehistoryofthegreatlakes.ca/documents/BlackRockFerry/default.asp?ID=c1.

"Obit—Thomas Root of Pekin, NY, 1903." http://boards.ancestry.com/surnames.root/843/mb.ashx.

Official Index to the Unconsolidated Laws, Being the Special, Private and Local Statutes of the State of New York from February 1, 1778 to December 31, 1919. "State of New York, Ferries Authorized, Year 1811." Index to Unconsolidated Laws, Niagara River, Youngstown, Year 1811, Chapter 246, pp. 460, 1033. Albany, NY: J. B. Lyon, 1920.

Official Index to the Unconsolidated Laws, Being the Special, Private and Local Statutes of the State of New York from February 1, 1778 to December 31, 1919. Albany, New York: J. B. Lyon Company, 1920.

"Old Welland Canal Fields Guide, The." http://oldwellandcanals.wikidot.com/the-deep-cut.

Onen, James. To *The Youngstown News*, December 24, 1908, titled "Recollections of James Onen. Youngstown's Early Days." Town of Porter Historical Museum. Also a notice of Vee Housman, Town of Porter Historian, N.D. http://www.newspaperabstracts.com/link.php?action=detail&id=28591. http://archiver.rootsweb.ancestry.com/th/read/NY-OLD-NEWS/2006-09/1157310292.

"Orleans County Towns." http://orleanshistory.org/general-information. http://en.wilipedia.org/wiki/File:Niagara_County_NY_map_labeled.png.

Orr, J. W. *Full Directions for Visiting the Cataract and its Neighboring Scenes. Illustrated by Numerous Maps, Charts, and Engravings, From Original Surveys and Designs*. Glegg, Thomas. Buffalo, NY: Press of Salisbury and Clapp, 1842.

Orr, J. W. *Pictorial Guide to the Falls of Niagara: A Manual for Visitors, Giving and Account of this Stupendous Natural Wonder; and All. The Objects of Curiosity in its Vicinity; With Every Historical Incident of Interest.* Buffalo, NY: Salisbury and Klapp, 1842.

Oswego Commercial Times and Buffalo Morning Express, September 16, 1847.

Oswego Free Press, November 28, 1832; December 4, 1833.

"Our Rights as Men." William J. Watkins. Harvard Black Abolitionist Archives 13923. Harvard University Widener Library Anti-Slavery Pamphlets. http://research.udmercy.edu/digital_collections/baa/Watkins_13923spe.pdf.

Palmer, John C. *The Morgan Affair and Anti-Masonry*. Whitefish, MT: Kessinger Publishing, Rare Reprints, 1924.

Parker, John P. *His Promised Land: The Autobiography of John P. Parker, Former Slave and Conductor on the Underground Railroad*. Edited by Stuart Seely Sprague; New York, NY: W. W. Norton, 1996.

Percy, John W. *Buffalo-Niagara Connections: A New Regional History of the Niagara Link*. Buffalo, NY: Western New York Heritage Press, 2007.

Percy, John W. "Pioneer Preacher Glezen Fillmore: A 200-year Heritage on the Niagara Frontier 1809 – 2009." *Western New York Heritage* (Winter 2009): 56-63.

Perez, Marjory Allen. *Final Stop, FREEDOM! The Underground Experience in Wayne County, New York*. Rochester, NY: Heron Bends Productions © Marjory Allen Perez, 2017.

Pettit, Eber M. *Sketches in the History of the Underground Railroad*. Westfield, NY: Chautauqua Region Press, 1879. Introduction by Willard McKinstry. Reprinted with an "Introduction" and "Notes to Pettit's *Sketches*" by Paul Leone. Westfield, NY: Chautauqua Region Press, 1999.

Phillips, Mrs. 614 Main Street, Youngstown, New York. Interview with Dennis Duling.

Pierce, Preston E., *"And who was she anyhow?" Sarah Hopkins Bradford, Biographer of Harriet Tubman*. Canandaigua, NY: Ontario County Historical Society, 2009.

Pierce, Visit, and Clarence Bolden. "The Summative History of the Episcopal Church Policies Regarding Slavery and Segregation." North Pole, AK: St. Jude's Jubilee Center, 2006.

Plaindealer, The (New York, New York), December 3, 1836.

Pool, William, editor. *Landmarks of Niagara County, New York*. Syracuse, NY: D. Mason and Co., 1897.

Power, Michael, and Nancy Butler (with Joy Ormsby). *Slavery and Freedom in Niagara.* Niagara-on-the-Lake, ON: The Niagara Historical Society, 1993. Reprint 2000.

Power, Michael. "Simcoe and Slavery." Pp. 9-39 in Michael Power and Nancy Butler (with Joy Ormsby). *Slavery and Freedom in Niagara.* Niagara-on-the-Lake, ON: The Niagara Historical Society, 1993. Reprint 2000.

"Railway Suspension Bridge, The." *Bridges Over Niagara Falls: A History and Pictorial.* http://www.niagarafrontier.com/bridges.html#b2

Ranke, Leopold von. "Vorrede der ersten Ausgabe, Okt. 1824." Geschichte der romanischen und germanischen Völker von 1494 bis 1514 zur Kritik neuerer Geschichtsschreiber, 5.vii. 3rd edition. Leipzig, Germany: Verlag Duncker und Humblot, 1885.

Reflector (Norwalk, Ohio), August 16, 1853.

"Researching the Underground Railroad. Part 2. Using Primary Sources: The Historians' Toolbox." National Park Service Links to History. http://www.nps.gov/parkhistory/online_books/ugrr/exugrr3.htm.

Reynolds, James, and Jim Smith, with Phebe Appleton and Terry Boulton. "Niagara-on-the-Lake." Pp. 79-121 in Gretchen A. Duling, *et al. From the Mouth of the Lower Niagara River: Stories of Four Historic Communities, Commemorating 200 Years of Peace on the Border.* Niagara Greenway Approved Projected funded by the Niagara County Host Community Independent Publication. Buffalo, NY: Goulah Design Group, 2012.

Rhodes, Jane. *Mary Ann Shadd Cary: The Black Press and Protest in the Nineteenth Century.* Bloomington, Indiana: Indiana University Press, 1998.

Richards, Leonard L. *Who Freed the Slaves? The Fight Over the Thirteenth Amendment.* Chicago, Il: The University of Chicago Press, 2015.

Riddell, William Renwick. "Slave in Upper Canada." *Journal of Criminal Law and Criminology* 249 14/2 (May 1923 to February 1924), Article 6 (1923): 249-78.

Riley, Kathleen. *Lockport. Historic Jewel of the Erie Canal.* Charleston, SC: Arcadia Publishing, 2005.

Robertson, John Ross. *Landmarks of Toronto: A Collection of History Sketches of the Old Town of York from 1792 until 1833, and of Toronto from 1834 to 1895.* Toronto, ON: J. Ross Robertson, 1896.

"Rochester Ladies Anti-Slavery Society and Papers 1851-1868" (Watkins letter). William L. Clements Library Manuscripts Division, University of Michigan, Ann Arbor Michigan. http://quod.lib.umich.edu/c/clementsmss/umich-wcl-M-2084roc.

Rome Daily Sentinel (Rome, New York), August 9, 1853.

Romney, Virginia, *Intelligencer.* N.D.

"Ross, Harriet (originally named Araminta) ([Harriett] Tubman; Davis)." *Dictionary of Canadian Biography.* http://www.biographi.ca/en/bio/ross_harriet_14E.html.

Sackets Harbor Courier, November 15, 1832.

"Saga of Brock's Monument, The." Archives of Ontario, Ministry of Government and Consumer Services. http://www.archives.gov.on.ca/en/explore/online/1812/saga.aspx

"Samuel Ringgold Ward. American Abolitionist." *Encyclopedia Britannica*, editors. http://www.britannica.com/biography/Samuel-Ringgold-Ward.

"Samuel Ringgold Ward. American Abolitionist." *Wikipedia.* https://en.wikipedia.org/wiki/Samuel_Ringgold_Ward.

Santayana, George. *The Life of Reason or the Phases of Human Conquest;* Introduction and Reason in Common Sense. New York, NY: Charles Scribner's Sons, 1905; reprint 1920.

Scadding, Henry. *Toronto of Old; Collections and Recollections Illustrative of the Early Settlement and Social Life of the Capital of Ontario.* Toronto, ON: Adam, Stevenson & co., 1873. Online text: http://www.ebooksread.com/authors-eng/henry-scadding/toronto-of-old-collections-and-recollections-illustrative-of-the-early-settleme-hci/page-53-toronto-of-old-collections-and-recollections-illustrative-of-the-early-settleme-hci.shtml.

Schultz, Christian. *Travels on an Inland Voyage through the States of New-York, Pennsylvania, Virginia, Ohio, Kentucky, and Tennessee, and through the Territories of Indiana, Louisiana, Mississippi, and New-Orleans, Performed in the Years 1807 and 1808*. New York, NY: I. Riley, 1810.

Scott, Dewey. Docent, John P. Parker House, Ripley, Ohio. Interview with Dennis Duling.

Shumway, G. R. H. To *The Friend of Man,* October 17, 1836, *printed* November 3, 1836.

Schwartz, Barry. "Social Change and Collective Memory: The Democratization of George Washington." *American Sociological Review* 56/2 (1991): 221–236.

Scott, O. *The Ground of Secession from the M. E. Church, or Book for the Times: Being an Examination of Her Connections with Slavery, and also her Form of Government*. Revised and Corrected. To Which is added "Wesley Upon Slavery." New York, NY: C. Prindle, 1848.

Scoville, Dan, and Jim Kennard. "Shipwreck Explorers Discover 1850's Schooner in Lake Ontario." YouTube. https://www.youtube.com/watch?v=NAWEHGrAtYw.

Sernett, Milton C. *Harriett Tubman: Myth, Memory, and History*. Durham, NC; London, UK: Duke University Press, 2007.

Severance, Frank Hayward. *Old Trails on the Niagara Frontier.* Buffalo, NY: The Matthews Northrup Co., 1899; Cleveland, OH: Burrows Brothers, 1903.

Shadd, Adrienne, Afus Cooper, and Karolyn Smardz Frost. *The Underground Railroad: Next Stop, Toronto!* Toronto, ON: Natural Heritage Books, 2002. (Youth).

Sharpe, Teresa. "Children Vow to Continue Murphy's Devoted Work." *The Buffalo News* (June 1, 2014). http://www.buffalonews.com/city-region/all-niagara-county/children-vow-to-continue-murphys-devoted-work-20140601.

Sharpe, Teresa. "Take a Step Back in Time at Historic McClew Farmstead in Burt." *The Buffalo News* (Sept. 1, 2013). http://www.buffalonews.com/city-region/all-niagara-county/take-a-step-back-in-time-at-historic-mcclew-farmstead-in-burt-20130901.

Shaw, Donald C., and June P. Zintz, compilers. "Niagara County Purchasers Under Land Contracts in 1835." *Western New York Genealogical Society Journal* 3/4 (March 1977): 161.

Sheer, Mark. "Work Begins on the Double Tree Hotel Downtown." *Niagara Gazette* (November 25, 2014).

Shomette, Donald G. "Heyday of the Horse Ferry: A Long-forgotten Animal-powered Craft is Discovered on the Bottom of Lake Champlain." *National Geographic* 176/4 (1989): 548-556.

Siddall, Bill. "Samuel Chubbuck." *Find a Grave*. 2009. http://www.findagrave.com/cgi-bin/fg.cgi?page=gr&GRid=39961693.

Siebert, Wilber H. The Underground Railroad from Slavery to Freedom: A Comprehensive History. New York, NY; London, England: The Macmillan Co., 1898; reprint Mineola, NY: Dover Publications, 2006.

Siebert, Wilber H. "The Underground Railroad in Massachusetts." *The New England Quarterly* 9/3 (1936): 447-67.

Siebert, Wilbur H. "Light on the Underground Railroad." *The American Historical Review* 1/3 (1896): 455-63.

Siener, William H., and Thomas A. Chambers. "Crossing to Freedom: Harriet Tubman and John A. Roebling's Niagara Suspension Bridge." *Western New York Heritage* 13/1 (Spring 2010): 8–17.

Siener, William H., and Thomas A. Chambers. "Harriet Tubman, the Underground Railroad, and the Bridges at Niagara Falls." *Afro-Americans in New York Life and History* 36/1 (2012): 34-63.

Sinha, Manisha. *The Slaves Cause: A History of Abolition.* New Haven, CT: Yale University Press, 2016.

Six Degrees of Separation. A film. 1993. Based on John Guare, *Six Degrees of Separation*, a play. Directed by Fred Schepisi and starring Stockard Channing, Donald Sutherland, Ian McKellen, Anthony Michael Hall, and Will Smith.

"Slaves." Index to *Journal of the Legislative Council of the Province of New York*. Albany: Weed, Parsons & company, printers, 1861. P. 259. https://books.google.com/books?id=BMT04vmAoR8C&pg=PA2066&lpg=PA2066&dq=%22An+Act+for+the +suppression+and+punishment+the+conspiracy+and+insurrection+of+Negroes+and&source=bl&ots=Cezc G0BFux&sig=H6rtS7R7eBfTXoGrE8iomC4TmB8&hl=en&sa=X&ved=0ahUKEwi8_PS1nfbPAhUBMz4KHdyHD bIQ6AEIKDAC#v=onepage&q&f=false.

"Slave to Free Before General Emancipation. Selections from 19th- & 20th-Century Slave Narratives." National Humanities Center Resource Toolbox. The Making of African American Identity: Vol. 1, 1500-1865. http://nationalhumanitiescenter.org/pds/maai/identity/text2/slavetofreenarr.pdf.

Smedley, Robert Clemens. *History of the Underground Railroad in Chester and the Neighboring Counties of Pennsylvania*. Lancaster, PA: John A. Herstand, 1883. https://archive.org/stream/historyundergro00smedgoog#page/n10/mode/2up.

Smith, Mrs. Andrew M. To Clarence O. Lewis in Clarence in O. Lewis, "Old County Communities Located." *Niagara Falls Gazette* (February 5, 1964), 8.

Smith, Gene Allen. *The Slaves' Gamble: Choosing Sides in the War of 1812*. New York, NY: Palgrave Macmillan/St. Martin's Press LLC, 2013.

Snodgrass, Mary Ellen. "Cuyler, Samuel Cornelius (1808—1872) and Cuyler, Julia Speed (1812--?)." *The Underground Railroad: An Encyclopedia of People, Places, and Operations*. New York, NY; London, UK: M. E. Sharpe, Taylor & Francis, 2008; London, UK: Routledge, 2015.

Snodgrass, Mary Ellen. *The Underground Railroad: An Encyclopedia of People, Places, and Operations*. New York, NY; London, UK: M. E. Sharpe, Taylor & Francis, 2008; London, UK: Routledge, 2015.

Snyder, Charles M. "The Antislavery Movement in the Oswego Area." Eighteenth Publication of the Oswego County Historical Society, Oswego County. Oswego, NY: Palladium-Times, Inc., 1955 (February 15), 4, 7-12. http://ochs.nnyln.org/ochs-issues/ochs-issue-1955.pdf.

Sokolow, Jayhme A. "The Jerry McHenry Rescue and the Growth of Northern Antislavery Sentiment during the 1850s." *Journal of American Studies* 16/3 (December 1982): 427-45.

Souvenir History of Niagara County, New York. The Pioneer Association of Niagara County, 1902.

St. Catharines Standard, December 11, 1914.

Still, William. *Underground Railroad, with a Life of the Author William Still. A Record of Facts, Authentic Narratives, Letters, &C., Narrating the Hardships, Hair-Breadth Escapes and Death Struggles of the Slaves in Their Efforts for Freedom, as Related by Themselves and Others, or Witnessed by the Author*. Philadelphia, PA: William Still, Publisher, 1872. https://books.google.com/books?id=KD9LAAAAYAAJ&pg=PA269&lpg=PA269&dq=Suspension+Bridge,+Ni agara+Falls,+Methodist+church&source=bl&ots=yeGlIX_WTr&sig=l9b_b3PoX21MJYYLMKr1AbG4D9A&hl= en&sa=X&ved=0ahUKEwiguOzni9vOAhVD1B4KHSdFBDcQ6AEIPTAG#v=onepage&q=Suspension%20Bridge %2C%20Niagara%20Falls%2C%20Methodist%20church&f=false. Revised as *Underground Rail Road Records: With a Life of the Author: Narrating the Hardships, Hairbreadth Escapes and Death Struggles of the Slaves in their Efforts for Freedom: Together with Sketches of Some of the Eminent Friends of Freedom, and Most Liberal Aiders and Advisers of the Road*. Philadelphia, PA: William Still, 1879; 1886. Project Gutenberg e-book. http://www.gutenberg.org/files/15263/15263-h/15263-h.htm. See also a partial reprint, William Still, *The Underground Railroad. Authentic Narratives and First Hand Accounts*. Edited with an Introduction by Ian Frederick Finseth. Mineola, NY: Dover Publications, Inc., 2007.

St. Louis Daily Union, November 2, 1846.

Stone, Phillip. "How the Methodist Church Split in the 1840s." *SC United Methodist Advocate* (February 2013); reprinted in *Wofford College. History Document and Photos from the Archives*. http://blogs.wofford.edu/from_the_archives/2013/01/30/how-the-methodist-church-split-in-the-1840s/.

"Story of William Morgan, The." *The Times*, Centennial Edition. Batavia, New York, 1918. Fulton History.com.

Stowe, Harriet Beecher. *Uncle Tom's Cabin*. Dover Thrift Editions. Mineola, NY: Dover Publications, Inc., 2005 (1852).

Strand, Ginger. *Inventing NIAGARA: Beauty, Power, and Lies.* New York, NY: Simon and Schuster, 2008.

Swain, Sarah. "Appendix II. The Bloody or Two Mile Run and its Relation to Local History." Revised. *The Town of Porter 1776-1976—A Bicentennial History.* The Town of Porter Historical Society, 1976.

Switala, William J. *The Underground Railroad in New York and New Jersey.* Mechanicsburg, PA: Stackpole Books, 2006.

"Theodore Weld." Wood engraving. Library of Congress. http://www.loc.gov/pictures/item/2006687237/.

Thomas, E. A. *Buffalo City Directory.* Buffalo, NY: Franklin Steam Printing House, 1868.

Tillery, Tyrone. "The Inevitability of the Douglass-Garrison Conflict." *Phylon* 37/2 (1976): 137-49.

"Timeline. 1800-1900." *Black History Canada.* Historica Canada.
        www.blackhistorycanada.ca/timeline.php?id=1800.

Times (Batavia, New York), 1918, 14.

Times-Pecayune, The (New Orleans, Louisiana), August 4, 1841.

Toplin, Robert Brent. "Between Black and White: Attitudes toward Southern Mulattoes, 1830-1861." *The Journal of Southern History* 45/2 (1979): 185-200.

Toronto Daily Leader, The, August 4, 1853.

Town of Porter Historical Society. *The Town of Porter 1776-1976—A Bicentennial History.* Youngstown, NY: Town of Porter Historical Society, 1976.

"Trial of Alexander McLeod for the Murder of Amos Durfee, The." *Gould's Stenographic Reporter; Published Monthly in the City of Washington, and Devoted to the Recording of Important Trials, or Treason, Murder, Highway Robbery, Mail Robbery, Conspiracy, Riot, Arson, Burglary, Seduction, Etc., also Miscellaneous Speeches.* Vol. 14, 1841.

True Wesleyan (New York, New York), August 14, 1850.

Turner, O. *Pioneer History of the Holland Purchase of Western New York.* Buffalo, NY: Jewett Thomas & Co., 1849.

Twelve Years a Slave in 2013. Academy Award-winning film. Directed by Steve McQueen and starring Chiweter Ejiofor. Based on Solomon Northup, *Twelve Years a Slave*, as told to David Wilson, an 1853 memoir and slave narrative. See "Twelve Years a Slave," https://en.wikipedia.org/wiki/Twelve_Years_a_Slave.

Twenty Third Report of the American Home Missionary Society, The. New York, NY: William Osborn, 1849.

Underground Railroad Free Press. Summary of the Wellman Scale. http://www.urrfreepress.com/#Scale.

The Underground Railroad in Oswego County. A Driving Tour. Oswego Country Freedom Trail, Site 10. Based on research by Judith Wellman's team written up in Wellman, "Survey of Historic Sites Relating to the UGRR, Abolitionism, and African American Life in Oswego County." http://visitoswegocounty.com/wp-content/uploads/UGRR.pdf.

United State Census Bureau. "Measuring Race and Ethnicity Across the Decades: 1790–2010." Online at http://www.census.gov/population/race/data/MREAD_1790_2010.html

U.S. Supreme Court. Scott v. Sandford. 60 U.S. (19 How.) 393 (1856). Justia US Supreme Court.
        https://supreme.justia.com/cases/federal/us/60/393/case.html.

Van Cleve, James. *Early Steamboating Reminiscences From the Ontario, Martha Ogden and United States. Oswego Palladium.* Oswego, NY, April 4, 1876. In Early Steamboating Reminiscences. Maritime History of the Great Lakes. http://images.maritimehistoryofthegreatlakes.ca/66322/data

Van Cleve, James. *Reminiscences of the Early Period of Sailing Vessels and Steamboats on Lake Ontario with a History of the Introduction of the Propeller on the Lakes and Other Subjects with Illustrations.* Buffalo, NY: Manuscript at the Buffalo History Museum, 1877.

Van Cleve, James. *The Great Northern Route. American Lines. The Ontario and St. Lawrence Steamboat Company's Hand-Book for Travelers to Niagara Falls, Montreal and Quebec, and through Lake Champlain to Saratoga Springs. Illustrated with Maps and Numerous Engravings.* Buffalo, NY: Jewett, Thomas, & Co.; Rochester, NY: D. M. Dewey, 1852.

VanDeusen, Anna S. "Life of John P. VanDeusen by his Daughter Anna S. VanDeusen (1931)." In Christopher Davis, Museum Director of the Newark-Arcadia Historical Society and Museum. A Letter to Gretchen Duling, December 19, 2014.

VanDeusen, John P. Diary. 1855. Newark, NY: Newark-Arcadia Historical Society Museum. Transcribed by Gretchen Duling, Oct. 22, 2014.

Vaughn, William Preston. *The Anti-Masonic Party in the United States 1826-1843*. Lexington, KY: University Press of Kentucky, 1983. Paperback 2009. Chapter 1, "The Morgan Affair and Its Consequences."

Versailles, Elizabeth Starr. *Hathaway's of America*. Northampton, MA: Gazette Print Co., 1970; Supplement, Hathaway Family Association, 1980.

Vinal, Theodora. *Niagara Portage from Past to Present*. Buffalo, NY: Foster and Stewart, 1949; Henry Stewart, 1955.

Walsh, Edward. "A View of Fort George, Navy Hall and New Niagara, taken from the Un. States' Fort of Old Niagara." Watercolor, 1804. In E. Walsh, M.D., 49th Regiment, *Sketches from Nature made in Upper Canada in the Years 1803, 1804 and 1805*. William L. Clements Library, University of Michigan, Ann Arbor, Michigan.

Ward, Samuel Ringgold. *Autobiography of a Fugitive Slave: His Anti-Slavery Labours in the United States, Canada, & England*. London, UK: John Snow, 1855. Schomburg Center for Research in Black Culture, Manuscripts, Archives and Rare Books Division, The New York Public Library.

"Ward, Samuel, Ringgold." *Dictionary of Canadian Biography* IX (1861-1870). http://www.biographi.ca/en/bio/ward_samuel_ringgold_9E.html.

"Ward, Samuel Ringgold." *Encyclopedia of African- American Culture and History*, 2nd ed. Edited by Colin A. Palmer. Vol. 5. Detroit, MI: Macmillan Reference USA, 2006. http://www.encyclopedia.com/article-1G2-3444701276/ward-samuel-ringgold.html.

"War of 1812 Heroine: Betsy Doyle." http://www.nyusd1812.org/our-ancestors/betsy-doyle.html.

Warren, Tanya Lee. Compiler, *Freedom Seekers, Abolitionists, and Underground Railroad Helpers,* Cayuga County, New York. Historical New York Research Associates. http://www.cayugacounty.us/portals/0/history/ugrr/report/pdf/consolidated.pdf.

Watkins, Wm. J. To Mrs. Armstrong, N.D. "Rochester Ladies Anti-Slavery Society and Papers 1851-1868." William L. Clements Library Manuscripts Division, University of Michigan, Ann Arbor Michigan; cited in Wellman, "Site of the International Suspension Bridge, 1848, 1855," *Niagara Falls Underground Railroad Heritage Area Management Plan Appendix C,* 171-72.

Webster, Donavan. "Traveling the Long Road to Freedom, One Step at a Time." *Smithsonian Magazine* 27/7 (October 1996), 48-50. Also at United States Embassy Digital. http://www.smithsonianmag.com/ist/?next=/history/traveling-the-long-road-to-freedom-one-step-at-a-time-1-43841138/; http://iipdigital.usembassy.gov/st/english/texttrans/2005/06/20050606101156pssnikwad3.773135e-02.html#ixzz3oZ5VmeDk.

Weiskotten, Daniel H. "The 'Great Cazenovia Fugitive Slave Law Convention' August 21 and 22, 1850 at Cazenovia, New York." http://www.rootsweb.ancestry.com/~nyccazen/Shorts/1850Convention.html.

Wellman, Judith, and Marjory Allen Perez, Manager, with Charles Lenhart, Milton C. Sernett, Angela A. Williams, and others. *Uncovering Sites Related to the Underground Railroad, Abolitionism, and African American Life in Wayne County, New York, 1820-1880*. Sponsored by and located at the Wayne County Historian's Office, Peter Evans, Wayne County Historian. Funded by Preserve New York. Lyons, NY: Wayne County Historian's Office, 2008.

Wellman, Judith, and Tanya Lee Warren, Manager. Database: People and Sites Relating to the Underground Railroad, Abolitionism, and African American Life, 1820-1880, Niagara Falls and Niagara County. New York Historical Research Associates, Inc., for edr. Companies and Niagara Falls Underground Railroad Heritage Area Commission. http://www.niagarafallsundergroundrailroad.org/assets/Uploads/Niagara-Falls-Underground-Railroad-Project-Database.pdf.

Wellman, Judith. Articles listed below in Niagara Falls Underground Railroad Heritage Area Management Plan Appendix C: Survey of Sites Relation to the Underground Railroad. Abolitionism, and African American Life in Niagara Falls and Surrounding Area, 1820-1880. Historic Resources Survey Report (April 2012). Part II. http://www.niagarafallsundergroundrailroad.org/assets/Uploads/NF-HAMP-Report-Appendix-C-1.pdf. **Twenty-seven descriptive, survey articles on various sites. Hereafter Appendix C.** Most of these articles are also listed at the Underground Railroad Heritage Area, "UGRR SITES." The following is a selection. http://www.niagarafallsundergroundrailroad.org/, "UGGR SITES."

Wellman, Judith. "Lewiston Landing." *Appendix C,* 181-92.

Wellman, Judith. "Site of the Augustus and Letitia Porter Home." *Appendix C,* 42-44.

Wellman, Judith. "Site of the Cataract House." *Appendix C,* 48-79.

Wellman, Judith. "Site of the Eagle Hotel and International Hotel." *Appendix C,* 79-84.

Wellman, Judith. "Site of the Ferry Landing at Youngstown." *Appendix C,* 177-81.

Wellman, Judith. "Site of the Home of Peter A. Porter, Elizabeth Porter, and Josephine

Wellman, Judith. "Site of the Home of William H. Childs." *Appendix C,* 100-103.

Wellman, Judith. "Site of the International Suspension Bridge, 1848, 1855," *Appendix C,* 160-72.

Wellman, Judith. "Site of the Peter Buell Porter House." *Appendix C,* 44-48.

Wellman, Judith. "Site of the Whitney-Trott House." *Appendix C,* 103-11.

Wellman, Judith. "Solon and Francis Drake Whitney House." *Appendix C,* 133-36.

Wellman, Judith. "The Site of the Ferry Landing [Niagara Falls]." *Appendix C,* 142-60.

Wellman, Judith. "How Do we Separate Fact from Fiction in Underground Railroad Sites." In "Uncovering the Underground Railroad in the Finger Lakes." http://www.co.seneca.ny.us/wp-content/uploads/2015/02/Uncovering-UGRR-in-Finger-Lakes.pdf.

Wellman, Judith. "Larry Gara's Liberty Line in Oswego County, New York, 1838—1854: A New Look at the Legend." *Afro-Americans in New York Life and History.* https://www.questia.com/read/1P3-494776751/larry-gara-s-liberty-line-in-oswego-county-n.

Wellman, Judith. "Oral Traditions and Beyond: A Guide to Documenting the Underground Railroad." Unpublished manuscript, August 18, 2015.

Wellman, Judith, Marjory Allen Perez, with Charles Lenhart and others. "Uncovering the Underground Railroad, Abolitionism, and African American Life in Wayne County, New York, 1820-1880." Sponsored by the Wayne County Historian's Office, Peter Evans, Historian. Funded by Preserve New York, a program of the Preservation League of New York State and the New York State Council on the Arts. 2009.

Wellman, Judith, Project Coordinator, and Tanya Warren, Project Researcher. *Discovering the Underground Railroad, Abolitionism and African American Life in Seneca County, New York, 1820-1880.* Sponsored by and located in the Seneca County Historian's Office, Walter Gable, Seneca County Historian. Funded by Preserve New York, 2005-2006. Seneca Falls, NY: The County of Seneca, New York: 2006. http://www.co.seneca.ny.us/wp-content/uploads/2015/02/discovering_ugrr.pdf.

Wellman, Judith Survey of Historic Sites Relating to the UGRR, Abolitionism, and African American Life in Oswego County. Originally online at SUNY Oswego.

Wellman, Judith. *The Road to Seneca Falls: Elizabeth Cady Stanton and the First Women's Rights Convention.* Urbana and Chicago, Il: University of Illinois Press, 2004.

Wellman, Judith. "This Side of the Border: Fugitives from Slavery in Three Central New York Communities." New York *History* (October 1998): 359-92.

Wellman, Judith. "'Unspeakable Joy': Religion, Reform, the Underground Railroad and African American Life in the Burned-over District of Wayne County, New York." In Historical New York Research Associates, *Databases. Sites Relating to the Underground Railroad, Abolitionism, and African American Life in Wayne County, New York.* Lyons, NY: Wayne County Historian's Office Preserve, 2007—2009.

Wellman, Judith, with assistance from Milton Sernett. "Bibliography." Uncovering the Freedom Trail. The Underground Railroad, Abolitionism, and African American Life Syracuse and Onondaga County, 1820-70. Project sponsored by the Preservation Association of Central New York, with funding from Preserve New York, 2001-2002.

"When Did Slavery End in New York?" New York Historical Society, Museum and Library. http://www.nyhistory.org/community/slavery-end-new-york-state.

White, Alan. "Origins [of the Underground Railroad]." http://www.undergroundrailroad.org.uk/ur-origins.htm.

White, Deborah Gray. *Ar'n't I a Woman. Female Slaves in the Plantation South*. Revised Edition. New York, NY; London, UK: W. W. Norton and Co., 1999.

"William Lloyd Garrison. 1805 – 1879." PBS Online Resource Bank. http://www.pbs.org/wgbh/aia/part4/4p1561.html.

"William Lyon Mackenzie." *Dictionary of Canadian Biography*. http://www.biographi.ca/en/bio/mackenzie_william_lyon_9E.html.

"William Morgan - Revenge of the Freemasons." *Murder by Gaslight*. http://www.murderbygaslight.com/2009/12/william-morgan-revenge-of-freemasons.html.

"William Morgan Digital Library." http://olivercowdery.com/morganhome/morgtxt.htm.

Williams, Edward T. *Niagara County New York . . . A Concise Record of Her Progress and People, 1821-1921*. 2 vols. Illustrated. Chicago, Il: J. H. Beers & Company, N.D. (ca. 1921).

Williams, Lillian Serece. *Strangers in the Land of Paradise. The Creation of an African American Community, Buffalo, New York. 1900-1940*. Bloomington and Indianapolis, IN: Indiana University Press, 1999.

Williamson, Jenn. "J. W. Loguen (Jermain Wesley), 1814-1872. Summary." *Documenting the South*. http://docsouth.unc.edu/neh/loguen/summary.html.

"William Still." Femi Lewis article at *About Education*. http://afroamhistory.about.com/od/africanamericanwomen/a/WilliamStill.htm;

"William Still: An African-American Abolitionist. Timeline. The Life and Times of William Still." Temple University Libraries. http://stillfamily.library.temple.edu/timeline/william-still.

"William Watkins (b. circa 1803 - d. circa 1858). Biographical Series. " Archives of Maryland. http://msa.maryland.gov/megafile/msa/speccol/sc5400/sc5496/002500/002535/html/002535bio.html. https://www.facebook.com/whynotsuspensionbridge/posts/736396376465307

Wilner, Merton M. *Niagara Frontier, A Narrative and Documentary History*. Chicago, Il: S.J. Clarke Pub. Co., 1931; Volume IV. Provo, UT: Ancestry.com Operations Inc., 2005.

Wilson, David. *Twelve Years a Slave*. Auburn, NY: Derby and Miller, 1853.

Wilson, Mrs. Daniel. "Not So Long Ago." *The Youngstown Centennial Magazine 1854-1954.Youngstown Centennial. Youngstown 1854—1954*. Youngstown Historical Society, 1954. Pp. 41-45.

Yee, Shirley J. *Black Women Abolitionists: A Study in Activism, 1828-1860*. Knoxville: Univ. of Tennessee Press, 1992.

Yetman, Norman R. *When I was a Slave*. Dover Thrift Editions. Mineola, NY: Dover Publications, Inc., 2002.

Youngstown and some of its citizens related to the UGRR are also on the site at http://www.niagarafallsundergroundrailroad.org/assets/Uploads/Niagara-Falls-Underground-Railroad-Project-Database.pdf.

Youngstown and Town of Porter, Census Record Booklets. 1820; 1830; 1840; 1850; 1860; 1865. Youngstown, New York: Town of Porter Historical Society and Museum.

Youngstown Historical Society. *The Youngstown Centennial Magazine 1854-1954*.

Youngstown News (Youngstown, New York). Microfilm. 1880's and scattered issues to 1909 – Niagara Falls Public Library.

INDEX

D

Daily Evening Transcript (newspaper), Boston, viii, 222–223

Daily Journal, Lockport, 171, 268, 277–278, 279, 329, 382, 393, *400*

Daily Leader, Toronto, 217–219, 463

Daley, James, 448

Daniel (fugitive slave, father), viii, 126, 171, 235–265, 267, 278, 326, 329, 372, 374–375, 380, 388, 393, *395, 398–400, 402, 403. See* James (fugitive slave, son)

Dann, Norman K., xix, 36n, 37n, 223n, 323n, 448

Davids, John, 435

Davids, Tice (fugitive slave), xxiii

Davis Brick Block, x, 153n, 251–253, 264, 278–279, 307–312, 315, 326–327, 372–374, 376–377, 380, 388, *399–400,* 410. *See also* N.D. Haskell Building

Davis family and properties, 307–312

Davis grist mill, 104, 309, 370n, 371–375

Davis, Bradley D. ("B.D."), ix, 120, 122, 186, 252, 308–312, 326, 372, *400, 406*

Davis, Christopher, xviii, 239, 249n, 431, 434n, 448, 453, 464

Davis, Daniel L., xviii, 109n, 113n, 116n, 117n, 448

Davis, Dernoral, 60n

Davis, Elvira. *See* Haskell, Elvira Davis

Davis, Estella. *See* Hutton, Estella Davis

Davis, Gordon, 308

Davis, J. W. (letter to Siebert), 269–270, 393, *400*

Davis, Jason, 18, 308, 309, 311–312, 372

Davis, Martha Hathaway (wife, B. D. Davis), 309

Davis, Martha Hathaway (wife, Jason Davis), 308

Davis, Nelson R., 67, 73, 279, 308, 311, 312, 326, 372, 382, *401–401, 405,* 411

Davis/Haskell Home, ix, 186, 308–312

Davison, G. M. (Tour Guide), 146, *147,* 159, 448

Dawn Settlement, Ontario, Canada, viii, 206–207, 284n

Decatur, William, 418

Declaration of Sentiments of American Anti-Slavery Society, 31–32

DeCroix, Douglas, xix

Deeds of Manumission. *See* Certificates of Manumission

Democratic Mirror (newspaper), Sandusky, Ohio, 217, 221n, 448

Dennis W _____ . *See* W___, Dennis

Densmore, Christopher, xx, 49n, 211, 222, 290, 296, 299n, 448

Deputy husbands, 169. *See also* Doyle, Betsy; Greensitt, Agnes

Detroit, Michigan, 22, 125, *224*

Devil's Hole Massacre, 1763, 290, 446

Diaries. *See* VanDeusen

Dieling, Caroline, 68

Dieling, Daniel (Prussian shoemaker), 68

Dieling, Henry, 68

Dieling, Kate, 68

Dieling, Lena, 68

Dieling, Mary (daughter), 68

Dieling, Mary (mother), 68

Dietz, Suzanne Simon, xix, 55n, 88n, 130n, 137n, 138n, 139n, 159n, 160n, 161, 184n, 185, 372n, 381, *405,* 448, 449

Director for Life of American Home Missionary Society, 377, *399*

Distances to Youngstown, 331–332

Dittrich, Nicole C., xx

Dix, Barbara, 229

Dog, Kim Kelsey's, 97

Douglass, Frederick, v, 19, 27, 35–37, 44–46, 48–49, 58, 74, 179, 183, 198, 199n, 211, 215, 216, 282n, 308, 312, 321–322, 326, 341n, 346n, 383, *401, 403, 408,* 429, 430, 446, 449, 450, 451, 452, 463. *See also The North Star,* Anti-Slavery Society and, 35–36

Doyle, Andrew, 167

Doyle, Betsy, 158n, 167–169

Dred Scott, 14, 28, 58, 75n, 80

Dred Scott v. *Sanford,* 28, 75n, 80

Drew, Benjamin, 10n, 207–208

DuLaney, Cora Woodward (Anderson), 249n, 456

Duling, Dennis C., xvii, xxi, 6, *7, 11, 38, 39, 40,* 80n, 124n, 189, *201, 224, 229, 236, 238, 255, 256, 265,* 276, *310,* 314n, *315, 319, 324, 331, 333, 337, 339,* 356n, *359, 363, 364,* 366-369, 373, *388, 417,* 448, 450, 452, 455, 458, 459, 461, 485, *488*

Duling, Gretchen A., xxi, xxv, 9n, 52, 80n, 143n, 169n, 229n, 236n, *240,* 240n, 242, *243,* 313n, 303n, 313n, 316n, 318n, 322n, *353,* 371, 372n, *380, 385,* 386-*388, 398,* 418, 447, 448, 449, 464, 485–488

Dunlap, Orrin E., 117, 450

Dunn, Edward T., 120n, 450

Dunnigan, Brian Leigh, xix, xx, 77, 124n, 359n, 364, 365, 450

Durfee, Amos, xi, 440, 441, 442, *443,* 452, 455, 463

Durham (Schenectady) boats, 87, 90

Palmyra, viii, ix, xxvin, 25, 178, 226n, 236, 240, 242n,
    244–248, 250, 254, 257, 259–265
    Female Anti-Slavery Society, 246–247, *398*
Palmyra Whig, 242n. *See also Wayne County Whig*
Pardee, Cynthia A. (Wilcox), 254, 259–260, 261, 262,
    265, 307, 377–380, *400*. *See also* Myron J.
    Pardee; Harriett Wilcox; Pardee/Wilcox
    home
Pardee, John, 262
Pardee, Myron J. ("Mr. Pardee"), iii, ix, 39n, 145n,
    146, 153, 154, 157, 171, 226n, 227, 235–
    236, 240, 244, 250–265, 278, 279n, 307–
    308, 311–312, 323, 326–327, 329, 352, 372,
    374, 377, 378, 380, 388, 393, *395, 399, 400,*
    407–410, 412, 416. *See also* Pardee &
    Pomroy; Pardee/Wilcox home
    as real estate broker/agent, 39n, 226n, 259, 378
Pardee, Rebecca C., 260n
Pardee, Richard G. (R.G.), 244, 250, 254, 260–262,
    264, 326, 374, 377, *399*
Pardee, Richard S., 261n
Pardee, Ward C., 260n
Pardee, William W., 254, 262, 265, 377, *399*. *See also*
    Pardee/Wilcox home
Pardee & Pomroy (Pomeroy), 153, 154, 251–254,
    257, 258, 259, 260, 262, 264, 265, 278, 307–
    308, 310–311, 326–327, 372, 374, 377, 380,
    388, 393, *399, 400,* 4010
Pardee/Wilcox home(s),
    In Youngstown, 145n, 146, 257, 259–260, 261,
    262, 264, 278, 307, 377–380, 383, 388,
    399–400, 400, 409
    In Palmyra, 254
    In Lancaster, 262
Parker, John P., vi, xviii, 58, 61, 63–64, 454, 459, 461
Parker, Theodore, v, 29–30
Parsons, Charles, vii, *114*
Parsons, Levi, 259
Philadelphia Female Anti-Slavery Society, 31
Perez, Marjory Allen, xxxi, 235n, 459, 464, 465
Peterboro, New York, v, vii, xix, 36–38, 195–198,
    206, 245, 254, 323n, *409,* 448, 452. *See also*
    Smith, Gerrit
Peterboro Presbyterian Church, 37
Pettit, Eber, iv, xxivn, xxvi, xxxi, xxxiv, 55n, 85n, 281–
    282, 289, 291n, 296, 299, 300, 394, 410,
    422–424, 426
    Sketches, 283–289, 300. *See* Cassey.
Philadelphia Female Anti-Slavery Society, 31
Phillips Academy, 42

Phillips, Harry W., 69, 135, 150
Phillips, John, 67, 69, 74, 105, 129, 131–135, 141–
    145, 150, 158n, 159–160, 163, *402, 405*
Phillips, John G. (= John?), 69, 135, 150
Phillips, Patricia, 378, 379n, 459
Phillips, Thomas, 418
Phillips, Wendell, 30
Pillars Mansion, 315
Pittavino, Michael, xviii, 97
Pluto (locomotive), 112–113
Pomroy, D, 152
Pomroy, J., 152
Pomroy (Pomeroy), E. P., ix, 153, 154, 257–259, 262,
    264, 307, 311, 377, *399*. *See also Pardee &*
    Pomroy (Pomeroy)
Pomroy (Pomeroy), Elizabeth, 262
Pomroy (Pomeroy), Julia, 262
Pomroy (Pomeroy), Lydia, 262
Pomroy (Pomeroy), Mary L., 262
Pomroy (Pomeroy), Perry, 262
Pomroy (Pomeroy) residence, 253n, 258n, 259–260
Pool, William, 65n, 87–88, 121, 136n, 137n, 138n,
    150n, 153n, 158, 160, 184n, 185n, 189–190,
    251n, 304n, 308n, 313n, 314n, 335n, 336n,
    339n, 340, 357n, 380, 385n, *405, 406, 407,*
    409, 459
Porter, A. H., 112n
Porter, A. S., 112n
Porter, Judge Augustus S., 55, 112n, 129, 290, 291
Porter, Elizabeth, 46n, 112n, 282n, 291–292
Porter, John (Youngstown clerk), 120, 122, 186;
    schooner named, 96, 97
Porter, Josephine Matilda (Morris), 282n, 291, 292n.
    See also Porter home
Porter, Minerva. 431. *See* VanDeusen, Minerva
Porter, P.B., 112n
Porter, Col. Peter Augustus, 46n, 282n, 290–292,
    296, *402*. *See also* "Col. P__"; Porter home
Porter, Peter Buel, 8–9, 112n ("P.B."), 129n, 290–
    292, *404*
Porter, Town of (New York), xvi–xvii, xix, xxvii, xxi,
    xxxv, 25, 40n, 41, 52–81, 87, 96, 120–121,
    405, 408. *See also* Porter Historical Society;
    Youngstown, Village of; *specific public*
    officers by name
    African Americans in, iii, 52, 53–56, 69–70
    Bicentennial History (1976), 95–97, 124, 137n,
    184, 453, 454, 463
    Book of Records of the Town of Porter, vii, 138n,
    159–160, 161–163, 161n, 169, 185

ABOUT THE AUTHORS

This book is the second official, collaborative research and writing project by Gretchen and Dennis Duling, both published authors, but in different academic fields. Gretchen initially launched the project in 2009. In 2010, she presented a Powerpoint program to the Town of Porter Historical Society on the connection between Youngstown, New York, and the Underground Railroad based on the status of her research at that time. After that public presentation, she continued her research and writing. As with most couples, Dennis and Gretchen (married for over fifty-seven years) had always discussed, edited, and shared their research and writing projects. They held each other to high standards and did not always agree. This project was different because over time Dennis, who was engaged in other research projects and was only copyediting Gretchen's earlier drafts, found himself becoming more and more interested in the topic. Eventually, he became directly involved in the research and writing. By 2015, Gretchen had encouraged and convinced him to officially come on board as a co-author.

Gretchen has always had a serious interest in the Underground Railroad. She grew up in a small Ohio River town named Gallipolis (French: "City of the Gauls") in Gallia County along the Ohio River. The town was an Underground Railroad crossing site. Ohio, just north of the Mason-Dixon Line, was not a slave state and it had the most Underground Railroad routes of any state in the nation. Some Freedom Seekers passed through Gallipolis on their way north; some settled there. The Emancipation Proclamation has been celebrated and observed in Gallia County, Ohio, continuously since 1863, one of the longest continuously running celebrations of the historic event in the United States.

Gretchen's early degrees were in music education (B.A. and M.A. Chicago Musical College at Roosevelt University), Creative and Gifted Education (M.A. Buffalo State College), and Educational Administration and Supervision (M.S. Canisius College, Buffalo, New York). With her husband, she was a *Haus Villigst* Exchange Student at Heidelberg University, Germany. In research for her doctoral dissertation for the New York State University at Buffalo (Ph.D.) she used both traditional historical and oral historical methods,[1] included oral interviews of elderly one-room school house teachers, the majority of whom attended one-room schools in southern, rural Ohio, and all of whom began teaching in the early 1900s. Two of these teachers were African American women. One had relatives who were manumitted slaves escorted by their former master to Gallia County; the master purchased land for them there and stayed long enough to get them settled. The other African American woman's heritage stemmed from fugitive slaves who escaped across the Ohio River and settled in the rural area outside of the town of Gallipolis. Both of these women were from families who wanted their children to be well-educated; both attended Rio Grande College, which is now Rio Grande University, near Gallipolis; and both shared oral accounts about how they managed campus racial restrictions and about those college faculty persons who educated them in their homes. Their experiences left a lasting impression on Gretchen (currently a retired career teacher) and generated many unanswered questions about the history of the UGRR.

Dennis spent his early years in Coshocton, a small town in east-central Ohio. Coshocton and nearby Roscoe Village are situated where the Walhonding and Tuscarawas rivers meet to form the Muskingum River, which flowed south to the Ohio River. It was a major north-south Underground Railroad Corridor. From this UGRR station, fugitive slaves could continue north via the Ohio-Erie Canal and on to Canada. Dennis graduated from the College of Wooster (B.A.), McCormick Theological Seminary (B.D./M.A.), became an ordained Presbyterian minister, and continued at the University of Heidelberg (with Gretchen) and the University of Chicago (M.A.; Ph.D.) and has done post-graduate research at Yale, Yeshiva, and Heidelberg Universities. Dennis is a T. B. Blackstone Fellow (ancient Greek), a University of Chicago Fellow, and a National Endowment for the Humanities Fellow (at Heidelberg). He has authored books and

---

[1] Gretchen A. Duling, *Voices From The Recitation Bench: Oral Life Histories of Rural One-Room School House Retired Career Teachers from Southeastern Ohio* (Lewiston, NY: Edwin Mellen Press, 1997).

technical studies in his field, held offices in professional societies, given academic presentations in the United States, Europe, and South Africa, and spent time in the Middle East. He is Professor Emeritus, Canisius College, Buffalo, New York, where he was a recipient of the Kenneth L. Koessler Distinguished Faculty Award for teaching, concern for students, service, and scholarship (publications http://www3.canisius.edu/~duling). He was a local "Environmentalist of the Year" (2013), and plays golf and keyboards in a jazz group, the Water Street Quartet.

Dennis and Gretchen lived in Youngstown for twenty years, from 1997 to 2017. Their Youngstown home had (and still has) has a magnificent, panoramic view of the Niagara River and Canada from the Brock Monument in distant Queenston, Ontario, to Fort George, Niagara-on-the-Lake, Ontario, and Lake Ontario. It is not surprising that they became deeply absorbed in local history along the lower Niagara River and that this interest blossomed into research on the history of the Underground Railroad in their adopted community.

Since 2017 the couple has lived at Fox Run, a retirement community in Orchard Park, New York. Yet, based largely on their research, Dennis, Gretchen, a local Youngstown historian Dr. Karen Noonan, and Pauline Goulah of Goulah Design Group, Inc., in Buffalo, New York, have teamed up to create a Graphic Rail illustrating Youngstown's pivotal role in the Underground Railroad. On September 5, 2020, the Graphic Rail was dedicated in a formal ceremony at the upper level of Youngstown's Constitution Park, below which the Youngstown Ferry House likely stood on the bank of the Niagara River.

Panorama of Niagara River and Canada from the Duling Backyard, Youngstown, New York
Photo Dennis Duling
Image 19.1

Dennis and Gretchen at Home
Photo *Buffalo News*
Image 19.2

Pauline Goulah (graphic designer), Gretchen and Dennis Duling (authors), Karen Noonan (historian)
Underground Railroad Crossing Graphic Rail Dedication
Constitution Park (Main Street, Across from Falkner Park)
Youngstown, New York, September 5, 2020
Design based on Gretchen and Dennis Duling, *A Final River to Cross*
Image 19.3